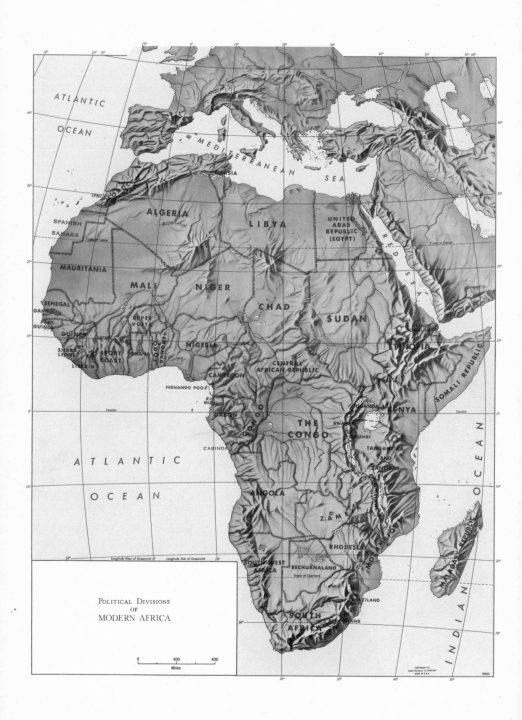

POLITICAL DIVISIONS
OF
MODERN AFRICA

0   400   800
Miles

Independent Black Africa

Independent Black Africa

The Politics of Freedom

Edited by

WILLIAM JOHN HANNA
MICHIGAN STATE UNIVERSITY

RAND McNALLY & COMPANY
Chicago

RAND M^CNALLY POLITICAL SCIENCE SERIES

Morton Grodzins, *Advisory Editor*

Eldersveld, *Political Parties: A Behavioral Analysis*
Fiser, ed., POLICY BACKGROUND SERIES
    Clawson, *Land for Americans*
    Clawson, *Land and Water for Recreation*
    Sufrin and Buck, *What Price Progress? A Study in Chronic Unemployment*
Froman, *Congressmen and Their Constituencies*
Goldwin, ed., RAND M^CNALLY PUBLIC AFFAIRS SERIES
    America Armed: Essays on United States Military Policy
    A Nation of States: Essays on the American Federal System
    Why Foreign Aid?
    Political Parties, U.S.A.
    100 Years of Emancipation
Golembiewski, *Behavior and Organization: O & M and the Small Group*
Hanna, ed., *Independent Black Africa: The Politics of Freedom*
Milbrath, *The Washington Lobbyists*
Peabody and Polsby, eds., *New Perspectives on the House of Representatives*
Press, ed., *The Polity: Selected Essays by Norton E. Long*
Schmidhauser, ed., *Constitutional Law in the Political Process*
Schubert, ed., *Judicial Behavior: A Reader on Theory and Research*
Singer, ed., *Human Behavior and International Politics*
Strauss, *The City and Man*
Strauss and Cropsey, eds., *History of Political Philosophy*
Ulmer, ed., *Readings in Political Behavior*
Williams and Press, eds., *Democracy in Urban America: Readings on Government and Politics*

To
D.C., J.C., I.H., D.M., V.O.,
H.L., E.S.,
Judy and Anne

Preface and Acknowledgements

Independent Black Africa is that part of the continent which has a predominantly Negro population and is not under European rule. Bounded by the Atlantic Ocean on the west, the Indian Ocean on the east, and roughly by latitude 20° north and 10° south, Independent Black Africa is an area of great diversity. The annual rainfall varies from under ten inches to over eighty, the population density ranges from uninhabited wastelands to overpopulated urban centers, and vegetation types include tropical rain forest and desert shrub. There are traditional chiefs and modern presidents, rural mud huts and capital-city luxury hotels, naked warriors and sophisticated Dakarois, ancient kingdoms and new states.

Despite this diversity, the people of Black Africa, their imperial pasts, the revolutionary changes they have experienced, and the contemporary problems they face are remarkably similar. There is unity of race and, at least in the opinion of some Africans, a unity of culture.[1] Most of the countries of Black Africa have become independent in the 1960's after experiencing centuries of foreign slaving and at least a half century of European rule. The countries have all undergone a metamorphosis as a result of the giant forces of change launched by European contact. They share the problems of deep social divisions, fragile governments, and underdeveloped economies. Because of these similarities, Black Africa has been chosen as an area for study. Two analytical foci for this study have been established: the *modal* political system and the factors which have contributed to its development. Thus my concern in this reader is with both systematic and developmental analysis.

Contemporaneous with changes in Africa have been changes in Africanist scholarship. Paternal stereotypes and fixations on the exotic, common during the period of imperial rule, have been giving way to comparative research guided by, and designed to contribute to, contemporary social theory. Attracted by the opportunities for comparative research, inter-disciplinary cooperation, contributions to policy, and the excitement of change, scholars from all the social sciences have swelled the ranks of specialists on Africa (and the developing areas in general). African scholars are now among those making important contributions.

[1] See *L'Unité des Cultures Négro-Africaines* (Paris: Présence Africaine, 1959).

vii

The backgrounds of the authors represented in this reader, the original publication dates of their papers, and, of course, the papers themselves are indicators of the developments in Africanist scholarship. The backgrounds include anthropology, economics, history, political science, sociology, practical administration, and practical politics. A majority of the papers were originally published in the 1960's, and those published earlier were considered landmarks in their disciplines. The papers themselves represent our current understanding of Black Africa in particular and, to a lesser extent, the new states in general. But despite the developments in Africanist scholarship, there are enormous gaps in our understanding of politics in Black Africa. This can vividly be seen by comparing the literature available on Black Africa and on the United States. It is my hope that this reader will stimulate research that will fill some of the gaps.

By way of acknowledgement, I would first like to thank my many African friends and acquaintances. They have helped me to understand their part of the world, and they have developed in me a sympathy I feel it is worthwhile to share. In addition, I wish to thank the Office of International Programs, Michigan State University, for sponsoring a review of the literature on African politics[2] which led to the conclusion that this reader was both necessary and possible; the authors and publishers of the included papers for their permission to reprint; the photographers and information services for the permission to reproduce the included photographs; Victor du Bois, Alvin Magid, K. W. J. Post, Aristide Zolberg, and Judith Lynne Hanna for helpful comments on various drafts of the manuscript; and Rand McNally and Company for support and patience. With such help, the errors are obviously mine.

William John Hanna

Mbale, Uganda
November, 1963

---

[2] William John Hanna and Judith Lynne Hanna, *A Selective Bibliography of Periodical Literature on the Politics of Black Africa* (East Lansing: African Studies Center, Michigan State University, 1964).

Table of Contents

PART FOUR: FORGING TERRITORIAL UNITY: I

PART FIVE: FORGING TERRITORIAL UNITY: II

PART SIX: A LARGER UNITY

Illustrations following page 308

Independent Black Africa

Introduction: The Politics of Freedom

WILLIAM JOHN HANNA

Black Africa, to many outsiders, is savage and pagan, and its contemporary politics are chaotic. Despite the enormous changes which have taken place in recent years, murder in the Congo is considered representative of all Black Africa. Africans in business suits and skyscrapers in bustling African cities are not fully integrated into the image of Africa. Commenting on impressions such as these, one observer writes:

> Of all the obstacles in the way of understanding the African situation the most serious is this curious collection of intellectual junk with which we are still burdened—the colonial stereotypes which, in varying degrees, trouble the minds of all of us.[1]

These stereotypes have developed because Africa and Africans have been assessed ethnocentrically and out of context. Similarities are dismissed and differences emphasized. But the problems of building a united Europe or a strong and stable United Nations are similar to the problem of integrating many ethnic groups within a new African state. Charles de Gaulle's self-image and its effect upon French policy are similar to the self-image of Kwame Nkrumah and its effect upon Ghanaian policy. Violence in the Congo, skyscrapers in Nairobi, single-party politics in Tanganyika, and anti-intellectualism in Ghana are the results of change and the forging of a new national unity.

Perhaps the greatest differences between the cultures of Europe and the cultures of Africa are the sources of information and energy—and their corollary, might. There is no certain explanation for these differences (most research indicates no inherent racial inequality), but several situational factors appear to be relevant. (a) The vast, hot Sahara Desert, the forbidding coasts, and the interior plateau partially isolated the people of Black Africa, thereby restricting cultural and genetic exchanges.[2] It should be noted, however, that camel caravans pro-

[1] Thomas Hodgkin, "What Future for Africa?—I," *Encounter*, XCIII (1961), 8.
[2] In *Race and Culture* (Paris: UNESCO, 1958), p. 34, Michel Lieris suggests that Europeans "owed their cultural lead to the opportunities they have long had of frequent contacts among themselves and with contrasting peoples."

1

vided a link between Africa north and just south of the Sahara beginning early in the Christian era, and the Indian Ocean has long linked East Africa with parts of Asia and the Middle East. (b) The dense tropical rain forests and bordering sparse savannas inhibited intra-continental communication, causing further isolation and limiting (with some notable exceptions) the scale of social, political, and economic systems. (c) The heat and disease of the tropics drained potential energies and kept the density of the population low. One African writes, "Over vast areas of Africa, the challenge of natural conditions and habitat is so severe, and technology is so inadequate and inefficient, that whole families have to work hard all the year round to provide for a bare subsistence."[3]

Despite these handicaps, African cultures developed impressively before early European contact and the beginning of European slave trade in the fifteenth century. (Arabs and Africans previously traded slaves.) In the Western Sudan, the kingdoms of Ghana, Mali, and Songhai rose and fell. Timbuktu, which reached its zenith in the fourteenth century as the capital of Mali, was a thriving center of trade, administration, scholarship, medicine, law, and religion. The emperor, Mansa Musa, made a pilgrimage to Mecca in 1324 that left a profound and favorable impact upon the Middle East. In East Africa, Great Zimbabwe, feudal capital of the Monomotapa Empire, flourished for five centuries beginning in about 1250 A.D. Located in what is now Southern Rhodesia, it is known to have had stone buildings of advanced construction and design, irrigation dams, a specialized division of labor, and trade across the Indian Ocean.

From the mid-fifteenth through the mid-nineteenth centuries, the slave trade took from Black Africa an estimated 25 million people, primarily young men and women who in most societies are responsible for a major portion of the physical and creative effort. (The effectiveness of the slave trade, it should be noted, was due to the active cooperation of African middlemen.) "What the full effects of it really were is difficult and perhaps impossible to say. They were ruinously destructive of society and civilized growth. At many points they were probably fatal to both."[4]

The nineteenth century marked the decline of European slave trading and the maturation of other interests in Black Africa. To "civilize" Africans and assuage the guilt of Europeans, missionary activity was expanded. The satisfactions of fatherhood (Africans were equated with children), the prestige of power, the wealth of new resources and

[3] K. A. Busia, *The Challenge of Africa* (London: Pall Mall Press, 1962), p. 61.
[4] Basil Davidson, *The Lost Cities of Africa* (Boston: Little, Brown and Co., 1959), p. 132.

markets, and the need to protect these new activities brought additional administrators, traders, and soldiers. By 1884, the year the Congress of Berlin began, European slave trading had been almost completely stopped. By then, however, slaving and other disturbances had interrupted the development of indigenous African cultures.

Before the Congress began, European control in Africa was limited to the coastal areas, although their claims were not. The Congress of Berlin was called by Bismarck to prevent or resolve major disputes among the European states over African territorial claims. Because the Congress made effective control the test of title, the continent was rapidly occupied and divided. The boundaries which were drawn, based upon European interests and opportunities rather than indigenous needs, resulted in a Balkanization which has caused difficulties ever since. The tensions arising from the Somali people living in Ethiopia and Kenya, and the Ewe people split between Ghana and Togo, are reminiscent of the tensions which have arisen in the Balkans from equally questionable boundary-making.

CHANGE

European occupation launched forth giant forces of change[5] (intended and unintended) and these in turn have inexorably led to the rise of nationalism, the restoration of independence, and many of the challenges which face the present leaders of Black Africa. As Tom Mboya puts it:

A vision of Africa—present and to come—is impossible without being armed with a background and a history of Colonial Africa—its impact, effects, and the problems it has generated for the future Africa.[6]

The most politically important changes occurred in perspectives (values, truths, and identifications) and controls (social, economic, and political).[7] The total impact of change was, and continues to be, the metamorphosis of Black Africa. The principal means of change have been the European elite, new schools, new communications media, new opportunities for travel, new towns, new economic systems, and new political systems.

[5] Excluded from the discussion are changes not primarily caused by European contact and occupation.

[6] "Vision of Africa," this volume, p. 515. Busia, *op. cit.*, p. 52, writes: "Colonialism drew Africa into the orbit of modern history."

[7] Rupert Emerson, *From Empire to Nation* (Cambridge: Harvard University Press, 1960), p. 6, makes the prediction that imperial rule will, from a future vantage point, be viewed more as "the instrument by which the spiritual, scientific, and material revolution . . . was spread" than as the instrument of "oppression, exploitation, and discrimination."

THE EUROPEAN ELITE

Until recently, many Africans thought that Europeans were omnipotent and omniscient—demigods who had a special right to rule. The Europeans were conscious of their exclusiveness and pre-eminence, and they were deferred to and imitated by Africans. The Europeans were, in other words, social elites,[8] and as such they were models of behavior. Imitation of the models, in a conscious or unconscious attempt to partake of their power and wisdom, has been broad in scope and great in depth. In remote villages steaming in the tropical heat there are women wearing heavy European gowns. Some townsmen practice Parisian accents and mannerisms so that they will appear to be as "civilized" as Frenchmen. Imitation has included religious practices, work techniques, use of leisure time, and, later, political formulae and practices. Sometimes imitation has extended to basic values and beliefs. (Of course, some Africans independently arrived at styles, values, and beliefs which are similar to those of Europeans, and others evaluated alternatives before adoption.) Many Africans had limited contact with Europeans, however, and they retained most of the old ways. It was the limited few who could be called, even disparagingly, "black Frenchman" or "black Englishman." Nor has imitation been complete, either for the individual or for the society. Political independence is now bringing forth a more rational evaluation of alternatives leading to a new synthesis. Or as Nnamdi Azikiwe, the President of Nigeria, might put it, the day of mental emancipation is slowly arriving.

NEW SCHOOLS

Europeans established schools in Africa primarily to train the personnel needed to support European administrative and economic projects, and to convert Africans to Christianity. The teaching, mostly done by Christian missionaries, often featured appeals to authority and emotion rather than appeals to evidence and reason. Europe and its ways were good and "civilized"; Africa and its ways were bad and "primi-

[8] Cf. "African Elites," *International Social Science Bulletin,* VIII (1956), 413–98, especially the contributions by S. F. Nadel and K. A. Busia. In some cases imitation was probably based upon the mechanism of personality defense called "identification with the aggressor." Anna Freud reports the following incident: "The boy identified himself with the teacher's anger and copied his expression as he spoke, though the imitation was not recognized. Through his grimaces he was assimilating himself to or identifying himself with the dreaded external object." Anna Freud, *The Ego and the Mechanisms of Defence* (London: The Hogarth Press and the Institute of Psycho-Analysis, 1937), p. 118. This passage is also suggestive with reference to African leadership after independence.

tive." Students learned European history, but African history was limited to such subjects as "the pacification of primitive tribes." Christian hymns were practiced, traditional African folk songs repressed. Yet, an ever greater number of parents sent their children to school, or went themselves. Some were forced, some wanted to imitate, and others were fascinated by the secrets of European power and wisdom, or were opportunists who realized that a European education was the key to new power, wealth, and prestige.

The changes caused by the new schools were profound, although they had often not been foreseen by the Europeans. The gap between European rulers and African ruled was narrowed. The ideas of freedom, equality, and popular sovereignty, learned in a European context (reflecting the democratization of Europe), were applied to Africa and used to justify nationalism. Modern intellectuals (including such men as Nnamdi Azikiwe, Kwame Nkrumah, and Julius Nyerere) [9] emerged and became the vanguard of nationalism. And a *lingua franca* was provided which made it possible for educated Africans in all parts of a territory, as well as in different territories, to communicate with each other. The new schools, however, were for the fortunate few. Most countries of Black Africa, upon their attainment of independence, had literacy rates under 20 per cent and over one-half their children under seventeen were not in schools. Education is now the largest single budget item in Black Africa.

NEW COMMUNICATIONS MEDIA

By word of mouth or drum, news can travel rapidly through a village. But until the arrival of Europeans, the substance of some messages and the distances over which they were transmitted were limited. Modern communications media, often established for the benefit of Europeans, have brought the residents of towns and villages closer together, and put both into contact with the larger world. In some territories Africans were allowed to run their own newspapers, and these were important in their nationalist movements. Newspapers and books require the receiver to be literate (many illiterates receive printed news indirectly), but radio broadcasts and cinema shows can communicate new perspectives to all. However, newspapers, books, radios, and cinema houses are concentrated in the large towns, where even television may be available. (Television is

[9] As with many of the modern intellectuals who were at the forefront of the nationalist movements in their respective territories, these three men were educated overseas: Azikiwe at Storer College, Howard University, and Lincoln University; Nkrumah at Lincoln University, the University of Pennsylvania, and the University of London; and Nyerere at the University of Edinburgh.

a national status symbol as well as an emergent medium of communication.) Some towns and virtually all rural areas have not received the full benefits of new communications media, and it is in these places that traditional perspectives and controls have their strongest hold.

NEW OPPORTUNITIES FOR TRAVEL

In some parts of old Africa hostile tribes made long trips dangerous, and the physical environment made them difficult. To develop trade and improve personal safety, Europeans created order and built transportation networks within the newly formed territories. Many towns and villages are now serviced by tarred roads, railway lines, and even airports. The increased safety and speed of travel has made it easier for Africans to leave their homes for distant towns and villages, where new comrades can be found and new perspectives can be obtained. However, there are still villages that can only be reached by dirt paths, and their inhabitants remain partially isolated from the outside world.

NEW TOWNS

With few exceptions (e.g., Yorubaland in Western Nigeria), there were no towns in Africa before the arrival of the Europeans. People usually lived in ethnically homogeneous villages or clusters of villages. The Europeans established new towns throughout Black Africa to facilitate administration and the new economy. Soon, Africans began to come to the towns and urban population explosions occurred. (Leopoldville, for example, has increased in population from approximately 400 to 400,000 in the past eighty years.) Some Africans came as part of forced labor projects, some sought work to pay their taxes, and others came voluntarily to obtain education, to make money for purchasing modern conveniences, to participate in the excitement of town life, or to escape from the bonds of their villages.

Whatever their reasons for coming, Africans in the new towns found themselves in many new situations, faced with many new decisions, but without some of the security or control of home or tradition. Those who survived this ordeal developed a new sense of security and a new ability to innovate. Nationalist movements obtained support primarily from the Africans living in towns who found in the movement the needed sense of security. Of course, the transformation of most townsmen was far from complete. Ties with the home village remained relatively strong both socially (through kinship associations) and psychologically. In several sample surveys recently conducted by this author, a large majority of those in new towns considered some village "home" and expected to return there someday.[10] Moreover, most Africans have stayed in the rural areas where, bound by tradition, they remain the objects of innovation.

NEW ECONOMIC SYSTEMS

Natural resources, land alienation, and money were three important aspects of economic change. (a) Although resource discoveries have been localized (e.g., copper in Katanga and Northern Rhodesia), the resultant industries have drawn to employment centers thousands of Africans from homes scattered over a large area, led to the development of transportation and power systems, and linked Black Africa with the world economy. (b) The alienation of land by European settlers and entrepreneurs, especially in parts of East and Central Africa, created some land pressure and more resentment among Africans. Excluding southern Africa, where the pattern of land alienation is somewhat reminiscent of the North American experience, territorial percentages were low (e.g., Kenya: 7 per cent) but "best land" percentages were high (e.g., Kenya estimate: 30 per cent). Resentment of land alienation contributed to several outbreaks of violence, among them "Mau Mau." (c) Territorial money economies have been the most significant economic means of change. (Some African societies, e.g., the Ibibio of Nigeria, had developed rudimentary money economies before European occupation, but barter was more common and wealth was often in the form of cattle or communal land.) Introduced by Europeans to raise revenue, facilitate trade, develop cash crops, and regulate behavior,[11] territorial money economies have disrupted individual ways of life and traditional social systems, while imposing new controls. Individuals became more independent because their holdings could be converted to money and taken with them. Money became a new basis of power and respect, challenging tradition. Individuals were motivated to aggrandize and economize because of the benefits of wealth, they could engage in many impersonal transactions by using money, and they were exposed to the vicissitudes of territorial and world markets.

Some Africans have become very rich and somewhat independent. They now have automobiles and modern homes and work in air-conditioned offices. (Air-conditioning raises work potential exponentially and, moreover, has become an individual status symbol in Africa.) However, there are many subsistence farmers, herdsmen, fishermen, and hunters

[10] William John Hanna and Judith Lynne Hanna, "Leadership and Politics in the New Towns of Africa" (manuscript, 1964).

[11] An interesting discussion of colonial intentions appears in Kwame Nkrumah, *Africa Must Unite* (London: Heinemann, 1963), Chapter III.

who have hardly felt the impact of the new economic systems. The bonds of family and tradition remain strong for them. The reported situation in Kumasi, Ghana, applies throughout Black Africa: "The rich live very well indeed, but the poor are very poor."[12] The poor live at the subsistence level—or below.

NEW POLITICAL SYSTEMS

The Europeans enclosed many traditional political systems within the boundaries of a new territory, or split them between two or more territories, and established new central territorial political institutions. Two methods of rule were advocated by the Europeans. The British favored an "indirect" method in which traditional political systems were used as units of local administration and traditional leaders were used as links between the European rulers and the African masses. This contrasts with the "direct" method favored by the French and the Portuguese, which bypassed or repressed traditional political systems and leaders. The Belgians favored a mixture of the two methods. In practice, however, these differences were of slight degree rather than of kind. The traditional political systems could not be completely destroyed, because they were fused with ethnic groups. However, many traditional African leaders were to some extent bureaucratized (or deposed and replaced by "collaborators"), and new administrators representing the central authority were posted. Often, the chiefs who survived the upheaval were more agents of the new administration than spokesmen or rulers of their people.

Despite the new administrators and the attempts to co-opt traditional leaders, there was little depth to the new territorial systems. The new institutions formed a super-structure which sometimes channeled protest or in other ways had to be taken into consideration, but generally only passive acceptance of it was demanded and given. Few Africans became actively involved in the politics or administration of the territory or thought of all the people within its boundaries as "we." Most Africans retained their traditional political perspectives and were only active in village politics. Since the Second World War, important modifications in this pattern have begun to take place. But even in contemporary independent Black Africa, territorial politics are just beginning to penetrate meaningfully to the grass roots level.

DIVISIONS: OLD AND NEW

Most African countries have deep horizontal and vertical divisions. The horizontal divisions are the result of the enclosure of many ethnic

[12] Dennis Austin and William Tordoff, "Voting in an African Town," *Political Studies*, VIII (1960), 133.

groups within a territory. These divisions are a source of friction when historical rivalries exist or when the members of one kinship group domi-nate the political life of a new country.[13] Most vertical divisions have been caused by the uneven change which followed European occupation. To summarize these divisions—some of which overlap—it is useful to con-sider two polar "ideal types" of individuals who live in contemporary Black Africa: (a) The *modern man* has been introduced to a variety of new perspectives by European schools, travel, and modern communica-tions media. His style of life resembles the European's. He lives in a new town where he has developed a sense of autonomy, an ability to innovate, and new sources of security. Money has made him somewhat independent of his extended family and he has learned to economize. He takes part in modern territorial politics and understands the new ad-ministration. He has also been subjected to a new set of social, economic, and political controls. (b) The *traditional man* is oriented to subsistence. Whether a farmer, herdsman, fisherman, or hunter, his life is enveloped by his village or kin. His contacts with modernity have been limited to taxation, occasional administrative regulation, the use of some imported goods, the experience of having seen a European and an automobile, and the stories of relatives returned from a town. He may vote in an election, but the act is more social than political. His contacts with modernity have had little effect upon his style of life or world view.

Most of the new leaders of Africa are modern men, although this group constitutes a small fraction of the population in all the newly inde-pendent states. For the most part the African people lie between the ideal type of modern man and traditional man, although they are closer to the latter. They tend to be passive, marginal citizens of their new states rather than active participants. It should be added that there are few Africans who are completely modern, in the sense that tradition is completely excluded from their lives, or completely traditional, in the sense that modernity has not affected them. This means that they are likely to be cross-pressured by the two worlds of which they are a part, and, as a result, they have developed some insecurities. At the social level, they serve as links between the modern men and the tradi-tional men,[14] and they are, therefore, bases of unity and legitimacy for both the modern and the traditional.

[13] The contemporary role of ethnic groups is further discussed on pages 18–25.

[14] "They make up the social bridges between otherwise distinct and separated political subcommunities." The authors, Bernard R. Berelson, Paul F. Lazarsfeld, and William N. McPhee, were writing about a comparable group, cross-pressured voters in Elmira, New York. The quotation is from their *Voting: A Study of Opinion Formation in a Presidential Campaign* (Chicago: University of Chicago Press, 1954), p. 131.

REACTION TO CHANGE

The changes brought about by European occupation disturbed many Africans. New decisions, new conflicts, and new demands for innovation arose. A feeling of inferiority was caused by the obvious superiority of some aspects of European culture. Perhaps Africans experienced a "sense of humiliation upon realizing their own retarded position among the peoples of the world."[15] At the same time, the security of traditional life weakened. The search for security and equality first led some Africans to join together in voluntary associations. Later, it led to the quest for freedom in the form of territorial independence.

VOLUNTARY ASSOCIATIONS

Because change has been greatest in the new towns, they have been the setting for the formation of most voluntary associations. Tribal unions, alumni groups, and dancing societies are among the variety of associations which have helped to fulfill the need for the psychological and social security that family and village no longer provided and that the new territorial administrations have been unable or unwilling to provide. The most common basis of association has been kinship, because a way of meeting kinship obligations is provided and "attachment in terms of common language and culture gives comfort in the midst of a highly segmental intertribal field."[16] The voluntary associations have offered security to their members in a variety of ways. These may include medical and burial insurance financed by membership dues, scholarships, literacy classes, technical training, counseling, and dispute mediation.

Until World War II, there were few manifestly political voluntary associations. But even those which were non-political taught their members new values, alerted them to the potential of organization, and trained their leaders in administrative and agitational skills. Many contemporary African political leaders served apprenticeships as officers in voluntary associations, and several political parties grew out of one or more voluntary associations which became politicized with the emergence of nationalism. Today, however, many voluntary associations are either arms of a government, arms of a political party, or they are protective associations which seek preference only in law enforcement. Pressure groups similar to those found in European and Anglo-American states are still in their infancy in Black Africa.

[15] Margery Perham, "The Psychology of African Nationalism," this volume, p. 177.
[16] A. W. Southall, "Introductory Summary," in Southall (ed.), *Social Change in Modern Africa* (London: Oxford University Press, 1961), p. 2.

NATIONALISM

The concept "nationalism," as used with reference to Africa, has usefully been defined by Coleman. "Modern nationalism," he writes, "includes sentiments, activities, and organizational developments aimed explicitly at . . . self-government and independence . . . as a nation-state existing on a basis of equality in an international state system."[17] In this book attention is directed to modern political nationalism, but it should be recognized that earlier forms of political nationalism, as well as nationalism in other spheres, have been and are present in Black Africa. (A non-political nationalism in many ways similar to its political counterpart is *négritude,* an attempt by Africans to gain self respect and the respect of others in the cultural sphere.) The partial exclusion in this book of nationalisms other than modern political nationalism is the result of analytical focus, not the segmentation of African behavior.

Africans were rarely treated as equals or allowed to integrate with Europeans during the period of imperial rule. This forced, unequal treatment ("forced," in the sense that Europeans had the power to enforce it), within a setting of personal insecurity, rising aspirations, and some feeling of political efficacy, was the most important cause of African nationalism except for occupation and change themselves.[18] The qualification of personal insecurity is important because under such circumstances an individual is likely to seek precisely what a nationalist movement has to offer, namely, the strength that identification with a leader offers, the support that fellow members provide, the sense of purpose which a crusade affords, and the feeling of achievement gained from activity.[19] Rising aspirations are important because they are the bases for the realization of deprivation and then the desire to change the status quo. "Colonial nationalism," writes Emerson, "is far less a response to oppression or neglect than to the widened horizons opened up by progressive colonial governments."[20] Two of Lasswell's hypotheses provide

[17] James S. Coleman, *Nigeria: Background to Nationalism* (Berkeley: University of California Press, 1958), pp. 169–70.

[18] In a similar vein, Ivo K. Feierabend *et al.* developed indices of social frustration and political stability and concluded that "a relationship between these two variables . . . is ascertained in corroboration of the general hypothesis postulating high (low) want formation and low (high) want satisfaction as the condition of political instability (stability). "Correlates of Political Stability" (paper delivered at the 1963 Annual Meeting of The American Political Science Association), p. 14.

There is, it must be emphasized, no clear consensus on the contributing causes of nationalism or the rank order of the causes. See James S. Coleman, "Nationalism in Tropical Africa," this volume, *passim.*

[19] Cf. Sigmund Freud, *Group Psychology and the Analysis of the Ego* (London: Hogarth Press and the Institute of Psycho-Analysis, 1922), especially pp. 41–51 and 110–11.

[20] Emerson, *op. cit.,* p. 45.

a broader frame of analysis: "The power seeker . . . pursues power as a means of compensation against deprivation." "Compensation is favored when the deprivation is not overwhelming."[21] Finally, some sense of political efficacy is important because it makes political solutions possible.[22] If the only result of political action is increased deprivation, the most common response is withdrawal.[23]

Until fairly recently, most Africans had limited non-traditional aspirations and little feeling of efficacy in the territorial political system. As a result, acceptance of European occupation and inequality was widespread, either in the active "collaborationist" sense or in a more passive way.[24] (This passive acceptance has been attributed to a need to be dependent.) [25] Africans began to resent the enforced inferiority when they realized that Europeans were not even demigods and in many cases were less intelligent, less skilled, and less moral ("Christian") than they were.[26] The crucial lesson, according to Quaison-Sackey of Ghana, is "not only that the former colonial powers are not omnipotent, but, indeed, that they are not omniscient—that they are, in short, fallible or, in another sense, only human."[27] Perhaps the most profound indicators of inherent equality were the overseas experiences of African students and troops.

[21] Harold D. Lasswell, "Power and Personality," in Heinz Eulau, Samuel J. Eldersveld, and Morris Janowitz (eds.), *Political Behavior* (Glencoe: The Free Press, 1956), p. 98.

[22] Cf. Angus Campbell, Gerald Gurin, and Warren E. Miller, *The Voter Decides* (Evanston: Row, Peterson and Company, 1954), pp. 187–94.

[23] Cf. Morris Rosenberg, "Some Determinants of Political Apathy," *Public Opinion Quarterly*, XVIII (1954), 349–66.

[24] There have, of course, been instances of active opposition to the Europeans throughout the history of European-African contact.

Georges Balandier suggests the acceptance-opposition, active-passive dimensions of response in his "Contribution à une Sociologie de la Dépendance," *Cahiers Internationaux de Sociologie*, XII (1952), 47–69.

[25] A. Mannoni, *Psychologie de la Colonisation* (Paris: Ed. du Seuil, 1950).

[26] The developmental pattern of low aspirations and efficacy changing to resentment bears a suggestive resemblance to the pattern reported by Greenstein in another setting: favorable attitude towards authority and few interests outside the immediate circle changing to realism and cynicism. Fred I. Greenstein, "The Benevolent Leader: Children's Images of Political Authority," *American Political Science Review*, LIV (1960) 934–43. The resemblance may be due to the equivalent broadening of perspectives.

[27] Alex Quaison-Sackey, *Africa Unbound* (London: Andre Deutsch, 1963), p. 56. Similarly, Ndabaningi Sithole of Southern Rhodesia writes, "The emergence of nationalism, in many ways, represents the degree to which the white man's magic spell, which at the beginning of the nineteenth century had been cast on the African, is wearing off." *African Nationalism* (Cape Town: Oxford University Press, 1959), p. 156. And Ayo Ogunsheye asserts, "Before the African could come into his own, he had to break out of the shell in which others had sought to contain him; he had to destroy the stereotype idea of himself as an inferior being." "The African Personality: Ideology and Utopia" (paper presented to the International Symposium on African Culture, Ibadan, Nigeria: mimeographed, 1960), p. 1.

There they saw the "primitive" state in which some Europeans lived, how Europeans killed each other in "tribal" wars, and how some of their women could be purchased and dominated sexually. They also realized the underprivileged condition of Africans and learned the war's moral lesson: the domination of one country by another is wrong.

Had change been accompanied by equal opportunity and integration, African territories might now be autonomous parts of inter-continental Euroafrican communities. But even after some Africans learned the "secrets" of European power and wisdom by going to schools, churches, and even universities, their aspirations were frustrated because they continued to be treated as inferiors. The educated African was less respected than his European counterpart, the best jobs were not open to him, and his pay scale was relatively low.

The European appears to Africans to be guilty of turning them out of their lowly hut of contentment, or at least of unconsciousness, erecting at its doors the glittering house of his own civilization, and then forbidding him entry except to the kitchen and the workshop.[28]

Africans often write and talk about unequal treatment. A Kenyan asserts that in his country "there was a wholesale disregard for the human dignity and little respect for anyone with a black skin."[29] A Nigerian university student writes about "the damage done to the personality of the individual by the imperial master over several years of bondage and servitude."[30] And Nkrumah charges that "Europeans relegated us to the position of inferiors in every aspect of our everyday life," adding that the nationalist movement began only when Africans started to question that position.[31]

Early protests against the inferior status were made by intellectuals, especially the lawyers, journalists and teachers. It was they who felt the enforced inferiority most and therefore wanted equality most. At first, the protests were relatively defensive and apolitical. Next, there were voiced particular and more political demands for such satisfactions as entry into the civil service or consultative councils. Nationalism, the final stage of protest, emerged in most territories of Black Africa during or after the Second World War. It was the creation of aspiring modern African intellectuals who had risen as high as was possible in an imperial

---

[28] Perham, this volume, p. 182.
[29] Josiah Mwangi Kariuki, *"Mau Mau" Detainee* (London: Oxford University Press, 1963), p. 21. The author's objectivity has been questioned by some Kenyan observers.
[30] Obiajunwa Wali, "Lesson from Ghana," *The Beacon* (Easter, 1958), p. 2.
[31] Nkrumah, *op. cit.*, p. 32.

territory, who were developing the idea that equality could be achieved through the freedom that independence was to provide, and who were beginning to gain satisfaction from political activity. In a way, "the development of African nationalism is a progressive metamorphosis of what would be acceptable as an adequate expression of racial equality."[32] From a different vantage point, "A man who can improve his position one rung does not resent the man who starts on a different ladder half way up."[33] Modern African intellectuals believed that they were on the last rung permitted them and that they needed to be free to get to the top of the ladder.

The satisfactions intellectuals gained from political activity ranged from a feeling of accomplishment, to a sense of identity, to a release of tension. The cross-pressures upon the intellectuals, added to their concern with authority, made it relatively likely that they would seek political solutions and displace private tensions on to public objects.[34] As nationalist momentum developed, Nkrumah articulated the ever more popular belief, "Seek ye first the political kingdom and all things shall be added unto you."[35] Thus the final stage of protest was a direct attack upon imperial rule itself. Out went the cry for Free-Dom, for *Uhuru.*[36]

In its early stages, nationalism was the province of a few modern intellectuals. Many of their confreres were content with the status quo or lacked the necessary courage and energy. The masses, with few exceptions, continued passively to accept European rule. The mature stage of nationalism was reached when the active few, accused by the Europeans

[32] Ali A. Mazrui, "On the Concept of 'We Are All Africans,'" *American Political Science Review,* LVII (1963), 96.

[33] Robert E. Lane, "The Fear of Equality," *American Political Science Review,* LIII (1959), 50.

[34] Cf. Harold D. Lasswell, *op. cit.* Shils suggests, "extremist nationalism is often an unconscious expiation for guilt-generating but status-enhancing xenophilia." The relevance to intellectuals is clear. Edward Shils, "Intellectuals, Public Opinion, and Economic Development," this volume, p. 478.

[35] Kwame Nkrumah, *Ghana* (New York: Thomas Nelson and Sons, 1957), p. 163.

[36] In some parts of Africa, especially the Portuguese territories and South Africa, the search for a political kingdom was so unrealistic that it could not be acted upon. The slightest political activity was met with physical repression. Africans often coped with this situation by seeking the kingdom of heaven through fervent religious activity. (The parallel with the southern United States is apparent.) In what is now independent Black Africa, physical repression was infrequent; thus, an important barrier did not exist and nationalism could develop early and along non-violent lines. In general, the violence of nationalism varies with the degree of repression attempted, up to the point where repression turns energies into non-political channels. Thus Mau Mau could be viewed as "merely an extension of the deepest springs of African nationalism to which ordinary [i.e., non-violent] expression had been denied." Kariuki, *op. cit.,* p. 80.

of engaging in a hobby and representing only themselves, began a campaign to mobilize support for independence. The nationalist movements which emerged, usually led by a "political messiah" (movements and messiahs are discussed on pp. 29–32), strove to make the masses aware of their unequal position, to generate resentment, to instill self-confidence, and to gain the allegiance of the masses in the fight for independence. In Tanganyika, for example, Nyerere states that "the first task of the nationalist movement was to renew the self-confidence of a people who had old and bitter memories of ruthless suppression of revolt."[37] Nkrumah recommends a leadership policy which will eliminate the people's fears, voice their assumed unarticulated desires for freedom, give them a sense of self-confidence, and bring them actively into the nationalist movement.[38] The success of the mass campaigns was related to the satisfactions provided by a movement which offers meaning and organization to the insecure;[39] it signalled, in all the now independent states, that the most important battle was won and the transfer of sovereignty was only a matter of time.

External factors also contributed to the rise of nationalism. American Negroes began articulating slogans such as "Africa for the Africans" in the nineteenth century, and their organizational and ideological efforts have had an impact upon African conferences and nationalist movements. Other outside voices were, before World War II, effectively kept out of Black Africa by imperial insulation. President Woodrow Wilson's call for self-determination, and the demands of some socialists in the Soviet Union and elsewhere, had little effect—and seemed to have little applicability—in Black Africa. This situation changed dramatically during and after World War II. Most Allied leaders articulated the principle of self-determination, and Africa, because of idealism or the need for war support, was occasionally included. Wartime defeats of the British and French indicated relevant weaknesses. In the post-war period, inspiration for Black Africa was provided by the 1947 independence of India, the 1956 failure of the Anglo-French attack upon Egypt, and the 1957 independence of Ghana. In general, the more territories that obtained independence, and the more the signs of imperial weakness, the greater the pressure for independence in the remaining territories. Finally, the United Nations must be mentioned. Spearheaded by members from the Soviet Bloc, Africa, and Asia, the organization has, with increasing vigor,

[37] Julius K. Nyerere, "A United States of Africa," *Journal of Modern African Studies,* I (1963), 9.

[38] Nkrumah, *Africa Must Unite,* p. 50.

[39] It is useful to compare the African nationalist movement with other ideological and mobilizational movements. See, for example, Gabriel A. Almond, *The Appeals of Communism* (Princeton: Princeton University Press, 1954), especially Chapter 10.

backed the application of the principle of self-determination to non-white territories throughout the world.

The pace and character of nationalism have varied considerably throughout Black Africa. Ghana achieved independence with relative quiet in 1957 after a long period of nationalist activity; three years later, after a relatively short period of nationalist activity, the independence of Congo (Leopoldville) triggered violence throughout the new state; and a violent nationalist battle is just beginning in the Republic of South Africa, the Portuguese colonies, and Southern Rhodesia. Much of this variation probably depends upon the prospects for the future articulated by the imperial rulers and the number of non-Africans resident in the territories. Other differences, such as education and political license, are largely derivative.

European policy underwent many changes, the last usually being active support of independence. However, it was the prospects for the future articulated by Europeans during the earlier periods of imperial rule, and the implicit corollary racial attitudes (a partial reflection of class attitudes in the metropole), which tended to channel the hopes and energies of Africans. Formally, French policy was "assimilationist," i.e., Africans were to be "civilized" and then integrated with Europeans as equals within a Euroafrican union. (There is also an implicit corollary of cultural inequality in French policy, which probably explains the later cultural assertion of French-speaking Africans.) In 1792, for example, a decree was issued which stated that "all men, without distinction of color, domiciled in French colonies, are French citizens, and enjoy all the rights assured by the Constitution." The Senegalese voted for a French deputy more than one hundred years ago, and in 1946 Leopold Senghor was the official grammarian of the French Constitutional Convention. There were also many infrastructural links between France and her African territories. In practice, however, assimilation was only applied in the old *communes* of Senegal, and it was later formally abandoned (except in the *communes*) in favor of the former *de facto* policy of "association," in which an educated African middle class assigned to subaltern positions was created to bridge the gap between the European rulers and the African masses. Association, it should be emphasized, did not mean self-government. Even in the post-war Fourth Republic, all French political groups "firmly rejected African self-government or independence as a legitimate end of policy."[40]

British policy, on the other hand, was designed to keep the African

[40] Thomas Hodgkin and Ruth Schachter [Morgenthau], "French-Speaking West Africa in Transition," *International Conciliation*, No. 528 (May 1960), p. 389.

territories and the metropole separate, but to work slowly towards self-government in some distant future. As with the French, there was a group to act as a bridge, but the British differed by using more traditional leaders in this role. The racial implication of British policy was inherent difference, not inherent equality.[41] The Belgians, until shortly before the independence of the Congo, did not have plans to relinquish their African territories, and the Portuguese probably still do not have such plans. Both had policies similar to assimilation, but, with the exception of early Portuguese miscegenation, they were implemented even less honestly than in the French territories. (Less than one per cent of the Africans in Angola and Mozambique have become *assimilados*.) It appears that assimilation focused attention outward and made it possible to hope for equality, whereas separation focused attention inward and made nationalism the only hope for equality. During the middle 1950's, when English-speaking West Africans were gaining independence and English-speaking East Africans were dreaming of or agitating for it, most inhabitants of the French territories (with the exception of Guinea) seemed content to remain within a Euroafrican community. As late as 1957, Houphouet-Boigny, now President of the Ivory Coast, could reject independence in favor of "equality and fraternity" within the French community.[42]

There was considerable variation in the number of non-Africans resident in the territories of Black Africa. The areas most attractive to immigrants had economic opportunities and moderate climates. Starting with the territory having the most non-Africans, the first six ranked in 1960 as follows:

Republic of South Africa	32%
Southern Rhodesia	8
Kenya	4
Northern Rhodesia	3
Angola	2
Mozambique	2

The policy of *apartheid* in the Republic of South Africa, the repressive European rule in Southern Rhodesia, Angola, and Mozambique, and the difficult fights for independence which are now being won in Kenya and

[41] It should be recalled that British policy at home was long based upon a similar social image. Striking parallels can be found in the overseas and domestic policies of all imperial countries.

[42] Felix Houphouet-Boigny, "Black Africa and the French Union," *Foreign Affairs*, XXXV (1957), 579.

Northern Rhodesia indicate a close association between the number of non-Africans, on the one hand, and the repression of Africans (accompanied by low aspirations and little sense of political efficacy) and the character of nationalism, on the other. In some of the territories with few non-Africans, African political activity, newspapers, and university educations were to some extent tolerated, and these were the territories in which the earliest nationalist movements arose. This can be explained in several ways. First, the non-Africans constitute the power and wealth elites. The more non-Africans, the more people who have vested interests which are threatened by the prospect of African rule. Second, the only claim to superiority that some non-Africans have is race. If equal access to values is permitted, this claim is nullified and they will be surpassed by those Africans who are more intelligent, more skillful, and so on.[43] Third, many of the non-Africans who came to the continent were misfits in their own societies (why leave a country where you are happy and successful?) who sought deference from the "inferior" Africans. When the needed deference is threatened, vigorous attempts to retain it are likely.

The fight for independence in Black Africa was, with few exceptions, non-violent. The transfer of sovereignty was smooth to the point of being uneventful. The first Black African territory to win independence was Ghana,[44] and since that eventful day in 1957 more than a score of territories in Black Africa have become independent. By the time this book is published, Kenya will be independent. The collapse of the Federation of Rhodesia and Nyasaland means that Malawi and Zambia will soon be on the map. The end of European occupation in southern Africa will raise the number of independent countries in Black Africa to over thirty.

CONTINUITY IN CHANGE

Despite the giant forces of change, a link between the Africa before European occupation and the Africa of today exists through the many elements of traditional life which have either had the vitality to resist change or have been maintained or revived by Africans concerned with their heritage. This continuity usually exists in modification, either of function or of structure. In general the new leaders of Black Africa are

[43] These first two explanations also apply to white-Negro relations in the United States.

[44] Of his independence day, one Ghanaian writes: "I felt that I had suddenly become a different person, that I had broken free from some shell or casing that had been preventing me from growing to full stature." Quaison-Sackey, *op. cit.*, p. 6.

Throughout Black Africa, traditional continuity means contemporary cultural duality. Both primary and secondary structures are present.[51] Barnard[52] and others have shown that both levels of a dual culture can be functional to a social organization. However, there are aspects of tradition which can threaten the stability—perhaps the very existence —of the new states of Black Africa. There is, for example, a danger involved in selective incorporation. Internally, a spillover effect may result from incorporating some traditional elements and inadvertently strengthening others. A traditional leader who is given a position in the territorial government may contribute more to ethnic identifications than to territorial identifications. Externally, since the new leaders may appear "primitive" to outsiders for having employed traditional symbols or rituals, they undermine their attempts to prove equality. When Nkrumah poured a libation several years ago, it was reported in the world press in denigrating terms. Perhaps the greatest danger of traditional continuity to state stability comes from identifications with kinship groups. In traditional African societies kinship was the nucleus of the social structure and the primary basis of identification. Other than the fact that kinship groups are being transformed into ethnic groups (in the sense that the importance of common culture for mutual identification is increasing), the same can be said today for many Africans and for many parts of Africa. This can be dysfunctional to the building of a territorial political community and therefore to the stability of the new states.

Identification with one's own ethnic group is a universal phenomenon; it is operative with the Irish of Boston, the Bagisu of Eastern Uganda and the French, Italians, and Germans of the emergent European Union. These identifications can be compatible with the interests of the state as a whole, but if they are predominant and not usefully channeled, they are probably dysfunctional to the community and the state. The situation becomes especially serious in a new state with fragile authority and identity.

Recognizing the dangers of these sub-territorial identifications in a new state, the new leaders of Africa almost universally condemn "tribalism" and "clannism." Many African conferences devote time to the denigration of tribalism. And African newspapers have attacked these

[51] Almond convincingly calls attention to the cultural duality of all contemporary political systems. See his "Introduction: A Functional Approach to Comparative Politics" in Almond and Coleman, *op. cit.*, pp. 20–23, *et passim*.

[52] Chester I. Barnard, *The Functions of the Executive* (Cambridge: Harvard University Press, 1938).

identifications in no uncertain terms, as these recent headlines suggest:

"NO UNITY WHILE TRIBALISM LIVES"
"OUR TRIBALISTIC INSTINCTS STINK TO HIGH HEAVEN"

(Of course Africans, like non-Africans, are sometimes prone to practice other than what they preach.) But despite the general condemnation, predominant identification with one's own ethnic group, accompanied by hostility to outgroups, appears to have increased in some African states since independence. The cause of this increase is probably the loss of a common enemy.[53] When Africans "find themselves associated with other Africans of different tribes in opposition to Europeans, they express their unity in racial terms and ignore the tribal differences." But "when Africans find themselves associated with fellow tribesmen in opposition to other groups they express their unity in tribal terms."[54]

There are a number of specific ways in which ethnic identifications can be dysfunctional to the new African state. First, ethnic identifications often create cross-pressures in governmental decision-making. They can be

a constant threat to the civil service norm of disinterestedness. The wide extension of kinship bonds means that a chief [or any other official] is frequently put into the position of having to choose between his obligations to favor particular kinsmen and his official duty to act disinterestedly.[55]

Put differently, "family and tribal loyalties . . . obscure . . . devotion to the national community."[56] The problem is intensified because in most African societies the powerful and wealthy members of an ethnic group are expected to provide for the less fortunate. A successful political candidate, for example, is

regarded by many of his constituents [frequently his kinsmen] as an investment, and he will be asked for jobs or scholarships or for help in local disputes often far beyond his capacity to satisfy all those who, having helped him to become an Assembly member, now expect something in return.[57]

[53] Current attempts to create new common enemies are noted on page 37.
[54] Michael Banton, "Race Relations in . . . Africa South of the Sahara," *International Social Science Bulletin*, XIII (1961), 209. The phenomenon is, of course, universal.
[55] Lloyd Fallers, "The Predicament of the Modern African Chief: An Instance from Uganda," this volume, p. 291.
[56] M. McMullan, "A Theory of Corruption," this volume, p. 501.
[57] Dennis Austin, "Elections in an African Rural Area," this volume, p. 359. See also Hanna and Hanna, *op. cit.*

As a result of these demands, government and party officials often give jobs to members of their ethnic groups without considering merit, and many are forced to accumulate wealth illegally to provide the money demanded of them for school fees, living expenses, business or pleasure.

Another aspect of the problem of cross-pressures is the effect they have upon a decision-maker. It has been argued, for example, that the cross-pressures of the traditional (including ethnic identifications) and the modern increase the likelihood of personality disorders. Recent evidence suggests, however, that personality disorders are not significantly high in Africa, despite the manifest cross-pressures. One psychiatric study, comparing a town and rural area in North America with a town and rural area in Nigeria, reports that "the similarity in the two samples is much more impressive than the differences. In view of the contrast between the cultures and life situations, this is truly remarkable."[58] There is little research in the area of cross-cultural intra-personal conflict resolution. But at least two fruitful areas for research may be indicated. One is the relationship between the need for intra-personal conflict resolution and the development of social institutions, such as nationalist movements. A second is the compartmentalization of potential conflicts, such as by being a Christian on Sunday morning and a "pagan" the rest of the week (another solution: creating a "new" religion).

Second, identifications with ethnic groups are often decisive in determining allegiance within the political system of the new state. In Black Africa, as in the United States, "The family is a key reference group which transmits, indoctrinates, and sustains the political loyalties of its members."[59] But in Africa the adult relies more on the ethnic group for identity; therefore deviance is more threatening or meaningful. One observer comments that "to some extent most people continue to relate themselves to political parties through a 'screen of kinship.' "[60] From another perspective, a Kenyan reports that most of his country's leaders depend for their political strength "on their acceptance by their own tribe."[61] One of the manifestations of this phenomenon is ethnic community solidarity in political campaigns.

The decision to support a candidate in a competitive election campaign is often made communally, and all members of the community are expected to adhere to the decision. Deviation may be considered

[58] Alexander H. Leighton *et al., Psychiatric Disorders Among the Yoruba* (Ithaca: Cornell University Press, 1963), p. 274.

[59] Herbert McClosky and Harold E. Dahlgren, "Primary Group Influence on Party Loyalty," *American Political Science Review*, LIII (1959), 775.

[60] Ruth Schachter Morgenthau, "Single-Party Systems in West Africa," this volume, p. 429.

[61] Kariuki, *op. cit.*, pp. 165–66.

an act of rejection. A report on the 1959 Nigerian federal election states, "for a man to support a political party different from the one supported by the rest of the community amounted almost to a repudiation of his own people."[62] This is the principal reason why a majority of the competitive political campaigns in Black Africa feature ethnic appeals. The report of the Nigerian federal election is again relevant: "when the local opinion leaders came to interpret political issues to the electors in their communities the simplest language they could use, and therefore the one most often used, was that of 'tribe.' "[63] Even higher education may have but slight effect upon this phenomenon, as this University of Ibadan student editorial indicates:

> *The events surrounding the last student presidential elections are, to say the least, most distressing. We were treated to a most shameless display of tribalism and sectionalism . . . if as the "undergrads" of Nigeria's only University, we cannot grow out of tribal loyalties and petty tribal prejudices, then there is very little reason for optimism in the New Nigeria of our dreams.*[64]

Third, identification with an ethnic group can compete totally with identification to the new state. This is the basis of separatist movements which have arisen in Kenya, Congo (Leopoldville), and elsewhere in Black Africa. The recent history of the Bakongo is illustrative. These people are located in Congo (Leopoldville), Congo (Brazzaville), Angola, and Cabinda, having been divided by European boundary-makers. The concern of the Bakongo about this division grew with their increasing awareness of the boundaries and their meaning. Believing that a modern Kongo state encompassing the area once controlled by the pre-European Kongo empire would solve their problems, several members of a Bakongo cultural organization proposed to the Belgian government in 1959 that such a state be established. The proposal was turned down. Then in June, 1960, thirty-two members of the Provincial Assembly who were in the cultural organization formed a "government" of the Republic of Central Kongo.[65] Although the government was dissolved in a matter of hours, this incident vividly illustrates the possible incompatability between ethnic and state identifications.

There are, however, some ways in which having a predominant identification with one's ethnic group may be functional to the new state.

[62] K. W. J. Post, "The Individual and the Community and the Communities and the Political System," this volume, p. 337.

[63] *Ibid.*, pp. 336–37.

[64] "Looking Back in Anger," *The Beacon*, I (March, 1960), 2.

[65] René Lemarchand, "The Bases of Nationalism among the Bakongo," *Africa*, XXXI (1961), 348.

The first of these is the enlarging of identifications.[66] The identification of an individual with his ethnic group may be considerably broader (i.e., include many more people) than all his previous identifications, which were probably at the lineage or village level. The Ibo people of Eastern Nigeria illustrate this phenomenon. Before European occupation, "we" was primarily at the lineage or village level, but their "we" now can include approximately ten million people. This extension may be a useful step on the way to identification with all Nigeria. The second way in which ethnic identifications may be functional to the state is as the basis of voluntary associations. These associations serve to facilitate the transition between village and town life and to improve the lot of relatives at home.[67] Finally, ethnic identifications buffer class and status differences by turning attention elsewhere. For example, rival clans or tribes can absorb projections and aggressions which might otherwise be directed toward government offices; the fragile state may be protected when office-holders are attacked only as members of an ethnic group. Of course, state-protective rivalry among ethnic groups can go too far, as the genocidal activities of the Bahutu of Rwanda against their Watutsi countrymen illustrates. Throughout Black Africa, there are minorities that fear, if not genocide, at least second-class citizenship.[68]

FORGING TERRITORIAL UNITY

Soon after the new leaders of Black Africa assumed power, they embarked upon programs of forging unity. The main elements of their programs (a political messiah, a mobilization movement, and a centripetal government) varied considerably from the European democratic model which they had inherited at independence and which the Europeans hoped would develop firm roots in the African soil. Yet a program of forging unity seems to be a natural outgrowth of the problems which faced the new states upon independence and the interests of their new African leaders.

PROBLEMS

Many of the problems facing the new African leaders have already been considered. Restated, the most important of these are (a) uneven change and ethnic identifications which have created deep social divi-

[66] Cf. Richard L. Sklar, "The Contribution of Tribalism to Nationalism in Western Nigeria," *Journal of Human Relations*, VIII (1960), 407–18.

[67] See Immanuel Wallerstein, "Ethnicity and National Integration," *Cahiers d'Etudes Africaines*, II (1960), 129–39.

[68] Cf. *Nigeria: Report of the Commission Appointed to Enquire into the Fears of Minorities and the Means of Allaying Them*, Cmnd. 505 (London: H.M.S.O., 1958).

sions, and (b) insecurities, rising aspirations, and feelings of political efficacy which have channeled demands toward new and as yet fragile states. There is yet another important problem, implied throughout the discussion of change, and that is underdevelopment. The independent states of Black Africa have low per capita gross national products and energy consumption rates, and relatively few town dwellers, literates, school children, doctors, vehicles, telephones, radios, and newspapers.[69] In general the people of Black Africa are relatively isolated, yet they must cope with the insecurities of a rapidly changing society. In the political arena, they tend to seek simple and sure solutions. "The less sophisticated and stable the individual," writes Lipset, "the more likely he is to favor a simplified view of politics, to fail to understand the rationale underlying tolerance of those with whom he disagrees, and to find difficulty in grasping or tolerating a gradualist image of political change."[70]

In an underdeveloped country there are also insufficient personnel and resources to provide for decentralized or autonomous centers of responsibility and power. This means, first, that a balance of power, which often "forces" a political system into the democratic mold because a concentration of power is unacceptable to any of the participant groups, is unlikely to develop. And second, it means that the ruling leaders must take it upon themselves to perform functions which, in more developed countries, are performed by others. In other words, "a new country, where there is strong national but limited local leadership and vigour, cannot afford to gamble. . . . A new country needs to initiate central nation-wide planning."[71]

Change from underdevelopment towards development has, throughout history, been marked by great social stress and strain. Because of the rapid timetable which has been prescribed by the new leaders (see below), the stress and strain in Black Africa has been especially acute. To hold the new states together, numerous control mechanisms are needed. To forge the greater unity that is demanded, even more of these mechanisms are necessary.

INTERESTS OF THE LEADERS

A number of the interests of African leaders have previously been indicated. These include improving the standard of African life, gaining respect, and proving to themselves and others that Africans are

---

[69] "Appendix," in Almond and Coleman, *op. cit.*, pp. 579–81.

[70] Seymour Martin Lipset, "Working-class Authoritarianism," *Political Man* (New York: Doubleday and Company, 1959), p. 115.

[71] Nkrumah, *Africa Must Unite*, p. 64.

not inferior.[72] In addition, the new leaders of Africa want to remain in power and they want to effect changes rapidly.

The new African leaders do not want to create a political system in which they can be voted out of office. This can be attributed to their charismatic self-image (see below), their sometimes disdainful view of the political judgment of the masses, and their vested interests in power. The leaders' disdain is a product of the gap between their modern style of life and world view, and the masses' traditional style and view. The political consequence of the decision is that, as Lipset hypothesizes, "the upper strata also tend to regard political rights for the lower strata, particularly the right to share in power, as essentially absurd and immoral."[73] This is similar to the view Europeans long held about all Africans. University students in Africa also tend toward this view, and as a result are "skeptical about the possibility or the advisability of democracy, at least in its parliamentary form," preferring a political system with "dynamic centralized leadership and a socialist state."[74]

The new African leaders also have vested interests in their positions of power. Vested interests are likely to be intense in societies where the difference between being "in" and "out" is great. African leaders now have the satisfactions and perquisites of power, including a sense of accomplishment and luxurious living. Out of office, all of this might be lost. Some observers interpret the leaders' efforts to retain power as confirmation of the charge Europeans made before independence, namely, African nationalist leaders are primarily interested in themselves. Another possibility is that the model of European behavior is still meaningful, for it was the Europeans who first fed their self-esteem and lived luxuriously in Africa. And Pye suggests that the "new countries are trying to be built upon the myth that if each strives to get ahead in government and politics, the public good will be served."[75]

"I am impatient," writes Nkrumah.[76] "In three or four years," Sekou

---

[72] Nyasaland, for example, "is currently placing first priority on instilling the vigor of self-respect into the minds of a people long accustomed to alien government." Robert I. Rotberg, "Malawi 1963," *Africa Report*, VIII (January, 1963), 7. At another level, Pye concludes that "fears of failure in the adventure of nation-building create deep anxieties." Lucian W. Pye, *Politics, Personality, and Nation Building: Burma's Search for Identity* (New Haven: Yale University Press, 1962), p. xv.

[73] Seymour Martin Lipset, "Some Social Requisites of Democracy: Economic Development and Political Legitimacy," *American Political Science Review*, LIII (1959), pp. 83–4.

[74] William John Hanna, "Students," in James S. Coleman and Carl G. Rosberg, eds., *Parties and Integration in Tropical Africa* (Berkeley: University of California Press, 1964).

[75] Pye, *op. cit.*, p. 3.

[76] *Africa Must Unite*, p. 83.

Touré asserts, "no one should remember the tribal, ethnic, and religious rivalries which, in the recent past, have done so much harm to our country and its people."[77] The new leaders of Africa want, within a few short years, to raise the standards of living and prove that they and their countries are equal to others in the world. They believe that to do this unity must rapidly be forged. The emphasis is upon mobilization and regimentation. Some political practices valued in Anglo-American countries are considered at best luxuries and at worst not applicable to Black Africa. Nevertheless, the political systems of the metropoles remain standards to be met or rationalized away. Thus, the policy of forging unity is said to be an emergency measure. Nkrumah, in his autobiography, writes, "A system based on social justice and a democratic constitution may need backing up, during the period following independence, by emergency measures of a totalitarian kind. Without discipline freedom cannot survive."[78]

THE PROGRAM

Faced with similar problems and having similar interests, the new leaders of Black Africa have embarked upon similar programs. They believe that "singleness of purpose, unity of action, undivided loyalty, a sense of participation, and a feeling of oneness among the masses are absolutely essential to the success and stability of a young government."[79] Designed to meet an emergency, the major elements of the program are similar to those used during emergencies in other parts of the world. The style of the program is aggressive, both because forging unity demands it and because threatening feelings of doubt need to be overcome. (English-speaking African leaders have been more politically aggressive partly because British imperial policy was more manifestly founded upon the assumption of inequality.) The program has been somewhat successful for many of the reasons that the nationalist movement was successful.

The three major elements of the program to forge unity had their heritage in the pre-independence period. The political messiah and the mobilization movement (in the form of the nationalist movement) had been used to win independence, and the centripetal government was developed by the imperial administration to facilitate rule by a few

[77] Sekou Touré, *Toward Full Re-Africanisation* (Paris: Présence Africaine, 1959), p. 98.
[78] *Ghana*, p. xvi.
[79] D. K. Chisiza, "The Outlook for Contemporary Africa," *Journal of Modern African Studies*, I (1963), 28. Put differently, they believe that the "participation and distribution capabilities" must be fused with the "integration and mobilization capability." Gabriel A. Almond, "Political Systems and Political Change," *American Behavioral Scientist*, VI (1963), 9.

representatives of the metropole.[80] However, the situation after independence was in some respects more difficult: there was no common enemy to unite the people in opposition, counter-elites arose to vie for the power that was now seen as immediate and obtainable, the legitimacy of the new government and its policies was not fully established, and it was the task of the new leaders of Africa to solve the problems facing their countries.

THE POLITICAL MESSIAH

Sékou Touré of Guinea, Kwame Nkrumah of Ghana, Kamuzu Banda of Nyasaland, and Jomo Kenyatta of Kenya are typical of Black Africa's political messiahs. To many, they are heroic, instilling in their followers a sense of mission, and sacred, appearing to be God-sent leaders. Having gained independence against odds which, a generation before, appeared insurmountable, they seem omniscient and omnipotent. They are sincerely dedicated to their mission;[81] their values are universal. They are *the* man and Everyman.[82]

The new African leaders are not unaware of the need for a political messiah. A single leader can penetrate the cognitive communications barrier with universally understood emotions and draw the population towards himself as a symbol of unity and security. "The lonely individual in transition," writes Davies, "becomes prey to the demagogue who promises simple solutions to complex problems and a vicarious, often spurious affection, and who imparts a sense of social solidarity to replace the comforts of family life in the village of the lonely one's childhood."[83] The correspondence between Mr. Chipembere and Dr. Banda, now Treasurer and President, respectively, of the Malawi Congress Party, is probably representative of the thinking of other leaders throughout Black Africa.

What was needed was a kind of savior: although it is wrong to be led by a single man placed in a powerful position, still "human nature" is such that it needs a kind of hero to be hero-worshipped if a political struggle is to succeed.[84]

---

[80] Busia, *op. cit.*, Chapter V, suggests that the development of centripetal governments has been encouraged by foreign businessmen trying to create stability so that their investments would be safer.

[81] Cf. Ernst Kris, "Some Problems of War Propaganda," *The Psychoanalytic Quarterly*, XII (1943), 381–99.

[82] Cf. S. Freud, *op. cit.*

[83] James C. Davies, *Human Nature in Politics* (New York: John Wiley and Sons, 1963), p. 99.

[84] Reported in *Cmnd. 814* (London: H.M.S.O., 1959), as quoted in Thomas Hodgkin, *African Political Parties* (Middlesex: Penguin, 1961), p. 137.

Today, Dr. Banda's picture appears on the front page of almost every issue of the country's national newspaper and he is written about in god-like terms.

Political messiahs are glorified throughout Black Africa. Houphouet-Boigny lives in a new multi-million dollar home that towers over the swank residential area of Abidjan. Tubman is building an equally expensive palace. In many ways the political messiahs are surrounded with pomp. Nyerere's recent order to "stamp out the disease of pomposity" is a rare exception to the rule.

The political messiah was not simply manipulated into being. Roots can be found in the traditional societies, the impact of change, and the success of the nationalist movements. (a) "Despite the obvious divergences between the traditional culture of the mass and the modern culture of the educated," the two share "an image of the concentration of charisma in those who rule the nation."[85] Chiefs were often considered intermediaries between God and the people; the political messiahs have in part inherited this position. In addition, the latter are "legitimized in their own eyes by their permeation with *the sacredness of the nation.*"[86] (b) When traditional ties are attenuated and a need for new psychological security develops, satisfaction is often provided by an omnipotent and omniscient father-surrogate in the form of a political messiah. (c) Political messiahs are, in a sense, saviours. Much of the credit for returning Black Africa to independence must be given to such men as Touré, Nkrumah, Banda, and Kenyatta. It is likely that messianism feeds on success, especially when the success has been achieved in the face of danger. Danger that is not overwhelming also tends to act as a coalescent for the masses and make mass persuasion easier to accomplish.[87]

THE MOBILIZATION MOVEMENT

Most countries in Black Africa are one-party states or are competitive but have no opposition parties with a real chance to win a national election. Leaders of the few politically competitive countries, such as Nigeria and Uganda, are at this writing proposing one-party or united front systems. Some of these "parties" are little more than associations among notables, but the more common pattern is an organization designed to mobilize (and therefore possibly *not* to represent) the population at large in support of the goals of the leaders. It is therefore conceptually useful to refer to these "parties" as "mobilization movements."

[85] Edward Shils, "The Concentration and Dispersion of Charisma: Their Bearing on Economic Policy in Underdeveloped Countries," this volume, p. 390.

[86] *Ibid.* Cf. David Apter, *Ghana in Transition* (New York: Atheneum, 1963).

[87] Cf. Robert K. Merton, *Mass Persuasion: The Social Psychology of a War Bond Drive* (New York: Harper and Brothers, 1946).

The unity of these movements, it should be noted, appears greater from the outside than from within. Internal factionalism is present in these movements, just as it is present in almost all contemporary political parties. Sometimes, the pattern of factionalism approximates, at the leadership level, the pattern of competition in a two-party system.[88] But from outside, the mobilization movement often appears monolithic.

Many movements, outgrowths of unified nationalist movements have been maintained and strengthened in the interest of forging unity. As Emerson observes, "it is in general more realistic to see the trend toward the authoritarian one-party system as deriving from the lack of national unity rather than as the expression of it."[89] The wide support given to these mobilization movements is partly due to the satisfactions of nationalist activity and the involvement in a new unity, previously discussed. Additional factors include the service activities of the movements, their patriotic images, and their control of wealth and power.

The service activities of some movements bear a striking resemblance to those of the political machines in urban America during the years of large immigration, although the movements have less per capita funds available than did the machines. (The Africans uprooted by change are in many ways similar to the immigrant Europeans in America.) The machines were, and the movements try to be, involved in the life of the people from the cradle to the grave, as well as being concerned with explicitly political matters. In Guinea, for example, the Parti Démocratique de Guinée "has become a dominating influence at virtually every level of human activity."[90] The situation in Guinea is extreme, but it represents the developmental pattern. In many African countries, the mobilization movements give bonuses to parents with twins or triplets, sponsor traditional dance festivals, mediate occupational disputes, donate money to waking ceremonies, and so forth.

Supporting the movement is often the equivalent of supporting the state, and opposition is considered unpatriotic. "Unity is the demand of the hour—and cooperation. Join the party and the nation can be free and prosperous. A house divided cannot stand."[91] Supporting the move-

---

[88] For the report of a comparable pattern in a one-party system, see Malcolm B. Parsons, "Quasi-Partisan Conflict in a One-Party Legislative System: The Florida Senate, 1947–1961," *American Political Science Review*, LVI (1962).

[89] Rupert Emerson, "Political Modernization: The Single-Party System" (paper presented to the Seminar in the Problems of the Emerging Nations, Aspen, Colorado: Mimeographed, 1963), pp. 24–5.

[90] L. Gray Cowan, "Guinea," in Gwendolen M. Carter (ed.), *African One-Party States* (Ithaca: Cornell University Press, 1962), p. 177.

[91] David Apter, "Some Reflections on the Role of a Political Opposition in New Nations," this volume, p. 459.

ment is also a way of giving thanks to the political messiah. To the question, "Why do you support the party?" a frequent reply is, "Because [the political messiah] brought us independence." Support of the movement is also linked to the legitimacy which it carries over from its successful fight for independence. One consequence of these factors is that, although elections continue to be held in all African countries, legitimation of the state and symbolic identification with the government, movement, or ethnic group may be their primary functions.

Through the government, the mobilization movement rewards strong supporters with wealth and power. Included are directorships on boards of government corporations (which have high salaries and provide the opportunity for "commissions" in return for favors), import licenses, and government contracts (even though the movement supporter's bids may be relatively high.) Continued loyalty and large donations to the movement, perhaps as a percentage of rewarded salaries or profits, are the repayments demanded.[92] Thus business "created new interests and relationships, new allegiances and obligations. It helped to bind together the major parties more closely, to attract to them the support of people who hoped thus to advance their business careers."[93]

The movement also controls advancement in the civil service. Civil servants are often elevated as much for political loyalty as for formal job efficiency. What has been said about opposition politicians applies equally to civil servants favoring the opposition: "the deprivation involved in their exclusion from a share of the power and opportunities that are afforded the governing group provides them with a powerful incentive to unity."[94] Yet Madeira Keita is probably right in stating that "the system of the unified party calls upon the leaders for greater honesty, greater disinterestedness, greater devotion,"[95] because there is no legal opposition to question decisions and propose alternatives.

THE CENTRIPETAL GOVERNMENT

Because the personnel and functions of the movement and the government have a relatively high degree of overlap and interchangeability in most countries of Black Africa, and both are arms of the new leaders, much of what has been said about the former applies to the latter. However, several characteristics of the government deserve special examination: politicization and the concentration of power in the government, and the adoption of "African socialism."

[92] Hanna and Hanna, op. cit.
[93] K. W. J. Post, "The Use of Power," this volume, p. 451.
[94] Gwendolen M. Carter, "Introduction," in Carter, op. cit., p. 8.
[95] "The Single Party in Africa," Présence Africaine, II, No. 30 (1960), 37.

Power is concentrated in the executive branch of African governments and all other branches are drawn towards this center. Government
is politicized and partisan. Nyerere writes, "The system of 'checks and
balances' is an admirable way of applying the brakes to social change.
Our need is not for brakes. . . . We need accelerators."[96] (Countervailing
power exists but its pattern is different than in the United States.) The
legislature debates and passes laws, but it almost invariably "rubber
stamps" decisions that have been made earlier by the executive. In
Liberia, for example, informants could not identify "one significant
measure which had emerged from the Legislature without presidential
approval" or "any major legislation which failed despite concerted and
sustained support from the Executive Mansion."[97] The primary functions
of the legislature are legitimation of executive decisions and communication. Some public opinion is brought to the attention of the executive
in debates and the public is informed of current decisions when the
legislators return to their constituencies. The *judiciary* of a few countries
is independent, but the more common pattern is for it to reflect and
legitimize the positions of the executive. The judiciary of Guinea, for
example, "is not regarded as independent; on the contrary, party officials
are encouraged publicly to denounce judges who fail to follow the party
line."[98] Thus it is usually futile to take an action against the government
to court, but the African leaders need not fear judicial derailment of
their programs. The *civil service* is not neutral because there is no
effective opposition to make it so (civil servants need not fear that the
opposition political party will win the next election) and because appointments are often based upon the spoils system. It should be noted
that a spoils system can add useful strength to a newly established
political party.[99] *Community development organizations,* widely employed for the purpose of social mobilization, are directed from the
center and often their duties include political socialization. In some
parts of Black Africa they provide one of the few links between the
village peasant and the territorial political system. The *police* are also
prone to favoritism. For example, party thugs may be allowed to do

[96] Julius K. Nyerere, "How Much Power for a Leader," *The Observer* (London), reprinted in *Africa Report,* VII (1962), 5. In a similar vein, Joseph LaPalombara writes, "A bureaucracy heavily encumbered by Weberian-derived norms may
for that reason be a less efficacious instrument of economic change." "An Overview
of Bureaucracy and Political Development," in LaPalombara (ed.), *Bureaucracy and
Political Development* (Princeton: Princeton University Press, 1963), p. 12.

[97] J. Gus Liebenow, "Liberia," in Carter, *op. cit.,* p. 354.

[98] Cowan, in Carter, *op. cit.,* p. 215.

[99] Cf. Fred W. Riggs, "Bureaucrats and Political Development: A Paradoxical
View," in LaPalombara, *op. cit.,* pp. 120–67, especially p. 128.

their work before they are arrested (if they are arrested), whereas political antagonists may be arrested on the slightest provocation and their homes searched as a "precautionary measure." The government has also co-opted many *voluntary associations* in order to prevent the development of the autonomous centers of power which usually accompany economic development.[100]

Most of the new leaders of Africa believe that industrial output and efficiency can best be raised by "planning, governmental initiative and even management, the deliberate application of scientific outlook and procedure to industrial problems."[101] The new leaders attempt to legitimize their approach by reference both to European socialism and to traditional African economic systems. The result, "African socialism" (other names that have been used include "dynamic socialism" and "communitarianism"), has been defined by Senghor as a "synthesis of Negro-African values, of Western methodological and spiritual values, and Socialist technical and social values."[102] Yet in the practical application of African socialism, emphasis has been placed upon social mobilization and central planning. The affected spheres of activity include community development, industrialization, agricultural production, and foreign trade. In addition, identifications are involved for it is the expressed aim of many African leaders to enhance loyalty to the state by means of socialism.

The prevalence of "African socialism" can be traced to causes other than the need for rapid development and the overall policy of forging unity. Socialists outside Africa have long articulated support for the independence of Black Africa, this support often being a mixture of positive concern for Africa and hostility towards particular capitalist states or capitalist institutions. African leaders tend to suspect the capitalist system because of its connection with imperialism (old or new),[103] and admire the Soviet and Chinese economic systems because of their

[100] "Totalitarianism," writes Kautsky, "grows out of the attempt to make the maintenance or even the acceleration of industrialization compatible with the prevention of the growth of such organizations, or their suppression [or co-optation] where they have already grown." John H. Kautsky, "An Essay in the Politics of Development," *Political Change in Underdeveloped Countries: Nationalism and Communism* (New York: John Wiley and Sons, 1962), p. 93.

[101] Shils, "Intellectuals, Public Opinion, and Economic Development," this volume, p. 474.

[102] Leopold Senghor, "Some Thoughts on Africa: A Continent in Development," *International Affairs,* XXXVIII (1962), 191.

[103] Edward Shils writes of "a derogatory conception of businessmen as either exploitative foreigners or money-grubbing, short-sighted, native manipulators of financial combinations." "Intellectuals, Public Opinion, and Economic Development," this volume, p. 474.

advertised rapid development. There are also several parallels between the socialism which the new African leaders now advocate and the economic systems prevalent in their traditional societies. For example, property (especially land) was often owned by the community, the profit motive was not prominent, and charisma was concentrated.

THE QUESTION OF OPPOSITION

Despite the political messiah, the mobilization movement, and the centripetal government, opposition to the ruling leaders exists in all the independent countries of Black Africa. Some of the factors which contributed to the rise of this opposition are common to all political systems. Others seem to be especially characteristic of newly independent countries. The latter include traditional elements, lack of civility, nationalist opposition, and disillusionment. (a) Some traditional leaders and ethnic groups are now centers of opposition. Virulent opposition is often manifested by those who ruled in old Africa but have little power in the independence regimes. (b) A sense of civility has only begun to develop in the new states. Individuals do not form a whole by virtue of transcending nation-wide identifications, and they do not have a concern for, nor a sense of responsibility to, the state and the nation.[104] (c) During the period of European rule, nationalist movements were in continual opposition. The administration was considered against rather than for, "they" rather than "we." Many Africans have carried these political orientations over into the independence period. (d) Independence has been followed by disillusionment among many segments of the population. (Notable exceptions are the bureaucrats and managers who have developed vested interests in the *status quo*.) The revolution of rising aspirations has far surpassed the evolution of standards of living. The charismatic relationships between leaders and masses are wearing thin, exposing the leaders to more realistic assessments. More specifically, the *masses* in some countries believe that the gap between themselves and their leaders is widening. In sample surveys recently conducted by the author, many urban laborers and village peasants complained that they were suffering at the hands of the politicians. Occasionally, a preference was voiced for European rulers.[105] *Many intellectuals* are disillusioned because their expectations for a democratic welfare state have not been met, nor have they been empowered to realize their utopia.[106] *Soldiers*

[104] See Edward Shils, "The Intellectuals in the Political Development of the New States," *World Politics*, XII (1960), 329–68.

[105] Hanna and Hanna, *op. cit.* (The preference for Europeans was voiced to African interviewers as well as to us.)

[106] For some parallels in the United States, see Lipset, "American Intellectuals: Their Politics and Status," *Political Man, op. cit.*

in some countries are upset because their pay is low, they continue to serve under European officers, and the policies of political leaders do not suit them. The military governments in Asia and the Middle East reveal possible future developments. *Disappointed nationalists* complain that their efforts in the fight for independence have not been rewarded.[107] *Disappointed applicants* complain because the successful applicants for jobs and scholarships are often related to the right person or have paid a "commission." The frustrations of *school-leavers* are building to explosive proportions because many remain unemployed or under-employed due to the slow rate of economic growth and the young age of job incumbents who, but a few years before, replaced Europeans or filled new jobs and now, unless there is a revolution, will block the advancement of those now leaving school for most of their adult life. *In all walks of life,* disillusionment has tended to develop from the attenuation of charisma, the realization that the good life has not come with independence, and the belief, common in some countries, that corruption and nepotism are rampant in the leadership.

Most political opposition which has arisen in independent Black Africa is not responsible and loyal according to Anglo-American standards. Rather, it cavils, disrupts, or plans secessions or *coups d'état.* This behavior can be explained by the factors which contributed to the rise of the opposition and also by the actions of the ruling leaders. In some countries opposition leaders have been detained or deported, properties owned by members of the opposition have been confiscated, electoral laws have been manipulated, those who publicly criticize have been charged with sedition, and even opposition itself has been made illegal. These actions seem to have been caused by concern for vested interests, some irresponsible and disloyal behavior by the opposition, and the ruling leaders' belief that they are patriotic whereas the opposition is devilish, treasonous, "sterile and fratricidal."[108] The ruling leaders *tend to believe that those who are in opposition are separated from them by fundamental and irreconcilable differences. They feel that they are the state and the nation, and that those who do not go along with them are not just political rivals but* total *enemies.*[109]

---

[107] This problem has been of special concern to Guinea's leaders. "[Former militants] believe that the services of veteran party members should be preferred to the utilization of the special skills of former political adversaries. This is an extremely dangerous tendency which must stop." *L'Expérience Guinéenne et l'Unité Africaine* (Paris: Présence Africaine, [1959?]), p. 356, quoted by Cowan, in Carter (ed.), *op. cit.,* p. 205. Alas, revolutionary agitators are often not the best suited to administrate the victory.

[108] Keita, *op. cit.,* p. 39.

[109] Shils, "The Intellectuals . . . ," *op. cit.,* p. 354.

This can in turn be traced to the concentration of charisma and the personality mechanism of defense called "splitting," by which the actor's world is sharply divided into good and bad.[110] As Middle Eastern and Latin American history suggests, it will probably take many years and several political upheavals before the repression-extremism, extremism-repression cycle is broken.

Although opposition is, by definition, the antithesis of the unity which African leaders are attempting to forge, it can often make a contribution to unity. During the fight for independence, a major factor contributing to solidarity was common opposition to the imperial rulers. A dynamic relationship of outgroup hostility and ingroup solidarity was clearly operative. All aggressions could be directed toward, or projected into, the rulers instead of being scattered among the African population. When the fight for independence was won, the convenience of this common opposition was lost. Attempts to give it a new birth under the name of neo-colonialism or neo-imperialism have not always been successful. Other external opposition has usually been avoided because of the danger of fulfillment. As a result, internal opposition has been created, identified, or magnified (sometimes beyond recognition). In Ghana university professors and students have been called "saboteur intellectuals" and several have been deported. In Zanzibar the Arabs are charged with being the source of all difficulties. Throughout East Africa the Indian population has been accused of ruining territorial economies. Of course, these target groups were not selected at random. "Usually, projections in general . . . are directed toward some point in reality where they are met halfway."[111] This situation is likely to increase in intensity as the potential for widespread opposition rises, goals are not achieved, and insecurities intensify.

THE QUESTION OF DEMOCRACY

The African leaders' choice of a system to forge unity was made with at least some knowledge of the usual meaning of democracy. Many traditional African political systems contained elements of classical democracy. In some villages, for example, decisions were made by the community as a whole. (It is noteworthy, however, that institutionalized opposition usually did not exist in old Africa.) Independence was won by nationalist movements that incorporated the ideas of freedom and equality. Hodgkin believes that democracy is "a primary datum for

[110] See William John Hanna, "Splitting: The Case of the Soviet Delegates in the United Nations Security Council," *American Imago*, XX (1963), 175–85.

[111] Otto Fenichel, *The Psychoanalytic Theory of Neurosis* (New York: Norton, 1945), p. 147.

almost all African parties."[112] Most African leaders received advanced Western education and from it have learned about the democratic political systems in the United Kingdom, France, and elsewhere. There seems to be a special awareness of electoral competition for power as a component of democracy. (Awareness or articulation do not, of course, imply commitment. It may be that some African leaders know what the "rich capitalists" of Europe and America want to hear!) On the subject of democracy, Nyerere writes:

> *The two essentials for "representative" democracy are the freedom of the individual, and the regular opportunity for him to join with his fellows in replacing, or reinstating, the government of his country by means of the ballot-box and without recourse to assassination. An organized opposition is* not *an essential element.*[113]

Although disagreeing on the necessity of an opposition, Mboya writes in the same tradition:

> *Opposition parties must develop not because the text books say so but rather as a normal and natural process of the individual freedom of speech and freedom to criticize government and the right of people to return a government of their choice by use of the ballot box.*[114]

The evidence which has been presented suggests that the political system which the new leaders of Africa are forging has been chosen after evaluating theoretical alternatives in terms of their countries' problems and their own interests. The choice may in one sense have even been the most democratic one that could have been made. The centralization of power by means of the political messiah, the mobilization movement, and the centripetal government may provide the most checks and balances —the most competitive system—that can realistically be achieved in contemporary Black Africa, given the conditions in which the system must exist. Perhaps only a mobilization movement can act as an organizational counterweight to a government made powerful by its dominant role in economic development. (This assumes that the two have not been completely fused under the messiah.) Perhaps only a political messiah can constrain such powerful organizations as the movement and the government. Perhaps only the combination of messiah, movement, and government can transform a fragmented society into a political community. And perhaps not. Another possibility is that opposition will continue to grow

---

[112] Hodgkin, *African Political Parties, op. cit.,* p. 155.
[113] Julius K. Nyerere, "The African and Democracy," this volume, p. 526.
[114] Tom Mboya, "Vision of Africa," this volume, p. 519.

until another revolution occurs, likely led by the military and the militant jobless youth. Future historians may identify the contemporary leaders of the new states as the Kerenskys of Black Africa.

A LARGER UNITY

. . . the aspiration of our people for strengthening of our brother-hood and creating solidarity in a larger unity transcending ethnic and national differences.[115]

The goal of African unity has been at the forefront of continental politics since independence has been expected or realized. (Its roots go back at least a century.) The All-African People's Conference (1958) condemned the "artificial frontiers drawn by imperialist powers to divide the people of Africa." The Conference of Independent African States (1958) "discovered . . . a common community of interest" and asserted that "Africanism binds us together." And the summit confer-ence of the African Heads of State (1963) created the Organization of African Unity, the first listed purpose of which was to promote "the unity and solidarity of the African and Malagasy States." Most African leaders believe that some form of unity is possible, and they publicly support it. One of them recently posed the question: "If Europe and America can create vast political, economic, and cultural units, why cannot Africa do it?" Yet African unity has hardly advanced beyond the discussion stage, for although some leaders honestly want it, some use it only as an emotional substitute in domestic politics for the inde-pendence which has now been realized, while others are against unity but afraid to denounce it publicly. These differences can be traced to a complex set of factors, some working for unity and some working against it. Writing about Europe, although it applies equally to Black Africa, Haas states, "The decision to proceed with integration or to oppose it rests on the perception of interests and on the articulation of specific values on the part of existing political actors."[116] The analysis of these factors provides insight into the nature of leadership and the process of change in Black Africa.

COMMON IDENTITY[117]

Returning from the 1963 African summit conference, one partici-pant exclaimed: "We have discovered our common identity!" The most

[115] *Charter of the Organization of African Unity* (1963).
[116] Ernst B. Haas, *The Uniting of Europe: Political, Social, and Economic Forces 1950–1957* (Stanford: Stanford University Press, 1958), p. 13.
[117] An important analysis of this factor occurs in Mazrui, *op. cit.*

manifest roots of this common identity are color, for it is easy to distinguish black "we" from non-black "they," and geography, for Black Africa is a contiguity. Color (perhaps it should be "difference") has overtly or covertly been mentioned as the basis of common identity by several leaders of Black Africa. Nyerere has said, "Africans, all over the continent, without a word being spoken either from one individual to another or from one African country to another, looked at the European, looked at one another, and knew that in relation to the European they were one."[118] But the roots go deeper, and it is probably correct to say that "their common identity has been forged in the flames of their common suffering."[119] In a similar vein, an editorial in the Nigerian government newspaper asserts that "the blood of Africans, who have suffered all forms of indignity in the hands of their foreign rulers, is thicker than the water of colonialism."[120]

Africans have shared many similar experiences: a village life with rudimentary technology, conquest, imperial rule, denigration by Europeans, and probably a feeling of inferiority. Some Africans claim that their people have developed a unique set of values, institutions, and styles of life; the terms *négritude* and *African personality* have been coined to identify this uniqueness. After traveling widely in Africa, a noted social psychologist reports "striking uniformities" and suggests: "People subjected to similar pressures are likely to develop somewhat similar forms of behavior. . . . Africans south of the Sahara live in the midst of similar pressures."[121] However, not all Africans accept the claims of uniqueness or uniformity. Balewa comments:

> *I do not believe in what some people call the African personality. There is no such thing as African personality. I believe in human personality. Africans belong to the human race and I say talk of African personality betray inferiority complex.*[122]

Of course, his statement contains support for both sides of the argument.

[118] Julius K. Nyerere in *Symposium On Africa* (Wellesley, Mass.: Wellesley College, 1960), p. 149.

[119] Rupert Emerson, "Pan-Africanism," *International Organization*, XVI (1962), 282.

[120] *Morning Post* (Lagos), May 28, 1963, p. 5. Elsewhere, Nyerere writes, "African unity is at present merely an emotion born of a history of colonialism and oppression." "A United States of Africa," *op. cit.*, p. 1.

[121] Leonard W. Doob, "The Psychological Pressure upon Modern Africans," *Journal of Human Relations*, VIII (1960), 465.

[122] Quoted in Allah-De, "Words, Words Galore!" *Sunday Times* (Lagos, Nigeria), May 26, 1963, p. 9.

THE NEED FOR GREATER STRENGTH

African unity is linked with independence and economic development. Many African leaders believe that the strength derived from unity will be able to maintain and broaden the freedom of newly independent countries and win freedom for those territories in which Africans (i.e., people indigenous to Africa) do not control the government. Thus there is an internal and an external aspect to the need for greater strength.[123] The African Heads of State were "determined to safeguard and consolidate the hard-won independence as well as the sovereignty and territorial integrity of our states, and to fight neo-colonialism in all its forms." Speaking at that conference, Kwame Nkrumah asserted:

> *Only a united Africa with central political direction can success-*
> *fully give effective material and moral support to our freedom fighters*
> *in Southern Rhodesia, Angola, Bechuanaland, Swaziland, Basutoland,*
> *Portuguese Guinea and other territories, and, of course, South Africa.*[124]

The African Heads of State also asserted that unity will be able "to harness the natural and human resources of our continent." Separately, the economies of most countries of Black Africa are weak. There is little industrialization, exports consist largely of one or a few crops, territorial systems of transportation and communication are rarely linked, and the countries compete against each other. African unity would permit the economics of scale. One observer writes, "It is the economic consideration which constitutes the strongest basis for a rational desire for African unity."[125] Realizing this, the African Heads of State decided to set up a preparatory economic commission to explore the possibilities of a free trade area, a common external tariff, a raw material price stabilization fund, transport coordination and development, a payments and clearing union, and a monetary zone. If these possibilities become realities, Africa will probably be able to industrialize more rapidly and compete more effectively in the world market.

HISTORICAL INHERITANCE

"We must start our quest for African unity," writes Julius Nyerere, "from the facts of our historical inheritance."[126] Different European ties

[123] Cf. Ernst B. Haas, "Regional Integration and National Policy," *International Conciliation*, No. 513 (May 1957), 381–442.
[124] *Nigerian Outlook* (Enugu), May 19, 1963, p. 1.
[125] N. A. Cox-George, "The Political Economy of African Unity," *Présence Africaine*, III, No. 31 (1960), 10.
[126] "A United States of Africa," *op. cit.*, p. 2.

and territorialized political behavior have made African unity more difficult to achieve. During the period of imperial rule, African life styles were influenced by the life styles of their rulers. This is dramatically illustrated by the contrast between French-speaking and English-speaking Africa. Many of the capitals of French-speaking African countries remind one of the provincial capitals of France. There are French restaurants and outdoor cafes, and many Africans speak French among themselves. In contrast, the capitals of English-speaking West African countries, despite their modernity, are strikingly African. There are African restaurants and bars in the downtown areas, English is rarely spoken when there is a common vernacular, and so on. (The capitals of English-speaking East African countries are more mixed in character because of the large number of resident Asians and Europeans.) The ties of independent African countries to their former European rulers go far beyond these examples of style. Political, economic, and social life is influenced by European models, and sometimes, even after the transfer of sovereignty, partially directed from Europe. De Gaulle's interventions in French-speaking Africa are illustrative. This direction continues because most African countries rely upon European development funds, trained personnel, protected markets, and military support. The reluctance of French-speaking African leaders to support Algeria's fight for independence against France has illustrated the effect of this reliance.

Within the European-established boundaries, rapid change has taken place, nationalism has arisen, and modern political activity is organized. The new leaders of Africa have been acting and thinking in terms of these territories rather than in terms of Black Africa (or Africa as a whole), and the institutions of these territories are now familiar to them. Some people in these territories are also beginning to think of themselves as Ghanaians, Senegalese, and so on, as a result of the years of nationalism and forging unity. Balewa is correct in stating, "However artificial [imperial] boundaries were at first, the countries they have created have come to regard themselves as units independent of one another."

VESTED INTERESTS[127]

Once a person has had great power or wealth, it is difficult for him to share or relinquish it voluntarily. This proposition applies to American presidents and chairmen of corporation boards as well as to African leaders. Although there are probably some African leaders who expect to profit personally from African unity, most look forward to a loss of

[127] Also see above, pp. 26–28.

power and wealth.[128] The situation is especially traumatic if the leaders are political messiahs who have charismatic self-images. Azikiwe is undoubtedly correct when he says:

> It would be capital folly to assume that hard-bargaining politicians who passed through the ordeal of victimization and the crucible of persecution to win their independence will easily surrender their newly-won power.[129]

In a united Africa present leaders could lose power both from above and from below. A supranational organization would draw power from individual African countries, and thus from their leaders. Divided ethnic groups would also be reunited and traditional leaders would be in a better position to rival the territorial leaders. This threat probably also accounts for the failure to adjust the boundaries of African countries after independence.

Although African unity would probably be economically advantageous to the continent as a whole, the wealthier countries might have their rate of development slowed because they would have to help the poorer countries and because they would lose some of their present competitive advantage. This consideration was important in the Ivory Coast's rejection of French West African unity and Katanga's secession from the Congo. The European experience proves that wealthier countries can profit from larger markets, but the economic effect of African unity is felt by some leaders to be uncertain.

THE POLITICS OF FREEDOM

Before the Congress of Berlin, the freedom of most Africans was limited by the traditions of relatively static societies. For the following seventy-five years, it was limited by imperial rule. The symbol of the nationalist struggle was freedom and the fruit of victory was independence. But only the future will determine whether Africans will realize freedom now that the opportunity is theirs.

[128] Chisiza, *op. cit.*, p. 26, believes that African unity is endangered by those who, "driven by excessive ambition, attempt to pose as *the* leaders of . . . Africa," adding that unity requires absolute equality, not "pride that apes humility."

[129] *Zik: A Selection from the Speeches of Nnamdi Azikiwe* (Cambridge: Cambridge University Press, 1961), p. 72. Quaison-Sackey, *op. cit.*, pp. 78–9, applies this point to the failure of the Sanniquellie Declaration. Similarly, with reference to French-speaking West Africa, Victor D. du Bois notes "the fundamental reluctance of each of the African leaders to submerge his own identity and that of his country in a more elaborate political grouping in which he might be obliged to yield first place to a rival." "A Note on French-Influenced West Africa," *American Universities Field Staff Reports*, VI, No. 5 (1963), 14.

PART ONE

Prelude and Change

African Personality and the New African Society

JOSEPH KI-ZERBO

Lycée d'Ouagadougou
Upper Volta

I, who am neither a philosopher nor a sociologist, but a historian and geographer, propose to make a few observations about African society. And it is first of all essential to underline the importance of this problem within the context of the theme chosen for this conference.

What is Africa? What ought Africa to be? Such are the basic questions to which the conscientious African or Africanist must find a reply. Africa must be defined. Now what is a country if not, above all, the human beings who live in it, are part of it, and transform it? For example, when we have returned home after this conference, people will ask us: "What is America? What is it like?" We shall speak of the people we have met here, their appearance, their gestures, their opinions, and so forth. And so it is with Africa; she is not merely the iron ore or the aluminum with which her soil is rich; she is not only her forests of ebony and mahogany and other precious woods. Africa is above all the African people—insofar as man creates his own history—and the Africa of tomorrow, the African personality of which the whole world is speaking, will be what the African people make it. The development of that personality is the ultimate aim of all our efforts, both in the political struggle and in the economic field. And in spite of the difficulty of the subject, it is therefore important to examine this final aim of our efforts, this African personality, this goal of all the efforts and the sacrifices of African nationalists, many of whose blood was spilled and who died for the development of this personality.

As we are speaking now, there are still thousands of Africans, especially in North Africa, who are continuing to give their all in order that this same African personality may evolve. It is thus most important to examine the emergence of this new African society whose positive characteristics will represent our contribution to the great meeting of civilizations. And may I, at the outset, make an observation: we would

Reprinted from The American Society of African Culture, *Pan-Africanism Reconsidered* (Berkeley and Los Angeles: University of California Press, 1962), pp. 267–282, with the permission of the compilers and the publisher.

be wrong to treat this problem from a purely academic viewpoint. Too many anthropologists and sociologists have wielded the scalpel on this subject, giving us analyses and descriptions of the past that are already outmoded and fossilized by the rapid evolution that is taking place. Certain sociologists for example, giving way to the convenient, are content to interpret the feelings of the present-day African toward his leaders as a mere transposition of the attitudes of tribalism into 1960. As if the African mind had not been touched by the new way of life! Africa is no longer the Africa of the Dogons; Africa is not a museum! It is a dough in full ferment. And the dialectic method is still the best method of approach to the sociological reality of Africa. In my opinion this approach could be made from the three following directions.

First, what are the main features of the social organization and conception of the traditional African society? Next, what are the principal elements of the present crisis? And finally, what prospects and what transcendent structure will emerge to create the new African society for her to attain a higher sociological level?

What are the main features of the traditional social organization and conception? Contrary to the colonial image, which presents precolonial Africa as a collection of tiny groups torn by internal strife and tribal warfare, sociologically frozen at the stage of a protozoan or an amoeba, African society was highly organized. Its principal features, in my opinion, were the following: first, the authority of the old people. You are all aware that in Africa the hierarchy of power, of consideration and of prestige, was in direct rapport with the hierarchy of age. When I was a shepherd, for instance, and we tended our goats, our little community was rigorously governed by the law of the hierarchy of age; I mean to say that it was the eldest who was the undisputed head, who assigned the day's work, and who, for example, designated the one among us who was to return to the village for provisions for all the other shepherds. Often enough, even today, one hears on the lips of Africans: "Don't talk to me in that tone of voice! I'm older than you." The council of elders in traditional Africa was the supreme political master of the city or the tribe. It was often this autocracy of the old that evolved into a veritable cult of ancestor worship. This cult closely identified ancestors with the main acts of the living—who were nothing but a tiny link in the giant chain of generations. The living were but a microcosm restricted to certain narrow duties in comparison with the tremendous cohort of those whose shades still peopled the ancestral home or the patriarchal or tribal territory. The African, even when emancipated of his metaphysical beliefs, still gives a large place to his ancestors. For him more than for any other, the famous statement of

Renan holds true: "The nation is made up of more dead than living." It is for this reason that, for the African, patriotism has a distinctive dimension. The word *fasso*, which means "ancestral home" in Bambara, evokes for the African not only territorial or ethnic overtones, but cosmic and metaphysical ones as well. The oath at the tomb of one's ancestors is the most binding in existence. Certain nationalist parties have taken advantage of this, and by drawing from their followers such an oath, have bound them ever closer. Some people have contended that this respect for one's ancestors and for the past has made of the Africans a people forever mired in the stereotyped repetition of the same ceremonies and congenitally unable to invent anything new. But such arguments, supported by the colonialists, are easily controverted by the many contemporary or historical examples of African creativity that we can all advance.

Another important characteristic of the traditional society is solidarity, and this point is too obvious to require any lengthy examination. I would, however, like to say that this solidarity is not just a phenomenon of the superstructure, a trembling of the spirit, or a tenderness of heart toward others. This solidarity is imprinted on the very basic structure of African culture, and especially in its economic organization. You know that in the traditional African society the notion of property was defined in terms of the family community or the village and not in terms of the individual. The concept of personal property in terms of the individual is generally alien to African social concepts. Fields are often common property and work is most often collective. Another social manifestation of this solidarity is hospitality, which, it is true, is obviously not an African monopoly but which nevertheless is particularly strong there; and here I am pleased to associate North Africa with the rest of the continent. How many times when I was a child did my mother prepare a hot meal for us; but strangers, travelers who stopped in to stay with us, arrived suddenly, and we had to content ourselves with a cold meal, while the hot meal that had just been prepared for us and which we were already enjoying in anticipation, was served to the guests. Even the white conquerors, when they arrived in Africa, were the recipients of this hospitality, of this African openness of heart, of this predisposition to kindness toward all new arrivals. Many conquerors who entertained unhappy thoughts for Africa in the back of their heads, were received with extraordinary friendliness, housed with the chiefs, fed, and generally surrounded with consideration and respect up to the very moment when they left this collectivity and considered themselves free of any obligations in this regard. In traditional Africa, there were no orphans—but, it must unfortunately be added, there was also no quarantine or segregation of even the contagious sick. In the African mind it was unthinkable that because one of the members of the family or the tribal group was ill, he should have been separated and isolated. We are dealing, therefore, with a solidarity with unlimited mutual responsibility.

Another important feature is the equalitarian character of African society. Naturally, I do not intend in any way to idealize or to present traditional Africa as the best of all possible or imaginary worlds. Africa has had its tyrants, as have other nations throughout history. But it must be stressed also that the traditional African society often included classes based solely on functional differentiation. There was, for instance, the mason class, the blacksmith class, the warrior class. But the fact that in Africa property was common, the fact that there was no class that accumulated the capital property and reduced others to the state of mere tenancy—mere peasants or farmers whose toil was used to amass profit—well, that fact proves that the exploitation of man by man never achieved the status of a system in the traditional society of Africa. And, moreover, by reason of the unlimited solidarity of which I have just spoken, the true principle of such a society was "To each according to his needs," to the extent of the complete utilization of common revenues, in which case, of course, everyone also participated in a common famine. And even in the political field, where it has become the custom to depict Africa as swarming with uncontrolled and bloody petty tyrants, power was in fact limited by custom. For example, the supreme chief of the Mossi tribe, the Moronaba, was invested with extraordinary power, even divine power, and was compared to the sun. At the Moronaba's death, the Griot (medicine man), who had to announce it to the people, merely said: "The fire has gone out" or "The sun has set." Well, even in that Mossi society, the Moronaba was not an absolute monarch; his power was restrained by a council of chiefs as provided by custom, that is, by a sort of unwritten constitution—and any Englishmen who are present will understand that concept. This council of chiefs was endowed with great power to brake, hinder, oppose or even to effectively veto the desires of the Moronaba. One could mention many other characteristics of the traditional African society. One could, for example, speak of its ideological tolerance. It is a constant in the history of traditional Africa that there were practically no wars of religion. There is a tolerance toward others which may perhaps be explained by the fact that African religion did not develop through a structural elaboration of a dogma but through the elaboration of a special social cadre of priests consecrated to the cult, the celebration of ritual, and liaison with the supernatural world.

You are aware that in traditional African culture the king generally
was the political leader and also the head of the society.

What are the principal elements of the present crisis? The historical
origin of this crisis was the gigantic trauma inflicted on the African personality by colonialism. Colonialism has not only been a tremendous
embezzlement of material wealth, but also a tragic sidetracking of the
African personality toward ideals and roles that have adulterated it.
Thus the African personality has become a sort of shipwreck towed
along by the thread of a history made and written by the European
conquerors. This is, moreover, especially true of the African of French
culture, where assimilation was one of the categorical imperatives, one
of the canons of colonization—the final aim of the colonizers being to
completely annex the mentality and concepts of the colonized people.
Education has thus become one of the main points, one of the most
important methods of colonization. And I believe that one could almost
make mention here, speaking of colonialist education, of a colonial
pact of minds. Now the origin of this trauma, of this cultural oppression, is the singleminded European conception of civilization: There
is only one Civilization with a capital C.

I should like here to tell a little story to help you understand how
far this mentality extends, even to children. When I was in Paris, I
was often received in French homes, and once, after dinner in the
living room, a little girl seemed uncommonly interested in my appearance. She began walking around and around me, felt my hair, and
finally took my hand. She turned it over and over to study it, and then
holding up this part of my hand, said to those present: "It's clean
here." You will see that already in that little head there existed a conception with regard to color. For her, that which was clean was white.
Obviously, from the African point of view and the black point of view,
you could also say that what is clean is black. This attitude is going to
drag out the crisis in the African personality—and it does not necessarily arise from a calculated colonial point of view.

Each time we have the contact of two civilizations, mutual perturba-
tions arise *ipso facto* and of necessity. A few examples: first, the introduction of money. In traditional society, money existed but its use was
restricted by reason of a closed economy—an economy based on barter. Well, the very presence of money in the capitalistic sense of the
word—that is, as a general equivalent, property that can be equated
with any other kind of property, merchandise with an extremely rapid
turnover and (according to the expression used by Aristotle and, I
believe, taken up again by Karl Marx) capable of begetting children
—money in that sense could not help but occasion profound upsets in

the traditional society. Accumulation becomes possible. For example, farms develop into individual landed estates; the worker, too, earns his salary on an individual basis; and new social cleavages, new social classes, are tending to develop in Africa today, as they did in Europe in the seventeenth and eighteenth centuries. In traditional Africa money did not afford the right to everything, as it does in the capitalistic system. For example, titles were not bought and sold. As in Europe in the Middle Ages, there was no artificial nobility; the only nobility was of the blood.

Similarly, another disturbing element is that of a city considered as a gigantic laboratory for a new humanity, where the West is on hand with its goods—which are, moreover, not always particularly useful for Africa. I am thinking of the immense quantity of alcohol that has been imported into Black Africa. Well, the West is on hand with its goods, its services, its publicity, its multitude of solicitations, and slowly and surely it penetrates the traditional civilization. It is said that when the Upper Volta was being colonized, a military column under Vonlay and Chauvine met an old African near Gonvadonjon. This old man had just left his village, along with a little child who was leading a goat; the old man himself was carrying a chicken, and was on his way to a funeral where the goat and the chicken were to be sacrificed. Brenton tells us that this old man did not lose his head. He went up to Vonlay and said: "I heard that you were supposed to come this way; everyone else has fled, but I decided to come and meet you and I have brought you this chicken and this goat."

It is certain that that was a meeting of two civilizations; the old man, pondering the traditional ceremonies he must perform and the formulas he must pronounce to ensure peace for the soul of his dead relative, is brusquely confronted by European civilization, as represented by material military power. Now, imagine an old man who leaves his village and goes to the city. This trip is not just a trip in space; it is also, and perhaps primarily a trip in time, across many centuries of evolution, which leads him from the sociological context of the Middle Ages, so to speak, to a completely different context: the context of the material, moral, psychological, and mental civilization of Western Europe.

Similarly, setting up a factory in Africa has sociological implications. Such was the case with the creation of Fria in Guinea; there were not just engineers, geologists, and geographers who set to work; there was also a team of sociologists to determine the possible social repercussions of this installation. Likewise with the development of unions and parties, which create new solidarities, sometimes stronger than the old. It has been determined, for instance, that after 1946, there were often quarrels among family relatives, and the subject of these quarrels was political struggle and divergencies. The result, you all know—it was well expressed by Frantz Fannon in his book *Black Skins, White Masks*—is imitation become a system; it is the uprooting, the disembodiment, and the calculated withering of a civilization; it is cultural genocide. I have seen people taking great pains to learn the French dictionary by heart, as if culture were a matter of pure accumulation of knowledge and not one of comprehension and communion. I have seen Africans wearing sunglasses in the middle of the night. I have seen colonized peoples don the colonial helmet as the sign and the test of social advancement. And since one's basic nature is always just under the surface and impossible to subdue completely, the end result is the drawing and quartering of conscience and the formation of serious psychological complexes. We have the rifleman, for instance: that very African soldier who struggles in the African armies for a policy external to Africa. And here I shall make a brief digression. With regard to Pan-Africanism and African unity, it is difficult to conceive that those black African soldiers who are now fighting in the colonial army against the emancipation of Algeria will not be retired from the front after the attainment of independence by their states; it is difficult to believe that those independent countries will not withdraw their soldiers so that their Algerian brothers, who are of the same continent, who often shared the same history, may free themselves and attain their political aspirations. Well, very often the soldier who tries to speak French as it is spoken in Paris will show you the talisman he wore in the fight for the liberation of France. Similarly, during electoral rollcalls, I have often seen candidates call upon both the voice of the people and the intervention of witch doctors.

But we must determine whether or not the present crisis is a fatal illness or if it is just a phase of disequilibrium in the coming blossoming—a sort of puberty. It depends mainly on the Africans themselves—and this brings us to the examination of the third and last point of this study: *What prospects and transcendent structures will emerge?*

What are the principles? What do we want? What sort of Africa do we desire? The African people themselves must answer these questions. There is no culture but that which is fixed in space. On his little island, Robinson Crusoe was perhaps educated, but it cannot be said that he was cultured. Cultured with regard to whom? Culture is a social idea. And the great inventor, the creator, the genius, is the people. Thus, the first duty of the social revolution is to free the people, to liberate man. This was well expressed in the slogan of the

Accra Congress of 1958: "Hands off Africa!" And I think it was Alioune Diop who pointed out that after the independence of Guinea the very fact of political freedom gave rise to extremely interesting lyric and epic poetry, especially in the Fonta area.

Of course, it is not up to an areopagus of sages or leaders to pre-organize or to prefabricate the future African personality. But the people often do need to be guided, especially after such a deep and fundamental trauma as the colonial era. You Americans are familiar with this experience, because immediately after the abolition of slavery —which was in itself a positive factor from the point of view of historical evolution—there was for a certain time an equivalent to the present total confusion among the black Africans; that is, certain deviations and aberrations occurred in the Negro society of America which was not accustomed to the breath of freedom or the free condition into which it found itself so brutally thrust.

So, the role of the leaders is to know what basic choices must be presented for the evolution of African culture and civilization—and here it is obvious that each has complete freedom of self-determination on the condition that he does not enter into flagrant contradiction with the recognized values of the original civilization. Within this framework of respect for traditional African civilization, there is still room for a great variety of choice. Hence the necessity of frequent meetings among political, union, and cultural African leaders, in order to localize and to illuminate the points of friction and opposition and to clearly present ideological problems. Failing this, we run the risk, after the precolonial clannishness and the colonial cloistering, of a sort of ideological tribalism in the independent nations, which would obviously be to the detriment of Africa as a whole. They tell the story of two African students in Paris—relatives, who did not get along and who did not even speak to each other because one considered the other a Trotskyite.

The possibility of opposition to Pan-Africanism does exist, as other speakers here before me have pointed out. The battle formation to counter such action, to direct the new African society, would, in my opinion be the following: first, decolonization of social values; next, self-examination leading to the suppression of certain customs and social factors in present-day African society, and, on the other hand, the invention of new social forms better adapted to our situation in the twentieth century—thus arriving at the progressive formation of a new Africa, sociologically and culturally speaking.

To be sure, a civilization is not a museum; it is a living organism—like a tree, which harbors positive and negative elements, young shoots and dead branches, blossoms and fruit. It is the role of the political and cultural leaders to make this new tree of African culture, of African personality, grow straight, by pruning the deadwood and the new shoots also. To begin with, one could start with the decolonization of social values, and specifically and above all the education of the masses. In the African tradition, education is not something apart from society but is intimately connected to the people. You are aware that in traditional Africa, different age groups acceded progressively to civic responsibilities, passing successively through the initiation stages, which were generally quite long. For instance, in Guerdé, the initiation stages for men generally lasted up to seven years—seven years of separation, during which the youths underwent very vigorous exercises, civic training and formation, and moral instruction—true education in the etymological sense of the word, that is, in the passing from an inferior state to a superior one. This education was aimed at making them into men completely a part of the city. Such education is not a superstructure; it is not an epiphenomenon in the social weave; it is, on the contrary, minutely integrated into the social body. There is thus in it the functional character of education to which our friend, Fofana, the Education Minister of Mali, has referred and which seems to us quite valid: the university, within the cadre of the traditional African society, cannot be an alien body in regard to the society, the state, or the government.

The same observation, in my opinion, could be made with regard to African art. It has often been said that African art has never been "art for art's sake." It was, for the most part, functional art—an art that was part of the principal acts and works of a society that had as its aim and its objective the augmentation of the vitality and the potential strength of the social body. It has, for example, been stated that African art is often utilitarian. It may serve as a weapon; and it can always serve as a weight, as can be seen in the art of Benin (Dahomey) on the Ivory Coast [sic]. There are small-scale weights that are fashioned according to a lost technique, and which are both useful and esthetically pleasing. It is thus necessary to restore African art to its traditional significance.

There is also another means—the transformation of society on an economic basis. You are aware that there is a process of classification in present-day Africa. In certain wealthy countries, especially those rich in export commodities, such as the Ivory Coast, a class system is obviously developing. This problem of the existence of classes in the traditional African society has long been debated, and I believe it is a basic problem, for on its solution depends to some extent the ideological choice that must be made. Is there segregation of classes in traditional African society? I personally believe not. As I have already mentioned, there was no class that exploited another through the accumulation of capital under a capitalistic system of economy; it might be said that there were social categories. There were not, in my opinion, social classes, and I believe this is the opinion expressed on many occasions by President Sékou Touré. It is also the opinion of a good many other African leaders, who believe that Africa reaps from this historical good fortune the benefits of a very rapid evolution, allowing us to become the masters of our destiny at a time when social classification has not yet crystalized and when, in spite of acceleration of the process in regions such as the Ivory Coast, we can still apply the brakes to this classification and avert in Africa the tragic experiences of the class struggle as it existed in Western societies. There are also developing, besides these classes based on economics, certain classes based on politics. Certain governments in power profit from the national revenue or the national budget to such an extent that they are little by little cutting themselves off from the masses through their special comforts, way of life, and income, and are becoming a sort of class. In certain countries of French West Africa, for instance, 120 people, who constitute only 1/30,000 of the population, are benefiting from 1/20 of the national budget.

The role of money and the problem of a fundamental economic choice should also be noted here. It is the problem of socialism. It is obvious that the choice of socialism is almost naturally and inevitably the end of African evolution. But, in my opinion, it is not the socialism elaborated by Marx on the basis of an analysis of a society fundamentally different from the traditional African society; for the society that Marx had before his eyes in nineteenth-century England was a class society. I think it would be a basic methodological error to transpose Marxism to Africa as the general philosophy of society. It would be an error of method because, as has been often said, if Marx were to reappear now he would probably not be a Marxist. So, it would be a basic error of method and also an error of principle. Some say that scientific Marxist socialism is valid as such everywhere and at all times. In my opinion, it is not sufficient to transplant socialism into the tropical latitudes of Abidjan, Conakry, or Dakar in order to have African socialism in Africa. African socialism must not be distinguishable only by the climate and the temperature of Africa. This socialism, if it is to be truly African, must be based on more solid foundations. If we purely and simply transplanted scientific socialism, it would constitute a new spiritual colonization, which, moreover, would not be justified by effectiveness. To be sure, there is a positive contribution in Marx-ism; no one can deny that Marxism, as a method of analysis of social factors, as an analysis of social dynamism, as a method of social and political action and organization as well, has contributed new things from which we can and should profit. But, in my opinion, it would be a lack of intellectual integrity to pretend, as Léopold Sedar Senghor did, that atheism is not essential to Marxism. It is apparent that athe-ism, the most fundamental materialism, is one of the essential charac-teristics of Marxism. One cannot declare oneself a Marxist and a spir-itualist at the same time, taking away from Marx everything that concerns social analysis pure and simple. I believe that the person who would go that far could not be a true Marxist.

The best approach, in my opinion, would be to begin from the con-crete socioeconomic structures of Africa itself. It is obvious that 80–90 per cent of Africans are peasants who still live and work under the system of collective property. Thus, we see that African society pre-sents an embryo, a form, perhaps primitive, of socialism. In this society, the revolutionary class is not the working class, for the good reason that it hardly exists in terms of numbers; it is very small, which does not mean that in the process of African emancipation the organized unions were not among the better elements, the better tools, and the better instruments of the political liberation. But as for the question of independence and the organization of the social revolution, it is obvious that the class upon which the transformation must be worked is the peasantry. The African peasant enjoys extraordinary enthusiasm for work, contrary to colonial depictions. You all know the role of the Negro in toil through the course of world history. One might almost say that the Negro has been the proletarian among nations. He was used for the accumulation of capital, not only here in America by the transportation of many tens of millions of the best Africans to American soil, but also in Europe, where the work of the Negro race made possible the amassing of capital and the industrial revolution, of which we are now seeing and admiring the effects. The Europeans, coming to Africa, pretended to be struck by the so-called laziness of Africans, and they suggested forced labor as the cure for this disease. In short, we must stress the role of the state in recapturing the traditional coöperative forms of labor, in modernizing them, by adding new ele-ments—for example, use of the concept of planned production, prelimi-nary studies, and so forth. It is a question of stopping the evolution toward a capitalistic society, for individualism and the systematic search for profit are not in the African tradition either.

There is another question it would be interesting to debate—chieftaincy. In any event, as far as the countries of French West Africa are concerned, chieftaincy seems to have terminated its role and should not be considered from a formalist point of view, but rather from a functional one. The chiefs who are useful as individuals must be rehabilitated—the institution itself being impossible to integrate into the new society. Besides, the sinister role often played by the chiefs during the colonial period must also be underlined. From the political standpoint, let us emphasize the role of the party as the transcendental structure; the old role of the council of elders, that is, the dream of the integration of all the living forces of the country, in order to realize a common program and common ideals. The question of the unity of the party should be resolved in that direction. The unity of the party ought not to be a system but should have a value of method, of utilization during a given phase, and thus a circumstantial value, in order that the centrifugal forces, which are numerous in a new country, may be restrained and braked, thanks to the existence of this powerful nerve center, which serves as a catalyst for all the values of integration. Thus, it is a question of breaking down tribalism, not as such, but as the political basis for possible parceling. The tribe as such can be the center of an artistic blossoming, for political unification does not mean the complete destruction of the tribe in its artistic, folkloric, esthetic, and cultural manifestations. For instance, in the long run, the French Revolution and the political and administrative integration brought about by Napoleon did not hinder an esthetic, folkloric, and artistic blooming in France, in Britain, and in the Netherlands. The same in Soviet Russia. But there is obviously a danger of institutionalization on the part of a single party. This danger is not fatal, as has had to be stressed; even in the political history of the United States there was a phase when the regime of the single party was in power for a long period.

The principal agents of this sociological revolution are, above all, the young, for the old are often incapable of incorporating new elements. Speak to an old polygamist and tell him to send away his other wives. He won't understand you; and he would be right to tell you that you are a bit late. There is in that an important factor; the disappearance, each day, each week, each month, of the old. There are many old people to whom, in the African tradition, we owe every respect and to whom we should address ourselves to learn the most about African tradition; but this does not alter the fact that the numerical decline of these old people renders it impossible for them to be leaders in the sociological transformation. What is tragic is that the young are often more impressed by the new than by the old traditions. For example, they are more sensitive to the cha-cha-cha than to normal African tradition. This is a great problem for sociological evolution. Other highly important agents of society are women. Women will be, I believe, among the best representatives of the sociological and cultural renewal. Why? Because they are very sensitive. This sensitivity allowed them to be mobilized during the struggle for political freedom. You know the role played by women's associations in Ghana, in Guinea, and so on. This sensitivity is also an important element as concerns attachment to the past. A man can more easily throw off the past than can a woman. Consequently, the role of women will be fundamental. Concretely speaking, this has already been translated, in French Africa, for instance, into practical innovations; in clothing styles, there have been inventions that have captured both the African and the Western style. Finally, the general philosophy of all this, as I have said, will not, in my opinion, be Marxism, except for certain aspects that I have already mentioned. Nor will it be capitalistic individualism, which is even less in the African tradition; the best approach will be to constitute a general philosophy of African society—personalism.

There is in Africa a particular conception of the human being as a member of a community with all its rights and privileges—remember the unlimited mutual solidarity of which I spoke—but also with very strict duties extending even to the sacrifice of one's life. For example, many youths have died in the initiation ceremonies of which I spoke. But the tribal framework of the personalism, which is the foundation of traditional patriotism, is too narrow; the frame will break. We must transcend this traditional framework of the microcommunities of the tribe to reach a higher level; hence, the utility of Pan-Africanism as a material basis for an economic substratum sufficiently strong to substantiate and sustain the new culture. But I must stress here a very great technical weakness: Africa could become a cultural disaster and microstates could only damage the formation of a new African personality. So, there is a foundation to this personalism; there is in Africa a common history through a common experience of oppression, particularly in the colonial period. And here, as a professor of history, I could not but stress the role of history in the edification of this conscience and this personalism. History, as it has been said, is the memory of nations, and one cannot live with another's memory or another's history. Consequently, we must rehabilitate our own history.

There are also common customs and attitudes—a common conception of the world. While the West adopts a position of separation from nature, a position of logical and technical analysis of nature in order to dominate her, the African has rather an attitude of participation in nature and thus an attitude of participation in the whole social body.

Dancing, for instance, is merely a technique of participation; there has thus developed in Africa an extraordinary blossoming of social relations. Africa tends rather more toward social relations than toward the exploitation of the world. When one travels in Europe or in America, one notices the presence of human intelligence; everywhere the landscape has been transformed and humanized; in this there is the expression of universal civilization, to the extent that man is called to dominate and organize nature. But one of the other important aspects of human civilization, in my opinion, is the organization of social relations, interpersonal and international rapport. And it seems to me that, in this domain, Africans are capable of making a contribution that no one else can make. The greatest asset to be saved, in my opinion, is the functionalism of African personalism. It is a great economic asset, which can, for example, be translated through human investment; it is a great political asset, consisting of a readiness to share the joys and sorrows of the entire world, to accept others, be they of the same race or not, be they of the same tribe or not. And, this, in my opinion, would be a great contribution to a world where aggression, still far from being eliminated, has become incalculably more dangerous owing to the technical means of destruction.

To conclude, I would say that negritude has been sufficiently sung and celebrated in story; it is time for a transformation—not for a new or so-called new, culture, consisting of a cloudy veneer over merchandise coming from the West or from the socialist countries. This new culture must stem from an African basis; it must resemble the great African trees, whose heads are thrust up into the civilization of the Universal but whose roots, on the other hand, plunge deeply into African soil.

Primitive Political Systems: A Preliminary Comparative Analysis

S. N. EISENSTADT

The Hebrew University, Jerusalem

INTRODUCTION: THE PROBLEM

This paper will present a general approach to the comparative analysis of primitive political systems and illustrate it by reference to some available material. The paper will not attempt to give a full inventory, or a full cross-cultural analysis, of all available data, but will only use some for purposes of illustration and analysis.

Despite the abundance of material, there have been few systematic works on comparative political systems of primitive societies. In the available literature, two main approaches can be discerned. The first, best exemplified by *African Political Systems* (Fortes and Evans-Pritchard 1940), is to differentiate between the "stateless," so-called segmentary societies and primitive societies with centralized governmental and political organizations. The essays analyzed the ways in which political activities are organized in each of these types, and also attempted to describe the conditions under which each of them exists.

After publication of this volume, papers appeared which tried to modify the dichotomy and to show that in reality a greater variety of forms of government existed among African societies. Barnardi's paper (1951) showed that in many of these tribes, age-groups perform certain governmental or political functions. Paula Brown (1951) classified West African societies according to the locus of governmental and juridical

Reprinted from *American Anthropologist*, LXI (1959), 200–220, with the permission of the author and the publisher.

This paper has been written at the Center for Advanced Study in the Behavioral Sciences, Stanford, California. I am indebted to my colleagues at the Center, David F. Aberle, Ralph Beals, Alex Inkeles, and David M. Schneider for criticisms and suggestions; to D. F. Aberle and Miss Miriam Gallagher for editorial help; to M. G. Smith of the University College of the West Indies for lending me the manuscripts of his essay on "Segmentary Lineage Systems," and for commenting on the paper; and to J. Middleton of London for comments.

functions, and showed that in addition to societies in which corporate lineages (segmentary societies) bear political functions and those with centralized chiefdoms and kings, there also exist societies in which most of the political functions are performed by so-called "association." These associations—the best examples of which are among the Yako, Ibo, and some Yoruba groups—seem to be somewhat intermediate cases between the segmentary and the centralized states. However, Brown did not deal with the conditions under which these types arise, nor did she investigate basic differences in the performance of governmental functions among them. Recently M. G. Smith (1956) has subjected the dichotomy to critical analysis, and showed that in it there is a tendency toward reification in that the analysis focuses on the concrete social units which perform the political functions and not on the functions themselves. He also claims that this approach has not differentiated sufficiently between different aspects of governmental functions— especially between the political and the administrative functions.

The second approach to the study of comparative primitive political institutions is best exemplified in the works of Colson (1954), Gluckman (1954a) and Peristiany (1954); and, from a somewhat different point of view, Hoebel (1954). While most of these works deal with only one tribe or society, they provide, either explicitly or by implication, possible comparative applications. Their main concern has been to show that in all primitive societies—ranging from small bands of hunters or fishermen to kingdoms such as those of Zulu, Swazi, and Dahomey—there exists some basic mechanism of social control which regulates the affairs of the tribe and resolves conflicts arising among its component groups. In the words of Gluckman (1954a:11), the most important among these mechanisms are "the inherent tendencies of groups to segment and then to become bound together by cross-cutting alliances."

The general assumption is that most of these mechanisms are in one way or another common to all types of primitive societies—whether "segmentary," centralized or some other. This approach poses the problem of the conditions under which various regulatory mechanisms operate, either without any specialized roles and organizations, or through specialized roles and organizations which are devoted mainly to the performance of regulatory tasks. Also implicit in some of these studies is the question of which area of life (economic, ritual, and so forth) makes such regulation most important and necessary. Hoebel's work on primitive law touches on some of these problems, mainly from the standpoint of the development of legal institutions.

The works summarized above have laid the foundations for the comparative study of primitive political institutions, but they are inadequate in several ways. First, there has been little comparative work using the criteria of comparison offered; second, some of these criteria have not been sufficiently systematic, as shown by Smith (1956); third, there has been too great an emphasis on the groups which perform governmental functions rather than on the functions themselves, and an inadequate differentiation between various types of governmental functions; and finally, there have been few attempts to relate the organization of various political functions to other aspects of the social organization.

The following sections will present a systematic scheme for the analysis of comparative political systems and of the social conditions to which they are related, and will illustrate it with several primitive societies. Before doing this, however, we must present some general considerations on the place of political institutions in the social structure.

POLITICAL INSTITUTIONS AS A SUBSYSTEM OF SOCIETY

Our basic assumption is that the political system is a specific subsystem of any society and that it can be most fully understood, and different political systems compared, through the analysis of its place within the society and its relation to other subsystems (economy, family ritual, status). This assumption has been used by several sociologists in analyzing characteristics of the political subsystem in the social structure (Levy 1952; Sutton 1955; Parsons 1956a).

The basic sociological characteristics of any political system are: it is the representative organization of a territorial society which has the legitimate monopoly of the use of force within the society which it regulates; in its representative function it uses this monopoly for the implementation of those goals which are held to be most important for the society by its influential members and groups and to some extent by all members of the society. The political system also organizes the general conditions for the maintenance of the society's solidarity and for the regulation of its members' behavior, especially potentially disruptive behavior. While many other parts of the society's institutional structure obviously contribute to one or another of these regulatory functions, the political system is characterized by its organization of these various functions in one subsystem and by its relating them within the framework of some common activity or organization. Because of this, the political system is dependent on other parts of the institutional structure for those activities and facilities which are necessary for its own operation and which enable it to make its specific contributions to other subsystems of the society.

Two aspects of the political system seem to be paramount. The first is regulation of power relations and mobilization of power for the implementation of various societal goals and for the maintenance of conditions necessary for such maximization. The second aspect deals with the processes of social control in the various groups and subsystems of a society, which are largely concerned with the prevention of deviant behavior. These enable us to understand some of the basic types of activities which are inherent, although in different degrees in different societies, in any political system and which largely determine the nature of its relations with other parts of the society.

Broadly speaking, political implementation of collective goals and maintenance of the proper conditions for this are closely related to the administrative and executive aspects of political activity. The administrative function of the political system deals principally with the organization of various technical aspects of collective activity, and with some regulation of the economic activities (e.g., maintenance of irrigation works). The executive functions are mainly concerned with articulation of major policy decisions concerning choices between different societal goals and allocation of obligations for the implementation of these goals.

With regard to the regulatory processes of a society, the functions of political institutions are in turn closely related to the mobilization of political support and the maintenance of the legitimacy of the system. Here the chief problems are (1) to maintain loyalty to the political system and to the bearers of political roles, especially basic loyalty to the main symbols of society and contingent loyalties to changing policies; (2) in this way to assure the flow of solidarity from the different groups to the political system, as well as the flow of necessary patterns of influence and demands from the political system to the other main centers of power in the society; and (3) to counteract any disintegrative tendencies within the society.

The problem of legitimation and loyalty exists in every society on at least two different levels. The first is that of legitimation of the political system as such—widespread identification of the members of the society with its major values and objectives and with its basic structural characteristics. This level of loyalty is maintained by any social system through a series of ritual and legal activities which emphasize identification of the political system with the basic values of the society, and its acceptance of responsibility for these values as well as of limitations in exercise of political power imposed by adherence to these values.

The second level of loyalty involves the manipulation of contingent support for changing policies and for different groups contending for positions of leadership. This has been called by Parsons (in discussion) the "party political" aspect of the political process; it is related to the regulation of shifts in the distribution of power in a society, and to the attempt to control such shifts. The party-political activities are usually oriented to the mobilization of support for varying, changing policies and for various people and groups contending for power and influence. The existence of party-politics assumes that within the society some measure of uncommitted, "floating" support exists which is not bound entirely to any group but can be manipulated by groups or individuals competing for power. These activities are the main focus of what may be called the *political struggle* for power and influence in a society, and they constitute an important aspect of all political organizations.

It is important to remember that political functions are an aspect of all groups and organizations in any society. All groups—family, locality, associations, and so on—have to deal with administrative problems, have to make decisions toward the realization of goals, have to be sure of the loyalty of members and of their support for various collective activities. The crucial point which differentiates the "total" political system from the political activities of various groups is the ultimate control of power and force within given territorial boundaries. This control is usually the monopoly of the central political institutions, which can endow with legitimacy any use of force by other groups in the society. But the very fact that political and regulatory aspects exist in all social groups poses one of the most important problems for comparative political research; namely, the extent to which the various subgroups within a society can regulate their own "political" problems and their political relations with other groups without recourse to the political subsystem itself. This problem is related to what Levy (1952) has called the distinction between concrete and analytical units of analysis. The political "element" is analytically present in all groups and societies, but the degree to which specific and concrete political roles exist differs from one society to another.

PROBLEMS OF COMPARATIVE ANALYSIS

This last problem, the extent to which there develop specific and concrete political roles, has been in the foreground of most of the comparative studies of primitive political systems, and the dichotomy between segmentary and centralized systems is largely derived from it. However, it is not the only problem and preoccupation with it can lead to neglect of other significant items of comparative analysis. It is our contention here that additional criteria are important for the comparative analysis of primitive political systems and that the development of special political organization cannot be fully understood without reference to these additional criteria. Among these, the following seem to be most important:

First is the relative emphasis within each political system on the four main types of political activity—the administrative, executive, "party-political," and juridical-cultural. While all are inherent in every political system, the degree to which each is emphasized and elaborated varies greatly and this variation constitutes one of the most important differences between political systems.

Second is the scope and nature of the political struggle in a society, particularly the nature of the dominant rules and norms which regulate the political struggle, their relation to the basic values and to the legitimation of the political system, and the degree of acceptance of these rules and norms by all who participate in the political struggle. This struggle should be related to the nature of the groups from which the different contenders organize their support, and to the types of rewards allocated through the political struggle.

Third is the extent and nature of changes possible within a given political system. While every political system has to deal with problems of change, the ability to cope with different types of change differs greatly. Some systems can regulate changes in personnel but not changes in structure, or can at best only multiply existing structural arrangements and groups. Other systems can contain structural modifications and some secondary orientations and values—but only to a limited degree. Others generate certain types of structural changes and may or may not have mechanisms which can accommodate and even foster a significant amount of such changes.

The importance of these additional criteria of comparison can be demonstrated in several ways. First, it can be shown on the purely descriptive level that they can focus our attention on many features of the political organization of primitive societies which otherwise may remain unnoticed. Second, and perhaps more significantly, it is only through the use of these variables that we can go beyond the purely descriptive and classificatory level and attempt to analyze the various social conditions which are related to different types of political organization.

The analysis of such conditions is, in my view, one of the most important problems in a comparative analysis of primitive (or, for that matter, of all) political systems. It has been perhaps the most neglected aspect in the existing literature on this subject. Some general assump-

tions have been made on the correlation between the development of
the political system and population density and modes of subsistence
(Fortes and Evans-Pritchard 1940; Lowie 1949; Schapera 1956), but
they have not been systematically analyzed or subjected to rigorous
examination.

In the following pages we shall attempt to demonstrate the utility
of the proposed criteria of comparison from both the descriptive and
analytical points of view. We shall describe the political systems of several types of primitive tribes and analyze the social conditions which
are related to these types. The description will emphasize the following
aspects: the system of role allocation, the extent of differentiation, the
extent of self-regulation of the major units of the society, and the major
goals and value orientations of the societies. On the basis of the general
theoretical considerations presented above, these aspects seem to be most
relevant to the study of political organization. The typology of the various tribes is based on the extent of articulation of political positions
and organizations. In this way it will be possible to see to what extent
such a typology is adequate, and what other aspects of political organizations are important for a comparative analysis. At the end we shall
propose some tentative hypotheses as to the relationships between
various aspects of political organization and of the social structure.

SOME TYPES OF PRIMITIVE POLITICAL SYSTEMS

We illustrate our approach through the analysis of several selected
cases: various types of "segmentary" tribes (mostly African, Apache,
Plains Indian, and Pueblo), African autonomous village-communities,
and some African centralized kingdoms. These societies do not constitute a systematic sample of primitive tribes (they are mostly African),
but since our purpose is only to illustrate the feasibility of our
approach, this can perhaps be excused.

The starting point of this analysis is the extent of articulation of
special political positions and organizations. The first broad group is
composed of tribes which seemingly have no specially organized, central
political authority or organization; political activity takes place within
the subgroups of the society and through their interaction. Beyond this
common denominator there are many differences between these tribes,
particularly in the nature of the main subgroups among which interaction takes place, and the extent of and the main social spheres of this
interaction (our sample does not include all variations, but those presented suffice for our preliminary analysis). This category includes: (a)
tribes with but rudimentary political interaction between various loose

bands, small family and territorial units (only cursorily mentioned); (b) segmentary tribes organized in corporate lineages between which there is extensive political and ritual interaction; (c) tribes in which, in addition to the organized kinship groups, other important groups and principles of social and political interaction exist, notably in those cases where various criteria of universalistic allocation of roles are manifested in age-groups and regiments; (d) those where association is based on particularistic criteria of membership and oriented either to ritual or collective (war) activities; (e) tribes in which the kinship and lineage groups interact on the basis of a special hierarchical stratification into classes (mostly in the ritual field), and finally (f) the so-called "acephalous villages" in which the importance of family and kinship groups diminishes in favor of various specialized associations based on the universalistic criteria of achievement and interacting chiefly in the economic and social spheres.

The next category includes those tribes among which central political authority and organization undoubtedly exist, subdivided according to the types of groups which bear the political action and positions. The first are (g) tribes in which kinship and lineage groups are the most important units that bear political action; the second are (h) tribes in which some universalistic groups also exist, such as regiments or age-groups, and the last are (i) societies in which various types of associations perform such central tasks.

While we call each type by a descriptive name, usually the one most commonly found in the literature, it should be borne in mind that they are not a series of discrete, discontinuous categories, but derive from the analytical criteria enumerated above.

I. TYPES OF SEGMENTARY TRIBES

A. Band organization. The simplest type of political and social organization can be found among "simple," noncentralized societies, such as Australian and Pygmy tribes, and tribes such as Jicarilla Apache (Bellah 195:212–41), and the Plateau Tonga (Colson 1953). They are composed of relatively undifferentiated, loose groups, families and territorial units. There is little division of labor, and the extent of interaction and interdependence is relatively small except for intermarriage. Roles are mainly allocated to members of the family and other small particularistic groups, and there is relatively little scope for individual initiative and achievement, except occasionally in the field of leadership. The main goal orientations are adaptive and ritual; i.e., adaptation to the physical environment, procurement of well-being for the tribe, and maintenance of its main patterns of life. These goals are attained through the internal activities of the main subgroups of the society and through their interaction. The system of stratification, insofar as it exists, is focused on these units, with status determined in terms of the common ritual values and to some extent in terms of the relative wealth between the various local and kinship groups. In these tribes, we find few fixed "political" positions and a high extent of self-regulation of the main component groups.

B. *"Classical" segmentary tribes.* The "classical" segmentary societies are best exemplified by the Tallensi (Fortes 1940, 1945, 1949) and Bantu Kavirondo (Wagner 1949) and less well by the Nuer (Evans-Pritchard 1940c). Among them, the basic lineage groups—the various maximal lineages—are the primary bearers of political roles and tasks. There is a high degree of organized interdependence and complementarity among the various component units. The main unit of social specialization is the lineage, i.e., a segment of the clan in which the members are genealogically related to one another. The lineages may be of various generation depths and may split off after some generations, but the common identification expressed in terms of common ancestry persists. The lineages and clans are usually localized groups with a strong corporate organization. Their interrelations are defined in corporate terms and the most important political, judicial, and ritual interaction of their members is carried on in the name of these corporate units, the individual members acting as their representatives. The mutual specialization and interdependence of corporate lineages and clans is manifest among the Tallensi in the two types of chiefdoms, the *na'am* and the ritual *tendaam* (Custodian of the Earth); the first is related to earth and the second endowed with rainmaking powers. Both of these offices are permanently vested in certain clans, and thus the main offices of leadership reside in corporate kinship groups. There exists some competition between the various lineages and their respective officers as to prestige and influence, although these relative positions are seemingly defined largely by tradition and the dominant ritual values of the society. The leaders of the society are concerned principally with ritual functions, and to a smaller degree with the settlement of disputes between the lineages. In most other respects, the single lineage is the unit of collective action. Most administrative-technical problems are settled and organized within the maximal lineages, and most collective action—such as the organization of fishing expeditions—is largely, if not entirely, within the province of the lineages. Most of the interaction between lineages—in addition to intermarriage and kinship ties—is concerned with ritual, and to a much smaller extent with economic activities. It is in the field of ritual that the main values of the society lie.

C. *Universalistic (age-groups) segmentary tribes.* The Nandi and Masai have usually been regarded as falling within the segmentary category, but nevertheless differ from the tribe just described (Eisenstadt 1954b; 1956: Ch. III, Bibliography). There are no corporate lineages: the clans and subclans are not territorial organizations, and the territorial groups are not composed of homogeneous kin and family elements. The kin group does not constitute the basic unit of the social division of labor, and the main political roles are allocated according to universalistic criteria of membership. There is also some achievement orientation with respect to excellence in warfare and, to a lesser degree, accumulation of wealth. The main goal and value orientations are in the fields of ritual and warfare, where social differentiation is highest. Interaction between the various subunits of these tribes is regulated by a purely local and territorial hierarchy, beginning with the smallest units and extending upward toward the wider and more inclusive ones. The judicial system is similarly organized. Quarrels which cannot be settled within a small local unit, or in which several such units are involved, are settled by representatives of larger territorial units; nowhere are these judiciary offices vested in representatives of lineages, clans, or other kin groups. The same holds true of ritual offices. The extent of self-regulation of the various kinship and territorial groups is somewhat smaller than in the former types, and there are groups of elders or "village" councilmen which, while they do not have great formal power, are an important factor in molding public opinion and in mediating and resolving conflicts. There also appear semiformalized leaders and chiefs with rather special positions. Unlike positions of leadership among the segmentary tribes, these are not necessarily vested in any lineage or other group but are achieved through individual attainment. Such leaders are important in making decisions regarding wars or raids.

The specific organizations for the implementation of warfare are the military regiments and the age-groups, which need not be identical but usually have a strong interrelationship (Eisenstadt 1956; op. cit.). They cut across kinship and local ties, and perform important functions in warfare and other collective activities such as the juridical process. In connection with these collective activities, as well as with some of the disputes that may arise, we find a certain amount of what we have called party-political activities. Disputes may arise as to the wisdom of a certain policy, initiation of a war-party, allocation of available manpower for tribal tasks, and there also may be informal competition between individuals for positions in the tribal council or tribunals.

D. *The "associational" tribes.* A type of tribe which does not have centralized political organization can be found among some of the

Plains and Pueblo groups, especially the Hopi, the Zuni (Eggan 1950; Titiev 1944), the Kiowa and other Plains societies (Lowie 1916; Bowers 1950). In most of these tribes with the partial exception of five Plains tribes which have a strong age-group organization and a larger extent of individual achievement orientation (Eisenstadt 1954a) the most important offices are vested either in members of hereditary kinship groups or in members of the various associations which are characteristic of these tribes. As a general rule, these associations perform important functions in integrating the various kinship and territorial groupings, and membership in them is largely determined on the particularistic grounds of kinship and personal relations. There are few full-fledged political offices and organizations which are distinct from other roles and groups. Some types of chiefs exist whose main functions are performance of rituals and mediation, and who usually have little coercive power or authority. On the whole, the various kinship, territorial, and associational groups are self-regulatory. These different types of groups tend to perform complementary functions in the integration of the tribe, although they may not always succeed in coping with all the tensions that exist and in regulating all the interrelationships between the component groups. The main goal and value orientations of these societies are similar to those of the tribes previously discussed, but some important differences exist between them. Among the Pueblos the main values are ritual-adaptive ones, while among the Plains tribes there is a greater emphasis on achievements in war and on pursuit of collective goals, and these have repercussions on the structure and goals of the associations.

The principal exception to this relative lack of coordinated activity is found among the Plains tribes, during the periods when the bands gather and engage in common efforts—especially in hunting and war expeditions. On these occasions, a relatively distinct leadership emerges, various associations perform basic directive functions, and their chiefs become fully authorized leaders of the tribe (Mandelbaum 1956). One association is delegated the task of directing the expeditions, another has the full policing authority. The emergence of specific executive and juridical positions is here closely related to the need to perform common collective tasks and to regulate the available manpower resources for their execution. The extent of party-politics was relatively small, although competition existed among various associations for prestige, for the performance of different ritual functions, and for ownership of various "bundles."

E. *The ritually stratified tribes.* The Annuak (Evans-Pritchard 1940b), the Shilluk (Butt 1952) and the Ankole (Oberg 1940) display many differences, but share common characteristics in political organization. Among them we find some degree of differentiation and stratification in the ritual-symbolic field, but very little in any other major field of social life. The main goal-orientations are collective-ritual, i.e., are expressed in attempts to "wrest" ritual power in behalf of various collectivities. These goals constitute the common tribal framework of interaction and afford the main criteria of stratification, according to which the lineages and kinship groups are judged. These groups are relatively self-sufficient economically and administratively but interact in ritual matters. In most of these societies, there are two "classes"—nobles and commoners. The nobles are the active competitors for the main political positions, which entail little actual authority and power. Their political systems can best be described as centralized, stratified, focused on competition for ritual positions, and with minimal administrative and juridical organization. The chiefs and nobles may distribute any surplus to their followers. They have little juridical power, and most subunits of the society (lineages, villages) enjoy relative autonomy and regulate most of their own affairs. The main value of political positions is symbolic-ritual and, in the words of Evans-Pritchard (1940b: 138) "it is the acceptance of a common value, and not corporate action, which constitutes the policy." Around these ritual positions a continuous struggle is waged between nobles of different lineages, who try to mobilize support among the commoners. Thus, we find a rather intensive pattern of party-political activities which gives rise to a special type of political intermediary—a member of the class of commoners who is in the political service of a noble or chief, organizes his supporters, and comes to his aid in various quarrels. Beyond these activities, focused on the ritual-political field, there are few specialized, administrative, or executive activities or organizations.

F. Acephalous, autonomous villages. The so-called acephalous villages are best exemplified by the Yako (Forde 1939, 1950), Ibo, Ibibio (Green 1947), and some Yoruba groups (Lloyd 1954). Their main specific characteristic is the presence of so-called associations that have an especially important place in their life. The graded titles and membership positions in these associations are not hereditarily vested in families, lineages, or other descent groups, but are acquired individually, although perhaps with the help of the families. Thus, the main principles of role allocation are here universalistic, achievement-oriented, and to some degree specialized. Most of the specialization is especially prominent in the activities related to the attainment of instrumental gratification and economic and social goals, which are also the main values of the society.

Among the Yako, the most fully described of these peoples, the village (or town) is divided into several wards which form the basic administrative units of the society. Within these wards several family groups and patri-clans live together, while other members of the same patri-clans may be found in other wards. Except on the lower, family-unit level, the organization of the ward is not based on the corporate interaction of the family and kin groups. The patri-clan has certain corporate functions and its heads perform both ritual and judiciary roles, but this is true only with respect to members of other patri-clans, members of a ward, or to the common economic enterprises and ritual observances which bind the village together. The common affairs of the ward are supervised by various officers, elected not on the basis of kin affiliation or membership but on the basis of wealth, age, wisdom, and various other personal qualities and attainments.

Among the Yako we also find a relatively more complicated governmental system than in the former types. The main centers of power are the ward and village councils, and the associations divide among themselves, as it were, many functions of government and social control. Quite strong competition exists between individuals over the attainment of positions within the associations, semipolitical positions as ward heads or members of the village council, and between some of the associations as to their relative influence in village life. Here is high degree of group interaction, especially in the economic field. Each group is to a large extent dependent on the labor force of other groups, and many economic tasks are undertaken in common by a ward or village. The extent of economic activities also explains the great importance of various technical-administrative activities within the structure of governmental framework. Thus, we find that one of the main concerns of the "central authorities" is to arrange for common economic activities, maintenance of the water supply, or clearing of the bush. Most activities are performed by members of various age groups, and are directed by village and association officials.

As has already been implied, most of the higher "political" positions are closely related to positions in associations, but at the same time certain more specialized political, and especially administrative, positions also tend to develop. Here are special administrators of the various wards or of the village councils, who are usually in charge of the administrative works performed by the age groups.

II. CENTRALIZED CHIEFDOMS

The so-called centralized chiefdoms are best exemplified by the Zulu (Gluckman 1940), Ngoni (Barnes 1955), Swazi (Kuper 1947), Tswana

(Schapera 1955), Bemba (Richards 1940), Ashanti (Busia 1951), Pondo (Hunter 1936), and Khoisa (Lestrade 1937). The most important characteristics shared by these chiefdoms is that within their kingdoms, the political sphere is distinct from that of lineage and kinship relations, and political positions acquire a certain degree of autonomy. The relative importance of corporate descent groups, lineages, clans and the like for the definition of the territorial units of society and for the general political life of the tribe is smaller than among the various segmentary tribes, with the possible exception of the Ashanti.

. In most of these societies there is also less self-regulation of internal affairs and fewer mutual interrelations of the major subgroups of the society.

G,H. Centralized and federative monarchies. But beyond this common characteristic there are certain important differences among them. The chiefdoms mentioned above can be roughly divided into two types: The first (to be called the centralized monarchy) is illustrated by Zulu, Ngoni, Swazi, and Tswana; the second (to be called the federative monarchy) is illustrated by Bemba, Ashanti, Pondo, and Khoisa.

The distinction between the two types of "primitive" kingdoms may be said to be broadly that of a difference in the degree to which (a) the major groups regulate their own affairs in various spheres, and (b) the extent to which the major political offices are vested in various ascriptive groups or, conversely, the extent to which the political sphere is organized on a level different from that of local kin and economic spheres.

If we compare the two groups of peoples according to these criteria, we find some broad and striking differences. First, we find that in general the extent of self-regulation of territorial and kin groups in economic, juridical, and ritual matters is much smaller in the centralized than in the federative monarchies. Second, among the centralized monarchies, the most distinguishing characteristic is universal membership in the widest political unit of the tribe through direct allegiance to the king. Although the king's relationship to his subjects is couched in kinship terms (manifest in the national royal ritual), from the standpoint of membership this relation is distinctly universalistic, i.e., open to anyone who will swear allegiance and attach himself to the chief. Moreover, allegiance to the chief and membership in the political community are not necessarily dependent upon membership in any intermediary group. The contrary is true of the federative monarchies, which are usually composed of amalgamations of lineages, clans, or local kin groups which have been incorporated as groups within the total social unit, with membership in the latter attainable only through these subunits.

In the centralized monarchies, the king may approach his subjects directly in judicial matters, and especially in exacting tribute and calling up the army for either military exigencies or "public works," and the king has ultimate authority over the various heads and local chiefs. In the federative monarchies, the king's ultimate dependence on the lesser chiefs and on the organized, corporate activities of the various kin and territorial groups is most clearly evident among the Ashanti and somewhat less so among the Khoisa, Bemba, and Pondo.

Differences in the composition of the king's council are also important. Truly enough in both types, the council is composed of certain members of the royal clan (family), heads of certain leading clans and families, and certain personal favorites of the king. However, the relative importance of these elements, especially the last two, varies considerably among the societies. Among the centralized monarchies, the commoner members of the council are not merely private advisers and favorites of the king, but full members of the council, holding central offices. Among the federative monarchies, the advisers are usually more limited in number and act in a more private capacity. In these latter societies, the council is composed principally of heads of the various territorial units, clans, and lineages, who have an inherent membership right and without whom the council cannot properly act. Among the Swazi and Zulu such hereditary councillors, although important, are not as independent of the king's will in holding their offices as they are among the federative monarchies.

Differences also exist between the two groups in relation to the major goal emphases. Among the centralized monarchies, there is a strong emphasis on collective goals (war, expansion), and many ritual activities are even geared to these goals. Among the federative monarchies, there is a much stronger emphasis on adaptive-ritual goals.

There are corresponding differences between the two types in the organization and articulation of various governmental activities. First, as has been implied in the earlier discussion, in the centralized monarchies we generally find a greater articulation of specific political positions and organizations. As we have seen, the various positions on the king's council, in the royal courts, and so forth, are more independent of membership in other groups (lineages, clans) than in the federative monarchies, and there are also more positions of this kind in the first type than in the second. Further, in the centralized monarchies there are many more organized collective activities, common to all the tribes and directed by the main chief. The two most important are military expeditions and various kinds of public works. These public works are usually performed for the benefit of the central authorities or for the maintenance of efficient networks of communication. While some such activities are also organized in the federative monarchies, they are usually more limited and confined to local enterprises and are directed by heads of lineages or clans. In the centralized monarchies, most such activities are performed by specific organizations, namely, the various age-groups or age-regiments. The age-regiments cut across the existing lineage and territorial units, and are directed by the king or his representatives. There are no age-regiments in the federative tribes, and most military and public works activities are performed by lineages and clan groups.

Another important characteristic of the centralized monarchies is the relative intensity of party-politics, although some party-politics can also be found in the federative monarchies—most of it centering around the struggle of various lineage and kinship groups for positions of influence and prestige in the political framework. The Ashanti confederation perhaps shows the greatest amount of such conflict, but it can also be found among the Bemba, Pondo, and others. In these tribes, however, political conflict has been largely between corporate groups, with little room for individual or subgroup activities. In the centralized monarchies, there is much more intensive party-political activity; there is strong competition between the king and members of his own clan, between king and local chiefs, between various councillors and between kinship and local groups versus the central authorities. In certain respects this intensity of party-political activities resembles that of the segmentary tribes of the Nandi type. Here, as in the tribes of the latter type, we also find relatively little administrative activity directed toward the organization of economic activities and conditions.

I. Monarchies based on associations and secret societies. A distinct type of centralized chiefdom found among the Mende and other tribes of Sierra Leone and Liberia (McCulloch 1950; Schwab 1947) resembles the Bemba and Ashanti, in that most political positions are vested in members of hereditary groups. But here an additional factor intervenes—namely, the existence of many associations, most of the "secret society" types. The best examples of this are the Poro and the Zande associations among the Mende. These perform important political and administrative functions, especially in economic and cultural fields and in the general maintenance of social control. Here is also a greater elaboration of special political and administrative apparatus, some of which is under the control of the king and some under the control of the associations. In addition to this wide range of administrative functions which deal with the organization of certain economic activities, some degree of party-politics also exists. The party-politics usually center in the upper echelons of the secret associations and in the relations between the associations and the kings, and are not as public and open as among the Zulu or Swazi. Here also, the extent of self-regulation by the various subgroups of the society—kinship and locality groups—is very small, and more of the regulatory functions are performed by the central organs. This can be seen especially in the relatively centralized juridical organization of these tribes.

Of the societies studied here, the highest degree of centralization and of development of special political and administrative organs can probably be found among the Dahomey (Herskovits 1938). This society shows a highly centralized hereditary monarchy, based on a hierarchical organization of various hereditary subunits—localities, groups of families, and the like. Most secondary political positions are vested in such groups, but the various officials are to a considerable extent dependent upon the king, and do not have the semiautonomous status that such officials have among the Bemba and Ashanti. There is a relatively marked economic differentiation between the king and his entourage and other groups in the society. The administrative and centralized juridical activity is focused largely on the provision of adequate economic and manpower facilities for the king. The various subunits have little autonomy, and can regulate directly only a few of their own affairs and their interactions with other groups. There seem to be few "secret" associations among the Dahomey, and those that do exist are of a much more private nature than those of the Mende. Moreover, they do not play an important part in the political life of the tribe. However, relatively strong cult-groups seem to exist, and the heads of these have some political influence. Because of the highly authoritarian and ascriptive character of the political institutions, there is little party-politics, but such activities go on among the heads of cult-groups, the king's councillors, and the people holding the higher administrative positions. The elaborate and well-knit central administrative staff deals with the organization of economic activities, keeping the peace, and the maintenance of discipline and obedience toward the king, performing these functions on behalf of the subgroups of the society.

TYPES OF SOCIAL STRUCTURE AND OF POLITICAL ORGANIZATION: SOME TENTATIVE HYPOTHESES

We have described some of the main characteristics of the political organization and social structure of selected types of primitive societies. We may now inquire as to how these aspects of the social structure are related to characteristics of the political structures.

Social differentiation and levels of political organization. We may first inquire what the material presented tells us about the conditions under which different levels of articulation of political positions and organizations are found. Generally speaking, this material bears out the hypothesis that the greater the differentiation and/or the inability of various subgroups of a society to regulate their interrelations, the greater would be the development of special political organizations, other conditions being equal. As we have seen earlier, such an hypothesis is implicit in some of the existing discussions about comparative primitive political systems. It is in line with that advanced lately by Schapera (1956:219), although it aims at a more inclusive definition of the nature of differentiation. Such an hypothesis may seem to be tautological, since it may be claimed that obviously the more differentiated a society is, the more specialized will be its constituent parts of which the political system is one. But it need not be tautological if it can be shown that greater articulation of political organization will take place no matter in what sphere (e.g., economic, ritual, and so on) there is greater differentiation and specialization. In other words, the level of differentiation need not be the same in all subsystems of a society, and political subsystems (unlike other subsystems) are most sensitive to problems arising out of differentiation in any other parts of the society.

If we consider societies discussed above in the order of their differentiation, we find that in general this hypothesis is borne out. We have analyzed in each of the types the extent of differentiation and of self-regulation of the various groups of which the society is composed. We have seen in each category the number and type of groups found, the extent to which these groups manage their own affairs in the economic, ritual, and legal field, and their relations with other groups. We have also seen how many special political positions and organizations exist in each. These two variables—the extent of differentiation and self-regulation, and the extent of articulation of political positions—have been established by independent criteria. The less differentiated societies—the so-called segmentary tribes of different types—have minimal special political positions, but even among these there are significant differences. Tribes such as the Nandi and Masai, where some differentiation exists between spheres in which roles are allocated by universalistic or particularistic criteria, and where there is some stratification based on achievement, show a greater development of political roles than do such peoples as the Tallensi. Among the Annuak and Shilluk, where some differentiation of strata exists, we also find a few specific political offices, centered especially in the ritual field.

In the various autonomous villages, where we have seen much

greater differentiation and where wide spheres of life are regulated by universalistic and achievement orientations, and where a correspondingly complex system of groups and stratification is formed, we have also seen the greater existence of political organization. The same principle applies if we analyze the centralized chiefdoms, all of which have relatively greater differentiation. Among these kingdoms we also find that the societies which have strong universalistic and achievement orientations (such as the Zulu and Swazi) have a more complex system of political organization than do those whose division of labor is based on particularistic and ascriptive criteria.

Organization of different types of political activities. In general, the first hypothesis is borne out by the data presented here. A closer examination of these data, in relation to this hypothesis, shows several interesting facts: First, the dichotomy between "segmentary" and "centralized" primitive societies is not a true dichotomy. Rather, there is a continuum in the articulation of political positions and of organization of political activities. In all societies at least some of the basic political functions are performed by some specific roles or units and it is not possible to distinguish entirely between stateless and "state" societies. What distinguishes one society from another is not so much the existence or nonexistence of central political organization, but the extent to which different types of political functions are performed by different specialized units and the extent to which the functions are organized in various types of roles and organizations (Smith 1956).

Second, this hypothesis is too general to account for many significant differences in the political organization of the tribes analyzed here. It treats the concept of "differentiation" in too homogeneous a way and consequently tends to treat diverse political activities as a homogeneous unit. Neither does it take into account the fact that emphasis may be placed on different aspects of political activity. The data show that societies may differ in the extent of articulation of political roles and moreover may emphasize different aspects of political activities (as for instance, the strong emphasis on executive and party-political activities of the Zulu as against the emphasis on ritual and juridical activities of the Bemba). It is necessary to account for these differences.

We have seen that the main interrelations between the political and the other institutions of a society can be understood in terms of the functions which the political institutions perform, and in terms of the types of resources these institutions must mobilize in order to perform these functions. Thus, in any detailed consideration of the relation between the political structure and other aspects of the social structure, it is important to see what goals and needs the society emphasizes; what exigencies it faces; to what extent these goals and needs can be implemented and the exigencies dealt with by the various subgroups of a society without recourse to special political and administrative agencies, and where such agencies do develop, what kinds of resources are most important for them.

On the basis of these considerations and the material analyzed above, the following hypotheses can be proposed: That the relative emphasis on different types of political activities is dependent on the main goal and value-orientations of a society.

(a) An emphasis on collective goals, preoccupation with warfare, extension of collective power, or with other collective endeavors is closely related to executive activities which deal with the mobilization, manipulation, and organization of internal manpower resources. In such cases, the need arises to emphasize executive leadership and decision-making, and to enable such leadership to organize the available resources for the maximization of collective goals and for dealing with the exigencies which are created through the emphasis on them. Both the Nandi and Masai groups, and the Zulu and Swazi are good illustrations of this correlation. Interesting support for this hypothesis can be found among many of the Plains societies. Here executive leadership is operative only when the tribe is engaged in a collective endeavor—e.g., war raid, hunting party—and is not operative when the tribe is dispersed and its component parts are dealing primarily with adaptive problems. Also, many embryonic types of leadership found in simple bands and tribes seem to be closely connected with the performance of collective tribal tasks.

(b) Special emphasis on instrumental goals and economic gratifications seems to be more closely related to development of administrative functions. The implementation of such goals usually necessitates the organization of many technical aspects of common activities and creates many exigencies in the technical cooperative fields. The best illustrations of this correlation can be found among the Yako and Ibo, and to some extent among the Mende.

(c) A strong emphasis on solidary values and integrative goals seems to be related to a special articulation of party-political activities. Insofar as the society emphasizes maintenance of the basic solidarity of the collectivity, with the consequent regulation of all subgroups within its framework, it would also be necessary to manipulate those subgroups in such a way as to assure their allegiance to the common goal. As the maintenance of solidarity and integration is of some importance in all societies, some party politics can be found in all the societies studied. However, they are most evident in societies such as the Tallensi, Annuak, Shilluk, and Mende, which tend to emphasize the goal of solidarity.

Party-political activities also increase when the problems of maintaining solidarity become more complex and acute, especially insofar as many groups with differing principles of social organization participate in the political struggle.

(d) Also of interest is the special place of ritual activities, which must deal with the legitimation of the political system in terms of the society's values. Obviously such activities are closely related to an emphasis on cultural values. Some aspects of such values seem to be predominant in most of the primitive societies studied, and the maintenance of their given traditions and patterns of life is a common basic orientation of their values. In most of the societies discussed here, the performance of ritual functions which emphasize these orientations is therefore a basic part of the activities of holders of political positions, and there are few differences between them in this respect.

Social differentiation, societal goals and political organization. But the value orientations and goals predominant in a society are not the only determinants of the relative emphasis on different aspects of political activity. These goals tend to delineate the general orientation of the political activities of a society, but in themselves they do not determine the actual organization of these activities. It is entirely conceivable that a particular society may be able to implement its major goal and value orientation through the activities of its component groups, without recourse to any specific political organization, simply by special emphasis on this or that aspect of political activity. The hypothesis may be suggested that the full articulation of any aspect of political activity, in the form of special organizations, will be determined by: (a) the main goals and value orientations of a society; (b) the types of resources needed for their maximization; and (c) the extent to which these resources are not available through the internal work of various subgroups of the society.

In all the tribes discussed above, we saw examples of societies which could maximize goals with little recourse to specialized positions and agencies. The Tonga, Tallensi, and Pueblos are good examples of this.

In other tribes, however, a relatively great differentiation and consequent lack of self-regulation of various subunits exist in areas of social life which are most closely related to the main goals of the society. Among the "universalistic" segmentary tribes (e.g., Nandi, Masai) and among the centralized monarchies (e.g., Zulu, Swazi) the existence of both universalistic and particularistic principles of role allocation has repercussions on the availability of resources which are necessary for the maximization of their collective goals. The most important of these is the fact that such resources—manpower, wealth, group loyalties—are not "given" by various ascriptive subgroups, but have to be mobilized through special political-executive and party-political activities.

Among the Pueblos, executive leadership arises on occasions when the goal-emphasis is shifted to collective tasks which cannot be performed by the self-regulated interaction of various subunits. Among the Annuak, the special articulation of political-ritualized positions is found in relation to the relatively great differentiation and stratification in the ritual-solidary field and to the high level of rather unregulated competition between the subgroups in this field.

Among the Yako and Ibo, the special organization of administrative activities is closely related to the strong interdependence (and the relative lack of self-sufficiency) between various local and family groups in the economic and instrumental fields. Significantly enough, in those areas of social life where such differentiation does not exist and/or which are not related to the main goals and value-orientations of the society, the articulation of special political positions is smaller. Thus, among the universalistic-segmentary tribes and centralized monarchies, there are few purely administrative positions which deal with organization of economic and instrumental activities; among the autonomous villages there are few special executive positions, and so on.

While many more illustrations could be given, those given above suffice to demonstrate the feasibility of the approach presented here. At this stage of analysis, this approach does not presume to say anything about the historical development of different political institutions or to deal with the problem of what mechanisms these institutions develop under certain social conditions. It aims only to establish meaningful correlations between different aspects of social structure and political organization.

We have here attempted to present a new approach to the comparative study of primitive political institutions and to introduce some new variables in such studies. We have not dealt with all the problems of such an analysis, specifically not with the political process and its relationship to processes of change. It is not claimed that this approach in general, or our discussion in particular, is definitive. There are many other significant variables for comparative analysis. Moreover, the data presented here will have to be modified and elaborated through application to wider and more representative samples of primitive societies. At present, the main purpose of the study has been to illustrate the feasibility and value of such an approach.

BIBLIOGRAPHY

BARNES, A. J.
> 1955   Politics in a changing society. Oxford, Oxford University Press.

BARNARDI, B.
> 1952   The age-system of the Nilo-Hamitic peoples. Africa 22:316–332.

BELLAH, R. N.
> 1952   Apache kinship systems. Cambridge, Harvard University Press.

BOWERS, A.
> 1950   Mandan social and ceremonial organization. Chicago, University of Chicago Press.

BROWN, P.
> 1951   **Patterns of authority in West Africa. Africa 21:261–278.**

BUSIA, K.
> 1951   The position of the chief among the Ashanti. Oxford, Oxford University Press.

BUTT, A.
> 1952   The Nilotes of the Anglo Egyptian Sudan. London, International African Institute.

COLSON, E.
> 1953   Social control and vengeance in Plateau Tonga society. Africa 23:199–212.

EGGAN, F.
> 1950   Social organization of the Western Pueblos. Chicago, University of Chicago Press.

EISENSTADT, S. N.
> 1954a   Plains Indian age groups. Man 54:6–8.
> 1954b   African age groups. Africa 24:100–113.
> 1956   From generation to generation—age groups and social structure. Glencoe, The Free Press.

EVANS-PRITCHARD, E. E.
> 1940a   The political structure of the Nandi speaking peoples of Kenya. Africa 13:250–267.
> 1940b   The political system of the Annuak. London, London School of Economics, Monograph in Anthropology.

1940c The Nuer. Oxford, Oxford University Press.

FORDE, C. D.
1939 Government in Umor. Africa 12:129–162.
1950 Ward organization among the Uakö. Africa 20:267–289.

FORTES, M.
1940 The political system of the Tallensi of the northern territories of the Gold Coast. *In* African Political Systems, ed. by M. Fortes and E. E. Evans-Pritchard.
1945 The dynamics of clanship among the Tallensi. Oxford, Oxford University Press.
1949 The web of kinship among the Tallensi. Oxford, Oxford University Press.
1953 The structure of the unilineal descent group. American Anthropologist 55:17–41.

FORTES, M. and E. E. EVANS-PRITCHARD
1940 African political systems. Oxford, Oxford University Press.

GLUCKMAN, M.
1940 The kingdom of Zulu. *In* African Political Systems, ed. by M. Fortes & E. E. Evans-Pritchard.
1954a Political institutions. *In* The institutions of primitive society, ed. by E. E. Evans-Pritchard. Glencoe, The Free Press.
1954b Rituals of rebellion in S. E. Africa. Manchester.

GREEN, M. M.
1948 Ibo Village affairs. London, Sidgwick and Jackson.

HERSKOVITS, M.
1938 Dahomey. New York, J. J. Augustin.

HOEBEL, E. A.
1954 The law of primitive man. Cambridge, Harvard University Press.

HUNTER, M.
1936 Reaction to conquest. Oxford, Oxford University Press.

KRIGE, E. J. and J. D.
1943 The realm of the Rain-Queen. Oxford, Oxford University Press.

KUPER, H.
1947 An African aristocracy. Oxford, Oxford University Press.

LESTRADE, G. P.
1928 Some notes on the political organization of the BeChwana. South African Journal of Science 25:427–432.

LEVY, MARION J.
1952 The structure of society. Princeton, Princeton University Press.

LLOYD, P.
   1954   The traditional political system of the Yoruba. Southwestern Journal of Anthropology 10:361–384.
LOWIE, R.
   1916   Plains Indian age societies: historical and comparative summary. Anthropological Papers of the American Museum of Natural History, Vol. 11.
   1948   Some aspects of political organisation among the American aborigines. Journal of the Royal Anthropological Institute 78:17–25.
MANDELBAUM, D.
   1956   Social groupings. *In* Man, culture and society, ed by H. L. Shapiro. New York, Oxford University Press.
McCULLOCH, M.
   1950   The peoples of Sierra Leone Protectorate. London, International African Institute.
OBERG, K.
   1940   The kingdom of Ankole in Uganda. *In* African Political Systems, ed. by M. Fortes and E. E. Evans-Pritchard.
PARSONS, T.
   1956a Economy and society. Glencoe, The Free Press.
   1956b Sociological approach to the theory of organization. Administrative Science Quarterly 1:63–86.
PERISTIANY, L. W.
   1954   Law. *In* The institutions of primitive society, ed. by E. E. Evans-Pritchard. Glencoe, The Free Press.
RICHARDS, A.
   1940   The political system of the Bemba tribe, Northern Rhodesia. *In* African political systems, ed. by M. Fortes and E. E. Evans-Pritchard. Oxford, Oxford University Press.
SCHAPERA, I.
   1955   A handbook of Tswana law and custom. Oxford, Oxford University Press.
   1956   Government and politics in tribal societies. London, Watts.
SCHWAB, D. W.
   1947   Tribes of the Liberian Hinterland. Papers of the Peabody Museum, Vol. 31.
SMITH, M. G.
   1956   Segmentary lineage systems. Journal of the Royal Anthropological Institute 86:II, 39–81.
SUTTON, F. X.
   1955   Social theory and comparative politics (mimeographed).

TITIEV, M.
    1944   Old Oraibi. Papers of the Peabody Museum, Vol. 22.
WAGNER, G.
    1949   The Bantu of North Kavirondo, Vol. 1. Oxford, Oxford
            University Press.

Some Social Concomitants of Industrialization and Urbanization

JOSEPH A. KAHL

Washington University, St. Louis

The transformation of society by industrialization and urbanization is currently of great concern to men of affairs and to men of science.[1] Since the second World War the rate of industrialization has increased as people in previously isolated or tradition-bound societies have entered the main stream of world history to demand the material benefits of modern technology. They often seek those material benefits while hoping to retain their traditional cultures, yet, since England pointed the way in the eighteenth century, experience indicates that their hopes are utopian, for a radical change in the mode of production has profound repercussions on the rest of culture. This generalization is as sure as any in all of social science, but it is so abstract as to offer little guide to one who wants to know what the specific consequences of industrialization are likely to be. Some recent research helps us to do better.

The process of "development" involves a series of intertwined economic changes: 1) the integration of previously isolated, self-sufficient rural economies into a single national economy with strong ties to the international economy; 2) the dominance of production for sale over production for barter or for use, thus the increasing emphasis upon money; 3) the introduction of new technological devices in farming and in manufacture which are based on world-wide science and involve large capital expenditures; 4) a tremendous growth of the means of communication and transport; 5) a steady growth of towns and cities (through internal migration from the farms) as bases of manufacturing, trade, and political control which become consumers of surplus food produced on the modernized farms; 6) a steady development of special-

Reprinted from *Human Organization*, XVIII (Summer, 1959), 53–74, with the permission of the author and the publisher.

[1] The author takes pleasure in recording his indebtedness to students in two seminars who have given bibliographic assistance, and to several of his colleagues from Washington University and beyond it who read the first draft of this paper and offered useful critical comments.

ization in the division of labor between occupations, between farm and city, and between regions.[2]

Although economic development, industrialization and urbanization can be conceived of as separate variables, in most real instances the three unfold as an over-all complex. The changes listed in the preceding paragraph occur together, and no country can go far along the road to development unless they occur in a fairly harmonious pattern. Consequently, the sociologist can take the entire complex as a given, and seek its repercussions upon social organization in the growing cities. For present purposes, I shall concentrate upon changes in family, career, education, and stratification, and shall pay little attention to changes in politics and religion or to the modernization of the countryside.

The questions raised here are old ones: they have been at the center of social theory since Karl Marx. Consequently, many of the ideas discussed in this paper have a long and worthy tradition. But in the postwar years there has been a florescence of research data that carry us considerably beyond the traditional formulations, which were mostly based upon historical studies. The new data can be grouped into two classes: direct field studies carried out in rapidly-growing cities, and national statistics from censuses or from series of vital statistics. My purpose is to organize the new data into a meaningful pattern, relying upon those of the older theoretical ideas which are most congruent with the empirical results. No attempt at a complete survey of the new literature is implied; I shall discuss only the major monographs, and at times will sample from among them. A selected and annotated bibliography is appended, and it includes references to more complete bibliographies.

I am going to stress the general, the universal—those social effects of the development process which tend to occur regardless of the traditions of the particular culture under consideration. Obviously, local traditions make a difference, and the final outcome will show a compromise between the ecumenical social forms of modern, industrial society and the local forms of a given culture. We do not yet know how much "leeway" exists, how much variation around the central theme of industrial society is possible. It is one of the prime tasks of current comparative research to find out.

POPULATION GROWTH

A traditional society composed of isolated, self-sufficient villages has a very slow rate of population growth: it takes at least a century for the

[2] For background in economics the author relied principally upon Buchanan and Ellis, 1955.

population to double, and ordinarily the counteracting forces of plague and famine decimate the growth almost as fast as it occurs. Economic development changes that picture: better means of transport make it possible to move food from areas of plenty to areas of scarcity; economic resources become available which permit the basic devices of sanitation, namely, fresh water and adequate sewage disposal; and contact with the outside world permits the rapid importation of cheap devices, such as DDT and penicillin, for the control of contagious disease. When economic development goes a bit further, and the general standard of living rises and provides better nutrition and medical care, the reduction in the death rate is dramatic.

Population growth is obviously the result of an excess of births over deaths. Economic development affects both the birth rate and the death rate, but at different periods in the development process. During the early industrialization of Europe, improvements in transport, urban sanitation, and general nutrition reduced the death rate slowly over a long period of time; when the great discoveries of modern medicine appeared in the 19th century and further cut the death rate, the birth rate had *already* begun to decline as a result of those gradual changes in family life which generally lead urban people to prefer fewer children than do rural people. But nowadays the rate of change is faster and the sequence of steps is different: during the earliest stages of modernization, a country simultaneously improves its transport and communication, increases its food supply, cleans up its cities, and introduces scientific medicine by importing it from advanced countries. All of these changes can occur *before* any important alteration in the average size of family takes place as a result of urbanization. The consequence is a rapid reduction of the death rate, the maintenance of a high birth rate, and a population explosion (Davis, in *Annals,* 1956).

Recent data from Mexico, the one developing country with which I have firsthand experience, illustrate this process of sudden growth (for statistical details, see Iturriaga, 1951; Germán Parra, 1954; Duran Ochoa, 1955). The pre-conquest population of Mexico is estimated at around nine million. The conquest in the early 16th century and its immediate aftermaths reduced the population by about one-half; thereafter, a stable though stagnant social system emerged and a very slow growth in population resulted. There were some six million by 1800, and twelve and a half million by 1895. Industrialization began under the Diaz dictatorship; just before the overthrow of his regime in 1910, the population reached 15 million. The severity of the civil war during the decade of the 1910's reduced it by almost one million people.

Thus, 400 years after the conquest the population had only grown by about 60 percent.

In the 1920's peace was restored and a new surge of economic and social development began. The result was an unprecedented spurt in population: 16,553,000 in 1930; 19,654,000 in 1940; 25,791,000 in 1950; 33,000,000 in 1958.

The birth rate has probably been between 40 and 46 per thousand per year since the end of the revolution, but the death rate has steadily declined: it was over 30 before the revolution, about 25 during the 1920's and 1930's, about 20 in the 1940's, and is about 12 now.[3]

The disparity between the birth and death rates produces the annual rate of natural increase, and note its trend: from about 14 per thousand before the revolution, to about 19 in the 1930's, about 25 in the 1940's, and between 31 and 34 now (that is, a compounded growth of between 3.1 and 3.4 percent per year).[4] The current rate of natural increase is sufficient to double the population *in less than 24 years* instead of in 400 years as was previously the case. But Mexico, although close to the top of the list of the countries of the world in current rate of increase, is by no means a special case. Other countries in Latin America, the Near East, and Asia are experiencing roughly the same phenomenon.

If a country is to progress in the economic sense—to raise the standard of living of its people and to have a surplus available for capital investment—it must increase its agricultural and industrial production faster than it increases its population. For the years since the second World War, Mexico has been able to expand production about twice as fast as the growth of population; as a result, she currently has a tremendous "boom." But it is of recent origin; from the revolution to the war, population growth appears to have outstripped production increase.

Those countries which are industrializing now, and as a result are having a population explosion, face a problem that is much greater than the one faced by Europe or the United States during their periods of rapid development. For example, Great Britain's population increased at an annual rate of about 1.4 percent during the first half of the 19th

[3] Much of the decline in the death rate is due, of course, to diminishing infant mortality. The latter rate (deaths in the first year of life per thousand live births) has fallen from 317 in 1895 to 95 in 1953.

[4] All statistics in Mexico are suspect, and that is particularly true of vital statistics until recent years. Consequently, the estimates of natural increase given in the text have been adjusted somewhat to reflect growth as measured by the census, which is more accurate than growth measured by vital statistics. See Germán Parra, 1954, Table 23. Immigration has been negligible since the 17th century.

century, and 1.1 percent during the second half. The United States had an annual rate of increase of about 2.4 percent during the second half of the 19th century (including immigration), and its present rate of growth, despite the continuing postwar "baby boom," is about half that of Mexico's. The current rates for such countries as India and Russia are similar to that of the United States.

General industrial development and deliberate government action in sanitation and medicine can reduce a death rate from forty per thousand to close to ten per thousand in a generation's time. Birth rates usually go down much more slowly. The availability of mechanical devices for birth control, plus the forces of urban living which caused a desire for smaller families (which will be detailed below), had, by World War II, slowly cut the birth rates in countries in Western Europe and in the United States until a stable population was reached or expected. Since then, there has been a slight increase in birth rates but the resulting population growth is slow compared to what is happening in the newly developing countries. The data available so far indicate that Latin American and Asian cities do show reductions in birth rates over their surrounding rural districts, but there is as yet no assurance that the family size will ever go down as low as it has in countries of northwestern European culture (Smith, 1958). And we cannot yet predict the course of population in Negro African cities.

Time is a crucial factor. For the development process to occur, a surplus must be available for capital investment. Factories must be built, mines sunk, farm machinery and fertilizers bought. Cities must be created as centers of industry and as sources of jobs to absorb the excess population from rural areas. Also, highways, railroads, schools, and hospitals have to be constructed. And to make matters more tense, the people, once aroused from a traditional way of life which assumes a fixed standard of living, start demanding new consumption goods; they institute a "revolution of expectations." Consequently, a country that once initiates the changes that lead it toward modernization must, to maintain self-sustained growth, increase its production considerably faster than its population; merely keeping even is impossible without chaos and revolution. There exists a critical period of rapid population growth which must be met by rapid industrialization before the gradual effects of urbanization can produce a decline in the birth rate and thus initiate a later period of slower growth.

FROM RURAL TO URBAN

The traditional world is a rural world, seventy percent or more of the people live on farms, and the surplus of food which they grow with their crude techniques of production can support but a few urbanites. Each village is self-sufficient in most of its needs, and engages in only a small amount of trade with the outside world.

But the modern world is an urban world. Less than ten percent of the population (given good farmland and scientific techniques of production) can feed ninety percent living in towns and cities. Even if the urban proportion is smaller than ninety percent, urban control in science, commerce, manufacturing, mass media, and politics comes to dominate. Modern culture originates in cities and spreads outward to farms.

During the period of rapid development, there is an enormous flow of young people from farm to city. If a farmer has eight children who reach maturity, only two may remain on the farm, if a stable rural population is to be maintained. Actually, in the early stages of development, there is usually a slow growth in the rural population as new lands are opened for exploitation and as old ones become more crowded (in the later stages of development, the absolute size of the rural population is likely to shrink, for farms become larger and are worked by machinery instead of by hand). But a slow growth in the rural population is not enough to absorb all of the farmers' children; many of them must move cityward when they are young adults to seek urban jobs.

Once again, Mexico can serve as an illustration: 22 percent of its population lived in urban places in 1910, but 43 percent did so by 1950.[5] In those forty years the rural population grew from 10,812,000 to 14,808,000, an increase of 37 percent. But the urban population expanded from 4,348,000 to 10,983,000, or an increase of 153 percent. The growth rate of the nation's capital, Mexico City, has been phenomenal: from 721,000 in 1910 to 3,050,000 in 1950. In 1958, its population was estimated at 5,000,000, and its current growth rate at 7 percent per year, or a doubling in less than 12 years. Almost half of its inhabitants are migrants from farms and from smaller towns and cities.

Cities are large and heterogeneous (Wirth, 1938). The contacts between men tend to be contacts in specialized roles rather than as total personalities. Workplace is different from home and both are different from worship-place. At each, a man has different associates. Salesman and customer, teacher and student, fellow members of the Society for the Preservation of Ancient Choral Music, even "neighbors," interact for particular purposes and do not allow themselves to become totally involved with one another: there is not enough time, and it would interfere with the efficiency of the specialized interaction (for example, a

[5] In 1910, an urban place was classified as one with 2,000 or more inhabitants; in 1950, the more standard definition of 2,500 was used.

teacher is not supposed to consider "family background" in awarding grades to students—or, to use an overworked phrase, "business is business"). The immediate family and very few "close friends" are the limits of social relationships based on long contact, personal rather than business attitudes, emotional rather than rational purpose, total rather than specialized and thus superficial involvement.

The link between men in the city is mediated by money: urbanites buy and sell goods and services, and they play in ways which cost money so that only those with similar incomes can play the same games and join the same clubs. Even one's neighbors are determined by money, for the economic competition for space sorts out neighborhoods according to "quality" or cost. The cash nexus tends to replace kinship and local community as the main determinant of social position and consequently of social relationships.

It is often said that life in the city is "individualistic." This term is to me one of the vaguest and least useful in the social science lexicon. It is true that many people in the city are lonesome; it is true that the clan is non-existent, the extended family is weak, and the neighborhood is amorphous, thus the individual has a range of free choice in his decisions which goes beyond that of the peasant or tribal member. But it is not true that the individual is lacking in group ties. The key to city life is the multiplicity of group ties: each may have strong influence on the individual, but each is limited to a specific area of behavior and is balanced by others. In the folk society, the family group generally controls property, marriage, work, and much of religion. The individual is a member of a *single* small group whose activities cover all the important aspects of his life. In the city, the individual interacts with many groups: he has his own personal career and he meets on the job a team of workmates; at home, he sorts the claims of parents, extended kin, wife, and children into different compartments; he may belong to a church which tells him that the goals of business are not the only important ends of life, etc. He has a great range of choice, and can use one group to offset the other. He must manipulate their various claims by means of rational decision, and thus may at times seem like an extreme individualist organizing his life to suit himself. But the fact is that his own goals are taken over from various of these groups; he follows group codes, gets emotional satisfaction from group memberships, thinks in terms of maximizing group performance. Work groups, recreational cliques, nuclear families—these are "tight" groups which bind the individual to them, shape him in their image. The typical urbanite is not an isolate; he is a group member whose total involvement in collective life is very great but whose involvement in any one group is limited.[6]

As long as the rapidly growing cities contain so many citizens who are migrants from rural areas, we must distinguish between their transitional way of life—combining rural and urban traits—and the more adapted pattern which eventually develops among those born and reared in city environments. Persons in transition may cling to many rural characteristics, such as devotion to the extended-family system, which give them security in their new situation. Indeed, many new city workers are temporary workers, leaving families behind in the villages. On the other hand, some transitional individuals throw over the rural patterns before they have time to learn functionally adapted urban ways, and their lives show the "disorganization" noticed in many urban studies. But neither rural survivals nor temporary disorganization last through time; if we are to predict the future, we must concentrate on the city-bred persons who have turned their back on the farms and are committed to an urban style of life.

FROM LOCALISM TO NATIONALISM

The creation of a modern economy demands a large market. There must be a division of labor and an exchange of produce from one region to another. Modern means of communication and transport are constructed to facilitate this exchange.

The social effects of these new means of communication are enormous—I think it was Ralph Beals who remarked that one road is worth twenty schools as a stimulus to social change. The harmony of tribal and even of peasant society is based on small communities which are at least partially isolated, for isolation produces inbreeding of genes and ideas and leads to the stability of a fixed tradition. (Redfield, 1947).

The new economy breaks down local isolation. Not only goods but men and ideas move freely from one region (and one country) to another. The powers of local landlords, local chieftains, local clans, and most important, local traditions, are weakened. This sets men free to

[6] Perhaps some of the overemphasis upon individualism, even on isolation, in urban society stems from the attempts of Park's students in Chicago to find and portray "extreme" types of urbanites, like taxi dance hall girls and rooming house inhabitants. But such extremes cannot be used to construct an "ideal-type" of life in the city. Durkheim, in discussing his model of modern society, emphasized *both* the loosening of the old social controls of rigid tradition in small communities *and* the emergence of new social controls in terms of segmental groups functionally adapted to the urban milieu.

experiment, but it also isolates them from their previous bases of personal security (Fromm, 1941). If you do not belong to a village, where
your family has lived since time began, who are you?

The answer is: you are a member of a nation. The national state
must exert its supremacy over local districts if a large market is to exist
in security and order. Those countries which developed an effective
national government and sense of national identity before they industrialized, such as England and Japan, had an enormous advantage over
those countries which are trying simultaneously to create national unity
and modernize their economies, such as Indonesia and Ghana. The fact
of national economic and political dominion goes hand in hand with
the spirit of national belongingness. Perhaps the test question is this:
for whom will you fight unto death? Your family, in the spirit of the
blood feud? Your tribe? Your region? Your country? An alliance of
like-minded countries?

The spirit of nationalism which sweeps new countries thus stems
from a combination of a rational impetus toward the building of a
new society, and an emotional need to replace the broken sense of local
identification with new symbols of group membership (often reinforced
by the desire for freedom from colonial overlords). These are powerful
forces of mind and heart, and, until they are spent, we should not
expect a new identification with the world community, despite the
obvious fact that both economic and political realities are now pushing
us toward international rather than national bonds of organization.

The breakdown of a sense of local identity and its replacement by
a national (and occasionally international) view results from a double
process: the actual movement of men from the village to the city, and
the spread of the mass media throughout the cities and eventually into
the villages. This latter process has been studied through sample surveys of some 300 respondents in each of six countries in the Middle
East by the Columbia University Bureau of Applied Social Research.
The surveys they did in 1950 have recently been synthesized by Daniel
Lerner in *The Passing of Traditional Society*, 1958. This book is worth
our special attention, for it reports a pioneer effort to study the transition from a situation focused on the murmurings of old men, who recite
from memory the ancient traditions of the local folk, and deduce therefrom permanent rules of conduct, to a situation focused on the voices of
young men who are excited about the national happenings of today and
tomorrow, and seek new rules of conduct for a new world they hope to
build. In this new world, the mass media are crucial, and with the
arrival of radio and movies, no longer depend completely upon literacy;
Nasser has shown us the power of the electronic voice. And let it be

remembered that the mass media originate in the cities, from the centers of power; they represent the national, the urban, the sophisticated points of view, and they give people something to think about that carries their minds beyond the implications of the immediate locality.

Lerner maintains that modernization in communication involves a single package of interrelated phenomena, and he demonstrates, for over fifty countries, high correlations among the following variables: urbanism, literacy, participation in elections and media participation (newspaper circulation; cinema attendance; radio ownership). The effects of this package upon individual mentality, upon a man's sense of identity, are described as follows (pp. 50–51):

Traditional society is nonparticipant—it deploys people by kinship into communities isolated from each other and from a center; without an urban-rural division of labor, it develops few needs requiring economic interdependence; lacking the bonds of interdependence, people's horizons are limited by locale and their decisions involve only other known people in known situations. Hence, there is no need for a transpersonal common doctrine formulated in terms of shared secondary symbols—a national "ideology" which enables persons unknown to each other to engage in political controversy or achieve "consensus" by comparing their opinions. Modern society is participant in that it functions by "consensus"—individuals making personal decisions on public issues must concur often enough with other individuals they do not know to make possible a stable common governance. Among the marks of this historic achievement, which we call Participant Society, are that most people go through school, read newspapers, receive cash payments in jobs they are legally free to change, buy goods for cash in an open market, vote in elections which actually decide among competing candidates, and express opinions on many matters which are not their personal business.

Especially important, for the Participant Style, is the enormous proportion of people who are expected to "have opinions" on public matters—and the corollary expectation of these people that their opinions will matter.

Lerner calls the ability to have opinions about many things beyond one's immediate personal business the capacity for *empathy,* and he measures it by the simple device of the number of questions answered with an opinion instead of a "don't know" in a battery of semi-projective questions that ask people to take the roles of others, such as:

If you were made editor of a newspaper, what kind of a paper would you run?

Suppose that you were made head of the government. What are some of the things you would do?

If for some reason, you could not live in our country, what other country would you choose to live in?

On the basis of the index of empathy, in combination with certain other key characteristics, Lerner sorts the respondents into five basic types:

Modern—literate, urban, high media participation, high empathy
Transitional:

    A. Non-literate, urban, high media participation, high empathy

    B. Non-literate, rural, high media participation, high empathy

    C. Non-literate, rural, low media participation, high empathy
Traditional—non-literate, rural, low media participation, low empathy

Note that the transitional individuals are persons who are beginning to leave the complete mental isolation of the village but only by partial steps: they may still live in the village, but they show an interest in the outside world and develop opinions about it. Once this interest is aroused, they tend to pay attention to the mass-media, particularly the radio and the cinema. The next step is for them (or their children) to learn to read and perhaps eventually to migrate to the city. There are not many cases of Type B in most villages, but they are of very great importance for they are carriers of the new viewpoints and have much influence on their neighbors.

The contrasting viewpoints of dwellers in the old society and participants in the new are vividly shown by some quotations from the interviews (pp. 319–345):

Bedouins believe that having to travel far from one's country and relatives and friends is a curse that descends from the forefathers to the child. . . . We Bedouins don't need the cinema. Those who go are not real men. They are useless and have lost all value of morals. . . . Those who read are politicians and trouble seekers.

If you don't read you are far away from trouble and the government. . . . The U.S.? What is it? Where is it? . . . We don't like to hear about war in far away countries. When Bedouins start a fight among themselves, they never bother other people about it. So why should we bother about what other countries have to go through whether in war or peace. . . . I am interested in news about my household and my camel because these are my life and my link with this world. I don't care for anything else because what is outside my concern I am not supposed to care for.

Radio is a very good friend at home who is very loyal and useful. I consider it my best friend. . . . Movies are the best means of communicating a people's culture and civilization to the other parts of the world. It is a mirror of a country's advance in life. Movies are one of the modern means of entertainment which is quite indispensable as a part of our daily life. I couldn't imagine how flat life would be without the movies. It has become very essential that everybody should go to movies and learn many things about the secrets of life.

Lerner suggests that much of the instability in the Near East can be linked to a development process which is out of phase and has not achieved harmonious rates of progress among its interrelated elements. For example, in some areas the authority of the village elders has been weakened but no new elite has arisen which is tied to the national scene but keeps roots in the local villages and offers an alternative to the traditional elders as a source of guidance and support. In other places, an urban elite of university graduates has emerged before there are places for them in the new division of labor—lacking jobs and a future, they are a source of revolutionary agitation. In some countries, urbanization has moved too fast, for the rural excess population flocks to cities which have no industries and therefore no jobs.

Lerner's book is a rich collection of data, insights, and theories. Unfortunately, they are not well put together, for the surveys in the various countries were originally analyzed separately by different interpreters, and Lerner does not succeed in completely unifying the results. Furthermore, Lerner tries to present between two covers a general theory of development, a series of case studies of six countries in flux, and a report of a specific sample survey. Nobody could have synthesized all of this into a neat monograph. But nobody else raises such pointed questions about the role of communications and of self-image in the transition from village identity to national consciousness.

NEW DIVISION OF LABOR

An urban population supported by industrial and commercial activity develops a division of labor markedly different from that of a rural population. The latter contains farmers plus a very few specialists (artisans, merchants, priests, soldiers, governors). The former contains thousands of different specialists (the United States Government catalogues over 20,000 in the Dictionary of Occupational Titles) whose existence is dependent upon an intricate system of exchange which integrates the labor of bricklayer, machine-tool maker, automobile assembly worker, and clerk, so that all end up with complete houses and automobiles. The occupational division of labor is the economically determined skeleton on which the flesh of modern social organization develops; it is somewhat analogous in function to the kinship system which is the base of much of primitive society. Therefore we can use the division of labor as a convenient index of the degree of industrialization-urbanization reached by any given society—it is probably the most meaningful index for sociological purposes.

The division of labor is conventionally portrayed by two distributions: that among branches of activity (industry, agriculture, and services, including commerce), and that among socioeconomic levels (professionals, clerks, laborers, etc.). Let us examine both measures. If we use the historical experience of the United States as a model (and it appears that other countries tend to follow the same general trends), we find that economic development involves a steady shift from an early period in which agricultural labor predominates, with a secondary emphasis upon industry and services, to an intermediate period in which there is a shift from agriculture into both industry and services in equal proportions, to a later period of maturity when industry stops growing and the remaining shift is from agriculture into services. In other words, there appears to be a limit upon the need for industrial labor, for as the system matures the machines get more efficient and increases in production can be obtained without increases in manpower (Clark, 1957). However, services cannot so easily be mechanized, and they continue to absorb excess agricultural workers. The data for the United States since 1860 are given in Table I.

TABLE I

AMERICAN LABOR FORCE, BY TYPE OF ACTIVITY, 1860–1950

| | Percent of Labor Force | | |
	1860	1900	1950
Agriculture, fishing, and forestry	59	38	12
Industry, construction, and mining	20	30	33
Services (professional, administrative, transport, and commerce)	20	31	53
Other	1	1	2
Total	100%	100%	100%
Number in labor force (in thousands)	10,530	29,070	56,239

Sources: *Historical Statistics of U.S. 1789–1945*, p. 64; *Statistical Abstract of U.S.* (1954), p. 208.

If we turn our attention to the distribution by socioeconomic levels, we get a complementary picture (see Table II). Here we notice that as

TABLE II

AMERICAN LABOR FORCE, BY SOCIOECONOMIC LEVEL, 1870–1950

	Percent of Labor Force	
	1870	1950
Professional persons	3	9
Proprietors, managers, and officials:		
Farmers	24	7
Others	6	9
Clerks, salespeople, and kindred	4	19
Skilled workers and foremen	9	14
Semiskilled workers	10	22
Unskilled workers:		
Farm laborers	29	4
Laborers, except farm	9	8
Servant classes	6	6
Not reported	—	2
Total	100%	100%
Number in labor force	12,924,000	56,239,000
Percent of labor force, female	15%	30%
Total population	39,818,000	150,697,000

Source: Kahl, 1957, p. 67; based on the U.S. Census.

the industrial system matures, there is a greater need for professional and technical people (they almost tripled in proportion from 1870 to 1950), and for clerks and salesmen (they increased fivefold). There is a smaller need for more workers at the semiskilled level (they doubled). The skilled workers increased by a still smaller amount (about fifty percent), and the unskilled workers not at all. Thus there is a constant up-grading of the labor force as the system matures: from blue-collar to white-collar work, from lower levels to higher levels of technical competence.

The implications of these shifts in the labor force are far-reaching. For instance, it becomes less likely that a boy will become a farmer like his father and learn his occupation within the family context; instead, he follows a personal career and prepares for it by going to school, and that takes him out of the home (and often away from the community) and thus weakens the family while it strengthens the system of formal education. Furthermore, since many urban occupations are open to women, they are no longer thought of solely as daughters, wives and mothers, but become individuals who can pursue careers.

Finally, the interactions of city life become, as was suggested above, contacts between specialists acting in their occupational roles rather than human beings as total personalities. If the trading of the market-place is the framework for the interaction, cold-blooded rationality and pursuit of personal gain will come to the fore. If entrepreneurship in long-range enterprises based on substantial capital is the focus, then attitudes of planning, of husbanding of resources, of efficiency in the use of expensive time and equipment will predominate. If bureaucratic organization is emphasized, the relationships between people will take on the coloration of attention to the rules, limitation of authority to the specifics of the job, a conservative and cautious approach toward life (Merton, 1949). If the interaction is between professional and client, then the traditions of intellectual mastery, of pride, of devotion to the traditions of the professional group and its ethics will largely govern behavior (Parsons, 1939). If assemblyline workers are observed, a rou-tinization of behavior and a psychological alienation from work will be noted. In general, the more specialized the job is, the more bureaucra-tized the organizational context in which it occurs, and the bigger the price tag on the product or service, the more narrowly is the interaction likely to be confined to the business at hand.

We can explore some of the implications of a changing division of labor through recent research reports on areas that are currently industrializing.

The best survey of new industrial workers that we have was pro-duced by faculty and students of the University of Dacca (East Pak-istan). The fact that it was executed by unpaid volunteers in a short space of time shows what can be done with limited resources under powerful leadership. The study was directed in 1953–54 by A. F. A. Husain and reported in his two volumes entitled: *Human and Social Impact of Technological Change in Pakistan,* 1956. The first volume tells of the statistical survey; the second contains sixty-eight case studies, averaging some four pages in length, which summarize the results of open-ended interviews with workers representing various types of ad-justment to industrial impact: those who have moved from farm to factory, those whose traditional crafts were displaced by factory produc-tion and who may or may not have themselves taken up factory labor, those who continue to work the farms but in areas where factories have entered, etc. The cases are often referred to as illustrations of statistical findings, an innovation in method worthy of emulation.

East Pakistan is just starting its industrialization: of its forty-two million people, over eighty percent are agriculturalists. The dominant pattern of life is village life, often on lands that have been tilled by ancestors for many generations. But population is increasing rapidly, and many families who are landless, or whose fields are inadequate to support them, are sending sons to seek paid employment. The most progressive and educated of these are the ones who end up in factories.

Husain surveyed the workers in nineteen factories of various types, some located in cities and others in rural areas. For the most part, these factories were large establishments which processed agricultural products: cotton, jute, rubber, etc. About half were newly established since the partition of India and Pakistan in 1947, the rest having a longer history. In each factory, 3.5 percent of the workers were chosen on a random basis and were interviewed from a fixed schedule. In addition, the bicycle-rickshaw drivers of Dacca were sampled (by a less formal method). In all, the sample included 471 workers and 90 drivers.

Only a quarter of the workers came from villages close to the factory where they worked; the rest travelled great distances to find work. Less than ten percent of these men had fathers who were industrial workers. Most of the workers were young men under thirty-five, four-fifths were Muslims, and slightly more than one-half were literate (compared to 20 percent of the total population). Most workers were assisted in getting jobs by a relative or fellow-villager who already worked in the factory. They were trained in a haphazard manner, often just by standing next to their relatives and watching.

Slightly over one-half of the workers were living away from their families (despite the fact that seventy percent of those living away from their families were married). Those who lived with their families were mostly those who worked in factories within commuting distance of their native villages. Thus the predominant pattern of this labor force is one of young men, mostly married, who leave their homes in order to earn money. Their wives and children are taken care of under the joint-family system, for eighty percent of the workers belonged to such joint families made up of brothers and often the father, together with their respective wives and small children, all living in a single household. The workers sent remittances of about one-third of their pay home to help support their families. Only in the relatively rare instances where a worker took his wife and small children away from the village and to the factory site did the joint-family system disintegrate.

A recurring theme in Husain's report is the ease with which this new industrial labor force was recruited (essentially as a result of overpopulation on the land, for those with enough land preferred to remain farmers) and the small amount of change in social life that followed the switch to factory employment. The joint-family system, deep belief in religion and execution of its responsibilities in prayer and in daily life, a conservative, peasant outlook on life permeated with fatalism—all of these continued for the majority of workers. Yet the seeds of more radical change were planted. There were some workers, particularly those who took their spouses with them to the city, who began to change their outlook. They weakened in religious belief (at least they modernized their religious views and ceased to follow the detailed instructions of reactionary religious leaders). They reported that contact with many other workers had stimulated their minds and showed them the "stupidity" of merely following tradition. They believed in the practicality of the nuclear as against the joint family, and a few began to practice birth control. They learned new methods of cooperation through union activity. They began to plan and to agitate for a better future rather than accept what fate might bring.

And even in the villages where the conservative social structures continued to operate without much alteration, some changes were beginning. People saw that educated men got better factory jobs, and a general belief in the value of education (even for women) was growing. Literacy brought contact with the outside world and with modern medicine and science, weakening the belief in some aspects of tradition.

Husain's report on East Pakistan is convincing evidence of the degree to which early industrialization is compatible with much of family-centered and village-centered traditionalism.[7] But it also suggests that when people move permanently to the city more radical changes begin, for without a close tie to the land and the total village community, the older social structures weaken.

Some thirty-three studies of the effects of wage-labor on social life in Africa have recently been summarized by Merran McCulloch (in International African Institute, 1956). He indicates that there are important variations from one region to another, especially with respect to the policies of the various colonial powers and to the proportion of white men in the different populations. Nevertheless, there are striking similarities stemming from the universal problems arising from the imposition of colonial rule upon native peoples. The colonial powers at first were interested in the profits from mines and from plantation agriculture. They needed abundant supplies of cheap native labor. The workers were recruited at times by force but more frequently by the establishment of head and hut taxes which had to be paid in cash. Young men left the villages to work for a period of a few years in the mines and on the plantations to earn enough money to pay the taxes

---

[7] For a detailed study of how a single factory can enter a well-organized village community and find ways of accommodating to its culture with few disrupting effects, see Nash, 1958.

for their families. They worked, therefore, *as representatives of the group,* and they went home as soon as possible. They lived on the job in male barracks, and were either unmarried or would leave their wives in the villages, for the fields had to be tilled at home and there was no work for women in the mines. This system has been in operation for two or three generations, and is widespread throughout Negro Africa; indeed, the migration is often across colonial frontiers.

In recent years, however, the system has started to change. The natives have learned new tastes which depend upon money and they thus demand cash beyond the needs of taxes—cash for clothing, cigarettes, beer, bicycles, sewing machines, phonographs. In many areas, the traditional "bride-wealth" paid by the groom to his father-in-law has been changed from cattle (contributed by the relatives of the groom) to cash (usually earned primarily by the young man himself). In some areas, increasing population is creating a pressure on the land that "pushes" people out. Furthermore, increasing proportions of the natives are going to work in the towns and cities rather than on the mines and plantations, and some of them want to stay once they have tasted the joys of city life. The trade and service industries of the cities, the political staffs centered in them, and the emerging light consumer-goods industries which they stimulate, all demand a different type of labor. They need workers who are more educated, more skilled, and more stable. A three-year hitch by an ignorant boy from the bush may be a suitable system for hiring a miner or possibly an unskilled factory hand, but it does not work for an automobile mechanic, a teacher, or a clerk.

The United Nations estimates that about six percent of the Africans south of the Sahara currently live in large cities of over 20,000, though many more live in them from time to time. In 1953, some five million workers (out of a population of some 160 million) were dependent upon wages for their livelihoods (U.N., 1957, p. 152). About 38 percent of these were in the Union of South Africa and another 17 percent in the Belgian Congo. Moreover, some 50 percent of the men in most areas were thought to be dependent upon wages during some period of their lives.

The cities are growing so fast that it is not unusual to find that three-quarters of the inhabitants were born elsewhere (in smaller towns or villages). Furthermore, these are usually male cities, with a very high disproportion of men over women, and they are young cities, with the bulk of the population being young men between 15 and 45. There are few children, few women, few old people. McCulloch writes (International African Institute, 1956, p. 210):

Some children are brought up in the country and then come to town; others know no other environment except the town; numbers of young men and women live between two worlds; others are settled in towns; old people remain in the country and become increasingly estranged from their children. Perhaps one of the most fundamental results of this situation is that it hinders the emergence of an urban public opinion—which would set norms of behavior between the sexes, within the family, and within the community.

Some details on life in one of these new towns can be had from a survey made in Jinja, Uganda, by Cyril and Rhona Sofer, 1955. Jinja grew from 8,400 to 20,800 persons in the few years from 1948 to 1951. It had a high proportion of males to females, and most of the men did not anticipate permanent settlement. There were almost 15,000 Africans, some 5,000 Asians, and about 800 Europeans. The latter dominated the administrative positions in government and business, and also included some skilled workers (especially those brought in to aid in the construction of a new dam which was to supply cheap electric power). The Asians dominated trade and many of the skilled and clerical occupations. The Africans occupied the lower-level jobs. This racial division tended (despite protestations that only skill mattered) to create job ceilings which limited the advancement and consequently the motivation, of most of the Africans and some of the Asians.

The Sofers conducted a sample survey which included 15 percent of the African households, 33 percent of the Asian, and all of the European. They found that four percent of the Africans were professional and clerical workers, six percent traders, thirty percent artisans, forty-five percent unskilled, six percent military or police, and nine percent held other types of jobs. Regarding age and sex, three-quarters of the Africans were between 16 and 45; two-thirds were men. About half of the men were married, but 40 percent of the wives were still living in the villages. The men came to town to earn tax and bride money, plus cash for a few simple objects useful on the farm, but, once there, they found that food alone took more than 70 percent of their earnings, leaving little for saving. Furthermore (Sofer, p. 56):

In the town horizons shift and standards are raised. The African who enters the town does so largely because of his need for an increased supply of cash to supplement the subsistence economy of his rural home, but he develops many new wants in the town for more or better Western-type goods and urban facilities. Many Western consumption items such as soap, sugar, salt, have already become conventional necessities even in the countryside. To these are gradually added others such as lamps, paraffin, cycles, watches, cameras, brick houses and European-style clothing. Desires to possess these articles increase incentives to participate in the urban economy.

The single man who comes to town lives in a barracks with several men to a room, usually assigned according to the convenience of the landlord rather than the preferences of the tenants. Thus men from various regions and tribes become mixed. Later on, if he marries and brings a wife to town, he has difficulty in finding adequate quarters, and usually continues to think of himself as a temporary resident even though he may be in town for many years. The result is poor care of housing and a lack of interest in local politics or community affairs. Even voluntary associations are lacking. Indeed, other than the immediate family which exists for a small portion of the men, the only social groupings of significance are informal networks of friends, clansmen and tribesmen who provide sociability and mutual assistance (p. 108):

Extending to aid in times of unemployment and illness, this informal system of help constitutes, in the absence of formal community agencies and of tightly integrated kinship groups, the basic form of "social security" locally available to the urban African.[8]

The theme of the works thus far reported is that changes in the division of labor draw people from farming to urban jobs, and that wage-work has repercussions on the rest of life. Three areas of special importance will be noted below: education, social class, and family.

EDUCATION

A complex division of labor demands a system of formal education to prepare men for their jobs—apprenticeship is too conservative, too slow, too clumsy. Consequently, instead of walking beside his father at the plow, a young man prepares for life by going to school.

A modern school system, like modern industry, tends to emphasize norms of impersonal efficiency: promotion is based upon demonstrated performance. As industrialization proceeds and men begin to recognize the extent to which formal education is the key to their careers, the

---

[8] For additional details on factory labor in Jinja and in the near-by town of Kampala, see Elkan, 1956. Probably the most detailed—and least synthesized—study of work in a new African city is the report on Stanleyville by Clément, Pons, and Xydias (in International African Institute, 1956).

demand for schooling grows, as well as the feeling that it ought to be available to everybody regardless of his position in society. Thus the state is led to establish free public schools, and progressively to adapt their curricula from the old-fashioned subjects which were designed to perpetuate the traditional lore of the local culture among the upper classes (i.e., to prepare the elite for a life of leisure, or of governance or theology) to the new-fashioned subjects designed to prepare men for industrial and commercial careers.

Modern schools tend to separate young men from their fathers (in ideas and skills, if not in space); they lead the minds of the young outward from the locality to the nation; they teach a *personal* skill which can be sold anywhere. Such schools unfreeze the social class order by permitting, even encouraging, geographical and social mobility. They make inherited capital and inherited family status less important as the determinants of a man's career, and make intelligence, personality, and will-power more important.

Each level of education is designed to prepare students for an appropriate level in the occupational hierarchy. Thus, university education leads toward professional, technical and executive positions, secondary education toward skilled and clerical jobs, primary education toward semi- and unskilled jobs.

Mexican statistics show the extent of the transformation in education brought about by industrialization. In the old society before the revolution, the upper class sought literary education in Europe. Only a small number of professionals, mainly in the law, received university training in Mexico. Secondary schools were mostly private institutions which prepared a tiny segment of society for university education at home or abroad. The mass of the people were illiterate, for peasants needed no schooling.

In recent years, the entire school system has been changed. University training at home has gained in prestige, and the emphasis has shifted from literary toward technical and business subjects. Iturriaga (1951, p. 178) indicates that as many *titulos* (diplomas showing completion of a specialized university course often at the level of an American M.A. degree) were granted from 1938 to 1948 as in the whole period from 1901 to 1937. And notice these changes in subjects: 60 percent of the lawyers got their degrees in the earlier period, but over 80 percent of the chemical engineers and 95 percent of the economists graduated after 1937. In 1930, there was a medical doctor for every 3,451 persons in the nation; in 1950 there was a doctor for every 2,274 persons. In 1930, there were four small universities in the country; in 1948, there were twelve universities with a total enrollment of over 30,000 students.

And, by 1954, the National University in Mexico City alone had 22,000 students, while the Instituto Politecnico in that city had an additional 5,000 (*Anuario Estadistico,* México, 1954, pp. 282, 287).

Similarly, public secondary education has enormously expanded. Before the revolution, it was almost non-existent; in recent years, terminal secondary education has become the route to jobs at the level of skilled manual work and clerical positions. By 1950 there were 1,091 schools above the primary level with 176,000 students (*Anuario Estadistico,* México, 1951–52, pp. 228–308).

Primary education is changing the character of lower-class life. The proportion of the population classified by the census as "alphabetized," or able to read and write, rose from 26 percent in 1900 to 57 percent in 1950. In 1930, there were 11,349 primary schools; in 1950, there were 24,075 of them, serving three million students (who constituted about one-half of the children in the country between the ages of 6 and 14); most children now start school, but the drop-out rate in the first few years is very high (*Ibid.*).

The educational levels of the Mexican and the American people are compared in Table III, which shows the number of years of schooling completed by the population over 25 years of age in 1950. A little over one percent of the Mexicans had had some college training, versus

TABLE III

Years of School Completed, Persons 25 Years of Age or More

Mexico, Mexican Federal District (Mexico City), and United States, 1950

Years Completed	All Mexico	Federal District	Years Completed	United States
0	43%	16%	0–5	14%
1–6	45	60	5–6	11
7–9	3	9	7–8	35
10–12	2	6	9–11	15
13 or more	1	5	12	14
Unknown	6	4	13–15	6
Total	100%	100%	16 or more	5
			Total	100%

Note: Mexican primary education extends from grades 1 through 6; secondary through grade 9; college preparatory through grade 11; university training in specialized careers begins with grade 12. U.S. primary education extends from grades 1 through 8; secondary through grade 12; university "general education" through grade 14; university training in specialized careers usually begins with grade 15.

Sources: *Censo General* (1950), *Resumen General,* p. 56; *Statistical Abstract of United States* (1953), p. 115.

eleven percent of the Americans; an additional five percent of the Mexicans had gone to secondary school, versus twenty-nine percent of the Americans. Mexico is making educational progress, but the demands of an industrial society will force her to go much further.

In Africa, education for Negroes is just beginning, but the passion to obtain it is already intense. One pupil in the Belgian Congo said (International African Institute, 1956, p. 333):

> *I should be happiest of all if I could continue my studies. I think of this every night as I lie in bed counting the leaves in the roof of the room, I think of it all the time . . . for I see that I am slowly moving toward civilization.*

The available education in the French and Belgian Congo regions is mostly limited to primary school (the first university is now being organized), and the teaching is usually under the control of Catholic missionaries. They still emphasize the older literary tradition in both content and method. The limitation on higher education leads many Africans to suspect that the whites do not wish to "reveal all their secrets" to the natives. But once schools are established, the natives are quick to respond, for they wish to learn the secrets, to move toward civilization, and to obtain better jobs. Miss Xydias, in her report on Stanleyville, writes *(Ibid.,* p. 333):

> *School attendance is gradually taking its place among the customs of the Congo. Whereas formerly the children came forward at 9, 10 or 12 years of age, a marked change has been recorded during the last few years. In Stanleyville they are now brought to school at the age of six or seven, and on enrollment day the parents queue up at dawn outside the director's office to make sure of a place for their children. All teachers in the town testify to the regular attendance of their pupils; those absenting themselves without due cause are rare.* To a far higher degree than in Europe, *the young folk of all ages are fired with a keen desire to learn* (emphasis added).

SOCIAL CLASSES

A truly "primitive" society has no class system: all families live at about the same socioeconomic level. As agricultural production grows, and the society transforms itself into a settled, peasant-type of structure, a surplus of food is produced which is used to support landlords, priests, and rulers. Ordinarily, there exist only two classes: those who work with their hands, and those who engage in administrative or ritual activities and enjoy leisure. There may exist the germs of an in-between group of clerks and merchants who are aids to the leisure class, but they are relatively insignificant.

The development of a commercial civilization enormously expands the role of trade and thus the in-between group grows into an independent middle class. Industrialization speeds this process for it increases the flow of goods which are traded, it up-grades many handworkers into skilled machine-tenders who have middle-class educations and incomes, and it produces enough surplus wealth to support many people in service activities which enrich the leisure hours of the majority of the people rather than just the upper class.

The new industrial class order is divided into a series of groupings which overlap with one another; there are no sharp divisions, and the terms we use such as "upper class," "middle class," and "working class" are but convenient rubrics, rather than precisely denotative classifications. There are gradations of occupation, education, and life-style within each broad class, and there is considerable mobility from one level to another. Instead of the great gap between landlord and peasant, we get the series of small gaps between factory worker, skilled laborer, foreman, engineer, plant manager, and company president, with young workers aspiring to be foremen and young engineers dreaming of the presidency. This series of small gradations means that communication from one level to another is easier and class-consciousness is weaker. Marx was wrong: industrial capitalism does not simplify the class order into two antagonistic groups, but rather makes it much more complex.

Stable city life is dependent upon a social class system. Public opinion in cities—that substitute for firm tradition maintained by the social controls of an homogeneous village—is never a single entity, but rather a series of opinions, each adapted to the needs of a given class level, and supported by networks of overlapping cliques which articulate basic values and teach them to new members. Ideals of family life (including the size of family desired), patterns of expected education for children, attitudes toward work and career, modes of consumption in matters of dress, food, house furnishings, and to some extent religious and political beliefs, all these emerge within the framework of relatively homogeneous strata of society which share a given level of education and a given type of job and income. The conversations of men on the job, and women and children in the area of residence (which is segregated by ecological competition according to income), create an appropriate style of life or class sub-culture.

The changing class pattern in Mexico has been analyzed through the use of occupational and income statistics by Iturriaga. Unfortunately, his data (shown in Table IV) go only to 1940, and it is likely that there has been as much change in the 19 years since as in the 45 years preceding that date.

TABLE IV

MEXICAN SOCIAL CLASS DISTRIBUTION, 1895 AND 1940

	1895	1940
Upper Class:		
Urban	0.4%	0.6%
Rural	1.0	0.5
Total	(1.4)	(1.1)
Middle Class:		
Urban	6.1	12.0
Rural	1.7	3.8
Total	(7.8)	(15.8)
Lower Class:		
Urban	14.2	22.4
Rural	76.6	60.7
Total	(90.8)	(83.1)
Total	100.0%	100.0%

Source: Iturriaga (1951), p. 28.

As a result of the revolution, the power of the rural upper class—a small number of families who owned great plantations or *haciendas*—was broken; many fled to the city and some succeeded in reinvesting a portion of their capital in new commercial enterprises. In recent years, a new upper class of big businessmen has grown, but their point of view looks forward to further industrial growth rather than backward toward the maintenance of a life of leisure based on rent.

The middle class in Mexico doubled from 1895 to 1940, according to Iturriaga's calculations. This means that there were far more people with secondary and university educations, with steady incomes derived from profits, salaries, and professional fees, and with standards of consumption which offered a regular market for industrial goods and for sophisticated services.

The lower class decreased in size and shifted toward urban concentration. Generally, the urban proletariat are a bit better educated and have a slightly higher level of consumption than their peasant cousins.

Shifts in the distribution of the population among the class levels are of considerable importance. For one thing, it is misleading to calculate the consumption gains from industrialization and to ignore this factor. One cannot compare the lot of peasants in 1895 with peasants in 1940, or of clerks in 1895 with clerks in 1940, and get the full picture of the change that has occurred (indeed, when inflation is considered, some groups are not a great deal better off now than they were then). One must realize that there are, relatively speaking, a lot more clerks and a lot fewer peasants than there used to be. Furthermore, shifts in class distributions open up new markets for industrial goods (e.g., peasants drink native brews, city people drink bottled beer and Coca-Cola), they shift the balance of political power,[9] they change the "tone" of a culture by altering education, taste, even the style of interpersonal relations.

So far, there has been a very slow emergence of class differences among Negro, urban Africans. The cities are new, the populations include many transients, the old people tend to remain in the villages. The net result is what McCulloch called the lack of an "urban public opinion."

An additional reason for the amorphousness of social class differences in Africa is the widespread backwardness of women. Education is primarily for men, and is thought of as preparing them for jobs. Women are usually illiterate and are more likely to engage in petty trade than to work for wages. Consequently, an educated man who becomes a skilled clerk finds it hard to secure a wife who can be a good companion, who can intelligently budget the use of money, who can entertain his friends, who can create the kind of home that the husband thinks is appropriate to his new status (one that is modeled after European middle-class patterns).

Of course, the continuing attempts in many areas by the European masters to limit Negro workers to low-level tasks in order to preserve European superiority is a basic fact which prevents the emergence of a fully differentiated class structure. In South Africa, even the skilled trades are reserved, where possible, for white men, and until recently higher education and professional careers in French and Belgian Africa were closed to Negroes.

The struggles in Africa for a class culture and a personal sense of identity—and the two are closely linked—are well portrayed by Georges Balandier in *Sociologie des Brazzavilles Noires*, 1955. This book, like most of those reported here, is a general survey of a new city, and contains demographic statistics, a sampling of public opinion, a comparison

[9] For an account of the effects of class changes on politics in Latin America, see Kling, 1956.

of aspects of town culture with surrounding village culture, a history of the city, etc. But Balandier adds something more: considerable attention to detailed case studies with attention to the changing attitudes of citizens who are becoming urbanized—what he calls the "psychological" approach. Balandier focuses upon the *évolués*, the evolved natives who seek an entirely urban way of life. He writes (p. 235):

The évolué *can be defined as an individual projected outside of his customary milieu by reason of a system of education in which he finds himself or by reason of his participation in economic and administrative processes established by the colonizer, conscious of the fundamental changes taking place in his milieu, and becoming suspect by the elders of his own society, and by European society, as a result of his modernist spirit.*

The *évolué* is a man in search of a self-image. He looks up to European culture as being "advanced"; he looks down upon village culture as being "backward, uncivilized, outmoded." But he learns of European culture through a language, studied in school, which never becomes fully comfortable. He has as his models Europeans who are playing the special role of "colonizer" and thus do not behave as they would at home. Furthermore, those Europeans do not accept him as an equal regardless of his degree of acculturation. For instance, every new group activity is scrutinized by the colonial officials for possible "subversive" political tendencies. And many of the European modes of behavior are not functional in a tropical town that lacks a firm economic base. Thus the *évolué* is constantly seeking and never fully finding; he has turned his back on one culture and is unable—in fact, not allowed —to create an adequate new one by imitation or by invention.

Balandier sketches the plight of the advanced native with warm insight; unfortunately, he does not give a systematic account of the new culture which is being created (weak though it may be) because he concentrates upon the difficulties more than the successes, and he emphasizes the disintegration of the old more than the reintegration of the new. I say this despite his many pages on new urban associations—occupational, religious, political—for what he fails to do is to show how these combine to create a social system for the urbanized individual which has a sense of pattern comparable to the pattern of kinship in the village.

The problem of the *évolué* is ordinarily the problem of a nascent middle class. The working-class individual is less likely to move so far from the native culture, for he has less education, and his job is precarious and provides little income beyond the needs of barest subsistence according to the native pattern. It is only when some individuals gain more education and have an economic stake in the new order which really promises something substantial that they begin to turn their backs upon the old ways and seeks to identify with the new ones.

Once class culture begins to appear, it is passed on from one generation to the next. Thus sons born of urban fathers, and especially of urban middle-class fathers, have a great advantage in the occupational world over sons born in the rural villages. The report on Stanleyville, previously cited, gives us a rare statistic on African occupational inheritance (International African Institute, 1956, p. 267): 43 percent of the white-collar men, 26 percent of the skilled and semiskilled men, but only 16 percent of the unskilled men had fathers who were wage earners rather than subsistence cultivators. The white-collar men, incidentally, earned three times as much as the unskilled men; and 83 percent of the former, but only 14 percent of the latter, had achieved four or more years of schooling.

EXPECTATIONS OF AN INCREASING STANDARD OF LIVING

Partly because of the new wealth produced by industrial techniques, partly because of the greater fluidity in the class system which encourages people to try to move up in the hierarchy and thereby redistribute existing wealth, there grows among men in modern societies an expectation of a constantly increasing standard of living. This is a radical shift: in the old society, the consumption standards were fixed for each segment of the hierarchy, and men did not expect to move from bottom to top. Good times were times when the customary standard could be reached; bad times were times when a man was unable to live the way he and his parents had always lived. A fixed expectation induced a man to work hard until the customary level of income was achieved; after that, he rested, and he was likely to be satisfied whatever the actual income happened to be.

Modern man is constantly expecting more. New gadgets are invented, and advertising turns them from novelties into necessities. If a man has a "lower-middle" income, he begins to reach for an "upper-middle" income. To be satisfied implies a lack of ambition, an acceptance of failure. Much of the emotional restlessness of modern society stems from this new notion of a constant increase in consumption goods, as well as much of the drive that makes man work hard and produce much. Under the new conditions, political and social unrest cannot be thought of as results of "poverty," for there is no fixed line between "poverty" and "plenty." Dissatisfaction, rather, stems from a discrepancy between what people have and what they want and feel they are entitled to, and the impact of industrialization raises standards of expectation at a very rapid pace—often faster than production itself goes up. Thus, we see the paradox: the more people get, the more they demand.[10]

THE FAMILY[11]

In general, urban-industrial society is conducive to the nuclear rather than the extended-family system; it tends to equalize the power of the sexes and the generations; it reduces the economic functions performed by the nuclear family to a minimum, and instead centers it upon sex, companionship, and the socialization of the very young. Let us examine these trends and their causes in some detail, and also note certain exceptions and countertrends.

In African rural life, the domestic unit frequently consists of more than one nuclear family. The members of the extended family cooperate in herding or agriculture, in the raising and distribution of the dowry or bride-wealth that permits young people to marry (thereby uniting not just individuals but family lines), in religious ceremonies (including ancestor worship), in the education of adolescents and its symbolization in *rites-de-passage*, in social control which keeps individuals from straying from the path of customary virtue, in political organization. All of these activities are based on the assumption that the crucial family members (the lineage, howsoever it be defined, and the spouses of its members) live and work in the same area; through the structure of kinship is organized the life of a homogeneous community. There results a strong sense of kin obligation and dependence: one shares with his relatives, one grows strong and safe through having many family ties that are actively functioning. One submits to family discipline because it pays off (and because there is no alternative).

At first, the urban migrant clings to the old family values. Indeed, he often goes to the city as a young man to raise money for his parents and expects to send cash home at regular intervals. But he quickly finds that the cost of housing and food absorbs most of his income, leaving little for remittance home. If he stays in the town and learns a skill which brings a higher income, he may be able to get a wife and settle

---

[10] The early stages of adaptation to modern habits of consumption are discussed by Elizabeth E. Hoyt, "The Impact of a Money Economy on Consumption Patterns," in *Annals*, 1956.

[11] This section has greatly benefited from my conversations with my colleague Irving Kaplan.

down as an urbanite. Then he finds that rural relatives expect him to house them without pay when they come to town for a visit or a job; sometimes they send their children to him for schooling, or he sends his young children to the village to keep them from being "spoiled" by the undisciplined ways of city youth.

As long as it manages to stay alive during the period of transition from rural to urban life, this system of kinship obligations has several effects: it slows down the emergence of class differences, for wealthier men are called upon to give more to their relatives than are poorer ones; it blurs the distinctions between town life and village life, for it stimulates interchange between them; it serves as a system of social security providing benefits during times of illness or unemployment. *Particularly during the period of transition*, while individuals brought up in the villages are trying to adjust to the demands of the city, are they likely to lean upon the family for help. Jean Comhaire stresses this theme in "Economic Change and the Extended Family" (in *Annals*, 1956), and shows the continuing strength of certain family ties. Indeed, he suspects that these will continue beyond the period of transition, but the evidence he cites mainly concerns behavior which shows a way of life which is partly rural, partly urban. He says that often the bride-wealth continues to be expressed in cattle, and the urban dweller is dependent upon his rural relatives for care of the beasts. He indicates that often the young man expects his kinsmen to help him raise the necessary price for a bride (but note that Mair, below, stresses the increasing tendency for the groom to raise the price himself and pay it entirely in cash). Comhaire continues (*Ibid.*, p. 47):

In Leopoldville, the capital of the Belgian Congo, the growth of the nuclear family and of a native middle class is impeded by low wages as well as by the absence of private property for African residents. The extended family thus remains a necessary institution for security and for educational and religious purposes. The newcomer in town and the unemployed both expect from their cousins some help, which they will be prepared to return when fortune changes. Children born in town are often sent to relatives in the rural home who can more easily take care of them and who educate them in customs which include the recognition of kinship ties up to the level of ancestor worship. On the other hand, prosperous native farmers send their children to Leopoldville, where they receive school education while staying with relatives. Urban social life centers around matanga, week-long funeral proceedings which include both rites and entertainment, and to whose considerable cost distant relatives must contribute.

As time passes, kinship obligations are put under more and more strain. They grew out of a village way of life which integrated all the institutions into a functioning equilibrium. That integration weakens in the city *because the wage job is an individualistic affair, and because the members of the kingroup no longer live close together.* A man eventually comes to feel that his wage income belongs to him and his wife and children, and he resists the claims of relatives. This process is described by L. P. Mair in "African Marriage and Social Change," a summary of many field studies (in Phillips, 1953, pp. 152–55):

> *On the basis of the existing evidence it is possible to discern certain general trends. Many of these can be correlated with the general increase in freedom from control by personal authority which can be seen in every sphere of African life. This arises directly from the fact that the African village is no longer an almost isolated, self-contained world, within which each member is dependent on the good-will of the rest and must secure it by conformity with accepted rules, and which he cannot leave without considerable danger. The African of today depends for his material needs at least as much on sources of income outside the village as on the cooperation of his family and kinsmen, and colonial rule has established law and order which make it safe for him to leave his village, and means of communication which make it easy.*
>
> *One consequence of this situation is that marriage is becoming increasingly a matter of personal choice rather than an arrangement between groups in which the elders have a dominant say. . . .*
>
> *Where the marriage is made legal by a payment, the husband is coming more and more to be expected to provide for this from his own resources. . . . The substitution of cash for some or all of the gifts or services included in the marriage formalities has often had the consequence of introducing a mercenary element that was not present in the old days. . . .*
>
> *The family found in the towns is usually the elementary family. Circumstances rarely make it possible for a wider group of kinsfolk to live in close contact. As a result, the influence of the "family council" in maintaining the stability of the marriage is weakened or even removed. There is no longer any organization outside the family for inculcating accepted rules and values in the next generation, and it is difficult for the family to meet this need when mothers as well as fathers have to earn money. . . .*

Balandier, in the book previously cited, also stresses the weakening of kinship ties under the impact of urban individualism, and adds the further point that this tends to undermine the entire traditional social structure, for it was closely tied to kinship. Once resident in the city, the young man is offered many choices between a variety of alternatives which did not exist before. He can choose his work, his place of residence, his friends, his wife; the authority of the elders to control his life is broken. Balandier writes (*Brazzavilles*, 1955, p. 262):

We think that the determining fact, in the urban milieu, is the destruction (or alteration) of the framework of the family in which the individual is placed—even when he keeps some contact with his original kinship group. For kinship structures remain, in central Africa, above all after the reduction in number and efficacy of specialized associations, the social framework that defines and regulates traditional groups and behavior. In dislocating the family, urban society alters, then ruins, the last support of the traditional cultures. We have shown . . . how extended family groups only have a provisional existence and tend to create isolated, nuclear families. It is a movement that is part of the general "process of individualization" that the city creates and makes predominant. The fact of having to hire out one's capacity to work for money . . . plus the fact of the shortage of women . . . turn marriage and the relations between the sexes into individual more than group affairs. . . . Finally, the shrinking of social bonds—the solitude of the city —leaves to the individual a large range of choice with regard to new groupings that he may join which lack any element of constraint. . . . This double movement of weakening family and of general individualization is transforming the ancient cultures.

A recent monograph probably offers more detail than any other on the changing family pattern in urban Africa: Georges Forthomme, *Mariage et Industrialisation*, 1957. It is a study of railroad workers in Elisabethville, Belgian Congo, conducted in 1952. Forthomme gives minute descriptions of the various customs connected with birth, adolescence, courtship, marriage, divorce, and death as they were practiced in traditional village environments among the surrounding Baluba tribal peoples, and then offers point-by-point contrasts from the current trends in the city. Unfortunately, his data appear to be based on a limited number of informants who describe how things are "usually" done— there is insufficient information on the range of variation; furthermore, a list of traits does not always produce a picture of the urban family as a functioning institution.

Forthomme points out that the patrilineal clan structure and patrilocal extended-family ties begin to weaken the moment an individual moves out of the ancestral village to go to work in the city. Nevertheless, such individuals continue to follow many of the practices they had learned as children; the fundamental changes come among those who are born and reared in the urban environment (p. 17):

In the city, children grow up in groups that are not based on tribe or clan membership. Friendships are founded not only in the neighborhood but also in school. A friend is chosen according to certain common interests, and becomes a person in whom one can confide, from whom one expects aid in times of difficulty. With him, a helping hand is not so much an obligation but rather a sign of affection. When one can surround himself with such true friends, why sacrifice for a group that uses the tie of blood to put one at their mercy? It is not just a question of an exchange of services with clan members, but the fact that the aid they usually demand is in the form of money, that thing so hard to obtain, which is lost once it is loaned to a relative.

Besides, the elders use the blood tie in order to impose their authority. But that right can be asserted only in the age-group that recognizes it. That authority was justified formerly by all knowledge resulting from experience, but currently the occupational opportunities permit a young man to have a social role almost as important as that of an elder.

Such are the changing conceptions of those who are currently forming families. Although not excluding his parents, the modern young man primarily considers his family to be made up of his wife and children. Without doubt, he still hears the mystical voice of the clan: exogamy remains a vigorous principle, and one dares not break certain tabus, but the rules that were the base of the old social order appear old-fashioned and are progressively abandoned.

The native of the city, regardless of his tribe, is proud of his young independence which was won by work outside of the clan context. He no longer counts on the clan and if, in important decisions, he consults his father it is mainly a gesture of protocol for he expects his father's views to differ from his and he will follow his own inclinations. The cases of young people marrying against the wish of their parents are not rare.

Forthomme agrees with other observers of African life that the urban woman demands and receives much more independence from the authority of her husband (and before marriage, her parents) than does the rural woman. There is usually a shortage of women in the city, which gives them increased bargaining power; their ready contacts with other men during the day while their husbands are away at work offer them easy alternatives to spouses who may not satisfy; the possibilities of earning a living as a trader, a prostitute, or occasionally a factory worker or domestic servant free women from the economic necessity of having husbands. All of this means that women assert a greater degree of independence, including the right to easy divorce.

The mixture of young people of different tribal groups in the city leads to intermarriage. Forthomme reports that 17 percent of a sample of almost 2,000 married persons had crossed tribal lines; the percentage is higher in some other cities reported in the literature. Insofar as tribal customs vary, it is obvious that mixed marriages will show individualistic adaptation to current needs.

The most acculturated African sample discussed in the literature are the Zulu inhabitants of a government housing project in Durban, Natal, Union of South Africa. Almost all of the 118 households in the "Baumanville" project were interviewed in 1954 by a group from the Institute for Social Research of the University of Natal under the acting directorship of H. P. Pollack; the report was edited by Hallenbeck, 1955.

Despite the fact that the people of Baumanville are an old, settled and highly urbanized group with weak ties to rural culture, they continue to live in large households. I do not think it is appropriate to conclude that they have an extended-family system, though the statistics may so suggest: three-quarters of the "core" families (the nuclear family that rents the house) have relatives living with them. The latter are about equally divided between single persons and married couples (often with their children). The modal house has six to eight inhabitants, despite the fact that it contains but two rooms and often a makeshift porch added to the rear.

The authors suggest that the great overcrowding in Durban puts pressure on people to absorb relatives, and that there has emerged a cultural norm which assumes that a "normal" house will contain three or four persons per room. This pressure for space, plus the old traditions of family hospitality, lead to large households. However, these households are created for practical reasons, reflecting the space shortage, and are not functioning systems of extended families based on the norm that certain classes of relatives *should* live together and *should* cooperate on economic tasks. Indeed, in the city, there is a wide variety of arrangements for sharing in the rent and the household tasks, showing the lack of clear cultural patterning. It seems to me that we have a situation in Baumanville that is similar to that in the Negro ghettos in

American cities: great overcrowding and a flexible adaptation thereto, but not an institutional form of the extended-family, for when a particular nuclear family can afford separate accommodation, they are likely to seek it.

The practice of bride-wealth continues in Baumanville (along with Christian marriage) although it has been converted into a cash transaction. This has the effect of delaying the age of marriage for the boys, as they cannot easily raise the necessary money. The modal time for men to marry is from 26 to 30 years of age, for women, five years earlier. The delayed age of marriage is leading to a large increase in illegitimacy which the people find distressing but do not know how to control.

The various reports on African cities uniformly speak of weak control of adolescents by their parents and the community. Especially among first-generation urban families, young people feel that their parents' norms are poor guides to the future. Adolescent gangs wander the streets and perplex the older generation by their disregard for authority. But *none* of the reports tells us what happens to these adolescents as they grow older and take up regular occupations; *none* of the studies contrasts rebellious youths with those who obey and respect their parents. Do the latter come from those families in which the parents have made a more successful adjustment to city life and therefore can serve as realistic role models for their children? A careful analysis of the years of late adolescence and early maturity, based on a study of an urban group as they pass through the various stages of growth, with sub-samples representing families of different degrees of urbanization, and different levels of the class hierarchy, would add immensely to our understanding of the emerging urban culture.

In contrast to the foregoing studies, Oscar Lewis in "Urbanization Without Breakdown: A Case Study," 1952, offers an analysis of new urbanites in Mexico City which seems to contradict many of the trends thus far discussed. He reports his data against a background of findings from the United States which indicate that farmers who move to the city often experience family disorganization leading to divorce and desertion, adolescent rebellion against parental authority leading to delinquency, and personal disorganization leading to neurosis and psychosis. Lewis interviewed 69 families who had moved from the village of Tepotzlán (which he had previously studied in great detail) to the capital city. They included families who had moved before the revolution of 1910 and others who had come more recently; in occupation, they ranged from professionals to domestic servants. He summarized his findings as follows (pp. 40–41):

From our study of Tepoztecans living in Mexico City, we find that peasants in Mexico adapt to city life with far greater ease than do American farm families. There is little evidence of disorganization and breakdown, of culture conflict, or of irreconcilable differences between generations. . . . Family life remains strong in Mexico City. Family cohesiveness and extended family ties increase in the city, fewer cases of separation and divorce occur, no cases of abandoned mothers and children, no cases of persons living alone or of unrelated families living together.

How can these findings be reconciled with the usual picture of disorganization among new urbanites? Lewis himself suggests several ways, and I shall add a few more:

1. Lewis' sample is a special one. Tepotzlán is only two hours' bus ride from Mexico City, and the cohesive social structure of the village is reflected by the continuing ties of the urbanites to village life: over half of the city dwellers still own houses in the village, and visits back and forth are common.

2. The Mexican rural family system is better adapted to urban needs than is the African, and thus less change is produced when people move cityward. The Mexican rural family is essentially a nuclear family; there are patterns of aid among extended kin and ritual kin (*compadres*) based on mutual exchange, but these are flexible and much choice according to personal taste is permitted. The basic economic functions of farming and trading are carried on by nuclear families who have a strong sense of independence and a long acquaintance with money markets and personal gain. Residence is nuclear whenever economic conditions permit: 70 percent of the village families in Tepotzlán (and 67 percent of the Tepoztecans in Mexico City) lived in nuclear households. Furthermore, Lewis does not tell us of adaptations to urban needs that many parents probably made which allowed them to retain solidary ties with their children.

3. Catholic religious traditions in Mexico reinforce its family pattern. The homogeneity of Mexico City, which draws most of its immigrants from Mexican rural districts which have basically similar traditions of family and religion is in great contrast to the American cities with their many foreign immigrants and their many competing religious creeds, and it is in great contrast to the African cities where the strictly urban culture patterns are in large part imitations of European modes of behavior.

4. The statistics on disorganization—whether they be African, American, or Mexican—exaggerate the differences between the city and the country. Recordkeeping is much better in the city, so more cases of divorce, delinquency, and psychological illness are reported. The same differentials between urban and rural statistics exist in Mexico as in the United States; we cannot draw conclusions from a comparison of a small sample of solidary families in Mexico City with American national statistics on family disorganization.

5. Case studies of American urban families are rare, and are often interpreted through middle-class eyes. Consequently, certain patterns of adolescent sexual behavior, of "rebellion," of adult behavior that appear odd to middle-class observers, may represent differences in culture pattern and not necessarily "disorganization."

In summary, I think it clear that the evidence so far does suggest a general pattern, but we must specify in detail the circumstances in which the pattern holds. The pattern is an abstraction of tendencies noted in many cultures; in concrete fact, each situation will show a combination of the general trends and the local traditions—the very nature of abstraction involves the overlooking of some aspects of reality in order to emphasize others.

The urban family tends to be nuclear; women have considerable independence and there is a trend toward sexual "equality"; young people have considerable freedom to move about the city, make friends, seek their own careers and wives. Now, where the rural family patterns are at variance with these urban forms, there will be culture shock and strain when people first move to the city and until they have had time not only to break loose from the old forms but *to institutionalize the new ones*. These new forms grow out of the economic life of the city (just as the old ones grew out of the economic life of the country), and only when persons achieve stabilized careers will they be able to develop new patterns of stabilized family life. As Mair said in her report on African families previously cited (p. 155):

In the towns . . . most observers have found that an ideal of marriage and home life exists, and that great efforts are often made to attain it. If irregular unions are regarded with tolerance, yet legal marriage is still regarded as the ideal; homes are kept clean in the midst of slums, and children cared for as well as may be. Where higher standards of living are attainable, marriage is more stable, women stay at home and look after their children, and children go regularly to school. The answer here lies surely as much in the attack on African poverty as in moral exhortation.

Young people will respect their elders when the elders deserve respect. In rural cultures, the old people are wise in the ways of farming and in most matters of life, secular and sacred; furthermore, they control the land which is vital to the fate of their children. In the city, lower-class migrants from the farms tend to be ignorant people who know less about city life than do their children. But when parents adjust to the city environment, when they have good jobs with steady incomes, when they themselves have had city schooling, then they can serve as potent role models for their children. Eventually, working-class and middle-class cultures emerge which produce new stability within the nuclear family in the urban milieu.

Indeed, the noneconomic functions of the nuclear family are likely to be strengthened in the city. For example, it is this group that gives basic emotional warmth and support in an environment which tends to be impersonal and calculating; it is the agent of socialization, which becomes more conscious and deliberate as modern theories of personality-formation diffuse; it is a major center of consumption activities, and they grow in significance as the length of the work day diminishes; and for many members of the middle and upper classes, it is a group which shares career responsibility by aiding the father in his duties of entertainment of customers, clients, or fellow-executives.

The urban family tends to be smaller than the rural family. On the farm, children cost less to rear, for space is cheap, food is home-grown, and formal education unnecessary. From a young age, farm children contribute labor which is worth more than their upkeep. But, in the city, children are more expensive to rear and they do not start earning until a much later age. Especially in the middle classes, where economic wants (including the symbols of consumption necessary for upward mobility) tend to outrun income, children become a burden and parents gladly turn to methods of birth control.

I have stressed that individualistic jobs and geographic separation are the keys to the breakdown of close kinship solidarity beyond the nuclear family. But these two forces do not operate equally throughout city life. The urban proletariat (once stabilized) tends to be less geographically mobile than the middle class; working-class siblings may grow up in the same area and, when married, may exchange services such as baby-care or aid in housebuilding which tend to keep solidarity alive. These mutual exchanges can function well so long as social mobility is not present: if one of a pair of siblings climbs into the middle class, opportunity for equal reciprocity is lost, the less successful sibling feels awkward in the presence of the more successful one, and interaction declines. Thus, social mobility has effects similar to geographical mobility.

Family businesses often serve as ties between siblings and between generations. Especially where great property is present, as in the upper class, kinship solidarity is likely to remain strong.

In other words, it is only an approximation to use the shorthand phrase "urban life affects the family." One must specify the particular urban processes which are at work, and recognize that they operate with differential force among different groups. All urbanites are not alike.

ORGANIC SOLIDARITY

In *The Division of Labor in Society*, 1893, Durkheim developed a distinction between two forms of social solidarity. The simple rural or folk society is held together by similarity: there is very little specialization of function; there is a single, coherent, homogeneous, and sacred cultural tradition which tells everybody how to behave; there is a strong public opinion based on face-to-face interaction (perhaps the word should be "gossip") which brings deviants back into line. This type of social cohesion Durkheim labeled "mechanical solidarity." Based upon custom and the similarity of one man's life to that of another in a small community, it creates a strong but static society which continually reproduces itself without much variation.

Modern societies cannot be held together by such means. There is an elaborate dviision of labor which makes one man unlike another; men engage in systems of production and exchange which promote attitudes of rationality and calculation; there is constant economic and social change which weakens sacred custom. But Durkheim pointed out that the very elaborateness of the division of labor makes each man more dependent upon his neighbor than in the past: no one can be self-sufficient when he is a specialist in some one, minute task. This interdependence creates the conditions for a new form of social cohesion which Durkheim called "organic solidarity." Let us examine its components.

In part, organic solidarity is based on the sheer fact of interdependence in the market place. I am connected with the Brazilians who grew my morning coffee, with the assembly-line workers in Detroit who made my automobile, with the members of the world-wide organization of the Standard Oil Company which supplies my gasoline. Under ordinary circumstances, my dealings with these people are impersonal: I am interested in their goods and not their lives. I may, in objective fact, share with them a common destiny, but I do not subjectively feel a common identity. Our attitudes towards each other are attitudes of rational calculation of personal gain; our dealings are controlled by price competition.

However, market ties may become personalized through continued face-to-face contact. I begin to know my local gas station proprietor and become concerned about his health. I work not as an isolate but as a member of a team, and my teammates and I become mutually involved as individuals as well as participants in a common career.

And I have links to people not based on market relationships. My family is of central importance; I live in a local community and become conscious of the fact that my life is intertwined with the lives of my neighbors; I have interests in music, literature, the free life, and stand together with those who share such interests. I learn to have a concern for the maintenance of the type of society which permits me to live the kind of life I cherish. I may enlarge my sense of community beyond the immediate locality to my nation, my nation's allies, all the free world, humanity.

Organic solidarity is thus a complex thing of many parts. There is a dearth of research on how the parts fit together to make a whole, but some of the more important components can be listed in outline form:

1. Market interdependence.

2. "Rules of the game" or norms that regulate market dealings, such as honesty, fulfillment of contract, efficiency.

3. "Rules of the game" that regulate internal behavior within firms which operate in the market; that is, the norms of bureaucracy such as devotion to the benefit of the organization, limitation of authority to the proper confines of the job, elimination of private interests which conflict with those of the organization.

4. Occupational codes which create a subculture appropriate to each group, such as the professional ethics of the physician or the teacher, or the craftsmanlike creed of the skilled machinist.

5. Functioning face-to-face groups at work and in the residential community.

6. Organized interest groups which represent the concerns of occupational or regional segments of the society.

7. Legitimate structures of government which articulate and control the competing interests. There must evolve an emotional conviction in the supremacy of legal procedure, regardless of the content of particular decisions, to subdue the potential war of each against all. If a decision is reached legally, we must feel constrained to accept it even if it threatens our personal interests.

8. Ultimate values about the ends of life in society which are shared by all within it.

9. Rational awareness of common destiny and thus rational willingness to share for common good.

10. Organized public opinion based on a combination of long-term values, personal or group interests, and knowledge of current events. The mass media are the agents of opinion formation.

A smoothly functioning society based upon organic solidarity must somehow combine all of these elements into a totality. Obviously, it is a totality which is quite different from the mechanical solidarity of a rural village. This qualitative difference is of such magnitude that we ought to avoid analyses of urban society based upon rural models. Those who look toward urban society wearing glasses shaped in the villages see it as impersonal to the point of being inhuman, disorganized[12] to the point of imminent collapse, so distorting to innate human nature as to produce mass psychosis. I do not believe it. If one wishes to reverse the perspective and view village society with the glasses of an urbanite, one can call it stultifying to the personality because it shapes everybody into the same mold, repressive of creativity and innovation, exploitative of the labor of the many for the benefit of the few, so tightly organized

[12] The concept of "disorganization" is risky, for rarely is the comparative base of "organization" clearly specified. Particularly when we are studying social change must we be wary. Does the concept refer to a lack of close relationship between various segments of a culture, as Redfield defines it? Then what is the standard of proper integration?—a complex urban culture will, *when well organized,* show more variation, more alternatives, than a simple rural culture. Does the concept refer to social control over individual behavior? Then what is a proper standard of homogeneity within a given type of society and its various segments? American urban life is called disorganized by some observers, over-conformist by others.

and conservative that life lacks zest. One stereotype is as bad as the other.[13]

RESEARCH METHODS

There remains space for only a few comments on research procedures. Many of the books discussed above are "social surveys" of new cities. As such, they attempt to describe the situation as it exists at a given moment: How many people are there, what is the age and sex distribution, how many of them are married, where were they born, how long do they expect to stay in the city, do they send money home to villages, etc.? Only indirectly do these studies focus on the processes of change which are of central concern to the construction of general theory. For the latter purpose, the important data do not concern the proportion who appear to be committed to the new urban life at a given moment, but the processes which commit them and the changes which they undergo as a result of commitment. For an understanding of such processes of change, we need a number of detailed case studies selected according to a sampling scheme which draws upon all the crucial types of persons, defined according to combinations of the following variables: length of residence in the city, rural-born versus city-born, ties with rural life, education, occupation. The case studies must be cast in the form of life-histories, and must gather considerable data on behavior, on norms, and on feelings.

Simple transfer of traditional methods of anthropology or sociology will not serve adequately. For instance, the anthropologist usually seeks a "community." If he goes to the city, he may well concentrate on one small residential district under the impression that he is studying something analogous to the village community. However, he will be mistaken, for a residential area of a city—even in a slum where there appears to be much interaction among the neighbors—is but a pale imitation of a village community. The men (and many of the women) leave the area to go to work; the children leave to go to school; economic and much of social and religious life is not centered on the residential district. For the working-class, the factory is as much a community as the residential district, and for the middle classes, the network of clique ties which is rarely based on a single geographical district serves many community functions. *It is of the essence of urban life that*

[13] For the sake of simplicity, I speak of the village *versus* the city. Obviously, the urbanization of a society is a matter of degree. Early urbanization, a limited division of labor, a partially developed class hierarchy—such as in many African cities—will produce a social system quite different from the more advanced Mexican society. But I leave it to the reader to fill in the shades of gray.

interpersonal relations are based on several functions and groups and
these do not all overlap in a single small geographic center.

The currently fashionable methods in sociology are equally limited
for the problem at hand. They interrelate a small number of variables,
statistically measured, for a large sample. In most instances these variables all refer to a single moment of time. A great deal of previous
knowledge about the culture is assumed in such research; e.g., the American researcher has an enormous body of accumulated data that he takes
for granted in constructing his sample controls. When the culture being
studied is not well known, and when change through time under certain
defined circumstances is the focus of the research, the modern survey
methods are of limited use.

It seems to me that the appropriate procedure is to recognize that
the structure of urban life is based upon the division of labor. We
must sample systematically among various levels of the hierarchy and
then collect cases with full life-history data. We cannot rely upon a few
informants to tell us what the traditions are, for the traditions are
changing and informants have knowledge that is limited to their own
immediate social type. We must observe behavior and get detailed
verbal accounts of behavior in a large number of specific situations for
a large number of different types of persons. Then the scientific observer
can construct a picture of the general forms of behavior in such a way
that central tendencies and significant variations from them can be
described and analyzed and even explained. When he recognizes that
there is integration in urban society, albeit not based on the local
community, he will be able to relate the life-histories of the different
types of informants into a picture of the functioning totality. Of what
use is a knowledge of servants without an understanding of employers?
Of tradesmen without customers? Of political bosses without followers?
The division of labor integrates as much as it divides men from one
another. Durkheim was not using a meaningless phrase when he spoke
of "organic solidarity," and we must devise research procedures appropriate to its nature.

ONE WORLD, ALL ALIKE?

I have been stressing in this paper what seem to me to be the processes
of change which tend to create a universal way of life in modern industrial cities. No doubt some features that appear to me to belong to
this universal culture are only special aspects of Western European or
American life, and my own ethnocentrism has led me to generalize
them. I invite colleagues from other cultures to correct my biases.

I think the major research task in the years ahead is the design of comparative studies which will help us determine in a systematic way how the universal aspects of industrial civilization combine with local cultural traditions to create living societies. In other words, to what degree will all nations of the future be alike under the dictates of industrial life, and to what degree can they retain features of uniqueness? It is perfectly obvious that pre-industrial cultures must undergo drastic reorganization under the impact of industrialization and urbanization; it is impossible to adopt a new economy and retain an old society. But perhaps intellectual understanding of the minimum social prerequisites of an efficient industrial order will permit a planned readjustment which can keep strong those aspects of the various traditional orders which are compatible with the realities of the new one. To state a personal value of my own: I hope the intellectuals will join in leading such a readjustment, for I would not enjoy a world without diversity. Unfortunately, too many intellectuals, especially in the humanities, fight the new order blindly and without understanding, and thus lose the power to influence constructively the evolution of the emerging society.

A SELECTED AND ANNOTATED BIBLIOGRAPHY

A. *Journal:*
   Economic Development and Cultural Change, The University of Chicago.

B. *Bibliographies:*
   Comhaire, Jean, *Urban Conditions in Africa: Select Reading List on Urban Problems in Africa,* rev. ed., Oxford University Press, London, 1952.
   Classified, with some annotation; emphasizes social and administrative problems.
   Conseil International des Sciences Sociales, Bureau International de Recherche sur les Implications Sociales du Progrès Technique, *Consequences Sociales de L'industrialisation et Problèms Urbains en Afrique,* Paris, Septembre–Octobre, 1954 (mimeographed).
   A classified bibliography; not annotated; brief introduction and conclusion by Georges Balandier.
   Gilfillan, S. C., "Social Implications of Technical Advance," *Current Sociology,* I (1953), 187–266.
   Classified and annotated; considerable emphasis on causes and effects of inventions.
   Hazlewood, Arthur, *The Economics of Underdeveloped Areas,* Oxford University Press, London, 1954.

Annotated; covers mainly years 1930–53; 623 items.

Industrial Relations Section, Princeton University, *Manpower Problems in Economic Development,* Princeton, 1958.

Keesing, Felix M., *Culture Change: An Analysis and Bibliography of Anthropological Sources,* Stanford University Press, Stanford, 1953.

Smith, Robert J., "Comparative Studies in Anthropology of the Interrelations Between Social and Technical Change," *Human Organization,* XVI, No. 1 (Spring, 1957), 30–36.

A research review.

Trager, Frank N., "A Selected and Annotated Bibliography on Economic Development, 1953–57," *Economic Development and Cultural Change,* VI (July, 1958), 257–329.

Classified and annotated; 409 items.

United Nations, Department of Social Affairs, *The Determinants and Consequences of Population Trends: A Summary of the Findings of Studies on the Relationships between Population Changes and Economic and Social Conditions,* United Nations, New York, 1953.

A research review.

United Nations, Headquarters Library, *Bibliography on Industrialization in Underdeveloped Countries,* Bibliographical Series No. 6, April, 1956.

C. *Collections of Articles:*

American Journal of Sociology, Philip M. Hauser, ed., "World Urbanism," LX (March, 1955).

Annals of American Academy of Political and Social Science, "Agrarian Societies in Transition," Bert F. Hoselitz, ed., vol. 305 (May, 1956).

Annals of American Academy of Political and Social Science, "Contemporary Africa, Trends and Issues," vol. 298 (March, 1955).

Balandier, Georges, ed., *Le "tiers monde," sous-développment et développment,* Presses Universitaires de France, Paris, 1956.

Hoselitz, Bert F., ed., *The Progress of Underdeveloped Areas,* University of Chicago Press, Chicago, 1952.

International Social Science Bulletin, "Social Implications of Technical Change," IV (Summer, 1952).

Includes bibliography.

International Sociological Association, *Transactions of the Third World Congress of Sociology: Problems of Social Change in the Twentieth Century,* International Sociological Association, London, 1956.

Phillips, Arthur, ed., *Survey of African Marriage and Family Life,* Oxford University Press, London, 1953.

Shannon, Lyle, ed., *Underdeveloped Areas,* Harper, New York, 1957.

D. *General and Theoretical:*

Buchanan, Norman S. and Ellis, Howard S., *Approaches to Economic Development,* Twentieth Century Fund, New York, 1955.

A general survey of the economic literature, with chapters on the historical development of England, Russia, Japan, etc., plus analyses of main theoretical issues in "development economics." Good guide for the layman.

Caplow, Theodore, *The Sociology of Work,* The University of Minnesota Press, Minneapolis, 1954.

A general work on the division of labor and its consequences that synthesizes much empirical data, mainly American.

Clark, Colin, *The Conditions of Economic Progress,* 3rd ed., Macmillan, London, 1957.

Chapter IX, "The Distribution of Labour Between Industries," shows the pattern of world-wide trends in the division of labor under the impact of industrial development.

Cottrell, Fred, *Energy and Society,* McGraw-Hill, New York, 1955.

Measures development through the per-capita use of non-human energy and relates it to changes in social structure.

Durkheim, Emile, *The Division of Labor in Society,* trans. by George Simpson, The Free Press, Glencoe, Ill., 1947 (first published 1893).

Classic treatise on the distinction between "mechanical" and "organic" solidarity. Follows from the work of Maine, Spencer, and Tönnies, but is far superior to them.

Fromm, Erich, *Escape From Freedom,* Rinehart, New York, 1941.

Psychological analysis of the burden that individuals must bear when they break loose from traditional forms of society and seek individualism. In his more recent book, *The Sane Society,* Rinehart, New York, 1955, Fromm goes much further and damns modern society as being unsuited to human nature.

Hoselitz, Bert F., "The City, the Factory, and Economic Growth," *American Economic Review,* XLV (May, 1955), 166–84.

Good contrast of social structure in Asian cities with more familiar European-American cities. Indicates some ways in which "urbanism" responds to various cultural traditions and modes of economic organization.

Kahl, Joseph A., *The American Class Structure,* Rinehart, New York, 1957.

Analysis of the available empirical data on American stratification, set in the framework of a theoretical view that emphasizes the role of the changing division of labor.

Lynd, Robert S. and Helen M., *Middletown,* Harcourt Brace, New York, 1929.

The one first-class analysis of the transition from village to urban society in the United States; a model that current research might well follow.

Mead, Margaret, ed., *Cultural Patterns and Technical Change,* UNESCO, Paris, 1953.

A review of the literature on resistances to change and the effects of change among less-developed peoples; includes some case studies. Implications for mental health are stressed.

Merton, Robert K., "Bureaucratic Structure and Personality" in his *Social Theory and Social Structure,* The Free Press, Glencoe, Ill., 1949.

An essay on the pressures of bureaucracy that create a standardized "official personality" among its members.

Miner, Horace, "The Folk-Urban Continuum," *American Sociological Review,* XVII (October, 1952), 529–37; reprinted in Hatt and Reiss, eds., *Cities and Society,* The Free Press, Glencoe, Ill., 1957.

A re-evaluation of the Redfield concepts in the light of criticisms by Oscar Lewis and others as well as the new data from Miner's study of Timbuctoo.

Moore, Wilburt E., *Industrialization and Labor,* Cornell University Press, Ithaca, N.Y., 1951.

A systematic analysis of the reasons that draw workers from villages into industrial work, with the implications of the accumulated data for a general theory of labor economics. Also contains an empirical study of new industrial workers in Mexico.

Parsons, Talcott, "The Professions and Social Structure," *Social Forces,* XVII, No. 4 (May, 1939); reprinted in his *Essays in Sociological Theory,* The Free Press, Glencoe, Ill., 1949.

Elegant analysis of the code of behavior followed by professionals; good illustration of the degree to which norms enter the world of the marketplace and control behavior. This article contains an early statement of Parsons' important theoretical scheme of "pattern variables," later developed in his *The Social System,* The Free Press, Glencoe, Ill., 1951. See Theodorsen for an application of this scheme to the effects of industrialization.

Redfield, Robert, "The Folk Society." *American Journal of Sociology,* LII (1947), 293–308.

A succinct and powerful statement of an "ideal-type" of folk society that is implicitly contrasted to urban society. The scheme grew out of careful study of empirical data in Mexico plus the theoretical tradition of Maine, Tönnies, and Durkheim, as elaborated in Redfield's *The Folk Culture of Yucatan,* University of Chicago Press, Chicago, 1941. His position is controversial but very important and stimulating. See Miner, "The Folk-Urban Continuum."

Theodorsen, George A., "Acceptance of Industrialization and its Attendant Consequences for the Social Patterns of Non-Western Societies," *American Sociological Review,* XVIII (1953), 477–84.

An application of the "pattern variables" of Parsons to the process of industrialization-urbanization; Theodorsen considers the effects of industrialization on social structure to be universal.

Wirth, Louis, "Urbanism as a Way of Life," *American Journal of Sociology,* XLIV (July, 1938); reprinted in Hatt and Reiss, eds., *Cities and Society,* The Free Press, Glencoe, Ill., 1957.

A superb re-statement of the main trends of sociological thought on the characteristics of urban society. Draws heavily on Durkheim, Weber, Simmel, and Park.

E. *Recent Research Monographs:*

Balandier, Georges, *Sociologie des Brazzavilles Noires,* No. 67, "Cahiers de la fondation nationale des sciences politiques," Armand Colin, Paris, 1955.

A general report on the city of Brazzaville; contains more social-psychological material than most other monographs.

Banton, Michael, *West African City: A Study of Tribal Life in Freetown,* Oxford University Press, London, 1957.

A general report on Freetown; includes a sample survey of 1,042 persons with data on migration and household composition; also data from informants on family and religious life, and especially good analyses of voluntary associations and new political organizations.

Burnright, R. G., Whetten, N. L., and Waxman, B. D., "Rural-Urban Fertility in Mexico," *American Sociological Review,* XXI (February, 1956), 3–8.

A study of the 1950 census that shows a marked fertility differential according to size of place. (Yet the national birth rate remains at the same high level despite increasing urbanization.)

Caplow, Theodore, "The Social Ecology of Guatemala City," *Social Forces,* XXVIII (December, 1949), 113–33.

Begins with a summary of other ecological studies of Latin American cities; goes on to analyze the growth of Guatemala City, and shows that peculiar features of Latin American culture produce a growth pattern quite different from the one in the United States which is the base of much ecological theorizing.

Davis, Kingsley and Golden, Hilda Hertz, "Urbanization and the Development of Pre-Industrial Areas," *Economic Development and Cultural Change,* III (October, 1954), 6–26; reprinted in Hatt and Reiss, *op. cit.*

World-wide statistics on urbanization compared with data on the agricultural-industrial division of labor lead to conclusions on an "appropriate" rate of urbanization in relation to industrialization.

Duran Ochoa, Julio, Población, México; Fondo de Cultura Económica, 1955.

Detailed analysis of recent census statistics on Mexican population.

Elkan, W., *An African Labour Force,* East African Institute of Social Research, Kampala, Uganda, 1956.

Superficial study of the labor force of two tobacco factories, one in Jinja and the other in Kampala. See Sofer.

Germán Parra, Manuel, *La Industrialización de México,* Imprenta Universitaria, México, 1954.

A polemic against Tannenbaum. Contains many useful statistical series, set in the framework of a theory of unilinear evolution of industrialism. Powerfully argued, but the theorizing pushes the data too far.

Hallenbeck, Wilbur C., ed., (for Pietermaritzburg University of Natal), *The Baumanville Community: A Study of the Family Life of Urban Africans,* Institute for Social Research, University of Natal, Durban, 1955.

A thorough questionnaire survey of 118 households in a government housing project in Durban; emphasis on education, work, family.

Hoselitz, Bert F., "Urbanization and Economic Growth in Asia," *Economic Development and Cultural Change,* VI (October, 1957), 42–54.

Urbanization in Asia in relation to the changing division of labor.

Husain, A. F. A., *Human and Social Impact of Technological Change in Pakistan,* 2 vols., Oxford University Press, Dacca, Pakistan, 1956.

A meticulous survey of workers in 19 factories, plus rickshaw drivers in Dacca. Vol. I contains the results of the questionnaire survey; Vol. II contains brief but revealing case studies of different types of individuals.

International African Institute, London, *Social Implications of Industrialization and Urbanization in Africa South of the Sahara,* UNESCO, Paris, 1956.

Four parts: an introduction on the Africa of today (Forde); a summary and review of thirty-three research monographs on African cities (McCulloch); a detailed monograph on Stanleyville (Clément, Pons, Xydias); a report on a conference of experts held at Abidjan in 1954.

Iturriaga, Jose E., *La Estructura Social y Cultural de México,* Fondo de Cultura Economica, Mexico, 1951.

A general analysis, in large part statistical, of Mexican society.

Kling, Merle, "Towards a Theory of Power and Political Instability in Latin America," *Western Political Science Quarterly,* IX (March, 1956), 21–35.

Data showing that industrialization and personal political dictatorships by military men are inversely correlated; a theory of explanation is suggested.

Lewis, Oscar, "Mexico Desde 1940," *Investigación Economica,* XVIII (1958), 185–256.

A succinct statement of economic and social changes in Mexico since 1940, combining statistical and qualitative data; strong emphasis upon "Americanization."

Lewis, Oscar, "Urbanization Without Breakdown: A Case Study," *Scientific Monthly,* LXXV (July, 1952), 31–41.

Study of 69 families who have moved from the village of Tepotzlán to Mexico City; Lewis found few signs of personal or familial disorganization, which he considers proof that generalizations about such disorganization from United States data are not universally applicable.

Miner, Horace, *The Primitive City of Timbuctoo,* Princeton University Press, Princeton, 1953.

An ethnographic report on the three societies that live together in this city of 6,000 people that has had very little contact with the outside world. Designed as a test of the Redfield folk-urban continuum, it concludes that urbanization does produce secularization, individualization, and disorganization, but mainly between the three groups and only slightly within them. Timbuctoo is an example of a general type called "preindustrial cities"; see Sjoberg in *American Journal of Sociology* (March), 1955.

Nash, Manning, *Machine Age Maya, The Industrialization of a*

Guatemalan Community, The Free Press, Glencoe, Ill., 1958 (also published as Memoir 87, *American Anthropologist,* April, 1958). Study of the effects of a textile mill on a Guatemalan village. Conclusion: the effects have been surprisingly few.

Smith, T. Lynn, "The Reproduction Rate in Latin America: Levels, Differentials and Trends," *Population Studies,* XII (July, 1958).

Analysis of fertility data from 1950 censuses; although an urban-rural differential is widespread, only in Cuba and Argentina has it produced a marked effect on the national reproduction rates.

Sofer, Cyril and Rhona, *Jinja Transformed: A Social Survey of a Multi-Racial Township,* East African Institute of Social Research, Kampala, Uganda, 1955.

A general report on Jinja, mainly based on a sample survey. See Elkan.

Southall, Aiden W. and Gutkind, Peter C. W., *Townsmen in the Making: Kampala and its Suburbs,* East African Institute of Social Research, Kampala, Uganda, 1957.

A study of two proletarian districts in Kampala, with emphasis on social problems.

Tannenbaum, Frank, *Mexico: The Struggle for Peace and Bread,* Knopf, New York, 1950.

Analysis of the purposes, accomplishments, and failures of the Mexican revolution by a friend of President Cárdenas. Has a somewhat overly-romantic view of village life and an overly-pessimistic view of the possibilities of successful industrialization. See Germán Parra.

Textor, Robert B., *et al., The Social Implications of Industrialization and Urbanization: Five Studies of Urban Populations of Recent Rural Origin in Cities of Southern Asia,* UNESCO Research Centre on the Social Implications of Industrialization in Southern Asia, Calcutta, India, 1956.

Five studies: a digest of Husain; a pilot study of rickshaw drivers in Bangkok (Textor); a survey of 523 families in a housing project in Bombay (Prabhu); a survey of 959 migrant families in Madhya Pradesh, India (Deshmukh); a survey of 11,760 household heads in Djakarta (Heeren).

United Nations, *Report on the World Social Situation,* United Nations, New York, 1957.

A rich collection of data (mainly statistical) on population, nutrition, housing, etc., throughout the world, with a section on urbanization in Latin America. "Social problems" are emphasized.

West African Urbanization as a Social Process

KENNETH LITTLE
University of Edinburgh

It has been customary, until quite recently, to study the impact of Western civilization upon primitive society as a phenomenon of culture contact. Scholars like Herskovits and Malinowski, stimulated such research and a large number of studies were made in different parts of the primitive world, including Oceania and North America as well as Africa itself. Broadly, the aim of these investigations was to elucidate the particular Western traits and institutions adopted by the indigenous society concerned and their integration into the patterns of its culture.[1]

Methodologically, there is some justification for this kind of approach when the contacts in question involve no special reordering of social relationships. Thus, until well on in the 19th century, the contact that Europeans made with the native people of West Africa was almost entirely commercial. The two groups kept themselves apart and except for a few small Europeanised communities restricted to the coast, African society was not structurally affected to any degree.

The contemporary situation, however, is entirely different. As a result of the European colonial powers assuming political control over the hinterland and of the subsequent effects of two world wars, the West African region has undergone a political and economic transformation. It is now a part of an international system of economics and shares the same kind of technical and technological development as the world outside. To a large extent, therefore, Africans and Europeans are involved in the same institutions. In view of this, instead of regarding the social changes taking place in terms of the juxtaposition of two different cultures, we shall do better to conceive of them as a process of adaptation to new circumstances and conditions. Cultural contacts still go on, but between Westernized Africans and other Africans as well as between Westerners and Africans. In other words, what we have to con-

Reprinted from *Cahiers d'Études Africaines*, III (1960), 90–102, with the permission of the publisher.

[1] Cf. *inter alia* Melville J. Herskovits, *Acculturation*, New York City, 1938, Appendix, Outline for the Study of Acculturation, pp. 131–136.

sider is not so much a phenomenon of cultural contact as a social process. This is because the changes now occurring in the West African region are no different in kind from those within a single society.

The most significant form of this social process is urbanization. Urban growth results mainly from migration. Migrants, principally younger men and women, are attracted to the town and to the urban areas because it is there that money can be earned to pay taxes, to provide bridewealth, and to buy manufactured goods and appliances. Many of these people, therefore, are in search of a higher standard of living, but this is not the only motivation. A large number of the younger men are looking for further educational opportunities or are hoping to start a fresh career. Others move as a means of escaping from village restrictions, and some of the younger girls as well as the boys out of love of adventure and a desire for fresh experiences. The Mende of Sierra Leone have a saying: "A person who has not travelled thinks that only rice cooked by his mother is sweet," and a song popular in the French territories bordering Ghana: "Qui n'a pas été à Kumasi, n'ira pas au Paradis" sums up the general lure of the town.

Since European development was originally confined almost entirely to the coast and to the mouths of rivers, the first migration in colonial times was to the ports such as Accra, Lagos, Freetown, and Dakar. The export of palm products and other raw materials and the import of manufactured goods passed through these places. They also served as centres of administration. Later, the establishment of trading and transport centres upcountry and the exploitation of gold, manganese, tin, coal, and iron ore stimulated further waves of migration. In turn these commercial and industrial developments in the hinterland brought fresh urban communities into existence on the coast in such places as Port Harcourt which, today, has a population of over 50,000.

The rapid rate of growth of the above mentioned towns is well known and so there is no need to dwell upon the matter. The population of Lagos, for example, has trebled in 25 years. Enugu in Eastern Nigeria was founded in 1914 on an empty site, but, thanks to the development of nearby coal fields, its inhabitants now number more than 60,000. Cotonou grew from 1,100 in 1905 to 35,000 in 1953, while the principal towns of Senegal increased their populations by 100% between 1942 and 1952 and those in the French Cameroons by 250% between 1936 and 1952.[2]

Urbanism, as such, is far from being unique in West Africa. There were historical cities like Abomey, the capital of Dahomey, whose popu-

---

[2] Georges Balandier, "Social Change and Problems in Negro Africa," in *Africa in the Modern World*, edited by Calvin W. Stillman, Chicago, 1955.

lation was upward of 24,000 in 1772, and Kumasi which was estimated at between 20,000 and 25,000 in 1888. In 1931, some 28% of the Yoruba lived in 9 cities of 45,000 inhabitants, while 34% of the population were in 16 cities of over 20,000 inhabitants. Traditional towns of this kind were based largely upon agriculture and inhabited mainly by farmers whose farms are made on a belt of land surrounding the town. Since farming depends principally upon family and kinship, these institutions ensure that the pattern of urban life is essentially personal. The urban community itself is socially as well as economically self-contained.[3]

In contrast, however, to this *rus in urbe,* the modern African town is mostly a product of forces external not only to itself but to African society in general. This is because it has grown up mainly in response to the market economy introduced by European colonialism.[4] People have migrated and settled there to sell either goods or services. Though inhabited mainly by Africans, it is largely the creation of Europeans and its primary relationship is with Europe. It exists, therefore, not in its own right but because it serves a variety of administrative, commercial, and industrial functions having their origin in an outside system of economics.

It follows from this that a large proportion of the urban population depends upon the labour market for a living, the actual extent varying with the degree of industrialization. In Ghana, which is the most highly industrialized of all four countries with British connections, it appears to be greatest in Sekondi-Takoradi where, in 1955, 69% of all families had wage incomes. In Accra the proportion was 57% and in Kumasi 34%. In the last mentioned town, Kumasi, non-wage incomes, derived mainly from trading and crafts, were the principal source of livelihood and 63% of all families were dependent entirely upon these activities. During the month in which these matters were investigated wages constituted 90% of earnings in Sekondi-Takoradi, 67% in Accra, and 27% in Kumasi.

Migration is responsible for a relatively large proportion of the urban population being strangers to the modern town and its institutions. Thus, over one half the population of Lagos consisted in 1950 of people born elsewhere, and the 1948 census of Takoradi found that less than 15% of its population were born there compared with 48% in Accra, 58% in Cape Coast, and 59% in Kumasi. Less than 10% of

[3] William Bascom, "Urbanization among the Yoruba," *Amer. Jour. Soc.,* Vol. LX, No. 5, 1955.

[4] Cf. Georges Balandier, "Urbanism in West and Central Africa," in *Social Implications of Industrialization and Urbanization in Africa South of the Sahara* (ed. Forde), 1956.

the inhabitants of Poto-Poto, one of the three African towns of Brazza-ville, were born in that city. A good deal of this migration is from a short distance; nevertheless, the population of the modern city is tribally heterogeneous as well as non-indigenous. Thus, more than 65 different peoples and tribes are represented in Accra. The situation in Freetown is comparable in this respect and even the smaller towns, such as Sek-ondi-Takoradi, generally have at least a dozen different tribes repre-sented. Cultural heterogeneity is also increased by the presence of Europeans and Asians.

The fact that Europeans are engaged very largely in supervisory and managerial occupations and Asians in commerce is symptomatic of the general tendency towards ethnic and tribal specialization. Thus, in Accra the majority of fishermen and farmers are Ga and Adangme, semi-skilled and skilled workers for the manufacturing industry are supplied mainly from tribes from southern Ghana and Ashanti, while the educated workers in clerical, executive and administrative posts are provided by tribes from southern Ghana.* In general in West Africa, a very much higher proportion of women than men are engaged in trading.

Tribal diversity is reflected to some extent in turn in the spatial distribution of the population. Thus, the Ga, who are native to Accra, provide almost the entire population of the original settlement, Akan predominate in the neighbouring suburb, and Europeans in another district, while there is a *zongo* inhabited mostly by Hausa and other Muslims.[5] Similarly, in Freetown there are a number of neighbour-hoods in which one tribal people usually predominate. Residence is not determined wholly by tribe, however. In the larger towns there are frequently residential zones which are open only to members of the senior Civil Service. The result is that particular urban areas also reflect differences in earnings and income. A further very important demo-graphic effect of migration is the numerical preponderance of young people over old and of males over females. For example, only 2.4% of the population of Cotonou are over 60 years of age. In an area of Poto-Poto, where the average age of the population is about 25, there are only 515 females to over 1,000 males.

These and other circumstances are responsible for the modern town having a different social organization from that of traditional urbanism. Migrants come for employment, and in many cases come singly. If they bring their families with them, these normally consist of a wife, children, and perhaps one or more dependents. These factors,

---

* These statements should be interpreted as *relative* to the ethnic groups' num-ber of employable males living in Accra.—W.J.H.
[5] Cf. Ione Acquah, *Accra Survey*, London, 1959.

coupled with ability to pay rent and availability of accommodation, are the main determinants of household size. The average income is low. In Accra only 506 out of 2,332 heads of households had an annual income of £200 or more. Consequently, the urban family rarely consists of more than 8 or 9 persons, assuming it to be defined for practical purposes as a group of persons living and feeding together and forming a definite economic unit. According to data from such places as Sekondi-Takoradi, Kumasi, Lagos, Enugu, Ibadan, and Freetown its average size* is rarely larger than 4 persons. It follows from this that polygamy is much less common than it used to be. With the exception of Moslems and of men who have wives to help them in their work, most marriages in the larger towns are monogamous. This is particularly the case as educational standards improve. In West Nigeria, for example, monogamy is practically incumbent upon professional men, politicians, and senior civil servants, as well as upon Christian teachers and ministers.[6]

This decline in polygamy has as its corollary the growing importance of the conjugal bond and of the domestic group. One reason is that the companionate form of union is stressed by Western education as well as by Christianity. Nor is marriage any longer a matter for family groups to decide. A young man is in a position, nowadays, to earn money for himself and hence to provide his own payments for a wife. This tends to make marriage more of an individual affair which may be contracted in such circumstances without consulting the man's lineage. It is also relevant in this respect that women, too, are less dependent upon their relatives. They have increased opportunities of earning money by trading and, if educated, by working as teachers, nurses, and shop assistants. In the event of an unhappy marriage, therefore, a woman may be able to rid herself of it by repaying bridewealth out of her own pocket.

A more immediate reason, however, for the increasing primacy of the domestic group is to be found in the social effects of migration. In the first place, residence in the town removes one or both of the spouses from daily contact with their relatives. Secondly, getting a living in the town is an individual responsibility, and so very much more now depends upon the conjugal relationship itself than upon the ties which man and wife have with their respective kinsfolk. The fact, therefore, that the domestic group is economically independent of the lineage, means in turn that the latter have very much less say matrimonially than in the traditional circumstances. Their lack of control over the

* The average reflects *city-wide* distributions.—W.J.H.

[6] Kenneth Little, "Some Patterns of Marriage and Domesticity in West Africa," in *Soc. Rev., Urbanism in West Africa*, Vol. 7, No. 1, July 1959, and L. Masse, "Contribution à l'étude de la nuptialité et de la fertilité dans l'agglomération dakaroise," *in* "L'Agglomération Dakaroise," *Études sénégalaises*, No. 5, 1954, IFAN.

domestic group is shown in the increasing tendency of both spouses to spend money on, and to bequeath personal property to their children rather than relatives. This tendency is most evident in the case of people whose matrilineal system previously obliged a man to educate his sisters' children in preference to his own.[7] It would be a mistake, however, to imagine that loyalty to kin has entirely disappeared. Not only are the claims of kin upon one another's help strongly sanctioned by public opinion in all spheres, but economic interests themselves may give kinship ties an enhanced significance. This occurs when industrialization increases the value of land vested in descent groups.[8]

Along with the trend towards monogamy goes an increase in concubinage. Concubinage in various forms is a very common practise. It involves a union of varying degrees of stability, carrying less social prestige than marriage, but by no means necessarily considered derogatory.

One important reason for concubinage is to be found in the conflict between the European and the traditional conception of matrimonial law. Quite often, an educated man first marries an illiterate girl under Native Customary law. Later on, he is in a position to marry a literate girl under the Marriage Ordinance. He therefore divorces his illiterate wife or wives but resumes his relationship with them soon after his Ordinance marriage. This is the more likely to happen if he already has children by the first wife. Quite frequently, too, men marrying under the Ordinance already have wives married under Customary Law. They are therefore guilty of the crime of bigamy in the eyes of the law, but are not regarded as culpable by popular opinion.[9]

An Ordinance wife may not be happy about her husband's continued association with previous wives, but she is generally obliged to tolerate it. Whatever the Ordinance law may claim, the fairly popular tendency is to look upon a man's relationship with other women as acceptable polygyny. This includes, in Western Nigeria, the husband having an irregular union with a single woman. Such women are referred to as "outside wives" and the children born to them are always recognized as their father's children by all concerned.[10]

Concubinage also results indirectly from breakdown of the extended family under urban conditions. If a marriage comes to an end

[7] Kenneth Little, *op. cit.*

[8] Cf. P. C. Lloyd, "The Yoruba Town Today," in *Urbanism in West Africa, Soc. Rev., op. cit.,* 1959, and J. Comhaire, "Economic Change and the Extended Family," in *Ann. Amer. Acad. Pol. Soc. Sci.,* 1956.

[9] Cf. Tanya Baker and Mary Bird, "Urbanization and the Position of Women," in *Urbanism in West Africa, Soc. Rev.,* Vol. VII, No. 1, July 1959.

[10] Cf. Tanya Baker and Mary Bird, *ibid.*

in these circumstances economic reasons may make it essential for the man to seek another partner, and for the woman to do likewise. The man may be left himself with a number of children to look after. If, therefore, he has no relatives in the town with whom he can live, he must find a woman to cook and keep house for him. The woman may also find herself with the smaller children and without adequate support.[11]

Concubinage is also common among illiterate women who have left their husbands or families for the town. Many of these market women and hawkers combine petty trading with a semi-commercial form of prostitution. In the larger towns of the Coast, there are also groups of unattached girls who indulge in occasional prostitution. They work as sempstresses and in shops and offices during the daytime and dress smartly in European clothes. Girls of this kind frequent the hotels, dance halls, and bars of the town. Some of them are mainly out for a good time, and they rarely solicit for customers. Others, however, look upon their contacts as a method of supplementing their income and they have Europeans and Lebanese as well as well-to-do young Africans as regular patrons.

A public form of prostitution also exists in some of the coastal towns. In Accra it is carried on partly by women known as Tutu who cater widely for the migrant population. Migrants from the north, however, probably prefer to go to prostitutes of their own country, including Hausa, Fulani, Moshi, and Zerma women. The practice of these northern prostitutes, who are called by the Hausa term *Karua*, is to rent a small house in the *zongo* where they lodge, and feed their customers. These small "hotels" are also places where the young men meet to talk and play music. The attitude towards public prostitution varies. Prostitutes studied in Accra seemed to suffer little, if any, disapprobation. Prostitutes in Sekondi-Takoradi, on the other hand, are apparently ostracised by their kinsfolk with whom, in some cases, they have lost all contact.[12]

Few of the social services provided by the modern welfare state are available as yet in West Africa, and so people migrating to or living in the town are obliged to cater as best they can for their own needs. This, combined with the fact that a large proportion of the urban population are strangers to each other and live in relatively small household units, explains another important aspect of the new social organization. This consists in the growth of voluntary associations comprising a host of

[11] Kenneth Little, *op. cit.*
[12] Jean Rouch, *Migration into the Gold Coast*, 1954; and Acquah, *op. cit.*

tribal unions, friendly societies, church groups, occupational associations, mutual benefit societies, social clubs, recreational associations, and savings groups.

The members of these groups are people who have banded themselves together in order to pursue some economic, occupational, or other interest not served by the traditional organization of African society. Thus, many of the migrants who form tribal unions feel the necessity of keeping in touch with the towns and villages from which they moved as well as to provide themselves with protection in an alien situation. Other groups, which are not necessarily confined to persons of the same tribe, are concerned to further their common interests as traders; still others, to propagate their religion or to seek companionship and recreation. Common to all these men and women is the need for monetary assistance when ill and for assuring themselves and their closest relatives of a proper burial. Virtually every society and association, therefore, provides some form of mutual aid and benefit in addition to the other objectives it may have. A typical arrangement is for each member to pay a weekly or monthly subscription which entitles him or her to a sickness benefit ranging from a few shillings to about £1 per month. In the case of a member's death, his or her relatives are generally paid a lump sum by the society, which also helps to defray the funeral expenses.[13]

In addition to catering for the material needs of their members, some associations provide a certain amount of formal education. In the case of church groups this includes instruction in the Bible as preparation for admission into the Church. Church groups also organize classes in reading, sewing, housecraft, child care, knitting, and in useful hobbies. These are free to members, although paid for by the society. Tribal associations, in particular, are noteworthy for their support of education. They sometimes run their own schools and offer scholarships to deserving boys and girls.

As their activities imply, voluntary associations are largely an outgrowth of the ideas and institutions brought in by Europeans as missionaries, government officials, and business men. In addition, most of them combine in their practises and procedures the traditional interests and customs with which their members are more familiar. A typical example is an organization known as the dancing *compin* (Krio, "Company") in Sierra Leone. This is a group of young men and women concerned with the performance of "plays" of traditional music and danc-

---

[13] Kenneth Little, "The Role of Voluntary Associations in West African Urbanization," in *Amer. Anthrop.*, Vol. LIX, No. 4, 1957, and "The Organization of Voluntary Associations in West Africa," in *Civilisations*, Vol. IX, No. 3, 1959.

ing as well as with the raising of money for mutual benefit. An association of this kind has a complicated organization and a large number of officials many of whom bear European titles such as Doctor, Lawyer, Overseer, Sick Visitor, etc. Various new cults, also, display syncretistic features. For example, there are the *Atike* cults which within the last quarter century have been actively integrating with the Anlo culture of eastern Ghana and assuming local colour. The character of this religious movement is determined by two major "god" forms and a minor "goddess," but the rules of membership are in the nature of moral precepts somewhat like the Commandments of the Old Testament.[14]

Although the executive positions in these associations are held almost invariably by men, women play an important part in the general affairs of a society and are frequently its founders. They are also very much more numerous as members than men. For example, in Accra there were in 1954 some 70 societies which had between them a membership of 26,192 persons. Of these 23,400 were females and 2,786 males, representing about 75% of all females of 19 years and over and 10% of all adult males. Voluntary associations are popular with women not only because the savings groups and mutual benefits concerned help to raise capital for trading, but because membership of such organizations provides women with a social outlet. Only educated wives have the opportunity of a companionate marriage and the majority of women, although relatively emancipated economically, are still restricted to their own sphere by the traditional division of the sexes.[15]

In addition to raising loans, market women also form associations in order to control the supply or price of commodities in which their members trade. Some of the larger markets have a woman in charge, and each of the various sections which women monopolize, such as the sale of yams, cloth, etc., is also headed by a woman, who represents them in relation to customers and the market authorities. In Lagos market each such section has its own union, which discourages competition between women trading in that particular commodity. Unions of women concerned in a less orthodox way with the status and remuneration of their members include groups of Brazzaville prostitutes. Each group has its own name, such as *La Rose, Diamant,* etc., and is under a leader, an elderly woman, who can set a pattern of elegance and sophistication. Membership is limited and is regulated by a committee.

[14] Kenneth Little, "The Role of Voluntary Associations in West African Urbanization," in *Amer. Anthrop.,* Vol. LIX, No. 4, 1957, and "The Organization of Voluntary Associations in West Africa," in *Civilisations,* Vol. IX, No. 3, 1959; and M. P. Banton, *West African City,* London, 1957.
[15] *Ibid.*

There is also a common fund out of which members in financial straits are helped and their funeral expenses paid should they die.[16]

Fraternity and sociability are a particularly marked feature of voluntary association and this is expressed in the names which many of them bear, such as "Society of Brothers," "Society of Friends," etc. The reason for this is fairly obvious. The newly arrived migrant from the rural areas has been used to living and working as a member of a compact body of kinsmen and neighbours. He knows of no other way of community living than this, and his natural reaction is to make a similar adjustment to urban conditions. This adjustment the association facilitates by substituting for the traditional extended family a "functional kinship" grouping capable of meeting many of the needs formerly served by the lineage. For example, it provides the migrant with companionship, mutual aid, sometimes legal protection. It also assists in the adaptation of the migrant to urban life by imbuing him with new standards in dress and personal hygiene, and by teaching him habits of thrift and how to put his money to the best advantage. For the younger and more enterprising men, voluntary associations offer opportunities of social prestige and leadership denied to them in the tribal system as such. Finally, in the absence of kinship and other indigenous methods of consultation and arbitration, voluntary associations provide a means whereby personal difficulties and quarrels can be handled without the trouble and expense of modern litigation.[17]

A further aspect of the new social organization is its provision of roles to individuals possessing a Western outlook, education, and training. These new roles in politics, business, the professions, etc., give rise in turn to differences in wealth and social status, dividing the town's population into strata unfamiliar to tribal society. At the top are men who are important in national or local politics, the senior Civil Service, and the professional classes followed by the junior Civil Servants, teachers at mission schools, artisans, technicians, etc. Media of social prestige frequently include proficiency in Western social skills and rituals as well as fine houses, large motor cars, etc.

The total social system, however, is best conceived of in terms of a number of ethnic and tribal sub-structures. These result from the natural history of the town. Europeans, Lebanese and educated Africans as well as tribal Africans have all played a part in its development, and they all contribute culturally to its way of life. The consequence is that the town's population is largely segmented from the point of view of

[16] Georges Balandier, *Sociologie des Brazzavilles noires*, 1955.
[17] Little, *op. cit.*

social organization. Within the larger towns, male and female members of the élite meet regularly at public functions and clubs and visit each others' homes occasionally for cocktails or dinner. To the extent to which they share a common set of business, political, professional and other interests this group constitutes a community on its own.

Apart, however, from this highly placed class of westernised Africans and Europeans and Lebanese, there is no one focus for sentiment or unitary scale of values. The situation is rather that social relations are conceived of primarily in terms of the ethnic group to which a person belongs rather than according to social or economic criteria. In other words, a person thinks of himself in the first place as a European, as an African, as a tribesman, or as a Lebanese, and not as a member of a social class. The latter kind of distinction, where made, is confined to intra-group relations, and within the European ethnic group individuals are socially rated broadly according to the same criteria which serve for the system as a whole. Thus, a European holding a senior position in the civil service is regarded on a higher social plane than Europeans who are foremen or technicians and with whom he has little to do outside business hours.[18]

Within the African group, however, the social system is complicated by the fact that additional factors—kinship and tribal affiliation—also play a part which becomes increasingly important as literacy decreases. Thus, although spending most of his time in the company of other wealthy and well-educated Africans, a member of the élite is likely to have one or more illiterate relatives living permanently in his household. The same individual, moreover, is unlikely to receive much attention from a group of tribal people unless he is a fellow tribesman and has shown himself willing to conform with their ideas of etiquette so far as the sharing of food, forms of address, respect for age, etc., are concerned.

There is also a certain amount of vertical as well as horizontal overlapping in the system as a whole. An individual African whose way of life is Western so far, primarily, as monogamy, food and eating habits, and general observance of etiquette are concerned, may be accepted in the European group, although more readily among its upper than lower strata. Similarly, an individual European of comparative rank may be admitted into westernised African society. The principal criterion in the latter case is the European's attitude towards Africans. He should show no conscious sense of superiority either towards them as a race or towards their culture. In other words, factors of personality and

[18] Cf. Banton, *op. cit.*

social behaviour are important in this respect and they also pre-determine the European attitude towards the African[s].[19]

These considerations hold for the larger towns. In the smaller towns, the social system is broadly the same, but the size of the élite is smaller, its composition somewhat different, and the social distance between it and the rest of the town's population somewhat less. It tends to consist principally of resident officials of the central government, school teachers, and the richer traders and merchants. The native ruler of the town and his family, particularly if educated, may also be counted as members of this group.

West African urbanization as a social process may be summed up, then, briefly as follows. There has been an adaptation of the tribal system to the factors and forces introduced by European colonialism. This has involved a specialization of the older traditional system in terms of the embryonic development of social classes[20] and of the modern functions of voluntary association and of the nuclear family.

The modern West African town is the concrete expression of this adaptation. It is the product of outside forces, but its principal links, socially as well as culturally, are with its own hinterland. From the latter, the town draws its vitality as well as its population and hands over in return the new institutions which have developed in the urban environment. These exchanges take place through trade and through the movement of migrants in and out of the town, involving town and countryside in a far-stretching network of personal ties and reciprocal obligations.

The result is that West African urbanism is a part of a much wider social process than the settlement or re-settlement of large groups of individuals under new conditions of life and labour. It is the nucleus of a whole corpus of customs and practices which is gradually enfolding rural society within the same social system as that of the town.

---

[19] Kenneth Little, "The African Elite in British West Africa," in *Race Relations in World Perspective* (ed. A. Lind), 1955.

[20] The general question of African social classes is discussed *inter alia* by Paul Mercier, "Aspects des Problèmes de Stratification Sociale dans l'Ouest Africain," in *Cahiers Internationaux de Sociologie*, XVII, 1954, and by Georges Balandier, *op. cit.*, 1956, pp. 501 et seq.

PART TWO

Reaction to Change

Factors of Decolonisation

F. VAN LANGENHOVE
L'Université de Bruxelles

Decolonisation has become one of the dominant facts of our times. Little wonder then that it should also be a bone of contention. Some people cannot visualise any discussion of the subject without apportioning praise and blame. If no one should be denied the right to form opinions on the matter, it ought to be permissible also to abstain from doing so, to approach such a subject from a scientific point of view and with the objectivity which this demands. How, in any case, are sound opinions to be formed without first of all acquiring an exact knowledge of the facts, judging their significance with the necessary detachment and seeking to understand their connection. This is the spirit in which I have tried to make a contribution, however modest, to the understanding of present-day decolonisation and to find the principal factors of which it is the product.

While decolonisation has acquired an obvious importance in our times, it is not however a new phenomenon. In the past it had profound effects on the world's political structure. This was certainly the case with the revolutionary decolonisation which gave birth to the United States in the second half of the XVIII century and the Latin American States in the first half of the XIX century; likewise with the progressive, peaceful emancipation of the British dominions over the best part of a hundred years.

The decolonisation which has just been mentioned has one outstanding peculiarity to which I have had occasion to call attention in earlier studies.[1] It results from the reaction of a population of white colonists against a state of dependence on a metropolitan power of the same race. The declaration of independence of the United States of 4 July 1776 emanated from Britishers for whom their compatriots were,

Reprinted from *Civilisations*, XI (1961), 401–423, with the permission of the author and the publisher (translation).

[1] Cf. F. Van Langenhove: *Le problème de la protection des populations aborigènes aux Nations Unies* (Collection of courses of The Hague Academy of International Law, 1956, pp. 350 et seq.); *Conscience tribale et nationale en Afrique noire* (Institut royal des Relations Internationales, 1960, pp. 128 et seq.).

in their own words, "our British brethren." They were resisting the "despotism" of their ruler; and a few decades later the creoles of Latin America were to do the same, more or less as the peoples of the Low Countries in the XVI century, or later on the Belgians, Greeks and Yugoslavs resisted the authority of their rulers: the King of Spain, the Emperor of Austria, the Ottoman Sultan. . . .

Having gained independence or self-government, the white Americans started, throughout the length and breadth of the continent, a colonial expansion which was carried out, as that of Russia in Siberia and Central Asia, not overseas but on adjacent territory[2]; their emancipation did not abolish, and in fact often aggravated, the state of dependence of the aboriginal populations, the exactions which they suffered, or the danger of extinction which threatened several of them.[3]

The twentieth-century freedom movement in Africa and Asia, on the other hand, results from the reaction of coloured peoples against a white authority with a different and far higher culture. It is of much more recent date. With the exception of the independence of Haiti at the threshold of the XIX century, we hardly find any typical examples before the XX century.

Whether it is a question either of white settlers and creoles or of indigenous Afro-Asian peoples, decolonisation is carried out under the impulse of a national sentiment generated principally by the colonial system itself. It is this system which creates the colony's political unity and opens the way to its later accession to the status of an independent State. This is essentially, in Africa at any rate, an artificial creation; it results in fact from territorial partitions carried out by European Powers as a function of particular situations of their own, having nothing in common with the indigenous peoples.[4]

The colonial Powers have moreover made a major contribution to the formation and development of national feelings through the opposition which they have provoked. In the settler colonies this opposition results from the tyrannical, abusive, arbitrary or iniquitous character attributed to a distant metropolitan power and from a subordinate position deemed vexatious and inadmissible. In the Asian and African colonies it results from the kind of "colonial situation" which Mr. Balandier has defined, viz. from the domination of a racially and culturally different minority.

By its arbitrary implantation of the western civilisation from which

[2] Cf. R. Grousset, *Colonisations, Chemins du Monde, Fin de l'Ere Coloniale*, p. 21.

[3] F. Van Langenhove, 1956, *op. cit.*, pp. 353 et seq.

[4] I elaborated this point in a communication to the Belgian Royal Academy (Classe des Lettres, session of 6 November, 1961) on "The genesis of nations in the XX century."

it stemmed this minority threw into confusion the autocthonous social structures. The shock produced by this clash reached its highest degree in those immense regions of Africa by-passed until the end of the XIX century by the main stream of civilisation. The resultant crisis shattered the traditional framework of their populations; it undermined the sacred character of basic institutions, weakened the authority of chieftains and revolutionised the hitherto predominantly subsistance economy.

In countries with ancient civilisations such as India, Japan or North Africa the shock, although less violent, had none the less profound effects. Feudal structures, time-honoured traditions were shattered; in a few years capitalism had overturned a still mediaeval economy. The anti-foreign reaction which this shock provoked in Japan and China was attended by an effort at adaptation, so prompt and vigorous in Japan that within a few decades this mediaeval State itself became a formidable imperialist and colonial power. This is what China has in its turn now become too. It was the work of a numerous intellectual "élite" which was trained by drawing heavily on western sources of thought and technique. Having taken the lead, Japan served as a go-between: in 1907 there were 15,000 Chinese in Japanese universities, and it was among them that the Kuo Min Tang was set up.

The penetration of western ideas and techniques into the Arab world likewise gave birth to an "élite" destined to pursue its modernisation either by refurbishing Moslem traditions or by forsaking them to the benefit of western culture. But the Arab unity which this revival implied was based, in the thinking of its animators (Shekib Arslan in particular), on the independence of each Arab State. When the first world war replaced Ottoman domination by the domination of the European colonial Powers, it was in opposition to the latter that Pan-Arabism (and, within the frontiers they had drawn, the particular nationalism of each Arab country) continued to develop.

The intellectual "élite," permeated with western civilisation, which exercised a preponderant influence on the revival of Japan, China and the Arab world, was to play no less a role in the national liberation movements of the African and Asian dependent territories. Personalities such as Jawaharlal Nehru, educated at Harrow, Cambridge and the Inner Temple; Leopold Sedar Senghor, a graduate and fellow of the Sorbonne; Kwame Nkrumah, a student of the London School of Economics and lecturer at Lincoln University (Pennsylvania); Habib Bourguiba, a graduate of the Paris Schools of Law and of Political

Science: these are certainly exceptional. In Paris, London or Philadelphia, they belonged however to those groups of young students who had flocked in thousands to study at the principal seats of western learning; they became permeated with it to the point that several of them now express themselves more easily in French or English than in their native language.

I have shown elsewhere how they took over the values produced by this civilisation over the course of centuries: freedom, patriotism, national sovereignty, democracy, equality, the rights of man, the rights of peoples. . . .[5] They transposed and applied them to the situation created in their countries by the colonial system.

They were soon to find, however, that even after reaching the intellectual level of the Whites they were still denied equality with them by legal or practical barriers which also forbade them access to prerogatives enjoyed by the colonisers; their intellectual advancement, which offered them no escape from their position of inferiority, made their humiliation even more acute. Evidence of this comes from all quarters. "In North Africa," says Mr. Julien, "the European settlers, even if illiterate, treated young Arabs, university graduates, with condescension if not with contempt."[6] In Morocco the intellectuals, conscious of their worth, insisted on being shown due respect.[7] In Algeria, whatever their views or leanings, they were unanimous in making equality with the French the basis of their claims.[8] The Belgian parliamentary commission entrusted with the task of investigating the disorders which had broken out in Leopoldville at the beginning of 1959 collected similar evidence: "many Congolese are embittered because of the humiliations they undergo."[9] The British judge who sentenced the nationalist leaders prosecuted as the instigators of the Mau Mau rebellion said in his summing-up: "most of the accused have travelled overseas to Europe and have lived there; Kenyatta, in particular, is a most widely travelled man having spent several years in different countries in Europe and I feel that some of the underlying causes for their action is their obsession about what is called the 'colour-bar' or alleged racial discrimination."[10]

When the Indian National Congress was set up in 1885 among an intellectual middle class, which the British administration itself had called into being and reared on English culture, it set itself as its main aim to help in the revival of the country. Scarcely twenty years had

---

[5] F. Van Langenhove, 1960, *op. cit.*, p. 262 et seq.
[6] C. A. Julien, *L'Afrique du Nord en marche*, 1952, p. 37.
[7] *Ibid.*, p. 151.
[8] *Ibid.*, p. 128.
[9] Chamber of Representatives, 1959, Report 100, No. 3, p. 9.
[10] M. Slater, *The Trial of Jomo Kenyatta*, 1955, p. 239.

passed, however, before much less moderate tendencies became evident. Secret societies grouping young people of good family, students and intellectuals had sprung up in many parts of Bengal; their aim was to liberate India from the foreign yoke; they were still only a tiny minority but, with them, terrorism entered the scene. At the Congress session held at the end of 1916 at Lucknow the radical elements carried the day against the moderates; the slogan became "swaraj," meaning freedom or self-government.

The Indian national movement had thus entered a new phase, which the other nationalist movements that had appeared in the colonial territories were successively to enter in their turn. Hitherto confined to a relatively limited middle-class circle, it became a mass movement. This was mainly the work of Gandhi, who, like Nehru twenty years later, was a barrister trained at the Inner Temple. Returning to India in 1915 after an absence of almost a quarter of a century spent for the most part in South Africa, he appealed to the peasantry and spoke a language they understood. Although he preached non-violence, riots broke out in 1919. A bloody repression had the effect of heightening the revolutionary character of the movement and its leaders, who were jailed more and more frequently: Mr. Nehru seven times for a total of ten years.

The same broadening of the nationalist movement, also limited in the first place to the middle-class intelligentsia, was to take place in North Africa between the wars; in Africa south of the Sahara after the second world war. In the process the leaders took their example from the communists and other totalitarian parties: a close-knit organisation covering the country with a network of cells, sections, local committees; regimentation of the masses; propaganda methods designed to strike the imagination: processions, insignia, uniforms, songs, huge mass meetings. As in India, the demands became more and more radical. The programme Mr. Nkrumah got adopted in 1949 was summed up in two words: *"Independence now!"*

By this stage nationalism no longer manifests itself in spontaneous reactions of revolt; but in organised movements, having influential leaders and a doctrine, conscious of their strength and lacking any inferiority complex with respect to the colonial Powers; they are often accompanied by strikes, terrorist acts, ambushes and guerrilla warfare in the bush.

Anti-colonialist nationalism has thus become one of the main revolutionary forces of our times. Its virulence has grown in the course of recent years to the point of subjecting the colonial Powers, both within and without their non-self-governing territories, to a pressure which—failing recourse to totalitarian methods—tends to become irresistible. The process of decolonisation has been thereby speeded up.

Until the last world war the pressure from within was, if not the only kind, at least by far the most powerful and irrespective of whether it took the form of armed insurrection, as in the American wars of independence in the XVIII and XIX centuries, or exerted itself in peaceful ways as those which progressively led up to the emancipation of the British dominions.

In the case of the Indian Empire, whatever interest for its independence may have been shown by the United States government, the determining factor certainly remains internal pressure. The British government had long envisaged its progress towards self-government. It had pursued this by stages from the beginning of the XX century and well before it seemed conceivable in other parts of the Empire.[11] The antagonism between the Hindu Congress and the Moslem League, as well as the second world war, had delayed the final stake. But it does not suffice that decolonisation has been long prepared for it to take place in an orderly and peaceful manner.

In order to have some idea of the pressure to which the British government was subjected, one need only recall briefly the ever more critical events which came hastening after 1946. On 19 February a mutiny broke out in the Royal Indian Navy. The mutineers, who complained of discrimination, attacked British soldiers and officers, raised the Congress flag, and plastered the walls with slogans: "Quit India, Jai Hind." (Long live India.) The next day the mutiny spread to naval establishments in Karachi, Calcutta, Delhi and Madras; on 21 February about a thousand men of the Royal Indian Air Force staged a solidarity strike; on 22 February a score of naval vessels, including the vice-admiral's flag-ship, fell into the hands of the mutineers, who trained the guns on the city of Bombay. For four days this city was the scene of looting and arson. By 24 February official sources spoke of 187 killed and about a thousand wounded.[12] The leaders of the Congress and the League were in agreement in attributing the cause of the mutiny to racial discrimination and foreign domination. In January 1947 a British parliamentary delegation visited the country; it took note, not without surprise, of the extent and depth of the hostility to British rule. They were impressed by the explosive nature of the situation and their report contributed to speeding up the government's final decision.[13]

The conviction that independence was near, however, had the effect

---

[11] W. Macmillan, *The Road to self-rule*, 1959, p. 26.
[12] Cf. F. Moraes, *Nehru*, 1956, p. 314.
[13] *Ibid.*, pp. 315–316.

of sharpening the tension between Hindus and Muslims; it brought into play the forces of disintegration which, in accordance with an apparently general rule,[14] were to become manifest in the decolonisation both of Africa and of Asia. Some light has been thrown on this process in the Gold Coast by Sir Charles Arden-Clarke, the last British governor.[15]

In Calcutta on 16 February 1946 Hindus and Muslims clashed in a murderous frenzy which caused thousands of deaths in this one city.[16] This was only the start of a chain-reaction of murders and reprisals, of violence and counterviolence. Several regions became ungovernable and Lord Wavell, the Viceroy, was reduced to submitting a plan of military evacuation of the government.[17] In London, the British government, considering the use of force to be impossible but having decided to have done with it, fixed an irrevocable deadline: British sovereignty over India, it announced on 20 February 1947, would cease in June 1948 at the latest. Speaking in the Commons on 5 May, Sir Stafford Cripps declared on behalf of the government that it was out of the question from the administrative and military points of view to extend it beyond 1948.[18]

Lord Mountbatten, the new Viceroy, arrived in Delhi on 22 March 1947. He immediately realised the impossibility of bringing about the understanding between the Congress and League which had hitherto been the pre-condition of independence. In accordance with his advice, the government published on 3 June the partition plan dividing India into two States: the Indian Union and Pakistan. It was nothing short of a miracle that the Viceroy succeeded in gaining the assent of both the Congress and the League, thus narrowly averting the collapse of this vast empire into anarchy.[19] Lord Ismay, Churchill's military adviser during the war, who had been appointed Chief of Staff to the Viceroy, summed up the situation at the time in a suggestive figure of speech: "India, in March 1947, was a ship on fire in mid-ocean with ammunition in the hold."[20] There is only one thing to do in a case of this kind: abandon the ship as quickly as possible. The British government accordingly brought forward the date for the transfer of sovereignty, originally fixed for June 1948 at the latest, to 15 August 1947.

---

[14] Cf. F. van Langenhove, *Le Problème de l'intégrité nationale des Etats issus de la décolonisation* (Res publica, No. 2, 1960).

[15] Sir Charles Arden-Clarke, *Gold Coast into Ghana*, 1958, p. 55.

[16] Tibot Mende, *L'Inde devant l'orage*, 1950, pp. 642 et seq.

[17] A. Campbell-Johnson, *Mission with Mountbatten*, 1951, pp. 32, 64.

[18] *Ibid.*, p. 26.

[19] *Ibid.*, pp. 94 et seq.

[20] *Ibid.*, p. 221 (retranslated).

But the partition plan only increased the fury with which Hindus and Sikhs on the one side, and Muslims on the other, were engaged in killing each other. The crisis reached its crazy peak during the first months of independence. The "Times" correspondent described it as "infectious hysteria." A "war of succession" between the two new States was only avoided by a hair's breadth. The massacres continued until 1950; the dead were never counted: they have been variously estimated at several hundred thousand, even over a million. Whole populations took to flight; 15 million people were involved in the two-way exodus. The fighting which had broken out between India and Pakistan in 1947 was suspended on 1 January 1949; but, as a settlement of this conflict has never been found, the two armies still remain facing each other under the watchful eyes of United Nations observers.

While these events were taking place in India, the British government was subject to similar pressure in Burma. On 1 June 1945, as the war was nearing its end, it had drawn up a rational programme of decolonisation, taking account of the ordeal the country had undergone with the fighting and the Japanese occupation: the main objective was economic, social and political recovery; then, when the parties and the various sections of the population had been able to agree on a new constitution, self-government within the Commonwealth would be granted. But from the beginning of 1946, just when the British government was at grips with a serious mutiny and the threat of chaos in India, agitation, strikes, and disorder fomented by the nationalist movement assumed such proportions in Burma that it had to recognise the impossibility of keeping the country by force under British rule.

The agreement recognising the country's sovereignty and full independence, to date from 4 January 1948, was signed on 17 October 1947. Once the decisive step was taken, the troubles only grew worse and spread. Torn by civil war, the country was in danger of sinking into anarchy. While the red-flag and the blue-flag communist factions were fighting each other, the countryside was infested with bandits, national minorities such as the Karens, Shans and Arakans had taken up arms to secede and thus deprive the central government of its authority over considerable areas of the country. At one time its power was, in fact, virtually limited to the capital and its immediate surroundings. In 1950 the United States viewed its position as well nigh hopeless. Nevertheless the situation gradually improved in the end. In 1958, however, there was not a mile of railway track beyond the Rangoon suburbs which was not liable to insurgent attacks.[21]

[21] Cf. Tinker, *The Union of Burma: a study of the first years of independence*, 1959, pp. 97, 295.

In West and East Africa, as in India and Burma, the principal factor of decolonisation was still internal pressure. In Indo-China, however, the drama ceased to be played out only between the colonisers and the colonised: in the final phase the latter started to receive help from a third party; the internal pressure was now reinforced with strong external pressure. There is no need to recall in detail the awakening and development of Vietnamese national feeling: the successive rebellions and what Mr. Paul Mus has called "intolerance of colonisation in whatever guise it presented itself,"[22] the intellectual "élite," educated here too by the colonisers themselves, the blow to the prestige and authority of the latter due to the Japanese occupation during the second world war, the link-up of nationalists and communists, the breakdown in negotiations with Ho-Chi-Minh, the tragedy of Haiphong where thousands of civilians were killed in a naval bombardment on 19 December 1946, the start of the military phase, the belated concessions granted to Bao-Dai after earlier refusals but now beside the point. . . . On 14 December 1949, however, events took a new turn; communist troops appeared on the frontier: the question was now internationalised and tied up with the East-West conflict. In a desperate struggle, France threw in "the biggest army which she had ever—and at what price—maintained so far afield"[23]; up to the battle of Dien Bien Phu she was losing two thousand men a year and one third of the officers leaving military schools.[24] It was no longer a matter of re-establishing her authority, but of playing a role in a world conflict. As to this last phase, it is worth noting the importance which Mr. Mus attaches to it and which is so often lost sight of: "The time has passed —every day brings new proof of this—when a colony in any part of the world could remain a closed battleground where two nations, two ways of life, or even forces of occupation and of resistance measured their strength in single combat. Nowadays it is just possible for two nations to reach agreement unaided; but any conflict becomes public and sooner or later is joined by other nations."[25]

Decolonisation was proceeding simultaneously in Indonesia; here outside interference was of an entirely different kind: not concealed, but open and public; it took the form, not of military aid, but of diplomatic and economic pressure. It was carried on within the United Nations and by the Afro-Asian-Arab group of States.

The awakening of national sentiment at the beginning of the XX century had started, as elsewhere, among an intellectual vanguard which

[22] P. Mus, *Sociologie d'une guerre*, 1952, p. 49.

[23] *Ibid.*, p. 41.

[24] *Chronique de Politique étrangère*, Inst. des Relations Internationales, 1956, p. 488.

[25] P. Mus, 1952, *loc. cit.*, p. 62.

the colonial power itself had trained at metropolitan universities as well as in Indonesia; their radical tendencies had already led to repressive measures directed against several of their leaders.

The second world war had given a tremendous impetus to decolonisation; in a speech delivered on 6 December 1942, Queen Wilhelmina had hinted at the restoration of the Kingdom on the basis of a partnership, Indonesia joining a Commonwealth with complete autonomy in internal affairs. But the Japanese occupation had suppressed the colonial authorities for four years. When the Dutch returned to Java after the war they came into conflict with the nationalists who, on 17 August 1945, immediately after the capitulation, had proclaimed the independence of an Indonesian republic.

On the initiative of, and under pressure from, the United Kingdom, however, which had military responsibility at that time for the Dutch East Indies, an agreement was reached at Linggadjati on 15 November 1946.[26] The government of the Republic of Indonesia was thereby recognised by the Netherlands as the "de facto" government of Java, Madura and Sumatra and was invited to set up together with the States of Borneo and Eastern Indonesia a federal State which would form an indissoluble union with the Netherlands on an equal footing. This agreement was shortlived, however. On 21 July 1947 disagreement about its interpretation and application decided the Netherlands to launch a "police operation" against the Indonesian Republic. Hostilities having thus resumed, two States brought the matter to the notice of the Security Council of the United Nations on 30 July: India presented it as a threat to international peace and security (Chapter VI of the Charter); while Australia took the graver view of a rupture of the peace (Chapter VII). Meeting immediately, the Council adopted a resolution within 48 hours inviting the parties to cease hostilities at once. Until the Netherlands accepted the transfer of sovereignty to the Indonesian Republic two years later the Council was to exert increasing pressure on them.

Of the two States, India and Australia, which had taken the initiative of denouncing to the Security Council the use of armed force by the Netherlands, the first was moved by an anti-colonialism whose objective, in the course of a long and bitter struggle, had been national liberation; the anti-colonialism of the second was different: for them it was chiefly a matter of doctrine.

The latter aspect of anti-colonialism was not a recent apparition.

[26] A. Taylor, *Indonesian independence and the United Nations*, 1960, pp. 8 et seq.

The use of the word "colonialism" it is true, hardly dates back beyond the beginning of the XX century. The Encyclopedia Larousse at that time defined it as the term used by the socialists to designate and condemn colonial expansion.[27] But the thing itself had been an object for censure well before that.

In 1542 the "Very brief account of the destruction of the Indies" of Father Barthelemy de las Casas was an impassioned condemnation of the excesses committed by the Spaniards in their new American possessions.[28] Montaigne refers to it in the famous passage in his Essays where he exclaims: "Who ever set such a price on the service of commerce and traffic?" These accusations continued and developed among the XVIII century philosophers. As Mr. Gaxotte writes, "if there is a point on which they are in close accord and no longer at variance, it is the uselessness and danger of colonies."[29] Rivalling Montesquieu and Rousseau for the best-seller of the century was Father Raynal with his "History of the establishments of the Europeans in the two Indies," which condemns the destruction perpetrated there by the colonisers.[30] Colonisation tends to get equated with conquest, which is considered as improper and inhuman.[31] As early as 1748 Turgot said, referring, it is true, to the settler colonies, that "they are ripe fruit which, sooner or later, will drop from the parent tree."[32]

In Great Britain, as in France, colonies continued to enjoy very little favour during the first two thirds of the XIX century; the independence of the United States and the anti-slavery campaign no doubt contributed to their unpopularity. There was a strong current of opinion, mainly in the Liberal Party, against the acquisition of new territories. In 1866 Parliament adopted a formal resolution to this effect with Africa in view.[33] In 1865 a parliamentary committee had even envisaged giving up the Gold Coast; in its opinion the aim ought to have been the development of aptitudes among the natives in order "to allow us to transfer to them more and more the whole administration of government."[34]

Nor was colonisation any more in favour among the economists. In the sixties the intellectuals had little liking for it, while the public was simply not interested.[35] "When first edition of my book on colonisa-

---

[27] J. Freymond, *Colonialisme et Nationalisme* (Zaïre, 2 February 1957), p. 190.
[28] F. Van Langenhove, 1956, *loc. cit.*, p. 544.
[29] P. Gaxotte, *Le Siècle de Louis XV*, 1933, p. 245.
[30] J. Mollet, in *Le Tiers-Monde*, 1956, p. 30.
[31] R. Maunier, *Sociologie Coloniale*, 1932, p. 17.
[32] *Ibid.*, p. 73.
[33] Lord Hailey, *The future of colonial peoples*, 1943, p. 10.
[34] MacMillan, 1959, *loc. cit.*, p. 66 (retranslated).
[35] Ch. De Lannoy, *La colonistique, définition et méthode.* (Bulletin de la classe des Lettres de l'Académie de Belgique), 1913, p. 503.

tion appeared in 1874," wrote Paul Leroy-Beaulieu, "my publisher told me frankly that there was no sale for works on colonisation."[36]

There was a sudden change in the last decades of the XIX century. A general movement of expansion took place in which most of the European Powers were in competition. While the Russian Empire carried its colonisation across adjacent territory right to the Pacific, Britain and France were building new empires overseas. The United States had joined in by annexing the Hawaiian Islands and the Philippines and by extending their influence in Central America and in the West Indies.

But while colonial expansion had formerly had, so far as the State was concerned, essentially material aims—the growth of its territory and power, the enhancement of its economic interests, the exploitation of material resources—there now comes increasingly to be added a moral and humanitarian aim, that which had provided the Spanish publicists of the XVI century with their principal argument.[37] The colonial Powers had allotted themselves duties of trusteeship and a civilising mission in respect of the backward peoples under their administration. This was the idea behind "the white man's burden," and Lord Lugard's later "dual mandate." At the international level the signatory Powers of the Berlin treaty of 1885 undertook to look after the improvement of the moral and material conditions of existence of the populations. The idea of a mandate, of a mission, of trusteeship was to be included in Article 22 of the Pact of the League of Nations before it found wider expression in chapters IX, X and XI of the Charter of the United Nations.[38]

Prejudice against colonisation had not disappeared, however. In Great Britain Disraeli's expansionist policy, and later the Boer War, were condemned by a considerable section of public opinion as "imperialism" a word to which a book of J. A. Hobson, published in 1902, had given currency.[39] A new imperialism was to appear, however, after the first world war: that of fascist Italy, nazi Germany and, in the Far East, Japan.

It was the lot of the proletariat resulting from the industrial revolution in Western Europe which had inspired the socialism of Karl

[36] P. Leroy-Beaulieu, *De la colonisation chez les peuples modernes*, 1891, 1943, p. 10.

[37] Cf. C. Castañon, *Les problèmes coloniaux et les classiques espagnols du droit des gens* (Collected lectures of the Academy of International Law, 1954).

[38] Van Langenhove, 1956, *loc. cit.*, pp. 390 et seq.

[39] MacMillan, 1959, *loc. cit.*, p. 26; see also J. Mulenzi, *L'Internationalisation du phénomène colonial*, 1958, pp. 51 and 20.

Marx. The colonial question had almost nothing to do with it. Nevertheless socialist doctrine soon started to denounce colonisation as a
system of domination and exploitation. This is what the Second International did from the beginning of the XX century; the condemnation
of colonisation as a product of capitalism was taken up from congress
to congress[40]; anti-colonialism was likewise prevalent in the big trade
unions. "All that," wrote Léon Blum, "is in contradiction to modern
law and morality, all that belongs to a period in the history of humanity
which is finished. The retention of territories formerly colonised cannot
be continued against the will of the colonial peoples. Its aim is to guide
them until they are capable of governing themselves freely."[41] This
kind of attitude was a factor with which the democratic Powers were
going to have to reckon with on the home front and which was going
more and more to limit their ability to slow down and check the process
of decolonisation.

   For Bolshevism anti-colonialism is no longer a mere matter of
doctrine; it is a decisive factor in the triumph of the proletarian revolution. Lenin regarded imperialism as the extreme form of capitalism.
But at the same time he realised the advantage for Bolshevist strategy
of the fermentation which had started in Asia and the chance it offered
"of transforming the dependent and colonial countries from reserves
of the imperialist bourgeoisie into reserves of the revolutionary proletariat, of making them allies of the latter." Hence, concluded Stalin,
"the need for the proletariat to lend its resolute and active support to
the liberation movement of the oppressed and dependent peoples."[42] It
was in the East that the outlook was the most favourable. "Thanks to
the first world war," wrote Lenin, "the East has been definitely drawn
into the revolutionary movement, definitely swept up in the whirlwind
of the world revolutionary movement." In face of this fact, the victors
of the "capitalist war" were, according to Lenin, powerless. "What can
they do," he asked, "in India and China where the people are boiling
over? They are up against a population of 700 millions. If we included
the peoples living in the other Asian countries and in neighbouring
lands where the population is semi-Asian, there would be more than
half the world's population at stake."[43] In a lecture delivered at
Sverdlov University in April 1924 Stalin had summed up Leninist
theory in this respect in a few essential points: "the interests of the
labour movement in the developed countries and of the national libera-

   [40] Cf. Freymond, 1957, *loc. cit.,* p. 189.
   [41] J. Ehrard, *Le destin du colonialisme,* 1957, p. 130.
   [42] J. Stalin, *Marxism and the national and colonial question,* 1949, p. 63 (French
edition).
   [43] Stalin, *Leninism,* vol. 1, p. 234 (French edition).

tion movement in the colonies demand that these two aspects of the revolutionary movement unite in a common front of struggle against the common enemy, against imperialism; . . . the formation of a common revolutionary front is impossible without the direct and resolute support—by the proletariat of the oppressor nations—of the freedom movement of the oppressed peoples against metropolitan imperialism; . . . this support consists of demanding, of defending, of applying the right of the nations to separate, to exist as independent States."[44]

Stalin thus returned to the principle of self-determination of which President Wilson had been one of the chief supporters after the first world war. "Leninism, he said, has widened the concept of self-determination by interpreting it as the right of the oppressed peoples, of the dependent countries and of the colonies to complete separation."[45]

Until then the right of self-determination had scarcely been recognised as applying to the most backward peoples. Leninism was not alone, however, in defending their right to it. Churchill and Roosevelt had written it into the Atlantic Charter on 11 August 1941; while the former limited its scope to the peoples deprived of their independence by the Axis Powers, the latter declared, on the other hand, that it applied to the whole world. On 30 May 1942 the Under-Secretary of State, Sumner Welles, was explicit: "our victory," he said, "must lead to the liberation of all countries. . . . The age of imperialism is finished." A few weeks later, on 23 July 1942, the Secretary of State, Cordell Hull, set out the American position in terms which were to remain its official definition: "we have always believed," he said, "and we still believe today that all peoples, without distinction of race, colour or religion, who are prepared and willing to accept the responsibilities of liberty, are entitled to its enjoyment. . . . It has been our purpose in the past, and will remain our purpose in the future, to use the full measure of our influence to support attainment of freedom by all peoples, who by their acts, show themselves worthy of it and are ready for it."[46]

This statement of principle is in line with traditional American anti-colonialism. The overthrow of the colonial system in the New World had been the work of white settlers and creoles: with rare exceptions the native Indians had played no more part in it than they had benefited from it; that does not prevent America from keeping in respect to the colonial system prejudices which give it a feeling of solidarity with the coloured peoples of Asia and Africa still subject to

---

[44] Stalin, 1949, *loc. cit.*, p. 184.
[45] *Ibid.*, p. 179.
[46] *Postwar foreign policy preparation*, 1939–45, p. 109.

that system or who, having recently been freed from it, still bear a grudge against it.

The various anti-colonial currents came together in 1945 when the Charter of the United Nations was being drawn up. An amendment submitted by the three great Powers to their own draft introduced the right of the peoples to self-determination in articles 1 and 55. It is believed on good authority that the Soviet Union was the real author of this amendment.[47] Leninist theory and the conclusions which Stalin had drawn from it provide the explanation for this move. The first territorial settlements which had just been sketched out at Yalta showed that the population of territories in east and central Europe or Asia under Soviet rule or control would, in fact, be deprived of the right of self-determination, since for Stalin this was simply a tactical method of achieving the dictatorship of the proletariat.[48]

On the contrary, it was in particular the colonial peoples, formerly excluded from its application, who were now to benefit from the principle. The question was immediately posed as to how the right of self-determination could be implemented for them. In the United States this led again to talk of the idea, at least as a temporary solution, of their internationalisation which the British Labour Party had upheld during the first World War.[49]

Mr. Cordell Hull, the Secretary of State, had already proposed in July 1940 the introduction of a system of international trusteeship for all European dependencies in the Western Hemisphere.[50] There were even ideas of including all the other dependent territories; but the final outcome was that it would be limited to the League of Nations mandated territories and those taken from the enemy after the war. A draft declaration drawn up by Mr. Hull, however, would have bound the metropolitan Powers to fix dates as soon as possible for the accession of all their dependent territories to full independence.

In Great Britain, in spite of widespread sympathy for these ideas, the Government was opposed to them. At the San Francisco conference, however, they had the backing of the Labour governments of Australia and New Zealand; they were warmly supported, too, by most of the Latin American delegations and, above all, by those of the countries recently freed from colonial status or about to be so: India, which was to become their leader, the Philippines, the Arab States. The goal towards which they were going to bend their efforts was the accession of all non-self-governing territories to independence.

[47] Cf. Van Langenhove, 1952, *loc. cit.,* p. 3.
[48] *Ibid.,* pp. 12 et seq.
[49] J. Malenzi, *loc. cit.,* 1958, p. 53.
[50] *Postwar Foreign Policy Preparation,* 1939–45, p. 35.

In 1947 it was India which, together with Australia, brought the question of Indonesia before the Security Council; and she remained in the forefront of the struggle until the final victory of the Indonesian nationalists.

Australia was at that time a member of the Security Council; India was not, but in accordance with Art. 31 was admitted to take part in the discussion without the right to vote. At their request, the Philippines, Pakistan, Burma and Egypt were also subsequently admitted; the representative of the Indonesian Republic had been from the outset. The Netherlands had thus to answer the accusations not only of the two States which had summoned them before the Council but also of all those which had joined them to plead in favour of Indonesian independence, while the Soviet Union, together with the Ukraine and Poland, strove to outbid them all.

In December 1948, after the Netherlands had denounced the truce and undertaken new military operations in the course of which they had captured Indonesian leaders, the action of the Security Council became more energetic. Its injunctions followed each other in quick succession. Having called for the immediate cessation of hostilities and the release of the political leaders arrested, it took note four days later of the non-execution of its resolution and asked the Netherlands to submit a report within twenty-four hours. Although the latter had announced that hostilities would cease in Java on 31 December, it noted on 28 January that its resolution had still not been fully enforced. At the same time it took a decisive step forward: hitherto it had limited its intervention to measures of conservation and good offices; it now took up a detailed position on the main issue by recommending the creation of a Republic of the United States of Indonesia and the transfer of sovereignty by 1 January 1950 at the latest, together with the almost immediate formation of a provisional government, at the latest by 15 March.

The pressure exerted on the Netherlands was not limited to the Security Council. On the launching of the first "police operation" the Sydney dockers had refused to load Dutch ships until the cessation of hostilities, while it was due to Labour influence that the Australian government brought the matter before the Security Council.[51] The Arab League had hastened to recognise the Indonesian Republic; following the second police operation it called upon the Security Council to stop it. Ceylon, India and Pakistan closed their ports and airfields to Dutch ships and aircraft bound for Indonesia. India, which contested the right of European States to use armed forces in Asia, thus introducing a new

[51] Taylor, 1960, *loc. cit.*, p. 375.

Monroe doctrine,[52] convened a conference in New Delhi on 20 January 1949 in order to deal with the situation; fourteen Asian and African States sent delegates and three Asian States observers.[53]

In the United States there was also a lively reaction, especially in the Senate and in trade union circles. The U.S. government was exercising strong pressure on The Hague; it had withdrawn the benefits of the Marshall Plan from the Dutch East Indies and was threatening similar action against the Netherlands themselves.[54]

In these circumstances the view prevailed at The Hague that it was useless to continue the struggle. The government announced on 2 March that it was disposed to hasten the transfer of sovereignty. Yet the outcome of the fighting was in its favour; in this respect the situation bore no resemblance to that of France in Indo-China. The second "police operation" had achieved its military objectives, having encountered scarcely any organised resistance. But although the Dutch forces were in possession of the greater part of Java and Sumatra, the radical nationalists who now headed the Indonesian Republic were holding out, and their ranks had been swelled by the moderates who had at first come out in favour of the federal structure proposed by the Netherlands. External pressure, however, was becoming increasingly strong. Recourse to arms had not had the desired effect; on the contrary, it had resulted in the question being brought before the United Nations; its internationalisation had led to a series of measures which had finally forced the Netherlands to yield. "To have taken up arms again," said the Minister of Overseas Territories at The Hague in December 1949, "would have placed us in an untenable international position and bled our people white."

Since then anti-colonialist pressure has grown incessantly with the increasing number of States which have been freed from colonial rule in Asia and Africa. There were only seven such States members of the United Nations at the outset: Saudi Arabia, Egypt, India, Iraq, the Lebanon, the Philippines and Syria. In 1950 Pakistan, the Yemen, Burma, and Indonesia came to join them; in 1955 Cambodia, Ceylon, Jordan, Laos, Libya and Nepal; Morocco, Tunisia and the Sudan were followed in 1957 by Ghana and Malaya; in 1960 there arrived a compact group of 14 states from Africa south of the Sahara followed by Madagascar, Somalia and, in September 1961, Sierra Leone, while the admission of Tanganyika is expected in December of this year. Out of a total of 103 member states, the African group now numbers 27 and the whole Afro-Asian group 49.[55] The Soviet group has increased from

[52] *Ibid.*, p. 381.
[53] *Chronique de Politique étrangère*, IRRI, pp. 271 et seq.
[54] *Ibid.*, pp. 207, 210, 396.
[55] After Syria rejoined, and the admission of Mauretania and Mongolia.

5 to 10 members; with Yugoslavia and Cyprus it only needs the support of a few Latin American votes—that of Cuba being a certainty—for the anti-colonialist states to wield a two-thirds majority.

The Afro-Asian group, which had first met in January 1949 in New Delhi in order to study measures for dealing with the Indonesian problem, staged a striking demonstration of its importance at Bandung in 1955. Twenty-nine states took part in the conference held in that city; they represented almost half the population of the world. Its conclusions were published in a long statement in which colonialism in every form was denounced as "an evil which must be rapidly abolished." "The submission of the peoples to foreign domination and exploitation" were viewed as "a denial of basic human rights," as "contrary to the Charter of the United Nations," as "an obstacle to the maintenance of world peace and co-operation between the peoples." The conference proclaimed "its support for the cause of freedom and independence of all these peoples"; it appealed "to the Powers concerned to restore freedom and independence to these peoples."[56]

With the aim of strengthening Afro-Asian co-operation in "the Bandung spirit" an "Afro-Asian solidarity conference" met in Cairo on 26 December 1957. As distinct from the Bandung conference, the Cairo meeting brought together representatives not of governments but of political, social or cultural movements and groups which were supposed to be representative of the nations and peoples concerned. In fact, Egypt and the Soviet Union wielded an overwhelming influence, which gave a strong nationalist and the communist flavour to the conference.[57] It appealed, in particular, to the Afro-Asian peoples "to mobilise national and international opinion against imperialism in all its forms and manifestations"; it called for the recognition of the right of all colonies and protectorates to complete independence and insisted that the Powers concerned grant this right without delay; it recommended giving "all possible material aid to the peoples who are fighting in all parts of the world until they gain their incontestable right to freedom and complete independence."[58] It set up as an executive and co-ordinating agency, a Solidarity Council of Afro-Asian peoples, with a head-quarters' staff under the direction of a general secretary appointed by Egypt.

Ghana, which had just achieved its independence, took the initiative in convening a conference at Accra on 15 April 1958, of the eight independent states which Africa then had apart from the Union of South Africa. Considering themselves as "the vanguard dedicated to the

[56] *Chronique de Politique étrangère*, IRRI, 1955, p. 395.
[57] *Loc. cit.*, 1958, pp. 425 et seq.
[58] *Ibid.*, p. 435.

complete liberation of Africa," they pledged themselves to take the necessary measures for the accession to independence and self-determination of the African peoples.[59] A conference of the African Peoples' Assembly carried the campaign a stage further at Accra in December of the same year. As at the Cairo conference the previous year, it was not the governments which were represented but about 60 political movements and trade union organisations; the resolutions adopted sought to lay down a common revolutionary strategy against colonialism. A permanent secretariat was set up in Accra charged with the task of speeding up the liberation of Africa.[60] Three Congolese leaders, one of them Patrice Lumumba, who had taken part in the Accra meeting gave an account of its discussions to a stormy meeting of several thousand people in Léopoldville on 28 December 1958, and passed on the slogan of immediate independence; a few days later violent disorders marked the beginning of a period of agitation which was to lead 18 months later to the end of colonial rule in the Congo.

Anti-colonialism found the United Nations to be an excellent field for manœuvre. Its action was carried on in three main ways: the first was provided by chapters XI, XII and XIII of the Charter concerning non-self-governing territories and the international trusteeship system; the second by the principle of the right of peoples to self-determination which, thanks to the Soviet Union, had been inscribed in articles 1 and 55; the third by chapters VI and VII concerning international disputes and breach of the peace, which were invoked when a national liberation movement in a colony or protectorate had brought about disturbances and repressive measures that could be presented as a threat to international security.

The San Francisco conference in 1945 had not accepted proposals for the inclusion of all non-self-governing territories in an international system of supervision or trusteeship. This had been adopted only for territories previously under mandate of the League of Nations, ex-enemy territories or those voluntarily placed under this system by the States responsible for their administration (Art. 77). With tireless perseverance, however, the anti-colonialist governments were going to strive to achieve indirectly the objective which they had failed to attain at San Francisco.

In 1947, at the first session of the General Assembly the Indian delegation proposed that the powers administering non-self-governing

[59] *Ibid.*, p. 456.
[60] Cf. Van Langenhove, 1960, *loc. cit.*, p. 282.

territories be invited to transfer them voluntarily to the trusteeship system. Although adopted in committee, the proposal did not gain the necessary two-thirds majority in the plenary session. With the failure of this attempt to generalise the trusteeship system, the delegations which were carrying on the anti-colonialist fight had recourse to other means: they set out to change the system established by chapter XI of the Charter for non-self-governing territories not under trusteeship into a system of semi-trusteeship, in spite of the distinction between the two systems laid down by the San Francisco conference.[61] A joint committee of similar composition to the Trusteeship Council was thus set up and given the task, in like manner to the latter, of reporting on the information which members of the United Nations must communicate annually to the General Secretary on the non-self-governing territories under their administration (Art. 73 (e)). The administering authorities were consistently disparaged when representatives of the indigenous populations were invited to take part in the work of this committee, as in the Trusteeship Council, or granted a sympathetic audience, particularly when they came with their grievances against the administering authorities. In accordance with the interpretation of the Charter which the ever more numerous anti-colonialist states had been able to impose, only the few colonial Powers which had voluntarily accepted them were subject to the obligations of chapter XI. The new states, on the other hand, did not allow their own territories whose aboriginal populations were not completely self-governing to come under these rules. They could therefore, without prejudice to themselves, continually widen the scope of the obligations imposed on the colonial Powers, who, reduced to a handful, were incapable of any opposition. The provisions of the Charter which might rule out their proposals did not present any insuperable obstacle for the delegations dedicated to the elimination of the colonial system. When representatives of the administering Powers invoked these provisions they were reproached for their narrow-minded legalism; the others took their stand on a dynamic interpretation, as distinct from the static interpretation attributed to their opponents. Thus it was that in 1948 Mr. Romulo declared on behalf of his country to the General Assembly, of which he was soon to become the President: "The Philippines do not attach much value to so-called constitutional, legal or other considerations which could prevent certain powers from accepting United Nations supervision of their administration of non-self-governing territories." Quoting the example of the changes which had taken place in the British Empire, he believed that "many of the

[61] Cf. Van Langenhove, *La question des aborigènes aux Nations Unies*, la thèse belge, 1954, p. 99.

difficulties which chapter XI causes would disappear if this chapter were interpreted in the light of modern history. It could then be considered as a rough sketch of principles which are rapidly being implemented under the impulse of revolutionary forces."[62]

Such a point of view was bound to be revolutionary with regard to "respect for the obligations arising from treaties and other sources of international law" to which the United Nations dedicated themselves by the terms of the preamble to the Charter. Mr. Henri Rolin, who may be counted among the most advanced internationalists of our times, recently noted a similar declaration of an Indonesian minister, "according to whom, international law is only an invention of the West without any binding force for the rest of the world."[63]

The anti-colonialist pressure for the accession of non-self-governing territories to independence was exerted at the same time by virtue of the right of self-determination of the peoples. This began to figure ever more prominently in the discussions of the United Nations. After remitting it for study in 1950, the General Assembly decided at the beginning of 1952 to inscribe it in the international conventions on human rights which were under discussion; the allusion, in fact was to the dependent territories. A resolution adopted that year at the Assembly's 7th session expressly instructed the administering Powers to recognise the right of self-determination and to facilitate its exercise, the wishes of the peoples being determined by plebiscites or other recognised democratic means, preferably under the auspices of the United Nations. On 11 December 1957 at its 12th session, the General Assembly returned to the question to declare that "it is of international interest" that the Powers act in this way.

Preservation of peace and international security were the grounds on which India and Australia had acted in 1947 when they arraigned the Netherlands before the Security Council in connection with Indonesia. When, in 1951 and 1952, the six Arab states which were then members of the United Nations asked for the inclusion of the Moroccan question on the Assembly's agenda they accused France of violating the principles of the Charter and the Declaration of Human Rights at the same time insisting that Morocco was entitled to immediate independence. In 1953, together with other Asian and African states, they again had recourse to the General Assembly but also approached the Security Council on the grounds of a situation liable to threaten peace.

[62] General Assembly, 4th Committee, 55th Session, 12 October 1948 (retranslated).

[63] H. Rolin, *Le Droit des Gens en 1961*, Chronique de Politique étrangère, IRRI, 1961, p. 492.

The same group of states was responsible for further discussion of the Moroccan question at succeeding sessions of the General Assembly.

At the same time the Tunisian question was the subject of similar discussions raised by a group of eleven Afro-Asian states, more or less the same which had taken the initiative in the Moroccan question. They first presented it in 1952 to the Security Council as a threat to international peace. Having failed to secure its inclusion on the agenda, they tried without success to have an extraordinary session of the Assembly convened; the question was nevertheless broached by the Assembly at its 8th ordinary session and it continued to be examined at succeeding sessions until the Franco-Tunisian agreement of 1955 was reached.

Algeria, where in the meanwhile a rebellion had broken out, was to be the next objective of the Afro-Asian group. Already in January 1955 Saudi Arabia had drawn the attention of the Security Council to the matter. After a lively debate, the Afro-Asian group secured the inclusion of the question on the agenda of the Assembly's 11th session in the autumn of the same year, and the discussion was subsequently renewed from session to session.

In 1961 it was the turn of Angola. Following the disorders which had broken out there, the Liberian representative asked on 15 February for the matter to be placed on the agenda of the Security Council. On 20 February he presented the President with a request for a special session signed by 32 Afro-Asian states on the grounds of a "situation containing grave possibilities of friction liable to threaten international peace and security" requiring immediate action by the Council. The draft resolution submitted by Ceylon, Liberia, and the United Arab Republic having failed to gain the necessary seven votes, a group of 39 Afro-Asian states brought the question before the General Assembly. After a discussion on 20 April, the latter invited the Portuguese Government to envisage the urgent application of the resolution of 14 December 1960 calling for the immediate independence, without conditions or reservations, of peoples subject to foreign domination; a committee of five members was entrusted with any necessary investigation and to report as soon as possible to the Assembly. At the same time several African states broke off diplomatic relations with Portugal.

The new states recently emancipated from the colonial system have never, in any circumstances, ceased to show their solidarity with the peoples still subject to it whose lot they shared in the recent past. They have the feeling that the liberation of these peoples is their responsibility and that they have the duty of taking part in a crusade designed to bring this about without delay. Quite frequently, moreover, their own liberation seems to them incomplete, either because they claim territories which the former colonial power continues to administer, or because they insist on the evacuation of military bases which it continues to keep. The fight against the "vestiges" of colonialism is also carried on in another field: political independence does not abolish economic inferiority and dependence.

This is resented not only in the Afro-Asian countries but almost just as much in Latin America where it keeps alive—even if it does not always lead to the virulence of Castroism—their traditional anti-colonialism.

A great many of the developing countries thus harbour prejudices, suspicions, and resentment towards the colonial Powers, the strength of which the latter have often underestimated. "Colonialism" has become for millions of human beings a complex which passes the bounds of reason. It is enough that an action or a policy be denounced as "colonialist" to render it suspect and blameworthy. Many problems have had their terms simplified to the extreme by reduction to the antithesis: colonialism—anticolonialism. Thus colonialism was invoked not only in the dispute between Indonesia and the Netherlands over Western New Guinea or in that between France and Tunisia over Bizerta, but even in the Suez affair of 1956; it was as colonial Powers that France and the United Kingdom were accused by the Soviet Union, as well as by several Asian states and particularly by the Arab states; it was as such also that the Soviet Union brandished the threat of atomic rockets or bombs, of the intervention of an army of "volunteers" and of coercive measures. . . .[64]

In reducing problems to the summary antithesis of colonialism and anti-colonialism they are placed in an emotional atmosphere which lends itself neither to objectivity nor impartiality. The right of self-determination for example, frequently invoked against the Netherlands in favour of the Indonesian Republic in 1947–48, lost all its value in 1949–50 when it was invoked against the latter; having acceded to independence, it saw this only as a slight on its sovereignty. As Mr. Taylor has noted, the transfer of sovereignty had entailed a reversal of positions in this respect.[65]

In actual fact anti-colonialism is dominated by racial antagonism.

[64] Cf. Van Langenhove, *L'Anticolonialisme aux Nations Unies* (Revue générale belge, mai 1957).
[65] Taylor, 1960, *loc. cit.*, p. 417.

According to an eminent Indian publicist, "the Asian mind . . . has always equated colonialism with colour. Colonialism, to Asia and Africa, spells the domination of white powers over the coloured countries of the earth."[66]

The pressures to which the colonial powers are subjected in these different ways all converge towards one objective: immediate independence.

As previously in India, after the second World War this became the slogan of the militant national movements in the Gold Coast, Nigeria and the Congo, just as much as in Indonesia, Morocco, Tunisia or Algeria. It was too much in line with the theories of Lenin and Stalin for the Soviet Union not to join in the chase and even to encourage it with exaggerated demands.

Independence through the abolition of the colonial system had acquired a transcendent value; it had become the object of a mystic creed. Its strength was revealed when on 14 December 1960 the General Assembly adopted a resolution submitted by a group of 28 Afro-Asian states which was a replica, in more moderate terms, of a draft presented by Mr. Khrushchev himself a few weeks before. There were no votes against and only nine abstentions. In spite of the Congo crisis, which was under discussion at the same time and which had underlined the dangers of premature emancipation in a region of Africa which, unlike Ghana or Nigeria, was less than three generations ago still Stanley's "darkest Africa," the General Assembly declared in the resolution adopted that "inadequacy of political, social, educational preparedness should never serve as a pretext for delaying independence."

Things had come a long way since the mandates commission of the League of Nations made the independence of Iraq subject to detailed conditions of stability. The mystic attraction of immediate independence had become so strong that no State dared directly oppose this paragraph which was in flagrant contradiction with the basic article of the Charter in accordance with which member states with responsibility for territories whose populations are still not completely self-governing, "accept as a sacred trust the obligation to promote to the utmost, . . . the well-being of the inhabitants of these territories, and, to this end . . . to develop self-government, to take due account of the political aspirations of the people, and to assist them in the progressive development of their free political institutions, according to the particular circum-

[66] Moraes, 1956, *loc. cit.*, p. 465; see also Moraes, India Today, 1960, pp. 197 and 102.

stances of each territory and its peoples and their varying stages of advancement" (Art. 73).

The revolutionary forces thus set in motion are such that it has seemed pointless, even to the great Powers, to oppose them. Speaking to the nation on 12 July 1961 the French President declared that "the task which hitherto consisted of taking upon ourselves the government, the administration, the existence of colonial peoples is now out of date." This was due, he said, not only to the immense external effort required of France, but also to "the self-consciousness which the peoples have acquired and to their elemental desire for independence. . . . For many reasons," he concluded, "our direct national interest is therefore to free ourselves of costly and fruitless burdens and to let our former subjects decide their own future. . . . Commonsense, our aims, success, all call for decolonisation."

There is scarcely any colonial power today which has not come to the same conclusion, not without national feeling sometimes revolting against what looked like surrender, dismemberment, degradation.

But decolonisation, even deliberately decided, is not easily implemented. Due to the activity of the revolutionary forces which are pressing for it, it is rarely brought about in full accordance with any reasoned and methodical plan which may have been laid down. In the process critical moments arrive, imposing difficult choices; should the agreed plan be upheld as it stands, or should its execution be speeded up, skipping intermediate stages? In either case there are risks. This kind of decision had to be taken not only in the Congo in 1959–60, but even in the Gold Coast where decolonisation was crowned with success. If the British Government, following the violent disorders of February 1948 in Accra, carried through a daring constitutional reform, introduced universal suffrage and released Mr. Nkrumah from prison in order to make him prime minister overnight, it was because they had rejected the other alternative of bringing in troops and imposing their authority by force.[67] On the other hand, they did have recourse to force when the Mau Mau rebellion broke out in 1952, although its repression called for a great military effort, heavy losses in human life and the rigorous use of concentration camps. Even in French West Africa where the process was relatively peaceful it fell far short of conforming to plan. Even in Algeria, where the principle has long been accepted, and in spite of the exceptional quality of the statesman who is in charge of it, decolonisation is proceeding laboriously in a succession of painful ordeals. Even in India, where it had been the object of long and patient preparation, it ended up—in the figure of speech of Lord Ismay quoted

[67] Cf. MacMillan, 1959, *loc. cit.*, p. 219.

above—in the kind of panic flight in which a burning munitions ship is abandoned in mid-ocean.

Like all revolutions, while it solves old problems, decolonisation also raises new ones: international problems such as the war of succession between India and Pakistan over Kashmir which has been hanging fire for the last 12 years; conflicts over military bases between Egypt and the United Kingdom, or between France and Morocco or Tunisia; the tension between Indonesia and the Netherlands over Western New Guinea, or between Iraq and the United Kingdom over Kuwait; the cold war which is going on in Laos and which almost broke out in the Congo; internal problems of recently constituted states faced with forces of disintegration, set in motion by decolonisation, which threaten their national unity[68]; the breaking up of the former big territorial units of French West Africa and French Equatorial Africa and their regrouping into successor states; the threats of secession in Indonesia and the Congo, conflicts in Ceylon between Tamil immigrants and native Singhalese, the refashioning of the States of the Indian Union on linguistic lines; problems of political institutions, of the adaptation of the parliamentary system borrowed from the West, of the democratisation of ancient feudal structures; and, finally, the enormous problem of the social, economic and financial balance on which depend internal stability and the raising of living standards.

Many of these problems will no doubt continue to burden the world long after the colonial era has definitely closed.

[68] Cf. Van Langenhove, *Le Problème de l'Intégrité Nationale des Etats issus de la Décolonisation*, loc cit.

The Psychology of African Nationalism

MARGERY PERHAM
Nuffield College, Oxford

The political shape of Africa has been changing so rapidly in the last five years, with the pace accelerating during the last two, that Africa has at last caught the attention even of our distracted and endangered world. Interest is naturally concentrated upon the explosive force that is changing the political scenery as dramatically as the natural forces that produced the great rifts, mountains and lakes of this continent of extremes. But at this early stage in its appearance, African nationalism is still in a molten, plastic stage, and any opinions upon it must be offered as very provisional.

Nationalism is a protean word into which each of us reads our own historical or contemporary ideas. Some writers, despairing of an exact definition, conclude that, where a number of people make or accept a state within a given area, that is a nation. A variety of forces are seen to assist in welding the people together for this purpose and giving strength and durability to their association. Chief amongst these are common history, customs, language, religion and, at least in large measure, environment and way of life. Yet nations exist which lack at least one of these ingredients. The older nations have, in the course of centuries, enormously strengthened and enriched the common elements of their life, and, especially when seen from the outside, are judged to have developed something like a national character.

By re-stating these obvious truths we realize that most of the potential African negro nations lack every one of these components of nationalism except common land, and even this factor shows exceptional features. In British colonial Africa—to which this article will be mainly confined—the population was divided into hundreds, by some calculation of units into thousands, of independent tribes. The colonial frontiers within which, for the most part, Africans are aspiring to create nations, generally enclose large numbers of these tribes of varying size and character. Some of the larger of these so-called tribes lack any

Reprinted from *Optima* (published by the Anglo American Corporation of South Africa, Limited), X, No. 1 (1960), 27–36, with the permission of the author and the publisher.

political unity, though their peoples may be very close to each other in customs and language, but most territories enclose groups which are sharply distinct in both, and may have a long history of conflict with each other. There may be the deep ethnic and linguistic distinctions which divide Bantu from Nilotic. Upon the earlier religious distinctions found almost everywhere within these territories between Islam and the manifold pagan religions there will have come the further addition of Christianity. Common history, as distinct from misty tribal legend, is rare. Where it exists, as in parts of West Africa, it is very seldom a record of sustained unity for any group that could be classified as a nation.

The Asian dependencies showed large contrasts with the African. They had their divisions, their political weakness and, relatively to the modern West, their poverty. But they had populations which possessed large cultural and linguistic unity, even though they were often intermingled with other groups. These peoples had the pride that comes from a long history, a highly developed art, an ancient literature and famous and widespread religions of the book. It may be said that the origin of most nations could be traced back to congeries of tribes which were welded into unity through the centuries by conquest, external pressures and other forces. The difference between these older nations and those coming into being in middle Africa lies in the time factor. In Africa, the step from tribe to nation and from foreign rule to democratic independence is being taken within a very few years with conscious intention.

Denied so many of the things which have given birth and nourishment to nationalism elsewhere, Africans, it seems, are obliged to draw upon one main source. This is their sense of humiliation upon realizing their own retarded position among the peoples of the world. The political weakness resulting from their isolation implies, as the scientists now agree, no inherent inferiority but it allowed them to become the world's main source of slaves and, in modern times, brought them into quick subjection to European nations. Asians share in the Africans' sense of humiliation in some measure—was it not Mr. Nehru who added the fourth freedom "from contempt"?—but their sources of pride and their materials for unity assuage the hurt. African nationalism—we must use the word for convenience if not with exactitude—should be seen in its earlier stages as the sum of the sense of indignity felt by individuals. The humiliation has not been felt, with one or two possible small exceptions, in the context of anything that could be called a nation. It has been experienced by negro Africans not only separately but also as members of a race, a situation underlined because that race, in colour and form, had such very distinctive features. We may contrast the long subjected Greeks or Poles who could feel as a nation the shame of their status but who, as individuals, could feel the equals or the superiors of their rulers while they had no sense of racial inferiority or, indeed, of race. This contrast needs emphasis because some African propagandists, and those who have accepted their view, often talk as though the movements for independence in Africa were those of nations demanding no more than a return to a status of which they had been deprived.

It was, indeed, just because Africa was encountered in its tribal stage by the powerful nations of modern Europe that, for the most part, its annexation was so easy; and, it might be said, so unavoidable. Here and there a strong tribe, which like the Ashanti, the Zulu, or the Basuto, possessed in microcosm some of the elements of a nation, would put up a stiff resistance. But most of the tribes quickly accepted European rule as part of an irresistible order, one which brought many benefits, above all peace, and exciting novelties, railways and roads, lamps, bicycles, ploughs, new foods and crops and all that could be acquired and experienced in town and city. For the ruling classes, traditional or created, it brought a new strength and security of status and new forms of wealth and power. For many years after annexation, though there was much bewilderment, revolts were very few, and there does not *appear* to have been much sense of indignity at being ruled. It was not until a small minority, through their attainment of the higher levels of Western education, and above all through travel, came to understand something of the world at large and of their own place in it that the spell of acceptance began to be broken. Excited by the wine of these new ideas, and smarting, perhaps, from some experiences of the colour bar in Europe, and especially in Britain, the young African would return after some years to his own country. He would see its poverty and subjection with new eyes, and he was now ready to believe and to preach the idea that only by self-government could Africans escape from personal humiliation and win equality of status in a world of which they were at last becoming aware. This purpose had its adherents much earlier in West than in East Africa. The writer, in studying African affairs and visiting Africa in the 10 years before the second World War, could mark its rapid growth in the minds of Gold Coast and Nigerian students in Britain, and in the towns of the West Coast and the Sudan. But before 1939 the numbers of those whose education had reached the stage of world consciousness was still small, and the masses outside the few towns on or near the coast seemed to be unaware that their status was, as the young Press was beginning to declare, a humiliating slavery. But the next 10 war and post-war years saw a concentration of events and influences that spread the consciousness of "colonialism" as an evil, and raised hopes, especially along the West Coast and in the Sudan, that its supersession in Asia would be followed soon in Africa.

The view that African political consciousness is bred mainly from an individual reaction against an inferiority of status as a member of a race and not of a nation seems to explain some of the characteristics of African movements for self-government, especially in their early stages.

First, most basic and most obvious, comes the question of the area within which each of these young nationalisms has so far operated. The annexing powers marked out their boundaries upon the map of Africa in arbitrary fashion, very often in the chancelleries of Europe, before most of the regions concerned had been fully explored, still less demarcated on the ground. Yet, after not much more than half a century of European rule which, until very recent years, had done little to develop unity amongst the tribes thus enclosed, most of the African leaders find themselves obliged to begin the building of their nations within these boundaries. Doubtless, in time, the attempt will be made to re-draw frontiers more in accordance with the character and wishes of the peoples—the French colonies and Ghana are already experimenting in this way—but the point being made here is that there was a lack of any larger proto-national groups which could at once, at the very prospect of freedom, draw attention to their sense of unity.

This basic lack leads on to the second feature of African nationalism, and largely helps to explain it. This is the character of the leadership. In Africa, the general quiescence and passivity of the tribally divided masses under foreign rule has meant that leaders have arisen to create a movement rather than that a movement has thrown up a leader. The question arises at once as to why almost no traditional authorities have come forward as nationalists. It might have been expected that the almost universal and deep-rooted institution of chieftainship would have supplied, as it were, ready-made leaders. But the chiefs were chiefs of tribes, or of something even smaller than those more sizeable groups which that rather indeterminate word is generally used to describe. In most British territories, under the principles of indirect rule, chieftainship had been deliberately accepted, strengthened and developed in the sphere of local government. Where the chief was powerful and the group was large and coherent, and especially where it faced special dangers, there has been some tendency for embryonic nationalism to look to the chief for leadership. Part, at least, of the Ashanti people for a brief period hoped to build up their old kingdom under their Asantehene as a federal unit in order to preserve its distinction within the new Ghana. The three High Commission territories, dominated by fear of the overshadowing Union of South Africa, have naturally clung to their chiefs as symbols of continuity and identity. The Baganda, for all their small number, had perhaps more of the features of nationhood than most tribes of British Africa—a long history, a strong monarchical tradition, a ruling class, something very like a civil service, great tribal unity and pride and, relatively to African standards, a prosperous economy. Here the new spirit of assertion tended to find a centre in the chief, the Kabaka, with resultant complications at which we must glance again.

In most parts of Africa, however, chieftainship is tending to wither at the first breath of a national movement. Against most British expectations the impressive Indian princely states, expressive of autonomy and rooted in separatism, melted away before the nationalist movement. The African chieftainships are rooted in tribalism, and represent the principle of division; the nationalist must, therefore, set to work to destroy at least their political content. African chiefs were mostly much less autocratic and elevated than most of the Indian princes, but they suffered even more than these from being not only associated with, but even integrated within, the ruling power. As its agents in day-to-day administration they merged their own traditional authority with the new, irresistible colonial government. This partnership, which has to its credit some 40 years or more of economical and fairly effective local government, tends to be automatically dissolved by the onset of self-government, leaving the chiefs, in the eyes of the new leaders, more or less tainted by the association. In the Sudan, in Ghana and in Nigeria, there has been perplexed debate about the position of chiefs in the new situation, and a debate on March 19 last year in Nigeria's Western Region House of Assembly showed minds torn between their lingering respect for the social and customary status of the chiefs and doubts as to whether they could, or should, play any part in politics and administration in the new democratic order. Where chiefs were no more than agents appointed by the government, as in Kenya, they have not even the aura of tradition to protect them from the bitter antagonism of the new leaders, who see in these authoritative types the projection of colonial power, competing with their own new bid for influence right down to the level of sub-district and village.

Who, then, are these new leaders? It follows from what has been said that they must be entirely self-constituted. The first few educated men nominated by governments to sit in the legislature or in other advisory positions are generally disqualified as would-be democratic leaders by their dependence upon government or by moderation either of nature or as the fruit of experience. Tribalism and chieftainship are seen as barriers. Yet there is no wider community than the tribe with precedents or traditions that can be utilized. The masses, except perhaps in the towns, or in regions most exposed to Western influence, are probably unawakened in any effective political sense. The new leader must, therefore, by his own initiative build his own platform, and jump upon it. He must build it, in the main, of imported materials which he has most probably begun to collect during his travels abroad, in Britain or the United States, or both. His response to the political vacuum in which he must operate is naturally to build himself up as a striking personality, and this not only in the metaphorical sense, since he must keep up the interest and emotion of the masses by combatant acts and attitudes against the rulers. He cannot afford to be moderate lest he be outflanked by some more dramatically belligerent figure. Sociologists have applied the word "charismatic" to this new type of leadership, which emphasizes itself with new ceremonies, slogans and symbols.

These necessities of the leader become clearer when we look more closely at the other side of the partnership, the people to whom he is appealing. Since, in most contexts, he dare not make use of the only existing solidarity, that of the tribe, he must make a direct appeal to the individuals. The appeal is first of all to their sense of grievance. Causes of discontent, tangible, psychological and imaginary, are many. The apparent acceptance of colonial rule tends to wear thin, in proportion to the varying intensity of that rule in time and place, after some 40 years. The older generation, which was overwhelmed, whether in a military or a psychological sense, by the first impact of the European, dies out. Familiarity has eroded awe and admiration. The growing disharmonies in tribal, family and economic life become identified with, and are rightly charged to, the disintegrating effects of the White man's rule. Towns, large and small, draw peasant men and women into a difficult and often an impoverished and demoralizing life. An increasing number of children educated in European schools are coming to maturity with high expectations, based upon their new qualifications, which, in many cases, are doomed to a disappointment that can now be vocal. Government policy, through ignorance or inefficiency, may strike harshly. Even essential sanitary or agricultural controls necessitated by the new order may seem oppressive. The social colour bar, of which the African in the first few decades of annexation is hardly aware, begins to strike the rising and competing African and to infect its sufferers with an almost unappeasable hunger for equality.

In general it might be said—and this is especially true of the areas of White settlement—that the European appears to Africans to be guilty of turning them out of their lowly hut of contentment, or at least of unconsciousness, erecting at its doors the glittering house of his own civilization, and then forbidding him entry except to the kitchen and the workshop.

Discrimination was felt first and most bitterly by those who had reached to the very top of the Europeans' own educational ladder and had found themselves denied the same status and pay for which that arduous achievement seemed to entitle them. They saw no way of gaining it except by taking over, as Asians and Arabs had done, the government of their own country. To produce a potentially revolutionary situation in a very few years they had only to appeal to the half-conscious discontents and resentments felt in varying degree by the clerk, the wage-labourer and the peasant, with the assertion that all their ills were due to the colonial government, and that all their hopes could be met by freedom. "*All* their ills" because, though the historian must make the difficult attempt to judge between those due to the mistakes and even the crimes of the "colonialists" and those inherent in the sudden and belated penetration of industrial Europe into primitive Africa, the political leader need make no such distinction. His attitude is generally 100 per cent negative; he dare not admit one merit to the colonial régime.

But a sense of restlessness and inferiority, even when thus organized, and even when a millionfold or more, is not always enough out of which to make an immediately effective movement for self-government and to induce the colonial authorities to make the desired concessions. This is especially true of the more recent nationalisms. The leaders need to look outside the purely bilateral relationship within the colony and find extraneous support. This has come to hand in increasing quantity during the last 30 years or so.

The first external aid can be found in the political principles of the colonial powers themselves, especially, perhaps, of Britain. The contradiction between democracy at home and imperialism overseas had troubled the British since at least the time of Burke. The Indians, West Indians and West Africans, led or instructed by those who had reached the Inns of Court, quickly learned to borrow for their own use the liberties the British had so slowly and painfully acquired for themselves, and to employ them with powerful rhetoric and noble quotations. As Britain herself became more fully democratic so the possibilities in this field increased. The acquisition by Britain's own labouring class, first of powerful representation and then of majority power, was an immense encouragement to colonial aspirants for freedom. In major acts of policy it may not be easy to draw sharp contrasts between the records of Labour and Conservative cabinets, but there can be little doubt that the pronouncements of the Labour Party, whether in or out of office, and the personal encouragement, and even the tuition, given to colonial leaders by individuals in the party, greatly hastened an already moving current of liberalism in colonial policy.

A decisive point was the extension to the colonial dependencies of the general adult franchise so lately won in Britain. Acquired in Asia, extended to the West Indies, it could not, it seemed, be denied in Africa. Its sequence, by the irresistible logic of Britain's own democracy, was for leaders to organize the new electorate into parties, or a party, that would vote the colonial government out of the country. Furthermore, in countries of settlement, by the principle of "undiluted democracy," it could be hoped that dominant European and Asian minorities might, in the few days it takes to count the votes and summon the legislature, be swept out of the seats of political economic power.

If at the onset of the first waves of a freedom movement the colonial bastion remained unshaken by the weakness of its own inner contradictions, the new leaders could bring in from outside a second battering ram, perhaps the most powerful engine of all. This was the force of world opinion against colonialism. Changing components have made up this force. America's share in it was very strong before, during and for a few years after the war. To-day, for reasons, both of greater knowledge and more instructed self-interest, while by no means dead, this force has declined in power. The communist states offer a challenge of constant strength, but one in which the ingredients change. In the 'twenties and 'thirties the attack was mainly theoretical, aimed directly and also indirectly through the writings of left-wing socialists. This period was followed by a period in which it seemed that the communist system had achieved in Russia for a recently servile peasantry the exact results, both in character and in speed, which the Africans desired for themselves. Russia had even drawn strength from the same motive force as theirs, the desire to catch up rapidly with the West and escape the weakness of poverty and the stigma of inferiority. A new phase of communist influence has now developed, one in which Russia and China are entering into direct relations with African leaders, both independent and colonial, reaching out with diplomatic and economic feelers into their continent. Happenings in Hungary and Tibet are unlikely to offset the attraction of communist support since few Africans have yet a world view and their main concern is with their local imperialism. Those African leaders who have no desire to risk exclusive relations with Russia are naturally inclined to welcome other influences that seem to offset colonial power, and Colonel Nasser's balancing act may seem an attractive example.

A third and rapidly growing external force which gives strength to the nationalists is the massed attack on colonialism by the communist states and by the ever increasing number of ex-colonial powers at Lake Success. An analysis of the 83 members of the United Nations explains the order of battle. There are some 25 fairly recently emancipated dependencies, with more to come; 20 South American members who, with a few exceptions, tend to show their anti-colonial hang-over in their votes, and 10 communist states which give solid and automatic support to any anti-colonialist movement. There are 10 other states which for various reasons may feel a pro-dependency or anti-imperial bias. That leaves only nine states which are likely to take a truly independent attitude and the four older British Commonwealth states. The United States, with the greatest influence, has a somewhat ambivalent attitude, being herself an ex-colonial country, but she has increasingly supported the colonial powers as her North Atlantic Treaty Organization allies. Even so, the five colonial powers fight a losing battle in the international arena. It is true that, apart from Trusteeship matters, the struggle over the non-self-governing territories is for the most part one of words and paper. But these have a cumulative political effect. Above all they provide ideological sustenance of ever-increasing strength for an ever-diminishing number of dependent peoples. And the anti-colonial states can meet away from New York at Bandoeng or Cairo.

Fourth, and most recent as a stimulus to nationalism, is the activity of African political leaders in entering into contact with each other in Africa, in Europe or in New York. In this way they share experience—how much Dr. Nkrumah, the unofficial president of this club, must have to teach the new members!—and generate political energy. These councils encourage the more laggard colonies to aim at levelling themselves up to the stage reached by the advanced, and make it more difficult for moderates to fall below the standards of urgency set by their colleagues.

This attempt at drawing a composite picture of nationalism in British Africa means that the time factor is blurred and that no one territory is exactly portrayed. This demands some correction. The description of motive forces, for example, is more true of the later than the earlier stirrings of nationalism. Over the whole area of colonialism the pace has been quickening. India, by contrast with Africa, had a period of intervention and dependence that can be reckoned in centuries. Her nationalist movement was some 50 years in maturing, and her peoples' internal sources of strength and confidence meant that they had far less need for extraneous moral support which, in any case, only appeared in any strength, mainly from the United States, shortly before the attainment of independence. Egypt more slowly, the Sudan, the Gold Coast and Nigeria more quickly, have come first along the course for freedom in Africa. Egypt, hardly to be called an African dependency, stood alone in her ancient history as a nation. Among the others the Gold Coast had most cultural unity: the Sudan had experienced from the early nineteenth century an arbitrary political union imposed by Egypt, but neither Ghana nor the Sudan, until very recent years, showed much promise of nationhood: Nigeria, taken as a whole, might have been regarded as a hopeless non-starter in the race. All three, but especially the two latter territories, carried a large proportion of primitive tribes hardly reached by Western economic and political influences. The Sudanese had the unique advantage of the Condominium. This enabled their leaders, supported by the sophisticated dark Arabs of the three cities at the junction of the Niles, and of the Gezira, to win their freedom quickly and easily by playing off Britain and Egypt.

All these three territories needed, and could find, more external support than had the Asian dependencies. Yet all had partial sources of internal confidence greater than anything possessed by eastern and central African peoples. The northern Sudanese belonged to a great world religion and spoke the Arab language: the Gold Coast people, especially in the Colony, had long contact with Europe and a widely diffused Western education, while they shared with Ashanti both historic chieftainships and a prosperity based on cocoa. In Nigeria difficulties have been greater. The northerners were Muslim, but they were largely cut off from the world of Islam by a desert north and a pagan south. Moreover, their impressive political structure, reorganized and developed by the British, acted as a stabilizing and conservative force allergic to democratic nationalism. The Yoruba chieftainships, almost as sophisticated, with their civic development, as those of the Gold Coast, though not as wealthy, might have outrun their rivals to the freedom stakes if they had not been enclosed within a larger whole, the three parts of which have had harder work to come to terms with each other than with Britain. It is interesting, and a confirmation of the view expressed here about the major part played by the sense of inferiority as a motive force, that, while the Hausa and Yoruba peoples, with their long established city-states carefully recognized by the British, had little cause to feel this sense, it was the most primitive of the three main Nigerian groups, the Ibo and kindred peoples of the south-east who played the lead in the agitation for self-government. Through his

Press, Dr. Azikiwe ceaselessly spread the idea that the Nigerian peoples were enslaved and must follow him in the fight for freedom. This was his bludgeon, but he also made great play with darts of ridicule, raining these continually upon the government from the governors downwards, in order to destroy the Africans' sense of respect for the authorities they had so long obeyed. Among a numerous people who had no chiefs and no political unity outside the kinship group, he built himself up as a leader and saviour so that the women would drink the pools in which he had trodden.

Thus the peoples of these three African territories, each enclosing very contrasting elements of the advanced and the primitive, helped by increasing external encouragement, and by a quick response from Britain, were led forward by their intelligentsia to achieve their purpose in a far shorter period of agitation than the Asian countries whose just preceding emancipation had, indeed, helped by precedent to advance their own.

The three mainland territories under British rule in eastern Africa have not yet attained their independence. Possessing even less of the internal material for nationhood than the Asian and West African states, and with a shorter experience of European contact and government, their leaders are forced to rely much more upon the increasing external support. They have also a greater wealth of precedent, some of it now from negro Africa with even the Belgian Congo awakened from political somnolence. Furthermore, in the political climate of the world to-day, the remaining colonial peoples feel, or can be made to feel, even more acutely than their predecessors the stigma of their political subjection. These must be the reasons for the rapidity with which movements for independence have swept across the East African territories. This is especially striking in Tanganyika and Kenya since their arbitrary boundaries enclose scanty, ill-distributed peoples, showing great contrasts of culture and way of life, and inadequately linked by communications.

Uganda is more compact, and has been the scene of a rare attempt by a British governor to take the initiative in the creation of national unity and self-government. The failure so far, as already stated, has been due to the existence of one leading tribal group which distorts the usual pattern of colonial emancipation the other parts are trying to follow. The Baganda ruler and traditional leaders are torn between the desire to separate from the rest of the territory and the desire to dominate it, and the peoples of the other provinces are thwarted in their desire, which is also that of the British Government, to work for a united, self-governing and democratic Uganda.

By contrast Tanganyika, with its African population awakened to the first stirrings of political interest in a period that can be calculated in months rather than years, seems to be passing with ease and speed to the goal of majority rule and independence. At least one reason lies in the fact that Tanganyika, as a trust territory, is wide open to the influence of the United Nations, and once an African leader could evoke and represent the response of the people to this relationship, the end foreseen in the trust was in sight. In an impressive constitutional debate in the legislature on March 19 last year, the European and Asian representatives, quickly accepting the inevitable, vied with each other in their readiness to throw away the briefly held protection of parity of racial representation, and to line up behind the young African leader, Julius Nyerere, in his demand for democracy and self-government. His striking moderation may be due in part to character, but the ease with which, after a brief and able organization of support, he has reached the threshold of power, has relieved him from much temptation to extremism. The daunting nature of the task of making a nation out of Tanganyika and building an economy that can support and advance that nation may well incline him to cling to all the assets and all the allies he can find.

Kenya offers almost too many points of relevance to our scheme for us to examine them all. Of all African colonies it was, perhaps, the least well qualified to become a nation-state. Its characteristics were the exceptional isolation of the interior; a small population concentrated in a few widely separated parts of the large area; no political organization above the clan; and a coast with a history of its own under Arab influence. The Kenya of to-day has been created by British administration, by an arterial railway, and by the British settlers who have farmed the almost uninhabited highlands, and by the Asian craftsmen and traders. The Africans played the part of the unskilled labour force. Now they are learning skills, and Africans' agricultural production, with the first beginnings of their trade and industry, is playing a large and growing part in the economy. The Africans were stirred early into political consciousness by observing the struggle of the settlers to obtain full "self-government" from Britain. They felt a growing bitterness as they realized their own poverty and inferiority beside the apparently wealthy colonists, and contrasted their crowded reserves with the spacious European farms. Kenyatta, returning from many years of living in England, showed an almost mesmeric power in mobilizing the discontent of his Kikuyu tribesmen against government and settler. The tragic madness of the Mau Mau was the result.

The movement which has followed this has, so far, been purely political. Two able young men, Mr. Mboya and Dr. Kiano, the first educated at Ruskin College, Oxford, and the other at an American University, have taken the lead in trying to build up a national movement. Nairobi is necessarily its centre. In its spreading locations the consciousness of discontent welds the tribes and is reinforced by the tension over housing and employment, which fail to keep pace with the inflow from the districts. Faced by the entrenched settler position and the government's hesitation to surrender it to majority rule, the leaders here, more than anywhere else, seek compensating strength abroad. Mr. Mboya has travelled and lectured in Britain, Asia and America. He presided at the All-African Peoples' Conference at Accra in December, 1958. As president of the Kenya Trade Union Congress he draws help and advice from the International Confederation of Free Trade Unions and from Transport House. (He has not, it may be noted, so far used the trade unions for direct political action.) His problem will be to decide between a policy of moderation which could win the confidence of all races, or one of seeking quick results by trying to fuse tribalism with the strong emotion that each African feels, or can be helped to feel, at his political, social and economic subordination to the immigrant races.

In Central Africa, taken as a whole, the indigenous population was even more scanty and ill distributed than that of British East Africa. Nyasaland, though more populous than the Rhodesias, had been ravaged by the Arab slave trade and by the inter-tribal wars it fostered. A large proportion of its manhood was spending its energies scattered abroad as migrant labour. Education in the protectorate, well begun by the Scottish missions in the eighteen-seventies, had stopped short, and there were hardly any of the all-important returned graduates to give a lead. The sparse population of Northern Rhodesia had been dominated by the influence of the settlers and the mines. The apparent political backwardness of these two protectorates was, presumably, one reason why the governments concerned thought it possible to incorporate these territories in a federation dominated by the European colonists of Southern Rhodesia. But the very discussions that accompanied its inception woke the northern Africans to their being diverted, as they saw it, from the straight Colonial Office road to self-government into a by-road which, in their words, would lead them into slavery to the European settlers. Unable, the Devlin report tells us, to produce an adequate leader within Nyasaland, and aware now of the example of other colonies, the local nationalists invited Dr. Banda, then in Ghana, to come and lead them, with the expressed intention of building him up as the "political messiah" as this "would cause great excitement, and should precipitate almost a revolution in political thought." The importation was certainly effective, and is one more example of the speed with which the almost universal latent anti-government and anti-European feeling can be called into expression and action.

The conditions of Africa to-day act as a forcing house for the remaining dependencies. Since the British Government has made it clear that Tanganyika and Uganda have full scope to grow into self-government, the heat of pan-African and anti-colonialist feeling will increasingly be turned upon Kenya and, even more, upon Central Africa. There it will be concentrated especially upon the European minorities, who are now regarded by Africans as the main, if not the only reason, why the people in these territories are denied the same destiny as the rest of British Africa and, indeed, of kindred tribes just across an artificial border. The point will be driven home by the inability of France, because of the numerous *colons,* to grant Algeria the freedom so generously and dramatically given by De Gaulle to the rest of French Africa. South Africa is, of course, an even nearer warning to negro Africans, and the extreme polarization between the rapidly growing freedom of tropical Africans and the increasing repression in the Union, even if it is unlikely to produce much immediate effect upon the resolute Nationalists of that state, heightens tension throughout the continent.

The pot of racial controversy will be kept boiling by all the external influences we have reviewed, and the programme of African events for 1960, which includes the emancipation of Nigeria and of Somalia, the Kenya constitutional conference and the dispatch of the rather unwieldy commission which is to debate the Federation, will add their quota to the restlessness.

We have been looking at African nationalism mainly from the African side. The other side of the picture would be found in the character of the colonial governments and of the unofficial Europeans, settlers or business men, under whose control or influence that nationalism has been moulded and against whose policies it is now solidifying its form. This is outside our scope. But one thing remains to be said. An endeavour has been made to deal objectively with a subject that is highly controversial and which arouses deep feelings upon both sides amongst those who live in Africa or who are concerned with it. Let me then, in conclusion, offer my own opinion. African nationalism is not only the inevitable result of the forces working in our world and, indeed, in our own nation. To oppose it is to oppose these forces. The alternative is to endeavour to guide and assist it, a difficult task indeed. It may assist a right mental approach to remember that it is through no fault of the Africans, or, except to a marginal degree, of their European rulers, that this universal passion has reached Africans when they are so unready to give it constructive expression, and when it threatens the interests and achievements of European colonists. The desire to find relief from, and compensation for, a sense of inferiority is one that the psychologists identify in greater or less degree, in every human being, and which is reflected in the behaviour of groups, including almost all the nations of the world. It is the burden of the Africans that their history has bred in them this sense to a pathological degree, and it is the burden of the Western powers that they must pay for their century or more of domination over most of the rest of the world by being the object against which their former political or economic subjects must lever themselves up into the desired equality. The bond of humiliation extends outside the colonial people and links them psychologically with all who have had reason to hate or to fear the superiority of the so-called imperialist powers. Britain, for all her respect for native society and care for the masses, may suffer more at this stage than France which offered her African subjects, and especially the Westernized individuals, more equality of both social and political status.

Since at least the time of the Renaissance mankind has had to endure the excesses of nationalism which to-day threaten humanity itself, and some nations are already experimenting in the limitation of sovereignty. Yet it is difficult to see how Africans or other formerly dependent peoples can find the dignity and self-expression they need, with the experience of civic life and of economic development, except by following the rest of the world through the stage of nationhood. In political terms, which have been outlined here as realistically as possible, African nationalism inevitably leads to a struggle for power. We have, in fact, been witnessing a series of rebellions, but this reality has been veiled because of the growing readiness on the part of the colonial rulers to attempt by concessions to ensure that the rebellions shall be peaceful. It is, however, much to expect of young national leaders, whose impatience is encouraged from so many quarters, to conduct their movement at the permitted pace and strictly within the rules of law, the law of their rulers.

It would surely help our understanding of these movements if we could always remember that, though on the surface they are political, at a deeper level they are psychological and only psychological treatment will satisfy them. It is for this reason that even the attainment of independence does not complete the cure. British Africa's resources for nation-building, for immediately successful independence and, above all, for democracy are very deficient. True, much of tribal society was democratic in spirit. But this spirit, essentially tribal, has to be made inter-tribal by the sudden extension of the sense of social obligation. This need and the demands of unity and self-respect may serve to increase the tendency of the new nations, even when independent, to continue to exploit the negative impulse of anti-imperialism. This tendency is still present in some measure in the new Asian states. The Western nations, if they want to complete the emancipations which, voluntarily and involuntarily, they have set in motion, will have to go on paying the penalty of their former domination in patient understanding, in unrequited aid, largely through inter-national channels, and in such gestures of respect between equals as the British Sovereign has recently paid to Dr. Nkrumah. Altruism has, indeed, become the best policy. But something warmer than mere calculation will be needed to secure success, the realization that the achievement of African freedom is, or at least can be, a spiritual as well as a political gain.

The conviction of those who have lately become conscious that they are in subjection, that dignity and self-realization can be gained only, and immediately, in full political freedom clashes against the opposite conviction held by those in the "mixed" states, who believe that such freedom would bring disorder and poverty to all concerned, and therefore that African nationalism must be defeated, curbed or diverted— for the defenders are less united than the attackers. But whatever policy is devised to deal with an issue which is imminent and has no close precedent, it should be founded upon a reasoned measurement of the content of African nationalism in its various contexts and its growing strength.

Notes on Negro American Influences on the Emergence of African Nationalism

GEORGE SHEPPERSON
University of Edinburgh

The claims of no people . . . are respected by any nation until they are presented in a national capacity. (Martin R. Delany, *The Condition, Elevation, Emigration and Destiny of the Colored People of the United States, Politically Considered,* Philadelphia, 1852, p. 210.)

. . . it is not so much Afro-Americans *that we want as* Africans. (Casely Hayford, *Ethiopia Unbound,* London, 1911, p. 173.)

. . . on us too depends in a large degree the attitude of Europe towards the teeming millions of Asia and Africa. (William Edward Burghardt Du Bois, "The Present Outlook for the Dark Races of Mankind," *African Methodist Episcopal Church Review,* Philadelphia, XVI, 1900, pp. 102–3.)

It may be that the day is not far off when the new Negroes of Africa will be demanding that their blood brothers in the United States be treated with absolute fairness and justice. (James Weldon Johnson, *New York Age,* 12 May 1923.)

The first British Empire owed much to the triangular trade between Africa, the West Indies and North America. The last British Empire has not been uninfluenced by another triangular trade, a trade not of pocatille, slaves and molasses, but a commerce of ideas and politics between the descendants of the slaves in the West Indies and North America and their ancestral continent. Until the imposition of

Reprinted from *Journal of African History,* I (1960), 299–312, with the permission of the author and the publisher.

immigrant quotas by the United States in the 1920s, West Indian Negroes[1] contributed a distinct element to the coloured American's interest in and influence on Africa.

Edward Blyden, who was born in St. Thomas in 1832, went to New York in 1847 but was refused admission to an American university because of his colour and, therefore, emigrated to Liberia in 1850 to become a leading politician and pioneer theorist of the "African personality," is the outstanding example of this three-way process. At the peak of his powers, 1872 to 1888, Blyden visited America eleven times. He knew many Negro Americans and the sentiments he offered them are exemplified in his address at the Hampton Institute, Virginia, in 1883. Warning his Negro audience against European travellers' accounts of Africa, he declared that "No people can interpret Africans but Africans."[2] It was ideas of this kind which made the Gold Coast nationalist Casely Hayford dub the writings on racial questions by some Negro Americans as "exclusive and provincial" and led him to praise Blyden's conceptions as "universal among the entire race and the entire race problem."[3]

The two other outstanding West Indians in this ideological triangle are obvious: Marcus Garvey, the Jamaican Negro whose eleven years in the States, through his militant Universal Negro Improvement Association (U.N.I.A.), "awakened a race consciousness that made Harlem felt around the world";[4] and George Padmore of Trinidad whose last and best book, *Pan-Africanism or Communism?* (London, 1956) is one of the few studies which has recognized the existence of this triangle and tried to estimate its significance for Africa.

There are many lesser names which indicate that this is not inconsiderable: for example, the Barbadian Dr. Albert Thorne,[5] a precursor of Garvey, who tried from 1897 to the 1920s to launch in America a movement for the Negro colonization of Central Africa; the Antiguan

[1] With the exception of Ira De A. Reid's *The Negro Immigrant* (New York, 1939), there has been almost no serious study of West Indian Negro influence on Negro Americans.

[2] *Southern Workman* (Hampton, Va.), 1883, 9. See also Edward Blyden, *The African Problem and other Discourses delivered in America in 1890* (London, 1890).

[3] Casely Hayford, *Ethiopia Unbound* (London, 1911), 163: cf. Hayford's introduction to *Africa and the Africans. Proceedings . . . of a Banquet . . . to Edward W. Blyden, Ll.D., by West Africans in London* (London, 1903), especially p. 18. See also James S. Coleman, *Nigeria* (Berkeley, 1958), 175–6, 183–4, 452–3; L. J. Coppin, *Unwritten History* (Philadelphia, 1919), 316–17.

[4] Clayton Powell, Snr., *Against the Tide* (1938), 70–1. See also Edmund D. Cronon, *Black Moses* (Madison, 1955).

[5] *Illustrated Missionary News* (London, 1897), 70–2, 105, 113; *New York Age*, 12 Aug. 1922, "African Colonization Schemes."

George Alexander McGuire, first American Bishop in 1921 of the African Orthodox Church of the Garvey movement[6] which made its mark on independent African churches in South and East Africa; and the Jamaican Claude McKay whose militant verse of the "Harlem Renaissance" period has influenced emerging Negro literature everywhere. Thorne's belief that "Africa is the only quarter of the world where we will be permanently respected as a race"[7] illustrates one of the main factors linking the *avante-garde* of American and West Indian Negroes in a common interest in Africa.

Both groups shared a common challenge: the challenge implicit in such statements as that by a white sympathizer of the Negro in America in 1909 that "at the background of every Negro, however wise, or well educated, or brave, or good, is contemporary Africa which has no collective achievement . . . like other nationalities."[8] Two responses, at least, were possible: to recognize that this view was correct and to seek every means to lay a basis for African nationality and collective achievement; or to claim that it was wrong and to demonstrate this by searching into the African past for achievements which the biased eye of the white man had overlooked. In the intermingling of these two responses may be seen most of the elements in the Negro American's influence on Africa.

This influence would not be expected to make itself felt to any degree until after the American Civil War and the emancipation of the slaves. Nevertheless, some Negroes in America showed an interest in Africa before the 1860s—usually in the face of the criticism of black abolitionists such as Frederick Douglass who considered the African dream a dangerous diversification of energies which were needed in the fight for emancipation and civil rights at home[9]—which provided a basis on which coloured Americans' aspirations could build after the Civil War.

Liberia, of course, supplied them with a focus. Its American-style Constitution and Declaration of Independence in 1847 seemed to demonstrate "beyond all reasonable doubt that the Black Man is capable

[6] A. C. Terry Thomas, *The History of the African Orthodox Church* (New York, 1956). See also Cronon, op. cit. 69, 103, 160, 178–80, 189; *The African Yearly Register*, ed. T. D. Mweli Skota (Johannesburg, 1932), 128, 172, etc. G. A. McGuire (misspelt as "Maguire") is now immortalized as an "American Negro" in *Historical Survey of the Origins and Growth of Mau Mau* (Cmnd. 1030, London, 1960), 173: cf. also pp. 45, 174–5, 178.

[7] *An Appeal addressed to the Friends of the African Race* (c. 1896), 30, in Church of Scotland Papers, Miscellaneous Bundle, Pamphlets No. 1, National Library of Scotland.

[8] Edgar Gardner Murphy, *The Basis of Ascendency* (New York, 1909), 42.

[9] E.g. *Life and Writings of Frederick Douglass*, ed. Philip S. Foner (New York, 1950), II, 251–4, 387–8, 441–6.

of self-government"[10]—though there have been cynics, Negro as well as white, who have felt that the existence of Liberia has done as much to delay as to advance African self-government.[11]

But, for one of the major pre-Civil War Negro American exponents of the "Back-to-Africa" dream, Martin R. Delany, Harvard-trained physician and first Negro to be commissioned with field rank by president Lincoln, the Liberians were a "noble band of brothers."[12] He visited Liberia in July 1859 and saw in the proposed Liberian College "a grand stride in the march of African Regeneration and Negro Nationality."[13] Half a century later, however, Sir Harry Johnston castigated the "obstinate adhesion" of the Liberians and their College "to the ideals of New England" and warned that they "must turn their backs on America and their faces towards Africa, or they will dwindle to nothing."[14] That Delany was also seriously concerned with this problem of loss of identity was seen in September 1859 when he visited Abeokuta and concluded an agreement with the Egba chiefs. He criticized the Christian missionaries' habit of changing the names of their African converts on the grounds that this would lead to "a loss of identity."[15] For Delany, the only answer was "Africa for the African": with Blyden, he appears to have been one of the first to use this magnetic slogan.[16]

Delany's emphasis was political. Other Negro Americans looked for the joint regeneration of the coloured man in America and Africa through Negro-led Christian missions. As early as the 1790s, Negroes from America were interested in the independent churches of Sierra Leone. By the Civil War, the outstanding theoretician of the Negro missionary movement to Africa was Alexander Crummell,[17] Bachelor of Arts of Queen's College, Cambridge, and a coloured Anglican divine. It

[10] John Says, U.S. agent for liberated Africans in Liberia: Rhodes House Library, Mic. Afr. 349, Roll 10.

[11] George S. Schuyler, *Slaves To-day* (New York, 1931); Charles S. Johnson (Negro American member of 1930 League of Nations Commission on Forced Labour in Liberia), *Bitter Canaan*, unpublished typescript in C. S. Johnson papers, Fisk University. But cf. N. Azikiwe, *Liberia in World Politics* (London, 1934), 233 et seq.

[12] Martin R. Delany, *Official Report of the Niger Valley Exploring Party* (New York, 1861), 24.

[13] Ibid., 23.

[14] *Liberia* (London, 1906), 368–70.

[15] Delany, op. cit., 52.

[16] Ibid., 61. See also George Shepperson and Thomas Price, *Independent African* (Edinburgh, 1958), 504.

[17] Crummell's life is one of the great missed opportunities of American biographers, although most of his papers are conveniently collected in the Schomburg Collection of the New York Public Library. There is a brief sketch in William H. Ferris, *Alexander Crummell* (Washington, D.C., 1920). See also the moving tribute in ch. XII of W. E. B. Du Bois's *The Souls of Black Folk* (New York, 1955 reprint). An example of Crummell's interest in Africa is his *The Future of Africa* (New York, 1862).

was to be the connexion between the Negro churches of America and Africa which, after the Civil War, was to provide a channel for increasing numbers of Africans to gain an education in coloured American schools and colleges.

After the Civil War and the so-called Reconstruction of the Southern States, when the civil rights which the Negro had expected from a Northern victory were denied to him in many parts of the Union, numerous Negro Americans, despairing of a redress of their grievances in the United States, sought consolation in the "Back-to-Africa" dream. At the same time, the partition of Africa by the European Powers and the many overt injustices which this created, gave the Negro American, already highly conscious of injustice, the added incentive of rendering service in Africa to his "own people."

After the Civil War, as before, the "Back-to-Africa" movement was strenuously opposed by leading Negro politicians.[18] But it never lost its attractions. Up to the first World War, its major exponent was the African Methodist Episcopal Church Bishop, Henry M. Turner,[19] who urged Negro Americans passionately that it was their only way to salvation. For all its idealism, the movement did not lack its racketeers.[20] Nor was there any shortage of colourful characters, such as the Negro stockbroker, William Henry Ellis,[21] who led an expedition to Ethiopia in 1903, supported by Turner, which had the unusual effect of eliciting a letter in Amharic from Menelik II to thank Andrew Carnegie for his gifts to the education of "African Americans" in the United States.[22] All such schemes, fair or foul, kept the idea of Negro colonization and a roseate image of Africa alive amongst Negro Americans until the time was ripe for an outburst of Negro grievances which could make use of them.

This occurred immediately after the first World War when, as at the end of the Civil War, the raising of Negro hopes had proved abortive and fresh disillusionment ensued. Into this setting, in 1914, stepped Marcus Garvey, with a ready-made programme, the manifesto of his Universal Negro Improvement Association and African Communities

[18] A good example of modern criticisms is Charles I. Glicksberg's "Negro Americans and the African Dream," *Phylon* (Atlanta, Ga.), VIII, 4, 323–30.

[19] The best indication of Turner's interest in African colonization is his newspaper, *The Voice of the People*, 1901–7 (copy on loan in the library of Morris Brown College, Atlanta, Ga.). See also, for example, W. K. Roberts, *An African Canaan for American Negroes* (Birmingham, Ala., 1896), 18–19.

[20] E.g. Deluding the Negroes: "The United States and Congo National Emigration Steamship Company." A ticket to Africa and a Farm for One Dollar. From *"The (Washington) Post,"* 19 Jan. 1891 (Library of Congress).

[21] *Voice of the People*, op. cit., 33, 1 Oct. 1903; 3, 34, ? Nov. 1903, 1; *African Methodist Episcopal Church Review* (Philadelphia, 1903), xx, 302, "Menelik the Negus."

[22] The original letter and a small file about it are in the Carnegie Birthplace Museum, Dunfermline.

League which had been founded on 1 August 1914, in Jamaica. The U.N.I.A. stressed race pride and power and declared that it aimed "to strengthen the imperialism of independent African states."[23] At its 1920 New York convention a "Declaration of Rights of the Negro Peoples of the World" was drawn up which set out these aims in greater detail and demanded "Africa for the Africans at home and abroad."[24] If Garvey's "Back-to-Africa" scheme, his Black Star Line, collapsed when he was deported from America in 1927, his massive propaganda for pride, not shame, in a black skin left an ineradicable mark on African nationalism everywhere, all the criticisms which were made of him by men of his own colour notwithstanding.[25] Kwame Nkrumah has stated unequivocally that the *Philosophy and Opinions of Marcus Garvey* influenced him more than anything else during his period in America.[26] And Garvey's pride of colour, through his organ, *The Negro World,* reached out into West Africa, its independent church and nationalist movements;[27] into South and Central Africa, where it had some effect on the followers of Clements Kadalie of the Industrial and Commercial Workers Union of Africa and the remains of the Nyasaland Chilembwe-ite movement;[28] and into the messianic nationalism of the Kimbangu movement in the Congo.[29]

The 1920s, the main years of the Garvey movement, was the period when European governments in Africa were most wary of Negro American influences in their territories. Garvey's U.N.I.A., certainly, had brought this suspicion to a head: but it had much earlier roots. The phenomenon of "Ethiopianism"[30] in South Africa went back to 1896–8 when separatist South African churches had sought affiliation with the pioneer Negro American independent church, the African Methodist Episcopal Church,[31] and its fiery Bishop, H. M. Turner, had made his

[23] Booker T. Washington Papers, Library of Congress (hereafter cited as B.T.W.), Container 939, Miscellaneous Correspondence, 1915, E–H: Garvey to Washington, 12 April 1915.

[24] Raymond Leslie Buell, *The Native Problem in Africa* (New York, 1928), 11, 967.

[25] E.g. M. Mokete Manoedi (Basuto), *Garvey and Africa* (n.d.), in Schomburg Collection, N.Y.

[26] *The Autobiography of Kwame Nkrumah* (Edinburgh, 1957), 45.

[27] Coleman, op. cit., 189–91. See also correspondence between Akinambi Agbebi (Lagos Black Star line agent), E. M. E. Agbebi and John Edward Bruce in the John Edward Bruce Papers (hereafter cited as J.E.B.) in the Schomburg Collection, N.Y.

[28] Shepperson and Price, op. cit., 433–5, 504; *Nyasaland Times,* 24 Sept. 1926, 3.

[29] Efraim Andersson, *Messianic Popular Movements in the Lower Congo* (Uppsala, 1958), 250–6.

[30] Shepperson and Price, op. cit., passim.

[31] L. J. Coppin, *Observations of Persons and Things in South Africa* (Philadelphia, n.d.), 8–18. See also references to James Dwane in the A.M.E. Church, *Episcopal Handbook,* 1900, ed. B. W. Arnett, especially pp. 8–17.

trip to Africa.[32] Through such connexions, numbers of Africans from South Africa were to visit the United States, often in search of an education which seemed to them easier to obtain in Negro American colleges than at home. Three names stand out in this process: John L. Dube,[33] Solomon Plaatje[34] and D. D. T. Jabavu,[35] all of whom played important roles in the growth of the South African Native National Congress. The list could be extended considerably[36] until a pattern emerges which makes intelligible the South African Government's fear that Negro Americans were inflaming Bantu racial consciousness. This fear reached unreasonable heights at the time of the 1906 Natal Zulu

[32] His first trip was in 1892: see *African Methodist Episcopal Church Review* (Philadelphia), 1892, 446–98.

[33] Edward Roux, *Time Longer Than Rope* (London, 1949), 108, 117–18, 258, 260, 296, 306, 357; Shepperson and Price, op. cit., 91–2, 102, 145, 162, 203, 461; *Southern Workman* (1897), 141–2; John L. Dube, *A Zulu's Message to Afro-Americans* in J.E.B. Papers and *A Talk about my Native Land* (Rochester, N.Y., 1892).

[34] Roux, op. cit. 118–19; Shepperson and Price, op. cit., 202; Sol. T. Plaatje, *The Mote and the Beam* (New York, 1921) in Howard University Library; Sol. T. Plaatje, *Native Life in South Africa* (London, 5th edn., n.d.), 16, 286, 368, indicate the influence of W. E. B. Du Bois; Plaatje's pamphlet on the 1913 South African Natives' Land Act was sent to B. T. Washington's secretary, E. J. Scott, by Plaatje, 27 Aug. 1914 (B.T.W. Papers, Container 13, O–R) ; J. E. Bruce to Carter G. Woodson, 17 Jan. 1923, in Carter G. Woodson Papers, Library of Congress (hereafter cited as C.G.W.).

[35] Roux, op. cit., 65, 85, 182, 295–6, 299, 301, 306; D. D. T. Jabavu, *The Black Problem* (Lovedale, C.P., 1920), i, 25–96, 103.

[36] A representative list of some of the many South African Africans who visited America or corresponded with Negro Americans might include: The Lincoln University group—22 between 1896 and 1924 and none, apparently, thereafter (figures from an unpublished history of Lincoln University kindly supplied by Dr. Horace Mann Bond)—of which one of the most interesting was Livingstone N. Mzimba, son of P. J. Mzimba, separatist church leader (see *Lincoln University Herald*, Oxford, Pa., xiii, May 1909, 1–2, and L. N. Mzimba, "The African Church," 86–95, *Christianity and the Natives of South Africa*, ed. J. Dexter Taylor, Lovedale, 1927). A. K. Soga, editor of *Izwi LaBantu* (to Bruce, 23 Feb. 1907, J.E.B. Papers). Representatives of the "Ethiopian Church of South Africa" at 1912 Tuskegee Africa Conference, Reverends Henry Reed and Isaiah Goda Shishuba (C.G.W. Papers, Box 13, galley proof). P. K. Isaka Seme, initiator of the South African Native National Congress (see the reprint of his 1906 Columbia University address, "The Regeneration of Africa," 436–9, William H. Ferris, *The African Abroad*, I, New Haven, 1913). Columbus Kamba Simango, "The African and Civilization," *Southern Workman* (Hampton, Va., 1917), 552–5. Jeannie Somtuuzi, "African Contributions to Civilization," address at 34th annual meeting of the Negro National Baptist Convention, Sept. 1914 (in B.T.W. Papers, Container 12, L–N). Simbini Mamba Nkomo, *The Tribal Life of the People of South Africa* (Oration delivered at College Commencement, Greenville, Ill., June, 1917) in Howard University Library. Abraham Le Fleux, "who came to London to get justice for land out of which his people had been cheated" (letters sent by Alice Werner to Carter G. Woodson, C.G.W. Papers, Boxes 4 and 5); etc. It will be noticed that this very brief selection includes one African (P. K. I. Seme) who went to a non-Negro university. In general, such students often had deficiencies in their education made up at Negro American schools and colleges before proceeding to white institutions. A present-day example is Dr. Hastings K. Banda, who attended the Negro Wilberforce Academy at Wilberforce, Ohio, in 1928, before he went to Indiana and Chicago Universities.

Rebellion[37] and flamed up again in the 1920s, not only because of Garveyism but also because of the 1921 "Bulhoek Massacre" episode, for Enoch Mgijima, the leading figure in the affair, was known to have been in communion once with the primitive communistic Negro American Church of God and Saints of Christ.[38] If John Buchan's 1910 *Prester John* is the classical literary expression of this fear, Senator George Heaton Nicholl's hysterical novel *Bayete!* of 1923 shows it in its most frenzied form. It was a fear which manifested itself in British Central Africa from 1902, when two Negro American missionaries *en route* for Nyasaland were detained at Chinde for nine days,[39] until at least a decade after the 1915 Chilembwe Rising.[40]

If it was in South Africa and Nyasaland that the fear of Negroes from America disturbed most European Governments, other parts of Africa were affected by it. In the Congo, the Belgians, as early as 1878,[41] had shown interest in Negro Americans because of their long experience with the white man's methods of work. But by the 1890s,[42] although they were still interested, a critical attitude was developing amongst the Negro American intelligentsia towards the Leopold régime which was not calculated to ensure a warm welcome for the coloured American in the future by the Congo authorities. George Washington Williams, whose *History of the Negro Race* was one of the first historical studies by a Negro American writer to quicken the imagination of African nationalists,[43] played a small part in gaining American support for the Congo Free State; but in 1890, after a journalistic visit to the Congo, he became increasingly critical of conditions there.[44] Similarly, by the 1890s, the Negro American Presbyterian missionary, William Henry Sheppard, had begun his outspoken criticisms of the Belgian Congo régime which were to bring upon him a libel charge and eight months'

[37] Cf. C. S. Smith (A.M.E. Church Bishop in South Africa, 1904–6), *The Relations of the British Government to the Natives of South Africa* (Washington, D.C., 1906), 12–13; *Southern Workman*, 1906, 664–5.

[38] *Reports . . . relative to 'Israelites' at Bulhoek and Occurences in May, 1921* (Cape Town, 1921), 1; Elmer T. Clark, *The Small Sects in America* (Nashville, 1949), 151–3.

[39] *Review and Herald* (Seventh-day Adventist, Washington, D.C.), 18 Nov. 1902, 17: cf. George Shepperson, "The Literature of British Central Africa," *Rhodes-Livingstone Journal* (Manchester, 1958), xxiii, 42.

[40] Shepperson and Price, op. cit., 390–1.

[41] H. S. Sanford Papers in process at Tennessee State Archives, Nashville: H. M. Stanley to Sanford, Rotterdam, 20 Dec. 1878. See also Leo T. Molloy, *Henry Shelton Sanford* (Derby, Conn., private print), 27.

[42] Sanford Papers: Senator J. T. Morgan to Sanford, 19 ? 1890.

[43] Frederick Alexander Durham, *The Lone Star of Liberia* (London, 1892), xii.

[44] Paul McStallworth, *The United States and the Congo Question, 1884–1914* (Ph.D., Ohio State University, 1954), 196 et seq.; John Hope Franklin, "George Washington Williams, Historian," *Journal of Negro History* (Washington, D.C., 1946), xxxi, 1, 89–90.

imprisonment in 1908.[45] Beginning with Williams and Sheppard, an image of the Belgian Congo as the quintessence of European exploitation of Africa was created amongst Negro Americans which played no small part in shaping their attitude to Africa.[46] On the West Coast, the "Back-to-Africa" movement of "Chief Alfred Sam" and the Akim Trading Company seems to have had the effect, by 1914, of getting the Gold Coast to tighten up its immigration regulations in order to keep "undesirable" Negro Americans out of its area.[47] Altogether, by the mid-1920s, the problem of Negroes from the United States in Africa had become so serious that the 1926 International Conference on the Christian Mission in Africa addressed itself specially to the question.[48]

By the 1920s, the ideological influence on emerging African nationalism of the writings and political activities of such militant Negro Americans as W. E. B. Du Bois and Carter G. Woodson was making itself felt. Du Bois's role as a pioneer of Pan-Africanism through the Pan-African Conferences which he initiated or encouraged in 1919 (Paris), 1921 (London), 1923 (London and Lisbon), 1927 (New York) and 1945 (Manchester), to which Kwame Nkrumah paid tribute in his speech at the opening session of the 1958 All-African People's Conference at Accra, is relatively well known.[49] What is not so well known, however, is that the first so-called Pan-African Conference was held in London in 1900.[50] Although Du Bois was present at this Conference

[45] Ruth M. Slade, *English-Speaking Missions in the Congo Independent State, 1878–1908* (Brussels, 1959), 104–6, 254–6, 368–70; *Southern Workman* (1910), 8–12; *Africa in the World Democracy. . . . N.A.A.C.P. . . . 6 January 1919* (New York, 1919), 25–6.

[46] Samuel Barrett, *A Plea for Unity among American Negroes and the Negroes of the World* (Waterloo, Iowa, 1926), 65, copy in Howard University Library; Horace R. Cayton and St. Clair Drake, *Black Metropolis* (London, 1946), 720.

[47] Arna Bontemps and Jack Conroy, *They Seek a City* (New York, 1945), 171; Sydney H. French, "Chief Sam and His 'Back-to-Africa' Movement," W.P.A. paper, Schomburg Collection, N.Y.; *Sierra Leone Weekly News*, 23 Jan. 1915, 6–7, 9, 12; Rhodes House Library, Press Cuttings, 1914–15, "Back to Africa," Anti-Slavery Society Papers; *African Times and Orient Review*, 7 July 1914, 380, "Accra Native" letter.

[48] Milton Stauffer, *Thinking With Africa* (New York, 1927), 154–6. See also "The Contribution of the American Negro to Africa," *Christian Action in Africa, Report of the Church Conference on African Affairs held at Otterbein College, Westerville, Ohio, June 19–25, 1942* (New York, 1942), 140–1.

[49] See, for example, Padmore, op. cit. 89–170; Thomas Hodgkin, *Nationalism in Colonial Africa* (London, 1956), 21, 23–4, 161, 175, 181–2, 184, 188; Ch. du Bus de Warnaffe, "Le mouvement pan-nègre aux Etats-Unis et ailleurs," *Congo* (Brussels), May 1922.

[50] W. E. B. Du Bois, *The World and Africa* (New York, 1947), 7; George Padmore, *Pan-Africanism or Communism?* (London, 1956), 117–18. The fullest account is Alexander Walters, *My Life and Work* (New York, 1917), ch. xx. I am indebted to Mr. Harold Isaacs of the Centre for International Studies, Boston, for drawing my attention to Bishop Walters. See also *The Times* (London, 1900), 24 July, 7, 25 July, 15, 26 July, 11.

and became chairman of its "Committee on Address to the Nations of the World," it was started by H. Sylvester Williams, a West Indian barrister, and a moving spirit was Bishop Alexander Walters of the African Methodist Episcopal Zion Church, a neglected figure of Negro American history and a believer in the inevitability of a "Negro Cecil Rhodes."[51] The Conference sent a memorial to Queen Victoria protesting against the treatment of Africans in South Africa and Rhodesia and succeeded in eliciting from Joseph Chamberlain a pledge that "Her Majesty's Government will not overlook the interests and welfare of the native races."[52]

It was at the 1900 Pan-African Conference, in a memorial which he drafted to be sent "to the sovereigns in whose realms are subjects of African descent," that Du Bois first made the statement that "The problem of the Twentieth Century is the color line"—those famous words which, three years later, headed his influential book, *The Souls of Black Folk*.[53] It is important to remember that this often-quoted slogan started not in the opening paragraph to his first notable book but at the time of Du Bois's introduction to Pan-Africanism.

Until 1914, Pan-Africanism, if not forgotten,[54] was dormant amongst Negro Americans, probably because the increase of colour problems in the United States temporarily narrowed their horizons. The outbreak of the first World War, however, flung these horizons wide open again. In 1915, Du Bois published his important article "The African Roots of the War" in *The Atlantic Monthly*. Although he had not yet become converted to Marxism, Du Bois demonstrated in this article how close he was to its tenets. "The African Roots of the War" anticipates Lenin's thesis on the colonial origins of the War in his *Imperialism* and even uses the term "aristocracy of labor"[55] which is often considered to be Lenin's invention. Such writings stimulated a new interest in Africa amongst the members of the National Association for the Advancement of Colored People. As the editorials of James Weldon Johnson in the Harlem *New York Age* indicated,[56] the Negro in the United States felt that the 1914–18 War was crucial in his own struggle for greater civil rights. Africa and America joined hands. When James Weldon Johnson in a 1919 N.A.A.C.P. pamphlet, *Africa in the World Democracy*, con-

[51] B.T.W. Papers: Box 917, 1912 Conference, prospectus of Conference for Walters' paper.
[52] Walters, *Life*, op. cit., 257.
[53] In first paragraph of "Forethought" in 1903 ed.: vii in New York, 1953, reprint.
[54] J.E.B. Papers: ALS. Ms. 235, 1492, letter of 25 March 1907, "the Pan-African League Department of the Niagara Movement." Cf. Casely Hayford, op. cit., 179.
[55] *Atlantic Monthly*, May 1915, 711.
[56] James Weldon Johnson Collection, Yale University, Scrapbook X, see especially clippings for 7 Dec. 1918, and 11 Jan. and 8 Feb. 1919.

tributed an essay on "Africa at the Peace Table" and declared that "Self-determination will be secured only by those who are in a position to force it,"[57] he was speaking not only to the African in Africa but also—and perhaps primarily—to the Negro in America.

The association of these two motives was seen after the War when the N.A.A.C.P. sent Du Bois to Europe to collect material for a history of the Negro's part in the War and to call, if possible, a Pan-African Congress.[58] Out of this visit came Du Bois's ambitious plan, which the N.A.A.C.P. backed, for the internationalization of a great belt of Central African territory which would, in some measure, it was hoped, make up for the mistakes of the Scramble for Africa.[59]

Du Bois and James Weldon Johnson were not alone in their eloquence on the significance of the first World War for Africans. The Negro scholar, Benjamin Brawley, in his 1918 *Africa and the War* claimed that: "The great war of our day is to determine the future of the Negro in the World. Alsace-Lorraine, Belgium, the Balkans, and even Russia all become second in importance."[60] L. G. Jordan, Foreign Mission Secretary of the Negro American National Baptist Convention and mentor of John Chilembwe, leader of the Nyasaland Native Rising of 1915, rose to even more bitter heights of eloquence:

With 600,000 Africans fighting in the trenches with the allies and an equal number in arms in various parts of Africa under governments who have taken over the continent, it can never be hoped to again make the African a docile creature, to be dumb driven like a brute, which his oppressors have been 100 years or more in the making.[61]

How much such sentiments exercised a direct influence on Africans is a matter for speculation, though it should be remembered that coloured American soldiers, through their contacts with French troops in Europe, may have helped to disseminate them.[62] Similarly, in the present state of research, one can only speculate on the influence of the 1919 and 1921 Pan-African Congresses at which Du Bois and his Negro American colleagues associated with Blaise Diagne, the French Senegalese deputy, on the emergence of the Mandates System. Du Bois himself has claimed that:

[57] Op. cit., 15.
[58] Francis L. Broderick, *W. E. B. Du Bois* (Stanford, 1959), 129.
[59] Cf. Kelly Miller, "The German Colonies," *Southern Workman* (1919), 52–3.
[60] (New York, 1918), preface, p. i.
[61] Lewis Garnett Jordan, *Pebbles from an African Beach* (Philadelphia, 1918), 2.
[62] The problem of Negro American relations with French Africans is almost completely unstudied.

The Congress specifically asked that the German colonies be turned over to an international organization instead of being handled by the various colonial powers. Out of this idea came the Mandates Commission.[63]

No speculation, however, is necessary about the influence on emerging African nationalism of the cultural, as distinct from the organizational side of Pan-Africanism: pan-Africanism with a small rather than a large "p". Blyden, of course, was the pioneer of the Negro history movement: the search for roots, often romanticized, but a search which, without doubt, has brought to the surface important elements in the Negro and African past which the white investigator may easily overlook. Du Bois, like Blyden, realized that such a movement was necessary to bolster both Negro American and emergent African nationalist self-esteem. To this end, he produced in 1915 his little Home University volume, *The Negro*, the first of many books of its kind. Yet, as Rayford W. Logan, Du Bois's associate in the early post-1919 Pan-African movement has pointed out,[64] the popularization of the study of the African past probably owes more to one of the moving spirits of the Association for the Study of Negro History and the founder of the *Journal of Negro History*, Carter G. Woodson, than to W. E. B. Du Bois. Woodson's papers in the Library of Congress reveal an intense interest amongst early African nationalists in his work.[65] Aggrey of Achimota, for example, spoke enthusiastically of the importance of Woodson's efforts.[66]

But, if Woodson's contributions to that essential part of any nationalist movement, the myth—in the widest sense—of its past, are as great or greater than Du Bois's own immense efforts, one other name, hitherto grossly neglected by almost all writers on Negro history, must be mentioned: John Edward Bruce (1856–1924),[67] a New York Negro

[63] Du Bois, *World and Africa*, op. cit., 11. Cf. also Padmore, op. cit., 122–4; Rayford W. Logan, *The African Mandates in World Politics* (Washington, D.C., 1948), iv, 42; *League of Nations, Mandates, Second Pan-African Congress, August–September 1921;* George Louis Beer, *African Questions at the Paris Peace Conference* (New York, 1923), 285–6.

[64] Rayford W. Logan, "The American Negro's View of Africa," *Africa Seen by American Negroes,* ed. John A. Davis (American Society of African Culture, New York, 1958), 220.

[65] E.g. C.G.W. Papers: Box 5—from Amanzimtoti Institute, Natal, 13 March 1917; Box 6—from Kodwo Nsaaku, Gold Coast, 29 April and 21 July 1923, from Casely Hayford, 15 June 1916, and 11 Nov. 1917, from D. E. Carney, Sierra Leone, 19 Jan. 1921, from W. Esuman-Awira Sekyi, Gold Coast, 14 Oct. 1920, from Dada Adeshigbin, Lagos, 10 Jan. 1917, from Majola Agbebi, Lagos, 5 July 1916; Box 16—from Casely Hayford, 7 July 1923, and 4 Jan. 1924, from Dada Adeshigbin, 25 Sept. 1918; etc.

[66] C.G.W. Papers: Box 6—from Aggrey, 13 July 1927.

[67] There is a biographical sketch in J.E.B. Papers; see also Ferris, op. cit., 11, 862–3.

journalist who formed with Arthur Schomburg in 1911 the Negro
Society for Historical Research, which included amongst its original
honorary presidents, vice-presidents and members, Lewanika of Barotse-
land, Blyden, Casely Hayford, and Duse Mohammed Effendi,[68] who became later one of the leading ideologists of the Garvey movement, to
which Bruce himself subsequently gave his allegiance. Blyden, Hayford,
Dube[69] and numerous other Africans who visited America or who wrote
to Bruce, bear witness to his influence on their thought about the African past and their desire to gain from it a pride in their blackness.
Bruce's own pride in his colour was shown when he acted as American
agent for Casely Hayford's *Ethiopia Unbound*.[70] To Aggrey, Bruce was
"Daddy."[71] Furthermore, he maintained close relations with Majola
Agbebi,[72] Baptist Yoruba founder of what has been called "the first independent Native African church in West Africa,"[73] who was introduced
to Bruce by Blyden during a visit to America in 1903.[74] The importance
in the development of West African nationalism of Agbebi's inaugural
sermon to the "African Church" in Lagos on 21 December 1902, has
yet to be appreciated. Blyden believed that it showed that "Africa is
struggling for a separate personality."[75] Bruce responded enthusiastically, too, and asked Agebebi's permission to publish it in a Negro
American newspaper in a letter which shows that the African's address

[68] Ferris, op. cit., 11, 865. Cf. also C.G.W. Papers: Box 16—Bruce on Duse
Mohammed, 25 Jan. 1922.

[69] Blyden, Hayford, Dube items are well indexed in J.E.B. Papers, Schomburg
Collection, N.Y.: one interesting item in the Papers is a letter from James Cluny,
Sierra Leone, to Blyden, 21 June 1909, defending clithorodechtomy on "nationalist"
lines.

[70] Casely Hayford, *William Waddy Harris* (London, 1915), xi–xii.

[71] J.E.B. Papers: Aggrey to Bruce, 28 June 1922.

[72] There is a brief reference to Agbebi's paper, "The West African Problem" at
the London, 1911, First Universal Races Congress (in G. Spiller (ed.), *Papers on
Inter-Racial Problems,* London, 1911, 341–8) in Coleman, op. cit., 187. Agbebi remains, however, a neglected pioneer of Nigerian nationalism. In addition to the
references below, see Ferris, op. cit., 11, 822, 848; *Southern Workman*, 1896, 15; *An
Account of Dr. Majola Agbebi's Work in West Africa* (n.d.), copy in Howard University Library; *African Times and Orient Review* (London), Sept. 1912, 92, March
1914, 64; Majola Agbebi, *The Christian Handbook, New Calabar, West Africa*
(n.d.), copy in Schomburg Collection, N.Y.; letters by and about M. Agbebi and his
family in J.E.B. Papers, Schomburg Collection, N.Y. There is a photograph of Agbebi
in Lewis G. Jordan, *Negro Baptist History, U.S.A.* (Nashville, Tenn., 1930).

[73] *African Times (London)*, 5 July 1899, quoted in *Account of Dr. Agbebi's
Work,* op. cit.

[74] *Christian* (London), 27 Aug. 1903, quoted in *Account of Dr. Agbebi's Work,*
op. cit.

[75] Majola Agbebi, *Inaugural Sermon. Delivered at the Celebration of the First
Anniversary of the "African Church," Lagos, West Africa, December 21, 1902* (copy
in Schomburg Collection, N.Y.), 17.

had drawn out of him the full sentiment of *négritude:* "I am a negro and all negro. I am black all over, and proud of my beautiful black skin. . . ."[76] So enthusiastic was Bruce, that in 1907 he led a group of coloured Americans in New York, who sought to get 11 October observed each year by Negro Americans as "Majola Agbebi Day,"[77] "to immortalize in him an African personality." The very use of the last two words of this phrase suggests that the Ghanaian concept of "African personality" and its corresponding idea of *négritude* have complicated origins in the commerce of ideas over many years amongst peoples of African descent on both sides of the Atlantic. An honourable place in this commerce must be found for George W. Ellis, Negro American Secretary from 1901 to 1910 of the United States Legation in Liberia, who took as the aim of his pioneer study, *Negro Culture in West Africa* (New York, 1914), in the words of Edward Blyden: "To show the world —Africans helping in the work—that the African has a culture of his own—to explain that culture and to assist him to develop it."[78]

A less militant figure than those which have been examined must now be included in a brief examination of this commerce of ideas: Booker T. Washington whose self-help, educational ideal for coloured people had profound effects on African nationalism, particularly through its influence on Aggrey of Achimota[79] and John L. Dube of the Ohlange Institute, Natal.[80] (Not all the Negro American educationalists of the self-help school, however, exercised a "reformist," Booker-T.-Washington kind of influence on their African charges, as the effects of the militantly independent Principal of the Virginia Theological Seminary and College at Lynchburg, Gregory Willis Hayes, on John Chilembwe of Nyasaland indicate.) Sir Harry Johnston, who visited the Hampton Institute and Booker T. Washington's Tuskegee Institute when gathering material for his *The Negro in the New World* (London, 1910), saw the influence of this educational ideal and claimed correctly that it would "spread 'American' influence amongst the coloured peoples of the world."[81]

Booker T. Washington's interest in Africa has been disguised by the juxtaposition of his ideas with those of W. E. B. Du Bois in so many

[76] Ibid. 27.

[77] J.E.B. Papers: A.L.S. Ms. 167 (1493); see also A.8. (1504), 27 Aug. 1907, Agbebi to Bruce.

[78] Title page.

[79] Edwin W. Smith, *Aggrey of Achimota* (London, 1929), 121.

[80] B.T.W. Papers: Box 1060, 1912 Scrapbook, cutting from *South Africa,* 16 March 1912, and *The Trailer* (West Point, Pa.), 25 April 1912.

[81] 408. See also A. Victory Murray, *The School in the Bush* (London, 1929), 291–310.

works on Negro American history.[82] The great conference on Africa which he called at Tuskegee in 1912,[83] although it followed in the line of descent of the 1895 Africa Conference at the Negro Gammon Theological Seminary, Atlanta, Georgia,[84] shows that Washington was no Negro American isolationist.[85] This is also clear from his interest in coloured American business ventures in Africa, a good example of which is the Africa Union Company,[86] a carefully organized scheme for promoting trade between Negro America and the Gold Coast that was destroyed by the 1914 War's interruption of Atlantic commerce. Casely Hayford, whose 1911 *Ethiopia Unbound* had been sceptical of Negro American interest in Africa, by 1914 was welcoming this coloured American enterprise.[87]

The failure of the Garvey movement in the 1920s[88] and the coming of the Depression forced the attention of most Negroes in the United States closely upon their own country. Yet, if there was a decline in interest in Africa, coloured American influence on emerging African nationalism did not cease. Negro American missionary activity, orthodox and unorthodox, continued to influence the African political scene.[89] Negro American schools and colleges still attracted increasing numbers of African students. As in the period before the first World War, this was one of the main ways in which Negro American ideas and methods of political organization entered Africa. This is obvious from the careers

[82] Blyden knew better: see his article, "The Negro in the United States," *African Methodist Episcopal Church Review* (Philadelphia, 1900), XVI, 330.

[83] C.G.W. Papers: Box 13, galley proof. B.T.W. Papers: Box 917, Miscellaneous Correspondence (1912), CL, Conference CZ; Box 1060, 1912 Scrapbook. *Southern Workman* (1912), 347–86. *African Times and Orient Review* (London, 1912), I, 1, 9–12. Alfred Tildsley, *The Remarkable Work of Dr. Mark Hayford* (London, 1926), 33.

[84] *Africa and the American Negro*, ed. J. W. E. Bowen (Atlanta, Ga., 1896), passim.

[85] Cf. Washington's opposition to proposed 1915 U.S. Immigration Bill on the grounds that it was likely to keep out African students: B.T.W. Papers, Container 77, 1915.

[86] B.T.W. Papers: Personal Correspondence (Container 9), 1914–15, file on Africa Union Company; cf. "Afro-Americans and the Gold Coast," *African Times and Orient Review* (London, 1914), 21 April, 99–100.

[87] Hayford, " . . . marks the beginning of a new era here in the Gold Coast": B.T.W. Papers, Personal Correspondence (Container 9), 1914–15, extract in letter of Charles W. Chapelle to J. L. Jones, 15 July 1914. Hayford's attitude seems to have changed at the time of the 1912 Tuskegee Africa Conference: see his letter to the Conference in C.G.W. Papers, Box 13, press release of 17 April 1912.

[88] See Cronon, op. cit., 138–69.

[89] See Wilbur C. Harr, *The Negro as an American Protestant Missionary in Africa* (Ph.D., University of Chicago, 1945); Shepperson and Price, op. cit., passim; C. P. Groves, *The Planting of Christianity in Africa* (London, 1958), IV, 62–3, 79–80, 113–14, 128–9, 187. See also ref. 6 above.

of Kwame Nkrumah, Nnamdi Azikiwe and Hastings Kamuzu Banda. Furthermore, in South and Central Africa a glorified image of the Negro American as the liberator of Africa from European imperialism developed between the 1920s when Aggrey visited Africa with the Phelps-Stokes Commission and was seen as the spearhead of a coloured American invasion of South Africa[90] to the 1947 Madagascar Rising, when the rumour spread that Negro American troops had arrived to bring arms to the insurgents. But, amongst the emerging African middle-class, a more compelling image of Negro America has probably been that of the *Ebony* magazine variety, with its emphasis on respectable achievement.[91] What influence this may have had on African nationalism is an open question: for Du Bois, certainly, it seemed at one time to show "symptoms of following in the footsteps of western acquisitive society."[92]

No nationalism draws its strength from outside sources primarily, though a period of exile—if only in Harlem, Chicago or a Negro American college—has been a recognized mechanism for the political education of nationalist leaders at least since the 1848 revolutions in Europe. These notes make no claim that Negro Americans have themselves played a primary organizational role in African politics. But from the beginnings of Du Bois's interest in Africa and the 1900 Pan-African Conference, through the George Padmore period of African nationalism, to the 1959 London Kenya conference at which Thurgood Marshall, N.A.A.C.P. lawyer, acted as an adviser to the African delegation, they often appear to have acted at least secondary or tertiary parts. A more reliable measurement must await further research into all the avenues—unofficial as well as official, minor as well as major—of both Negro American and African history.[93]

Even in the present state of pioneering investigation into these fields, one thing is clear: Negro Americans, in a complicated Atlantic triangle of influences, have played a considerable part ideologically in the emergence of African nationalism: in conceptualization, evocation of attitudes and through the provision of the raw material of history. If, today, the new African nations may be said to be of more value to Negro America than Negro America to them, this should not be allowed to conceal the historical role of the coloured American in their emergence.

[90] E. W. Smith, op. cit., 181. See forthcoming paper, George Shepperson, "Nyasaland and the Millennium," *Comparative Studies in Society and History;* R. L. Buell, op. cit., 11, 603.

[91] Roi Ottley, *No Green Pastures* (London, 1952), 12.

[92] W. E. B. Du Bois, *In Battle for Peace* (New York, 1952), 154.

[93] Two useful guides to present-day Negro American interest in Africa are *Africa Seen by American Negroes,* op. cit., and Harold R. Isaacs, "The American Negro and Africa: Some Notes," *Phylon* (Atlanta, Ga., 1959), xx, 3, 219–33.

Nationalism in Tropical Africa

JAMES S. COLEMAN

University of California, Los Angeles

Postwar uprisings and nationalist assertions in Tropical Africa—that part of the continent south of the Sahara and north of the Union—have directed increased attention towards the nature and implications of the awakening of the African to political consciousness. Among scholars this neglected area has long been the preserve of the scientific linguist or of the social anthropologist; only recently have American sociologists, economists, and political scientists developed an active interest in its problems.[1] As a consequence, apart from certain efforts by anthropologists to popularize their findings and insights we have been obliged to rely primarily upon the somewhat contradictory accounts of colonial governments seeking to explain imperial connections, or of African nationalists determined to achieve self-government and the good life of which national self-determination has become the symbol.[2] Thus, we have been placed in the uncomfortable position of having to formulate opinions and policy and to render judgments without sufficient knowledge, or, what could be worse, on the basis of evaluations provided by participants in the nationalist struggle. There is, therefore, a very real need for independent and objective research regarding the character and probable course of African nationalist development.

I. WHAT IS AFRICAN NATIONALISM?

Not the least burdensome of our tasks is the problem of correlating or distinguishing between the generally accepted political concepts elabo-

Reprinted from *The American Political Science Review*, XLVIII (1954), with the permission of the author and the publisher. Adapted from a paper discussed at the Conference on Problems of Area Research in Contemporary Africa, held at Princeton University, October 14–16, 1953, sponsored jointly by the National Research Council and the Social Science Research Council under a grant from the Carnegie Corporation.

[1] Two notable prewar exceptions were Professor Raymond Leslie Buell and Dr. Ralph J. Bunche.

[2] As an excellent example of the application of the insights of anthropology to the problems of political development in this area, see William R. Bascom, "West and Central Africa," in *Most of the World*, ed. Ralph Linton (New York, 1949), pp. 331–405. For a historian's appraisal, see Vernon McKay, "Nationalism in British West Africa," *Foreign Policy Reports*, Vol. 24, pp. 2–11 (March 15, 1948).

rated with specific reference to developments in the Western World (i.e., state, nation, nationality, nationalism) and the conceptual tools developed by the Africanists. The latter have tended to feel that the traditional concepts and methods of the political scientist are unserviceable in the study of the political structure and life of pre-literate societies.[3] Yet notwithstanding the importance of the lineage, clan, or tribe; the role of the diviner, the chief, or the age-grade society; or the wide variations in the organization of power within such societies, the concept and the institution of the modern nation-state, towards the creation of which African nationalism tends to be directed, is distinctly Western in its form and content. It is as exotic to Africa as Professor Toynbee has suggested that it is to the rest of the non-European world.[4] Nevertheless, just as the Indian National Congress has largely created an Indian nation, so African nationalists are endeavoring to mould new nations in Africa (e.g., "Ghana," "Nigeria," and "Kamerun").

On the level of abstraction at which the political scientist is accustomed to roam, a nation is not a loose catch-all term denoting a larger grouping of tribes (e.g., Zulus, Basutos, Mende, Buganda, or Hausa); rather it is a post-tribal, post-feudal terminal *community* which has emerged from the shattering forces of disintegration that characterize modernity. This does not mean that the Hausa peoples of Northern Nigeria cannot become a nation, nor does it mean that the "national" consciousness of the ordinary Hausaman must reach the level of intensity of the average Frenchman before there is a nation. It does suggest, however, that there must be a much greater awareness of a closeness of contact with "national" compatriots as well as with the "national"

[3] *African Political Systems,* eds. M. Fortes and E. E. Evans-Pritchard (New York, 1940), pp. 4 ff. Insofar as *traditional* concepts and methods are concerned, ethnocentrism has been freely confessed by political scientists in recent self-criticism. See David Easton, *The Political System* (New York, 1953), pp. 33 ff.; also Report of the Inter-University Summer Seminar on Comparative Politics, Social Science Research Council, *The American Political Science Review,* Vol. 47, pp. 641–57, at pp. 642–43 (Sept., 1953). Amongst the modernists in political science one finds the argument that the political scientist should not be rejected too readily since he has developed skills and acquired insights that might well shed new light on the political process and pattern of government of pre-literate societies after the anthropologist has exhausted his resources. Another argument, rather different, is that such societies might profitably be regarded as microcosms in which the political scientist can discern with greater clarity the essentials of government that might be obscured in the more complex Western systems. A final argument might be found in the recent psycho-cultural studies, especially in terms of their implications for policy formulation. See Ithiel de Sola Pool, "Who Gets Power and Why," *World Politics,* Vol. 2, pp. 120–34 (Oct., 1949).

[4] Arnold Toynbee, *The World and the West* (New York, 1953), pp. 71 ff. It is difficult to accept without qualification Professor Toynbee's argument that the "national state" was a "spontaneous native growth" in Europe. One could argue that the centrally-minded, nation-building elites of emergent Asia and Africa are but the present-day counterparts of the centralizing monarchs of early modern Europe.

government.[5] This closeness of contact on the horizontal and vertical levels has been a distinctly Western phenomenon, for the obvious reason that it is the result of modern technology.

Not only is a political scientist quite precise in his use of the concept "nation," but in poaching on the insights of the Africanists he also finds it difficult to place under the cover of "nationalism" all forms of past and present discontent and organizational development in Africa. Thus, it is believed useful at the outset to distinguish the following:

A. TRADITIONALIST MOVEMENTS

1. Spontaneous movements of resistance to the initial European occupation or post-pacification revolts against the imposition of new institutions, or new forms of coercion, referred to herein as "primary resistance."

2. Nativistic, mahdistic, or messianic mass movements—usually of a magicoreligious character—which are psychological or emotional outlets for tensions produced by the confusions, frustrations, or socio-economic inequalities of alien rule, referred to herein as "nativism."[6]

B. SYNCRETISTIC MOVEMENTS

1. Separatist religious groups, which have seceded and declared their independence from white European churches either because of the desire for religious independence or because the white clerics were intolerant regarding certain African customs; hereafter referred to as "religious separatism."[7]

2. Kinship associations, organized and led by the Western-educated and urbanized "sons abroad" for the purposes of preserving a sense of identity with the kinfolk in the bush and "brothers" in the impersonal urban center, as well as of providing vehicles for pumping modernity—

[5] Royal Institute of International Affairs, *Nationalism* (London, 1939), pp. 1–7; Karl W. Deutsch, *Nationalism and Social Communication* (New York, 1953), pp. 1–14.

[6] Nativism is here used in its broad and universal sense, as defined by the late Professor Ralph Linton: "Any conscious, organized attempt on the part of a society's members to revive or perpetuate selected aspects of its culture." See his "Nativistic Movements," *American Anthropologist*, Vol. 45, pp. 230–40, at p. 230 (April–June, 1943). The concept thus includes traditionalist movements in either the European or non-European world. This point is stressed because of the understandable sensitivity of many educated Africans to the root word "native," which as a result of the colonial experience tends to carry with it the connotation of inferiority. See also A. LeGrip, "Aspects Actuels de L'Islam en A.O.F.," *L'Afrique et l'Asie*, pp. 6–20 (No. 24, 1953); Katesa Schlosser, *Propheten in Afrika* (Albert Limbach Verlag, 1949).

[7] Daniel Thwaite, *The Seething African Pot* (London, 1926), pp. 1–70; George Shepperson, "Ethiopianism and African Nationalism," *Phylon*, Vol. 14, pp. 9–18 (1st Quarter, 1953); Hilda Kuper, "The Swazi Reaction to Missions," *African Studies*, Vol. 5, pp. 177–88 (Sept., 1946), Jomo Kenyatta, *Facing Mount Kenya* (London, 1953), pp. 269–79.

including the ideas and sentiment of nationalism—into the rural areas.[8]

3. Tribal associations, organized and led by Western-educated elements—usually in collaboration with some traditionalists—who desire to resurrect, or to create for the first time, a tribal sentiment ("tribalism"), for the purpose of establishing large-scale political units, the boundaries of which will be determined by tribal affiliation (i.e., those who accept the *assumption* of common blood and kinship) and the forms of government by a syncretism of tribal and Western institutions.[9]

C. MODERNIST MOVEMENTS

1. Economic-interest groups (labor unions, cooperative societies, professional and middle-class associations) organized and led by Western-educated elements for the purpose of advancing the material welfare and improving the socioeconomic status of the members of those groups.

2. Nationalist movements, organized and led by the Westernized elite which is activated by the Western ideas of democracy, progress, the welfare state, and national self-determination, and which aspires *either:* (a) to create modern independent African nation-states possessing an internal state apparatus and external sovereignty and all of the trappings of a recognized member state of international society (e.g., Sudan, Gold Coast, Nigeria, and possibly Sierra Leone); *or* (b) to achieve absolute social and political equality and local autonomy within a broader Eur-African grouping (e.g., French and Portuguese Africa) or within what is manifestly a plural society (e.g., except for Uganda, the territories of British East and Central Africa).[10]

[8] James S. Coleman, "The Role of Tribal Associations in Nigeria," Proceedings of the Second Annual Conference of the West African Institute of Social and Economic Research, Ibadan, Nigeria, April, 1952. See also *East Africa and Rhodesia,* October 5, 1951, p. 106: "Nairobi is the happy hunting ground for the organizers of tribal associations, as there are to be found in the city representatives of practically every tribe in East and Central Africa." Also K. A. Busia, *Report on a Social Survey of Takoradi-Sekondi* (Accra, Government Printer, 1950).

[9] Most advanced amongst the Yoruba, Ibo, Ibibio, Ewe, Buganda, and Kikuyu peoples.

[10] The difference between the goal orientations of the two categories of movements is partly the result of the objectives of differing colonial policies (i.e., the British policy of self-government and differentiation versus the French, Portuguese, and in a qualified sense the Belgian policies of assimilation and identity) and in part the result of the presence or absence of a settled white population. Confronted with the overwhelming obstacles to the full realization of *African self-government,* African leaders in the second category tend towards the extreme either of accommodation (Union of South Africa) or of violence (Kenya). In the territories of the Central African Federation the leaders of the African Congress have tended not to define their ultimate objectives, preferring to act empirically. The strength and persistence of the autonomic drive is reflected, however, in their reported attraction to the original Gore-Brown partition plan adopted by the European Confederate party. See David Cole, "How Strong is the African National Congress," *New Commonwealth,* Vol. 27, pp. 5–10, at p. 9 (Jan. 4, 1954).

3. Pan-African or trans-territorial movements, organized and led by the Westernized elite, frequently in association with or under the stimulus of American Negroes or West Indians abroad, for the purposes of creating a global *racial* consciousness and unity, or of agitating for the advancement and welfare of members of the *African* race wherever they may be, or of devising plans for future nationalist activity in specific regions.[11]

Once these very arbitrary analytical distinctions are drawn it should be stressed that none of the categories can be treated in isolation. Each of the movements is in one way or another a response to the challenge of alien rule, or of the intrusion of the disintegrating forces—and consequently the insecurity—of modernity. The recent so-called nationalism in Central Africa has been a mixture of "primary resistance" by the chiefs and traditionalists of Northern Rhodesia and Nyasaland and the nationalist agitation of the Westernized elite. Until the project of Federation became an active issue, African movements in this area were confined principally to religious separatist groups, tribal associations, or, in the case of Northern Rhodesia, labor unions.[12] On the West Coast, where nationalism is far more advanced, traditionalist and syncretistic movements have not been and are not absent. In some instances, kinship associations and separatist religious groups have been the antecedents of nationalist organizations; in others they have provided the principal organizational bases of the latter (e.g., the National Council of Nigeria and the Cameroons was first inaugurated as a federation mainly of kinship associations, and the African National Congress of the Rhodesias and Nyasaland was the product of fusion of several African welfare societies). In certain cases unrest or protest of a nativistic flavor has been instigated by nationalists for their modernist ends; in others nationalists have claimed such uncoordinated uprisings, as well as purely economic protest movements, to be manifestations of "nationalism," when in reality the participants were unaware of such implications.

[11] For a variety of reasons these movements have thus far apparently accomplished little more than to dramatize their existence at infrequent *ad hoc* conferences. Until recently the initiative tended to be taken by Americans or West Indians of African descent (e.g., Marcus Garvey, W. E. B. DuBois, and George Padmore), although in the early 1920's there was a National Congress of British West Africa organized by the late Casely Hayford of the Gold Coast. Also, M. Blaise Diagne, a Senegalese, was President of the first Pan-African Congress in Paris in 1919. For recent pan-African nationalist activity in British West Africa see *West Africa*, Dec. 12, 1953, p. 1165; and for British Central Africa see Cole, *op. cit.*, p. 9.

[12] See Ian Cunnison, "The Watchtower Assembly in Central Africa," *International Review of Missions*, Vol. 40, pp. 456–69 (Oct., 1951).

One of the interesting differences between prewar and postwar nationalism on the West Coast of Africa is that in the former period nationalism tended to be—as Lord Lugard insisted—the esoteric pastime of the tiny educated minorities of Lagos, Accra, Freetown, and Dakar; whereas in the latter period these minorities—greatly expanded and dispersed in new urban centers throughout the interior—have made positive efforts to popularize and energize the nationalist crusade in two ways.[13] The first has been to preach education, welfare, progress, and the ideal of self-government among the masses, largely through the nationalist press, independent African schools, and kinship and tribal associations. The aim here has been, in the words of one of their leading prophets, Dr. Nnamdi Azikiwe of Nigeria, to bring about "mental emancipation" from a servile colonial mentality.[14] The second method has been to tap all existing nativistic and religious tensions and economic grievances among the tradition-bound masses, as well as the grievances and aspirations of the urbanized clerks and artisans, and channel the energies thus unleashed into support of the nationalist drive. The technique here has been (1) to make nationalism, and in particular its objective of self-government, an integrating symbol in which even the most disparate goals could find identification, and (2) to politicize—one would like to say nationalize—all existing thought and associations. Until recently, many observers—including colonial administrators—tended to live in the prewar climate of opinion and therefore underestimated the power which had thus been harnessed to the nationalist machine.

In the case of the Mau Mau movement in Kenya we are confronted with a complex mixture of nationalism, with a strong traditional bias on the part of the Westernized leaders, and nativism, manipulated by the leaders, on the part of the masses. Both have been generated to an especially high level of intensity as a consequence of the acute and largely unassuaged sense of frustration on the part of the Westernized elite, growing out of the very bleak outlook arising from the almost total absence, until recently, of meaningful career and prestige opportunities within either the old or the new systems, and of the masses, resulting from the land shortage and the overcrowding on the reservations. The presence of a sizable Asian "third force," which virtually monopolizes the middle-class sector, and which has been and is politically conscious, provides a new variable of no little significance in the total situation. The fact that the pattern of organization and the strat-

[13] Sir F. D. Lugard, *The Dual Mandate in British Tropical Africa* (London, 1923), pp. 83 ff.
[14] *Renascent Africa* (Lagos, 1937).

egy and tactics of the Mau Mau revolt indicate a higher level of sophistication than sheer nativism would imply suggests that our analytical categories need further refinement or qualification.

A particularly striking feature of African nationalism has been the literary and cultural revival which has attended it. A renewed appreciation of and interest in "African" culture has been manifested, in most instances by the most sophisticated and acculturated Africans (e.g., Mazi Mbonu Ojike's *My Africa,* Dr. J. B. Danquah's studies of the Akan peoples of the Gold Coast, Jomo Kenyatta's *Facing Mount Kenya,* Fily-Dabo Sissoko's *Les Noirs et la Culture,* Léopold Sédar Senghor's *Anthologie de la Nouvelle Poésie Nège et Malgache,* the French African journal *Présence Africaine* edited by M. Alioune Diop, and the writings of Antoine Munongo in the Belgian Congolese journal *Jeune Afrique).*[15] In some cases this cultural renaissance has had a purely tribal emphasis; in others it has taken a "neo-African" form, such as the African dress of Dr. Nnamdi Azikiwe, nationalist leader in Nigeria. It has usually been accompanied by a quest for an African history which would in general reflect glory and dignity upon the African race and in particular instill self-confidence in the Western-educated African sensitive to the prejudiced charge that he has no history or culture. In short, there has emerged a new pride in being African. In French areas, the accent until recently has been upon French culture and literature, but there are increasing signs of a shift to African themes amongst the French African literati. The important point is that African nationalism has this cultural content, which renders more difficult any effort to separate rigidly the cultural nationalism of the urban politician from the nativism of the bush peasant.

Yet the differences are important to the student of African nationalism. Primary resistance and nativism tend to be negative and spontaneous revolts or assertions of the unacculturated masses against the disruptive and disorganizing stranger-invader. They are a reflection of a persistent desire of the masses to preserve or recreate the old by protesting against the new. Syncretism is different in that it contains an element of rationality—an urge to recapture those aspects of the old

[15] See Rosey E. Pool, "African Renaissance," *Phylon,* Vol. 14, pp. 5–8 (First Quarter, 1953); Albert Maurice, "Union Africaine des Arts et des Lettres," *African Affairs,* Vol. 50, pp. 233–41 (July, 1951); Alioune Diop, "Niam n'goura," *Présence Africaine* (Nov.–Dec., 1947), pp. 1–3. The cultural revival is the product of four forces: (1) reflection and introspection on the part of educated Africans, frequently those confronted with the stimulating contrasts of a foreign environment while abroad; (2) the American Negro renaissance which commenced in the 1920's; (3) encouragement and sponsorship of European governments and unofficial organizations such as the International African Institute; and (4) support of missionary societies such as the United Society for Christian Literature in the United Kingdom.

which are compatible with the new, which it recognizes as inevitable and in some respects desirable. Whereas all forms of protest are politically consequential—at least to colonial administrators—only nationalism is primarily political in that it is irrevocably committed to a positive and radical alteration of the power structure. In brief, nationalism is the terminal form of colonial protest.

Another reason for distinguishing between the various categories of assertion, which are basically differences in goal orientation, is not only to provide some basis for judging the nature of the popular support of a nationalist movement during its buildup, but also to have some means of predicting the stability and viability of the political order established by the nationalists once they achieve self-government. The governments of Pakistan, Burma, India, and Indonesia have each been plagued by internal tensions arising from what are fundamentally South Asian variants of traditionalism and tribalism. If a colonial nationalist movement comes to power atop a wave of mass protest which is primarily or even in part nativistic in character, this would have a direct bearing upon the capacity of the Westernized leaders of that movement, not only to maintain political unity and stability but also to carry out what is at the core of most of their programs—rapid modernization by a centralized bureaucratic machine. Any thorough study of the anatomy of a nationalist movement, therefore, must seek to determine the linkages and compatibilities between the goal orientations of the several forces from which that movement derives its élan and strength.

II. FACTORS CONTRIBUTING TO THE RISE OF NATIONALISM

It is far easier to define and describe nationalism than it is to generalize about the factors which have contributed to its manifestation. Put most briefly, it is the end product of the profound and complex transformation which has occurred in Africa since the European intrusion. It is a commonplace that the imposition of Western technology, socio-political institutions, and ideology upon African societies has been violently disruptive of the old familistic order in that they have created new values and symbols, new techniques for the acquisition of wealth, status, and prestige, and new groups for which the old system had no place. The crucial point here is not that nationalism as a matter of fact happened to appear at a certain point in time after the "Western impact," but rather that the transformation the latter brought about has been an indispensable precondition for the rise of nationalism. Nationalism, as distinguished from primary resistance or nativism, requires considerable gestation. A few of the constituent elements have been:

A. ECONOMIC[16]

1. Change from a subsistence to a money economy. This change, consciously encouraged by colonial governments and European enterprise in order to increase the export of primary products, introduced the cash nexus and economic individualism, altered the patterns of land tenure and capital accumulation, and, in general, widened the area of both individual prosperity and insecurity.

2. Growth of a wage-labor force. This development has resulted in the proletarianization of substantial numbers of Africans, which has weakened communal or lineage responsibility and rendered those concerned vulnerable to economic exploitation and grievances.

3. Rise of a new middle class. Laissez-faire economics and African enterprise, coupled with opportunities for university and professional education, have been factors contributing to the growth of a middle class. This class is most advanced in Senegal, the Gold Coast, and Southern Nigeria, where it has developed despite successive displacement or frustration by the intrusion of Levantines and the monopolistic practices of European firms.

B. SOCIOLOGICAL[17]

1. Urbanization. The concentration of relatively large numbers of Africans in urban centers to meet the labor demands of European enterprise has loosened kinship ties, accelerated social communication between "detribalized" ethnic groups, and, in general, contributed to "national" integration.

2. Social mobility. The European-imposed *pax* coupled with the development of communications and transport has provided the framework for travel, the growth of an internal exchange economy, and socio-political reintegration.

3. Western education. This has provided certain of the inhabitants of a given territory with a common lingua franca; with the knowledge and tools to acquire status and prestige and to fulfill aspirations within the new social structure; and with some of the ideas and values

[16] L. P. Mair, "The Growth of Economic Individualism in African Society," *Journal of the Royal African Society,* Vol. 33, pp. 261–73 (July, 1934); Allan McPhee, *The Economic Revolution in British West Africa* (London, 1926); G. Wilson, *An Essay on the Economics of Detribalization in Northern Rhodesia,* Part I (Rhodes-Livingstone Institute, 1941). Cf. Karl Polanyi, *Origins of Our Time* (London, 1946); P. C. Lloyd, "New Economic Classes in Western Nigeria," *African Affairs,* Vol. 52, pp. 327–34 (Oct., 1953).

[17] J. D. Rheinallt Jones, "The Effects of Urbanization in South and Central Africa," *African Affairs,* Vol. 52, pp. 37–44 (Jan., 1953).

by which alien rule and colonialism could be attacked. It has been through Western education that the African has encountered the scientific method and the idea of progress with their activistic implications, namely, an awareness of alternatives and the conviction that man can creatively master and shape his own destiny.

C. RELIGIOUS AND PSYCHOLOGICAL[18]

1. Christian evangelization. The conscious Europeanization pursued by Christian missionary societies has been a frontal assault upon traditional religious systems and moral sanctions. Moreover, the Christian doctrine of equality and human brotherhood challenged the ethical assumptions of imperialism.

2. Neglect or frustration of Western-educated elements. Susceptibility to psychological grievance is most acute among the more acculturated Africans. Social and economic discrimination and the stigma of inferiority and backwardness have precipitated a passionate quest for equality and modernity, and latterly self-government. Rankling memories of crude, arrogant, or insulting treatment by a European have frequently been the major wellspring of racial bitterness and uncompromising nationalism.

D. POLITICAL

1. Eclipse of traditional authorities. Notwithstanding the British policy of indirect rule, the European superstructure and forces of modernity have tended to weaken the traditional powers of indigenous authorities and thereby to render less meaningful pre-colonial sociopolitical units as objects of loyalty and attachment. There has been what Professor Daryll Forde calls a "status reversal"; that is, as a result of the acquisition by youth of Western education and a command over Western techniques in all fields, there has been ". . . an increasing transfer of command over wealth and authority to younger and socially more independent men at the expense of traditional heads. . . ."[19]

2. Forging of new "national" symbols. The "territorialization" of Africa by the European powers has been a step in the creation of new nations, not only through the erection of boundaries within which the intensity of social communication and economic interchange has become greater than across territorial borders, but also as a consequence of the imposition of a common administrative superstructure, a common legal

[18] William Bascom, "African Culture and the Missionary," *Civilisations,* Vol. 3, pp. 491–501 (No. 4, 1953).
[19] Daryll Forde, "The Conditions of Social Development in West Africa," *Civilisations,* Vol. 3, pp. 471–85 (No. 4, 1953).

system, and in some instances common political institutions which have become symbols of territorial individuality.[20]

These are a few of the principal factors in the European presence which have contributed to the rise of nationalism. As any casual observer of African developments is aware, however, there have been and are marked areal differences in the overt manifestation of nationalism. Such striking contrasts as the militant Convention People's party of the Gold Coast, the conservative Northern People's Congress of Nigeria, the pro-French orientation of the African editors of *Présence Africaine,* the cautious African editors of *La voix du Congolais,* and the terroristic Mau Mau of Kenya are cases in point.

There are a number of explanations for these areal variations. One relates to the degree of acculturation in an area. This is a reflection of the duration and intensity of contact with European influences. The contrast between the advanced nationalism of the British West Coast and of Senegal and the nascent nationalism of British and French Central Africa is partly explicable on this basis.

A second explanation lies in the absence or presence of alien settlers. On this score the settler-free British West Coast is unique when contrasted to the rest of Africa. The possibility of a total fulfillment of nationalist objectives (i.e., *African* self-government) has been a powerful psychological factor which partly explains the confident and buoyant expectancy of West Coast nationalists. On the other hand, as previously noted, the tendencies toward accommodation or terrorism in the white-settler areas is a reflection of the absence of such moderating expectancy.

Certain African groups exposed to the same forces of acculturation and the same provocation have demonstrated radically different reactions. The Kikuyu versus the Masai peoples of Kenya, the Ibo versus the Hausa peoples of Nigeria, and the Creole and Mende of Sierra Leone are cases in point. It is suggested that the dynamism, militancy, and nationalistic élan of the Ibo peoples of Nigeria are rooted partly in certain indigenous Ibo culture traits (general absence of chiefs, smallness in scale and the democratic character of indigenous political organization, emphasis upon achieved status, and individualism). Much of the same might be said for the Kikuyu peoples of Kenya.

Differing colonial policies constitute another cause of these areal differences. Nationalism is predominantly a phenomenon of British

[20] See R. J. Harrison Church, *Modern Colonization* (London, 1951), pp. 104 ff.; Robert Montagne, "The 'Modern State' in Africa and Asia," *The Cambridge Journal,* Vol. 5, pp. 583–602 (July, 1952).

Africa, and to a lesser extent of French Africa. Apart from the influence of the foregoing historical, sociological, and cultural variables, this fact, in the case of British Africa, is explained by certain unique features of British colonial policy.

It was inevitable that Britain, one of the most liberal colonial powers in Africa, should have reaped the strongest nationalist reaction. A few of the principal features of British policy which have stimulated nationalism deserve mention:

1. Self-government as the goal of policy. Unlike the French and Portuguese who embrace their African territories as indivisible units of the motherland, or the Belgians who until recently have been disinclined to specify the ultimate goals of policy, the British have remained indiscriminately loyal to the Durham formula.[21] In West Africa, this has enthroned the African nationalists; in Central and East Africa, the white settlers.

2. Emphasis upon territorial individuality. More than any other colonial power, the British have provided the institutional and conceptual framework for the emergence of nations. Decentralization of power, budgetary autonomy, the institution of territorial legislative councils and other "national" symbols—all have facilitated the conceptualization of a "nation."[22]

3. Policy on missionaries and education. The comparative freedom granted missionaries and the laissez-faire attitude toward education, and particularly post-primary education, has distinguished and continues to distinguish British policy sharply from non-British Africa.

4. Neglect, frustration, and antagonism of educated elite. Not only have more British Africans been exposed to higher education, but the

[21] Regarding Belgian policy, see Pierre Wigny, "Methods of Government in the Belgian Congo," *African Affairs*, Vol. 50, pp. 310–17 (Oct., 1951). Wigny remarks (p. 311) that ". . . Belgians are reluctant to define their colonial policy. They are proud of their first realisations, and sure of the rightness of their intentions." Since this was written, there have been some very dramatic changes in Belgian policy, especially regarding the educated elite, the potential nationalists. The great debate in Belgian colonial circles on "le statut des Congolais civilisés" was terminated by four decrees of May 17, 1952, according to which educated Congolese are assimilated to Europeans in civil law. Regarding Portuguese policy, see Marcelo Caetano, *Colonizing Traditions, Principles and Methods of the Portuguese* (Lisbon, 1951). The keynote of the policy is the "spiritual assimilation" of the Africans to a "Portuguese nation dwelling in European, African, Asiatic and Indonesian Provinces." The African *civilisado* is thus a citizen of Portugal.

[22] Partly in response to nationalist pressures, the French Government has recently initiated certain measures of financial devolution to French West Africa. See G. Gayet, "Autonomies financières Française," *Civilisations*, Vol. 3, pp. 343–47 (No. 3, 1953). These measures may enhance the powers of the territorial assemblies to the point that the latter might ultimately become the foci for territorial nationalisms.

British government until recently remained relatively indifferent to the claims and aspirations of this class, which forms the core of the nationalist movements.

5. *Freedom of nationalist activity.* The *comparative* freedom of activity (speech, association, press, and travel abroad) which British Africans have enjoyed—within clearly defined limits and varying according to the presence of white settlers—has been of decisive importance. It is doubtful whether such militant nationalists as Wallace-Johnson of Sierra Leone, Prime Minister Kwame Nkrumah of the Gold Coast, Dr. Nnamdi Azikiwe of Nigeria, Jomo Kenyatta of Kenya, and Dauti Yamba of the Central African Federation, could have found the same continuous freedom of movement and activity in Belgian, Portuguese, and French Africa as has been their lot in British Africa.[23]

All of this suggests that African nationalism is not merely a peasant revolt. In fact, as already noted, nationalism where it is most advanced has been sparked and led by the so-called detribalized, Western-educated, middle-class intellectuals and professional Africans; by those who in terms of improved status and material standards of living have benefitted most from colonialism; in short, by those who have come closest to the Western World but have been denied entry on full terms of equality. From this comparatively affluent—but psychologically aggrieved—group have come the organizers of tribal associations, labor unions, cooperative groups, farmers' organizations, and—more recently—nationalist movements. They are the Africans whom British policy has done most to create and least to satiate.[24]

This brief and selective treatment of a few of the factors which have contributed to the African nationalist awakening suggests certain avenues which might be profitably explored and more fully developed by subsequent research. Specifically, what is the relationship between the nature and intensity of nationalism and the degree of urbanization, the degree of commercialization of agriculture, and the size and geographical distribution of the wage-labor force and salariat? In short,

[23] The stringent police measures adopted recently in Kenya and Nyasaland, the special press laws which have long been in effect in British East and Central Africa, and the obstacles to nationalist activity which have existed in the Muslim areas of Northern Nigeria, do not necessarily invalidate this *comparative* historical generalization.

[24] The thesis here is that there are at least four ingredients in the psychology of colonial nationalism, and that British policy in Africa has come closest towards inculcating or providing them: (a) an awareness of the existence or possibility of alternatives to the status quo, a state of mind produced by Western education and particularly by study and travel abroad; (b) an intense desire to change the status quo; (c) a system within which the major alternative to the status quo—self-government—has the status of legitimacy; and (d) an area of relative freedom in which that legitimate alternative may be pursued.

what is the causal connection between "detribalization" and nationalism? Certain aspects of such an inquiry could be subjected to statistical analysis, but the results could only be suggestive, and in some instances might be positively deceptive. In the case of urbanization, for example, the highly urbanized and acculturated Yoruba peoples of Nigeria for nearly a decade lagged far behind the Ibo peoples in nationalist vigor and élan. Ibadan, the largest urban center in tropical Africa, has been until recently one of the most politically inert towns of Nigeria. Again, in terms of the proletarianization of labor and urbanization resulting from European industrialism and commercial activity, the Belgian Congo is one of the most advanced territories, but one in which nationalism is least in evidence.[25] Freetown, Sierra Leone, one of the oldest non-traditional urban centers, became a haven of respectability and conservatism, being eclipsed by the less-developed Protectorate in the push towards nationalist objectives. Urbanization has been an important ingredient in the nationalist awakening, but it has been a certain type of urban development—mainly the impersonal and heterogeneous "new towns"—which has occurred in conjunction with other equally decisive factors.

In the case of the relationship between the degree of commercialization of land and labor and the degree of nationalism, the figures set forth for the Gold Coast in Table I suggest either a causal connection

TABLE I

COMMERCIALIZATION AND NATIONALISM IN CERTAIN AFRICAN TERRITORIES

Territory	Percentage of Cultivated Land Used by Africans for Commercial Production (1947–1950)*	African Wage Earners as Percentage of Total African Population (1950)†	Degree of Overt Nationalism
Gold Coast	75%	9.0%	Advanced
Belgian Congo	42	7.6	None
Nigeria	41	1.2	Advanced
Uganda	33	3.9	Nascent
Kenya	7	7.6	Nascent

* E. A. Keukjian, "Commercializing Influence of the Development of Exports on Indigenous Agricultural Economics in Tropical Africa," unpub. diss. (Harvard Univ., June, 1953); United Nations, Economic and Social Council (15th session). *World Economic Situation. Aspects of Economic Development in Africa.* New York, Document E/2377, March 20, 1953.

† United Nations, Department of Economic Affairs. *Review of Economic Conditions in Africa (Supplement to World Economic Report, 1949–50).* New York, Document E/1910/Add. 1 Rev. 1-ST/ECA/9/Add. 1, April, 1951, p. 76.

[25] The Belgian policy of stabilization of labor in the urban centers of the Congo, in which 83% of the men have their families with them, is one of the several factors which may help to explain this.

or a parallel development. Yet in turning to similar figures for other territories—especially the Belgian Congo and Nigeria—it is clear that the relationship between commercialization and nationalism, important though it may be, must be considered and interpreted in the light of other variables.

Again, the fact that the nationalist movements have been organized and led by intellectuals and the so-called middle class suggests a relationship between nationalism and the number of Africans with higher education, the size of per capita income, the degree of the individualization of land tenure, the size of middle-class and professional groups (i.e., independent traders, produce middlemen, farmers employing labor, druggists, lorry owners, lawyers, doctors, etc.), and the degree of vertical mobility within the emergent socio-economic structure. In any event, the insights of an economist are indispensable for a complete anatomy of African nationalism.

The Christian missionaries have been blamed frequently for their ruthless assault upon native religious systems and the thoroughgoing Europeanization, conscious or implicit, in their evangelization. This has suggested the formula: missionaries=detribalization=nationalism. Yet the postwar figures shown in Table II do not bear out this assumption.[26]

TABLE II
CHRISTIANITY AND NATIONALISM IN CERTAIN AFRICAN TERRITORIES

Territory	Percentage of Christians to Total Population	Percentage of Protestants to All Christians	Percentage of Catholics to All Christians	Degree of Overt Nationalism
Belgian Congo	37%	29%	71%	None
Nyasaland	26	49	51	Nascent
Gold Coast	15	58	42	Advanced
Angola	15	22	78	None
Kenya	10	51	49	Nascent
Nigeria	5	67	33	Advanced

Missionaries have been important catalytic agents in the transformation of African societies, but the causal connection between their activities and nationalist assertion cannot be established by mere quantitative analysis. The figures in Table II hint at a possible causal relationship between preponderant Protestant evangelization and advanced nationalism (viz., Gold Coast and Nigeria) and preponderant Catholic evangelization and the absence of nationalism (viz., Portuguese Angola and

[26] *World Christian Handbook* (London, 1949).

the Belgian Congo). Yet this connection must be examined in the light of other relevant factors, such as the degree of control and direction extended to missionary societies by colonial governments; the freedom allowed such societies to establish schools—particularly secondary schools —and to determine the curriculum; the tolerance accorded anti-white or anti-colonial sects (e.g., the Jehovah's Witnesses are permitted in most of British Africa but proscribed in non-British Africa); the latitude allowed African sects of a syncretistic, revivalistic, or puritanical character; the extent to which evangelical bodies have *Africanized* their church organization, the priesthood, and the propagation of the gospel; and, finally, the strength of Islam.

The corrosive influence of Western education has been a significant ingredient in the rise of nationalism. Yet the Belgian Congo claims a higher percentage of literacy than any other colonial territory in Africa.[27] In order to establish a relationship we must move beyond the superficial analysis of literacy statistics and ask the following questions:

1. The nature of the curriculum. Has it been and is it literary and based upon the model of a European grammar school, or is it practical and designed to train the student to be a good farmer, artisan, or clerk in European employ, and incidentally to limit his sophistication and contact with unsettling ideas? Is instruction conducted in the vernacular or in a European language?

2. Opportunities for post-primary education. Are secondary schools (particularly those operated by missionary societies or by enterprising and nationalist-minded Africans such as Eyo Ita in Nigeria or Jomo Kenyatta in Kenya) allowed to mushroom into existence, or are they carefully planned and rigidly controlled by the colonial government as to both number and curriculum? What are the opportunities for study in universities abroad? What is the latitude granted students to determine their own careers? Here we touch upon a crucial factor— in 1945, Freetown, Sierra Leone, and Lagos, Nigeria, each had more Western-type secondary schools than all of the non-British territories in Africa combined. In 1952 over 4,000 Africans from British territories were studying in universities and technical schools abroad and nearly 1,000 in territorial universities in Africa, whereas only a handful had such opportunity or inclination in Belgian and Portuguese Africa. This is in part a reflection of the existence of a larger African middle-class in British Africa, but it is also the result of the unique British attitude regarding the relationship between higher education and emergent

[27] United Nations, *Non-Self-Governing Territories.* Vol. III: *Special Study on Education.* New York, Document ST/TRI/SER.A./5/Add. 2, January, 1951.

African leadership. French policy and practice, despite differing assumptions, most closely approximate those of the British.[28]

3. Openings of careers for the talented. The stability of any political or social order is determined by this factor. Is there any planned relationship between the output of the schools and opportunities for satisfying employment or careers? In French and Belgian Africa, colonial governments have maintained a stringent control over the supply-demand situation as between *post-primary* schools and the requirements of government and the developing economy. In British Africa there are hundreds of thousands of unemployed or under-employed "Standard VI" boys clustered in the coastal towns and urban centers of the interior.

The most potent instrument used in the propagation of nationalist ideas and racial consciousness has been the *African-owned* nationalist press. In Nigeria alone nearly 100 newspapers or periodicals have been published by Africans since the British intrusion, of which 12 dailies and 14 weeklies—all African owned—are currently in circulation. The crucial role performed in the nationalist awakening by African journalistic enterprise on the British West Coast is well known.[29] Until the publication of *Afrique Noire* (organ of the *Rassemblement Démocratique Africaine* of French West Africa) there was nothing in non-British Africa which even closely approximated this development. And even this journal is no match for the pungent criticism and racial consciousness one finds in the pages of Dr. Nnamdi Azikiwe's *West African Pilot* in Nigeria.[30] Needless to say, the nationalist press is one of our

[28] By decree of April 16, 1950, the *Institut des Hautes Études* was established at Dakar; and on January 1, 1952, there were 1,640 scholarship holders in continental France, of whom 572 were pursuing higher education. *Civilisations*, Vol. 3, pp. 575–83 (No. 4, 1953). On British educational policy in tropical Africa see *African Education* (Oxford: The Nuffield Foundation and the Colonial Office, 1953). The Belgians within the past few years have dramatically reoriented their policy regarding higher education for the Congolese. Since 1952 Congo students have been admitted to the Albert I College at Leopoldville; the first Negro University of the Congo is scheduled for opening in 1954; and recently the Belgian press has drawn attention to the admission to Louvain University of a Negro student from the Congo. *Civilisations*, Vol. 3, pp. 599–602 (No. 4, 1953).

[29] Compare with the number of *African-owned-and-edited* dailies and weeklies (combined total) in the following territories: *British Africa:* Gold Coast (17), Uganda (8), Sierra Leone (7), Gambia (3); *French West Africa* (10); and none, insofar as is known, in Belgian, Portuguese, or Spanish Africa; or in Kenya, the territories of the Central African Federation, or in the Union of South Africa.

[30] On the other hand, there appears to be no newspaper in British West Africa comparable with the European-owned-and-edited journal of French West Africa entitled *Les Echos de l'A.O.F.*, which "week after week passionately attacks the administration. . . ." See Thomas Hodgkin, "The Metropolitan Axis," *West Africa*, January 9, 1954, at p. 6.

major sources of data regarding nationalist motivation, objectives, and organization. It is not the number of newspapers published which is significant, but rather the volume of circulation and areal distribution, the news and editorial content and the nature of the appeal, the types of readers, the existence of competitive papers sponsored by colonial governments, the financial stability of the paper, and other factors which would reflect its impact and influence upon the ideas, aspirations, and activities of those literate groups predisposed towards nationalism.

These are but a few of the more important factors in the rise of nationalism which require evaluation and weighting before the student of comparative colonial nationalism can go beyond the mere description of the history and anatomy of a particular nationalist movement. There is great danger in doing a disservice to scholarly research in Africa if one generalizes on the basis of observations made and data assembled in one territory. As has been suggested, there are certain general predisposing and precipitating causes of modern nationalism which are applicable to the whole continent; yet once these are mentioned, it is necessary to examine each area of nationalist activity for that special combination of factors which explains the origin, strength, and orientation of its nationalist movement.

III. FACTORS CONDITIONING NATIONALIST DEVELOPMENT

Normally, a colonial nationalist movement directs its efforts towards the attainment of two main objectives: (1) the achievement of self-government, and (2) the creation of a cultural or political sense of nationality and unity within the boundaries of the area of the nation to be. Nationalists are obliged to adopt the second objective because imperial powers either did not or could not establish political boundaries which embraced only one self-conscious cultural unit; and certainly those powers made no conscious effort to build nations. The nationalist dilemma is that in most cases pursuit of the primary goal (self-government) lessens the likelihood of achieving the secondary goal (cultural and political unity). Put another way, the drive behind African nationalism in many instances is not the consciousness of belonging to a distinct politico-cultural unit which is seeking to protect or assert itself, but rather it is the movement of racially-conscious modernists seeking to create new political and cultural nationalities out of the heterogeneous peoples living within the artificial boundaries imposed by the European master. Their task is not only to conduct a successful political revolution and capture power, but also the painful job of national political integration. And as Professor Crane Brinton has shown, the lessons of history are that nation-building is the product of both consent and coercion, and usually the latter.[31] It is the colonial power, of course, which has had a monopoly over the means of coercion.

The major factor conditioning the development of a particular nationalist movement, therefore, is the degree of internal politico-cultural unity, tolerance, or compatibility amongst the peoples of the area moving into its national era. Disunities can exist in a given territory for a variety of reasons:

1. Traditional pre-colonial hostilities and cultural incompatibilities such as exist between the Kikuyu and Masai peoples of Kenya, or the Ibo and the Tiv peoples of Nigeria. In some instances these have been exacerbated as a result of imperial policies; in others as a consequence of the mere fact of lumping them together and endeavoring to impose territorial uniformity.

2. Tensions between groups resulting from unevenness in development, acculturation, and the acquisition of modernity. These can be the product of original cultural differences (i.e., the variations between groups in their receptivity and adaptability to modernity—e.g., the Ibo and Hausa); historical circumstances (i.e., differences in the duration and intensity of the European impact—e.g., the Creoles of Freetown vs. the Mende peoples of the Protectorate of Sierra Leone); or of constitutional reforms pointing towards African self-government. One could argue that Ibo-Yoruba hostility in Nigeria is the product of all three factors. Just as the advance towards independence precipitated a cleavage between Muslims and Hindus in India, so has the development of nationalism and the move towards self-government in Africa brought to light a multitude of disunities. Fear of domination by the more advanced and acculturated groups—European or African—is one obvious explanation.

3. Tensions between the Westernized elite—the nationalists—and the traditionalists and the masses. This nationalist disability has tended to be exaggerated in the past, usually by imperial spokesmen endeavoring to repudiate the nationalists or to isolate them from the traditionalists. The intensity of the cleavage varies widely according to circumstances. In several areas such as the Protectorate of Sierra Leone, the Northern Territories of the Gold Coast, Western and Northern Nigeria, amongst the Kikuyu in Kenya, and in Northern Rhodesia and Nyasaland the educated nationalists and some leading traditionalists have cooperated in varying degrees.

[31] Crane Brinton, *From Many One* (Cambridge, Mass., 1948).

4. Differences within the ranks of the Westernized elite. These disagreements—and one is struck by their persistence, strength, and virulence—may arise from several causes, including normal competition for power and prestige or honest differences over aims, timing, or methods to be employed in the nationalist drive. Such differences as separate Messrs. Fily-Dabo Sissoko and Mamadou Konaté in the French Sudan; Lamine Gueye and Léopold Senghor in Senegal; Felix Houphouet-Boigny and Kouame Binzème in the Ivory Coast; Prime Minister Kwame Nkrumah and Dr. J. B. Danquah in the Gold Coast; the Sardauna of Sokoto, Obafemi Awolowo, and Dr. Nnamdi Azikiwe in Nigeria; Eliud Mathu and Jomo Kenyatta in Kenya; and Harry Nkumbula and Godwin Lewanika in Central Africa, have very materially affected the course and strength of nationalism in the territories concerned.

These nationalist disabilities are the product of a complex mixture of hard historical and cultural facts, of changes introduced and differentials created by the Western intrusion, as well as of the provocations of the nationalist drive itself. The success of any nationalist movement will in a large measure depend upon the extent to which these internal tensions are softened or dissipated. The latter will depend, in turn, upon the degree of repressive opposition, or unwitting or intentional cooperation, of colonial governments; upon the development of pan-territorial political associations, the membership of which is rooted in all ethnic groups and in which there is free vertical mobility into the "upper crust" which that membership constitutes; upon the emergence of pan-territorial economic-interest groups (e.g., middle-class associations or labor organizations); and upon many other sociological processes (out-group marriages, commonsality, etc.) which Professor Karl W. Deutsch has suggested are essential building blocks of any new national community.[32]

It would be naive and unhistorical to argue that a large measure of politico-cultural integration is required—as distinguished from being desirable—in order for a nationalist movement to succeed in wresting self-government from an imperial power. Most successful colonial nationalist movements have been organized and led by small minorities which have been able either to gain the support of the masses or to capitalize upon their inertia and apathy. It would be unrealistic, however, to contemplate the success of a movement which did not have at least a minimum of unity or tolerance within the "upper crust," even though it be of the sort displayed by the unstable truces negotiated

[32] "The Growth of Nations," *World Politics*, Vol. 5, pp. 168–96 (Jan., 1953).

from time to time between the Sardauna of Sokoto, Mr. Obafemi Awolowo, and Dr. Nnamdi Azikiwe, the regional leaders in Nigeria.

Some of these forces contributing towards integration are measurable and provide rough indices upon which the research scholar can base predictions of the development of a particular nationalist movement. In an interesting new theory regarding the growth of nations, Professor Deutsch has suggested certain criteria which might be profitably employed in seeking to determine the prospects of success of a nationalist movement in its nation-building endeavors.[33] His central thesis is that cases of successful political integration in history show a number of patterns which seem to recur. As he puts it, a nation "is the result of the transformation of people, or of several ethnic elements, in the process of social mobilization." The prospects of success are indicated by the completeness of that transformation and the intensity of social mobilization around the symbols of the new national community. A nation is not only a subjective affirmation of will of zealous nationalists; it is also the product of the operation of powerful objective forces, several of which have been mentioned.

Thus far it has been assumed that the leaders of nationalist movements in Africa will seek to build new national communities out of the diverse human materials located within the artificial boundaries of the existing colonial territories. This was precisely what happened in Latin America (Spanish imperial provinces), in the Middle East (European and Turkish regions), and in Southeast Asia (Dutch Indonesia, Burma, and in a qualified way, British India). In the case of British Africa, where nationalism is most advanced, this same tendency for nationalism to follow boundaries established by the imperial power rather than those coincident with pre-colonial socio-political groups is in evidence (e.g., Gold Coast and Nigeria). On the other hand, in many areas the situation is still relatively fluid. Togoland nationalism has been predominantly an Ewe affair, and the Ewes are a trans-territorial group stretching from the Gold Coast to Dahomey. Separatist sentiment in Northern Nigeria is an example, *par excellence,* of incomplete social mobilization. This, when coupled with growing Yoruba and Ibo self-consciousness, suggests that earlier pan-Nigerian nationalism may be eclipsed and Nigeria may ultimately become three or more states. Until the recent decision to give the Southern Cameroons greater autonomy within the emergent Federation of Nigeria, Cameroonian nationalists were wavering between remaining an integral part of the Eastern Region of Nigeria, or seceding and joining with the nationalists in the

[33] *Ibid.* See also Deutsch's *Nationalism and Social Communication* (cited in note 5), pp. 81 ff.

French Cameroons in an endeavor to create a Kamerun nation based upon the artificial boundaries of the short-lived German Kamerun.[34] In Kenya, Mau Mau and all earlier protonationalist movements have been predominantly Kikuyu endeavors, even though the name Kenya has been employed. In Tanganyika, the Chagga Cooperative movement may be the basis for a Chagga separatism; and in Uganda, it is questionable whether pan-Uganda integrative forces can erase the "national" separatism implicit in the Buganda Kingdom. Again, in Central Africa, will the territorial separatism symbolized by the Northern Rhodesian and Nyasaland National Congresses be eclipsed by the common sentiment and institutions growing out of the new Federation?

In the case of French Africa, dissimilarities in colonial policy (i.e., assimilation and direct rule) have tended to produce a somewhat different situation. Yet since the reforms of 1946, as a result of which each of the territories of the two federations of French West Africa and French Equatorial Africa received their own representative assemblies, territorial nationalist movements have tended to eclipse the pan-French African *Rassemblement Démocratique Africain* in much the same fashion as Nigerian, Gold Coastian, and Sierra Leonian nationalist movements have replaced the earlier National Congress of British West Africa. Thus one finds the *Parti Républicain de Dahomey, Parti Progressiste Soudanaise, Union Démocratique du Tchad,* and similar organizations in each of the territories. The future "national" orientation of nationalist forces in French Africa would seem to depend upon the extent to which pan-Federation forces and institutions, such as the *Grand Conseils,* or the assimilationist forces of the French Union, such as the metropolitan parties and labor movements projected overseas, operate to retard the growth of territorial symbols and sentiment. One thing, however, seems certain: French Africa—because of the French policy of assimilation and direct rule—is less likely to encounter such movements as the *Egbe Omo Oduduwa* of the Nigerian Yorubas, the Kikuyu Central Association in Kenya, and the *Bataka* movement of Uganda.

In general, it would seem that where nationalism manifests itself in considerable strength it is evidence that disintegration of the old and social mobilization around the symbols of the new order have occurred on a scale sufficient to weaken or destroy attachments and loyalties of the nationalists to pre-colonial socio-political units, either because they have been crushed and are beyond memory or because they are unattractive or manifestly unsuitable as "nations" in a modern world of nation-states. The European presence has done much towards the

[34] *West Africa,* January 30, 1954, p. 87.

creation of new nations, the "national" sentiment of the nationalists being a reflection of this.

A few of the many factors which might be observed and evaluated in order to determine the probable success, as well as the territorial implications, of an African nationalist movement or nation-building endeavor are as follows:[35] (1) the degree of internal social mobility, economic interchange and interdependence, intermarriage and commonsality, and the intensity and level of social communication among the ethnic groups comprising a given territory; (2) the location of population clusters and "core areas," as well as of "sub-national" regions of more intense economic interchange or of cultural focus; (3) the powers and functions of "sub-national" political institutions (i.e., regional, tribal, etc.), and the degree of *meaningful* participation in them by the Western-educated elements; (4) the rate at which "national" institutions and activities are capable of attracting and absorbing new social strata from all ethnic groups into the "national" life (e.g., the ethnic composition of the central administrative and technical services); (5) the centrality and nationalness of educational institutions, particularly the professional schools and universities; (6) the degree of pan-territorial circulation of nationalist newspapers and literature and the extent to which these play up "national" events and personalities; (7) the differentials in the material development, per capita income and wealth, the acquisition of modern skills and knowledge, and the concentration and capacity for accumulation of capital amongst the different sub-national areas and ethnic groups;[36] (8) the ethnic makeup of the Western-educated categories and particularly of the active membership of nationalist or proto-nationalist groups; (9) the development and extent of usage of a trans-tribal pan-territorial language, be it English, French, Portuguese, Swahili, or Hausa; (10) the compatibility of the "detribalized" basic personality types produced by the indigenous cultures; (11) the extent to which the territory concerned embraces total cultural groups, or, put another way, the degree to which artificial colonial boundaries have bifurcated ethnic groups whose division may be the source of later irredentism; and (12) the rapport between the Western-educated nationalist elements and the traditionalists, including

[35] For several of the concepts used here the author is indebted to the works of Professor Karl W. Deutsch, previously cited. See especially his *Nationalism and Social Communication*, pp. 15–45.

[36] It could be argued, for example, that apart from historical and cultural factors, the difference in the per capita income of the three regions of Nigeria (£26 for the Western Region, £16 for the Northern Region, and £23 for the Eastern Region) is of no little significance in the recent and current drive for greater regional autonomy. See A. R. Prest and I. G. Stewart, *The National Income of Nigeria*, abridged ed. (Lagos: Government Printer, 1954), pp. 14–16.

the existence of nativistic tensions or economic grievances which the nationalists could manipulate or exploit in their mobilization of mass support.

Results obtained from inquiries along these lines would go far to explain the present orientation of a nationalist movement, as well as possible future trends. And yet an emphatic note of caution should be sounded: objective forces of integration and disintegration are powerful determinants in the nation-building processes, but so also are subjective factors.[37] By all laws of geography and economics Northern Ireland should belong to Eire, and East Pakistan to the Republic of India; but they do not. By the same laws, the Gambia should belong to Senegal, French Guinea to Sierra Leone and Liberia, Mozambique to the Central African Federation, and so forth; and yet present trends suggest that such will not be the case. The principal forces currently operating to shape Africa's emergent nations are either tribalism or a nationalism following artificial imperial boundaries; and, with few exceptions, neither of these is directed towards the creation of political units which the geographer or economist would classify as ideal. In this respect, of course, Africa is not unique.

The foregoing raises the crucial question of whether it is possible for the peoples of Africa—in their own interest—to avoid the balkanization implicit in the full application of the national principle to their continent. So long as the rest of the world is organized according to that principle, and so long as the national idea universally embodies aspirations which cannot be satisfied by other forms of human organization, the answer would seem to be in the negative. The quest for racial equality and acceptance is as important an ingredient in the African revolt as is the desire to determine one's own destiny. Rightly or wrongly, self-government within the confines of the sovereign nation-state has become the supreme symbol of the equality of peoples. The only possible alternative would be broader Eur-African political groupings or self-governing plural societies in which emergent African leaders could play what they would feel to be an equal role. In the light of the persistence of national self-determination as a symbol, and particularly in view of the growing strength and contagion of African nationalism, the future of such multi-racial experiments will depend in a large measure upon the rapidity with which European governments and leaders provide for such a role.

[37] Given suitable conditions, including a politically favorable milieu and the proper techniques, there would seem to be no reason why subjective factors such as loyalties, attitudes, and attachments to national or "sub-national" symbols, could not to some extent be measured.

IV. SPECIAL PROBLEMS OF RESEARCH INTO AFRICAN NATIONALISM

There is perhaps no other type of research venture capable of evoking stronger feeling than an inquiry into colonial nationalism. The word "nationalism" in a colonial milieu has tended to be treated as the equivalent of sedition, or even treason. And this for good reason: by definition colonial nationalists are seeking to bring about a radical alteration in the power structure; namely, to evict the imperial power and to enthrone themselves. From the moment it makes its presence known, therefore, a nationalist movement is, in effect, engaged in a civil war with the colonial administration, the constitutionality of its methods varying according to the liberality of the colonial regime and the moderation of the nationalist leaders.

As regards colonial officialdom, an American undertaking a study of African nationalism is handicapped by the fact that in a large measure the African nationalist awakening is the product of American influences. Since the turn of the century, American Negro religious sects have contributed no little to religious secessionism, particularly in South and West Africa. The Garveyism of the early 1920's had an influence among sophisticated Africans which has tended to be overlooked or minimized. Since 1919 a growing number of American Negro intellectuals have taken an increasingly militant stand on African colonialism. Anti-imperialist sentiment in the United States, especially during the Second World War, was the source of considerable inspiration and delight to budding African nationalists, as well as the cause of no little acrimony between wartime allies. The Atlantic Charter, the Four Freedoms, and public statements by Mr. Willkie and President Roosevelt have bulked large in postwar African nationalist literature. The most important American contribution, however, has been the impact of our culture upon African students who have studied in America. Many of the important pioneers in the African awakening were profoundly affected by their American experience. Of this group the late Dr. J. E. K. Aggrey and Prime Minister Kwame Nkrumah from the Gold Coast, and Professor Eyo Ita and Dr. Nnamdi Azikiwe from Nigeria are the most prominent and best known. During the Second World War the number of African students in America was less than 25; since 1945 it has increased to over 500. With few exceptions these students have been and are strong nationalists, many of them having become leaders upon their return to Africa. In the eyes of colonial officialdom, therefore, an American inquiry into nationalism tends to raise certain doubts.

There has been a tendency in the past for American visitors making quick tours of Africa to rely mainly upon the white colonial administration for an appraisal of nationalist sentiment and activity. This is unfortunate in many respects. In the first place, it is most likely that any information bearing on nationalism is locked up in classified files. Secondly, most colonial administrators have tended to be anti-nationalists, even though many in British West Africa have adapted themselves to working with nationalists towards a mutually agreed goal of effective self-government. Their evaluation of nationalism is bound to be colored by their preconceptions and vested interests or by their honest fears regarding the welfare of the bush peasant, for whom they tend to have a preference and a strong paternal affection. Thirdly, circumstances have tended to place them too close to events or too far removed from the people. Their growing preoccupation with headquarters administration and development schemes, the social impediments—created frequently by the presence of white wives and families—to effective and continuous contact with the masses, and the almost total lack of rapport or confidence between nationalists and administrators, have given the latter many blind spots. Their past miscalculations of nationalist strength and trends tend to confirm this. In short, instead of being used as informants, a role they are not anxious to perform, they should be objects of study. Their fears, their adjustments, and their efforts to suppress, retard, manipulate, or encourage nationalism are all relevant in a complete study of the many interacting factors present in a nationalist situation.

Unlike the field anthropologist, who consciously seeks to work among the traditionalists, the student of political nationalism is concerned mainly with the attitudes, activities, and status of the nationalist-minded Western-educated *elite*. Here one is in a world very different from that of officialdom or the traditionalists. It is a world of great idealism, crusading zeal, and high resolve, as well as one of suspicion, hyper-sensitivity, and exaggeration. It has its careerists and opportunists, and its chronic nonconformists; but it also has its emergent statesmen, its enterprising industrialists, and its distinguished scholars. Only here can one get a partial glimpse into the depth of nationalist feeling, the sources of inspiration and ideas, and the key elements in nationalist motivation. Yet there are distinct limitations to the interview technique, not the least important of which is the possession of a white skin. Moreover, a colonial nationalist movement must have its *arcana* as well as its propaganda.

In the quest for knowledge regarding African nationalism, the most fruitful as well as unprovocative avenues to explore are those already indicated in earlier sections. African nationalism is something more than the activities of a few disgruntled journalists and frustrated intellectuals to whom Lord Lugard referred in his *Dual Mandate*. It is the inevitable end product of the impact of Western imperialism and modernity upon African societies; it is also the inevitable assertion by the Africans of their desire to shape their own destiny. Imperial systems are disintegrating, new nation-states are emerging, and new forms of political organization transcending the national state are under experiment. These political aspects of African nationalism, however, are but the surface symptoms of a great ferment about which we know very little. The study and analysis of the many complex factors in this unfolding drama provide not only a stimulating challenge to the social sciences, but also a compelling invitation to greater interdisciplinary cooperation.

A Note on the Language of African Nationalism

THOMAS HODGKIN
University of Ghana

I have been obliged to think recently about the language of African nationalism; in particular to ask what light the language of African nationalists throws on their theory; whether indeed there is what can reasonably be called a "theory" of African nationalism, which can be distinguished from other theories—and, if there is, what this theory asserts. My practical interest in these questions arose out of disagreement with two prevailing opinions: the view, expressed by the Prosecution in the South African Treason Trial, that in so far as those who talk the language of African nationalism are moved by any political theory it must be a "Communist" theory; and the view that African nationalism lacks any genuine theoretical basis—that such ideas as it makes use of are merely gadgets, borrowed to give an appearance of respectability. This note attempts to formulate, in a preliminary way, a different view.

For the most part African national movements have developed within the artificial frontiers determined by the European Powers—Britain, France, Belgium, Portugal, Germany, Italy, and, to a very minor extent, Spain—during the last quarter of the 19th Century. With the disappearance of Germany from the ranks of the colonial Powers after the first World War, and of Italy after the second, and given the lack of opportunity for political organization in the Portuguese territories, national movements in Africa south of the Sahara have in practice been largely confined to countries in which either English or French is the dominant language—for administrative, judicial, educational, journalistic, and similar purposes. (Somalia, within the zone of Italian linguistic influence, is an important exception.) In these territories indigenous languages are, of course, widely used for purposes of political agitation and debate, especially whereas in the case of Swahili in Tanganyika—a particular African language serves as a *lingua franca*

Reprinted from Kenneth Kirkwood (ed.), *African Affairs* ("St. Antony's Papers Number 10 [London: Chatto and Windus, 1961]), pp. 22–40, with the permission of the author. Passages which originally appeared in French have been translated into English by William John Hanna.

throughout a territory. But most of the literature of these national movements—newspapers, periodicals, pamphlets, broadsheets, programmes and policy statements, reports, biographical and autobiographical works, studies of specific problems—is in either English or French. (This generalization does not apply to Arab North Africa, where the Arabic literature is probably more important than the French.) Hence, although an adequate account of nationalist language would be bound to pay attention to material—in the form of speeches, songs, poetry, journals, et cetera—in the various African languages, a good deal can be learned from a study of the literature existing in English and French.

If one considers the output of national movements of sub-Saharan Africa only, whether in English or French, over the past fifteen years, one point is immediately clear: there is, to a large extent, a common political language; common themes continually recur. These themes might be summarized as follows:

(1) The people inhabiting a given colonial territory constitute a "nation," or a nation in process of becoming (Ghanaian, Cameroonian Tanganyikan, Congolese, for example).

(2) This "nation" is governed by an "imperialist" Power, which seeks its own, predominantly economic, interests and advantages.

(3) The relationship between the "imperialist" Power and the African "nation" is essentially one of "domination," in its political aspect; of "exploitation," in its economic aspect; and of "racialism," or "racial discrimination," in its human aspect. A system in which such relationships predominate is described as "colonialism."

(4) The members of a subject African "nation" have an "inalienable right" to govern themselves.

(5) In order to substitute "self-government," or "independence" for "colonialism," or "colonial bureaucracy," a "national liberation movement" has to be generated.

(6) The "national liberation movement" expresses itself through a political organization, which may be either a "Congress" or *Rassemblement* or a "Party," with linked functional associations—of women, youth, Trade Unionists, and the like. Though led by an élite, it attracts to itself "the masses," and seeks as its primary aim "the conquest of political power."

(7) The organization which serves as the instrument for national liberation possesses a double legitimacy. Historically it is the successor to the pre-colonial African States whose power was broken during the period of "imperialist" penetration. Morally it is the expression of the

"popular will," the will of the emergent African "nation." Thus, on both historical and moral grounds, it enjoys an authority superior to the merely legal authority, backed by physical sanctions, of the colonial state.

(8) In its effort to achieve "political emancipation," this organization will be bound to pursue, and justified in pursuing, a "dynamic," aggressive, strategy in its dealings with the colonial Government and Administration, involving, on occasion, the use of "positive action"—which should, however, as far as possible be "non-violent."

(9) Since the "national liberation movement" is, by definition, a "progressive" force, it will be bound also to seek to weaken, and eventually to eliminate, such "reactionary" forces as exist within the "nation" and are liable to retard the process of "political emancipation." The most important of these forces are restricted ethnic loyalties ("tribalism") and chiefly power, in many of its various forms (sometimes labelled "feudalism")—surviving from the pre-colonial period, but generally fostered by "colonialism," and liable to assert themselves in opposition to the organization expressing the "popular will" during the period of transition from "colonialism" to "independence."

(10) The new form of independent African state which the "national liberation movement" seeks to bring into being will be "democratic"—in the sense, particularly, that its government will be responsible to a popular assembly elected on the principle of "one man, one vote"; and "socialist," in the sense that it will develop a planned economy, in the interests of the "masses."

(11) The "national liberation movement" in any given African state should co-operate with similar movements in other African states, with a view to the total elimination of "colonialism" throughout the African continent, the avoidance of political fragmentation, or "Balkanization," and the realization, in the first place, of large and durable African systems—adequate to withstand external pressures—and, eventually, an "African Commonwealth."

The following quotations, drawn mainly from the nationalist literature of West Africa, provide some contextual examples of ways in which these propositions have been actually stated:

(a) National unity is necessary because the whole Congolese Population must, above all, become aware of its own national character and unity. . . . We are convinced that it is possible for pagans, Catholics, Protestants, Salvation Army members and Moslems to agree on a program

for the common good which respects the natural morality inborn in every man worthy of that name. . . . In the meantime, we invite our readers—both African and European—to write to us in order to undertake this dialogue. We would be especially happy to hear their ideas on the timeliness of the national popular movement which we propose . . .[1]

(b) We who live in this blessed country of Nigeria know that until we are in control of political power in our country, we would continue to be the footstool of imperialist nations, who are interested selfishly in their economic prosperity and social prestige. . . . If there is any doubt about the yearnings of Nigerians for self-government it should be dispelled forthright. We are fed up with being governed as a Crown Colony, which we are NOT. We are nauseated by the existence of an untrammelled bureaucracy which makes, administers and interprets our laws, without our knowledge and consent. The idea of our paid civil servants ruling and lording it over us is a challenge to our manhood, both as a nation and as a race.[2]

(c) The national liberation movement in the African colonies has arisen because of the continuous economic and political exploitation by foreign oppressors. The aim of the movement is to win freedom and independence. This can only be achieved by the political education and organization of the colonial masses. Hence workers and professional classes alike must unite on a common front to further the economic progress and indigenous enterprise of the people which is at present being stifled.[3]

(d) [The Seventh International Student Conference] acknowledges the right of students to strive for national independence by all legitimate means within their power; denounces colonialism, totalitarianism, imperialism, and any other form of regression or restriction which hinders the development of national cultures . . .[4]

(e) The Congress [of the RDA] believes that independence is an inalienable right of a people which permits them to make use of their sovereignty in the interest of the masses. . . . But interdependence is the golden rule in the life of these people, and it manifests itself in the

[1] Conscience Africaine, *Manifeste* (Leopoldville, July–August, 1956), p. 4.
[2] Nnamdi Azikiwe, *Political Blueprint of Nigeria* (Lagos, 1944), pp. 55 and 63.
[3] Kwame Nkrumah, *Autobiography* (Edinburgh, 1957), p. 47, summarizing the argument of his pamphlet, *Towards Colonial Freedom* (1947).
[4] COSEC, *Nigeria '57, the Story of the Seventh International Student Conference.*

20th century in the form of a constitution of great political and economic unities . . .[5]

(f) The Bloc Démocratique Sénégalais *is founded on the following principles: understanding and unity of action for all Senegalese workers regardless of race or religion; political and economic organization of all workers in order to banish classes and castes by the conquest of political power and the socialization of methods of production and trade. The* Bloc Démocratique Sénégalais *hopes to take its inspiration from the method of scientific socialism. Its aim is to eliminate capitalist imperialism. Its method is founded on the Black African tradition, modernized by European techniques. Only by following this tradition faithfully will the cultural values of Black Africa be singularly preserved. Its political future is to realize true democracy for Senegal . . .*[6]

(g) Freedom is our birthright, self-government our heritage as sons and daughters of the free men and women who inherited Africa for the Africans. It is, therefore, not only just but imperative that we restore our birthright which is freedom and our heritage self-government, for ourselves, our children, and our children's children. This we must do now . . . Every hour that passes means one hour more of subjection, degradation, exploitation, and humiliation by imperialists, white supremacists and foreign self-seekers.[7]

(h) I join the Sawaba Crusade because I believe in progress, not reaction; because, despite our shortcomings, I trust that an All-African Government for Nigeria could offer better opportunities and security and freedom to read and write, listen, think and talk and enjoy life to its fullest . . . I will fight, if need be, for Sawaba because it is my obligation, because oppressed and exploited people must struggle to be free . . . I will fight, if need be, for Sawaba, because colonial brand of fascism is menacing us as we have never before been menaced, because only craven will not struggle against establishment of a fascist government in Northern Nigeria . . .[8]

[5] *3ème Congrès Interterritorial du RDA (Rassemblement Démocratique Africain),* Bamako, 25–29 Septembre, 1957, Résolution Politique.
[6] *Bloc Démocratique Sénégalais,* Statuts du Parti (Dakar, 1952), Article 2.
[7] PAFMECA (Pan-African Freedom Movement of East and Central Africa), "Freedom Charter" (1958), quoted in Dennis Phombeah, *The Birth of a New Freedom Movement in East and Central Africa.*
[8] NEPU [Northern Elements Progressive Union], *Sawaba Creed* (Kano, 1956). ("Sawaba" is the Hausa word for "freedom" and one of the slogans of NEPU. It is also the name of the radical opposition party, at present illegal, in the new Republic of Niger, formerly French Niger.)

(i) By Positive Action we mean the adoption of all legitimate and constitutional means by which we can cripple the forces of imperialism in this country. The weapons of Positive Action are: (1) Legitimate political agitation. (2) Newspaper and educational campaigns, and (3) as a last resort, the constitutional application of strikes, boycotts, and non-cooperation based on the principle of absolute non-violence.[9]

(j) Whereas we strongly oppose the imperialist tactics of utilizing tribalism and religious separatism to perpetuate the colonial policies in Africa;
    Whereas we are also convinced that tribalism and religious separatism are evil practices which constitute serious obstacles to—
    (i) the realization of the unity of Africa,
    (ii) the political evolution of Africa,
    (iii) the rapid liberation of Africa,
    Be it resolved that steps be taken by political, trade union, cultural and other organizations to educate the masses about the dangers of these evil practices and thereby mobilize the masses to fight these evils . . .[10]

(k) By directing her struggle toward the creation of a United States of Africa, Guinea not only joins in the unique and true current of history; she also leads the evolution and emancipation of Africa. In proposing that the Republic of Guinea abandon her sovereignty, partially or totally, for the higher good of a government which would direct several territories or states, we have clearly defined the essential African basis for our political action. There is not—there cannot be for any African— an economic, social or political obstacle which would forbid or hinder the affirmation of this will to serve the just cause of his people.[11]

Much of this language, and the ideas which it expresses, belongs to the common stock of the Western democratic tradition; and can be traced back to the French and American Revolutions, the English Civil War, and, behind that, to mediaeval Europe. The conception of political liberty as a "birthright," for example, recalls the arguments of Mr. Edward Sexby, speaking in the Putney Debates in 1647:

[9] Kwame Nkrumah, *What I Mean by Positive Action* (Ghana Pamphlets, No. 1, Accra, 1949).
    [10] *Resolutions of the All African People's Conference* (Accra, 1958), Resolution on Tribalism and Religious Separatism, published in *Current History*, XXXVII, 215, July, 1959, p. 44.
    [11] Sékou Touré, broadcast of 30th November, 1958, published in *Republique de Guinée, L'Action Politique du P.D.G.–R.D.A. Guinée pour l'Emancipation et l'Unité Africaine dons l'Indépendence*, Tome 2, pp. 149–150.

*. . . I see that though liberty was our end, there is a degeneration from
it. We have engaged in this Kingdom and ventured our lives, and it was
all for this: to recover our birthrights and privileges as Englishmen; and
by the arguments argued there is none. There are many thousands of us
soldiers that have ventured our lives; we have had little propriety in the
Kingdom as to our estates, yet we have had a birthright . . .*[12]

This same idea, derived directly or indirectly from the 17th Century
Levellers, recurs in other contemporary African contexts, e.g. in Dr.
Nkrumah's speech on the Motion for Independence to the Gold Coast
Legislative Assembly, on July 10, 1953, quoting Mr. George Padmore:

*When the Gold Coast Africans demand self-government to-day they are,
in consequence, merely asserting their birthright which they never really
surrendered to the British who, disregarding their treaty obligations of
1844, gradually usurped full sovereignty over the country.*[13]

Or in one of Mr. Eyo Ita's pamphlets:

*Politicians must re-focus the truth that liberty is sacred, that for every
man or race it is a birthright, that the African is human and must enjoy
this divine birthright unconditionally.*[14]

Certain terms, on the other hand, such as "Fascist" or "totalitarian,"
used to describe the colonial system, belong to much more recent strata
of political language. Indeed, one marked characteristic of African
national movements is their eclecticism—their habit of taking over ideas
and terms which seem appropriate to their needs wherever they happen
to find them. An illustration is the use of the terms "Uncle Tom" and
"quisling"—the one taken from American 19th Century literature, the
other from British wartime usage—sometimes in juxtaposition, to refer
to individual Africans who are regarded as collaborating with the
colonial administration. The extent of borrowings from Indian, particularly Gandhist, sources also deserves attention—e.g. as regards the whole
notion of "non-violent non-cooperation" as a technique of nationalist
action. In the case of national movements in predominantly Muslim
territories, language and modes of thought derived from Islamic and

[12] A. S. P. Woodhouse, *Puritanism and Liberty* (London, 1938), p. 69.
[13] George Padmore, *The Gold Coast Revolution* (London, 1953), p. 35. The
full text of Dr. Nkrumah's speech is given in George Padmore's *Pan-Africanism or
Communism?* Appendix III. Although Dr. Nkrumah's quotation (on p. 407) differs
slightly from the original wording the substance is the same. (Ed.)
[14] Eyo Ita, *The Assurance of Freedom* (Calabar, n.d.), p. 29.

from Western sources are liable to be found in combination, as in the following passage from a document circulated within the Algerian FLN:

The FLN, by its very essence, violently opposes the cult of personality. In its historic proclamation of November 1, 1954, it officially condemned messalisme . . . as a system of government and control from the dark ages which Islam, formerly, and the 20th century, today, condemn unceasingly. . . . The first caliphs after Mohammed, in their daily reports to the citizens, rigorously applied this verse of the Koran: 'Problems are solved in common.' Realizing the fallibility of man, the only remedy to this weakness and the will of Providence is consultation with others, exchange of ideas, and free discussion of all problems. The advantages of such a form of government, at every level of our organization, are immense . . .[15]

Granted eclecticism as a general phenomenon, an interesting question which is sometimes raised is—How far, on the evidence of their literature, do African national movements appear to have been influenced by Marxist theory? This is the type of question, obviously, which has to be answered differently for different movements and organizations at different phases of their history. One generalization, however, seems worth making at the outset. The influence of Marxist ideas and language is much more evident in French-speaking than in English-speaking Africa, for good historical reasons. The institutions of the Fourth Republic were such as to encourage, initially at any rate, close relations between African parties and one or other of the major French Marxist parties—Socialists (SFIO) and Communists (PCF). The French intellectual tradition stimulated an interest in theory among African party leaders. Furthermore, for a large proportion of the post-war generation of party leaders, the *Groupes d'Etudes Communistes,* established from 1943 on in the main centres of French West Africa, provided the only form of political education available, and introduced them to the Marxist classics.[16] The post-war political leaders of English-speaking Africa, on the other hand, were confronted with a situation in which the only Marxist party, the British Communist Party, was relatively uninfluential; with which their relationships, where they existed, were

[15] FLN [*Front de Libération Nationale*], *Le bannissement du culte de la personnalité, le principe de la direction collective et le centralisme démocratique.* (The term "messalisme" means the cult of the personality of Messali Hajj, formerly the dominant figure in the Algerian national movement.)

[16] See Ruth Schachter [Morgenthau], *Some Aspects of the Development of Political Parties in French West Africa* (Oxford doctoral thesis, 1958), pp. 217–23.

casual and short-lived. As students they came in contact with the strongly anti-metaphysical (in the sense of "anti-system-building") British intellectual tradition. As regards their political education, the ideas by which they were most profoundly influenced were pan-African, rather than Marxist—the school of thought which had its origin in America and the West Indies rather than in Europe, and included the sharply differing standpoints of Marcus Garvey, W. E. Burghardt Du Bois, and George Padmore.[17] Of course, many English-speaking African leaders developed an interest in aspects of Marxist theory: Dr. Nkrumah has described how the Fifth Pan-African Congress, at Manchester, in October 1945, which he helped to organize, "adopted Marxist Socialism as its philosophy"[18] (the phrase itself is a good example of nationalist eclecticism). But they did not, like their French-speaking contemporaries, have the experience of a basic training in Marxist modes of thought.

In some cases African nationalist borrowings from Marxist sources are scarcely more than linguistic: echoes, without any particular political significance. It is indeed natural that the rhetoric of Marx, the prophet of the doom of capitalism, should be easily adaptable to the requirements of the contemporary prophets of the doom of imperialism. Two such echoes from *The Communist Manifesto* occur in the concluding sentences of Dr. Nkrumah's early pamphlet, *Towards Colonial Freedom:*

Thus the goal of the national liberation movement is the realization of complete and unconditional independence, and the building of a society of peoples in which the free development of each is the condition of the free development of all. PEOPLE OF THE COLONIES, UNITE: the working men of all countries are behind you.[19]

Similarly, the opening sentence of the original manifesto of the *Rassemblement Démocratique Africain,* from 1946 until 1958 the dominant anti-colonial organization in French Africa, "The reaction is creating fear of the Africans' striving toward liberty,"[20] is reminiscent of the opening sentence of *The Communist Manifesto:* "A spectre is haunting Europe—the spectre of Communism." More important is the use of Marxist categories of explanation. One obvious example is the concept of "imperialism." The theory that "the imperialist powers need the raw

[17] See George Padmore, *Pan-Africanism or Communism?* (London, 1956), chs. V–IX.

[18] Kwame Nkrumah, *Autobiography*, p. 53.

[19] Kwame Nkrumah, *Towards Colonial Freedom* (republished London, 1957), pp. 32–3.

[20] RDA, *Manifeste* (Paris, 1946), published in *Le Rassemblement Démocratique Africain dans la Lutte Anti-imperialiste* (Au Service de l'Afrique Noire, 1948), p. 23.

materials and cheap native labour of the colonies for their own capitalist industries; through their system of monopolist control they eliminate native competition, and use the colonies as dumping grounds for
their surplus mass-produced goods," that "the whole policy of the
colonizer is to keep the native in his primitive state and make him
economically dependent,"[21] and that this form of "economic imperialism" at the same time corrupts the European masters and degrades
the African servants, is "a cult which is just as offensive as the abuse
of the leopard society"[22]—this theme, or some variation upon it, recurs
constantly in the literature of African nationalism. I suspect that there
are few radical nationalists who would not agree with the essentials
of the argument. It is, however, important to note that what is accepted as the assertion that there is a direct causal relationship between
capitalism—or, more specifically, "monopoly capitalism"—and modern
imperialism; not the orthodox Leninist account of the genesis of imperialism in its entirety, with its thesis that it is primarily the pressure
of "finance capital" for new outlets for investment that generates the
imperialist drive to dominate colonial and semi-colonial territories.[23]
Rosa Luxemburg's standpoint, which places the main emphasis upon
the search for new markets and sources of raw materials, is usually
preferred. This point has been explicitly made by the Senegalese nationalist leader and intellectual, M. Abdoulaye Ly:

*Rosa Luxembourg, Lenin's contemporary, as much a Marxist as he and
certainly less a formalist, had meanwhile shown the way to a proper
analysis explaining imperialism and capitalism, even before the appearance of* Imperialism . . .

*Bourgeois "civilization," fruit of expanded bourgeois production,
could not exist without constant support of the "savages," "indigenous
peoples," "natives," or the colonials who are surely not the parasites
that one might imagine. . . .*

*In reality, there is, in the capitalistic system of production, a
chronic:*

*(a) under-production relative to the means of production (of one
nature or another) which makes imperialism (seeker of the sources of
raw materials) a necessary condition for the expansion of production;*

*(b) over-production relative to the use of consumer goods (of one
nature or another) resulting in imperialism (seeker of outlets and of*

---

[21] Kwame Nkrumah, *Autobiography*, pp. 46–7.
[22] Nnamdi Azikiwe, *"Before Us Lies the Open Grave"* (Lagos, 1947).
[23] V. I. Lenin, *Imperialism, the Highest Stage of Capitalism.*

*consumers with an 'outside source of revenue,' in accord with the cap-
italistic system).*

*The economic necessity of imperialism is found in this chronic
disorder.*[24]

Another important field in which the leaders of African national movements have made use of Marxist, or more precisely Leninist, ideas is
that of organization. The common conception of a nationalist party as
a "vanguard" or "avant-garde" is clearly influenced by Lenin's view of
the role of a revolutionary party:

*The CPP was not merely a mass movement. Mass movements are well
and good, but they cannot act with purpose unless they are led and
guided by a vanguard political party . . .*[25]

*The magic story of human achievement gives irrefutable proof that as
soon as an awakened intelligentsia emerges among so-called subject
people, it becomes the vanguard of the struggle against alien rule.*[26]

The same basic idea has been expressed, more elaborately, by M. Sékou
Touré:

*In the framework of society, what is it that motivates action? What con-
ceives and directs initiative? It is nothing else but the organization and
orientation of the thought of the total intelligence of a group. This
organization and orientation must be assumed by the Party at every
level. At the village level, it is the committee; at the district level, it is the
section; and at the level of the nation, it is the whole Party.*

*Thus, it is the Party that determines and directs the action of the
nation, the districts, the villages, collections of groups, and individual
groups.*

*Putting this fundamental idea into practice, we have adapted politi-
cal and administrative structures to the democratic structures of the
Party. . . .*

*Thus we declare that, everywhere, the Party has pre-eminence;
everywhere it must think, act, direct and control the action of the
working masses . . .*[27]

[24] Abdoulaye Ly, *Les Masses Africaines et l'Actuelle Condition Humaine* (Paris, 1956), pp. 47–9.
[25] Kwame Nkrumah, *Autobiography*, p. ix.
[26] Kwame Nkrumah, *op. cit.*, p. 91.
[27] Sékou Touré, *Cinquième Congrès Nationale du Parti Démocratique de Guinée*, Rapport de Doctrine et de Politique Générale (Conakry, 1959), pp. 40–1.

Another Leninist concept which has come into current African use is "democratic centralism." This principle, which, since its foundation in 1946, has had a profound effect upon the structure of the RDA and its constituent parties, was reaffirmed as the basis of party organization at the RDA's Bamako conference in 1957.[28] It was endorsed and defined by Dr. Nkrumah, Life Chairman of the CPP, at that party's tenth anniversary rally in 1959:

> . . . In our Party all are equal regardless of their race or tribe. All are free to express their views. But once a majority decision is taken, we expect such a decision to be loyally executed, even by those who might have opposed that decision. This we consider and proclaim to be the truest form of Democratic Centralism—decisions freely arrived at and loyally executed. This applies from the lowest to the highest level. None is privileged and no one shall escape disciplinary action . . .[29]

Here again, while there has been borrowing, there has also been adaptation. For Dr. Nkrumah it is the African intelligentsia, not the working-class, which furnishes the "vanguard" to lead the anti-colonial struggle. M. Sékou Touré seems on the whole to share this view, though he is careful to explain that to be an "intellectual" in the contemporary African context does not necessarily imply the possession of formal educational qualifications:

> Do we not constantly affirm that the PDG is the party of men who place their intelligence at the service of the masses? When we say "intellectuals," it is in the true sense of the word. It is not a question of those who know how to read and write, but of those who base their actions upon concrete study. . . . of men and women who search for truth starting from history and fact, at the same time orienting their actions toward assigned objectives.[30]

Moreover, the nationalist parties which conceive of themselves as "vanguard" parties are at the same time "mass" parties, which seek, as far as possible, to embrace the entire nation in their ranks. They are not small picked bands of professional revolutionaries. (The CPP has in fact recently decided to organize within the party a selected and trained

[28] 3ème Congrès Interterritorial du RDA, Bamako, 25–29 Septembre, 1957, Résolution d'Organisation.
[29] Accra Evening News, June 16, 1959, p. 4, para. 33.
[30] Sékou Touré, Cinquième Congrès National du Parti Démocratique de Guinée, Rapport de Doctrine et de Politique Générale (Conakry, 1959), p. 15.

élite of "Vanguard Activists"—a "vanguard within the vanguard," so to speak.[31]) Thus too the term "democratic centralism"—while it is certainly intended to emphasize popular participation in decision-making on the one hand, and the accountability of the lower organs of the party to the higher, the ultimate authority of the central committee, on the other—has in general a looser kind of meaning in the African, than in the original Leninist, context.[32]

The question—how far has Marxism served as a quarry, from which African national movements have been able to extract terms and ideas? —might clearly be further pursued. It may, however, be more useful to look at the matter from another angle, and ask—what are the points in regard to which, to judge from the literature, there is a marked opposition between African nationalist and Marxist doctrines?

The idea of "Pan-Africanism" is a point of this kind. According to Mr. George Padmore:

In our struggle for national freedom, human dignity and social redemption, Pan-Africanism offers an ideological alternative to Communism on the one side and Tribalism on the other . . .[33]

True, the idea can be expressed in a variety of ways. Its exponents do not necessarily claim that it should be given the status of an ideology. But, reduced to its simplest terms, "Pan-Africanism" involves the assertion that there are certain special ties, giving rise to a special sense of solidarity, among the African peoples, and a special historical direction in which they must travel, including, as an ultimate objective, the realization of an "African Commonwealth." This, from a Marxist standpoint, is a somewhat exclusive attitude, which conflicts with the notion of a more embracing kind of solidarity, between the colonial, semi-colonial, and ex-colonial peoples in general, the working-classes in the economically advanced countries, and the Socialist states. The conflict between the "Pan-African" idea and orthodox Marxism becomes more evident when—as sometimes occurs in the case of national movements in Africa south of the Sahara—the political objectives of "Pan-Africanism" are supported on the metaphysical foundations of *Négritude.* Here again there are variations in the doctrine. But, broadly speaking,

[31] *Accra Evening News,* June 16, 1959, paras. 34–8.

[32] For Communist interpretations of "democratic centralism," see R. N. Carew Hunt, *Guide to Communist Jargon* (London, 1957), pp. 53–6.

[33] George Padmore, *Pan-Africanism or Communism?* p. 379.

what is asserted is that there are certain essentially Negro-African values, which can be discovered by an inspection of the Negro-African past; that these values, suitably reinterpreted, should be made the basis of the Negro-African societies of the future; and that Negro-African civilization has its own specific contribution to make to humanity—by renewing itself it can renew the world.[34] Such ideas have been expressed with particular emphasis by the parties in which M. Senghor has played a leading role, for example the former *Convention Africaine,* which called for

. . . one great unified Party, inspired by Socialism, to maintain the autonomy of Black African thought, and to integrate Black Africa's cultural values.[35]

A variation on this theme recurs in the works of M. Sékou Touré:

Let us take a typical example of the social behavior of Africans compared with Europeans. . . . From the social framework and its conditions, solidarity is developed to a level of which you are all well aware. But the demands of the industrial era have deprived Europeans of that sense of solidarity which characterizes life in a community with all its freely accepted reciprocal obligations. Europeans are therefore individuals to the extreme. . . . In Europe, money has become, subjectively, the basis of estimating a man's value. In Africa, social values are the distinguishing factors, and contribute to the estimation of man's qualities. This is a human wealth which we must safeguard from all interference, and use for the development of our society . . .[36]

From a Marxist standpoint this insistence on the need to reassert traditional African values is surely characteristic of petty-bourgeois romantic nationalism.[37]

Another significant point of divergence is in regard to social classes. In general, African nationalists deny or ignore the existence of a "class-

[34] See Jean-Paul Sartre, *Orphée Noir* (Preface to Léopold Sédar Senghor, *La Nouvelle Poésie Nègre et Malgache,* Paris, 1948).

[35] Convention Africaine, *Congrès Interterritorial de Regroupement des Partis Politiques Africains,* Dakar, 11–13 Janvier, 1957, p. 48.

[36] Sékou Touré, *Texte des Interviews accordées aux Représentants de la Presse* (Conakry, 1959), pp. 124–5.

[37] See, for example, the criticisms by Albert Franklin, in *Négritude—Réalité ou Mystification?* (Présence Africaine, *Les Etudiants Noirs Parlent,* Paris, 1953).

struggle" within the African "nation" whose liberation they demand, while placing exclusive emphasis on the struggle between this "nation" and its colonial rulers. The assertion that classes do not as yet exist in African society—or, though they may exist in embryonic form, are totally without political importance—occurs frequently in nationalist literature:

CGTA [the Confédération Générale du Travail Africaine] . . . rejects the class struggle because of African social groups' identity of living conditions and lack of differentiation into antagonistic classes, and because of the economic and political alienation to which the peoples of tropical Africa are at present subjected.[38]

Actually, Africa has no bourgeoisie; its population is 85 per cent peasant; it lacks national financial capital; nor does it know "social classes" or the struggles born of their contradictions.[39]

This widely accepted view of African society is sometimes stated with a rider, to the effect that where, as in parts of the Sudan (in the traditional sense) or in Mauritania, social differentiation on a basis of "castes," or "estates," still survives, these divisions are tending to break down, under the impact of economic and educational developments and the levelling activities of nationalist parties. It is, understandably, in such societies, where a pre-colonial aristocracy continues to enjoy political power, that the language of the class-struggle is sometimes used by radical opposition parties, as in the following "Declaration of Principles," issued by the Northern Elements Progressive Union of the Northern Region of Nigeria:

Owing to this unscrupulous and vicious system of Administration by the Family Compact rulers, there is today in our society an antagonism of interests, manifesting itself as a class struggle, between the members of that vicious circle of the Native Administrations on the one hand and the ordinary 'Talakawa' [commoners] on the other . . . All parties are but the expression of class interests, and as the interest of the 'Talakawa' is diametrically opposed to the interest of all sections of the master class, the party seeking the emancipation of the "Talakawa" must naturally be hostile to the party of the oppressors . . .[40]

[38] *La Liberté* (Conakry), December 11, 1956, *Resolution on CGTA Doctrine* (translated).
[39] *Sékou Touré, Texte des Interviews*, p. 127.
[40] The NEPU Party of Northern Nigeria, *Declaration of Principles*.

The distinction here drawn between the "Family Compact rulers" (i.e. the predominantly Fulani ruling class) and the *Talakawa,* the commoners, is clearly a distinction of a pre-Marxist, early 19th Century radical, type. NEPU's conception of a fundamental antagonism between an oppressive "feudal" aristocracy on the one hand, and the "common people," the "industrious section of the population" on the other, is closer to the thinking of James Mill than of Marx.

A third point of difference is the tendency of African nationalist leaders to throw overboard the metaphysical aspects of Marxism: to disinterest themselves entirely in the propositions (or presuppositions)—that whatever exists is material; that consciousness is an emergent attribute of material organisms; that change occurs as a consequence of contradictions; that technological and economic change determine other types of social change; that "freedom is the understanding of necessity," and so forth. This attitude, of rejecting or ignoring the presuppositions of Marxism, is quite explicit in the case of M. Sékou Touré, who makes more use than almost any other nationalist leader of its sociological concepts. Marxism, he argues, has been shorn of those of its characteristics which did not fit the facts of the African situation:

I would be lying to you if I did not say that I have read many works of Mao Tse Tung, and many works of the great Marxist thinkers. I believe that Marxism contains important theses on the history of humanity. Dialectical materialism or philosophical materialism presents an interpretation of social or economic facts which might lead, for example, to a denial of the existence of God. But you will not find one man or one woman in the countries of Africa (especially Guinea) who does not believe in God. . . .

In Marxism, the principles of organization, democracy, control, and movement—find perfect methods of adaption to present-day conditions in Africa. . . . It is not philosophy that interests us. Our needs are too real . . .[41]

This is not the only possible way of looking at things. M. Senghor, a metaphysically-minded Catholic, resolves the problem of reconciling the use of Marxist categories with African theism rather differently from M. Sékou Touré, a Muslim pragmatist. Taking Marx's early idea of the

[41] Sékou Touré, *Texte des Interviews,* p. 108.

"alienation" of man under capitalism as his starting-point, he argues that "Marx's atheism can be considered as a reaction, Christian in origin, against the deviations of historic Christianity":[42]

Let us summarize the positive contributions of Marx: the philosophy of humanism, economic theory, the dialectic method. To that we would add, as means, *syndicalism and planning. Also federalism, mutuality, and the cooperation which come down to us from the idealistic French socialists—Saint-Simon, Proudhon, Fourier . . .*[43]

The upshot is similar in both cases: the metaphysical aspects of Marxism are either discarded or adapted to suit the needs of the African situation, as nationalist leaders understand them.

So far the argument has been somewhat negative, merely seeking to define the extent to which Marxist ideas have been embodied in African nationalist theory and expressed in its literature. Is it possible to say anything more positive about the content of this theory? Consider some of its basic ideas: the conception of an undifferentiated African people as the legitimate source of power; the emphasis upon the moral purposes which government should seek to realize (the restoration of African "dignity," for example); the strongly egalitarian, levelling outlook—"il n'y a pas des surhommes"[44]—the insistence on equality of rights for Africans, Asians, and Europeans, commoners and chiefs; the notion of the nationalist party, and thus the state—once the party has taken hold of it and remoulded it according to party principles—as the expression of the popular will; the idealization of the pre-colonial, pre-capitalist, collectivist African past; the linking of the ideas of national renaissance and international, particularly inter-African, brotherhood. The analogies with some of the central theses of Jean-Jacques Rousseau seem remarkably close. I would not argue that Rousseau's direct influence has been of special importance: I would doubt whether, even in the case of French-speaking African leaders, this is so. It is rather, perhaps, that a certain kind of historical situation, certain fundamental human problems to be resolved, tend to stimulate a particular way of thinking

---

[42] L. Sédar Senghor, *Congrès Constitutif du PFA (Parti de la Fédération Africaine),* Dakar, 1–3 Juillet, 1959, Rapport sur la Doctrine et le Programme du Parti (Paris, 1959), p. 54.

[43] L. Sédar Senghor, *op. cit.,* p. 64.

[44] From Sékou Touré: compare J-J. Rousseau—"Man is the same in all ranks; that being so, the ranks which are most numerous deserve most respect."

about the situation and the problems. Nor, of course, is African nationalist theory simply Rousseau tranplanted, any more than it is simply Marx transplanted (though it is certainly less misleading to regard it as the former than the latter). I would argue only that it belongs to a family of theories—which might be labelled "revolutionary democratic theories"—and that within this family Rousseau's teachings occupy a special and original place. In order to be able to say what are the distinctive characteristics of the various versions of African nationalist theory—how they differ from one another and from other non-African members of the family—a great deal more exploration would be necessary.

PART THREE

Continuity in Change

The Role of Traditionalism in the Political Modernization of Ghana and Uganda

DAVID E. APTER

University of California, Berkeley

Social analysts have long been preoccupied with those features of traditional culture and belief which affect the direction of change and the receptivity of a society to innovation. In spite of the very considerable literature concerned with acculturation, there have been few efforts to examine different types of traditional systems with respect to the problems they pose for political modernization. We attempt this form of analysis here. The plan is to examine two countries, Ghana and Uganda, which are engaged in the effort to build a national society. Each is experimenting with constitutional forms and each has had to deal with the problem of traditionalism. Indeed, the central problem of those concerned with building national, as distinct from local, political institutions has been to create overarching political parties, voluntary associations, and governmental forms that bridge older parochialisms. Moreover, just as tradition is a source of parochial strengths and social pride, so its characteristics vary widely. There are some who argue that any understanding of modernity in Africa must be based on an examination of the variants of the traditional systems.

In this article, we shall compare recent political events in Ghana and Uganda, and try to show how they have been shaped by the nature of traditionalism. By this means we can illustrate the implications of two different kinds of traditionalism and the problems they pose for modern nation-builders.

Reprinted from *World Politics*, XIII (1960), 45–68, with the permission of the author and the publisher. In an earlier form, this article was presented at the Dobbs Ferry Conference of the SSRC Sub-Committee on Comparative Government in 1959.

Research by the author in West Africa was first made possible through the generosity of the Social Science Research Council in 1952. Subsequent work was done in West Africa under the auspices of the West African Comparative Analysis Project, a Carnegie-supported research project that is still under way. Work on Uganda was undertaken in 1955–1956 through a Ford Foundation Area Research Training Fellowship. None of these agencies is responsible for the opinions expressed in this article.

I. TRADITIONALISM

The importance of traditional factors in change was not the discovery of Max Weber, as some have thought. Such antecedent greats as Marx and Coulanges sought to link to the problem of modernization those stable symbols, artifacts, and values transmitted by the people of a society through generations. Marx was particularly concerned with its economic aspects; Coulanges with its religious aspects. Since that time, the study of tradition has been either directly or indirectly brought into the most contemporary concerns. Most recently, Lerner has observed the behavioral consequences and durability of tradition by exploring degrees of participation in mass media of communication. Fallers has dealt with it in terms of bureaucracy. My own concern has focused on the functional implications of traditional political forms for modern ones.[1]

Nor is interest in tradition a peculiarity of social scientists. Politicians, no less than academics, recognize that traditional factors which under some circumstances seem to create immobilities in social structure, and abort or minimize innovation, at other times can open the door to an entirely different range of behaviors. Administrators who in Mali Federation (formerly Senegal and French Sudan) for years sought with only small success to establish effective local units of government, possessing cultural and solidary features satisfying to the population, now find the very same measures enthusiastically taken up by African leaders and interpreted as peculiar to the genius of Africans. Under the ideology of *negritude*, the meaning attached to community development, cooperation, and communalism has been transformed into a living and continuous feature of the African past. By this means, innovation has been "traditionalized" and made comfortable. Change is not strange or foreign, requiring new roles or learning. Traditionalism puts novelty on trial rather than the people that novelty is supposed to serve. The lesson of Mali is that contemporary administrators and political leaders in Africa who can learn to enlist traditionalism in the service of innovation will indeed be contributing to successful political modernization.

Traditionalism, as distinct from tradition, we can define as validations of current behavior stemming from immemorial prescriptive norms. It is not that traditionalist systems do not change, but rather that innovation—i.e., extra-systemic action—has to be mediated within the social system and charged to antecedent values. Modernism, in con-

[1] See D. Lerner *et al.*, *The Passing of Traditional Society*, Glencoe, Ill., 1958; L. A. Fallers, *Bantu Bureaucracy*, Cambridge, Eng., 1956; and D. E. Apter, *The Gold Coast in Transition*, Princeton, N.J., 1955.

trast, presupposes a much remoter relationship between antecedent values and new goals. Modern systems, with their complex and highly differentiated social structures, value change itself.

These distinctions between modernism and traditionalism, valid as they are, leave unanswered the question why some traditional systems can innovate more easily than others. Answers have been sought in the structural features of traditional societies, while traditionalism has remained a more or less undifferentiated concept.

The discussion here accordingly distinguishes between two types of traditionalism. The first can be called *instrumental;* the second, *consummatory.*[2] Each kind exhibits certain structural tendencies. The combination of value type and structural tendency determines the problems that confront political leaders as they seek to build modern nations. We shall examine these combinations in Ghana and Uganda.

As we are using the term, instrumental systems are those which can innovate easily by spreading the blanket of tradition upon change itself. In such systems, those who are called upon to arbitrate in matters of custom, and to interpret in some official capacity, are easily persuaded to find traditional counterparts in contemporary events. Such systems can innovate without appearing to alter their social institutions fundamentally. Rather, innovation is made to serve immemoriality. The characteristic structural expression of instrumental traditionalism is a military type of system, with hierarchical authority stemming from a single king or command figure.[3] Appointive ranks in the system tend to under-

---

[2] As we are using the terms, "instrumental" systems are those characterized by a large sector of intermediate ends separate from and independent of ultimate ends; "consummatory" systems are those characterized by a close relationship between intermediate and ultimate ends. The terms are derived from Parsons' categories of "cognitive-instrumental meanings" and "expressive-integrative meanings." See T. Parsons *et al., Working Papers in the Theory of Action,* Glencoe, Ill., 1953, p. 105.

In our sense, the difference between instrumental and consummatory values can be illustrated by the following example. Consider two traditional systems, one consummatory and the other instrumental in value type. Both are short-hoe cultures and an effort is made to introduce new agricultural techniques, particularly the use of tractors. In the consummatory system, changing from the short hand-hoe system will so corrupt the ritual of hoe-making, the division of men's and women's work, the religious practices associated with both, and the relationship between agricultural rituals and the authority of chiefs that it would be impossible to consider a tractor only in terms of increasing agricultural productivity. In the instrumental system, by contrast, the tractor would simply be viewed in terms of its ability to expand agricultural output and would not affect the ultimate ends of the system. In the first instance, such an innovation represents a threat to the system. In the second instance, it is far likelier to strengthen the system by increasing farm income.

[3] For a discussion of hierarchical authority, see A. Southall, *Alur Society,* Cambridge, Eng., 1956, esp. ch. 6. See also D. E. Apter, *The Political Kingdom in Uganda: A Study of Bureaucratic Nationalism,* Princeton, N.J., Princeton University Press, 1961.

write the king as the central source of authority. A heavy reliance on performance is a characteristic of office and the chief who fails to serve his king loyally and well is subject to removal or death. Religion is decidedly secondary in such a system, whose primary value is service to the king or state. Examples of such systems are Morocco, Ethiopia, and Buganda.[4]

The traditionalism of consummatory systems is much more complex. They were first described by Fustel de Coulanges when, deploring the simplistic interpretations of Greece and Rome as prototypes for modern societies, he wrote that examining the institutions of those two systems without a knowledge of their religious notions left them "obscure, whimsical, and inexplicable." He went on to say: "A comparison of beliefs and laws shows that a primitive religion constituted the Greek and Roman family, established marriage and paternal authority, fixed the order of relationship, and consecrated the right of property, and the right of inheritance. This same religion, after having enlarged and extended the family, formed a still larger association, the city, and reigned in that as it had reigned in the family. From it came all the institutions, as well as all the private laws, of the ancients. It was from this that the city received all its principles, its rules, its usages and its magistracies."[5]

Thus society, the state, authority, and the like are all part of an elaborately sustained, high-solidarity system in which religion as a cognitive guide is pervasive. Such systems have been hostile to innovation. Change has produced fundamental social upheavals such as migration to towns. Broken are the warmth and intimacy of custom. Not only were ancient Greece and Rome examples of such systems, but so was Ashanti.[6]

Our general hypothesis is that the instrumental-hierarchical type of system can innovate with ease until the kingship principle is challenged, at which point the entire system joins together to resist change.

[4] The reader should note that the name Uganda refers to the entire country, the Uganda Protectorate, which includes many different tribes; Buganda is a tribe within Uganda; the Baganda are the people (plural) of Buganda; a Muganda is a single member of the Buganda tribe; and Kiganda is the adjective form.

[5] Fustel de Coulanges, *The Ancient City*, New York, Doubleday Anchor Books, n.d., p. 13.

[6] Such systems can innovate, however. Indeed, the philosophy prevailing in Senegal today is similar to that described by Coulanges, but the religious system is pervaded by humanistic socialism. Hence to build upon traditional solidarities, the emphasis on family, corporatism in institutions, personalism, and the like go hand in hand with joint participation in communal economic efforts. By this means, work is ennobled and given new meaning in traditional terms. See, for example, the expression of this point of view by M. Mamadou Dia in *L'Economie africaine*, Paris, 1957, and "Economie et culture devant les élites africaines," *Présence africaine*, Nos. 14–15 (June–September, 1957), pp. 58–72.

In other words, such systems are highly resistant to political rather than other forms of modernization, and in particular cannot easily supplant the hierarchical principle of authority with a representative one.

Consummatory values are most significantly rooted where the structural expression of authority is pyramidal rather than hierarchical. Pyramidal structure means that patterns of subordinacy and superordinacy are limited to such activities as war or court appeals. For most purposes a chief or political leader is responsible to his social group rather than to a senior chief or official. The chiefs at each level of the pyramid thus have similar powers and are relatively autonomous of one another. Such a structural form relies heavily on semi-segmental kinship relationships. The autonomy of the chief or political leader is thus a reflection of the autonomy of the kinship unit itself.

The consummatory-pyramidal systems are highly resistant to all forms of innovation, and the consequences of change are external political groupings that form as new solidary associations cutting across the older ones. In other words, new social structures with a political focus emerge, with the object of tearing down the older ones. Let us examine these processes in Ghana and Uganda.

II. TWO TRADITIONAL SYSTEMS

Buganda, one of the most important kingdom states in the lake area of Eastern Africa, was regarded very favorably by Europeans who first came upon the country in the latter half of the nineteenth century. First Arabs, and then British and French missionaries, were welcomed by the king, or *Kabaka*, of Buganda. Kabaka Mutesa I encouraged competitive performances by the three religious groups—Muslim, Catholic, and Protestant. Although he died a pagan, he was intensely interested in Christianity.

To the Baganda, adoption of Christianity came to denote a superior technological and educational status. The older religious system, associated with the institution of clanship which was itself giving way to a hierarchical chieftaincy system, disappeared without producing much internal strain. Christianity easily passed muster as an aid to the Baganda in maintaining their society. The only point of concern was the fact that missionaries, in gaining adherents, tended to usurp the functions of chiefs. Since the latter remained responsible to the Kabaka, while the missionaries were not, a disturbing element was introduced into the political system.

Competition among religions, however, resulted in religious wars. These were eventually resolved by allocating fixed numbers of chieftaincies to Catholics, Protestants, and Muslims. The religious factions became tantamount to political parties within Buganda.

The missionaries themselves commented on how quickly the Baganda took to education and became ardent religionists as well.[7] After British intervention and the establishment of the Protectorate over Uganda, regular Catholic and Protestant school systems were established. The chiefs were the best-educated group in the population. Catholic chiefs were products of Kisubi, the Catholic school, and Protestant chiefs were products of King's College, Budo. Both were modeled after British public schools.

Moreover, freehold land tenure was introduced and 8,000 square miles were distributed among 1,000 chiefs and notables, who thereby became a kind of squirearchy. The recipients of the land were mainly Catholics and Protestants.

Whatever the innovated structure, whether civil-service chieftaincy, a parliament and council of ministers, modern education, or freehold tenure, it strengthened the system. The instrumental quality of hierarchical kingship was never defeated. The innovations that were most easily accepted were those that strengthened the Buganda government and also facilitated the individual's efficiency within it.

As a result, the organization of political life, which had been the crucial social structure in Buganda, was regarded as continuing from the past, with each innovation simply perfecting and strengthening an established system. All novelty came to be regarded as a device for strengthening tradition. As we shall indicate below, the main form of nationalism which emerged was that of a modernizing autocracy in which the government of the Kabaka and the Kabaka himself represented effective nationalism.

In Ashanti, on the other hand, responses to innovation were relatively complicated. Chieftaincy, despite its tiers of relatively autonomous powers with respect to various units of government, was nevertheless hemmed in with restrictions. Chieftaincy faced inward to the people to whom, by lineage and totem, the chief or headman was related. Instead of the individual atomism of Buganda, which was held together by regard for the Kabaka and the external force of hierarchical authority, the Ashanti chief was linked with an elaborate system of religiously sanctioned self-restraints on behavior. When land alienation began to occur in undue measure, for example, chieftaincy was affected and the stable confines of the social system were undermined. When Christianity was introduced, it helped to weaken the traditions of chieftaincy and

[7] See R. P. Ashe, *Chronicles of Uganda*, London, 1894; and A. R. Tucker, *Eighteen Years in Uganda and East Africa*, London, 1908, *passim*.

removed the control that the dead ancestors exercised over the living. The result was excesses by chiefs, who turned to British authorities for their support. When education was introduced, chiefs had to be ordered to send their children to school. While they could not disobey the orders of district officers, they often sent the children of their slave lineages rather than the children of royal blood. The succeeding generations of chiefs were thus by no means the best educated. The support required for the authority of the chiefs violated customary restraints on behavior. The excesses of the chiefs soon came to be regarded as perversions of traditional society, from which younger and more educated elements began to disaffiliate. Christianity helped ease the process of disaffiliation and there developed, along with an increase in urbanization and the growth of villages, the phenomenon of the urban village Christian and the rural village pagan. Most important, a series of wars between the British and the Ashanti was a token of the inability of Ashanti to absorb those innovating effects of a system of colonial rule which was basically common to both Buganda and Ashanti. In the end the *Asantehene,* or king of Ashanti, had to be exiled. Indeed, from 1901 to 1935, the Ashanti Confederacy did not exist as such.[8]

Within the context of the term "traditional," both Ashanti and Buganda were traditional systems. Both required validations of current behavior by appeal to immemoriality. Both had myths of origin involving a powerful figure associated with the formation of the society, and with whom the king had claims to ancestry. In the case of the Ashanti, the powers of origin descended to the Golden Stool rather than to a person. In Buganda, descent was reckoned through the line of kings, or Kabakas. That the preservation of power and continuity should reside in an object in the case of Ashanti—as distinct from a person, as in Buganda—is not without significance. For, in Ashanti, those in power serve the present by serving the past. It is a symbol of ancestral concern which is the visible repository of authority. In Buganda the king was, as both Roscoe and Fallers have called him, despotic.[9] While there was— and still is—pomp and ceremony around the king, he was not regarded as a descendant of living ancestors. He was rather the punishing, aggressive, and virile representative of a dynamic people expanding their military hegemony in the Lake Victoria region. Hence the essentially religious and theocratic nature of the Ashanti state, and the more secular and military character of Buganda.

There were other important differences between these societies. In

---

[8] J. N. Matson, *Warrington's Notes on Ashanti Custom,* Cape Coast, Prospect Printing Press, 1941 (2nd edn.).

[9] See, in particular, John Roscoe, *The Baganda,* London, 1911, p. 232.

Ashanti, the system of political organization had its prototype in the extended family, which included up to a hundred members, possessing strong solidary affiliations. Families lived together in villages and it was unusual for an Ashanti to live alone or with only his immediate family.

In addition, the Ashanti had an elaborate lineage system whereby recruitment to office and the allocation of rights and duties were organized. The core political unit was the village. The largest unit was the division, over which there was a paramount chief. Kumasi, which established a compact with the other Ashanti divisions in a historical episode veiled in mystery and magic, became the center of a Confederacy. An elaborate balance of checks and controls on authority extended from the village level to the division, including restrictions on the exercise of power by the Asantehene, or king of the Ashanti Confederacy.

The system in Buganda was much simpler in one respect, and much more complex in others. Unlike the chief in Ashanti, who was a religious figure, a lineage figure and, moreover, elected to office, the chief in Buganda was appointed by the king, or Kabaka, and was responsible to him. The chief was subject to summary dismissal at the pleasure of the Kabaka. Much closer to the Ashanti pattern was an earlier, pre-Kabaka, clan system which continued to play a part in subsequent periods. The king was both *Sabataka* (head of all the clans) and Kabaka.

Every Muganda is a member of a clan. Clans are hereditary. The elders of clans had responsibilities over the family, the social conduct of individuals, and inheritance. Chiefs, who were appointed, reflected the powers of the Kabaka. Clan elders, who were elected from eligible lineages, reflected religious and immemorial powers. These two principles of authority were in constant conflict. Increasingly, performance in serving the Kabaka and thereby the state became the basis of chieftaincy. Performance and service became readily identifiable since Buganda, as a military system, was in process of expanding at the expense of her neighbors.

The acceptance of hierarchical authority thus was associated with successful national aggrandizement and the pure authority of the Kabaka was not mitigated by any other countervailing principle. Tension within the system was produced by conflicts between clanship and chieftaincy. But the Kabaka represented the central authority in both systems—i.e., Sabataka or head of all the clans, and Kabaka or head of all the chiefs.

Two effects were immediately observable from the twin systems of organization in Buganda united by a system of autocratic and hierarchical kingship. Clans were scattered throughout the country. In any area an individual on the move could find a clansman and receive certain benefits from him. This not only facilitated mobility but also ensured considerable uniformity of custom and behavior throughout the system.

The chiefs, who were territorial governors for the king, were also military leaders. Their followers were loyal to the chief because the chief reflected the Kabaka's authority. This military-administrative system of organization included a massive network of military roads converging, radially, upon the center or capital. Yet the capital itself was often moved, so that there was no "center" and "hinterland."

The result was a "suburban" pattern of life in which clanship counterpoised chieftaincy in daily life, but each man's eyes centered upon the king. In time of war, which was often, the military administrative system required almost no modification. The necessary mobilizations took place under the chiefs. Food continued to be produced, and family life managed to go on quite well. In contrast, Ashanti had to shift to a quite different military formation in time of war, and then returned to their peacetime pyramidal organization when war was over.[10]

What were some of the controversial issues which the Kiganda system was unable to absorb? The most characteristic one was an inability to adjust to any permanent limitation on the power of the Kabaka. Whether a Muganda were chief or peasant, educated or not, he maintained the same unabashed veneration for the office of the Kabaka. Or, to put the matter another way, the principle of national aggrandizement was never lost, and the Kabaka was its symbol. Each of the major conflicts which aroused the Baganda and posed serious problems for the Protectorate government centered around possible dangers to the autonomy of Buganda or diminutions of the authority of the Kabaka.

In contrast to Ashanti, then, the Baganda have instrumental values. Ends are relatively well defined and essentially patriotic.

Both Baganda and Ashanti developed their own forms of tribal parochialism. The former were adept in retaining considerable political autonomy, and the Uganda Agreement of 1900, which stipulated the relations between Baganda and British, became a legal bulwark of ethnic nationalism and political parochialism. In Ashanti, where no

[10] Ashanti had a complex hierarchy of chiefs. At the pinnacle of the hierarchy was the *omanhene,* or divisional chief. Independent in his sphere of authority, he was nevertheless hedged about with restrictions. His was a religious role symbolizing lineage relationships to ancestors, and only members of a founder's or royal lineage were eligible to be elected to chieftaincy. The same held true for village chiefs and headmen. During war a division chief and others would take a position in the army and a more hierarchical system of authority would come to prevail. See E. Meyerowitz, *The Sacred State of the Akan,* London, 1951, especially ch. 10

such constitutional relationship existed, internal conflict was widely manifested throughout the entire area, creating instabilities which eventually led to mass nationalism. In more contemporary terms, in Buganda nationalist politicians have so far been able to make little headway and are regarded by the Buganda government as malcontents and ne'er-do-wells. One finds there an absorbing situation, in which the British authorities are anxious to see nationalist political parties develop on an all-Uganda pattern as the solution to building a modern state.[11] In Ghana, the party nationalists have become tantamount to the state itself, regarding chiefs dimly, to say the least. Not only have they taken active steps to break the chief's power, but the Asantehene, the paramount chief of Ashanti, has been their particular target. In the last encounter between the Asantehene and the party government, it was the former who had to admit defeat. The quasi-religious character of traditional society has been replaced by the quasi-religious character of modern nationalism in Ghana. We can analyze these developments more closely.

III. CONTRASTING EFFORTS AT POLITICAL MODERNIZATION

Uganda and Ghana are in the process of modernization. Practically, this has meant establishing parliamentary institutions by means of which the whole country is governed. Ghana achieved the level of political development in 1950 which Uganda now hopes to achieve. In other respects as well, Ghana has developed more rapidly. National income per head in Ghana is double that of Uganda. More effective internal transport and trade facilities are found in Ghana and Africans participate actively in all aspects of technical and commercial life. In Uganda, Asians and Europeans still monopolize the more important sectors of the economy and are the predominant racial groups in the civil service. In contrast, Africanization of the civil service in Ghana is virtually complete, with only a few senior positions and technical services still performed by Europeans, and these mostly on contract.

Ghana is economically well off for an African country.[12] Since 1951,

[11] See *Report of the Constitutional Committee, 1959* (Wild Report), Entebbe, Government Printer, 1959, pp. 33–35.

[12] A population of approximately 5 million in an area of over 90,000 square miles is divided into several main tribal groups. The northern peoples are chiefly grouped in Muslim kingdoms. The central group is the seat of the once-powerful Ashanti Confederacy. The southern groups—Fante, Ga, Ewe, and others—have had the longest contact with Western commerce and education. There are old families inhabiting the former "factories" of early traders who intermarried with the local people and established their own family dynasties. See J. Boyon, *Le Ghana*, Paris, 1958, pp. 7–10.

80 per cent of its internal savings has been based upon a single cash crop, cocoa. Other sources of income are gold, bauxite, manganese, industrial diamonds, and timber. It has advanced economically under a series of development plans, the first of which was primarily concerned with expanding basic transportation facilities. Railways were extended, a deep-water port built at Takoradi. The principle of a reserve fund for economic contingencies was established early. The first ten-year development plan was launched at the end of World War I and, except during the period of the world depression, Ghana has been development-conscious. Both under the later stages of colonialism and under her present nationalist government, she has been a social-welfare state.

What was the effect of innovation? Traditional chieftaincy and social organization increasingly became a focus for internal resentments. Bitter conflict over land developed. The pattern of self-restraints on behavior was upset. Land alienation in the form of concessions was common. Considerable friction developed between chiefs who took their seats not only in traditional councils, but on the legislative council and other conciliar bodies set up by the government, and the urban, educated elites which emerged with the spread of modern commerce. Each emerging group thought itself destined to inherit political power. The result was cultural withdrawal which prepared the ground for mass nationalism in Ghana after the Second World War. The chiefs, failing to consider the sources of mass nationalism, regarded it as simply an event in a long and stable cultural tradition which would only help to restore chieftaincy to its proper role.

The Western-educated elites regarded the nationalists as usurpers of their roles. The British viewed them as dangerous malcontents, subversive of public peace and good order. Such rejection gave fervor to the nationalists of the Convention People's Party (CPP), who by adherence to the party gave a new coherence to Ghana as a national society. They brought about a closer integration of the different peoples making up the territory, and they made economic and political institutions African rather than foreign by using them in the interests of self-government. Politics had already become polarized between traditional and secular authorities during the colonial period. Now the fundamental issues of traditionalism and modernity became wrapped up in more complex conflicts over democracy itself.

The major achievement of the CPP in Ghana was the organization and maintenance of an effective mass political organization. This resulted in centers of communication in the towns and villages, requiring members who could co-ordinate the activities of others. By building the CPP into a social group, a fraternity of the disadvantaged was encouraged to mold society in its favor by means of national political institutions and political freedom. A widely diverse membership was provided with a feeling of confidence in the future. Self-government was the goal. New opportunities were to be achieved thereby. A vision of a new society which was as vague as it was powerful was the moral claim of the CPP.

Yet in creating a mass political organization devoted to achieving independence, the CPP incorporated elements which had no long-run natural inclinations toward one another. More particularly, traditional groupings formed centers of opposition to Dr. Nkrumah both inside and outside the party. The main source of opposition was Ashanti. The Asantehene and his council helped plan the organization of an opposition, the National Liberation Movement (NLM), which itself renewed an old alliance between intellectuals and traditional authorities.[13]

With demands for a federal system of government, the situation rapidly grew dangerous. One Cabinet minister, a leading CPP figure from Ashanti, was ambushed outside his house and his sister killed. Government leaders did not dare to go to Ashanti for almost two years. Moreover, the appearance of successful traditionalism in Ashanti encouraged other opposition groups to form. In Accra, in Nkrumah's own constituency, there was formed an Accra people's movement which was essentially parochial and anti-Nkrumah. Everywhere traditionalism and the natural organization of the ethnic and tribal group seemed the only possible alternative to party rule by the Convention People's Party.

The conflicts over traditionalism and the future of democracy were sharpest during the period just prior to independence. In the general election of 1956, the candidates of seven parties and 45 independents ran for office. In spite of the fact that the NLM was able to put only 39 candidates in the field, and the CPP was well enough organized to contest all 104 seats, the latter received only 398,141 votes and the combined opposition received 299,116. This opposition vote was extremely high, considering the fact that a vote for the CPP was considered a vote for independence. Approximately 50 per cent of the electorate voted. In the post-independence period, the opposition was smashed. A series of acts rushed through Parliament were designed to break the power of

[13] In 1957 the NLM joined with other tribal parties like the *Ga Shiftimo Kpee* to become the United Party. The former leader of the party, Dr. K. A. Busia, is currently in Holland, Ghana's first real political exile.

traditional authorities. So successful were these efforts that, when elections to the Kumasi Municipal Council were held in February 1958, the CPP won 17 out of 24 seats—a remarkable achievement.

In attacking traditionalism, movements of the CPP type take on the characteristic of inviolability. They have a tendency to brand splinter groups and the opposition as playing into the hands of the "feudal" elements in society. The idea of party fealty is stressed more than any other.

The pattern which can be clearly seen in this conflict between traditionalism and modernism is thus the continuous affiliation to and disaffiliation from powerful social groupings that each make total claims on the allegiance and support of its members. The clear loser in such a situation is the opposition. In crucial respects, therefore, countries like Ghana find that in attacking tradition and supporting modernity they become one-party systems. It is not that there is no opposition, but that organized party opposition finds itself in difficult circumstances. Traditionalism, which serves the opposition as an effective rallying ground for popular support, is branded as subversive.[14] Indeed, at the Accra African Peoples' Conference in December 1958, tribalism and religious separatism were defined as evil practices by Africa's leading nationalists. It was resolved that "those African traditional institutions whether political, social, or economic which have clearly shown their reactionary character and their sordid support for colonialism be condemned."[15]

What, then, has political modernization meant in Ghana? Attacking tradition has resulted in the development of an "organizational weapon" type of party which, constantly on the attack, probes for weaknesses in the system. It seeks to jostle the public into functionally useful roles for the pursuit of modernization. To prevent the loss of power, and to modernize as rapidly as possible, are the basic goals of those who have inherited the mantle of British power. Modernization has come

[14] At the same time, the parliamentary opposition in Ghana has been effective on occasions. There are times when the CPP backbench threatens to bolt party whips and vote with the opposition. Such a threat has been a useful means of modifying the position of the government on several issues, not the least of which was modification of the Emergency Powers Bill, while the constitutional changes of early 1957 were incorporated under pressure from the opposition. Bitterly contested decisions which often resulted in suspensions of parliamentary sessions have been those involving basic liberties. Three such measures were the Ghana Nationality and Citizenship Bill, the Emergency Powers Bill, and the Deportation Bill. For an excellent study of Ghana's parliament, see D. G. Austin, "The Ghana Parliament's First Year," *Parliamentary Affairs*, xi, No. 3 (Summer 1958), pp. 350–60.

[15] All-African Peoples' Conference, Resolution on Tribalism, Religious Separatism, and Traditional Institutions, *Conference Resolutions*, Vol. 1, No. 4, issued by the Conference Secretariat, Accra, 1958.

to require a host of attitudes of mind and social organizations anti-thetical to traditional ways of doing things. Political modernization therefore attacks head-on traditional ways of believing and acting.

In these respects, the Ghana government has been unable to make use of traditionalism to support innovation. The past has become a dead weight on the present government, which by the use of induce-ments, and by occasional kicks and blows as well, seeks to drive people toward a new way of life. Because of the government's loss of support in the traditional sectors of society, the burdens of modernization on Ghana have become more intense. Unlike Senegal, where the blending of traditionalism and modernity has eased the transition to new politi-cal and economic forms, in Ghana traditionalism has not provided a genuine source of pride and inspiration. Unlike the French African con-cept of *negritude,* the slogan "African personality" has remained largely devoid of content.[16] Ghana, in assuming the heavy burdens of moderni-zation without the supports of traditionalism, has become a relatively autocratic system.

Uganda shows a completely different political pattern. Unlike Ghana, which is a maritime nation, Uganda is situated inland on the shores of Lake Victoria.[17] It is roughly the same size as Ghana, with an area of 80,000 square miles and a population of approximately 6 millons.[18]

By virtue of its superior institutions and successful collaboration with the British, Buganda was made a privileged area. The Uganda Agreement of 1900 formally recognized these privileges, and elsewhere in the country the Kiganda pattern of territorial organization was established—a three-tiered system of local government, each with a chief and a council (*Lukiko*) and ranging in scope from the parish to the county. The British retained an appointive chieftaincy system, but one which followed the practice of a regular civil service, with chiefs being promoted, transferred, and retired. Theirs was the task of maintaining peace and good order, collecting taxes, and otherwise taking care of the areas under their jurisdiction. Buganda, as a province, formed the

[16] It is interesting to note that while the term "African personality" is widely attributed to Nkrumah, it is in Nigeria that an effort is being made to give it content. Examples of such efforts are the journals *Black Orpheus* and *Odú,* which, as cultural and literary journals, seek to give a philosophic and cultural significance to the term.

[17] Blessed with an exceedingly good climate and well-distributed rainfall, most of Uganda is fertile agricultural country. To supplement her two main crops, cotton and coffee, she needs more diverse export commodities, and copper and other raw materials are being successfully exploited on an increasing scale.

[18] See *Colonial Report,* Entebbe, Government Printer, 1959. Buganda represents approximately 20 per cent of the population of Uganda.

model for the other ethnic groups to follow in the districts. In more recent times the parliament of Buganda, the Great Lukiko, has been the model for the district councils, which have become the object of considerable tribal parochialism in the districts outside of Buganda.

The three races, African, Asian, and European, live in uneasy proximity. Asians are involved in petty commerce, and increasingly in larger commercial enterprises in urban centers such as Kampala, while Europeans generally remain in charge of major commercial operations. Few Europeans were successful in farming in Uganda, where a situation comparable to that of the white settlers in Kenya never developed. Asians and Europeans have always tended to collaborate in representing the commercial interests of the country.[19] Asians were represented on the Legislative Council along with Europeans from the very onset, after World War I. No Africans were represented on the Legislative Council, nor was it regarded as desirable that they should be, until after the Second World War. It was widely held that Buganda's own Lukiko served as her political outlet, and the same situation was thought to prevail in the districts. It was regarded as essential to the interests of Africans that the principle of trusteeship, the mainstay of administration during the interwar period, should be maintained through the Governor and his staff.[20]

Until the present day, nationalism in Uganda* was largely expressed through the Buganda government "establishment." There is now stirring the kind of "modern" nationalism which is increasingly inclined to limit the powers of the Kabaka and make of Uganda a united, self-governing nation. But modernism as an ideology is confined to a very few. Indeed, it has been largely pre-empted by the Buganda government. Let us examine the process by which this occurred.

Although the Baganda did not suffer national defeats as did the Ashanti, religious wars in the latter part of the nineteenth century resulted in the deposition and restoration of the Kabaka by Europeans on two occasions. The Baganda have never gotten over that. Given the special position of the Kabaka in the structure of Kiganda society, cavalier treatment of them on the part of the Europeans deeply wounded and aggrieved the Baganda. Even during the period of their closest collaboration with the British (roughly from 1900 to 1926), such grievances were nursed. A singular touchiness has thus characterized relations between the British and the Baganda. Unlike the more typical

* I.e., Buganda.—W.J.H.

[19] The Indian Association and the Uganda Chamber of Commerce were instruments of that co-operation.

[20] For a discussion of this period, see K. Ingham, *The Making of Modern Uganda*, London, 1958, *passim*.

case in the districts, changes in political organization have, if they originated with the Protectorate government, been stoutly resisted. The Kabaka as a symbol of modern nationalism has been continuously strengthened and now has more power than at any time since British control.

When the Agreement of 1900 was signed, the Lukiko, or African parliament, dominated by the chiefs, was empowered to distribute land on a freehold basis to the most important people in Buganda. The three chief ministers received the largest estates (with the exception of the Kabaka himself), while others were given land according to their chieftaincy rank, or their general status.[21] Few pagans received any land.

Since chieftaincies had been divided up according to religion, both Protestants and Catholics of wealth came to have a considerable stake in the modified system. By fixing the proportions of chieftaincy along religious lines, family wealth and position were distributed in the same manner. Both Protestants and Catholics had some wealthy families in possession of land, and in important positions in the community. The Muslims suffered most of all the religious groups, while paganism quickly disappeared.

Those in the clan system who had been traditionally entitled to certain burial estates or clan lands, and who lost those lands during the parceling-out of freehold, became the first political force in Buganda. The clan system thus formed the "natural" opposition to a government of chiefs. This resulted in considerable internal dissension. Gradually the *bataka*, or clan groups, came to represent the *bakopi*, or peasantry. Land holding had become almost synonymous with prestige and social position.[22] Indeed, it appeared for a time that the system would become based on dynastic land-holding families, and the principle of easy access to political office and performance would be eliminated. Yet other innovations helped to prevent this. For example, the expanded educational system, which was enthusiastically supported by the Baganda, did not limit facilities to the children of chiefs, but included peasant children as well. Education was regarded as a major basis for entry into the political hierarchy (which remained the only major social organization throughout Buganda).

[21] Uganda Agreement of 1900, para. 15. See *Laws of the Uganda Protectorate, Native Agreements and Buganda Native Laws,* London, 1936, pp. 1380–81.

[22] Important in preventing such dissension from assuming proportions of "class conflict" was the fact that peasants could, and did, buy freehold land. Moreover, no landless peasantry was created. Everyone could get a leasehold property at a nominal and fixed rental. This deterred migration to towns, and no urban-rural cleavage developed. Buganda remains a rural "suburbia." See A. W. Southall and P. C. W. Gutkind, *Townsmen in the Making,* East African Studies No. 9, Kampala, East African Institute of Social Research, 1956, *passim.*

The instrumental values of the Baganda, colliding with a threatening monopoly of political roles by families of the senior chiefs who had received land, or by important Protestant and Catholic leaders, prevailed over both elites without altering the autocratic principle of hierarchical kingship. This allowed progressive modification of the Lukiko and greater opportunities to the public as a whole. Unlike the consummatory system of Ashanti, where individuals had virtually to withdraw from the traditional system in order to seek new careers and opportunities in a different kind of society, the Kiganda system was modified in practice, while posing few contradictions in principle.

Although the Buganda government was often in conflict with the peasantry, such conflicts appeared in the guise of government and its loyal opposition. The British, through a Resident, built up the influence of the chiefs and the ministers of the Buganda government. They regarded them as modern because of the ease and alacrity with which they learned to collect taxes, adapted themselves to methods of bookkeeping, and were able to control the public.

Thus the autocratic principle has prevailed in Buganda until the present. Innovations, it is widely believed, have come not from an alien source, but through the Buganda government itself. With the country's leaders able to maintain social discipline, because to act irresponsibly is to act against the Kabaka, a sense of awe and formality in social relations has helped retain public support. To keep the public "on the alert" and politically conscious, skirmishes against the intervention of the Residency are constantly fought.

As a result, the Baganda have regarded themselves as exceedingly blessed in a state of political autonomy. The Buganda government has been the most successful nationalist "party" in the country. Success in the economic field as well, particularly with the cotton and coffee crops, brought the Baganda considerable wealth as compared with the rest of Uganda. To add to their complacency, they had, by such visible indicators as tin roofs on their houses, number of bicycles, number of laborers from elsewhere working for them, and number of educated people, the highest standard of living in the Protectorate. They were able to absorb new forms of income, and to accept the standards of education, knowledge, skill, and training as requirements for a job such as chieftaincy, while retaining the essential character of their political system.

The freehold system, the chieftaincy system, the method of recruitment, the standards of selection, the acceptance of cash crops, all helped to make Buganda extremely modern in many ways. *But the prerequisite to accepting any modern feature on the political level was that some real or mythical traditional counterpart had to be found for it.* Hence, if the Lukiko was now a regular council with minutes, committees, and a budget, it was nevertheless regarded as an age-old institution. If chiefs were now almost invariably large landowners or related to the original holders of freehold, in custom those responsible for the control over "heads," i.e., over families and soldiers, were found to be the equivalent.

In 1955 several important measures were passed. In the districts, the District Councils Ordinance gave the councils both executive and legislative powers, enabling them to make bylaws on a wide range of subjects.[23] In Buganda, after the deportation of the Kabaka for refusing to co-operate with the Protectorate government (part of his effort to retain autonomy for Buganda), a new Agreement was signed which enhanced the powers of the Lukiko, made the Kabaka in effect a constitutional monarch, and gave the Baganda three new ministries—Health, Education, and Natural Resources—in addition to the three they already had (Prime Minister, Chief Justice, and Treasurer).[24] These reforms in effect gave to Buganda and to the district governments substantive warrants of authority and responsibility to attend to most of the economic and social schemes which are regarded as necessary to modernization. In Buganda the autocratic nature of the system has now come under attack—but the attack is still exceedingly mild. Elsewhere, in the districts, the effort to achieve local autonomy is regarded as the essence of political modernity.

What the system in Buganda cannot resolve are challenges to the principle of autocratic or hierarchical kingship. Resisting the first direct elections to be held in Buganda in 1958, the Baganda saw themselves threatened by devolution of authority to an African national government. Opposed to the nationalism of political parties, they regard representative government on an all-Uganda basis as tantamount to the destruction of their own society. In a pamphlet justifying the position of Buganda, the *Katikiro*, or Prime Minister, recently pointed out that the "peaceful growth of Western democracy in Buganda has been possible because the Baganda's customs and traditions are adaptable to new ideas which do not seek to uproot their fundamental political conceptions. . . ." Yet the pamphlet also warns that "The Baganda cannot exist as a people unless the Kabaka is the Head of the political structure in his Kingdom. Therefore, any constitution which envisages placing any other ruler or any foreign monarch in the position of the Kabaka of Buganda has no other intention but to cause the Baganda to cease to be a nation." More importantly, he concludes: "From time

---

[23] See *District Councils Ordinance, 1955*, Entebbe, Government Printer, 1955.
[24] See *Buganda Agreement of 1955*, Entebbe, Government Printer, 1955.

immemorial the Baganda have known no other ruler above their Kabaka in his Kingdom, and still they do not recognize any other person whose authority does not derive from the Kabaka and is exercised on his behalf."[25]

As a result of this position, it is the Protectorate government and British officials who are trying to build a modern national state in Uganda. How well they have succeeded is indicated by the fact that in the first direct elections in 1958, Buganda refused to participate, as did several other districts.[26]

Still more recently, a constitutional committee has recommended the establishment of responsible government at the center, with a legislature possessing 72 elected seats.[27] The Buganda government voiced its bitter opposition, but non-Baganda see in it the possibility of a political society not dominated by Buganda. With the Baganda anxious to secede from Uganda entirely if that is necessary to maintain the position of the Kabaka and the Buganda kingdom, there is bitter conflict between the Buganda government, on the one hand, and party politicians allied to British authorities, on the other.

There is now emerging among many Baganda an awareness that the absorptive capacity of the traditional system and its instrumental values has been reached. This is taken by the traditionalists to indicate a need for secession if the system is to be preserved. Younger groups are anxious to build a larger national society, a united Uganda. These are regarded as traitors by the traditionalists. However, the traditionalists are not anti-modern. Quite the contrary, as we have seen, they have built up a modern if miniature state in Buganda and now that very modernity is used as a justification for autonomy.

The result is that political parties remain largely ineffective both in Buganda and in Uganda as a whole. Recently, in an effort to gain popular support, several parties induced anti-Asian riots aimed at reducing the economic and commercial power of Indians. But in spite of such efforts, political parties remain weak and the Buganda government continues to be the main source of parochial nationalism. Political party leaders hope that when responsible government develops at the center and the financial resources of the country are allocated on the basis of popular government, the strength of the Buganda government will be diminished. The struggle to obtain parliamentary institutions is less

[25] M. Kintu, *Buganda's Position,* Information Department, Kabaka's Government, Kampala, Uganda Printing and Publishing Co., 1960, pp. 1–2.

[26] See C. P. S. Allen, *A Report on the First Direct Elections to the Legislative Council of the Uganda Protectorate,* Entebbe, Government Printer, 1959, Appendix J.

[27] See the Wild Report, *op. cit.,* which anxiously notes the need for political parties in order to create effective central government.

concerned with Britain or the colonial administration than was the case in Ghana. Rather, it is directed against the Buganda government because of its unwillingness to subordinate hierarchical authority to the principle of representative government. Thus the ethnic nationalism of Buganda remains the most important political obstacle to self-government and has crippled political party growth, rendering the political heart of the country virtually lifeless.[28]

As has been pointed out above, however, non-Baganda groups are developing a new political party that has been launched by recently elected African representatives of the Legislative Council. They seek to make the Legislative Council the crucial political organ in Uganda, and are reluctant to be tied to the tail of Kiganda parochialism. Thus the possibility presents itself that the central conciliar institutions of Uganda will now tend to favor the rest of the country. Grants in aid, development plans, and educational schemes can now become the target of competitive nationalism, fought out in the context of competing parochialisms. In that event, neither the traditional institutions nor their insularity will long be maintained.

Moreover, direct elections to the Buganda Lukiko will bring party politics strongly into the Buganda sphere.[29] It is possible that competitive nationalism can be transformed into federal government at the center. Federal government is a compromise system brought about by conflict among the constituent states, and conflict is necessary for its vitality. What is possible in the Uganda situation is political modernization in a federal system, in which the several traditional states will be allowed to modernize their institutions on their own terms. In the demand for federalism all groups see some hope for their survival. Federalism itself has come to mean political modernism.

IV. CONCLUSION

In both Ghana and Uganda tribal or ethnic parochialism has persisted with widely varying results. Kiganda parochialism has itself been a form of modernism. Civil-service chieftaincy and bureaucratic norms

---

[28] It must be pointed out, however, that in Uganda, unlike colonial Ghana, everyone knows that self-government is forthcoming. Lack of such certainty helped to develop an effective nationalist movement in Ghana, where to remain outside the party was tantamount to being pro-colonialist. In Uganda, all groups know that the country will eventually get self-government, and there is far more effort on the part of each of them to retain and expand their influence and power. Foreknowledge of self-government, in that sense, has helped to diminish the urgency of nationalism.

[29] Already in the new Lukiko, elected in 1959 (without direct election methods), five political parties are represented, a predominantly Catholic party supplying 80 per cent of all party representatives. The Buganda government has accepted the principle of direct elections but has steadfastly refused to implement it

have bolstered the kingdom. Indeed, the Buganda government is widely regarded as the most progressive force in the country. Hence, for the Baganda, to be modern is to be parochial.

In Ashanti, modernism clashed directly with traditionalism. The religious aspect of the traditional political and social structure was an important part of a network of suitable restraints on behavior. When these were disrupted by innovations in commercial enterprise and colonialism, traditional authority was quickly undermined. Yet because traditional authority was so much a part of daily life and custom, those who broke with tradition found themselves in drastic need of new and powerful social affiliations, for to break with tradition was to break with family, lineage, and ancestral fidelity.

In contrast to Ashanti, Buganda remains the most powerful solidary association possible. Social satisfactions are still achieved within Buganda and its government for all those who belong to the kingdom. In Ashanti the formation of a new political party was itself a process of forming new and powerful symbolic attachments. The Ashanti members of the CPP became fiercely devoted to the organization. The messianic role of the leader was based on the development of a new morality to supplant the old. Hence the deep cleavages in society which remained after self-government had been obtained posed the problem of nation-building after independence rather than before it.

We can summarize some of the more salient points of contrast between the two systems as follows:

(1) *Absorption of innovation.* Ashanti, with its consummatory-pyramidal system, was unable to control the effects of innovation. Ashanti tended to shrink from contact with the modern world. Early missionaries were imprisoned. The Ashanti wars were efforts to expel the British, as a foreign body, from the body politic. The effects of contact loosened the hold of traditionalism, although it remained a powerful force.

Buganda was able to control innovation. The European presence was absorbed and rendered useful. By careful planning and the use of modernizing agencies, the Buganda government increased its autonomy and control as time went on, rather than suffering partial decay.

(2) *Internal divisions and discontinuities.* What had hitherto been reinforcing social institutions of the consummatory system of Ashanti rapidly broke down into competing power groups and sources of internal antagonism and weakness. Thus the development of conflicts between youth and age, royals and non-royals, slaves and non-slaves, were all examples of conflict over the continuing strength of particularistic criteria which could be reconciled only so long as older religious and

institutional checks were sustained. Such social controls were highly internalized, with authority variously distributed. As soon as the continuity of past and present was disrupted, the various groupings rapidly came to compete.

In Buganda the internal conflict continued, as in the period prior to contact, between clanship and chieftaincy—all, however, under the umbrella of the king as both Sabataka, head of all the clans, and Kabaka, or king. The advantages of appointive chieftaincy had long been apparent in the military undertakings of the kingdom and a secular tendency inherent in the system was simply reinforced by contact with the British. The system was able to modify itself to restrain the old conflicts sufficiently so that the principle of hierarchic kingship did not require substantial alteration. Allegiance did not become confused.

(3) *Competition for affiliations.* Internal conflict in Ashanti produced widespread attitudes of guilt. Cleavages divided the extended and nuclear families. Social breaks which meant modifying one's religious practices and sundering ties with the past (and one's ancestors) led to migration of individuals to urban areas which supported very different patterns of social life. These created more fundamental differences in outlook between urban and rural groups who, within one generation had grown apart but were still not socially distant. The Ashanti were able to retain affiliations among those who represented orthodoxy. However, breaking such affiliations could not be resolved by the simple acceptance of heterodoxy. Rather a new orthodoxy had to be posed against the old. Thus the new affiliations of the political party assumed the proportions of a militant church movement.

In Buganda, there was relatively easy adaptation of internal cleavage to serve the larger purposes of the state. As a result, no Baganda repudiated their chiefs or the Kabaka. The Buganda government was itself a source of modernism, and no incompatibility between modernism and traditionalism resulted in the enforced disaffiliation of discontented groups. No discontented urban groups emerged, anxiety-ridden and seeking drastic change.

(4) *Legitimacy conflicts.* Just as innovation could not be controlled in Ashanti, so the secular authority of the colonial government was posed against the traditional authority of the chiefs. Immemorial prescriptive rights clashed with concepts of efficiency and performance as a basis of authority. In Buganda, the autocratic principle prevailed and two oligarchies, British and Baganda, worked alongside one another. They were in constant competition, but they did not challenge each other's legitimacy. Both were oriented to efficiency and performance.

In Ashanti almost any outside activity, by being resisted, posed an ultimate legitimacy problem. So closely interrelated were the elements of social life and belief that they conformed nicely to Durkheim's concept of a fragile and mechanical society. Ultimately all threats were threats against legitimacy. Hence not only was colonialism viewed as a threat to traditional legitimacy, but nationalism was even more so. The conflict between lineage and ancestral sanction (immemoriality) for current acts and secular forces was introduced by colonialism, and helped to produce the nationalism which then had to break the power of traditionalism and its residual hold upon the public. Thus modern nationalism in Ghana is essentially an effort to create a wider legitimacy which introduces some of the same instrumental characteristics which Buganda possessed traditionally. *The result is a growth of an autocratic principle of leadership in Ghana*—the organizational weapon serving as its own justification.

In contrast, in Buganda, the conflict over legitimacy never emerged in sharp form in the colonial-Buganda government relationship. Indeed, even when the Kabaka was exiled, early in the relationship, or more recently when the present Kabaka was deported, the principle of the Kabakaship was not questioned by the Protectorate government authorities.

However, now that the problem of building wider affiliations has been tackled effectively by the Protectorate government, political parties are challenging the principle of hierarchical authority. *They are seeking to supplant hierarchical authority with representative authority* as a means of building a modern nation. They do not, however, need to create attitudes of universalism and performance as the basis of political recruitment since these are already widespread and traditional.

Where the consummatory-pyramidal system prevailed, there developed fierce competition between traditional and secular leaders to monopolize allegiance. This was expressed by the latter in efforts to build overarching and autocratic institutions which by autocratic means fostered egalitarianism in political recruitment and the exercise of authority. The problem was to prevent social atomism while mobilizing those resources of the society which could capitalize on change itself. This put exceedingly heavy burdens on political nationalists, whose need for organizational control and support became all important.

In the instrumental-hierarchical system prevailing in Buganda, change has aided parochialism and modernism of a local sort, making political modernism of the national state more difficult to achieve. Where consummatory values prevail in the traditional sector, the political leaders lose the advantages of traditionalism. Their need is to find new ways and means of employing it to ease the burdens of political development. Where instrumental values prevail, the local and national forms of modernism need to be brought into some kind of useful identity so that instrumental traditionalism can reinforce political modernization at the national level.

Ghana shows the effects of a single-party unitary government and its difficulties in modernization. Can a modernizing nation be created through a federal system of government in which the parts will reinforce the whole? In this respect, Uganda represents a potential alternative to the Ghana pattern. Out of regard for instrumental traditionalism, Uganda may find a political compromise proximate to the needs of the public, achieving modernity with both prudence and freedom.

Modernism and traditionalism have become key political issues. Buganda has retained both her tribalism and her separatism, penalizing the political advance of the country as a whole. Ashanti, the last stronghold of tribalism in Ghana, has been defeated by modernism in the form of nationalism. Buganda and Ashanti, Uganda and Ghana, both facing similar problems in different ways, shed some light on the politics of modernization in contemporary Africa.

The Predicament of the Modern African Chief:
An Instance from Uganda

LLOYD FALLERS

Princeton University

The role of the modern African chief poses difficult problems of analysis because it is a role which is played out in a matrix of diverse and often conflicting institutions. Perhaps it would be better to say that the chief occupies many roles. On the one hand, he has a series of roles in the indigenous institutions of African society. On the other hand, he occupies roles in the imported institutions of colonial government. Of course, in various parts of Africa institutions of African and European origin have met under widely varying circumstances and have interpenetrated in varying degrees, but nearly everywhere the effect is confusing and bizarre. In Uganda, for example, if we were to visit a chief we might find him attending a committee meeting, helping to work out a budget for the coming fiscal year. If we ask for an appointment, we will be received in a modern office equipped with typewriters, telephones, filing cases, and the other apparatus of modern bureaucracy. If by chance we had called on another day, our chief would have been unavailable. He would have been meeting with his clan mates in the thatched hut of his paternal uncle, and the talk would have been of genealogical refinements and the wishes of the ancestors. If we are invited to have tea at the chief's house in the evening, we will be introduced to his several wives, and this may surprise us because we have heard that he is a pillar of the local Anglican parish and a patron of the Boy Scout troop. I have chosen a rather extreme, though not unreal, example. Reading the literature on the various areas of modern Africa, one is impressed by the patchwork character of the chief's social milieu. It appears to be a collection of bits and pieces taken at random from widely different social systems. Modern African society as a whole fre-

Reprinted from *American Anthropologist*, LVII (1955), 290–305, with the permission of the author and the publisher. This is a slightly revised version of a paper read before a conference on "Stability and Change in African Societies," jointly sponsored by the Social Science Research Council and the National Research Council, at Princeton, New Jersey, October 14 through 16, 1953.

quently gives this impression, but in the case of the chief the effect is heightened because his role is so often the meeting point, the point of articulation, between the various elements of the patchwork.

It is perhaps because of this confusing diversity of elements in the chief's social world that relatively few attempts to analyze his role in systematic terms are to be found in the social science literature on Africa. There are, of course, important exceptions, notably the papers by Gluckman and his colleagues of the Rhodes-Livingstone Institute on the village headman in British Central Africa (Barnes 1948; Gluckman, Mitchell and Barnes 1949; Mitchell 1949) and Busia's recent (1951) book on the chief in present-day Ashanti. Probably there are others. Generally, however, such published material as is available is of two sorts. First there is the large and growing body of official and semiofficial literature dealing mainly with what might be called the ideal structure of African politics as conceived by colonial governments. Notable here are Lord Hailey's (1950, 1953) five volumes on the British dependencies and much of the content of the *Journal of African Administration*. This is the literature of what is called in British territories "Native Administration," and it is concerned with those institutions which are the result of explicit planning on the part of the administering power. Sometimes these institutions embody many elements of indigenous institutions; sometimes they are wholly, or almost wholly, new. Everywhere they represent attempts by colonial governments to erect intervening institutions, manned by Africans, between themselves and African peoples. Familiarity with this literature on native administration is of course essential to the student of African politics, but by its very nature it seldom reaches deep levels of subtlety in the analysis of political process. It is concerned with formal arrangements, with the ways in which power *ought* to flow, and it treats such arrangements in quite general terms, emphasizing that which is common to native administration over wide areas often containing great diversities of indigenous social structure. It seldom concerns itself with the ways in which such indigenous diversities combine with the formal, official institutions to form the real pattern of politics within a tribal or ethnic area.

The second type of material generally available is that gathered by anthropologists in the course of investigations into the traditional structure of African societies. Such studies are most often concerned with the role of the chief in the *traditional* political structure and tend to treat those features of his role which are the result of modern conditions as peripheral to the main focus of study. If the official literature on native administration looks at the chief as he *ought* to be, or as the

District Officer hopes he will be tomorrow, the bulk of the anthropo-logical literature looks at him as he was yesterday. There are reasons for this emphasis. Rightly or wrongly, anthropologists have frequently seen their primary task to be the documentation of the full range of varia-tion in human society. They have therefore devoted themselves to the analysis of precisely those features of African society which existed be-fore contact with Europeans. Modern developments are usually men-tioned in monographs but most often only as representing the destruc-tion of the integrated social systems which existed before. Judged by the task which they have set themselves—the analysis of indigenous institu-tions—the work of anthropologists in Africa has been a high standard indeed, representing perhaps the richest body of monographic literature possessed by anthropology today. However, such studies do not often yield full analyses of the present-day role of the African chief.

The reason why we have so few adequate studies of the modern chief's role may be found, I think, in certain characteristics of the conceptual schemes commonly applied by students of African societies. African studies have been the home par excellence of structural socio-logical or social anthropological analysis, a tradition founded by Durk-heim, elaborated by Radcliffe-Brown, and more recently applied so brilliantly to empirical research by Fortes and Evans-Pritchard. The virtues of this frame of reference are obvious and familiar to anyone acquainted with the real classics of social science which have been its fruits. Its primary concern is to analyze the ways in which institutions dovetail with one another to form an integrated whole—the ways in which, to put it another way, the institutional demands made upon individuals are harmonized so that the demands of institution X do not run counter to the demands of institution Y, but rather complement and support them. As a result of such studies we now have, for exam-ple, excellent detailed analyses of the relationships between political and religious institutions among the Nuer (Evans-Pritchard 1940, 1951, 1953) and the Tallensi (Fortes 1945, 1949).

The difficulty which arises when this point of view is applied to the present-day role of the African chief or, indeed, to many other features of modern African society, is that much of what we observe appears, as I have said before, to be a patchwork of diverse and conflicting ele-ments. Institutions are constantly getting in each others' way, and indi-viduals are constantly being institutionally required to do conflicting things. If our point of departure is a conception of the integrated social system, we can say of such situations only that "society has under-gone disorganization" or that "cultures have clashed." We can say rela-tively little, I think, about why the particular kinds of disorder which we observe occur. Increasingly, however, we want knowledge of precisely this kind.

One key to the escape from this dilemma lies, I think, in a recognition that the notion of "social order" or "social system" can have two referents, both of which are quite valid, but which must be distinguished. One consists in order or system in the sense of harmonious integration, the notion which I think structural social anthropology has stressed. Order in this sense exists to the degree that institutions making up a social system mutually reinforce and support one another. The other referent is order in the sense that the phenomena observed may be subjected to systematic analysis leading to greater understanding by the analyst of the connections between events, whether these events relate to harmony or to discord. This meaning corresponds, I think, to the natural scientist's notion of "order in nature," leaving aside the philosophical question of whether the order really exists in nature or only in the scientist's head. In this latter sense, a society which contains major elements of disharmony or conflict may be studied just as fruitfully as one characterized by a high degree of internal integration. It would perhaps be better to say that the *disharmonious elements* of a society may be studied just as fruitfully as the harmonious ones, since presumably no society is ever either completely integrated or completely at odds with itself.

If I am right in thinking that there are these two possible conceptions of order or system in social life, then it follows that the second conception, that of social life as subject to systematic analysis without regard to its harmonious or disharmonious character, is the more fundamental. It is in the nature of a first assumption which we must make if we are to study the disharmonious elements in societies. The first conception then, that of order in the sense of harmony, finds its place in our frame of reference at the next stage and it defines a range of variation. The elements making up a social system will be harmonious or disharmonious in varying degrees and ways, and we will require concepts for talking about these various degrees and types of disharmony.

On the most general level, concepts of this kind are not hard to find. Delineating the elements involved in the *integrated* or *harmoniously functioning* social system has been one of the major preoccupations of social scientists, and lists of such elements may be found in almost any text or theoretical volume. All that is required in order to utilize such a list in the study of relative harmony-disharmony is to treat each of the characteristics of the integrated social system as subject to variation. Perhaps the most generally agreed-upon characteristic of the integrated social system is the sharing of a common system of values by its members. If the actions of the individuals who are members of the system are to be mutually supporting, these actions must be founded upon common conceptions of what is right and proper. Actions which are in accord with the common norm will be rewarded, and those which run counter to it will be punished. Sometimes it is useful to distinguish "means" from "ends" within the general field of common values. Or one may find it useful to distinguish between situations in which value integration requires actual sharing of common values and those in which it requires merely that values held by groups within the system be compatible. Further distinctions under this general rubric might be drawn, but it is clear that integration among the values held by its members is one of the characteristics of the harmoniously functioning social system. It is also clear, however, that in actual social systems the degree to which value system are integrated is subject to wide variation.

A second general characteristic of the integrated social system is a sharing of belief or a common system of cognition and communication. Persons must share not only a common system of means and ends but also a common system of symbols enabling them to interpret each others' behavior, as well as other events, in a common way. For traffic to flow smoothly on a crowded street, drivers must not only share the common value of obeying the law, but must also interpret red lights and green lights in the same way. Again, however, the sharing of symbols is by no means always complete, and we may expect to find social systems in which malcommunication is a common occurrence.

Again, the integrated social system is one in which the motivations of its component individuals are to a high degree complementary with the shared systems of value and belief. Actually, this is merely the other side of the social coin. To the degree that values and beliefs are actually shared, persons will "want" to do the "right thing" and will believe the "correct thing" and will be responsive to rewards and punishments which nudge them in this direction. The common values and beliefs of the social system will be built into the personalities of its members so that they will be adequately motivated to do the things others expect them to do. Where the system of value and belief is held in common and its parts harmoniously integrated, persons will not be expected to do incompatible things. All this, however, is also clearly subject to wide variability in concrete social systems. Individuals may be insufficiently motivated to socially valued behavior, or they may have placed upon them conflicting social demands.

I have been at some pains to spell out a point which may seem obvious to some and irrelevant to others because I believe it has a direct bearing upon the prospects for fruitful research into the role of the chief in modern Africa. In many areas the chief lives in a disordered and conflict-ridden social world, and it is important, if we are to reach some understanding of this chief's position, that we be able to talk about this conflict and disorder, if I may so put it, in an ordered way. In many regions of Africa today, and indeed in many other colonial and semicolonial areas, the situation is not simply one of two radically different social systems colliding head on and, as it were, holding each other at bay. Though in some areas something approaching this situation may exist, it is not generally so. More commonly, African and European social systems have interpenetrated with the result that new social systems embodying diverse and conflicting elements have come into being. We must therefore be prepared to analyze systematically situations in which incompatible values and beliefs are widely held by members of the same social system, where individuals are regularly motivated to behavior which in the eyes of others is deviant and where other individuals have conflicting motivations corresponding with discontinuities among the values of the social system. We must be able to think analytically about these elements of relative disharmony and to determine their consequences for the functioning of such systems as wholes.

Something of what I have in mind may be illustrated by the situation of the chief today in the Busoga District of Uganda, where I have been engaged in field research under the auspices of the East African Institute of Social Research and of the Fulbright Program. Conditions in Busoga, and, indeed, in Uganda as a whole, have provided perhaps the optimum situation for the harmonious mutual adjustment of African and European social systems. The absence of extensive European settlement has meant that there has been little or no competition for land. The successful importation and cultivation on small peasant holdings of cotton, coffee, and groundnuts have provided a cash crop economy upon which a rising standard of living could be built without detriment to food crop cultivation. Administrative policy has stressed the recognition and gradual remolding of indigenous political institutions without sharp breaks with the past. In this situation, European and African institutions have, indeed, merged to a striking degree, but the result remains a social system containing major elements of disharmony and conflict. In large measure, the role of the chief is the focus of this conflict.

Peoples of Uganda Protectorate

Busoga was "discovered" by Europeans in 1862 and came under British administration in 1892; the temporal base line for the analysis of change in the Soga political system therefore lies in the latter part of the nineteenth century. At this time, Busoga was not a political entity. It did have sufficient linguistic and general cultural unity to mark it off from the other Bantu-speaking areas of southern Uganda so that in 1862 John Hanning Speke, the first European explorer of the area, was told that "Usoga" comprised the area bounded by Lake Victoria, Lake Kyoga, the Nile, and the Mpologoma River. These are the boundaries of the present-day Busoga District. (See map.) The inhabitants of the area, the Basoga, appear to have numbered some half-million. They were sedentary subsistence cultivators and livestock breeders, relying for staple foods mainly upon their permanent plantain gardens and plots of millet, sweet potatoes, and maize. The country is described by early travelers as being extremely fertile and closely settled, particularly in the south along the Lake Victoria shore.

Politically, Busoga was divided among some fifteen small kingdom-states, which varied widely in size but which shared a fundamental similarity in structure. The elements of this common political structure may be seen in three key institutions: *patrilineal kinship, rulership,* and *clientship.*

In its fundamentals, Soga kinship followed a pattern common in East Africa. Descent was traced in the patrilineal line, and kinsmen sharing common patrilineal descent formed corporate groups which were important units in the social structure. Kinship terminology was of the Omaha type. The most important unit formed on the basis of patrilineal kinship was the lineage, comprising all those persons within a local area who were able to trace the patrilineal genealogical relationships among themselves. This lineage group was important in land-holding, through the rights which it exercised over inheritance and succession by its members. An individual was free to choose his heir from among his sons, but his testament was subject to confirmation or revision by the council of his lineage-mates, which met at his funeral. The lineage played a prominent role also in marriage. Most young men were unable to meet from their own resources the marriage-payment demanded by the bride's kinsmen and so had to depend for aid upon their lineage-mates. Such dependency gave the lineage at least a potential influence over its members' choice of marriage partner and an interest in the stability of marriage. Finally, the importance of the lineage in temporal affairs was matched and complemented by its role in relation to the supernatural. The most prominent feature of Soga religion was the ancestor cult, founded upon the belief that patrilineal ancestors maintained an interest in and influence over the well-being and good behavior of their living descendants. Common descent thus involved a common sacred interest in the ancestors, and this in turn, through the ancestor's graves, which were the focus of the cult, reinforced the lineage members' corporate economic and legal interest in the land.

Units other than the lineage were also formed upon the basis of patrilineal kinship. The individual homestead was located in space by the practice of patrilocal residence, and where extended family homesteads were formed, these took the form of a small lineage group composed of a man and his sons together with their wives and children. Beyond the lineage, groups of lineages which were known to be related patrilineally but which were unable to trace the precise genealogical links among themselves formed clans which were unified by a common clan name, common totemic avoidances, and the rule of exogamy. Patrilineal kinship thus defined a large sector of the individual's life; it controlled inheritance and succession, structured marriage, gave form to religion, and strongly influenced the spatial distribution of homesteads.

Soga society was not, however, a segmentary society in which unilineal kinship constituted the only principle of organization. Through the institution of rulership, members of many patrilineal groups were bound together to form kingdom-states in which membership was defined, not in terms of kinship, but in terms of territorial boundaries and common allegiance to the ruler. In each of the kingdom-states there was a royal clan or lineage (in the case of the royal group, clan and lineage tended to be coterminous because royal genealogies were better remembered), which was set above commoner groups as having higher rank and an inborn fitness to rule. The ruler's position was hereditary within the royal clan. He was the active head of the kingdom and the overlord of all other holders of authority. He was also the chief priest for, as the ancestors of commoner lineages were thought to both assist and control the behavior of their descendants, so the royal ancestors were in a sense *national* ancestors who took a similar interest in the affairs of the nation as a whole. The ruler, being their descendant, was supported and controlled by them in his conduct of national affairs and was the intermediary through whom they might be approached on behalf of the nation. Inherited regalia and a courtly style of living centering around an impressively constructed capital symbolized and enhanced the ruler's political power.

To complete this outline of traditional Soga political structure requires the addition of the third of the institutions noted above—that of clientship. The administrative staff through which the ruler in each of the kingdoms governed was recruited neither through patrilineal kinship in commoner lineages nor through membership in the royal group. The ruler's leading lieutenants—the prime minister and the chiefs of territorial divisions—were commoners bound to the ruler by personal loyalty. Often they were chosen from the many servant boys, sons of ordinary peasants, who were sent to serve in the palace and to seek social advancement. This mode of recruitment to positions of subordinate power was a partial solution to a problem which apparently afflicted most Bantu kingdoms in the Great Lakes region. All members of the royal group shared in some measure the inborn fitness to rule, but within the royal group there was no clear-cut rule of seniority.

Throughout the kingdom there were princes—junior members of the royal group—in control of villages or groups of villages, and these persons were a potential threat to the paramount authority of the ruler. When the problem of succession arose, any member of the royal group who could command a measure of support might assert a claim to rulership and fighting not uncommonly broke out. The institution of clientship, through which commoners of administrative and military ability were raised by the ruler to positions of authority and thus were bound to him as personal followers, provided an administrative staff which could be trusted with power. Not sharing the inherited rank of the princes, they were not potential usurpers. At times of succession, the major clients under the previous ruler participated along with members of the royal clan in choosing a new ruler and thus exercised a disinterested and stabilizing influence upon the ambitious princes. They also acted as a check upon the ruler's power, since if he failed to govern within the limits set by custom they might combine in support of a rival prince and drive him from his position.

Traditional Soga society thus took the form of a hierarchy. At the top was the hereditary ruler—the paramount holder of authority and the central symbol of the kingdom's unity. At intermediate levels were the princes administering villages or clusters of villages and, counterbalancing them, the ruler's administrative staff of client-chiefs administering other villages or village clusters in the name of the ruler. Forming the broad base of the society were the communities of commoner agriculturalists organized into corporate patrilineal groups. Commoner and royalty, kinsman and kinsman, patron and client, were bound together by highly personal rights and obligations. Subordinates owed superiors economic support through the payment of tribute, military support in war, the recognition of judicial and administrative authority, and personal loyalty. Subordinates in turn received paternalistic protection and aid.

The sixty years which have passed since the establishment of the British Protectorate in Uganda have seen the radical reconstruction of this political system, to a great extent as a consequence of explicit planning by the administration. Innovations were introduced gradually, however, and under circumstances which contributed greatly to the willingness of the Basoga to accept them. During the early years, little was changed in the formal structure of Soga political institutions, though their day-to-day functioning was substantially altered. Initially, the aims of the administration were limited to the establishment of "law and order," which meant an end to warfare, and the creation of a system of revenue and trade. In the pursuit of these limited aims, the indigenous political structure was simply taken over intact, given new tasks, and allowed to continue functioning under the supervision of administrative officers. The rulers of the various kingdoms continued to hold hereditary office and to recruit their administrative staffs through personal clientship. The judicial and administrative powers of rulers and chiefs were recognized, and even enhanced, by Protectorate legislation which made them statutory judges and gave them the authority to issue administrative orders having the force of law. They continued to be supported by tribute paid by the commoner population. In recognition of the authority of the colonial government, they were required to collect taxes, to assist in public works, and to submit their judicial decisions to review by administrative officers. The one major structural innovation was the setting up of a District Council composed of the rulers of the several kingdoms.

Even during this initial period of limited aims, however, important developments were taking place within Soga society. Though the additional functions which were imposed upon the indigenous political structure were minimal, they involved one important change. This was the introduction of literacy. Tax collection involved bookkeeping and administrative supervision over the courts required the keeping of written records of litigation. Every chief or ruler now either had to be literate or required the services of a literate clerk. This development was made possible by, and in turn stimulated, the development of mission education. Soon the sons of important rulers and chiefs, and ultimately the rulers and chiefs themselves, were mission-educated and largely Christian.

The loss of political independence and the innovations which accompanied it were made much more palatable to the rulers and chiefs by the support which they received from the administration and by newly developed sources of wealth. As I have noted above, the position of the ruler or chief in traditional Soga society was not particularly secure. Warfare was more or less endemic and the threat of revolt served as a constant check upon the ruler's exercise of power. Now, not only were the traditional authorities backed by the superior power of the British administration, but they were also able to enhance their economic position. Cotton was introduced at about the time of the first World War and it soon spread rapidly as a peasant cash crop. Tribute could now be collected in cash or in labor upon the rulers' and chiefs' cotton plots. Within a few years there developed a new chiefly style of life, which included imported consumption items such as European-style clothing and houses, automobiles, and, incidentally, mission education, which required the payment of fees.

This early period thus saw the development of a new kind of elite position for the traditional political authorities in Soga society. With greater power and an enhanced wealth differential, they now stood above the common people in ways which had not been possible for them in pre-administration times. This situation was very rewarding to them. It goes far to explain, I think, why they were so very ready to accept the supervision of administrative officers and why, later on, they were willing to accept much more profound innovations in the political structure. They had in large measure committed themselves to the new conditions.

The initial period, characterized by limited administrative aims and by the building up of the traditional authorities, came to an end in the nineteen-twenties and -thirties. The new policy of the administration came to be one of remolding the traditional political system in the direction of European-style civil service bureaucracy and electoral democracy. In a series of stages between 1926 and 1936, tribute was abolished and the chiefs and rulers began to be paid fixed salaries from a native administration treasury. The loss of tribute was painful to the chiefs and rulers, not only because it meant a reduction in monetary income, but also because tribute was in itself an important symbol of their power and prestige. Nevertheless, in part for the reasons I have mentioned, the change was accepted. A further fundamental change was introduced which concerned the basis of recruitment to office. Over a period of years, the administration came to insist more and more upon the recruitment of chiefs upon the basis of objective competence, and during the nineteen-forties it became established that not only chiefs but also the rulers themselves, who had previously been hereditary, would be chosen upon this basis.

Since, at first, rulers' and chiefs' sons tended to monopolize the mission schools, "recruitment on the basis of competence" meant, essentially, recruitment of the most competent from this group. With more widespread education, the group from which chiefs were recruited became wider. Again, no serious opposition was encountered. What had previously been a hierarchy of hereditary rulers, princes, and client-chiefs thus became in a strict sense a hierarchy of civil service bureaucrats, recruited upon the basis of competence, increasingly as indicated by formal education; paid fixed salaries out of revenue from general taxation; subject to bureaucratic transfer and promotion; and pensioned upon retirement.

Within recent years, this bureaucracy has tended to proliferate, as the Uganda Government has pushed forward its policy of devolving more and more responsibility upon the native administration, now known as the African Local Government. The hierarchy of civil servant chiefs which replaced the traditional hierarchy of rulers and client-chiefs has been supplemented by specialist officials concerned with taking over from Protectorate Government departments responsibility for matters such as finance, public works, agriculture and forestry, public health, and law enforcement. Concerned that this bureaucracy not become an irresponsible monolith, the Government has also encouraged the growth of elected councils, leading up to a District Council which is responsible for advising the bureaucracy, framing legislation, and preparing an annual budget. The strength of this trend toward devolution of responsibility upon the African Local Government may be seen in the fact that the share of direct taxation allocated to the African Local Government treasury is now four times that collected for the Protectorate Government. In 1952, the African Local Government Budget called for the receipt and expenditure of more than a quarter of a million pounds.

During the period of British administration, Soga political structure has been radically altered by the introduction of new institutional forms, which have achieved widespread acceptance by the Basoga. The new civil servant chiefs are granted great respect and are popularly regarded as legitimate heirs to the former authority of the traditional rulers and client-chiefs. Appointment to the civil service is regarded as a highly desirable goal for the ambitious young man. The acceptance of new institutions does not mean, however, that a harmoniously integrated social system has resulted. In many cases traditional institutions which are in large measure incompatible with the new ones have survived. The result is a social system which shows major deviations from harmonious integration in its value system, in its system of communication and belief, and in the social personalities of its members.

Traditional Soga political institutions emphasized the value of particular personal rights and obligations, a pattern which Parsons (1951) has described by the terms *particularism* and *functional diffuseness*. Relations were particularistic in that they emphasized personal loyalty between individuals who stood in particular status relations with one another, for example, as kinsman to kinsman, patron to client, or royal to commoner. One owed particular loyalty to *one's own* kinsman, to *one's own* patron or client, or to one's ruler *as a person*. Relations were functionally diffuse in that they involved a wide segment of the lives of the persons involved. Kinsmen, for example, were expected to stand together as total persons and to take a legitimate interest in the most intimate aspects of each other's lives. A patron was similarly related to his client, as is indicated by the difficulty of distinguishing a political subordinate from a personal servant and by the common practice of linking client to patron through affinal ties. The basic virtue was personal loyalty between particular individuals.

The value system associated with bureaucratic organization is in most respects in opposition to this pattern. Here the guiding norm is, as Max Weber has expressed it, " . . . straightforward duty without regard to personal considerations. . . . Everyone in the same empirical situation is subject to equality of treatment" (1947:340). Relations in such a system are to be, in Parsons' terms, *universalistic* and *functionally specific*—universalistic in that universally applicable rules, and not particular statuses, are to be the determinants of conduct, and functionally specific in that they relate to specific contexts and not to the whole of individuals' lives. As a civil servant, one ought to treat everyone alike without regard to particular status considerations. One applies general rules and procedures. One's competence is severely limited to what are called "official matters" and one is enjoined not to become involved in, nor even to know about, the personal lives of those with whom one has relations *as a civil servant*. This norm of disinterested service is of course the constant goal of all Western political systems, and it was the aim which led the British administration to introduce the civil service system into Busoga.

In Busoga, these two value systems today exist side by side, and both are represented in major institutions. The patrilineal kinship system is very much a going concern, in large part because its stronghold, the traditional system of landholding, has remained intact. Corporate lineage groups continue to exercise jurisdiction over inheritance and succession and this keeps the ties of kinship alive and strong. The strength of kinship ties is, however, a constant threat to the civil service norm of disinterestedness. The wide extension of kinship bonds means that a chief is frequently put into the position of having to choose between his obligation to favor particular kinsmen and his official duty to act disinterestedly. He may, for example, be asked to favor a kinsman in a legal case or to exempt him from taxation. Again, the institution of clientship survives and leads a *sub rosa* existence within the civil service. Although formally civil servants are chosen for their objective competence, in fact opportunities may arise for building up personal followings of clients. Senior members of the African Local Government, through their influence with the administration, are able to exercise substantial influence over the appointment and promotion of subordinates and are thus able to build up personal political machines.

I want to emphasize that *both* these value systems are institutionalized in Soga society and that both are accepted by most Basoga as, in a sense, legitimate.

The system of belief and communication is also a focus of disharmony within the social system. Relatively widespread primary education and exposure to mass communications media have produced a situation in which at least two sets of symbols and two views of the nature of the world are current in the society. Again, as in the system of values, it is not so much that different individuals interpret events differently as that the same individuals are trying to work with two sets of symbols at the same time. A chief may, for example, read a newspaper and have a good working knowledge of world politics, but he may still not be quite certain that Europeans are not cannibals or that witchcraft does not really work. Again, these disharmonies in the system of belief and communication center upon the chief because it is he who is most simultaneously involved in the two systems through his relations with European officers on the one side and with peasants on the other.

Discontinuities in the systems of value and belief are reflected in inconsistencies in the social personalities of persons playing roles in the system. Since both the civil service norm of disinterestedness and the personal ties of kinship and clientship are institutionalized, both are also internalized in the personalities of individuals. It appears to be the case, though it is somewhat difficult to think about, that chiefs and most other Basoga hold both value systems and both systems of belief at the same time. This results in frequent conflict, both between persons and within persons. In social interaction, an individual is likely to uphold the value or belief which seems advantageous to him in a given situation. The kinsman of a chief is likely to expect preferential treatment in court and to bring the pressure of the lineage group to bear upon the chief if such preferential treatment is not granted. The same individual is outraged, however, if someone else does the same thing. Similarly, a chief is likely to exercise "pull" through a highly placed patron, if he can, in order to secure promotion, but complains bitterly about such behavior on the part of others. A chief who is requested to exercise favoritism on behalf of a kinsman or a friend is put into a literally impossible position. Both his internalized values and the sanctions impinging upon him from society pull him in opposite directions. Whichever way he jumps, he will be punished, both by his own remorse at having contravened values which are part of his personality, and by sanctions applied by others.

One of the consequences of these conflicts and discontinuities is a high casualty rate among chiefs. Where conflicting demands pull him in opposite directions, it becomes very difficult for the chief to avoid falling afoul of sanctions. The administration, of course, strongly upholds the civil service norm. If a chief is caught engaging in nepotism or embezzlement, he is dismissed. But he may also be dismissed for upholding the civil service norm. If he offends a prominent superior by refusing to grant particularistic demands, he may find that charges of corruption have been "framed" against him, and he may be dismissed for the very thing which he has refused on principle to do. The poor communication prevailing between the Basoga and the administration and the consequent dependence of the latter upon senior chiefs for information make it unlikely that such fabrications will be exposed

Thus, from the point of view of the chief acting in his role, the discontinuities in the Soga social system impose severe burdens. It is possible to view these discontinuities also from the standpoint of their consequences for the system as a whole. From this point of view, it would appear that some of the conflicts noted above act to stabilize the system in a period of radical institutional change. I have stressed the point that these conflicts do not consist primarily in discrete groups of persons holding opposed systems of value and belief; they consist rather in the *same persons,* to a great extent throughout the society, holding two incompatible systems of belief and value. They appear *in action* in the form of conflicts between persons. A chief acts in terms of the civil service norm of disinterestedness and he is punished by others who wish him to act in terms of particularistic obligations. The *persons* in such situations, however, are interchangeable; on another occasion, the same chief may act to fulfill particularistic obligations and may have sanctions brought to bear upon him by the same persons who now, however, wish him to act disinterestedly. This *taking into* the social personalities of individuals of conflicts which might otherwise express themselves in conflicts between discrete groups of persons acts, I suggest, to maintain some unity and stability in the system. Very often— perhaps most often—in societies undergoing rapid change, the latter situation has developed. The society has divided into intransigently opposed factions or parties with the result that consensus can be reestablished only through the defeat, often by violence, of one group by the other. Of course, which of these alternatives one considers "better" depends entirely upon one's value position.

I have described the Soga political system only in outline as an example of the sort of disharmonious situation which I think we must be prepared to study if we are to reach greater understanding of the present-day role of the African chief. The situation is of course much more complex than I have been able to indicate. If there were more

time, I should like to say something about what appear to be some of
the consequences of the kind of institutional dilemma I have described
for the personalities of chiefs. There are indications that for chiefs who
do contrive to avoid falling afoul of sanctions, and who remain in
office, this success is achieved at considerable psychic cost. The East
African Institute of Social Research is currently engaged in a program
of research into a number of contemporary East African political systems and we hope, through a combination of institutional and personality analyses, to throw some light upon the reactions of personalities
to such situations as well as upon other aspects of political process in
these systems.

I should like to add just a word about the situation which I have
described in a comparative perspective. This situation, which in its
broad outlines is typical, I think, of Uganda as a whole, is probably
rather unusual in the broader African picture. In Uganda, there have
been few occasions for open conflict between European and African
social systems as such. Economic conditions have been beneficent and
administrative policy has emphasized gradual and orderly, though
steady, change. The result has been a really astonishing degree of
African acceptance of things European and a readiness to plunge into
radical institutional change. New institutions have been quietly incorporated alongside old ones and conflicts between new and old institutions have been taken into the personalities of individuals who play
roles in them. At considerable cost to its component individuals, the
social system has come through radical transformation without splitting
into opposed factions and without a serious showdown with the European innovators.

Elsewhere in British Africa, two other types of situations appear
to be more common. In the classical "indirect rule" territories, such as
the Gold Coast and the South African High Commission territories,
there was also, as in the early stages in Uganda, a recognition of indigenous political institutions, but it appears that there has been much
less emphasis in those territories on remolding such institutions and on
devolving new responsibilities upon them. The traditional political
systems have been preserved in more nearly their original form so that
when new political institutions do develop the traditional ones tend to
be bypassed and to remain as centers of conservative opposition. Such
a process seems to have occurred in Ashanti where, one gathers, the
Youngmen's movement arose as a "progressive" opposition to the "conservative," government-supported chiefs and ultimately contributed substantially to a self-government movement which was even more hostile
to traditional political institutions. Another type of situation seems to

exist in areas such as the Union of South Africa, parts of Central Africa, and in Kenya, where policy has stressed the rapid adaptation of Africans to the requirements of European settler communities. There again one sees African societies split into conflicting groups: traditional authorities who have had little recognition and who have gradually lost position and influence, government appointees who are often looked upon by others as stooges, and, occasionally, charismatic leaders of radical movements who oppose both the others. Comparisons with French and Belgian Africa should prove illuminating, though I am too little familiar with those territories to attempt such comparisons. One has the impression, however, that the French policy of "assimilation" and the Belgian emphasis upon economic as against political development have produced situations substantially different from those found in British territories (see, for example, Delavignette 1950).

I should like to end with a plea for more empirical studies of contemporary African politics. The great complexity and diversity of political phenomena there provide a fertile field for social scientists of many interests and disciplines.

REFERENCES CITED

BARNES, J. A.
  1948 Some aspects of political development among the Fort Jameson Ngoni. African Studies VII: 99–109.

BUSIA, K. A.
  1951 The position of the chief in the modern political system of Ashanti. London, Oxford University Press.

DELAVIGNETTE, R.
  1950 Freedom and authority in French West Africa. London, Oxford University Press.

EVANS-PRITCHARD, E. E.
  1940 The Nuer. London, Oxford University Press.
  1951 Kinship and marriage among the Nuer. London, Oxford University Press.
  1953 The Nuer conception of the spirit in its relation to the social order. American Anthropologist 55:201–14.

FORTES, M.
  1945 The dynamics of clanship among the Tallensi. London, Oxford University Press.
  1949 The web of kinship among the Tallensi. London, Oxford University Press.

GLUCKMAN, M., J. C. MITCHELL and J. A. BARNES
  1949 The village headman in British Central Africa. Africa XIX:89–106.
HAILEY, LORD
  1950, 1953 Native administration in the British African territories. London, Her Majesty's Stationery Office.
MITCHELL, J. C.
  1949 The political organization of the Yao of Southern Nyasaland. African Studies VII:141–59.
PARSONS, T.
  1951 The social system. Glencoe, Ill., Free Press.
WEBER, M.
  1947 The theory of social and economic organization, ed. and trans. T. Parsons. New York, Oxford University Press.

Traditional Authority and Social Action in Former British West Africa

ST. CLAIR DRAKE
Roosevelt University

A multi-dimensional revolution is sweeping the continent of Africa in this, the second half of the twentieth century. Economic, social, and political changes are occurring at a pace which evokes the politicians' metaphors such as "a raging hurricane," or prophetic book titles such as *Africa: Continent of the Future*. The social and economic factors underlying this process of change were isolated and analyzed by a number of sociologists and anthropologists prior to the outbreak of the series of political explosions which have occurred during the past ten years[1]—"Positive Action" in the Gold Coast; Mau Mau in Kenya; Defiance Campaigns in South Africa; riot and rebellion in the Congo. Few social scientists, however, realized the extent to which a political revolution was maturing, or foresaw the extent to which new social formations—African political parties, cliques of radical intellectuals, and pressure groups based upon sentiment and interest—would crystallize out of the social process and become catalysts of change as well as independent factors in a complicated process of social disorganization and reorganization.

Once the great nationalist upsurge had occurred, however, it became grist for the mill of the political scientists, some of whom have addressed themselves to the problem with skill and insight.[2] Comparative analyses and case studies of political action in Africa have begun to appear, and the groundwork is being laid for a sociology of African

Reprinted from *Human Organization*, XIX (1960), 150–158, with the permission of the author and the publisher. Dr. St. Clair Drake is Professor of Sociology at Roosevelt University, Chicago, Illinois and Visting Professor of Sociology at University College of Ghana. He is co-author, with Horace Cayton, of the classic study, *Black Metropolis*.

[1] See, e.g., B. Malinowski, *Dynamics of Culture Change;* Monica Hunter, *Reaction to Conquest;* G. Balandier, *Sociologie Actuèlle d'Afrique Noire;* and the publications of the Rhodes-Livingstone Institute, particularly the works of Max Gluckman and Clyde Mitchell.

[2] Note David Apter, *The Gold Coast in Transition* and James S. Coleman, *Nigeria: Background to Nationalism* as examples.

politics. In the meanwhile, descriptive studies of various aspects of the
political process may provide raw material for analysis as well as problems which can be refined for more thorough research and analysis.
This is the *raison d'être* for this brief study which involves a small
portion of West Africa.

THE SHIFT IN POWER IN WEST AFRICA

All of the former British and French colonies and trust territories in
West Africa are now sovereign states or have entered upon the final
stages of transition toward independence. The process began in 1952,
when Kwame Nkrumah became the first African Prime Minister of the
Gold Coast. After five years of quasi-independence, the Gold Coast became fully independent in 1957, and was renamed Ghana. Independence
then followed rapidly for Guinea, Senegal, Soudan, and Togoland.
Now Nigeria, with its thirty-five million inhabitants, will become independent in 1960, Sierra Leone following in 1961, while the tiny colony
of Gambia is making constitutional changes and discussing its future.
The Ivory Coast, Dahomey, Niger, and the Upper Volta are currently
negotiating with France for an independent status. All of the leaders of
West African states are talking of "closer union," and Ghana's prime
minister is stressing the desirability of merging the West African territories into a single state.

The entire West African area is poised for "a leap into The
Twentieth Century." In each territory, plans are being made and
implemented for the expansion of educational and health facilities, for
the improvement of agriculture, and for eventual industrialization.
There is recognition everywhere, too, of the fact that the new governments will have to meet the rising level of popular expectations if they
are to survive after the high emotional pitch of the "anti-imperialist
struggle" and the unifying force of "a common enemy" have diminished.
The term "socialism" has become a popular verbal symbol of the
promised welfare state.

In each territory, power has shifted from the hands of a governor
and his civil-servant bureaucracy into the hands of an African prime
minister and his cabinet of ministers representing a mass political party
which elects both the executive and the legislators. Since party machines
depend upon the support of a mass of illiterate voters, a skillful use of
personal, visual, and verbal symbols is necessary to organize consent and
to legitimatize the new rulers and the conciliar institutions. Most
leaders consider "strong government" a necessity for attaining development goals.

The new elite has inherited a skein of knotty problems from the colonial regimes. Not the least important of these problems is that of how to secure effective collective action on the part of a bewildering diversity of ethnic groups at varied levels of economic development and social complexity, and with differential degrees of exposure to, and acceptance of, Western values. No colonial regime ever tried to solve this problem through the instrumentality of representative government. The new elite, however, is trying to do so. The presence of a "traditional order" presents problems as well as opportunities.

THE STRUCTURE OF TRADITIONAL AUTHORITY

In each of these states, Western-type executive, judicial, and legislative institutions exist side by side with "traditional" institutions—familial, religious, economic, and political.[3] A process of adjustment and fusion of these two types of political and social institutions is evident everywhere, a process which began in the days of colonial rule and which still remains. This process is inexorable and irreversible.

While local and regional variations exist throughout West Africa, it is possible to construct an ideal-type formulation of the major characteristics of "traditional authority" as it existed prior to colonial contact:

1) The controls of kinship groups were basic. Within kinship groups (family, extended family, or clan), although lineage or clan leaders had extensive executive and judicial authority, there was a wide measure of discussion and consultation by adults of both sexes when crucial decisions were involved. *Legislation was not a primary issue. The rules of life were largely set by custom.* Discussion centered around the expediency of concrete actions within the framework of customary rules; rules were reinforced by sacred sanctions.

2) At the village or town level, even though "chiefs" or other wielders of authority and power might come from designated families or clans, the commoners often had some say about the selection of individuals, or where they did not, they frequently had the power to oust them. Where this power was not directly given to the populace, it was often vested in representatives of kin or "ward" groups, elders, or other types of councils. Decisions—executive, judicial, and

[3] Succinct surveys of traditional institutions in English-speaking West Africa may be found in the Ethnographic Survey Series of the International African Institute, edited by Daryll Forde. Surveys are available for the peoples of Nigeria, the Gold Coast, and Sierra Leone.

legislative—when taken by chiefs were normally decisions by "chiefs-in-council," not their lone dictatorial decisions. Chiefs had ritual power as well as political power.

3) In the more complexly organized societies, covering wider geographical areas, there were "tiers" of political power. Sometimes a paramount chief existed as a ritual and political head, over subordinate groups of chiefs who formed his council, and these, in turn, were the representatives of groups of villages and clans whose interests they were inclined to protect, and which they sometimes represented as delegates.

4) Among some West African peoples, corporate groups existed which served as checks upon the abuse of power by chiefs. Cases in point would be the *asafo* groups or *mmerante* among the Akan peoples; or some of the so-called "secret societies" in various places, one of the best known of which was the Poro Society among some of the Sierra Leonian and Liberian tribes. Where the political power of cults and societies was not direct, such institutions always influenced political decision-making indirectly.

Autocrats occasionally subverted this primitive democracy, and there were, of course, undemocratic elements in traditional African societies. Nearly all West African societies were characterized by a heavy male bias even when they were matrilineal, and many of them placed limitations upon the rights of "strangers" or had depressed strata as an integral part of their structure. The prevailing *ethos* put the accent upon *age* as a primary attribute of power holders, and, therefore, limited the full utilization of intellectual talent or the verve of youth.

The prevalence of animistic beliefs and of a mystical attitude toward nature inhibited social innovation as well as technical inventions, while the widespread belief in witchcraft (*juju*) introduced an element of tension into group life that is not present in interpersonal relations in those cultures where the source of evil is located in a devil who exists outside the boundaries of the social group, or where one's destiny is attributed to Providence, Fate, the planets, or "accident."

Finally, no elements were present in these societies leading toward self-generated change in the direction of individualism and equalitarianism, as was the case in the capitalistic and rationalistic societies of Europe and America. African societies had to wait for the introduction of such elements from without. Traditional authority operated to buttress all of these conservative tendencies, for the merging of ritual and secular power (whether it resided in lineage elders or in chiefs and kings) stabilized the society by inhibiting social change.

However, there are some observers and leaders who feel that, at the rural local level, the still viable *communal ethos* of African cultures brings powerful reinforcement to the carrying out of contemporary development plans, and that the existence of extended family obligations obviates the necessity for devising elaborate social security systems. They would strive to retain these features, which are sometimes referred to as aspects of "African Socialism."

The old pattern of mandated authority and of frequent consultations between leaders and the led is also frequently cited as a feature worth preserving; but the new imperatives of budget making or the provision of sanitary services and village planning, require a degree of speed and efficiency of administration with which prolonged deliberation and a system of "going back" for consultation before taking action is inconsistent. Few defenders of African traditional societies would contend that they can cope with the totality of demands imposed by the goals of democratization and modernization.

TRADITIONAL AUTHORITY AND COLONIAL RULE

Colonial rule in West Africa began less than two hundred years ago despite over five hundred years of trade relations with Europe and America, and of contact with missionaries among coastal peoples. Native rulers, even along the coast, preserved their hegemony throughout most of this period and a process of state-building, similar to that which occurred in post-neolithic Mesopotamia, began throughout the whole area bounded on the north and east by the Niger River. A pattern of "traditional authority" had become stabilized in this entire area by 1840, involving three "tiers" of political structure:

a) A few "royal families" and their retainers exercising sovereignty over relatively large areas which included the ancestral homeland of the specific ethnic group from which the ruler came and the territory of tributary ethnic groups (e.g., the Asantehene in Ashanti-land or the King of Dahomey, ruler of the Fon people);

b) A larger number of "kings" of city states and their immediate hinterlands (e.g., the Obas of the Western Region of Nigeria);

c) "Paramount Chiefs" over smaller ethnic or regional areas often owing allegiance to rulers of types (a) and (b).

d) Thousands of local chiefs at the village level;

e) Chiefs and headmen exercising authority over enclaves of "strangers" residing within towns or villages.

The pattern of "indirect rule" in British areas made full use of this structure as an agency of administration.

The technique of colonial rule was essentially the same throughout the area, namely to install a small but highly efficient army and police force to "keep the peace"; to find allies among traditional rulers (chiefs, emirs, and "kings") wherever possible, and to allow them to function very much as before but with the moral, financial, and military backing of the European power.[4] Where it was not possible to enlist the aid of the traditional rulers, it was the policy to replace them with other African leaders who were cooperative (warrant chiefs or appointed chiefs). In each territory, a civil service bureaucracy was established, with Europeans in the top control spots, but with Africans trained to serve in the minor posts. In every case, too, a great deal of ritual and pageantry created and maintained the *mystique* of the Governor and his immediate circle in order to impress and overawe the African population with the power of the metropole.

Traditional rulers were rather generally relieved from the checks imposed upon them in traditional society. Efficiency of administration in the interests of organizing local populations for such ends as supplying labour for European homes, mines, and plantations; for the recruiting of soldiers, the collecting of taxes, and for suppressing certain aspects of local cultures which outraged the moral sentiments of those back home; the suppression of violent conflict between ethnic groups— these were the ends for which *restriction* rather than *expansion* of indigenous representative government was often deemed necessary. A loyal chief was considered more dependable than a recalcitrant council or a reluctant constituency. Money, power, prestige, and patronage could often secure the loyalty of a chief or elicit a commercial concession from him, and these new relationships freed chiefs from the nuisance of popular restraints.

Yet, in coastal urban areas throughout British West Africa, the advisory Legislative Council, with members nominated from among cooperative traditional leaders and "safe" educated Africans, became, under pressure from the Africans, an institutionalized increment which

[4] E.g., Kofi A. Busia, *The Position of the Chief in the Modern Political System of Ashanti*, Chapters VI and VII on "British Rule and the Chief."

formed the basis for eventual evolution into fully elected legislative assemblies.

Throughout West Africa, traditional authority has survived the impact of colonial rule. "Chiefs," the traditional rulers in West Africa, continue to settle cases of disputes according to customary law and to control the allocation of land in their role of custodians of the people's patrimony. They also have religious duties to perform; they have sacred as well as secular roles. Their right to tax and to dispose of tax monies was jealously guarded in the days of colonial rule and is still conceded. Their position, quite understandably, still gives them great prestige in the eyes of the illiterate people who are the bulk of their subjects.

TRADITIONAL AUTHORITY AND THE NEW ELITE

The accession to power of the educated African elite has meant a threat to the status of, and to some extent to the power and privileges of, the traditional rulers who, in a sense, were "protected" by the colonial governments. They would not have been human had they not all been apprehensive over their fate, and had not many of them taken positive steps to protect their position. The extent to which, even today, traditional rulers resist pressure from the new elite may be illustrated by an extreme case, that of the small British colony of Gambia.[5] In this territory, with a population of only three hundred thousand people, there were, in 1958, thirty-five paramount chiefs in the hinterland protectorate. Of these, only five were literate. The town of Bathurst and the immediate environs constitute "The Colony" and it possesses a small elected legislature and a pattern of party politics. It is customary for the protectorate chiefs to hold an annual conference, and when they did so in 1958, they invited the Bathurst politicians to come and meet with them to discuss constitutional changes which were impending.

Three of the four Bathurst parties had proposed a Legislative Council for the Gambia of twenty-seven seats. They had made the concession of suggesting that twenty seats be allotted to the Protectorate, all of them to be filled by election with universal suffrage. They wished to have a cabinet of nine ministers chosen by the victorious party. The chiefs made counter-proposals, asking that eight of the twenty seats be reserved for persons nominated by the chiefs' conference rather than thrown open for election. They also insisted that women not be allowed

---

[5] "Chiefs in Gambia Politics: I," *West Africa* (October 18, 1958), 987 and "Chiefs in Gambia Politics: II," *West Africa* (October 25, 1958), 1017; and *West Africa* (March 15, 1958), 251.

to vote in elections to fill the other twelve seats. The chiefs also wanted no party politics in their areas and wished to have the nine ministers chosen on a *regional* basis.

The chiefs were scornful of all the city politicians' compromise proposals, causing one exasperated urban political leader to say,

Although universal adult suffrage is desirable for the Protectorate, we don't want to force it down the chiefs' throats. But if we find this is the only way of getting them to accept political parties in the Protectorate, we would have to insist.

The last speaker for the chiefs' side said,

We won't be forced into anything we don't like and no one can force us.

Some Gambia chiefs have, upon occasion, said that they would prefer to remain under colonial rule rather than to accept leadership from the new elite.

The problem of accommodating the structure of traditional authority to the new conciliar structure is one to tax the ingenuity and mature judgment of every West African statesman. Two years ago, the editors of the publication, *West Africa,* published a leading article, "Chiefs in Transition," in which, after discussing the position of chieftaincy in a number of West African countries, it was stated that,

. . . the diversity of West Africa is in no way better shown than in the differing functions of chiefs in the different countries today. One test of the skill and maturity of West African politicians is their sucesss in finding a place for chiefs in the new West Africa. There is no single answer and the different positions in which chiefs now find themselves in different territories is due as much to the basic differences in the institution itself as to the degree of radicalism with which the politicans approved of it.[6]

The fate of traditional authority will be finally settled primarily in terms of the extent to which traditional rulers can be rendered innocuous as a power threat to the new governments or can be turned into a positive asset; and to the extent to which traditional authority and political practices can be fitted into a situation which demands the quick release of productive energies, and efficient, expeditious decision-making on economic and political questions. Since traditional rulers do,

[6] *West Africa* (November 29, 1958), 1129–1130.

in fact, often have considerable prestige and do wield power, the initiative is, by no means, entirely with the new elite. Adjustments and compromises must be made which are not entirely satisfactory to either side, but the ingenuity of the compromises, the diversity of the systems of accommodation, and the new patterns of stabilization are indeed impressive. The Western Region of Nigeria has been studied as a case in which redefinition of the role of chiefs has proceeded most smoothly. Ghana, on the other hand, presents a case where redefinition has been more difficult. Due to limitations of space only the Ghana case can be discussed in this article.

THE RESOLUTION OF THE CHIEFTANCY CONFLICT IN GHANA

Ghana, with a population of between six and seven millions, is a new nation, formed by the knitting together of four discrete regions which had formerly been administered by Britain as "The Gold Coast."[7] The coastal southern area was called "The Colony." Here, the dominant tribes were the Fantes and Akwapims, among whom chieftaincy was highly developed and cherished; and the Gas, among whom the institution was somewhat less influential. The British colonial government organized the paramount chiefs of this area into an advisory and consultative body known as the Joint Provincial Council of Chiefs (JPC). By 1958, a year after independence, the JPC had fifty-nine members. In the center of the Gold Coast, an ethnically homogeneous area—Ashanti —preserved proud memories of the days when its people formed a powerful military machine and offered stubborn resistance to British conquest. Over the Ashantis, a "Paramount of Paramounts," the Asantehene, exercised great influence in his role as custodian of the Golden Stool, which was believed to embody the soul of the Ashanti Nation. Fourteen Asantehenes had occupied the stool since 1700 when it "descended from the heavens." In 1958, the Asanteman Council, presided over by the Asantehene, was made up of forty-nine paramount chiefs, each of whom had under him a group of sub-chiefs distributed throughout his territory, at the village level.[8] In the far north was an area, The Northern Territories. which was not only the most underdeveloped area, but which had been isolated from the rest of the coun-

[7] Dennis Austin gives a clear succinct account of constitutional development in Ghana up to 1957 in an article, "Institutional History of the Gold Coast/Ghana," in *What are the Problems of Parliamentary Government in West Africa?* The Hansard Society for Parliamentary Government, 1958.

[8] An indispensable work for understanding traditional authority in Ashanti is Dr. Kofi A. Busia, *The Position of the Chief in Modern Ashanti*, Oxford University Press, 1951. See also Robert Lystad, *Ashanti; A Proud People*.

try during most of the colonial era. Here, village chiefs gave allegiance to one or the other of several paramounts (each bearing the title, Na). These chiefs had never had a unifying institutional structure binding them together as in Ashanti and The Colony. The fourth region was the former British trust territory of Togoland, where chiefs existed among the Mamprusi, Dagomba, and the Ewes, but which also did not have a highly organized council of chiefs.

The problem of nation-building in Ghana involves the development of a national consciousness to replace ethnic and regional consciousness, as well as the adjustment of the institution of chieftaincy to the new Africanized civil service and the machines of political parties. It also involves, as one political leader phrased it, "showing them where power lies." The present pattern of relationships between traditional authority and the new elite represents a balance of forces arrived at after a decade of struggle.[9]

When the Convention Peoples Party came to power in 1951, in the transitional period prior to independence, most of the traditional rulers preferred to support the more conservative United Gold Coast Convention rather than the radical populist C.P.P. The C.P.P. embarked upon a two-pronged programme of dealing with traditional authority at the local level: 1) encouraging the younger, more radical elements, and all of those with grievances against the then incumbents, to find legitimate means for "destooling" chiefs who were not "progressive"; and 2) embedding democratically elected Local Councils in the heart of every local community. There was such a wave of destoolments that even the C.P.P. eventually attempted to slow down the process. At the beginning, Local Councils were set up with two-thirds of the members being elected and one-third being appointed by the traditional authorities. It was also usual for the chief to preside over meetings. Local councils had the power to collect taxes for local improvements of their own choice.[10]

Local councils have had their difficulties but still remain an integral part of the new Ghana. By 1959, however, a series of Acts had removed chiefs from the councils. The extension of magistrates' courts was also narrowing the area in which chiefs could exercise judicial authority. They were being urged to "support the government of the day" but to confine their activities to the carrying out of ritual functions related to the religious life of the people and to functioning in a quasi-judicial capacity by settling disputes involving breaches of cus-

---

[9] David Apter's *The Gold Coast in Transition* is the only scholarly, well-documented study available on these problems, although its primary focus is upon other aspects of the movement toward independence.

[10] See Kwame Nkrumah, *Ghana* and George Padmore, *The Gold Coast Revolution* for background on the early phases of C.P.P. government. Padmore discusses the village-level struggle in some detail.

tomary law. They were also to serve as spokesmen of the needs of their people. They were to be "The Fathers of the People." Because most of rural Ghana is illiterate and folk, and because traditional religion is still viable, the prestige of chieftaincy as an institution remains high, and a "good chief" still commands loyalty, affection, and respect.

Most chiefs, quite naturally, resented the gradual encroachment upon their area of power and influence, and their resentment reached its climax on the eve of independence between 1954 and 1956, when it was given expression through a National Liberation Movement which arose in opposition to the C.P.P.[11] This movement, centered in Ashanti, demanded the organization of a federal state rather than a unitary state. It proposed that each region should control its own finances, and should have its own civil service, as well as a bicameral legislature, the senior body of which would be a House of Chiefs. The N.L.M. also asked for a bicameral *national* legislature with a House of Chiefs in addition to the Legislative Assembly. The C.P.P., which had a legislative majority, refused to accept these demands. The issue was joined.

The struggle was fought out in a pre-independence national election, as well as on the streets in the villages and towns of Ashanti between "action squads" representing both sides. The C.P.P. won the elections, but traditional authority would not concede.

A series of conferences was held to define a desirable constitutional structure, but the N.L.M. boycotted these. Finally, a British constitutional adviser suggested that a unitary state was best for a small country like Ghana, but that in each region there should be an elected Regional Assembly and a House of Chiefs. He advised against a House of Chiefs at the center, however, and against the devolution of too much legislative and financial power to the regions. It took a visit from the Colonial Secretary himself to win the assent of the N.L.M. to this constitution with which Ghana began its independent existence.

In the two years since independence, the government of Ghana has revised the constitution so as to eliminate the elected Regional Assemblies. It has given a guarantee, however, that the Houses of Chiefs will remain. It has then proceeded to reorganize the structure of relations among paramount chiefs. Ashanti has been split into two regions, each with its own House of Chiefs, thus reducing the Asanteman Council to twenty-seven members. The Joint Provincial Council has been replaced by an Eastern House of Chiefs with fifteen paramounts as members; and a Western Region House of Chiefs with twenty-six members. A

[11] See St. Clair Drake, "Prospects for Democracy in the Gold Coast," *Annals of the American Academy of Political and Social Science* (1956) for a discussion of the growth of the NLM and an analysis of its early activities, as well as a summary of the constitutional conferences which followed. The issue of chieftaincy was only one of several issues which gave rise to the NLM.

Volta Region House of Chiefs, with thirty-seven members, has been formed in what was once British Togoland and a small section of the eastern Gold Coast. A Northern House of Chiefs with twenty-four members was also organized. Thus, between 100 and 150 paramount chiefs have been grouped into six collegial bodies reflecting regional and ethnic interests and sentiments. The number of important posts open to chiefs within their own organizations has been increased. These houses of chiefs lack any effective legislative power, but they do have substantial budgets at their disposal which may be used both for local regional development and for enhancing the prestige of the institution of chieftaincy. The whole formal structure of chieftaincy at all levels is now under the supervision of Regional Commissioners and District Commissioners, political officers who represent the central government.

The victory over those who supported greater power for chiefs through a federal structure was accomplished by a series of astute political maneuvers on the part of the government.[12] The magnitude of the victory is best illustrated by noting the present position of the Asantehene, whose linguist (spokesman) founded the National Liberation Movement and whose chiefs had sworn the Great Oath of Ashanti to support the N.L.M. and to oppose the C.P.P. The Asantehene has not only repudiated his supporters of the N.L.M., but has expressed his determination to support "the government of the day." His relations with the Prime Minister are now warm and cordial.[13] His sub-chiefs are, one-by-one, falling in line for once the holder of the Golden Stool had shown his willingness to accept a new role vis-à-vis the new African elite, the backbone of chiefly opposition was broken. On the other hand, another famous chief, the paramount of Akim Abuakwa, refused to support "the government of the day" even when his area had shifted

---

[12] First, there was a strong show of police power to restore order. This was followed by a judicial investigation of the affairs of the Asantehene which uncovered certain irregularities in the use of palace funds, including the diversion of some money to support the NLM. The Asantehene was then persuaded to repudiate those who had "misled" him. In the meanwhile, his power to dispose of stool land revenues was curtailed. The large Ashanti Region was then split, a separate region being formed among paramount chiefs who had historical reasons for antagonism toward the wide powers of the Asantehene. Throughout all of these events, the Asantehene was given a chance to preserve his dignity and his stool.

[13] On the occasion of the Independence Day celebrations in 1959, the Asantehene was permitted by his elders to break custom and to fly in an airplane to Accra. He was greeted with courtesy and deference by the prime minister. While in the capital city, he presented a trophy to a winning football team, crowned a beauty queen, attended state dances, and was photographed dancing the high life with Miss Ghana. He visited a number of development projects before returning home. The Asantehene is a man in his sixties, of limited formal education, but with wide experience. He has been knighted and likes golf; but he also takes seriously his role as mediator between Ashanti ancestral spirits and the living. He wears his evening clothes with as much dignity as he does his kente cloth.

its electoral majority to the C.P.P. He was eventually destooled, arrested for refusing to hand over stool property to his successor, and banished from his state to the capital city of Accra. With the pattern of these two great chiefs before them, other chiefs could chart their courses. Some have resisted governmental enticements and pressures. Others have calculated the costs and the rewards, and made either quiet or ostentatious readjustments. One of the Northern Chiefs, who was an Opposition member of Parliament, crossed the floor in 1960, embarrassing everyone with his announcement that his chiefs-in-council had advised him to join the C.P.P.[14] Notes such as the following appear frequently in the Ghana press:

DONYINAHENE JOINS C.P.P.—One hundred years old Nana Yaw Nimo, Donyinahene (Ashanti) has resigned from the United Party and joined the dynamic CPP. . . . The Donyinahene stated, inter alia, "I am declaring with my soul and heart that I and my people wholeheartedly support Dr. Nkrumah and his party. . . . We have been deluded well and long enough. Now our eyes are open. . . . I do not think that the fatherly heart of Dr. Kwame Nkrumah will refuse to accept us even though we might have been late.[15]

BEREKUM STATE SUPPORTS GOVERNMENT POLICY—One of the notable resolutions passed in recent times was the one passed by the Berekum State Council at an emergency meeting held on the 14th of April, 1960 . . . "in view of the fact that we have full confidence in the Government of Ghana headed by Osagyefo President Kwame Nkrumah we support the Government in all matters that are deemed suitable for Ghana."[16]

Over eighty percent of the people in Ghana are illiterate. Personal symbols and relationships phrased in terms of kinship carry great meaning to the illiterate masses. Terms of praise which sound extravagant to Western ears are a normal day-by-day aspect of relations between chiefs and their followers, an integral part of courteous ceremonial. Loyal chiefs receive such praise from the politicians. Politicians, in turn, receive it from the chiefs and their people. To a certain extent, the

[14] The situation was embarrassing because, technically, a member of Parliament represents a *geographical* constituency and a political party, and he would not be expected to take orders from a council-of-elders. His honest admission of the forces which impelled him to change his political colours brought temporarily into the open a situation which is of considerable interest to political scientists, namely, the extent to which traditional factors affect election procedures and the activities of parliamentarians, in a country such as Ghana.

[15] *Evening News,* June 7, 1960.

[16] *Ibid.,* April 29, 1960.

Prime Minister is viewed by the illiterate masses as a "Paramount of Paramounts" and the new evolving structure tends to institutionalize some of these appraisals of the new role of Chief of State.

Chieftaincy in Ghana is not a feudal institution. Land is held in trust by the chief for his constituents in some cases and there are some stool lands administered by chiefly families. But most land is owned by family and lineage groups. Occupational prestige and wealth are not the basic criteria in the selection of chiefs. Quite humble men and women may be enstooled as Chiefs and Queen Mothers. Most chiefs are people who have shown leadership abilities, who know customary usages, but are illiterate.

There are significant exceptions, however.[17] The Ghana government has attempted to open up opportunities for literate chiefs to play

[17] No comprehensive study is available of the social characteristics of chiefs in Ghana. The following table lists all of the chiefs whose names appeared in *Ghana Yearbook*, 1958 (which contains a short Who's Who in Ghana). These are the more progressive and better educated chiefs, or the ones of national political importance. It will be noted that, as a group, they are not highly educated, although the younger men are better educated. The important thing about all chiefs is that they are not a class set apart from the rest of the population and that, upon their death, their children or their nephews do not necessarily inherit their status.

Age	Ed.	Occupation	Honours	Age	Ed.	Occupation	Honours
85	—	—	—	50	P	lorry driver	
82	—	produce buyer	—			and owner	—
72	P	business man	—	50	P	road overseer	—
68	—	—	—	48	P	clerk	—
68	P	storekeeper	KBE	44	T	teacher	—
61	P	civil servant	QMC	44	P	—	—
60	S	cocoa broker	—	42	P	clerk	—
60	S	engine driver	—	41	P	driver-mechanic	—
59	P	policeman	CM	36	C	teacher-clerk	—
58	—	trader-farmer	—	35	B	shorthand typist	—
58	P	civil servant	KMC, OBE, KB	33	P	tax collector-typist	
				33	—	—	—
55	P	—	—	30	C	—	—
51	P	clerk	KMC	29	PG	teacher	—

Education	Honours
P—Primary school	KBE—Knight Bachelor of the Empire
S—Some secondary school	QMC—Queen's Medal for Chiefs
T—Teacher training school	CM—Coronation Medal
C—Some college work	KMC—King's Medal for Chiefs
PG—Post-graduate work	OBE—Order of the British Empire
B—Business school training	KB—Knight Bachelor

A dash indicates that no data were given. The assumption is that if no schools were mentioned, the chief probably had no formal education. Hobbies mentioned by chiefs ranged from poultry farming to stamp collecting; from hunting to reading; from gardening to golf.

a more active role in non-traditional sectors of government. One well-educated chief is ambassador to India. Another has served as a delegate to the United Nations General Assembly. Another, who holds a doctorate in anthropology from Oxford, is Cultural Adviser to the Ministry of External Affairs. Others serve on important boards and commissions. There is nothing to prevent a chief from running for the Legislative Assembly if he has the requisite qualifications, but only two, both from the North, have been elected to the Assembly.

Chiefs in Ghana have been encouraged to retain the dignified ceremonial and colourful attire which surrounds the institution. Chiefs, moving in state with their linguists and stool bearers, under multicoloured umbrellas, and with their corps of drummers, are familiar figures on all types of ceremonial occasions ranging from dances at the State House to the dedication of church organs, from the opening of new factories to the proroguing of Parliament. They still hold the colourful durbars which were once "laid on" for visiting queens, kings, and governors, but which now honor the African Prime Minister and other governmental dignitaries. As "Fathers of the People" they are urged to play an active part in mobilizing the people for economic and social development. When they do, they are praised and honoured. When they do not do so, they may be denounced as "unprogressive," or, in extreme cases, their destoolment is arranged.

TRADITIONAL AUTHORITY AND COMMUNITY DEVELOPMENT

Since 1948, Ghana has evolved a Department of Social Welfare and Community Development which has made available to towns and villages an experienced corps of Community Development Officers trained to carry out programmes at the village level. Through the years, community development has included such diverse projects as a concerted attack on illiteracy through mass education; organization of the Roof Loans Scheme which encourages the replacement of thatch roofs with metal roofs; the organizing of home economics training for women, and of young farmers clubs; assisting in the building of roads, schools, post offices, maternity centres, etc. The department also has carried out educational campaigns for various ministries making use of all varieties of visual aids. The wide range of projects is due partly to the fact that the programme emphasizes the voluntary selection of projects by villagers themselves, the basic philosophy of the programme being that:

. . . the initiative should come from among the people themselves [and that] there must be a process of stimulation by the community development organization to break down apathy and to show people that what *they want can be provided if they are prepared to listen to new ideas and to help themselves.*

Self-help, in the form of voluntary labour and substantial financial contribution, has been at the heart of the programme.[18]

Enlisting the cooperation of local traditional authorities takes very high priority in community development projects for, in hundreds of situations, they have the power to "make or break" a programme once it is under way, or to prevent ideas of self-help programmes from emerging within their areas at all. One Community Development Officer, writing upon the order of his procedures in mounting an illiteracy campaign, begins his field report as follows:

(a) Cinema van arrived in a town or village to spend two days.
(b) Mass Education workers talked to the chief, elders and literate leaders about the establishment of literacy classes.

"Talked to the chief and his elders" would be the first item in most development officers' notebooks as they give an account of the "softening up" process. Of one very difficult project, the Director of the Department of Social Welfare and Community Development wrote:

In 1947 the Department was brought in to carry out a land resettlement scheme among the Frafra, who occupy a very crowded area in the North. In this case pure logic should long ago have driven them elsewhere to earn a living from the land. It was the attachment to the soil and the powerful vested interests of chiefs and fetish priests which prevented this. The first step was, therefore, to achieve, if not the support, at least the tolerance, of the chiefs and fetish priests towards any move. Conducted visits, photos and films of success in the new area were arranged and a start was made in a small way with eight families—more than had been persuaded to move in the last three years. Eighty families have now been resettled and there is a waiting list.[19]

[18] For a detailed account of the history, philosophy and organization of the programme, see Peter du Sautoy, *Community Development in Ghana*, Oxford University Press, 1958.

[19] du Sautoy, *op. cit.*, p. 151. A similar situation arose in the attempt to persuade a group of villagers at Tema to move about a mile away from their traditional fishing site to a new fishing harbour and village. A new city was being built in what is to be Ghana's major sea-port and the village site was needed for a central business district. In this case, education was not enough. It was necessary to use the threat of the bulldozer and to exploit dynastic feuds and other internal divisions until a "cooperative" segment of the traditional structure would support the resettlement plans. The traditional rulers were helped in saving face by governmental cooperation in a large and impressive quasi-religious ceremony just before the move.

As a community-development or mass-education project proceeds, securing the active participation of a chief, as well as his blessing, becomes very desirable. It is perhaps a rare situation in which it can be reported, as in one case of road building, that:

Encouragement has been given by the Paramount Chief of the area who sometimes personally drove the tractor.

But, throughout Ghana, it has become the pattern for the chief to associate himself with the projects through participating in money-raising activities, "gracing the platform" when literacy certificates are being handed out, or making a ceremonial inspection tour. In construction projects at the village level, the cooperation of the chief is essential in securing a full and regular turnout of "communal labour."[20] The chief's role in community development will vary, of course, with the personality of the individual. Sometimes he initiates an activity, more often, perhaps, he simply climbs upon the bandwagon which the more literate or energetic of his subjects have set a-rolling. But there is general agreement that a chief's support, whether in the form of quiet approval or active participation, is essential to the successful outcome of most projects.

Within the last year Local Development Committees and Regional Development Committees have been particularly active, for Ghana is just beginning a new long-term development plan. While this programme will utilize the self-help activity of the Department of Social Welfare and Community Development, it is likely that much of the stimulus will now come from the new corps of District Commissioners who are scattered throughout the country. The C.P.P. press, during the past year, has given constant publicity to the activities of local development projects and these news notes reveal the role of chiefs in the process. One finds, for instance, an occasional news items such as this:

The newly appointed District Commissioner was officially presented to the chiefs and people of the Nanumba State on Tuesday. The District

[20] Communal labour for community projects is a general custom in West African societies. The colonial powers used such labour in the early days of colonization for carrying out public works. Undoubtedly, considerable pressure was sometimes used by chiefs to secure a labour turn-out. Today, compulsion is frowned upon, and a chief must rely mainly upon his prestige and persuasive powers. Insofar as there are C.P.P. "party activists" in a village his efforts are reinforced. Notes like the following occur frequently: "Work on the construction of a £1,700 Post Office Building at Mamfe is almost completed. . . . The cost of the project was met by the people themselves through voluntary contributions and with free labour and the Central Government gave a grant in aid." (*Evening News*, June 10, 1960)

Commissioner appealed to the chiefs and people to co-operate with him in his duties. . . .[21]

Older chiefs do not always find it easy to adjust to the presence of what one elderly Northern chief called "The New White Men"—the African District Commissioners who represent the C.P.P. government and are sometimes quite young. But adjust they do, and notes such as the following are by no means rare:

An £800 meat house for 'Kete Krachi built with funds provided by the Buem-Krachi Local Council, supplemented by communal labour, has been opened by the District Commissioner. At the ceremony was Nana Kofi Deduagya II. . . .[22]

Sometimes the ceremony at the conclusion of a project celebrates a long period of cooperation between chief and District Commissioner or chief and the Department of Social Welfare and Community Development. District Commissioners may stimulate Town Development Committees to take action and can secure aid for them from the central government. For example, quotations in the press show how chiefs, with the aid of Town Development Committees, led their people in projects for construction of roads, for clean-up campaigns, or for constructing street drains with communal labour. As custodian of stool lands, some chiefs are also in a position to give concrete assistance to agricultural projects such as experimental poultry farming or other types of agricultural experiments. Many of the current activities of chiefs are purely ceremonial, in the sense of putting in an appearance to lend sanction to some activity, but more often they are drawn in as presiding officers for conferences. These conferences are variously organized by the Peoples Educational Association, the Ghana Women's League, the Junior Red Cross, the United Ghana Farmers Council, and other similar organizations. And, occasionally, there is a beauty queen to be crowned.

The contest for power between traditional authority and the new elite is virtually over in Ghana, and, in some cases, chiefs have become what an Opposition Party newspaper calls "C.P.P. chiefs," that is, those who, in addition to serving as "Fathers of the People," supporting "the government of the day" and aiding social development, also go a bit further, as in the following case:

[21] *Evening News,* March 31, 1960.
[22] *Ashanti Times,* June 4, 1960.

The Nkrumah Eastern Progressive Association had been formed at Akwapim with Nana Atropa Amoa II, Ankobeahene of Larteh Kubease, as President. Besides being a charitable organization with an object of raising the economic standards in Akwapim, it also aims at propagating and explaining the Republican form of Government.[23]

Opposition chiefs are developing a sense of national patriotism which rises above the local village, the region, or the tribe.

THE 1960 CENSUS AS A CRUCIAL INSTANCE

That chieftaincy can respond to the challenge of a national effort was illustrated in the case of the 1960 census which was taken in March. Because of their close ties with the people, had chiefs been indifferent to this national effort, or hostile to it, a complete enumeration of Ghana's population could never have been carried out. In addition to the normal suspicion of rural, unsophisticated folk about an inquiry as to their ages, marital status, employment, etc., there were other factors in the situation which could have made census-taking in some areas extremely difficult. Insofar as some opponents of the Government party chose to define the census as "a C.P.P. party project" and this definition found acceptance, sabotage of the census could be considered one form of "loyal opposition." At crucial points, however, the top officials of the United Party spoke from a joint platform at mass rallies with C.P.P. speakers, appealing for cooperation. In some areas there was bitterness over deportations and Preventive Detention.[24] Here, too, refusal to cooperate might have been expected. It was impossible, also, to prevent the rise and spread of rumors—that the census was to count the people for compulsory military conscription; that the data would be used for deciding to shift people from one part of the country to another; that it was a part of a project to increase taxes; that it was a prelude to confiscation of property, etc., etc. These rumors had to be scotched as they arose and the meaning of the census explained in detail.

The evening of March 20, 1960, was officially proclaimed "Census Night" in Ghana. The Office of the Government Statistician, with a U.N. expert who had come to help set the census up, planned to at-

---

[23] *Evening News,* March 21, 1960.

[24] At certain points in the political struggle, influential Muslim aliens, who were encouraging bloc voting against the C.P.P., were deported to the French areas and to Nigeria. Ghana law allows citizens accused of subversive activities to be detained for up to five years. Most detainees are charged with conspiracy to commit overt acts of violence.

tempt a complete enumeration of the Ghana population. School teachers, clerks, and other available literates took intensive training courses so that every house in Ghana could be visited within a fortnight after Census Night in order to secure a list of every person who had slept in the house on that night, along with certain basic information about each person.

In addition to other administrative committees, a Census Education Committee was organized to publicize and explain the census over a period of almost half a year. Special films were made and census cinema vans toured the countryside. Films were run in the theaters. Thousands of leaflets and posters were distributed. Special radio talks were made and mass meetings held. Elaborate preparations were made to fix the attention of the whole population upon a date—MARCH 20—and to burn into the people's minds memories of where they spent that night and who stayed in each house on that night. "A Night to Remember" became the slogan.

From the outset, the Census Education Committee gave high priority to enlisting the cooperation of traditional rulers. In the initial stages of the work it became clear that their assistance was needed in helping to locate and map every dwelling within each enumeration unit. As planning proceeded, it became equally clear that their authority and prestige would be needed in most non-urban areas for securing confidence in the operation and for motivating people to tell the truth. Chiefs were asked to emphasize to the people that, in order to get schools and hospitals, it was necessary for the government to know how many people there were of both sexes and all ages, so that, like a good father, government could plan for the national household.

As census day drew near, an intensive educational campaign was launched. The regional Houses of Chiefs received deputations from the Census staff and were encouraged to give public collective endorsement to the census. Newspapers circulated widely the pictures of paramount chiefs meeting to endorse the census. The members of some Houses of Chiefs held meetings within their own states and these were also reported widely in the press. One paramount announced that anyone who did not get himself counted would be banished from his state and would be numbered among the living dead! The President of the Denkeyira State Council convened an emergency meeting of all chiefs in his state three days before the census to urge cooperation upon them. The week before, the Beposo State Council "adopted a resolution supporting education of the people on the forthcoming Census." In addition to these pronouncements, many paramount chiefs went on tours of their areas to explain the census and to call for cooperation. Newspaper accounts gave prominent display to these activities:

The Omanhene of Suma State addressed about 50 representatives of voluntary organizations to round off his fortnight's census education tour of his state.

The Omanhene of Shama State, Nana Kwaw Fraiku III, Vice President of the Western Region House of Chiefs, addressed census rallies. He explained the operations and asked for cooperation.

At Sunyani, several thousand people attended a census rally in a public park presided over by the Sunyanhene, Nan Kwaku Ababio.

Nana Kojo Anyimah II, Krontihene Sefwi-Anhwiasco State and Nana Osei Bonsu of Bibiani have completed their tour of towns and villages in the State to educate the people on the census. They had earlier visited 13 villages.

Kwadjo Nyako II had completed a six-day census education tour of his area during which he addressed mass rallies and spoke to some of his sub-chiefs and individuals. He urged his people to take the census seriously and to help the census officers in their duties.

Throughout the country, too, in hundreds of villages, local chiefs acted as did the Omanhene of Mompata, who, in his efforts to make March 20 "A Night to Remember,"

. . . made arrangements for traditional drumming and dancing, a candle light procession and pealing of church bells.

The author has been told by census officials that the cooperation of chiefs was indispensable in carrying out an operation which they deemed to have been highly successful—the enumeration of the population.

SUMMARY AND CONCLUSION

Throughout West Africa the new African elite and the chiefs are in the process of adjusting their relations to each other. The tendency of the new states in British areas is not to abolish chieftaincy but to redefine the role of chiefs and to educate them where possible, and to force them where it is impossible, to accept the redefined status. In Ghana, a struggle for power ensued which was eventually won by the new elite. In all areas, chiefs are exchanging roles of power for those of prestige. The data presented suggest the fruitfulness of a carefully documented study of the process by which chiefs have become accommodated to their new status, isolating the factors which have made for ease of adjustment in some situations and difficulty in others, and assessing their relative importance in the process of planned economic and social development. A thorough analysis of the types of traditional sanctions which are still effective would contribute to our understanding of the process of social change.

The Individual and the Community

and

The Communities and the Political System

K. W. J. POST

University of Ibadan

THE INDIVIDUAL AND THE COMMUNITY

On November 29th, two weeks before polling day, the *Sunday Times* published a column headed "You and Your Vote," which attempted to explain certain basic facts about the election. After pointing out how important it was that registered electors should take part in this crucial election it went on:

*But it is even more vital that your vote is the one that
completely satisfies your [sic] PERSONALLY.
Not the one that pleases your tribe or anyone placed higher than
you in your work.*
*BUT THE ONE YOU HAVE CHOSEN FROM YOUR OWN
FREE CONVICTION.*
*That is why the election is secret,
You vote and no one sees you.
The candidate for whom you vote has earned your confidence,
either because you trust him personally or because you believe
in his party.*[1]

These remarks, with their special emphasis upon personal choice, were directed, of course, at a particular audience—the relatively few people who could read them. Amongst people who could not read and write the emphasis was a different one:

Reprinted from *The Nigerian Federal Election of 1959* (London: Oxford University Press for the Nigerian Institute of Social and Economic Research, 1963), pp. 376–399, with the permission of the author, the publisher, and the Institute. Several minor contextual changes have been made.

[1] Layout and capitals as in the original.

"They say it is the NCNC we shall vote for, and I will vote for them" (illiterate nightwatchman, aged 41–45).

"The other time we were told to vote, we were told to drop in our ballot papers into the box with the cock emblem" (illiterate farmer (female), aged 41–45).

"I do not know the candidates, but it has been said that Azikiwe and his people are the ones we shall vote for" (illiterate farmer, aged 51–55).

"The only person we know in our constituency is Azikiwe and he is our candidate. We have all raised our hands for him" (illiterate farmer, aged 56–60).

"I just intend to do what others, especially Ibo men, are doing. Many a time I have seen people going to vote, but I have never voted before. According to public opinion in my area, every grown-up young man is expected to register for (the) election" (illiterate truckpusher, aged 26–30).

All these remarks were made during interviews in public opinion surveys carried out in two Ibo constituencies.[2] Though they are thus limited to one area and one people there can be little doubt that certain ideas implicit in these answers were held by the majority of electors in all parts of Nigeria. For most electors the choice between candidates was not one to be made individually, but as a member of a community. Sometimes indeed, as in the third and fourth quotations above, it was regarded as something to be made by the community as a whole.

How, then, are we to define community? Primarily, it may be suggested, as the place to which a man felt himself to "belong," where he had both rights and obligations, where his ancestors were buried, where his family had land—in the words of the electoral regulations ". . . the place to which he intends to return when away therefrom." Even if he moved away, the ordinary man still regarded the place he had left as his home, to which he would probably return one day, and where he might begin to build a house long before he actually returned. There were few "detribalized" people in Nigeria. Most of the "strangers" who lived in the growing towns—places like Sapele, Warri, Aba, Port Harcourt, Jos, or the Sabon Gari in Kano—were born elsewhere.[3] Their interests were still rooted in their birthplaces, often through a branch

[2] For more on these see the author's paper on "Some Pre-Election Public Opinion Polls in Eastern Nigeria, 1959," in the *Nigerian Institute of Social and Economic Research Conference Proceedings December 1960,* Ibadan, The Institute, n.d.

[3] In an opinion poll carried out by the author in Aba, 97.4 per cent of those interviewed were born outside the town.

of their community's local improvement union, formed by them and their fellow exiles. Everyone from the locality would belong, whether lawyers or businessmen, craftsmen or labourers.

This recognition of a common origin and interest meant that a man was identified by his membership of a community and was interested in preserving its cohesion. In this respect it resembled S. F. Nadel's "group"—

. . . a collection of individuals who stand in regular and relatively permanent relationships, that is, who act towards and in respect of each other, or towards and in respect of individuals outside the group, regularly in a specific, predictable and expected fashion.[4]

In Nigeria, then, a man was likely to be governed in his behaviour by the fact that he was a member of a community. This is not necessarily so in a "developed" political system, where

Man is essentially defined by his roles. From infancy onwards he thinks through his identifications. Some of them are his family, his school, his locality, his factory, his army company, his political party, his church and his country. His personality can be considered as a welter of overlapping affiliations, complementary to one another in most cases, conflicting in other cases.[5]

In Britain or the U.S.A. the individual's membership of different interest groups may expose him to strong cross-pressures when he is called upon to vote. A registered Republican who is a Roman Catholic may be asked to choose between a Protestant candidate from his own party and a Roman Catholic Democrat. In Nigeria the elector tended to vote with his community in 1959, according to its interests as he and the other members saw them, keeping this new identification as an elector within the community as all the others had been.

As it has been defined so far a community was obviously a basic unit. It might be a village, a ward in a town (especially a town with a long history, as in Yorubaland), or a lineage tracing its ancestors back for several generations: kinship would, in fact, form the foundations of almost any community, as the term is used here. It might, however, be

---

[4] S. F. Nadel, *The Foundations of Social Anthropology*, London: Cohen & West, 1953, page 146.

[5] Alfred de Grazia, "Research on Voters and Elections," *Research Frontiers in Politics and Government* (The Brookings Lectures, 1955), The Brookings Institution, Washington, D.C., 1955, page 120.

larger than that, a group of villages with a traditional alliance, a clan made up of several lineages, with a mythical common ancestor. Under pressure from outside the feeling of community of interest might be wider still: appeals might be made on a "Pan-Ibo" or "Pan-Yoruba" basis, or all Ibadans might be called on to vote against the "Ijebu" Action Group. Such a "community of interest," however, is not a community as it has been described here, though the appeal which gave rise to it might often be phrased in terms of kinship. The feeling was unlikely to persist for any great length of time, though in some cases, such as that of the Tiv, it had lasted throughout a number of elections.

Interestingly enough, it seems that those communities which in the past had no feeling of relationship with one another, sometimes even speaking different dialects of the same language, have been able to come together more effectively in a modern election than those which traditionally had been contained within some larger political unity. The Yoruba kingdoms, for instance, had internal differences which could sometimes be exploited by rival political parties. Groups like the Tiv or the Ibo, on the other hand, showed themselves to be extraordinarily solid in their support for their chosen party. In Tiv Division 84 per cent of the total votes cast were for Action Group, and Tiv accounted for nearly a quarter of that party's Northern votes and more than a quarter of its seats. It appears that those societies whose traditional political systems were on a small scale, and least hierarchical, were those which in modern elections were best able to come together in support of a particular party. It would certainly appear that where there was a tradition of chieftainship, hierarchical organization, and the association of power with office the way was opened to all sorts of disputes which might be taken up by the parties.[6] It might also be argued that where these elements were historically present the area involved was itself a political system, or "state," made up of many basic communities which commanded a prior loyalty. In the emirates, on the other hand, something resembling a "class struggle" seemed to be taking place. . . . In the societies which traditionally lacked centralized authorities there appeared to be a greater ability to assume a unified aspect when faced by what was thought of as a challenge from outside. Why this should be the case cannot be explained until much

[6] Perhaps the best single example of this is the case of the former *Alafin* of Oyo, sent into exile by the Western Region Government in 1955 and deposed in 1956. See articles in *West Africa*, June 25th and August 6th and 13th, 1955, and *Five Elections in Africa*, op. cit., pages 79–85.

more work has been done by anthropologists and sociologists on the behaviour of different societies in a modern political context.[7]

If the reaction of most individuals in Nigeria when called on to make a voting decision was to fall in with the consensus of opinion expressed in their community, the problem that arises is to discover how that consensus was reached. Very early in this study reference was made in talking about the "new men" in the East and West to the "interpretative function" which they performed, explaining the demands of the modern world to those whose lives were still conducted in the old ways.[8] Since these men were usually also the local political leaders, they assumed an extra importance during the election campaign, acting as the "opinion leaders" for their communities.

Often this function was assumed by the new men in their capacity as leaders of the local union. Accustomed to act as mediators between the community and the administration in pressing for more wells, schools, roads, and dispensaries, the unions were also involved in making the community's political decisions. The ways in which they were involved are difficult to describe. Once again these unions have as yet been little studied.[9] They were to be found in all parts of Nigeria, except in the Muslim states of the North, and were especially strong in Iboland and parts of the Middle Belt and other "pagan" areas of the North. In Yorubaland their strength varied. Sometimes, as in the case of the Ogbomosho Progressive Union, their hold over their home area

[7] So far they have tended to concentrate upon the classification of traditional political systems, and on the response of these to modern administration. See, for instance, *African Political Systems*, edited by M. Fortes and E. E. Evans-Pritchard, London: Oxford University Press for the International Institute of African Languages and Cultures, 1940: *Tribes without Rulers*, edited by John Middleton and David Tait, London: Routledge and Kegan Paul, 1958: *Bantu Bureaucracy*, by Lloyd A. Fallers, Cambridge University Press for the East African Institute of Social Research, n.d.: and *From Tribal Rule to Modern Government*, the 13th Conference Proceedings of the Rhodes-Livingstone Institute for Social Research, edited with an introduction by Raymond Apthorpe, Lusaka, 1959.

[8] See *The Nigerian Federal Election*, p. 48.

[9] See, however, Simon Ottenberg, "The Development of Village Meetings among the Afikpo People," *Proceedings of the Second Annual Conference of the West African Institute of Social and Economic Research (Sociology Section)*, University College, Ibadan, 1953, and "Improvement Associations among the Afikpo Ibo," *Africa*, Vol. XXV, No. 1, January 1955: a summary of a paper by J. S. Coleman on "The Role of Tribal Associations in Nigeria" in *Proceedings of the First Annual Conference of the West African Institute of Social and Economic Research*, University College, Ibadan, reprinted March 1957: and Abiodun Aloba, "Tribal Unions in Party Politics," *West Africa*, July 10th, 1954.

was very strong. Sometimes they might be opposed to the traditional ruler, as in the case of the *Egbe Omo Ibile Ife*. Occasionally they might split under some extreme pressure, as the *Egbe Omo Ibile* in Akure was reported to have done in 1959, one faction supporting the NCNC, the other Action Group.

This tendency to split under pressure from the political parties was not confined solely to Yoruba local unions. The Urhobo Progress Union, which had been founded for the advancement of all Urhobos, particularly in the field of education, and had been instrumental in the founding of the Urhobo College at Effurun (just outside Warri) in 1947, found itself in difficulties in 1959, with a NCNC President-General and an Action Group President of the Warri Branch. To make matters worse, another local union, the Urhobo Renascent Convention, which was closely linked with the NCNC (it had been affiliated to the party since the 1940s, and its Assistant Secretary was the NCNC Divisional Organizing Secretary) was competing for the allegiance of the Urhobos.[10]

It would appear that the local unions themselves often tended to be strongest and least prone to internal dissension in societies with no tradition of centralized political control. The strength of the Tiv Progressive Union and of the multitude of Ibo clan, town, and village unions seemed to point to this. The first organization, which was intended to include all Tivs, was solidly behind Action Group. The vast majority of Ibo local unions supported NCNC, and from the middle of November until the eve of the election the *West African Pilot* continually published affirmations of loyalty to the party made by their branches, along with some from Yoruba and other unions. The Ibo State Union, which was supposed to include all Ibos and encourage a feeling of unity among them, also backed the NCNC, as it had done since its foundation in December 1948.[11] Indeed, one Action Group newspaper columnist was moved to lament the failure of *Egbe Omo Oduduwa* to unite Yorubas in the way that the Ibos had been united:

. . . the Ibo Union . . . is organised on a mutual insurance basis. As long as you contribute your Ibo mite [sic] to a tribal union fund wherever you may be situated, your local union is prepared to exert all efforts to get your financial aid from the parent union.

[10] An Urhobo writer in a local newspaper ended a review of the situation by asking if the Union was to be allowed "to drift until it unredeemably founders in the Urhobo political abyss or completely disintegrates on the rocks of party strife to the chagrin of all and with the loss of all that is dear in the Urhobo nation." *Mid-West Echo,* June 13th, 1959.

[11] An Ibo Union (Lagos) had existed since June 1936, re-forming as the Ibo Federal Union in 1944 (Coleman, *Nigeria: Background to Nationalism,* op. cit., pages 340–1).

But it is not so among the Yoruba. Even the Egbe Omo Oduduwa in its short span of existence and enthusiasm cannot be said with confidence to embrace all and sundry, rich and poor, profesionals [sic] and houseboys.[12]

It is notable that nearly all the union branches whose resolutions were reported in the *West African Pilot* were established by people who had left their homes to seek their fortunes elsewhere; some of them were as far off as Takoradi and Accra in Ghana. It was quite frequently announced by such "exile" branches that they had formed a team which was to return home and join in the campaign there. It was felt by those who had travelled that they had a duty to inform their less sophisticated brethren, and to ensure their electoral solidarity.[13] This was the political aspect of the general function of these unions—to protect the interests of their communities amid the changing conditions of modern Nigeria. The local union was the community organized to deal with the intrusive outside world, in political as well as in social matters.

There was not always a local union, however, and if one did exist it was not always united on political matters. As in the case of Urhobo Division there might be several unions, each supporting different parties. Whether there was a local union or not, there had to be individuals who were capable of supplying the community with the information it needed to make its decision and of influencing it towards that decision. In the developed political systems the function of opinion leaders has been extensively studied. The conclusion reached by the authors of one such study, made in the U.S.A., was that

For leadership in political discussion people mainly turn to others like themselves. The banker and mayor and union officer may be "opinion leaders" in a distant sense, but ordinary voters listen to near-by in-

---

[12] "Charles Bishop" in the *Nigerian Tribune*, November 15th, 1958.

[13] See, for instance, a letter in the *West African Pilot*, September 24th, 1959: "The Divisional Secretariat of the NCNC Ogoni calls on all Ogoni Youths abroad to help in organising the masses in Ogoni for the forthcoming election.

"No doubt most of these innocent people had been deceived and misguided. When we go out to educate them they want to know the COCK. They want to know if these are not the Palm Trees who deceived them before. We all have a duty to save Ogoni from the AG grip of fear.

"If you are an Ogoni son or daughter abroad this is the time to show your love for your motherland.

"Visit home. Tell them. Teach them. Talk to them at night. Talk to them in the day time about the NCNC.

"Go from house to house and tell them to vote for the NCNC. Tell them to push their ballot papers into NCNC ballot boxes."

fluencers. For this reason, one might properly speak less of leaders than of a complex web of opinion-leading relationships.[14]

Nevertheless, there is reason to believe that in Nigeria in 1959 the opinions of a few "leaders" carried a great deal of weight in each community. National politics were still very remote to most people, and without personal contact with political leaders many electors tended to know very little about what was going on—"I do not know any of the parties you have mentioned and their leaders because they have not been coming here" was a typical reply in a rural area. The ordinary electors relied therefore upon the few individuals who were able to grasp some of the ideas of the national campaign and pass them into circulation at a local level. This meant that although opinion leaders might sometimes be chiefs or others with traditional authority—village heads, say, in parts of the North—more often they were educated men. Where an illiterate person's occupation gave him the opportunity to pick up news verbally over a wider area than his immediate home he might be a leader of opinion. One illiterate motor conductor remarked that "in politics nobody is more important than we motor boys." In general, however, people looked to the literate members of the community for a lead.

This dependence upon the literate members of the community meant that in the new sphere of party politics the traditional superiority of age was often no longer recognized. Usually it was the young men (and sometimes women) who were educated, and in political matters their seniors deferred to them. As one illiterate woman put it in an interview:

We have no idea what you younger ones are planning now. You know more than your parents, so we look to you people for any side you take us.[15]

Bodies like the "Shagamu Social Elite," or the "Social Government of the Federation of Ijebu-Remo" (with its motto of "Socialism, Integrity, and Power") were organizations of "youngmen" who came together intentionally to act as opinion leaders in their communities.

What functions, then, did these literate opinion leaders perform? First of all they acted as their communities' contacts with the outside world, with the new political system developing in Nigeria. They were

[14] *Voting*, by Bernard R. Berelson, Paul F. Lazarsfeld, and William N. McPhee, University of Chicago Press, 1954, page 109. For a similar study in an English context see *Marginal Seat*, by R. S. Milne and H. C. Mackenzie, London: Hansard Society, 1958.

[15] The interviewer in this case was a senior schoolboy from the local grammar school.

the sensitive contacts which fed information into the "unending circuits of leadership relations running through the community, like a nerve system through the body."[16] In describing the campaign two levels of communication between the parties and the electors were distinguished, the national level—that of the newspapers, the radio, and the "keynote" speeches—and the constituency level, that of face-to-face meetings between the politicians and party enthusiasts and the people whose votes they were seeking. In terms of seats to be won the second level was by far the most important, since it represented the only chance of the illiterate electors to get information about the parties and their leaders.

The opinion leaders in the constituencies represented, therefore, a channel through which the ideas generated during the national campaign passed on their way to the electors. This mediatory function is, of course, common in all "Western" political systems. However, as one recent study of politics in the developing systems has pointed out,

The opinion leader in the United States receives information from the mass media and interprets it for his "opinion followers." These opinion followers tend to speak the same language, share the same values and have cognitive maps similar to the ones conveyed in the mass media. The politician or interest group leader in an Indian urban area faces a far greater gap between the communication content of the literate modern sector of the Indian city and the illiterate and traditional sector. . . . What has been said of the communication gap in the urban areas of a country like India is true to an even greater extent of connections between the urban and rural and village areas. Here the problem of interpretation is a massive one. The interpreter, whether he be bureaucrat, interest group leader, or party leader, cannot readily find equivalents in language, values, and cognitive material to make an accurate translation.[17]

In Nigeria in 1959 this meant that the elaborate programmes and policies which formed the substance of the national campaign reached the constituencies only in a much simplified form. Sometimes a national issue never reached the constituencies; there were no indications, for instance, that the different views of the parties on foreign policy and pan-Africanism ever became an issue at the local level. If an idea did filter through to the constituency it was translated by the opinion leaders into local terms, and reinforced by local prejudices.

The campaign of the Northern People's Congress, in particular,

---

[16] *Voting,* op. cit., page 110.
[17] Gabriel A. Almond and James S. Coleman (ed.), *The Politics of the Developing Areas,* Princeton University Press, 1960, pages 50–51.

tended to be conducted almost entirely on the constituency level. There was far less generation of ideas at its centre, and no party newspapers by which they might be communicated.[18] Much more responsibility was laid on the local politicians to formulate and spread their own ideas, and in consequence these were usually in the form of appeals to Islam and tradition, and attacks on Southerners. It must be remembered also that many of the leaders of opinion in the North derived their positions from different sources of authority, and operated in a different way, from those in the South. In the emirates a NPC candidate was often a person of importance in the Native Administration, and expected to be voted for out of deference to his authority. In the South people expected to be visited and asked for their votes.

This brings us to the second function of the opinion leaders in helping the community to make its voting decision. Not only did they circulate the ideas and information, in whatever form, which were necessary for this; they also gave a lead to the community in making up its collective mind. They could not directly order electors to vote for a particular party—the relationship between them, even when the opinion leaders were traditional chiefs, was far more subtle than that. They had to convince people by virtue of their personal prestige within the community. Sometimes the community would actually meet in solemn conclave to decide which party its members would support— "We have raised our hands for (Azikiwe)," as the farmer quoted at the beginning of this chapter put it. In Orlu Division in the East the Umuchu Improvement Union allowed Dr. Mbadiwe time to present his case against Dr. Azikiwe. After taxing him with transferring their post office to another village when he was Federal Minister of Communications and with not having visited them before, the members of the Union finally decided that they "would not for any cause join in a dance started with a wrong foot."[19] In other communities the general opinion would merely "become known" by a process of casual conversations and the exchange of views—"They say it is the NCNC we shall vote for. . . ." Very often there was no question of choice between parties, merely one of reaffirming an old allegiance—"Look, I am heart and soul for Zik, and it is annoying for you to ask me about other political parties or their foolish leaders," as one man put it when interviewed. Yet in all this someone had to give a lead.

The parties were quite open in stating that "a strong man bought up in each village is sufficient for the purpose of winning all the votes

---

[18] This was also true, of course, of those minority parties whose appeal was to a purely local interest.

[19] *West African Pilot*, September 16th, 1959.

in each town or village."[20] The Action Group in particular laid stress on this factor in 1959. Frequent notices appeared in the party newspapers announcing that "NCNC Pillar joins AG," or "2 NCNC Pillars now support AG," as more and more influential people were alleged to have seen the error of their ways and changed their allegiances. On November 26th the *COR Advocate* carried the headline, "15 DAYS TO GO: 1,591 RESIGN FROM NcNc IN IKOT EKPENE," and then printed the names of the defaulters, including the man "who planted NCNC in this our area." The NCNC was forced to counter this by such claims as "AG Bulwark in Oyo Joins NCNC," or the allegation of Chief Oweh that his opponent in Urhobo West had published a picture of "his immediate relations and friends" and alleged it to be of Urhobos who had resigned from NCNC and joined Action Group.[21]

The importance of a few opinion leaders in shaping the community's decision meant that often the ideas passed on were judged not in the light of their own merit, but according to the status of the opinion leader.[22] This association of opinion with status meant that the parties sought to gather together as impressive a body of campaigners as they could. At one NCNC meeting in Urhobo Central the platform was adorned by Chief J. S. Mariere, the renominated candidate; the Member of the Western House of Assembly for the area; the NCNC Divisional Organizing Secretary; the local District Council member, who was a master at Urhobo College; and the President-General of the Urhobo Progress Union, who was a Director of the new Central Bank of Nigeria.

The sources of the influence of leaders of opinion in the different communities varied considerably. Sometimes it was drawn from some traditional authority. A local chief might throw his weight behind a party, very often the party in power in the Region, since ultimately his position now depended upon the Regional Government. In the West the *Egbe Omo Oduduwa* kept the interests of the Yoruba *obas* identified with those of the Action Group. The *Oba* of Benin was also very active in supporting Action Group in 1959, speaking on behalf of the party at meetings. . . . The Eastern Region Government's nomination of fourteen First-Class Chiefs in the Region on August 26th was perhaps intended to ensure their loyalty to the NCNC. In the North the support of the emirs

---

[20] *West African Pilot,* November 12th, 1959.

[21] Chief Oweh's allegation appeared in a letter to the *West African Pilot,* May 23rd, 1959. He won in Urhobo West, and Action Group in the three seats in Ikot Ekpene Division.

[22] On this point see Lucian W. Pye, "Communications Patterns and the Problems of Representative Government in Non-Western Societies," *Public Opinion Quarterly,* Vol. XX, No. 1, Spring 1956.

was a great asset to the Northern People's Congress, while District and Village Heads were able to speak with the weight of the Native Authority behind them. In all three Regions the opposition parties claimed that the traditional rulers should keep out of politics, since they were the fathers of all their people, irrespective of party. In practice the external pressures upon a ruler were such as to make it almost impossible to refuse to throw his weight behind one party or another.

The "new men" who were the most important group of opinion leaders in the South and the Middle Belt derived their authority from non-traditional sources in the main, though some of them did have titles, usually awarded in recognition of their achievements.[23] In their own communities they were the main leaders of opinion. Admired because of their success and the ease with which they moved in the modern world, their views on politics were sought and their opinions trusted. Yet the relationship between them and the ordinary electors was not entirely one of dependence. A man who sought to influence opinion had also to have been active in the affairs of his community and in promoting its welfare. At a meeting in Orlu North the Provincial Commissioner for Degema, who was a Member of the Eastern House of Assembly for Orlu Division, accused the DPNC candidate of placing a curse on the land and preventing wells being sunk in the area by the NCNC Regional Government. He was also reported as asking his audience whether the DPNC candidate had contributed "any common idea" to the local Improvement Union or Youths Organization on the development of his community. The reply was, "We do not even see him at home or at any progressive meeting."[24]

More tangible proof of a man's interest in his community than ideas might also be sought. An opinion leader might promise to endow scholarships to the local school. In this way his own reputation and that of the party he supported would be much enhanced. In its editorial comments on November 24th the Action Group's *Mid-West Echo* remarked scathingly that it was easy for NCNC leaders to announce that they were awarding scholarships out of their own private earnings, but "not quite so easy to find any of them demonstrating their love for the common man in any practical way as Action Group leaders do everywhere." It went on to describe how:

Only a short while ago the Action Group candidate for Benin Central, Mr. Agidigbi Uwagboe, visited Obajere Village in Ogba area in the

---

[23] Conversely, a traditional chief might be educated and active in some "modern" sphere. However, the broad distinction holds.
[24] *West African Pilot*, October 28th, 1959.

normal course of his work. It was a raining day and what he saw did not only revolt him, it stirred in him that spirit of sympathetic one-ness that has characterised everyone of Action Group's welfare programmes.

Obajere market, a market for which the NCNC-controlled Benin City Council is responsible, was quite appaling [sic]—wretched 'stalls', swampy ground and a mass of suffering, woe-be-drenched humanity going by the name of 'market women'. An NCNC campaigner would have turned his nose up at the sight and hurried away into a car that he obtained by foul means.

But Mr. Agidigbi Uwagboe returned to Benin and purchased iron sheets for the rebuilding of the market. And today, if nothing else, the market women in Obajere have permanent protection from the sun and the rain—they can trade in comfort. That is the stuff of which the Action Group is made.

The position of the new men when acting as opinion leaders was therefore a delicate one. They could not in the main rely upon some traditional source of prestige, and so had to draw upon the capital of their reputation, acquired through their success in dealing with the demands of modern life. A failure to maintain that success, or to come up to the general expectation in some matter, might mean the end of their influence. This failure could include a political misjudgement; sometimes individual opinion leaders had to become followers, if they found themselves out of key with the rest of the community. As one headmaster of a Roman Catholic school in Orlu Division wrote in his letter of resignation from his office as secretary and auditor of the local branch of DPNC:

I am resigning from the DPNC and declaring for the NCNC because membership of the DPNC makes a really influential person very un-popular.[25]

THE COMMUNITIES AND THE POLITICAL SYSTEM

So far we have considered the immediate setting in which an elector was asked to make up his mind and choose between rival candidates. It has been seen that particular groups of men acted as opinion leaders, while these same men provided the leadership of the political parties and stood as candidates in elections. There was, however, another wider setting within which the voting decision was made. An individual made his or her decision as part of a community, the communities made

[25] Quoted in the *West African Pilot*, October 6th, 1959.

theirs as part of the new Nigerian political system. When the individual cast a vote he was participating directly in the political system, and, incidently, affirming his faith in it as a form of government.

The number of people who realized this, or saw it in these abstract terms, must have been very small, even among the opinion leaders. Yet the act of voting was not in itself a very sophisticated way of participating in the political system. It involved two quite simple things—an appreciation by the individual of where his own interests lay, and the understanding that he was called upon to choose someone to represent these interests. It would seem that the majority of electors in Nigeria in 1959 at least understood that there was something called "Government" (though they might be unsure of its exact location), and that they were being called upon to choose someone to act as their spokesman in dealing with it. To this extent, then, people were aware that they were part of a larger political system. The ways in which this affected their voting decision will be considered in the following pages.

THE IDEA OF REPRESENTATION

Two things would be associated with "Government" in peoples' minds—power and the bestowal of benefits. Government had police and soldiers and could make people do things—cease raiding their neighbours, for instance. It could also, if it wished, give them such desirable things as wells, schools, roads to enable them to sell their surplus crops outside the community, and all manner of aids to comfort and prosperity. Anyone who was elected, therefore, was expected to be a "representative" in the full sense of the term. He was expected to know the area, to understand its needs, and to be prepared to secure for it as many benefits as he could.[26] Thus it was rare for a man to stand for election in a constituency which did not contain the community in which he was born. It did not matter if he had been educated elsewhere and had his business interests outside the community in which he was born, so long as he regarded it as his home. He would still be a better representative for it than someone who came from outside, who could not even speak the same tongue. Even in modern towns like Aba and Port Harcourt the candidate was expected to speak the predominant language.[27] If he was to fulfil the "interpretative function" properly he must be able to understand the needs and desires of his constituents, to speak their language in both the literal and the metaphorical sense, so that he might be "advised."

[26] As one literate Ibo carpenter put it, "I will not vote for a Hausa or a Yoruba man whom the NCNC wishes me to vote for. However bad an Ibo man is, I shall vote for him. If he does not represent us well, we will advise him."

[27] Nevertheless, in May 1961 Ibrahim Imam, a Kanuri, was elected as Action Group Member of the Northern House of Assembly for a Tiv constituency.

In the popular view, when a man was elected he agreed that in return for being given a position of influence, with a salary, a car loan, and the opportunity to further his own interests through the contacts he made, he would do all he could to further the interests of the communities which made up his constituency.[28] The elected man belonged, of course, to only one of these communities, but he would be expected to help all of them, if they had supported him. It has already been seen in discussing nominations that a Member of a legislature who had apparently favoured only his own people ran a grave danger of failing to be renominated by the local party. He also provided the opposition with an excellent weapon to use against him if he succeeded in getting the nomination once more. Indeed, this accusation of neglect was often levelled at any renominated Member by his opponents. In a speech in Benin City at a meeting at which the *Oba* of Benin presented the new Action Group Divisional Chairman to the crowd, J. U. Isuman, the party's Assistant Principal Organizing Secretary in the Mid-West, launched a bitter attack on Chief Omo-Osagie, the *Otu Edo* leader. In it he asked:

Here in Benin, how many people has Omo-Osagie, who asked you to vote for NCNC, put in the Federal or Eastern boards where NCNC is in power?

How many farmers has he helped financially or otherwise?

How many of your young ones has he employed in the services of the Federal and Eastern Governments where NCNC is in power?

How many market women has he helped through the African Continental Bank where NCNC dumps its Government's money?[29]

Whatever the party or organization which nominated him, in fact, a candidate would be judged in this light. If he was a man who was respected in his own community, who was thought worthy to represent it and the rest of the constituency in the world outside, and was believed to be able, by reason of his influence with the powers-that-be, to secure benefits for the constituency, he was in an advantageous position from the beginning of the campaign.

THE PARTY IN POWER

The parties were not backward in exploiting this attitude on the part of the electors. We have already had occasion to mention the advantage which each of the major parties enjoyed in controlling a

[28] During the 1959 election campaign an organization known as the Nigerian Tenants' Association actually called on candidates to enter into an undertaking with their constituents that should they fail to keep their election promises within three months they would be voted out of office or brought before a court of law.

[29] *Mid-West Echo*, June 8th, 1959.

Regional Government, the policies of which had a much more direct effect upon the lives of the ordinary people than those of the Federal Government.[30] The Nigerian political parties had a well-developed sense of the value of power. It was made very clear in 1959 that no development could be expected in any area rash enough to vote against the party which controlled the Regional Government. For the NCNC, the Action Group, and the Northern People's Congress it was most important that in the Region which they controlled they were, and called themselves, "the party in power."

All this meant that there was great confusion in the minds of the ordinary electors between Federal and Regional elections, or, to be more precise, the distinction between the various governments was not understood.[31] The fact that this was a Federal election, and that provision of things like wells and dispensaries was a Regional concern, meant nothing to people whose everyday contact was with agents of the Regional governments. Sometimes the parties tried to draw the distinction themselves, but only when it suited them. The *West African Pilot,* for instance, describing a tour made by the Provincial Commissioner for Degema, stated that

At Kugbo where a request was made for a Post Office, the Commissioner stated that since this was a Federal concern, it was necessary that the community should vote en bloc for NCNC candidates through whose efforts, backed with the Regional Government, the new Federal Government could hasten to give a Post Office to Odual clan area.[32]

In a speech made to an Action Group conference in Asaba East constituency Nduka Eze, one-time leader of trade union support for Dr. Azikiwe, now President of the Action Group in Asaba Division, also made the distinction, but with a different emphasis. Whatever happened at a Federal level, he said,

. . . the Western Regional Government will continue to remain inviolate and sovereign in matters within its executive and legislative competence. This means therefore the Action Group will continue to be the Government that you and the disgruntled NCNCers will have to call upon for many more years to come to provide you with water, hospital, dispensary, maternity, loans and all those immediate requirements of your everyday life.

[30] See *The Nigerian Federal Election,* Chapter II *et passim.*

[31] In the opinion polls conducted by the author a number of people gave as the reason for the election being held the fact that "the Western House has been dissolved."

[32] *West African Pilot,* November 25th, 1959.

*If by any stroke of the misjudgement of the people of this Con-
stituency they cast their votes for a worthless NCNC candidate, the
regret will be theirs and theirs for a long time. Imagine what is happening today in Asaba because the people decided to recognise their Government. Observe the phenomenal rate of development within so short
a time that has poured into Asaba. They are almost unbelievable—almost
unbelievable, but the developments are there for everyone to see and
this was achieved in under two years.*

It is for you to make up your minds as did Asaba people.[33]

It is interesting that these remarks were directed at people who
were potential opinion leaders in their communities. Everywhere it was
naturally such individuals who were most aware of this factor in the
relationship between their communities and the political system at
large. When Chief Awolowo visited Bonny, part of Degema constituency in the East, on one of his campaign tours he was presented with
an address signed by the *Amanyanabo* and seven of his chiefs. In it they
observed that "It is interesting to note that you have come on your first
visit to Bonny only during this federal election," and went on to say
that they did not support the Action Group idea of a "COR State," but
wanted a "Rivers State": "This we hope to achieve conveniently with
the co-operation of the NCNC Government of the East." The address
then listed eight benefits which had been bestowed upon Bonny by the
NCNC Regional Government, including a grant of £2,500 for a rural
health centre and recognition of the *Amanyanabo* as a First-Class Chief,
and remarked that "With the foregoing, you will agree that we have
nothing to lose from our co-operation with the NCNC East Regional
Government." The address ended with a request to Chief Awolowo to
convey the thanks of the signatories to Dr. Azikiwe![34]

Sometimes the argument that there was everything to gain by supporting the right party would be specifically directed at influential individuals. At a campaign meeting in Okigwi Central constituency in the
East Dr. Azikiwe attacked the Independent candidate, expressing surprise that "those who were helped by the NCNC had in most cases paid
the party with disobedience." The Premier then went on to list the
benefits the ingrate had enjoyed—membership of the Board of the
Eastern Region Development Corporation, and later of the Federal
Tariff Board. Here he was alleged to have earned £400 a year—one
shilling a mile transport allowance and five guineas a night when attending Board meetings. His son had also had a scholarship to study

[33] *Daily Service,* September 4th, 1959. In the local government elections of
April 1958, Action Group had captured Asaba Urban District Council from NCNC,
and Eze had become Chairman of the Council.

[34] *West African Pilot,* October 21st, 1959.

engineering. Yet "Mr. Ibeagi became so ungrateful that he decided to disobey the party which had done so much for him."[35]

Mr. Ibeagi got 362 votes out of a total of 23,754. Elsewhere the argument that it was foolish to oppose the party in power in the Region was not so efficacious. Degema returned an Action Group candidate, Asaba East one from NCNC. On the other hand, Ilorin Division showed signs of a swing back to the Northern People's Congress, whose Regional Government had invested a great deal of money in the area. The argument was most important in ensuring the major parties' continued dominance in the areas of their own Regions where they were already strongest. There was a force, however, which, especially in the ethnic minority areas, was stronger even than the appeal to immediate self-interest, and which even those who were potential opinion leaders had to respect. This force, loosely known as "tribalism," was a factor in the voting decision which must be considered at some length.

THE APPEAL TO SENTIMENT

When Nigerian politicians were asked what it was that made people vote the way they did they almost invariably answered "sentiment." The "sentiment" expressed was usually that of "tribe." It has already been mentioned that under what appeared to them to be pressure from some external force communities with certain things in common—language, cultural traits, traditions—would come together and act as a concerted political force. This pressure from outside was usually something which appeared to threaten their existence as communities. Political power had passed, or was about to pass, into the hands of strangers, people who would not understand their needs because they did not even understand their language. This had to be resisted at all costs. Since 1951 the smaller ethnic groups had become aware that they were in danger of perpetual subjection to the larger within the Regions. As we have seen, this gave openings to the major parties to gain stronger footholds in their opponents' Regions. It gave rise also to the demand that the new political system be changed in form, with the creation of new states for these minorities. By 1959 the acceptance of the report of the Minorities Commission as the basis of future constitutional discussion had made this impossible. The ordinary electors were unaware of this, and those politicians who were did not make it widely known. The creation of new states was thus an important issue in the 1959 election.

How did this affect the question of the voting decision? Put as simply as possible, it meant that when the local opinion leaders came to interpret political issues to the electors in their communities the simplest language they could use, and therefore the one most often used,

[35] *West African Pilot*, December 1st, 1959.

was that of "tribe." Thus the different parties were associated in people's minds with different ethnic interests—NCNC was an "Ibo" party, Action Group was "Yoruba," the NPC represented the Fulani. The attitude of the community to these parties was therefore a reflection rather of its attitude to other ethnic groups than to parties as such, an extremely important point when it is remembered that political parties are one of the main channels through which the individual can associate his interests with the political system. Most electors tended to judge the parties not by their activities as part of the political system, but by the much more fundamental yardstick of the supposed relationship between the elector's ethnic group and others. In these circumstances there was little freedom of choice between parties, since for a man to support a political party different from the one supported by the rest of the community amounted almost to a repudiation of his own people.

Comparisons between parties tended therefore to be very strongly expressed, in places where enough was known about them to make comparisons possible. In Aba, for instance, the following remarks were made about the different parties:

NPC . . . "A party of yesmen. It is partially influenced by the imperialists and is trying now to come to limelight by copying the ideologies of NCNC" (literate Ibo electrician, aged 21–25).[36]

Action Group . . . "Autocratic, vindictive, partial. I can't find enough adjectives to qualify this party" (literate Ibo clerk, aged 31–35).

DPNC . . . "Is strictly not a party but an association of Mbadiwe's brothers and hired officials" (illiterate Ibo silversmith, aged 31–35).

NCNC . . . "If I tell you all the good qualities of this party and its leader you will be tired of writing. In fact it is the only true political party in Nigeria. All others are just late-comers and opportunists. Zik is our light and my household and I must vote solidly for the NCNC because of him. I am not prepared to talk about any other party because I don't regard them as parties. I know all their leaders, but don't disturb me, there's no need mentioning them because it is no asset to know them. It is enough to know Zik and I am happy I have lived up to this time to see the fruit of his labour" (literate Ibo pensioner, aged 61–65).[37]

In the rural constituencies, the vast majority of the 312, the possibility of a choice between the parties for the individual elector was even more remote. In the towns there was access to such sources of in-

[36] So much for the "alliance" between NCNC and NPC.
[37] These answers were given to the question"What do you know about these political parties: the NCNC; the Action Group; the NPC; NEPU; the DPNC? Can you give the names of their leaders?" Few people knew anything about NEPU.

formation as newspapers and radio sets, and far more literate opinion leaders willing and able to pass information on to the rest. The rural communities had only a few opinion leaders through whom basic information about the parties could be channelled, and these were usually fully committed to one party or another. When this lack of an adequate flow of information from the centre of the political system to the periphery was added to the community's awareness of its "tribal" affiliations and to its group pressures on the individual, it is easy to see how one may speak of a "community vote," rather than individual decision. In such a situation it became "necessary and advisable for every reasonable person to vote for (the party)," as one illiterate male trader in Aba put it.

All this goes far towards explaining the bitterness with which politics were conducted in Nigeria, and the animosity felt towards those who "crossed the carpet." Yoruba supporters of Action Group felt that all "good" Yorubas should back their party. In the minds of most Ibos it was a moral obligation to support NCNC. Dr. Mbadiwe was regarded as the worst kind of traitor in 1958, at any rate after attempts to reconcile him and Dr. Azikiwe through a traditional Ibo oath-taking ceremony had failed. In an attempt to find an explanation for Mbadiwe's behaviour many Ibos blamed his treachery on his Aro blood. The Aros were looked on with some dislike by other Ibos because of their power over much of Iboland in the past. Dr. Mbadiwe was from Aro-Ndizuogu, in Orlu Division, one of the Aro settlements to be found along the old trading routes. The Obioha brothers were also "Aros abroad," and V. K. Onyeri, DPNC Member of the Eastern House of Assembly for Port Harcourt, was from an Aro settlement in Awka. Many Ibos therefore regarded the new DPNC as a kind of "Aro plot." In an article written by the Government Chief Whip in the Eastern House during the election campaign in 1959 the other communities of Orlu were exhorted not to vote for "a handful of Aro members of DPNC" who "look down upon the neighbouring towns."[38]

For some of the minority groups, support for an opposition party after 1951 had appeared to be the only means of salvation in a Region controlled by their "enemies." With the election of 1959 signs began to appear of a slow and painful change in attitude on the part of a few of them. For others pride in themselves as a "nation" was still to be equated with support for the political party in opposition in the Region. At a campaign meeting in Urhobo Central a speaker referred to the appointment of a prominent Urhobo as a Director of the new Central Bank of Nigeria. The fact, he said, that the NCNC had made it

[38] *West African Pilot*, October 30th, 1959.

possible for the signature of "the respected leader of the Urhobo nation" to appear on the new Nigerian currency "was in itself a demonstration of NCNC's appreciation of unremitting loyalty, a tribute to the Urhobos and an acknowledgement of their priceless contribution to the fight for the country's freedom."[39]

In Benin Division in the Mid-West Action Group campaigners made strenuous efforts to associate NCNC with the Ibos in the minds of the Bini electors, hoping in this way to break the hold over them which the *Otu-Edo—NCNC* Alliance had had since 1951. Many Ibos, particularly from Aboh and Asaba Divisions, had settled in Benin Division, attracted by opportunities of work as rubber-tappers or timber-cutters. It was felt by many of the Bini people that their ancient glories were past, and that, sunk in sloth and apathy, they would be overrun by the more vigorous Ibos. In a pamphlet published in 1953 a local observer lamented that

Take a short tour to Benin and districts, it would be regrettable to note that 75% of the inhabitants are foreign natives, i.e. Ibos. This tribe has tapped the natural resources of this nation. From the tapping of rubber trees in the morning, selling of its dead wood for fire in the afternoon, to the hawling [sic] of timber in the forest and gaming, belong to these people. In the markets they are, in the majority of cases Ibos. To this, our nation with unnecessary pride, can be said 'pride goes before destruction.' Visualising it could be seen that within a very short space of time, if care and precaution are not taken now, the Benin nation would be totally extaminated [sic] from the list of economic nations with the speed we allow leases of landed property to these foreign natives.[40]

In 1959 feeling between Binis and Ibos was still high. We noted that there had been fighting between them in Iyekovia District during registration,[41] but quarrels between Bini farmers and Ibo rubber-tappers were common enough at any time. Action Group supporters tried to exploit these quarrels, and more especially the feeling that the once-glorious Bini "nation" was being destroyed. Letters appeared in the local party newspaper complaining about the alleged activities of Ibo prostitutes in Benin City, who were "corrupting young men."[42] On December 12th, however, memories of the rule of the "Ogboni" group before 1951 and affection for the *Otu Edo*, which had destroyed the

---

[39] *Mid-West Champion*, July 14th, 1959.
[40] G. A. Obano, *Path to National Unity in Benin*, Ibadan, 1953.
[41] *The Nigerian Federal Election*, Chapter VI.
[42] *Mid-West Echo*, June 8th, 1959.

Ogboni power, proved too strong for the attempt to identify NCNC with purely Ibo interests. What would have happened if the support for NCNC had not been based on its alliance with a local minor party is difficult to say. In August 1960 Action Group was, in fact, able to defeat the Alliance in one of the four Regional seats in the Division, the party's first victory there in a parliamentary election.

Tanganyikan village
Courtesy Tanganyika Information Services

Part of a Ghanaian market
Courtesy Ghana Information Services

Women's dancing group at a fund-raising event for their clan
Photographed in Eastern Nigeria by Judith Lynne Hanna

Political speech in Ghana
Courtesy Ghana Information Services

Political rally in Tanganyika
Courtesy Tanganyika Information Services

Queuing up to vote in Tanganyika
Courtesy Tanganyika Information Services

Voting in Kenya
*Courtesy Kenya
Government
Information
Services*

Election results scoreboard in Nigeria
Courtesy Information Division,
Nigerian Ministry of Research and Information

The Honourable A. M. Obote and his prospective cabinet
after news of electoral victory
Courtesy Uganda Department of Information

The home of M. Houphouet-Boigny, President of the Ivory Coast
Photographed by William John Hanna

Uganda National Assembly in session
Courtesy Uganda Department of Information

Demonstrating against a European administrator in Nigeria
Photographed by William John Hanna

Ghanaian youth on the march
Courtesy Ghana Information Services

Friction between Nigeria and Ghana
Courtesy Information Division,
Nigerian Ministry of Research and Information

Industry in Uganda
Photographed by William John Hanna

Modern architecture and the money economy in Uganda
Photographed by William John Hanna

Street scene in Dakar, Senegal
Photographed by William John Hanna

Dar es Salaam
Courtesy Tanganyika Information Services

Elections in an African Rural Area

DENNIS AUSTIN

University of London

What happens when an African tribal community is suddenly brought within a parliamentary system based on adult suffrage? On the surface, the process is a familiar one: an election date is announced, parties begin to be active, candidates are chosen, a government information van goes round to explain the procedure of voting, polling day arrives, and the member for X constituency is declared returned. The electorate has made its choice and the new member takes his seat in parliament. But, in substance, what happens? What are the issues on which the electorate divides—supposing there is a contest? How does a candidate put himself forward? What should he do, or have in his favour, in order to win? And—the most difficult question of all: how *real* are such contests in terms of local understanding of what the election is about? The following account is an attempt to answer these questions for one part of West Africa: the Kassena-Nankanni North and Bongo constituencies in northern Ghana during the 1954 and 1956 general elections.

Before turning to the election campaigns in these two constituencies we should recall briefly the progress of events in the country generally leading up to independence in 1957. The first general election was held in February 1951. Nkrumah was still in prison but a strong tide of nationalism still carried the country along with it. The Convention People's Party was overwhelmingly successful in the popularly contested constituencies and Nkrumah became, first, Leader of Government Business and, then, Prime Minister in the new Legislative Assembly. Further constitutional reforms were proposed and a second general election was held in June 1954 for an all-African Assembly under a constitution which gave the country internal self-government. The C.P.P. won 72 seats out of a total of 104, and it looked as if the party had a clear run before it with only the formal negotiations to be got through before the

Reprinted from *Africa*, XXIX (1961), 1–17, with the permission of the author and the publisher. No authorities are cited in this article, the evidence being based on fieldwork carried out during a number of visits to the area between 1954 and 1960. However, I should like to thank Dr. Lucy Mair for enabling me to see more clearly the social-anthropological situation of the societies whose problems I have tried to describe.

final handing over of power. But immediately following the election, a strong Ashanti opposition movement arose, in alliance with similarly based regional and ethnic groups in the north and Togoland. The British Government insisted that there should be a third election, and a "reasonable majority" in a new parliament to decide (among other issues) the question whether the country was to enter independent life with a unitary or federal constitution. The election took place in July 1956. The C.P.P. was returned with a more than two-thirds majority and independence followed in March 1957.

In the northern region, political development was swift from 1954 onwards. The 1950 constitution enfranchised the north only indirectly: the region returned 19 members through a central Electoral College in Tamale based on District Councils. Then in 1953 the Van Lare *Commission on Representational and Electoral Reform* divided the area into 26 single-member constituencies; this was one-quarter of the proposed new Assembly: a rich electoral prize. Parties appeared: the C.P.P., which already had a regional office in Tamale although little more than that, and the Northern People's Party. The latter, in its early stages, was hardly a party in the usual sense of the term—it had very little formal organization outside the Northern Territories Council—and in the northern constituencies in 1954 each candidate, whatever party label he adopted as his election symbol, fought his own battle on his own terms. After 1954, however, the scene changed rapidly. Branches of both parties began to be opened in the larger centres of population, and the extent to which parties won support among the educated minority in the north can be seen by a comparison between the number of Independent and party candidates who stood for election in 1954 and 1956.

	INDEPENDENTS				PARTY NOMINATIONS			
	Candi-dates	Seats	Votes	% of Total Vote	Candi-dates	Seats	Votes	% of Total Vote
1954	36	6	60,328	31.3	44	20	132,351	68.7
1956	10	0	8,665	5.8	52	26	140,994	94.2

The two constituencies, which form the particular subject of this paper, are in the extreme north of the northern savanna belt—in the poorest area of the least-developed region. The district was cruelly laid waste in the half-century before the extension of British rule to the north, the local tribal peoples—Kassena, Nankanni, Frafra, and kindred groups—being constantly raided by armed mounted adventurers under Songhai and Mandingo leaders. Today the district is thickly populated.

One estimate places the population per square mile of farmable land in Bongo at over 450,[1] and the thin top soil, over-cultivated and under-fertilized, yields barely sufficient millet and guinea corn to maintain even a subsistence economy; in recent years, food has had to be imported from neighbouring settlements. A characteristic feature of the district is the spread of homesteads, each with its 30 to 40 relatives, living inside a walled compound of neatly thatched huts of puddled mud, and tilling a small acreage of farmland. There are "towns"—Paga, Chiana, Mirigu, Bongo, and others: but with the exception perhaps of Navrongo and the nearby large trading town of Bolgatanga they hardly warrant the name; properly speaking they are market centres which have grown in the shadow of the chief's compound and the District Commissioner's office.

Election campaigning in such an area calls for skilful understanding. Arguments must be couched in local terms; they must contain points that the elders can weigh carefully, for emotional appeals in the name of "Self-Government" or "Africa" or "Freedom" are likely to meet with a blank response. What *is* important is the support of influential groups, and a candidate will try and enlist on his side the chief, the *tendaana* (or *tigatu* among the Kassena), the clan elders, heads of compounds, the popular young men, and the few wealthy individuals who, because of their wealth, command respect. It means vigorous propaganda through a maze of sandy paths stretching from one homestead to another, sitting down patiently to drink and talk with the elders, gaining approval by coming if possible as the emissary of the chief, enlisting sympathies and arousing emotions along familiar lines of argument, and showing yourself to be a generous, open-handed person.

There is one particular group to win over: the handful of educated young men in each locality. In Bongo in 1954–6 there were only about 20 to 25 altogether who could claim to have had any schooling, but they were of enormous importance in the election campaign. In Kassena-Nankanni there were many more thanks to the work (over nearly fifty years) of the White Fathers' mission. In both constituencies this educated minority acted as voluntary propaganda agents who were listened to by the illiterates as having the mystique of belonging to the outside literate world, and because they held positions of key importance in local affairs—clerk to the local council, registrar of the native court, teachers, catechists, letter-writers, and so forth. The more active among them had sniffed the nationalist air from the south in the early 1950's although without knowing quite what to do about it: a "Frafra Youngsters' Organization" was formed in 1951 which met irregularly in the

[1] T. Hilton, Department of Geography, University College of Ghana, 1958.

large market-town of Bolgatanga and held debates on "modern topics" —"the reform of native authorities," "parliamentary democracy," "monogamy, polygamy, and Christian teaching," and the like; but it was not until the first party administration was formed under Dr. Nkrumah between 1951 and 1954 that parties began to stir in the district.

THE KASSENA-NANKANNI DISTRICT

As the name implies, we are dealing with two communities—the Kassena and Nankanni peoples. The district was brought together in 1936 as a Native Authority of ten confederated chiefdoms of which five were predominantly Nankanni—Navro, Kologo, Naga, Mirigu, Sirigu—and five predominantly Kassena—Page, Chiana, Kayoro, Katiu, and Nakon. The ten chiefs were co-equals within the federation, a president being elected every three years from among their number; none of the ten was officially accorded "paramount" status: that is, none was gazetted or received the salary of a paramount chief.

This was the official position of the federation, and the official status of its member chiefs. However, the chief of Navrongo in the southern area of the district gradually gained the ascendancy over the others. Navrongo is a good market centre where the main road from the south divides west to Tumu and Lawra along the northern boundary of Ghana, and north to Wagadugu* in Upper Volta; partly for this reason the town became the administrative headquarters of the whole Kassena-Nankanni area where the British District Commissioner had his office and court house. Because of the presence of the D.C. and the large market, Navrongo was also the earliest centre in northern Ghana of mission activity by the White Fathers, who moved there from Wagadugu in 1906. The Navropio (*pio* = chief) naturally benefited. Chief since 1945, an astute, self-educated ex-government servant (a P.W.D. Station Foreman) of great strength of will, he did everything he could to emphasize the *de facto* superiority of his state over the other nine states of the confederacy. The difference between Navrongo and the other "towns" became more and more marked. Strangers who arrived in the district believed it to be the local "capital." Litigants came to have their cases heard at the District Commissioner's court. Christians bicycled in to hear mass at the mission church. The market outgrew all other markets in the neighbourhood, the lorry park was always crowded with vehicles making the journey between Wagadugu, Tamale, and Kumasi.

Navropio's fellow chiefs watched this growth of Navrongo with a jealous suspicion. And early in 1951 their fears were increased when

---

* Usually spelled Ouagadougou.—W.J.H.

L. R. Abavana, a close associate of the Navropio, was one of the nineteen successful candidates from the Northern Electoral College to the new Legislative Assembly. After an initial period of "neutral support" for the government, Abavana joined the Convention People's Party. This was with the support of the Navropio, who had very early learned the advantage of being a good government man. To the other chiefs, Abavana's election, his membership of the party, and his appointment in February 1954 as a ministerial secretary, looked like a succession of major triumphs for the Navropio—further evidence that the latter wished to raise himself above his nominally co-equal chiefs.

We must now look at the north constituency within the Kassena-Nankanni district.

KASSENA-NANKANNI NORTH

The Van Lare *Commission on Representational and Electoral Reform* divided the Kassena-Nankanni into two constituencies with electoral sub-districts corresponding to local council areas. The north constituency was delimited as follows:

	Population
Paga local council area	12,077
Chiana local council area	9,059
Kayoro, Katiu, Nakon area	7,826
Mirigu, Sirigu area	18,594
1948 Census figures	47,556

The constituency comprises the five Kassena chiefdoms—Paga, Chiana, Kayoro, Katiu, and Nakon; and two Nankanni chiefdoms—Mirigu and Sirigu. It is the most densely populated of all the 26 northern constituencies and one of the smallest in area: the distance from east to west is approximately 15 miles, from north to south only 6 miles.

The announcement of a date (June 1954) for the second general election saw the C.P.P. and the newly formed Northern People's Party compete for candidates in the north, although neither had any great knowledge even of its own supporters in the region. The C.P.P. National Executive members, meeting in Accra, decided that Abavana was the obvious candidate for Kassena-Nankanni South; but they were less sure of what to do in the north constituency and had neither the time—with over a thousand applications to consider for Ashanti and the southern constituencies—nor the detailed knowledge to assess the situation in so remote an area as Kassena-Nankanni North. Presumably, they took Abavana's advice, and they offered their support to J. E.

Seyire, a local store-keeper. Seyire had been one of the handful of early C.P.P. supporters in the Navrongo district, who in 1951 felt that loyalty and service should now have their reward. But the reward he wanted was the party's nomination in his own area—Kassena-Nankanni *South,* in place of Abavana. The National Executive continued to support Abavana and told Seyire that they would support him only in Kassena-Nankanni North. He refused, being quite certain that he would lose there; and like a great many other party members throughout the country in 1954 he filed his nomination papers as an Independent. The result of the election in Kassena-Nankanni South was L. R. Abavana, C.P.P. 5,796; J. E. Seyire, Ind. 3,344.[2]

This brief account of events in the south constituency has a direct bearing on the election in Kassena-Nankanni North. Here, the C.P.P. was unlucky, for early in 1954, C. K. Tedam, a young head-teacher in Paga and one of Seyire's friends, was also considering standing for the party in the north constituency. (This was one reason why Seyire refused to stand there.) Tedam had been attracted to the C.P.P., partly because of Seyire's own advocacy of the party, partly because he was beginning to be interested in nationalist ideas. He had already made a name for himself as a member of the local Kassena-Nankanni District Council by bitter attacks on the Navropio, successfully resisting the chief's attempt to become both President and Chairman of the council— an attitude which would have earned him the party's commendation in other parts of the country at this time. When he heard that Seyire had been told to stand in Kassena-Nankanni North, he was understandably offended. And, like Seyire, he decided to stand as an Independent. The C.P.P. was thus left high and dry. But it was determined to have a candidate in every one of the country's 104 constituencies, cast about for a willing victim, and eventually persuaded Mr. Alban Logozure, a local bar-keeper, to stand. He was not a very active candidate and the result was never in doubt:

C. K. Tedam, Ind.	6,880
A. Logozure, C.P.P.	950
(Registered voters: 13,755—57% poll.)	

Support for Tedam came from every part of the north constituency. At the adoption meeting of District Councillors within the constituency he was proposed by the Chianapio, a Kassena chief from the west, and seconded by the Sirigunaba (*naba,* like *pio,* means "chief") a Nankanni

[2] Two other Independent candidates each polled between 600 and 700 votes.

chief in the south. He himself was the half-brother of the **Pagapio**, the most important chief in the northern section. The strength of his position lay partly through his own efforts—as we shall see he is an indefatigable campaigner—partly because of his championship of local interests against the Navropio. The argument used, and well understood, was: the Navropio, Abavana, and the C.P.P. are in league and must be checked, and Tedam is a good man to do it.

However, in the interval between the 1954 and 1956 elections, the balance of forces within the constituency altered considerably. Tedam joined the Northern People's Party and began to play an active part on the opposition benches. But, within his own area, cracks appeared in the solid wall of support given him in 1954. The division was not, as might have been expected, between the Kassena and Nankanni areas but between his own area, Paga, and a rival Kassena group based on Chiana. The list of candidates for the 1956 general election read:

> C. K. Tedam   N.P.P. half-brother to Pagapio.
> E. K. Ayagitam C.P.P. half-brother to Chianapio.
> V. A. Agongo   Ind.

The election campaign in July 1956 was fought as a struggle for power between the Paga and Chiana peoples with the Nankanni area of Mirigu and Sirigu as a "third force." What had happened?

The outburst of Ashanti and northern "nationalist" emotion in the period between the two elections had left the Kassena-Nankanni peoples unmoved, despite comparisons drawn by the N.P.P. between the C.P.P. and the slave-raiders of the last century. What had impressed them was the outcome of the C.P.P.'s victory in 1954 in the south constituency. Abavana was a "big man" in the government, and he spent much of his time when in the constituency impressing the local elders and chiefs with the fact of government power: there were broad hints that the Navropio would soon be recognized as a paramount chief, although nobody seemed to know how far his authority would extend. Such, it was pointed out, was the reward of those who supported the government. . . . True, argument along these lines could cut both ways: it might be said that there was now all the more reason to oppose the Navropio, and that the simplest way to do it was to go on backing Tedam. But, others began to question whether it was really sensible to go on opposing the C.P.P. Surely it was not too late to turn about? And if the Navropio was to be made a paramount over the Nankanni area— as some suggested—perhaps there was the possibility of a similar reward in the northern Kassena chiefdoms. Quite apart from the advantages which would accrue, and the possible dangers that would be averted, by being on the side of government, a change of allegiance might have the effect of checking the Navropio by his own methods.

It was in these terms—it is alleged—and with these arguments, that the Chianapio, a comparatively young, primary-school-educated chief, was approached and won over by the local supporters of the C.P.P. He thought it improper as a chief to stand as a candidate himself but agreed to support his brother, E. K. K. Ayagitam, a teacher in the local primary school. In this way, by the time of the third general election— the second to be fought on a constituency basis in the north—the long arm of the C.P.P. reached into Kassena-Nankanni, and it is instructive to note how quickly the correlation of party and government power was made. What were Ayagitam's—and the C.P.P.'s—chances of success?

Tedam had the weight of population on his side, for his own chiefdom, Paga, numbered 12,000 against Chiana's 9,000. The Chiana people expected to have the support of their western neighbours, the three small chiefdoms of Kayoro, Katiu, and Nakon (population 8,000) to whom they were linked by marriage and proximity. But Paga had *its* near neighbours, the Nankanni chiefdoms of Mirigu and Sirigu, with over 18,000. The Chiana camp knew therefore that, to succeed, it must somehow divide its opponents. Its first move was to try and gain the support of Namon, a wealthy cattle trader in Paga, who had twice contested the chieftaincy against the present Pagapio's family. But, at this particular juncture, Namon was not to be persuaded. The Chianas, ably led by Ayagitam and an energetic fellow teacher, Patrick Amipare, then turned to the Nankanni area. Here they had an initial triumph. Playing on local ambitions they persuaded the son of the Mirigu chief to stand. In this way a serious threat developed to Tedam, who looked upon the Nankanni chiefs as natural allies. A deputation was sent from Paga, meetings were held with the elders, the traditional gifts of kola and drinks were offered, and the Mirigu chief told: "You are an old man. What will happen to you and your family with your son away in Accra, even supposing he won? And if, as is likely, he doesn't win, he will weaken support for Tedam. Then you will see Chianapio become like the Navropio, always trying to assert his authority outside his own chiefdom. Is this what you want?" With such arguments, the Paga delegation persuaded the chief to withdraw his support from his son, who then agreed to stand down.

However, the Chianas were not quite finished. A little before the closing date for nominations they put up Mr. V. A. Agongo, a Nankanni from Sirigu, who was then clerk to the Chiana local council. Agongo stood as an Independent and chose as his election symbol a white fish on a blue background. This was thought to be a subtle move, for Tedam had used the symbol in 1954 and it was hoped that some might vote for the same symbol, believing it to be Tedam's, in 1956.[3] It was clear by the results of the election, however, that Agongo came much too late to disturb seriously the Paga-Nankanni alliance.

C. K. Tedam, N.P.P.	5,775
E. K. Ayagitam, C.P.P.	4,528
V. A. Agongo, Ind.	302

(Registration 17,422—67.4% poll.)

We turn now to the actual conduct of the campaign.

Polling was carried out over two days in both 1954 and 1956. This was to enable the regional administration to make the best use of its meagre staff of presiding officers and polling assistants. But it also had the effect of intensifying the campaign by allowing a concentration of effort by both sides, first in the west, then in the north. The thoroughness and energy with which the two party candidates set about the campaign can be seen from the account by one of Tedam's supporters:

Things were not as easy in the election as they were in 1954. It was very difficult to forecast the winner.

We set to work at once, called all the councillors[4] in Paga, got bicycles from the N.P.P. Tamale headquarters. One jeep was given to us to use in the Kassena-Nankanni North and South constituencies, Builsa and Bolga.[5] We had little use for the jeep as it is not easy to travel to the remote places with a car. The councillors and some young men of Paga helped us a great deal, expecting no reward. We made it an issue that it was a fight between the Chianas and the Pagas. We will not like the Chianas to be paramount over us. We would have to walk to Chiana for court cases and pay our levies to them; we made it known that if we allowed the Chianas to win, that means Chianapio would be made a paramount and would dictate to our chief in Paga.

Owing to this news the whole of Paga went haywire. Enthusiastic representatives from all sections volunteered to help Paga win the elections so that we might not become servants to the Chianas but masters of our own.

Some of these volunteers who had their daughters married to the Nankannis and other sides tried to influence their in-laws to vote for Paga as it would also take them a longer time to go to Chiana for their cases.

---

[3] Tedam used the clenched-fist symbol of the N.P.P. in 1956.
[4] Of Paga Local Council.
[5] I.e., Bolgatanga.

*Kola was sent out per leaders of groups for customary greetings . . .
to the headmen in the district. . . . In the Nankanni area our aim was
to convince the headmen who were very influential. In Sirigu especially
we had an assurance from the chief of support. We were not sure in
Mirigu until the last two days to the elections. Most of the headmen in
Mirigu supported us but were waiting for a word from the chief who
had not made up his mind as to whom to vote for. The reason why he
does not want to tell us his mind was, he said: "the highest bidder will
win the elections." He said he heard that when they elect M.P.s to the
Assembly, we rather go to find fortune for our benefits. That for every
mile we travel we claim allowance and because of that he would not tell
us his mind. . . .*

It was felt to be useless to canvass in Chiana chiefdom itself "as
they were all under Chianapio's command." But, just as the Chiana had
hoped to divide Paga and Mirigu, so Tedam and his agents tried to
wean some of the Katiu, Nakon, and Kayoro compounds from Chiana.
A key chiefdom was Kayoro. Ayagitam had a strong foothold there
through Patrick Amipare, brother of the Kayoro chief. But Amipare
had at one time contested the chieftaincy against his brother, and the
Pagas believed that this might help them:

*On market day we had a rally in the market with the Kayoro chief
as chairman. We invited all the Headmen, young men and some influential leaders in the area. We bought about three pots of pito. . . . The
rally was a success. . . . We slept in the town for two days and at night
called on the Headmen and explained what Chianapio was trying to
do. . . .*

The election was fought in acrimonious terms. Close personal ties
linked the candidates and their supporters—Amipare was actually
Tedam's brother-in-law; the small group of teachers, clerks, and store-
keepers had all been to school together in Navrongo or to the Training
College in Tamale; they were all Catholics meeting together each Sunday, coming together, too, for the extra-mural class at Navrongo, or for
tennis in the evening, or the rare cinema show during visits of the mass
education teams. Both Ayagitam and Amipare had been active on
Tedam's behalf in 1954; their defection—as it looked to Paga—in 1956
aroused bitter feeling.

The course of events after the 1956 election confirmed the worst
fears of those who disliked the Navropio and his allies. Abavana, who
had defeated Seyire again in Kassena-Nankanni South, was made a
minister in Nkrumah's third cabinet. Fifteen months later (1 November

1957), he was appointed the first party Regional Commissioner for Northern Ghana—a swift rise to fortune: a local school-teacher until 1951 and, six years later, the political/administrative head of the largest region in the country. The Navropio did not lag behind. He was recognized by government as a paramount chief in December 1957. Then in November 1958, at the first meeting of the Northern House of Chiefs in Tamale, the Navropio (seconded by Chianapio) was elected the constitutional Head of the Region, defeating the once powerful Yabumwura of Gonja and the equally powerful Ya-Na of the Dagomba. The Navropio, too, had come a long way since 1951.[6]

THE BONGO CONSTITUENCY

Although only 10 miles from the large market-town of Bolgatanga the Bongo constituency is a remote one, lying off the main trunk routes. Its peoples speak one of the many cluster dialects of Frafra, and from 1932 until 1952 formed part of the Frafra confederacy of five chiefdoms as an area committee of the large Mamprusi Native Authority. In the latter year, the Bongo sub-native authority was replaced by a Bongo local council as part of the Frafra subdivision of the Mamprusi District Council. At the end of 1957 the Mamprusi district was divided into three separate councils: the South Mamprusi, Kusasi, and Frafra District Councils.

The Bona—the chief of Bongo—is chosen from two "royal" or chiefly lineages—the Anafobissi and Abagnabissi—each of which has a number of subdivisions. The earlier settled peoples live in what one might call the outer, "rural" area of Bongo, farthest from the eponymous capital—Bongo; it is they who, subject to the chief's authority, provide the *tendaana* of the area. These lineages with their subdivisions are important not only in tradition but in modern party political conflicts, and something should be said of the traditions surrounding the origins of the Bongo chieftaincy.

The legend usually recited is of the wandering warrior Awobgo to

[6] The Na-Yiri of Mamprusi, traditionally the most important chief in the north, was also put forward as a candidate but failed to find a seconder. Voting was: Navropio 15, Yabumwura 6, Ya-Na 6. The Chianapio, too, as a member of the regional House of Chiefs, might be considered to have done well for himself. In his inaugural address the Navropio appealed "not only to you, Members of the House, but to each and every one in this Region to give our Government his or her unfailing support and loyalty in all matters. If we support the Government, the Government will help us in all our needs; but if we don't, we should not expect the Government to help us. God helps those who help themselves." The concentration of power in Kassena-Nankanni was still continuing when I revisited the district early in 1960: one of the Navropio's relatives was the party-appointed District Commissioner, another was the acting superintendent of the local Builders' Brigade camp, a third was the newly appointed lay Magistrate for the area.

whom the powerful chief at Nalerigu gave a horse and a boy called
Anambiliga to help him in his wanderings. Leaving Nalerigu they came
to Borigo near Bongo. The man died; the boy grew up and married a
woman of the area. Later she sat under a Bagne tree to rest with her
bundles of firewood and there gave birth to twins; a male child whose
teeth were already formed, whom she named "Anafo," meaning "like a
cow" (that is, born with teeth), and a female whom she named
"Abagne" after the tree. From these two children are believed to be
descended the two "royal" lineages—Anafobissi and Abagnabissi (*bissi*
means "descendants of"). Within memory, nine chiefs have come from
the Anafobissi side, five from Abagnabissi; four of the latter have come
from one particular subdivision—the Asankabissi of Abagnabissi.

One further point of recent history: in 1942 the Bona, Anane
Salibiga, ran into misfortune. A cattle-thief was caught near the township of Bongo and brought into the chief's compound. Following customary practice, all those who came to visit the chief took their turn in
beating the man, who collapsed and died. The chief was held responsible, tried in the assize court at Tamale, and sentenced to a year's
imprisonment with hard labour followed by ten years' exile at Bakoldo
in south Mamprusi. In his absence his brother's son, Akumolga—like
Anane, of the Asankabissi lineage of Abagnabissi—was appointed
Regent. Anane was allowed to return in 1947 although not to act as
chief until 1952. The former Regent, Akumolga, continued to be a
powerful figure in the background as president of the native authority
court.

THE 1954 AND 1956 ELECTIONS

Forty-two delegates attended the Northern Electoral College from
Mamprusi in 1951, and of these 6, including Mr. J. A. Ayinibisa from
the neighbouring Tallensi area, were elected to the new Assembly. The
election caused very little stir in Bongo and it was not until the first
direct elections in June 1954 that parties and candidates appeared. The
final list of nominations for the Bongo constituency was:

> W. A. Amoro Ind.
> Kofi Akumolga N.P.P.
> D. G. Akologo C.P.P.

To understand the growth of party affiliations in Bongo one must
go to Bolgatanga, with its great market (held every three days), its row
of trading stores, District Council offices, police station, hospital, middle
school, and Catholic mission house. A branch of the C.P.P. was formed

in 1950 by R. B. Braimah (a store-keeper) and Jerome Ayema (a letter-writer) and their friends about the same time as the Frafra Youngsters' Organization and a local branch of the People's Educational Association. The small number of educated Bongo young men used to cycle into Bolga' on market days to talk and gossip in the pito bars and to attend meetings of the F.Y.O. or an extra-mural class. They met fairly regularly each Sunday to attend mass. In this way political ideas spread into Bongo, and eventually a branch of the C.P.P. was formed there. In these early days, however, it was more like a social club than a political organization; it would have been difficult to say who was or who was not a member until the election in June 1954 forced this small group of teachers, clerks, traders, and the local catechist into two opposing factions which looked round for support.

Kofi Akumolga, the son of the former Regent and treasury clerk to the local council, listened to the arguments of Mumuni Bawumia, clerk to the Mamprusi District Council and Vice-President of the newly formed Northern People's Party, liked what he heard, and sympathized with the new party's aim of defending northern interests. He wanted to stand for election and agreed to stand for the N.P.P. in Bongo. He knew that he had the support of his father and of those who hoped to benefit should Chief Anane die and be replaced by the former Regent. William Amoro also sympathized with the aims of the N.P.P. and might well have stood for the party but for Kofi Akumolga's prior candidature. An able, energetic former teacher, and now clerk to the Bongo local council, he too wanted to go to the new Assembly. He was also a casual member—as indeed was Kofi Akumolga—of the very loosely organized C.P.P. branch in Bolgatanga and Bongo, but he knew that one of the arguments used with good effect by the N.P.P. against the party was that it was "anti-chief." Having good hopes of enlisting the support of Chief Anane, who was suspicious of the Akumolga family, Amoro decided to play safe and stand as an Independent. The C.P.P. label (in 1954) would not bring him any votes and might lose him support. Once again, however, as in Kassena-Nankanni North, the regional and national headquarters of the C.P.P. decided that any candidate was better than no candidate, and they persuaded D. G. Akologo, a semi-educated farmer in Bolgatanga, to stand; they paid his deposit and gave him a small amount of money with which to canvass.

Akumolga and Amoro were the two most likely candidates by their personal standing, the close relationship which existed between Akumolga and the former Regent on one side, and the alliance between Amoro and the chief on the other. The elder Akumolga, while Regent between 1942 and 1952, had gained support in some areas by the appointment of a number of heads of subdivisions of the two chiefly lineages; there were those, too, among the Anafobissi—the rival royal lineage—who were willing to vote for Akumolga rather than for the chief's candidate. Both father and son could, of course, rely on their own close agnates. On the other hand, Amoro had the chief on his side, he was supported by his own Gunabissi lineage within Abagnabissi, and he had the greater number of educated young men with him. These included John Baptist Atubga, the catechist, perhaps the most deeply convinced supporter of the C.P.P. in Bongo, and John Abagre, a lively, intelligent local council employee, both of whom brought Amoro the support of their own kin—John Baptist Atubga from the Kuyelengobissi lineage of Abagnabissi, John Abagre from the Werigurigubissi lineage of Anafobissi. Amoro had the additional advantage of being able to enlist support on a wide basis, through his mother who is from the Zagsi people, in the outer "rural" areas, from whom the *tendaana* are drawn, and this gave him a valuable foothold among the non-chiefly—Namoosi, Yareba, and Zagsi—lineages.[7]

The picture is a bewildering, complicated pattern of lineage relationships in which the rivalry of Akumolga and Amoro was overlaid with the older rivalry between the Regent and the chief. The two royal lineages were divided not, as one might have expected, the one against the other—for both Amoro and Akumolga were from Abagnabissi—but between rival groups drawn from both, and arranged round the Akumolga family on one side and the chief's supporters on the other. The non-chiefly lineages in the more remote part of the constituency did not vote in large numbers; but, where they did vote, the majority supported Amoro through the influence of his mother's kin. The educated minority supported him on personal grounds. The result was a narrow majority for Amoro and a mere handful of votes—some quite possibly through error—for Akologo, who hardly put in an appearance in the constituency.

W. A. Amoro, Ind.	2,201
K. Akumolga, N.P.P.	1,856
D. G. Akologo, C.P.P.	317

(Registered Electors 8,208—53% poll.)

A little over a year after he was elected, Amoro—with the permission of the chief and his friends—crossed the carpet to join the C.P.P. Then, towards the end of 1955, chief Anane died and a fierce contest for the Bongo chieftaincy took place between the two royal lineages.

[7] But not in the Via district, where Kofi Akumolga had married the daughter of the Vianaba.

Three claimants came from Abagnabissi, two from Anafobissi. Traditionally, the Bongo chief is appointed by the Na-Yiri, the Mamprusi paramount at Nalerigu, after rival claims have been argued out by supporters of each contestant. Three months of canvassing and intrigue followed, with visits and traditional gifts to influential persons at Nalerigu. Finally, the Na-Yiri appointed the former Regent Akumolga. (It was immediately alleged that he had been influenced by his adviser, Mumuni Bawumia, in favour of Akumolga as the father of the N.P.P. candidate.) Once a chief is appointed, however, there is very little the defeated families do about it except retire and bide their time.[8]

Then in May 1956, a month after the instalment of Akumolga as chief, the Prime Minister announced in the Assembly that a third general election would be held in July. Amoro was greatly disquieted. Akumolga, the father of his political rival, was chief; Kofi Akumolga was now clerk to the Bongo local council—a very influential office. Amoro was further embarrassed at this time by the government's decision not to act on its own proposal to divide the large Mamprusi district council into three separate councils. The proposal had been welcomed by Amoro and opposed by the Akumolgas, father and son. It had aroused passionate controversy throughout Mamprusi, not least in the Frafra area, most of the chiefs and elders being in favour of retaining their traditional connexion with Mamprusi, most of the younger, literate citizens rather liking the idea of a greater local autonomy.[9] It was not difficult therefore to make Amoro and his colleagues appear as enemies of chiefly rule who had tried but failed to weaken the authority of the Na-Yiri, the Bona, and his fellow chiefs.

However, in Amoro's favour was the fact that the Akumolga family had overreached itself. The father was already ruling with a strong hand. It might be unwise to add to his power by sending his son to Accra. True, Amoro had lost the backing of the chief and this cost him some support: his vote in 1956 dropped below that for Akumolga in 1954. But the latter's vote also dropped and by a much greater extent. For some of the members of the Anafobissi lineage who had supported

---

[8] Mr. Amoro himself commented on this: "This practice of keeping mute even when dissatisfied is undergoing reform, and people are beginning to speak up for their rights." The idea of "destoolment" is spreading from the Akan area into the north under the gruesome title of "deskinning." Thus, charges were brought in 1959 against the Ya-Na of Yendi and a "deskinment case" committee of inquiry appointed to look into it.

[9] There was a certain administrative justification behind the proposal, Mamprusi being a very large district council area, but it was generally regarded as a political move aimed at Mumuni Bawumia and the Na-Yiri. A Commissioner was appointed to inquire into the merits of the case and his recommendations that the proposal be abandoned were accepted by the Government.

Kofi Akumolga in 1954 now held back. Having failed to wrest the chieftaincy from the Abagnabissi lineage in 1955, they did not see why— a year later—they should go on helping the Akumolgas and the Asankabissi division of Abagnabissi. There were others who were puzzled by the announcement that there should be a second election, for Amoro was still alive, and it hardly seemed time to change. Others again were impressed by the visit of Nkrumah during his quick pre-election tour of the north. So Amoro was again elected, although in a much reduced poll:

W. A. Amoro, C.P.P.	1,760
K. Akumolga, N.P.P.	1,225
(Registered Electors 8,435—35% poll.)	

GENERAL CONCLUSIONS

What does one need to win? This was one of the questions posed at the beginning. Is it possible now to answer for Kassena-Nankanni and Bogo?

The chief? Certainly his help is extremely useful. Tedam would have found it difficult to contest without Pagapio's support; so would Abavana in Kassena-Nankanni South without the Navropio. In these areas the chief still has authority over others and there is hardly any point in discussing whether or not chiefs should "take part in politics": he is there to give guidance and to represent the community in every-thing that affects it. But it is possible, as Amoro found, to run counter to the chief's wishes and still be successful. An able candidate can use local rivalries arising from personal jealousies and long-standing rival-ries between lineages. In Bongo especially, where the dispute took place within the area of a single chiefdom, Amoro was able to use a latent anti-chief attitude. The various lineages had a watchful eye on Akumolga in 1956. He was respected, obeyed, even feared, but a jealous suspicion was there below the surface and used by Amoro with good effect.

Money also is important. There is no law restricting the amount each candidate may spend, and the regulations prohibiting "treating" are ineffective. Most members of parliament will admit that elections are extremely expensive: you have to spend to win, and you have to pay back what you have borrowed whether you win or not. One estimate of election expenses incurred by an unsuccessful candidate in one of the northern constituencies came to £800 in 1954 and £600 in 1956. He would probably be considered in the south to have been fortunate to have escaped so lightly. But money is needed not so much to buy votes as to ensure goodwill. If a rally is held on market day the candidate must earn the approval of a lively crowd of possible supporters by supplying generous quantities of local beer; dancers, drummers, pipers may be asked to perform, and the candidates must reward them. Someone may have died—the relatives must be consoled in a practical way; someone's wife may have given birth—and the family must be honoured. These are customary practices, except that what may have been adequate even in recent times is no longer so today: the double handful of kola has to be supplemented by beer or minerals or, for the "big man," whisky. All this is very expensive, quite apart from the cost of transport and the maintenance of election agents. Practically nothing comes from the party headquarters—at least in Bongo and Kassena-Nankanni—except the loan of a propaganda van. Money for the election has to be raised locally. The area is wretchedly poor, but there are a few comparatively rich individuals, including of course the chief.

Religion? In neither election was religion of importance, except in one minor respect in Bongo, where the formation of the Frafra Youngsters' Organization and the C.P.P. was probably promoted by common membership of the Catholic church which helped to draw the educated and illiterate leaders together; association meetings were often held after mass on Sunday morning in Bolgatanga.[10] (Perhaps one should add that the church merely provided the opportunity for members to meet regularly together; in the north-west, in the strongly Catholic area of Nandom, a similar development happened *vis-à-vis* the formation of a branch of the N.P.P.) Despite fifty years of strong Catholic influence, traditional animist beliefs are still widespread. There is a belief throughout the area in sympathetic magic. Thus, every Kassena has his crocodile in the village pool at Paga. The creatures bask fearlessly at the water's edge and, with equal confidence, the women and children come to wash their clothes in the muddy water. It is believed that any injury to a villager means a similar injury to his crocodile; to shoot a crocodile would mean the death of somebody in the village. In the Kayoro area there is a river which has the magical property of bestowing wealth on any suppliant who is prepared, in exchange, to endure childlessness. But no one is sinister or naïve enough to try and use such beliefs for political ends. When, some time after the election, I suggested (light-heartedly) that one way to win might be for a candidate to try and seize his opponent's crocodile and keep it in seclusion until

[10] Bongo C.P.P. 1956:
   Chairman: Joachim Agilogo. R.C. illiterate farmer, grandson of a former chief.
   Secretary: Felix Anongyele. R.C. Teacher.
   Treasurer: John Baptist Atubga. R.C. Catechist.

after the election campaign, the chief laughed and said: "No, it doesn't work like that." Quite clearly, like many people, the Kassena-Nankanni have learned to live in two worlds, centuries apart in thought. Similarly Islam, although a minor political force in some northern constituencies, played no part either in Kassena-Nankanni or Bongo. There are perhaps thirty to forty Muslims in the two constituencies who are either "strangers" from Bawku or south Mamprusi, or cattle-traders who have entered Islam along with their profession. But they play no part in election politics.

Nor, surprisingly perhaps, do the women. The women vote in good number. In 1954 in Kassena-Nankanni North out of the 13,755 who registered nearly 5,000 were women. Many of them enjoy a measure of financial independence through the sale of garden produce and pito. Brewing is a woman's job. But it is asserted, even by the women, that generally speaking they vote the way the compound or village votes, the decision being left to the compound head and elders, the *tendaana,* the locally acclaimed leaders of the young men and other—male—sections of society.

Two final questions remain to be answered: the influence of parties, and the reality of elections by ballot in such areas.

Party *organization* was at a very elementary stage in both constituencies. In 1956 the party candidates had their deposits paid, and leading politicians of both sides paid visits to the two constituencies. But the candidates were still very much their own masters. Neither in Kassena-Nankanni nor Bongo was there any formal party machinery—no office, no paid officials, no local manifestoes. Amoro was the only regularly paid-up member in Bongo in 1956—having his party subscription deducted monthly from his salary as an Assembly member. The candidates relied on personal followers who were either their kinsmen or school-fellows (and often both). The following extract shows how one of Tedam's "agents" went about his self-appointed task:

> In Paga the clerk to the local council, half-brother to Tedam and also a Prince in Paga, acts as his agent. He is very influential. He goes round to the outlying villages on each of the market days to collect taxes from the people and takes the chance to tell the people what Tedam is doing and what would happen if they became C.P.P.ists.

Much depends also on the candidate. He, too, must go the rounds whenever he returns home—and in Ghana the candidate usually has his home and family in the constituency; he must visit the influential leaders of each group of compounds, hold a rally in the market place, and reward those who gave him their support.

The chiefs, tigatine, *the headmen and* biepio *take very little notice of what is happening in the National Assembly unless it is something concerning the Kassena-Nankanni area. They look forward to getting some presents such as drinks and cloth. The less you give the more you lose your popularity. The masses must be given pito and kola.*

Thus the successful candidate must try and live up to his campaign promises: he is regarded by many of his constituents as an investment, and he will be asked for jobs or scholarships or for help in local disputes often far beyond his capacity to satisfy all those who, having helped him to become an Assembly member, now expect something in return.

Yet parties were important. Although outwardly very similar, the two elections, from a party point of view, showed an important shift in emphasis. When, for example, Ayagitam in Kassena-Nankanni North wanted to stand for election everyone knew that he would stand for the C.P.P. Indeed, but for the party, he might not have stood. It was recognized by 1956 that parties were more than labels, that they were avenues to power not only remotely, in Accra, but in Kassena-Nankanni and Bongo. This awareness was quickened after 1956 when Amoro became a Ministerial Secretary in February 1958 and Abavana a Regional Commissioner at the end of 1957. From 1954 onwards we see the same process taking place on a small scale as took place throughout the country—we see the party rewarding its friends and making life uncomfortable for its opponents. Ideas move slowly in areas like Kassena-Nankanni and Bongo but the understanding spread that members of parliament are important people, particularly if they are on the winning side. There were many now, including chiefs like Pagapio, who began to argue that the sensible way to behave was to show one's loyalty to the new government by joining the party. "The C.P.P. is strong." "They can do anything." "They are the new white men." These were the sort of phrases used, and eventually they had their effect. In June 1958 Mumuni Bawumia, with two other N.P.P. members from Mamprusi, crossed over to the government side. They were followed later in the year by Tedam.

Secondly, the question of understanding: did they know, in Paga and Chiana and Bongo, what they were voting for? At first sight, one is inclined to say "no": there are not more than a dozen people in Kassena-Nankanni, and less than that number in Bongo, who could have explained the difference in 1956 between what the C.P.P. wanted, and what the Ashanti National Liberation Movement/N.P.P. alliance meant when it campaigned for federation. An attempt *was* made to explain the issue in Kassena-Nankanni North:

*In the 1956 election we had the backing of the N.P.P. We invited
some of their leaders to speak—the Tolon-Na, S. D. Dombo, Mumuni
Bawumia. They told the people that the C.P.P. were against the chiefs,
that the Northerners are going to be used as tools for the benefit of the
southerner. We should stand firm, otherwise the C.P.P. will use us as
Samory and Babatu did our forefathers in the olden days. It was the aim
of our leaders to get our own Assembly where we should have full
control of our money.*

This was as far as the federation-unitary argument went and, as we
have seen, the result in each constituency depended on conflicts born
of local disputes. Amoro himself was under no delusion. Having walked
out with the Opposition when the Assembly debated the appointment
of a *Select Committee on Federal Government and a Second Chamber*
in protest against its membership, he then decided to give evidence
before it. He was at this time in the process of moving over to the government side. The following questions were put to him by the Committee, and his answers give a very good picture of the level of understanding in his constituency:

1302. *Which constituency do you represent? . . . The Bongo constituency.*

1303. *Is this view of federalism your personal view or is it shared by
your constituency? . . . This is my personal view.*

1304. *What is the feeling of your constituency with regard to this matter? . . . The people of my constituency are almost all farmers
and have little idea of what government involves.*

1305. *Are you suggesting that they do not know what is going on at
all? . . . No.*

1306. *At least there are some who can understand government, though
perhaps only a few? . . . There may be.*

1307. *Are they not interested? . . . The few who can understand it may
be, and they may support or condemn federalism in accordance
with how they have been convinced by its advocates.*

1308. *In your opinion which view of federalism is supported by the
majority in your constituency? . . . I cannot judge.*

1309. *Do you mean you cannot tell us the general reaction of the people
in your constituency regarding these questions? . . . No, I am
afraid.*

1310. *What happens when you, as their representative in the Legislative*

> *Assembly, go back to explain to them any Government pro-*
> *gramme; don't they do anything to indicate their approval or*
> *disapproval of the particular Government plans or measures you*
> *talk to them about? . . . Sometimes they feel pleased with certain*
> *matters and at other times they feel displeased.*

1311. Yes; all we want to know is what they feel about these two ques-
tions of federalism and a Second Chamber? . . . Most of my people
favour a unitary system of government.

1312. Do you mean they agree with the views you express to them on
these questions and therefore favour a unitary system of govern-
ment? . . . Yes.

This paints the picture admirably. But it does not make the election meaningless. The candidates knew the national issues, the electorate knew—and knew intimately—the candidates. The idea of elections as a struggle for power between rival groups was well understood. Admittedly, the contest was fought within a local framework of references, with quarrels between chiefdoms and lineages given a fresh look and new vigour from the party conflict between Tedam and Ayagitam, Amoro and Akumolga. But these, in turn, gave depth to the struggle between the candidates. It might perhaps be argued that, even if elections are understood, the idea of representation is not; that, such is the nature of election contests in areas like Kassena-Nankanni and Bongo, the losing side, having lost, will feel that they have lost everything; that Tedam and Ayagitam, Amoro and Akumolga, were protagonists in a conflict which was irreconcilable. But this, too, was probably not the case. Traditional society had a great ability to "return to laughter" after a period of conflict, and there is no reason to doubt the ability of the Anafobissi and Abagnabissi sections, or the Paga and Chiana chiefdoms, to adjust themselves to the new fact of parliamentary contests. Already the suggestion is heard in both areas that if one section of the community supplies the members of parliament at one time, then the honour and office ought to go to the other side on future occasions, although whether such a solution may suit party headquarters is another matter.

Finally, a general point to be noted, of technical interest and of great importance to parties in Ghana, is the size of the electorate. Registration is not automatic: a would-be voter has to apply and make sure during the time allowed that his name is on the register. Much therefore depends on the zeal of the candidates' agents long before the election. In the 1956 Kassena-Nankanni election Tedam was out-generalled in this respect by his opponent, as the following table shows:

	(1) *Total* *Population*	*(2)* *Aged 21* *and Over*	*(3)* *Registered* *Voters*	*%* *(3) of (2)*
Paga	12,707	6,811	4,732	69.5
Mirigu/Sirigu	18,594	9,996	5,015	50.2
Chiana	9,059	4,856	3,973	81.8
Katiu, Kayoro, and Nakon	7,826	4,195	3,702	88.2
	48,184	25,858	17,422	67.4

Based on the 1956 *Digest of Statistics:* 21 and over $= 53.6\%$ of the total population in the north. The population figures are, of course, subject to the approximations made in the 1948 Census; the 1960 Census figures are not yet available on a district basis.

Thus, Paga and its allies, pro Tedam, with an eligible electorate of over 16,000 registered under 10,000 or 58 per cent. The Chiana group, pro Ayagitam, registered nearly 7,700 or 84.8 per cent. out of a possible 9,000.

In Bongo the vote is seen to be extremely small once the factor of non-registration as well as non-voters is taken into account.

1954	(1) 21 and over	21,591
	(2) Registered	8,208—38%
	(3) Voters	4,374—53% of (2)
		20% of (1)

1956	(1) 21 and over	21,591
	(2) Registered	8,435—39%
	(3) Voters	2,985—35% of (2)
		14% of (1)

Amoro owed his election to a narrow majority of a very small minority vote: in 1956 to a majority of 535 in a poll of under 3,000, or approximately 14 per cent. of the total eligible electorate.

There is clearly every possibility of change in both constituencies.

POSTSCRIPT

The April 1960 plebiscite on the draft republican constitution, and for Dr. Nkrumah or Dr. Danquah as president, showed that there are still two sides to political issues even in the remote north:

	For the *Constitution*	*Against the* *Constitution*	*For* *Nkrumah*	*For* *Danquah*
Kassena-Nankanni North	8,489	1,244	8,524	1,156
Bongo	3,001	774	2,953	783

Some Sources of Traditionalism among Modern African Elites

WILLIAM H. FRIEDLAND

Cornell University

The peak of the political revolution which began in sub-Saharan Africa with the independence of Ghana in 1957 was reached in 1960 when 18 nations achieved independence. This political revolution is not yet complete and it can be expected to continue until most of sub-Saharan Africa becomes free of colonial rule.

If the political revolution has largely been accomplished, the accompanying social revolution which is reshaping the economies and societies of the new African nations has only just begun. In most of the newly-independent states, educated and westernized elites are leading their countries into the modern world. In seeking modernization, these elites are undermining and subverting the traditional social and cultural systems that continue to be found among the multifarious tribes. Yet, in spite of the drive for modernization, many aspects of traditionalism continue to exist. Indeed, as pan-Africanism has emerged as an important ideology, leaders of the new African nations have sought increasingly to incorporate elements from traditional Africa into emergent Africa.

The student of African affairs discovers that the modernizing elites are simultaneously undermining traditional societies and cultures and adopting traditional elements that will contribute to a distinctive and unique Africa of the future.[1] The existence of traditionalism among

This paper was presented at the panel "Traditional and modern elites," Fifth World Congress of the International Sociological Association, Washington, D.C., Sept. 1962. The research reported here was conducted under a fellowship of the Ford Foundation. The views expressed are those of the author and not necessarily those of the Ford Foundation.

[1] ". . . we must assure a cultural base for the future Nation, by defining the essential characteristics of traditional Negro African civilization which, blending with European and French contributions, will undergo a renaissance." Léopold S. Senghor, *African Socialism* (New York: American Society of African Culture, 1959), p. 12. Thus, when Senghor proposes a plan for development of the nation, one of three elements which must be considered is "an inventory of our traditional civilization." *Ibid.*, p. 31. Similar sentiments have been expressed by Nkrumah, Sekou Touré, Nyerere, etc.

modern elites represents the continuation of the process of acculturation that has been studied by many anthropologists.[2] The present paper seeks to examine elements of traditionalism found among modern elites and elucidate their sources.

ELEMENTS OF TRADITIONALISM

What is most striking to the student of Africa at first glance is the predominantly modern outlook of most African leaders. The economic, political and social concerns of these leaders are identical to those found in other parts of the world: they are concerned with constructing viable, modern economies, nations with stable political systems, social forms compatible with modern society. Tribalism and other forms of parochialism are severely denigrated.

In spite of this, the presence of traditional elements is continually confronted. The most obvious example is the use of traditional dress. Even in East Africa, where "national dress" is an abstraction, attempts are being made to introduce Ghanaian-style clothes. Equally obvious is the presence of traditional religious elements. In Ghana, for example, most ceremonial occasions are marked by a sacrifice and the pouring of a libation (using modern gin or whiskey) to the shades.[3] The behavior of political and trade union leaders in Tanganyika also reflects the continued presence of traditionalism. Julius Nyerere affects the walking stick—symbol of age (which, in turn, is symbolic of leadership)—and his model is followed by other political and union leaders. Age is such a concomitant of leadership that youthful trade unionists will be addressed as *mzee* ("elder") by elderly workers.

More complex and subtler manifestations of traditional behavior can also be found. In Tanganyika, for example, modern union leaders use a consensus search to achieve decisions on important questions. While the bulk of the formal procedures by which decisions are made were borrowed from British models, the consensus procedures char-

[2] Space does not permit an examination of the literature dealing with acculturation generally or with the process in Africa, in particular. For a discussion, see Melville Herskovits, *Acculturation* (Gloucester, Mass.: Peter Smith, 1958); International Institute of African Languages and Cultures, *Methods of Study of Culture Contact in Africa* (London: Oxford University Press, for the International Institute of African Languages and Cultures, 1938), Memorandum XV.

[3] When Kwame Nkrumah returned from his 1960 visit to the United Nations in a modern jet plane, part of the ceremony included the pouring of a libation by the chief priest of the Ga state as well as the slaughter of a sheep. See the *Evening News* (Accra), October 6, 1960. Similarly, the Chief Justice of Ghana poured a libation on his arrival to attend the independence celebrations of Tanganyika in December 1961. See the *Tanganyika Standard*, Dec. 7, 1961.

acteristic of traditional societies are typically utilized when critical decisions are made.[4] On a somewhat different level, a number of attempts have been made to incorporate traditionalist ideas into modern manifestos.[5] These are but a few indications that illustrate the continued presence of traditionalism among the modern elites.

SOURCES AND FUNCTIONS OF TRADITIONALISM

The origin of traditionalist elements among modern elites is found with the formation of the anti-colonialist movements. These movements sprang to life as new ideas were formulated about the rights of Africans to freedom and independence. Until the time these ideas were expressed, the notion that Africans had particular rights (i.e., equal to those of Europeans) was undeveloped. The authority of the colonial power was accepted because of the right of conquest.

With the spread of democratic ideals during the second world war and with the example of the post-war Asian revolutions, a handful of Africans began to formulate ideas about national independence.[6] Political movements were created to provide a mechanism for the expression of these ideas. Beginning with a handful of educated and westernized fellow-thinkers, the leaders soon spread the ideas to the illiterate masses.

Following the war, these ideas began to have meaning to large numbers of people and the early nationalists emerged as leaders of mass movements. Although they generally had no claim to leadership on the basis of tradition,[7] their authority was validated because of their char-

[4] William H. Friedland, "Decision-Making in Africa: A Case Study," *Africa Today*, VIII, No. 10 (December 1961), 14–15.

[5] Cf., the case of the autonomous trade union federation organized in French West Africa in 1956 described by Ruth Schachter, "Trade Unions Seek Autonomy," *West Africa*, January 19, 1957, p. 55 and January 26, 1957, pp. 81–82. The manifesto of the organization, the Confédération Générale du Travail Africain, accepted the dialectic but rejected "the class struggle because of African social groups' identity of living conditions and lack of differentiation into antagonistic classes. . . ." Many other examples can be cited where ideological formulations are made incorporating ideas taken from traditional society into modern political manifestos.

[6] In Nigeria, African nationalism can be traced to 1922 when Herbert Macauley formed a political party aiming at self-government for Nigeria. It was not until 1944, however, that the first modern nationalistic party was founded. See Royal Institute of International Affairs, *Nigeria* (London: Oxford University Press, 1960), pp. 39–40. The anti-white character of Macauley's movement has been noted by Chief Obafemi Awolowo in his autobiography, *Awo* (Cambridge: The University Press, 1960), pp. 69–70.

[7] Many modern African political leaders, of course, do lay claim to authority on the basis of tradition. Thus, many modern Nigerian leaders are chiefs (i.e., Chief Awolowo, Chief S. L. Akintola, etc.).

isma.[8] In this context, their charisma consisted of the ability to express sentiments (whose expression was seen as hazardous) that were increasingly meaningful to the inchoate masses. The nationalist leaders were also "successful," in that the colonial authorities began disengagement with their African colonies: "success" is a crucial element necessary to sustain charismatic authority. In addition, the leaders were able to command certain requisite skills necessary for operations vis-à-vis the metropolitan powers—they were educated and westernized and could deal with the instrumentalities of modern administration. These factors contributed to the formation of a new authority which became embodied in the modernizing, nationalist elites.

Yet, while the nationalist movements were in the process of formation, elements of traditionalism began to be incorporated into them. This was because already-existing patterns of relationships between leaders and followers could be utilized upon which to model the relations between the masses and their new leaders. Existing patterns were meaningful to the more traditionalist, tribal followers of the new movements. In the interaction between leaders and masses, while many relationships were new, other elements of behavior originating in traditional society were incorporated into the mass movements. This was clearly reflected, for example, at mass meetings of the ruling political party and the trade unions in Tanganyika. The arrival of the "leader" was frequently marked by the organized ululation of the women's chorus. While the meetings were themselves *modern* in form with the leader utilizing modern propaganda techniques, the women's chorus, the patterns of deference to the leader, etc., represented an amalgam of elements taken from traditional societies.

Thus, the expectations of masses with respect to the leader (or leaders) and the leader's expectations with respect to himself represent a combination of new patterns of behavior necessary to handle a modern organization overlaid with elements taken from traditional society. The patterns of deference shown the leader also reflect a similar amalgam. This does not mean that traditional elements are taken over wholly or that traditionalism dominates the relations between leaders and followers. This could not take place because the leaders were not making appeals to single parochial groups (i.e., tribes) but to masses of people. The appeal was not on a tribal basis but was, instead, anti-colonial and anti-European. Role expectations and deference patterns had to be

[8] The basis for the charisma of African political leaders is discussed in my paper "Charismatic Leadership in a Developing Society" read to the 1962 meeting of the American Sociological Association.

modified so that they would fit the expectations of peoples coming from a broad variety of tribes.

Traditional elements could also be taken over quite consciously by the anti-colonialist movements in attempts to broaden the base of these movements.[9] These movements had originated with westernized Africans and adaptations had to take place as an appeal was made to more parochial and tribally-minded Africans in the rural areas. Thus, specific elements of traditional society were manipulated to broaden the appeal of the anti-colonialist movements.

Once independence was achieved, Europeans ceased to be a major factor in the organization of political relations.[10] Relations between different African groupings therefore came to the fore. Primary among these are, of course, tribal attachments which frequently had economic overtones. In Ghana, for example, much of the country's wealth was concentrated among the cocoa-growers of Ashanti. If the nation is to be created, a national economy must be formed and it was with the Ashanti that Nkrumah came into conflict in the process of nation-building.[11] The Ghanaian case is typical and similar conflicts can be found in other African states.

The basis of charismatic authority in the pre-independence period rested upon the ability of leaders to express inchoate sentiments held by masses of people. With independence, this authority was increasingly

[9] One of the modernizing movements, although not typical because of its Yoruba social base, was the movement created by Chief Awolowo, the Egbe Omo Oduduwa ("A society of the descendants of Oduduwa"). This Yoruba cultural association, which laid the basis for the Action Group, a modern political party, had the following aims originally.

"To study its [Yorubaland's] political problem, combat the disintegrating forces of tribalism . . . and generally infuse the idea of a single nationality throughout the region; . . . to foster education . . . the study of Yoruba language, culture and history." These aims were slightly revised when a branch of the organization was created in Lagos. These aims were ". . . to encourage . . . the pursuit of secondary and university education among Yoruba boys and girls; . . . to recognize and maintain the monarchical and other similar institutions of Yorubaland, to plan for their complete enlightenment and democratisation. . . ." Awolowo, op. cit., pp. 169–171.

[10] Indeed, as Mitchell has shown, the awareness of Africans as Africans is manifested primarily only vis-à-vis Europeans. In everyday relations between Africans, corporate consciousness is based upon tribal affiliation. Cf. J. Clyde Mitchell, The Kalela Dance (Manchester: Manchester University Press for the Rhodes-Livingstone Institute, 1956), pp. 18 ff.

[11] The conflict between Nkrumah and the opposition party in Ghana reflected the struggle between a nationally-oriented political leader seeking to draw upon the wealth produced by a parochially-based group. This was accomplished through the agency of the Cocoa Marketing Board which paid cocoa growers a fixed price for their product. Since the price on the world market was in excess of the price paid to the growers, the margin of "profit" could be utilized for national development (and, of course, for political purposes).

called into question as national leaders began to formulate policies damaging to parochial groups.[12] In these circumstances, leaders sought to manipulate traditionalist symbols to retain their authority. Since elements of traditionalism are important to people whose primary attachments are tribal, some traditionalist elements could be taken over by the leader and his coterie. It does little harm, after all, to appear in national dress, pour libations, etc. As long as these traditionalist elements are not damaging to the main drive to achieve modernization, such symbols can be useful.[13]

As the charisma of the leaders has become increasingly questioned they have turned not only to the manipulation of traditionalist elements but also to the creation of what might be called "pre-tradition." Thus, in recent years, attempts have been made to create a historic myth.[14] This is reflected in the revival of the names of two ancient African empires, Ghana and Mali. Claims are also being made to the existence of high-level culture on a grand scale; indeed, the contention has been registered that Africans invented many elements of modern civilization and bequeathed them to Europe.[15]

[12] The calling into question of charismatic authority can frequently be "managed" by maintaining the isolation of the leader and occasionally "purging" secondary leaders. Thus, the secondary leaders are assumed to have had the responsibility for formulating policies damaging to parochial groups. Followers come to believe that the leader "doesn't really know what is going on," etc. This serves to sustain charismatic authority when that authority engages in actions regarded negatively by masses.

[13] A concomitant of the process by which elements are borrowed from traditional society is found in the rejection of cultural elements originating in the metropolitan power that previously exercised control over the colony. Thus, the Ghanaians reject many elements "given" to them by the British. An example is found in the institutional eclecticism of the Ghanaian trade unions. The Trades Union Congress determined in 1957 that a change in the structure of the unions was necessary and a delegation was sent off to Europe to inspect the structures of the German trade union federation and the Israeli Histadruth. On their return, a structure was formulated which was largely based upon the Israeli model. See John Tettegah, *A New Chapter for Ghana Labour* (Accra: 1958), pamphlet. It is also interesting to note that the organization chart embodying the new structure of the trade unions is almost identical to an organization chart prepared by the German trade union federation. I am grateful to John Windmuller for calling my attention to the similarity between the charts.

[14] In arguing that there is now a tendency to create a historic myth, I am not contending that this myth is false. Much of the currently-existing myth about Africa was formulated by Europeans who came to believe that Africa had had no highly developed civilizations. The modernizing elites are now in the process of levelling that myth—basing themselves on some evidence which has been developed by scholars. The evidence is still not fully developed and considerable research will be necessary before the validity of many claims can be ascertained.

[15] The *Sunday Express* (London), October 16, 1960, depicts a number of postcards on sale in Accra. These cards showed various scenes with the following legends: "African teaching mathematics to the Greeks," "The science of medicine was originated by Africans in the ancient empire of Ghana," "Tyro, African secretary to Cicero, originated shorthand writing in 63 b.c.," etc.

CONCLUSION

Elements of traditionalism were incorporated into the nationalist African movements because of traditionalist expectations of followers who were responding to calls from modernizing leaders. The response was less in terms of modernization than because of the anti-colonialist aspects of the call. Once colonialism was brought to an end by the achievement of independence, the difficult work of building a modern nation was begun. This required the elimination, or at least the minimization, of parochial loyalties and as parochial groups felt themselves threatened, the charismatic appeal of the nationalist leaders became diminished. Traditionalist symbols were sought by the leaders to broaden their appeal to masses. Yet these symbols were carefully "chosen"— in the sense that elements of traditionalism are taken over which are not expected to impede the development of a nation in an economic and political sense. Thus, not all elements of traditional society can be adopted because many will impede modernization.

Elements of traditionalism will, in all likelihood, continue to be utilized as pan-Africanism spreads its appeal. The search for national and continental roots makes pan-Africanist leaders increasingly dependent upon African resources. Thus, while pan-Africanism represents that most modern of political ideas—continental federation—it can be anticipated that the acceleration of the political movement will increase the search for relevant elements of traditional society and culture to encompass larger and more diverse groups.

PART FOUR

Forging Territorial Unity

I

The Non-Western Political Process

LUCIAN W. PYE

Massachusetts Institute of Technology

The purpose of this article is to outline some of the dominant and distinctive characteristics of the non-Western political process. In recent years, both the student of comparative politics and the field worker in the newly-emergent and economically underdeveloped countries have found it helpful to think in terms of a general category of non-Western politics.[1]

There are, of course, great differences among the non-Western societies. Indeed, in the past, comparative analysis was impeded by an appreciation of the rich diversity in the cultural traditions and the historical circumstances of the Western impact; students and researchers found it necessary to concentrate on particular cultures, and as a consequence attention was generally directed to the unique features of each society. Recently, however, attempts to set forth some of the characteristics common to the political life of countries experiencing profound social change have stimulated fruitful discussions among specialists on the different non-Western regions as well as among general students of comparative politics.

For this discussion to continue, it is necessary for specialists on the different areas to advance, in the form of rather bold and unqualified statements, generalized models of the political process common in non-Western societies.[2] Then, by examining the ways in which particular

Reprinted from *The Journal of Politics*, XX (1958), 468–486, with the permission of the author and the publisher. This is a revised version of a paper presented at the annual meeting of the American Political Science Association on September 5–7, 1957.

[1] For two excellent discussions of the implications for comparative politics of the current interest in non-Western political systems, see: Sigmund Neumann, "Comparative Politics: A Half-Century Appraisal," *Journal of Politics*, XIX (August, 1957), 269–290; and Dankwart A. Rustow, "New Horizons for Comparative Politics," *World Politics*, IX (July, 1957), 530–549.

[2] The picture of the non-Western political process contained in the following pages was strongly influenced by: George McT. Kahin, Guy J. Pauker, and Lucian W. Pye, "Comparative Politics in Non-Western Countries," *American Political Science Review*, XLIX (December, 1955), 1022–41; Gabriel A. Almond, "Comparative Political Systems," *Journal of Politics*, XVIII (August, 1956), 391–409; Rustow, *op. cit.*, and also his *Politics and Westernization in the Near East*, Center of International Studies (Princeton, 1956).

non-Western countries differ from the generalized models, it becomes possible to engage in significant comparative analysis.

1. In non-Western societies the political sphere is not sharply differentiated from the spheres of social and personal relations. Among the most powerful influences of the traditional order in any society in transition are those forces which impede the development of a distinct sphere of politics. In most non-Western societies, just as in traditional societies, the pattern of political relationships is largely determined by the pattern of social and personal relations. Power, prestige, and influence are based largely on social status. The political struggle tends to revolve around issues of prestige, influence, and even of personalities, and not primarily around questions of alternative courses of policy action.

The elite who dominate the national politics of most non-Western countries generally represent a remarkably homogeneous group in terms of educational experience and social background. Indeed, the path by which individuals are recruited into their political roles, where not dependent upon ascriptive considerations, is essentially an acculturation process. It is those who have become urbanized, have received the appropriate forms of education, and have demonstrated skill in estab- lishing the necessary personal relations who are admitted to the ranks of the elite. Thus, there is in most non-Western societies a distinctive elite culture in which the criteria of performance are based largely on non-political considerations. To be politically effective in national politics, one must effectively pass through such a process of acculturation.

At the village level it is even more difficult to distinguish a distinct political sphere. The social status of the individual and his personal ties largely determine his political behavior and the range of his influence. The lack of a clear political sphere in such communities places severe limits on the effectiveness of those who come from the outside to perform a political role, be it that of an administrative agent of the national government or of a representative of a national party. Indeed, the success of such agents generally depends more on the manner in which they relate themselves to the social structure of the community than on the substance of their political views.

The fundamental framework of non-Western politics is a communal one, and all political behavior is strongly colored by considerations of communal identification. In the more conspicuous cases the larger communal groupings follow ethnic or religious lines. But behind these divisions there lie the smaller but often more tightly knit social group- ings that range from the powerful community of Westernized leaders to the social structure of each individual village.

This essentially communal framework of politics makes it extremely difficult for ideas to command influence in themselves. The response to any advocate of a particular point of view tends to be attuned more to his social position than to the content of his views. Under these conditions it is inappropriate to conceive of an open market place where political ideas can freely compete on their own merits for support. Political discussion tends rather to assume the form of either intracommunal debate or one group justifying its position toward another.

The communal framework also sharply limits freedom in altering political allegiances. Any change in political identification generally requires a change in one's social and personal relationships; conversely, any change in social relations tends to result in a change in political identification. The fortunate village youth who receives a modern education tends to move to the city, establish himself in a new sub-society, and become associated with a political group that may in no way reflect the political views of his original community. Even among the national politicians in the city, shifts in political ties are generally accompanied by changes in social and personal associations.

2.   *Political parties in non-Western societies tend to take on a world view and represent a way of life.*   The lack of a clearly differentiated political sphere means that political associations or groups cannot be clearly oriented to a distinct political arena but tend to be oriented to some aspect of the communal framework of politics. In reflecting the communal base of politics, political parties tend to represent total ways of life. Attempts to organize parties in terms of particular political principles or limited policy objectives generally result either in failure or in the adoption of a broad ethic which soon obscures the initial objective. Usually political parties represent some sub-society or simply the personality of a particularly influential individual.

Even secular parties devoted to achieving national sovereignty have tended to develop their own unique world views. Indeed, successful parties tend to become social movements. The indigenous basis for political parties is usually regional, ethnic, or religious groupings, all of which stress considerations not usually emphasized in Western secular politics. When a party is merely the personal projection of an individual leader it is usually not just his explicitly political views but all facets of his personality which are significant in determining the character of the movement.

In the past, the tendency for political parties to adopt world views was in some instances strongly encouraged by the desire of traditional authoritarian governments or colonial regimes to suppress all explicitly political associations, and such associations found it expedient to adopt a religious cloak to hide the character of their activities. In time, however, the religious aspect came to have genuine significance in determining the character of the group and maintaining its continuity. This was the case with most of the secret societies common to traditional Chinese society. The same development also took place in French Indo-China, where political activity took the form of organizing quasi-religious sects. Both the Cao Dai and the Hoa Hao began as political movements masking as religions, and, although they never lost their political character, they found a basis of integration in their religious aspects.

The history of the secular nationalist movements reflects a similar tendency for parties essentially to represent ways of life. Even after independence the tendency remains strong because such parties are inclined to feel that they have a mission to change all aspects of life within their society. Indeed, such parties often conceive of themselves as representing a prototype of what their entire country will become in time. Members of such movements frequently believe that their attitudes and views on all subjects will become the commonly shared attitudes and views of the entire population. Those committed to modernizing their societies can see few aspects of life which must not be altered, while those more attached to tradition have equally broad concerns.

3. The political process in non-Western societies is characterized by a prevalence of cliques. The lack of a distinct political sphere and the tendency for political parties to have a world view together provide a framework within which the most structured units of decision-making tend to be personal cliques. Although general considerations of social status determine the broad outlines of power and influence, the particular pattern of political relationships at any time is largely determined by decisions made at the personal level. This is the case because the social structure in non-Western societies is characterized by functionally diffuse relationships; individuals and groups do not have sharply defined and highly specific functions and thus do not represent specific interests that distinguish them from other groupings. There is no clearly structured setting that can provide a focus for the more refined pattern of day-to-day political activities. Hence, in arriving at their expectations about the probable behavior of others, those involved in the political process must rely heavily upon judgments about personality and the particular relations of the various actors to each other. The pattern of personal associations provides one of the firmest guides for understanding and action within the political process. Personal cliques are likely to become the key units of decision-making in the political process of most non-Western societies.

Western observers often see the phenomenon of cliques as being symptomatic of immoral and deviously motivated behavior. This may actually be the case. Considerations of motive, however, cannot explain either the prevalence of cliques in non-Western societies or their functions. It should also be noted that the fact that cliques are based on personal relations does not mean that there are no significant differences in their values and policy objectives. Since the members of a given clique are likely to have a common orientation toward politics, if their views were fully articulated they might appear as a distinct ideology that would be significantly different from those of the other factions.

In order to understand the workings of the political process in most non-Western countries it is necessary to analyze the character of inter-clique reactions. To ignore the importance of cliques would be comparable to ignoring the role of interest groups and elections in analyzing the behavior of American Congressmen.

4. The character of political loyalty in non-Western societies gives to the leadership of political groups a high degree of freedom in determining matters of strategy and tactics. The communal framework of politics and the tendency for political parties to have world views means that political loyalty is governed more by a sense of identification with the concrete group than by identification with the professed policy goals of the group. The expectation is that the leaders will seek to maximize all the interests of all the members of the group and not just seek to advance particular policies or values.

So long as the leaders appear to be working in the interests of the group as a whole, they usually do not have to be concerned that the loyalties of the members will be tested by current decisions. Under such conditions, it is possible for leadership to become firmly institutionalized within the group without the particular leaders having to make any strong commitments to a specific set of principles or to a given political strategy.

Problems relating to the loyalty of the membership can generally be handled more effectively by decisions about intra-group relations than by decisions about the goals or external policies of the group. So long as harmonious relations exist within the group, it is generally possible for the leaders to make drastic changes in strategy. Indeed, it is not uncommon for the membership to feel that matters relating to external policy should be left solely to the leadership, and it may not disturb them that such decisions reflect mainly the idiosyncracies of their leaders.

5. *Opposition parties and aspiring elites tend to appear as revolutionary movements in non-Western politics.* Since the current leadership in non-Western countries generally conceives of itself as seeking to effect changes in all aspects of life, and since all the political associations tend to have world views, any prospective change in national leadership is likely to seem to have revolutionary implications. The fact that the ruling party in most non-Western countries identifies itself with an effort to bring about total change in the society makes it difficult to limit the sphere of political controversy. Issues are not likely to remain as isolated and specific questions but tend to become associated with fundamental questions about the destiny of the society.

In addition, the broad and diffuse interests of the ruling elites make it easy for them to maintain that they represent the interest of the entire nation. Those seeking power are thus often placed in the position of appearing to be, at best, obstructionists of progress and, at worst, enemies of the country. Competition is not between parties that represent different functional specific interests or between groups that claim greater administrative skills; rather, the struggle takes on some of the qualities of a conflict between differing ways of life.

This situation is important in explaining the failure of responsible opposition parties to develop in most non-Western countries. For example, the Congress Party in India has been able to identify itself with the destiny of the entire country to such a degree that the opposition parties find it difficult to avoid appearing either as enemies of India's progress or as groups seeking precisely the same objectives as Congress. Since the frustration of opposition groups encourages them to turn to extremist measures, they may in fact come to be revolutionary movements.

6. *The non-Western political process is characterized by a lack of integration among the participants, and this situation is a function of the lack of a unified communications system in the society.* In most non-Western societies there is not a single general political process that is the focus of most political activities throughout the population; rather, there are several distinct and nearly unrelated political processes. The most conspicuous division is that between the dominant national politics of the more urban elements and the more traditional village level of politics. The conflicts that are central to the one may hardly appear in the other.

Those who participate, for example, in the political life of the village are not an integral part of the national politics, since they can act without regard to developments at the central level. Possibly even more significant is the fact that at the village level all the various village groups have their separate and autonomous political processes.

This situation is a reflection of, and is reinforced by, the communication system common to non-Western societies, where the media of mass communication generally reach only to elements of the urban population and to those who participate in the national political process. The vast majority of the people participate only in the traditional word-of-mouth communication system. Even when the media of mass communications do reach the village, through readers of newspapers or owners of radios, there is almost no "feedback" from the village level. The radio talks *to* the villagers but does not talk *with* them. The views of the vast majority of the population are not reflected in the mass media. Indeed, it is often the case that the Westerner has less difficulty than the majority of the indigenous population in understanding the intellectual and moral standards reflected in the media of mass communication, not only because these media are controlled by the more Westernized elements but also because the media may be consciously seeking to relate themselves more to the standards of the international systems of communication than to the local scene.

The lack of a unified communication system and the fact that the participants are not integrated into a common political process limit the types of political issues that can arise in non-Western societies. For example, although these are essentially agrarian societies in which industrial development is just beginning to take place, there has not yet appeared (in their politics) one of the issues basic to the history of Western politics: the clash between industry and agriculture, between town and countryside. Questions of agriculture usually arise in politics when the urbanized leaders advance plans for increasing production and developing village life. The values and concepts of the rural element are not effectively represented in the national political process largely because its fragmented character and the lack of a unified communications system leave the rural elements without a basis for mobilizing their combined strength and effectively advancing their demands on the government. It is possible that in time the rural masses, discovering that they have much in common, will find ways to mobilize their interests and so exert their full potential influence on the nation's political life. Such a development would drastically alter the national political character. In the meantime, however, the fragmented political process of the non-Western societies means that fundamentally agrarian countries will continue to have a form of national politics that is more ur-banized than that commonly found in the industrial West. In many cases one city alone dominates the politics of an entire country.

7. *The non-Western political process is characterized by a high rate of recruitment of new elements to political roles.*[3] The spread of popu-lar politics in traditional societies has meant a constant increase in the number of participants and the types of organizations involved in the political process. This development has been stimulated by the extraor-dinary rise in the urban population, which has greatly increased the number of people who have some understanding about, and feeling for, politics at the national level. A basic feature of the acculturation process which creates the sub-society of the elite is the development of attitudes common to urban life. It is generally out of the rapid urban growth that there emerge the aspiring elites who demand to be heard. In al-most all non-Western societies, there is a distinct strata of urban dwellers who are excluded from direct participation in national politics but whose existence affects the behavior of the current elite.

The more gradual reaching out of the mass media to the country-side has stimulated a broadening awareness that, although participation in the nation's political life is formally open to all, the rural elements actually have little access to the means of influence. In some places political parties, in seeking to reach the less urbanized elements, have opened up new channels for communicating with the powerful at the nation's center which may or may not be more effective than the old channels of the civil administration. In any case, the existence of mul-tiple channels of contact with the national government tends to increase the number of people anxious to participate in national decision-making.

8. *The non-Western political process is characterized by sharp dif-ferences in the political orientation of the generations.* The process of social change in most non-Western societies results in a lack of continu-ity in the circumstances under which people are recruited to politics. Those who took part in the revolutionary movement against a colonial ruler are not necessarily regarded as indispensable leaders by the new generations; but their revolutionary role is still put forward as sufficient reason for their continued elite status. As a result, in some countries, as in Indonesia and Burma, groups that were not involved in the revolu-tion feel that they are now being arbitrarily excluded from the inner circle of national politics. For these people, the current elite is claiming

[3] Kahin, Pauker, and Pye, *loc. cit.*, p. 1024.

its status on the basis of ascriptive rather than achievement considerations.

This problem in non-Western societies is further complicated by demographic factors, for such societies are composed of rapidly growing populations that have a high birth rate. In Singapore, Malaya, and Burma, over half the population is under voting age, and the median age in most non-Western countries is in the low twenties. There is thus a constant pressure from the younger generation, whose demands for political influence conflict with the claims of current leaders who conceive of themselves as being still young and with many more years of active life ahead. In most of the newly independent countries, the initial tendency was for cabinet ministers and high officials to be in their thirties and forties, a condition which has colored the career expectations of the youth of succeeding generations, who now face frustration if they cannot achieve comparable status at the same age.

This telescoping of the generations has sharpened the clash of views so that intellectually there is an abnormal gap in political orientations, creating a potential for extreme reversal in policy, should the aspiring elites gain power. Ideas and symbols which are deeply felt by the current leaders, including those relating to the West, may have little meaning for a generation which has not experienced colonial rule.

9. In non-Western societies there is little consensus as to the legitimate ends and means of political action. The fundamental fact that non-Western societies are engrossed in a process of discontinuous social change precludes the possibility of a widely shared agreement as to the appropriate ends and means of political activities. In all the important non-Western countries, there are people who have assimilated Western culture to the point that their attitudes and concepts about politics differ little from those common in the West. At the other extreme there is the village peasant who has been little touched by Western influences. Living in different worlds, these individuals can hardly be expected to display a common approach toward political action.

The national leadership, recruited from people who have generally become highly urbanized, is in a position to set the standards for what may appear to be a widely shared consensus about politics. However, more often than not, this apparent national agreement is a reflection only of the distinct qualities of the elite sub-society. The mass of the population cannot fully appreciate the values and concepts which underlie the judgments of the elite and which guide its behavior.

The lack of a distinct political sphere increases the difficulties in achieving agreement about the legitimate scope and forms of political activities. The setting is not one in which political issues are relatively isolated and thus easily communicated and discussed. Instead, a knowledge of national politics requires an intimate acquaintance with the total social life of the elite. The fact that loyalty to the particular group rather than support of general principles is the key to most political behavior strengthens the tendency toward a distinct and individual rather than a shared orientation towards politics.

The situation is further complicated by the fact that, since most of the groupings within the political process represent total ways of life, few are concerned with limited and specific interests. The functionally diffuse character of most groups means that each tends to have its own approaches to political action in terms of both ends and means. Under these circumstances, the relationship of means to ends tends to be more organic than rational and functional. Indeed, in the gross behavior of the groups it is difficult to distinguish their primary goals from their operational measures. Consequently, the political actors in non-Western societies tend to demonstrate quite conspicuously the often-forgotten fact that people generally show greater imagination and ingenuity in discovering goals to match their means than in expanding their capabilities in order to reach distant goals.

Given the character of the groups, it is difficult to distinguish within the general political discourse of the society a distinction between discussions of desired objectives and analyses of appropriate means of political action.

10. In non-Western societies the intensity and breadth of political discussion has little relationship to political decision-making. Western observers are impressed with what they feel is a paradoxical situation in most non-Western countries: the masses seem to be apathetic toward political action and yet, considering the crude systems of communications, they are remarkably well informed about political events. Peasants and villagers often engage in lengthy discussions on matters related to the political world that lies outside their immediate lives, but they rarely seem prepared to translate the information they receive into action that might influence the course of national politics.

The villagers are often responding in the traditional manner to national politics. In most traditional societies, an important function of the elite was to provide entertainment and material for discussion for the common people; but discussions in villages and teashops could center on the activities of an official without creating the expectation that discussion should lead to action. Thus the contemporary world of elite politics provides a drama for the common people, just as in many traditional cultures the popular forms of literature and drama stressed court life and the world of officialdom.

A second explanation for this pattern of behavior is that one of the important factors in determining social status and prestige within the village or local community is often a command of information about the wider world; knowledge of developments in the sphere of national and even international politics has a value in itself. But skill in discussing political matters again does not raise any expectations of actual participation in the world of politics.

Finally, many of the common people in non-Western societies find it desirable to keep informed about political developments in order to be able to adapt their lives to any major changes. Since their lives have often been drastically disrupted by political events, they have come to believe it prudent to seek advance warning of any developments which might again affect their lives; but it has not necessarily encouraged them to believe that their actions might influence such developments.

11. In the non-Western political process there is a high degree of substitutability of roles.[4] It seems that in non-Western societies most politically relevant roles are not clearly differentiated but have a functionally diffuse rather than a functionally specific character. For example, the civil bureaucracy is not usually limited to the role of a politically neutral instrument of public administration but may assume some of the functions of a political party or act as an interest group. Sometimes armies act as governments. Even within bureaucracies and governments, individuals may be formally called upon to perform several roles.

A shortage of competent personnel encourages such behavior either because one group may feel that the other is not performing its role in an effective manner or because the few skilled administrators are forced to take on concurrent assignments. However, the more fundamental reason for this phenomenon is that in societies just emerging from traditional status, it is not generally expected that any particular group or organization will limit itself to performing a clearly specified function. Under these conditions there usually are not sharply defined divisions of labor in any sphere of life. All groups tend to have considerable freedom in trying to maximize their general influence.

12. In the non-Western political process there are relatively few explicitly organized interest groups with functionally specific roles. Although there are often large numbers of informal associations in

[4] See Almond, *loc. cit.*, p. 30.

non-Western countries, such groups tend to adopt diffuse orientations that cover all phases of life in much the same manner as the political parties and cliques. It is the rare association that represents a limited and functionally specific interest. Organizations which in name and formal structure are modeled after Western interest groups, such as trade unions and chambers of commerce, generally do not have a clearly defined focus.

In many cases groups, such as trade unions and peasant associations that in form would appear to represent a specific interest, are in fact agents of the government or of a dominant party or movement. Their function is primarily to mobilize the support of a segment of the population for the purposes of the dominant group, and not primarily to represent the interests of their constituency.

In situations where the associations are autonomous, the tendency is for them to act as protective associations and not as pressure groups. That is, their activities are concentrated on protecting their members from the consequences of governmental decisions and the political power of others. They do not seek to apply pressure openly on the government in order to influence positively the formation of public policy.

This role of the protective association is generally a well developed one in traditional societies and in countries under colonial rule. Under such authoritarian circumstances, since informal associations could have little hope of affecting the formal law-making process, they tended to focus on the law-enforcing process. Success in obtaining preferential treatment for their membership did not require that they mobilize general popular support. On the contrary, activities directed to broadly articulating their views were generally self-defeating. They were likely to be more successful if they worked quietly and informally to establish preferential relations with the policy-enforcing agents of the government. Under such conditions each association generally preferred to operate separately in order to gain special favors. The strategy of uniting in coalitions and alliances to present the appearance of making a popular demand on the government, as is common in an open democratic political process composed of pressure groups, would only weaken the position of all the informal associations in a traditional society, for it would represent a direct challenge to the existing governmental elite.

This approach to political activity common in traditional societies still lingers on in many non-Western societies. Informal associations tend to protect all the interests of their members in relations with the government. At the same time, many interests in the society are not explicitly organized. Although the process of social change is creating the basis for new interests, the formation of explicit interest groups rarely moves at the same pace. Often the new groups turn to the more traditional informal associations and only very gradually change their character. In other cases interest groups that fundamentally represent the newly developing aspects of the society perform according to the standards of the traditional groups.

From this brief discussion we may note that when interest groups act as protective associations, focusing on the law-enforcing process and seeking special treatment for their members, they are likely to avoid articulating publicly their goals and are likely to base their requests for special favors on particularistic rather than universalistic considerations. In appealing to policy-enforcement agents, prudence dictates the desirability of framing a request as an isolated demand; for any suggestion that a request constitutes a widespread demand, consistent with the general interest or the public good, would threaten the preserve of the law-makers, who were presumed to be unapproachable in most traditional societies.

We may sum up these observations by formulating a general hypothesis that would read: "Whenever the formally constituted law-makers are more distant from and more inaccessible to the general public than the law-enforcing agencies, the political process of the society will be characterized by a high degree of latency, and interests will be represented by informally organized groups seeking diffuse but particularistically defined goals which will not be broadly articulated nor claimed to be in the general interest." The corollary of this hypothesis would, of course, read: "Whenever the formally constituted law-makers are less distant from and more accessible to the general public than the law-enforcing agencies, the political process of the society will be open and manifest, and interests will be represented by explicitly organized groups seeking specific but universalistically defined goals which will be broadly articulated and claimed to be in the general interest."

13. In the non-Western political process the national leadership must appeal to an undifferentiated public. The lack of explicitly organized interest groups and the fact that not all participants are continuously represented in the political process deprive the national leadership of any readily available means for calculating the relative distribution of attitudes and values throughout the society. The national politician cannot easily determine the relative power of those in favor of a particular measure and those opposed; he cannot readily estimate the amount of effort needed to gain the support of the doubtful elements.

It is usually only within the circle of the elite or within the administrative structure that the national leaders can distinguish specific points of view and the relative backing that each commands. In turning to the population as a whole, the leaders find that they have few guides as to how the public may be divided over particular issues. Thus, in seeking popular support, the politician cannot direct his appeal to the interests of particular groups. Unable to identify or intelligently discriminate among the various interests latent in the public, the political leader is inclined to resort to broad generalized statements rather than to adopt specific positions on concrete issues. This situation also means that, whether the question is one of national or of merely local import, the leadership must appear to be striving to mobilize the entire population.

The inability to speak to a differentiated public encourages a strong propensity toward skillful and highly emotional forms of political articulation on the part of non-Western leaders. Forced to reach for the broadest possible appeals, the political leader tends at times to concentrate heavily on nationalistic sentiments and to present himself as a representative of the nation as a whole rather than of particular interests within the society. This is one of the reasons why some leaders of non-Western countries are often seen paradoxically both as extreme nationalists and as men out of touch with the masses.

14. The unstructured character of the non-Western political process encourages leaders to adopt more clearly defined positions on international issues than on domestic issues. Confronted with an undifferentiated public, leaders of non-Western countries often find the international political process more clearly structured than the domestic political scene. Consequently, they can make more refined calculations as to the advantages in taking a definite position in world politics than they can in domestic politics. This situation not only encourages the leaders of some non-Western countries to seek a role in world politics that is out of proportion to their nation's power, but it also allows such leaders to concentrate more on international than on domestic affairs. It should also be noted that in adopting a supra-national role, the current leaders of non-Western countries can heighten the impression that their domestic opposition is an enemy of the national interest.

15. In non-Western societies the affective or expressive aspect of politics tends to override the problem-solving or public-policy aspect of politics. Traditional societies have generally developed to a very high order the affective and expressive aspects of politics. Pomp and ceremony are usually basic features of traditional politics, and those who are members of the ruling elite in such societies are generally expected to lead more interesting and exciting lives than those not involved in politics. In contrast, traditional societies have not usually emphasized politics as a means for solving social problems. Questions of policy in such societies are largely limited to providing certain minimum social and economic functions and maintaining the way of life of the elite.

Although in transitional societies there is generally a greater awareness of the potentialities of politics as a means of rationally solving social problems, the expressive aspects of politics usually continue to occupy a central place in determining the character of political behavior. The peculiar Western assumption that issues of public policy are the most important aspect of politics, and practically the only legitimate concern of those with power, is not always applicable to non-Western politics. Indeed, in most non-Western societies the general assumption is not that those with power are committed to searching out and solving problems, but rather that they are the fortunate participants in the central drama of life. Politics is supposed to be exciting and emotionally satisfying.

In part the stress on the affective or expressive aspect of politics is related to the fact that, in most non-Western countries, questions of personal loyalties and identification are recognized as providing the basic issues of politics and the bond between leader and follower is generally an emotional one. In fact, in many non-Western societies, it is considered highly improper and even immoral for people to make loyalty contingent upon their leaders' ability to solve problems of public policy.

In the many non-Western societies in which the problem of national integration is of central importance, the national leaders often feel they must emphasize the symbols and sentiments of national unity since substantive problems of policy may divide the people. It should be noted that the governmental power base of many non-Western leaders encourages them to employ symbols and slogans customarily associated with administrative policy in their efforts to strengthen national unity. The Western observer may assume that statements employing such symbols represent policy intentions when in fact their function is to create national loyalty and to condition the public to think more in policy terms.

16. Charismatic leaders tend to prevail in non-Western politics.[5]
Max Weber, in highlighting the characteristics of charismatic author-

[5] Kahin, Pauker, and Pye, *loc. cit.*, p. 1025.

ity, specifically related the emergence of charismatic personalities to situations in which the hold of tradition has been weakened. By implication, he suggested that societies experiencing cultural change provide an ideal setting for such leaders since a society in which there is confusion over values is more susceptible to a leader who conveys a sense of mission and appears to be God-sent.

The problem of political communication further reinforces the position of the charismatic leader. Since the population does not share the leadership's modes of reason or standards of judgment, it is difficult to communicate subtle points of view. Communication of emotions is not confronted with such barriers, especially if it is related to considerations of human character and personality. All groups within the population can feel confident of their abilities to judge the worth of a man for what he is, even though they cannot understand his mode of reasoning.

So long as a society has difficulties in communication, the charismatic leader possesses great advantage over his opponents, even though they may have greater ability in rational planning. However, the very lack of precision in the image that a charismatic leader casts, especially in relation to operational policy, does make it possible for opposition to develop as long as it does not directly challenge the leader's charisma. Various groups with different programs can claim that they are in fact seeking the same objectives as those of the leader. For example, in both Indonesia and Burma, the Communists have been able to make headway by simply claiming that they are not directly opposed to the goals of Sukarno and U Nu.

Charisma is likely to wear thin. A critical question in most non-Western societies that now have charismatic leaders is whether such leadership will in the meantime become institutionalized in the form of rational-legal practices. This was the pattern in Turkey under Kemal Ataturk. Or will the passing of the charismatic leader be followed by confusion and chaos? The critical factor seems to be whether or not the leader encourages the development of functionally specific groups within the society that can genuinely represent particular interests.

17. The non-Western political process operates largely without benefit of political "brokers." In most non-Western societies there seems to be no institutionalized role for carrying out the tasks of, first, clarifying and delimiting the distribution of demands and interests within the population, and, next, engaging in the bargaining operation necessary to accommodate and maximize the satisfaction of those demands and interests in a fashion consistent with the requirements of public policy and administration. In other words, there are no political "brokers."

In the Western view, the political broker is a prerequisite for a smoothly operating system of representative government. It is through his activities that, on the one hand, the problems of public policy and administration can be best explained to the masses in a way that is clearly related to their various specific interests and, on the other hand, that the diverse demands of the population can be articulated to the national leaders. This role in the West is performed by the influential members of the competing political parties and interest groups.

What is needed in most non-Western countries in order to have stable representative institutions are people who can perform the role that local party leaders did in introducing the various immigrant communities into American public life. Those party leaders, in their fashion, were able to provide channels through which the immigrant communities felt they could learn where their interests lay in national politics and through which the national leaders could discover the social concerns of the new citizens.

In most non-Western societies, the role of the political "broker" has been partially filled by those who perform a "mediator's" role, which consists largely of transmitting the views of the elite to the masses. Such "mediators" are people sufficiently acculturated to the elite society to understand its views but who still have contacts with the more traditional masses. In performing their role, they engage essentially in a public relations operation for the elite, and only to a marginal degree do they communicate to the elite the views of the public. They do not find it essential to identify and articulate the values of their public. Generally, since their influence depends upon their relations with the national leadership, they have not sought to develop an autonomous basis of power or to identify themselves with particular segments of the population as must the political "broker." As a consequence, they have not acted in a fashion that would stimulate the emergence of functionally specific interest groups.

The Concentration and Dispersion of Charisma
Their Bearing on Economic Policy in Underdeveloped Countries

EDWARD SHILS

University of Chicago

I

The countries with underdeveloped economies are primarily peasant countries and their national unity is quite new and fragmentary. The uneducated classes are rooted mainly in local territorial and kinship groups; sometimes they are the dependents of feudal magnates to whom are directed whatever wider loyalties they have. They do not have the strong sense of nationality which drives the leaders of their country, who are often the creators of the new nation and not merely of the new state. These leaders are strong and creative persons who have broken away from the bonds of the old order—the bonds of kin and family and local territory. Even when they claim to speak on behalf of the deeper traditions of those whom they would lead, they have departed from the actual traditions of the culture in which they originated. They are "nationalized" and "politicized" and therein lies their chief novelty. The majority in the state, by contrast, lives in sometimes unthinking, sometimes obstinate, attachment to its traditional symbols. Most of its life is "pre-national" and "pre-political." The nation does not always, thus far, include most of the members of the state, even to the degree of intermittent citizenship which is characteristic of modern states. It is unlikely therefore that the ideal of *national* economic development can provide sufficient, continuing motive power for the voluntary modification of traditional procedures, for the renunciation of leisure and consumption, for additional exertion, adaptive ingenuity, and initiative on the part of the ordinary peasant, craftsman, factory-worker, or small businessman. There is a great gap between the highly political outlook of the intellectual and public elite and the pre-political outlook of the mass of the population.

When the politicians seek to mobilize the human resources of their countries on behalf of mighty aspirations toward economic develop-

Reprinted from *World Politics*, XI (1958), 1–19, with the permission of the author and the publisher.

ment, they do so by attempting to arouse devotion to the nation. Yet, the continuous exhortations of prime ministers, politicians, and publicists from the seat of government, from the platform, from the broadcasting station, and from the pages of the press do not sink very far into the structure of motivation which impels economic development. It may here and there, and for a short time, stir tens of thousands of persons—most of whom are no longer engaged in agriculture—to an acutely and intensely developed sense of nationality, and these people may in their turn prod others around them into working harder. Even if these secondary leaders are successful, the range of their possible influence is narrowly confined and the effect on the motivation of most of the working population seems to be negligible. Nonetheless, much weight is laid by the ruling groups in these countries and by Western observers on *national* and *political* motivation of the actions required for economic growth.

This disjunction between the "politicized" leaders of the new state and the mass of the population is usually attributed to the detribalization, the uneven modernization (or Westernization) of the small educated elite, which is said to have lost or renounced its contact with the traditional culture of its compatriots. The relevant truth, however, lies elsewhere. Despite the obvious divergences between the traditional culture of the mass and the modern culture of the educated, in its "political" orientation the educated elite shows in one fundamental way an important affinity with the culture from which it is alleged to have been uprooted.

The political conceptions which are expressed in the prevailing notions of economic growth or development rest on a deep-lying image of the nature of society and of the right ordering of life. It is an image of the concentration of charisma in those who rule the nation. One of the central features of the dominant conception of economic development is that autonomous movement of the economic system is thought to be undesirable, even if possible. What are called "economic motives" are distrusted because it is believed that no intrinsic value resides in the economic sphere—in the way in which the religious and political spheres possess the intrinsic value connected with sacred things. The only truly respected motives are those generated by authority, the exercise of that sovereignty, religious or political, which entails communion with the sacred.

The political leaders who live in the modern sector of their respective societies, and who are usually less immediately involved in a traditional way with the sacred, are legitimated in their own eyes by their permeation with *the sacredness of the nation*. They feel themselves to be legitimate because they believe that they possess within themselves the spirit of the nation, that spirit which slumbered long and which is now awake in them. It is with this charisma—this sacred quality—inherent in nationality that they would infuse the ordinary peasant and workingman. Ordinary persons living in their tribal villages respond not to the charisma embodied in national authority, but to that which tradition locates in the authority of their kinship groups, in their feudal and royal rulers, and in their priests and magicians. Both modern leaders and the traditional mass are held in similar subjection by the charisma which is concentrated in authority.

Life in traditional societies is permeated by charismatic manifestations.[1] The traditional character of these societies, so often designated as their most prominent feature, testifies to the extent to which many things are infused with sacredness to such a degree that great care must be taken to maintain "right relationships" through stereotyped action. Many of the events of daily life in traditional societies have a charismatic significance which has become attenuated in modern "secular society."

Those strong personalities who break out of the round of traditional life cease their affirmation of the concrete forms of that life, but they retain the charismatic sensitivity which is essential to it. Indeed, that sensitivity is often heightened by the strain of living without the comfort of traditional surroundings and tasks. When they renounce loyalty to the tribe and the divinities of the tribe, their responsiveness to sacredness, their readiness to discern sacredness, does not necessarily die; instead it seeks new objects. In some cases, new, syncretistic reli-

---

[1] Max Weber's classification of types of legitimate authority suffers from its tendency to isolate charismatic authority from the traditional and rational-legal types. Its deficiency lies in its failure to acknowledge in a systematic and explicit manner that traditional and rational-legal authority both contain charismatic elements, and that a major difference among the three types consists in variations in the intensity of the attribution of charismatic properties to the incumbents of authoritative roles. (Cf. Max Weber, *Wirtschaft und Gesellschaft*, Tübingen, 1925, 2nd ed., I, pp. 124, 140–48; II, pp. 753–78.) His treatment of the transformation of charisma leaves unsettled the question whether charisma "evaporates" or becomes attenuated in the course of its transformation. Rudolf Sohm's *Kirchenrecht* (2 vols., 1892), a work of the very greatest relevance to contemporary social science, and one from which Max Weber learned much, also overstressed the disjunction between charisma and ecclesiastical organization. It is possible that some of the difficulties which arise from the acceptance of Sohm's and Weber's views are attributable to their inclination to see charismatic qualities solely as the possession of charismatic individuals. Rudolf Otto's conception of the "numinous" offers an excellent point of departure for a reconsideration of the nature of charisma, its generalization, and its fruitful application in the study of society. I have made a very tentative and preliminary effort in "Tradition and Liberty: Antinomy and Interdependence," *Ethics*, LXVIII, No. 3 (April 1958), pp. 155–57.

gions promise salvation; in others, a territorial symbol, assimilating some of the charisma formerly attributed to symbols of tribe and village, becomes the object of attachment. The continuity is as significant as the disjunction. Tribe is transcended, while the sacred earth retains its sacredness, its charisma, although it is no longer circumscribed by the area within which one's particular tribe—one's kinship and ethnic group—dwells.

Many of the leading politicians in these new countries have the traits of persons who have recently dropped their immediate tribal bonds, but not from indifference. They retain the unitary response to charismatic things—regardless of whether they are traditional or newly emergent—which is a feature of traditional societies or enthusiastic cultic associations. They are themselves almost always charismatic men in the conventional sociological sense—strikingly vivid personalities and extremely sensitive. They arouse the charismatic sensibilities of others and they do so largely because they pulsate in response to the symbols in which charisma is latent. They are charismatic because they are connected with "things" to which they (and others) ascribe charismatic significance. For the politicians and their zealous followers, charisma is resident not in tribes, or in elders and chiefs who possess the tribal charisma, but only in the nation. The nation becomes the charismatic object and it is only through their connection with it that charisma flows into persons. The rulers of a country are the most charismatic persons of that country, because they are closest to the source from which charisma radiates.[2]

These rulers have experienced the revelation of nationality. Hence, because the nation is the ultimately significant entity, only those who rule—in the first instance, the politicians and, derivatively, the civil servants—are endowed with the charisma of the nation. Those who do not share in this authority and, even more, those who do not affirm with vigor their membership in the national community are thought to share very little of this charisma. Tribal chieftains, traditional religious leaders, elders of kinship groups, merchants, cultivators, and craftsmen all fall outside this circle of the charisma of nationality

[2] As politicians who exercise authority in the state, and as party leaders, which they must be in order to achieve a position of authority in the state, their conduct naturally and frequently shows that other motives and images are at work in them. The conduct of office and the management of a party machine impose lines of action which are far from identical in spirit with the charismatic disposition. Compromise, manipulation, rational judgment, and acceptance of opportunities for self-aggrandizement are among the inevitable products of the exigencies of leadership in the state and party. Nonetheless, the preponderance of considerations of nationality is evidence of the persisting sacredness of the nation. The extreme nationalist sensibility of the rulers is not a demagogic mask to conceal self-seeking.

within which political leaders, agitational journalists and, to a lesser extent, civil servants find themselves.[3]

Thus the religious sensitivity which is common in traditional societies and in the traditional sectors of underdeveloped countries lives on in a transformed way in these societies as they move toward modernity. In its transmogrification, it penetrates into the life of the apparently "secular" state.

There is less conflict between this particular transmogrification of traditional life, with its displacement of the locus of charisma from the tribal to the territorial, and the modern education of many of the political leaders and higher civil servants than is generally asserted by those who emphasize the "ambivalence" and "uprootedness" of the educated elites of the new societies.

The prevailing attitudes toward economic policy disclose an intimate continuity with ancestral sensitivity to charismatic things. The modern leadership of the underdeveloped countries is very largely socialistic in its outlook. Fabian Socialists, Marxian Social-Democratic socialists, Gandhian socialists, fellow-traveling socialists, Trotskyite communists, Titoist communists, crypto-communist socialists, and outright Communists fill most of the political spectrum of these countries. Those who favor a traditionalist, religious state are usually socialists by implication. There are very few liberals in the economic sense, few who expect or wish to see their country make its economic progress through the "private sector." Although wealthy merchants have political influence, there is little moral sympathy with their activities or outlook. There are of course practically no proponents, except for tactical reasons, of the traditional tribal organization of society.

It is usual to attribute the socialistic orientation of the educated leadership of the underdeveloped countries to the atmosphere of the London School of Economics in the 1920's and 1930's, when so many of them studied there, to the personal and literary influence of the late Professor Harold Laski and Professor G. D. H. Cole, to Professor Tawney's *The Acquisitive Society and Equality,* to Mr. John Strachey's *The Coming Struggle for Power,* to the *New Statesman and Nation,* and the Left Book Club. More generally, great weight is given to the anti-imperialist attitudes of Socialist and Communist parties in the metropolitan countries. There is much truth in these assertions. More emphasis should perhaps be placed on the fundamental anti-bourgeois

---

[3] Of the modern professions and occupations, the law, because its practice is entwined with political authority and because it is so often the point of departure for a political career, and journalism, both under colonial rule and under conditions of sovereignty, seem to possess more of the charisma of nationality than any others.

attitude of that section of the British and, to a lesser degree, Continental intellectual classes which exercised such a fascination on the students who came to London, Oxford, and Paris from the then dependent
countries. The culture of the European intellectuals, whether it was
socialistic or not, was hostile to the ethos and activities of the businessman, large and small. However, the root of the attitude of the educated
elite in underdeveloped countries lies within their own traditional
culture.

The orientation toward the political sphere which derived from
the vicissitudes of native life and its immanent transformations, and
that which came from an admiring contact with certain features of
European and particularly British intellectual life, are thus more in
harmony than in conflict. Both move in the same direction. Both are
indifferent to, and even repelled by, everyday life and above all by an
economic life which is directed toward private gain. Both are impatient
with the humdrum of traditional life, with its inertness and compromise. Both wish to see life lived in accordance with an ideal emanating
from some creative source, from a genius, from a hero, from a lofty
and inspiring authority. A great difference between them lies in the
fact that the intellectuals of the underdeveloped countries have political
power. They are the sole modern class in their society; modernity rests
on them.

II

It is against this background that the intellectual political leaders of
the new countries conceive of economic progress. They envisage a system
in which the initiative, on the whole, will come from the politicians and
the civil service, while the populace, if made sufficiently enthusiastic on
behalf of the national ideal, will carry out their schemes. They conduct
a policy which aims to create socialistic, governmentally initiated, controlled, or operated enterprises, because they assume that the initiative
for productive economic activity is lacking in the population at large
and, above all, in the present and any prospective entrepreneurial class.
The politicians and civil servants are convinced that they must arouse
the present working-force from what they think is a state of torpor and
that they must train the prospective members of the working-force to
a readiness to accept goals beyond those they have been accustomed to
achieve. They believe that the motivation of the working population
will be adequate to their great national ideals only if it seeks to exceed
its present level of aspiration in work and mode of life. There are very
mixed feelings about the extent to which the workingmen or peasantry
should seek to enrich themselves, to improve their standard of living

and otherwise enhance their earthly pleasures. On the one hand, humanitarianism and national pride counsel improvement of the standard of living; on the other hand, nationality and its glory counsel abstention from consumption and so does an ethic of austerity.

The rulers of the new societies of Africa and Asia have no love for the maxim: *Enrichissez-vous,* or for those who follow it. They wish their people to be more efficient in the use of resources which they possess or which authority allocates to them. But that is as far as they will usually go in seeking the diffusion of the ideal of individual achievement in their societies, and they are not eager to have that ideal dependent on the desire for a continuously rising material standard of living. They seek efficiency without basing it on ambition and, above all, they have no interest in the specifically economic form of ambition—namely, *economizing* activity.

Ambition is a matter of motivation, efficiency is a matter of performance. A person can be efficient without being ambitious. Ambition is the aspiration to meet or conform with a standard which is not automatically achieved through the continuation of current practices. The ambitious person is one who tries to do something which he is not already doing. He wishes to enter into a role which he does not already occupy or, if he is in that role already, he seeks to conform more closely to a certain standard of performance than he already does. No stress is laid here on the conservation of means or resources, although such might well be a consequence of the actions of an ambitious person. In the economic sphere, it almost always is. It entails above all the individual's subjective attachment to a goal, regardless of whether he has chosen the goal through his own imagination and reason or has assimilated it from his culture. Ambition requires exertion, but not necessarily initiative. Ambition need work only along well-prescribed paths, while efficiency must seek, within a partially determinate framework, to find new ways of expending fewer resources to attain the *given* goals or to find new ways of expending a *given* quantity of resources in order to produce a maximum output. Efficiency in action is conformity with a given standard through the expenditure of as few resources as possible, or, with a predetermined quantity of resources, the production of as large an output as possible. It requires initiative or creativity, which ambition does not, but the initiative need not be that of the person performing the efficient action. He can be efficient by carrying out procedures which are stipulated for him by someone else, in order to attain goals which are also stipulated for him by someone else.

The attitude which is constitutive of economizing practice[4] is, in contrast to this, one to which little is sacred except results and, indeed,

[4] Weber, *op. cit.,* i, pp. 23–24.

no particular result except output in general. The economizing attitude is not simply interested in employing as few resources as possible in particular uses in order to get a fixed quantity of output of a particular commodity. It is interested in getting as much as possible from the available resources, and in increasing the resources. It is interested not just in increasing output of particular commodities, but in the optimal increase of total output.

The economizing attitude involves a boundless aspiration; its goal is not fixed in quantity at a particular point. There is no final resting place. It has no determinate and specific goals, other than the most general goal of maximizing returns which commits the acting person to neither particular procedures nor particular ends. The category or sphere within which the goal is sought within any given period of time is determined, but not the value or level to be achieved in that category; the more that can be achieved, the better. But if another category of goal offers a better return for resources invested, then the economizing attitude counsels a shift to that goal. Moreover, the goal is one which, from the standpoint of the economizing person, can never be attained. Each triumph leads to another goal a little farther off.

Here it differs from the goal of efficiency, which sets a target and attempts to use as little as possible of the available resources to achieve it, or which, with a fixed allotment of resources, seeks to achieve as much as possible of a specific set of ends. Efficiency pays no attention to alternative uses of the means or resources; it is concerned only with using what it has to achieve the end set or to exceed the standard within its own category. The economizing orientation is, however, a readiness to shift the use of a resource from, let us say, the raising of cocoa beans to the raising of groundnuts, should the latter use appear more profitable, or to sell up and to enter retail trade or manufacture, should action in those categories promise greater returns.

Economizing, since it seeks to maximize total income, is forced into a more comprehensive view of the field in which it must operate. Efficient action need not take such a comprehensive view of the field. Thus it is not economizing to build factories which produce goods which cannot meet competitive prices abroad or at home, however efficiently the factories are run. It is scarcely economizing to build steel mills in Burma or Indonesia or West Africa when foreign steel can be brought in much more cheaply from Japan or India or Europe, however efficiently labor works and management organizes in the former countries. Efficiency concerns itself with a narrower range of alternatives and opportunities. Economizing involves flexibility in the choice of goals and, above all, it involves maximizing output relative to input; it does not involve either maximizing absolute output of particular goods or producing any particular goods.

The disposition to act economically or "economizingly" disrupts received patterns of action. It is anomic,[5] in the sense that it knows no rules but its own. Although it too works within a tradition, its tradition is one which allows room for innovation and, indeed, presses for it. The economizing attitude is a creative attitude. As a creative attitude, it gives expression to the "genius"—i.e., the individuality—of its bearer. It expresses a charismatic quality.

The creativity of the successful business enterpriser is as unattractive to the political and intellectual elite of the underdeveloped countries as it is to the intellectuals of Western countries (disregarding for the moment certain economists)—and partly for the same reasons. The modern intellectuals in the West spurn the businessman in part because businessmen are hostile to or unsympathetic with intellectuals. On a deeper level of thought, they spurn the businessman because what he produces is thought to have only instrumental value. But even more basically, they spurn him because the intellectual, even the most secular, lives in a tradition which is historically of religious origin and which still retains much of the substance with which that origin endowed it. This tradition derives from a culture which believed charismatic qualities were concentrated in those who knew sacred texts, who cultivated or enjoyed sacred states of mind, meditations, and ritual actions, and in those who exercised authority and, in doing so, enunciated rules imbued with a charismatic or sacred quality.

Although it is a long distance from the modern Western intellectual's culture to that of the traditional societies of Africa and Asia, in this particular respect the line of movement is straight. The antichrematistic attitude of the modern intellectual is of a piece with the belief in the concentration of charisma which is held by the elites of traditional societies.

The creativity of the craftsman and the business enterpriser has thus been denied the status of true creativity. Great artists, great mili-

---

[5] Social scientists have tended to look askance at anomic activities, in accordance with their own tradition of the romantic ideal of a spontaneously "integrated" society. Although anomic actions are often pernicious in themselves and in their consequences, there are some which may be pernicious or immoral in themselves and most beneficial in their consequences. (This was the view of Mandeville and Adam Smith, but it has not entered very centrally into modern sociology and particularly into the ethical-political outlook of modern sociologists.) And, finally, there are anomic actions which are good in themselves—like works of art and scientific discoveries and the creation of new economic organizations—and which are also beneficial in their consequences. It is only the anti-business prejudice of social scientists which denies the accolade of creativity to economic activity.

tary leaders, great rulers, great saints, great scientists have been acknowledged as genuinely creative, but not the great innovators in business enterprise. Yet the daring imagination, the readiness to enter into *terra incognita* where the lessons of the past are insufficient, the deep conviction and the unrelenting persistence and intensity of effort would appear to make the achievements of the great businessman as creative as the achievements of a great ruler or a great captain.

In addition to the reasons mentioned above—namely, the instrumental nature of the products of the businessman's activity and their consequent unconnectedness with the ultimate powers and mysteries of the universe, such as life and death and sovereignty over them—there is another reason which is very pertinent to our concerns here. The activities of the businessman are carried on outside the domains of the prophet, the intellectual, the warrior, and the prince or statesman, in which it has been believed that charismatic manifestations are concentrated. From the standpoint of the traditional bearers who have claimed the monopoly of creative charismatic powers, the business enterpriser is an outsider, a pretender, a denier of the legitimacy of the monopoly. He has exercised *initiative* outside the sphere of legitimate creativity. The sphere within which he acts is thought to be repugnant to the appearance of charismatic qualities. Up to the present, economizing activity has almost always been outside the circle of concentrated charisma.

III

There is no logical necessity for the self-sustaining, self-developing economic system to be a capitalistic economy, working through the initiative of business enterprisers. It is logically and empirically possible that it could be socialistic. It is, however, most unlikely that it would be a centrally planned economy, run by government departments which monopolize all initiative at their higher levels. Electronic computers might permit the making of centralized decisions about optimal allocations of resources which would be beyond the powers of men unaided by such machines, and if this were to occur it might permit the economizing attitude to come into play without decentralization. But whatever the power of the machinery which they may employ, politicians and civil servants have little affinity with the economizing attitude.

Civil servants are interested in efficiency. Even when they become planners, that remains their preponderant consideration, and there are good reasons for this. They are always checked, at least in countries with parliamentary democracy, to see that they do not waste resources in achieving determinate goals; or, alternatively, they are expected to produce a maximum of a given end with a determinate amount of resources. Moreover, the strongly rooted departmental patriotism of even the best civil services, which makes for narrowness of outlook, militates against the operation of the economizing attitude, which requires comprehensiveness of outlook.

In addition, since so many important parts of government activity in any country require a pure efficiency orientation, it is very likely that civil services will continue to attract and select—and they will be fortunate if they get them—persons whose aspiration toward achievement presupposes externally prescribed goals. The flowering among civil servants of an economizing attitude, with all its flexibility and willingness to take risks, is further obstructed by the incapacity of politicians, parliamentary or oligarchical, to make economizing decisions for a whole society, as well as by the frequency of considerations of local advantage and of symbolic importance in political calculations. Even though a planning commission is full of experts, political necessities in fact play a great role. As a result, civil servants move within a narrowing framework which prevents them from acting as flexibly as the owners or directors of large firms, who are relatively little preoccupied with symbolic or local political concerns such as engage the minds of politicians.

In principle, a decentralized socialistic system of the type designed by Professors Lange and Lerner some years ago and now being canvassed in Yugoslavia could accommodate the expression of economizing attitudes. This seems to me to be improbable, however, not for technical reasons, but because the whole tradition of socialism is so permeated by belief in the inevitability and propriety of the concentration of charisma.

Now this does not mean that underdeveloped countries cannot make substantial improvements in the material conditions of their people, or that they are doomed to remain in their present economically retrograde condition. What is meant, however, is that the system is likely to remain dependent for its motive force on the decisions of politicians and civil servants and that the progress of the system will depend on the availability of exterior models and sources of technological and organizational knowledge. In other words, there can be economic growth with little self-development of the economy.

For a self-developing economy to emerge, there must be a dispersion of charisma from the sphere of political authority into other spheres—notably, the economic sphere. There must be an acknowledgment, throughout the significant sectors of the population, of the possibility that the "essential" spirit, the *sacred* of the society, can find expression in actions other than the exercise of authority on behalf of the territorial community and in the name of the nation. Herein rests the whole difficulty.

It is in the nature of the intense experience of charismatic qualities that their dispersal should be viewed with anxiety and repugnance. It is in the nature of charismatic authority that the universality which it seeks must emanate from a single center—its own. The same considerations which cause churches to frown upon the efflorescence of sectarianism make charismatic politicians resistant to the emergence of centers from which a charisma that does not emanate from them—which is, in a sense, a countercharisma—can flow freely. In turn, the most powerfully charismatic businessmen are no different from the politicians and the ecclesiasts. When, for a brief span of American history, charisma seemed to be concentrated in the great businessmen, everyone else was treated by the powerful industrialists as of secondary importance. Politicians and intellectuals were despised and churchmen were treated as handmaidens. In England and in Germany, during the periods of their greatest industrial expansion, a similar tendency was to be observed, offset only by the irreducible charisma of the court and the aristocracy which derived its charisma from the court. But these were only a brief diversion of the long course of history; on the whole, traditions do not favor the businessman.

IV

The spirit of economizing innovation is a scarce good and even the most dynamic economic system has only a minority of such spirits in its population. It is not necessary for more than a small proportion of the population to have an economizing disposition in order for that country to develop economically, as long as natural resources are available and other institutional conditions, economic, legal, and political, are favorable. A country in which everyone was of an economizing disposition would probably be such a cauldron of unrest and dissatisfaction that the orderly framework necessary for economic development would be injured. All that is necessary from the mass of the industrial and agricultural labor force is a certain measure of persistence, some sense of workmanship, and a preference for a higher income when the opportunity for it is available—i.e., a moderate amount of ambition to measure up to a standard and to obtain additional rewards. Such ambition is necessary not only for efficient performance but also because it is the psychological matrix out of which the economizing attitude emerges.

A host of tiny shops, working with antiquated hand- or foot-powered machinery or even with electrical power, do not themselves constitute the economic progress of a society. A large number of small farms, the proprietors of which are seeking to increase their incomes, does not sound very significant. Both of these are, however, indispensable for economic development. What they provide, aside from their contribution to output, is the recruiting ground and the atmosphere from which can come forward more vigorous, more foresighted, more creative entrepreneurial types.

The economizing spirit, with its readiness to enter markets and to adapt to the needs of the market, is as possible and necessary in agriculture as it is in industry and commerce. The fundamental components of the economizing disposition—the readiness to consider and follow alternatives, the location of goals in the remoter future, and the expansibility of goals—are the same for activity in agriculture as in industry and trade.

This is the chief utility of a very widespread, small-scale, economic activity. It creates an environment of sentiment and aspiration in which economizing activity comes to be taken for granted as a good.

There is no other way to form the economizing businessman or to select him. Higher commercial and technical colleges are important for providing knowledge of specific procedures and for training those who will become subordinates or executives in the middle of any hierarchy. The innovators who start new waves of activity moving throughout the society are products of much less contrivable processes. They cannot be deliberately created. They can only be provided with an area in which to work and be offered the necessary facilities, such as banking institutions, markets, transportation, a labor force oriented toward achievement, etc.

Of the modern types of aspirations toward achievement in under-developed countries, the most common are the ambition to enter the civil service, and to practice one of the liberal professions, with law in the lead. Of these, the ambition to enter an administrative career is probably the most fruitful for economic development, but it has serious limitations. It is of great advantage for a country like India to possess an outstanding body of administrators. It is not, however, unqualifiedly advantageous. Quite apart from the burden on economic life of an excessively large bureaucracy, which becomes more inefficient as it grows larger, the bureaucratic variant of ambition—namely, efficiency—is not conducive to economic progress. Ambition in the civil service is forced into the mold of striving to be more efficient, to deal with more files in less time, to do certain tasks with smaller funds. It encourages reluctance to risk public resources. Furthermore, it reinforces a cultural pattern which maintains the prevailing belief in the charismatic nature of the center of authority, and despises the occupations which pursue money and adventure. A great civil service, such as that of India or such as the Sudanese Civil Service is on the way to becoming, enhances the dignity of its country, and increases its respect for probity and devotion to the common good. Yet, there are other things in life, and a little reputation for corruption in a civil service, painful though it is to contemplate, probably has some advantages in making the populace less awe-struck before its ruling group and less inclined to believe in its monopoly of virtue and of charisma.[6]

V

How are ambition and its more complex variants of efficiency and economizing generated, and how can creativity in economic life be dispersed?

Ambition—least of all, ambition in the economic sphere—is not part of the culture of the underdeveloped countries. Ambition does not necessarily require a high degree of development of individuality. There are ambitions which have to be realized by an intense exertion to attain traditionally and authoritatively established ends through the use of similarly established procedures. The economizing attitude does, however, require some measure of individuality. Not perhaps great richness or integration, but at least a center of gravity which lies within the individual actor and not in the traditions or authorities which confront him. An amorphous ego which does not attach itself to objects or roles other than those immediately presented by the situation within the family is the very opposite of individuality. The person in such a situation, characteristic of life in traditional societies, is not allowed to discover his own path. It is laid out for him. He is forced into a state of dependence to the point where he cannot exert *himself* continuously and independently. Where marriages are arranged, where most associates are members of the kinship group, and where also there is little heterogeneity in the economic environment—as well as little opportunity for effective choice (even when the desire for choice exists)—the self or the individuality of the adolescent does not acquire a differentiated and determinate form. That incipient outward movement of the spirit which exists in every human being atrophies in early adolescence in traditional societies. Curiosity, inventiveness, realistic phantasy, expansive and disciplined self-assertion wither in the seed.[7] The authority of the elders and of the group as a whole is so strong that even when a person achieves eminence as a lawyer or civil servant, it is often because his elders put him on the road and pressed him to persist rather than because he was moved in that direction by an inner entelechy, by an intensely held internal image and standard.

We assert the hypothesis that this underdevelopment of individuality is in large measure a result of the extended family system. The loosening and even disruption of that system might help to create more favorable conditions for economizing action.

The disruption of the extended family system would certainly do more to a society than release ambition and facilitate economizing action. Professor Hoselitz points out that the "dissolution of traditional patterns of family organization may result simply in deep-going social disorganization, the creation of non-productive 'marginal' individuals who cannot make a creative adjustment but who suffer anomie or become criminals, gangsters, or mentally maladjusted."[8]

There is much truth in this proposition. Since, however, *anomie* and creativity are closely related to each other, the very situation which stimulates *anomie* also releases creative potentialities. Both consequences may coexist in the same individual; in any case, they are certainly likely to coexist within the same society. The suffering victims of *anomie,* whose lives become disordered without the supporting hands of a strong kinship group and strong traditions transmitted and observed within the group, are the painful and perhaps inevitable price which is paid for a process which liberates creativity by allowing individuality to develop.[9] Individuality in its higher forms entails aspirations toward the unknown, toward the performance of actions hitherto not performed in the imagination of the individual, toward roles the indeterminate content of which is their essential feature. The comprehensive dissolution of the family's control over the individual in some cases

[7] Other qualities such as kindliness, humor, generosity, which are less dependent on the formation of individuality, are not equally affected.

[8] "Social Structure and Economic Growth," *Economica Internazionale,* VI, No. 3 (1953), p. 20.

[9] This connection was first hinted at in American sociological literature by William I. Thomas and Florian Zaniecki in *The Polish Peasant in Europe and America* (2nd ed., New York, 1925) in their threefold classification of personalities as "Bohemian," "Philistine," or "Creative." Max Weber said as much when he declared that charismatic authority arises in times of crisis (*Wirtschaft und Gesellschaft,* I, p. 142). Of course, discussion of the affinities of genius and neurosis or genius and madness dates from antiquity and underwent a profound renewal in European Romanticism.

merely results in random and amorphous hostility toward authority; in other cases, it allows the individual who would otherwise have been repressed by authority to aspire toward the exercise of initiative which is entailed in authority. In strata which have been anti-economistic, and in cultures which are generally anti-economistic, the loosening of the hold of the ties of the extended family which is the chief bearer and mediator of tradition is essential, if any of the potentialities are to become economically productive. When this occurs, a necessary precondition for the dispersion of charisma has been achieved. The man who discovers his own capacities by exercising them comes to have a higher self-respect. He acquires an ego which can be esteemed.

Curiosity and inventiveness are more likely to flourish when the authority of elders has loosened its hold on the individual and allowed some of his libido to expand and to flow onto the objects involved in his work. Genuine pride and creativity in work can develop only with great difficulty where the power of the extended kinship group is so strong that it crushes the embryonic individuality of its younger members and prevents it from acquiring a differentiated form. Above all, the breaking of a system that inhibits the emergence of individual attachments to objects which fall within the lifetime of the individual, and which are nonetheless remote from the present, opens up the possibility of persistent striving toward a distant goal, just as it opens up the possibility of disorderly, discontinuous, and amorphous action.

The loosening of the authority and pervasiveness of the extended family system is a necessity, but the breakup of the family is not. The system now prevalent in so many parts of Africa and Asia, whereby a man leaves his immediate family—his wife and children—with his parents or his elder brother and goes off to a town where he remains for many years, probably does not contribute anything except the man's labor power to economic development. When the man leaves his family and lives alone for years, there result the conditions of which Professor Hoselitz is apprehensive. The individual acquires no organizing focus for his liberated energy, his life loses the regularity imposed on him in his village, and his activity is dispersed in an aimless and restless way. Economic development needs not only the orderly institutional environment which a reliable legal and administrative system can provide, but also an orderly personal environment to maintain persistence in motivation. The man who retains his nuclear family has, thanks to the stability and coherence of his immediate domestic environment, more chance to persist in his pursuit of a goal. Naturally, not many such persons will become creative enterprisers, but a small number in each community may do so.

One might venture the hypothesis that the more widespread the establishment of nuclear or immediate families outside of the range of the extended family, the more likely we are to encounter economizing behavior. The common practice of alternating periods of separation from the extended family and complete reimmersion in its atmosphere is likely to combine the worst of both worlds—the personal disintegration of which Professor Hoselitz has written and the periodic and intense reaffirmation of kinship values. What is therefore required is a continuous looseness of the wider kinship system and a continuous firmness of the nuclear family ties.

VI

The expansion of the market through better communications and transportation contributes to the removal of limitations on the range of perception and imagination. Entry into a larger market increases the opportunities and the competitive pressure for economizing; it does so by exhibiting a wider range of opportunities for the use of resources, especially personal or human resources. The expansion of the market weakens the extended family system by providing opportunities for some of its members to live outside its immediate presence and its pressing demands. This in turn permits the emergence of dispositions which react to the opportunities of the market more economizingly than is possible where markets are meager. The expansion of the market contributes to economizing not only because it widens the range of opportunity, but because it enriches and enlivens the imagination. It engenders the economizing attitude as well as enabling it to operate.

The learning of skills through organized education facilitates a more ready adaptation to the possibilities offered by the market, and thus works in the economizing direction. However, the stimulation of the imagination, the arousing of curiosity, the enhancement of individual self-esteem—in fact, the general stirring-up of the intellect and emotions—are far more important functions of education in underdeveloped countries. They awaken individuals to new occupational and social opportunities, to possibilities of life lived in styles different from their own. In short, such stimulation makes them restless about their village- and kinship-dominated life, with the result that a few of them, having learned to read and write and having become curious about a life wider and more exhilarating than their own, try to find a new path corresponding to their own inclinations. This is why the governments of underdeveloped societies which spend 10 or more per cent of their budgets on education are probably making a better investment in the capital equipment of their country, however intangible and vague the object, than those which spend only 3 or 4 per cent and which put the difference into factories for making machinery. Primarily vocational education and "basic education" will extend the boundaries of imagination less than general education in humanistic and scientific subjects and they will do less to enhance the self-esteem of their pupils.

Creativity, and the belief in one's charisma which goes with it, can be dispersed in a society only when those who bear it are self-confident, have a sense of their own intrinsic value, and are in consequence convinced of the intrinsic value of the actions they undertake.

The economizing orientation is sustained by the self-esteem and self-confidence of the enterpriser, by his conviction that he is doing something valuable. These are the products of his own personal expansiveness, his prior personal achievements in enterprise, the atmosphere of confidence and self-respect in which he works—i.e., the immediate culture of the entrepreneurial classes and the wider culture. Every known culture, even that of the United States, has strong anti-economizing components; there is furthermore a tendency within families in which the economizing disposition has once been strong for it to become enfeebled and to yield to the lure of the learned professions, politics, the civil service, the army, etc. Yet continuous economic development requires that both the structure of the society and at least some parts of the culture offer the stimulus which turns ambition into economizing and the legitimation which only cultural values can give. In most underdeveloped countries, this tradition is still to be created. It cannot of course be created deliberately. But it can be helped to grow by the establishment of favorable conditions. Successful enterprise will help to create it, but so will a sympathetic and appreciative public opinion. Such opinion scarcely exists today in the underdeveloped countries. Businessmen are distrusted—above all, by the educated in government, in education, journalism, and literature—and they are not highly prized by the traditions which survive even in the modern sector of the society.

Thus anything which raises the appreciation of the potential creativity of persons outside the circle of the traditionally consecrated bearers of religious and political charisma must in the long run make the economies of underdeveloped countries more dynamic. Political democracy, religious effervescence, universal elementary education, internal migration, the widening of the cognitive map through study and experience are all important in the transformation of the human being from a recipient of tradition and an object of authority into an independent, differentiated, initiating individual. For this, it is indispensable that men and women in underdeveloped societies come to feel and believe that a "spark of divinity" or some other manifestation of what is sacred to human life dwells as much in those who live outside the circle of authority as it does in those who live within it.

Authority and Authoritarianism in the New Africa

FRANCIS X. SUTTON

The Ford Foundation

The rushing surge that brought sixteen African nations to independence this year has caught up the world in the excitement of witnessing a great historical change, and it has mostly been a happy excitement. By becoming politically independent nations, the African peoples have done what most of the world felt they ought to do and 1960 could be unaffectedly a year of multiple celebrations. But there have also been reasons for anxiety about the new era that is beginning in Africa. The distressing events in the ex-Belgian Congo have been like the descent of a wicked fairy, marring the year's celebrations and threatening a troubled future. The Congo was scarcely born before it gave lurid illustration to doubts that independence meant free and secure citizenries within African countries or that the removal of foreign domination in Africa was a sure step toward a healthier international order.

The front-runners in African independence had already stirred doubts and misgiving before the 1960 independence rush. Ghana had been put to close scrutiny since 1957 for its deportation of people it found politically undesirable, for its Preventive Detention Act and for its alleged efforts to cripple or eliminate the political opposition. Guinea presented a one-party state to the world as a matter of principle, and found sympathetic echoes all across Tropical Africa, even in that apostle of moderation and good sense, Mr. Julius Nyerere of Tanganyika.

The West has strained to comprehend these early signs and to sympathize without condescension. There has been a vague willingness to believe African conditions are somehow different, and hence that a more authoritarian form of government may be called for. The possibilities of anarchy and disorder are one evident basis. The mutiny and tribal warfare in the Congo have only been the most noted examples. Scarcely any emerging African state has escaped some manifestation of potential explosiveness. There were, for examples, the disturbances in the southern provinces of the Sudan as independence approached in 1955, the Ashanti riots of 1956 in Ghana, and the persisting terrorism

Reprinted from *Journal of International Affairs,* XV (1961), 7–17, with the permission of the author and the publisher.

in the Cameroons; even Nigeria saw independence marred by the (probably unimportant) disorder among the Tiv people in the Northern Region. Scylla and Charybdis seem very close together for these new states, squeezing out any comfortable track between tyranny and anarchy for parliamentary democracy to follow.

On the international scene, the new African states have declared themselves firmly for neutralism or non-alignment. They do not immediately run to the Soviet bloc in their new freedom. But neither do they cling to the Western nations which have been their masters but have ultimately sought to bring them to independence in amity and good faith. Given the past intimacy of relations with Western countries, neutralism seems a withdrawal of loyalties. And it is a withdrawal that is no calm and simple assertion of autonomy, but is full of assaults on colonialism and capitalism, warnings against continued Western domination, and expressions of sympathy for the models of development seen in Communist countries.

These are the principal sources of disquiet about the African political future that show themselves among Western observers. Even when they have not seriously quieted the celebration of African independence, they have been troublesomely in the background. To understand what substance they may have, and how seriously one must view them, it seems essential to scrutinize recent history and actual conditions in Africa. One must not rest with a vapid assumption of historical difference but try to understand how the conditions of the era of colonialism brought forth nations with these characteristics. Understanding these nations in their genesis, one may try to assess the hopes and misgivings they arouse and distinguish their deep-running tendencies from mere rhetoric and passing circumstance.

THE SOURCES AND CHARACTER OF AUTHORITY IN THE NEW STATES

The recent history of Africa has a tidiness for which future generations of school children may be grateful. A neat seventy-five years measures the Era of Colonialism in Africa. The Berlin Conference of 1884–85 does very nicely to mark its beginning and 1960 does dramatically well to mark its close.

Most of the independence celebrations of 1960 were the culmination of a long course of preparation, deliberate or inadvertent. Some of this preparation can be given clear dates and descriptions as historical record. The evolution of the Nigerian constitution from the Richards constitution of 1946 through the MacPherson constitution of 1951 to the constitution of 1954 and its amendment in the succeeding constitutional conferences makes such a record. So do the long discussions in the U.N. of the Somalia Trusteeship. But there has also been another form of preparation of independence that lies deeper and has the intangibility of pervasive things. This is the process whereby the authority that was vested in European governors and administrators in Africa gradually fell into dispute between Europeans and Africans and ultimately has fallen to Africans. The ultimate shift of sovereignty from a European metropolitan power to a new African nation is the legal and political expression of a sociological shift that has gone on over many years.

The rule of the European nations in Africa was established by the assertion and exercise of superior European power. Not that the scramble for Africa was particularly harsh or bloody. In some places it was, but much was gotten by negotiation, and adroit displays of power or minatory gestures often were humanely substituted for plain force. Whatever the pattern of conquest, there was conquest nonetheless and the position of the colonial powers in Africa was that of powerful conquerors. Europeans assumed a special status as superior people with a claim to authority, and colonial governments established a firm control over African territories that will undoubtedly seem remarkable in retrospect. The pacification of Africa became so thorough that personal security for a white man in Africa was as good or better than it was in Europe or America. It was sometimes not as good for Africans but African populations grew sharply in many places through the sheer elimination of warfare and insecurity. Remarkable records of peacefulness were attained. In Southern Rhodesia, for example, a melancholy note for 1960 was the breaking of a more than 60-year stretch in which there had been no killings by police action.

The coming of African independence has depended upon a change in the structure of African societies whereby Europeans ceased to be the elite to whom the power of political control exclusively belonged. The history of African reaction to European social, economic, and political superiority is a complicated history taking many forms. For a long time the reactions of Africans to the European makers of empires could not be directly challenging without severe costs. Indeed—and this is a most important fact—the African had usually to react by accepting a subordinate and dependent position. In saying this, I mean to describe a reaction involving something more than calculated accommodation to the facts of European control and superior power. I mean something of the sort that psychologists have variously labeled "identification with the aggressor," "introjection of an authority figure," or "acceptance of a role model." That some psychological process of this sort should have happened seems clear, and it was an essential and inevitable step toward the ultimate emergence of African nations as we see them today. For it was through this process that Africans learned the values and practices and ideals of Europeans and shaped their own aspirations toward competing with Europeans in these terms. Sociological studies like those of Professor Clyde Mitchell and his associates at the Rhodes-Livingstone Institute for the Copper Belt of Northern Rhodesia,[1] or the now faintly tragic studies sponsored by UNESCO in Stanleyville in the former Belgian Congo,[2] have made clear the depth of African involvement in the influences brought by Europeans. While not ceasing to be African, increasingly large sections of African populations have imitated Europeans and learned in various ways to aspire to the same things.

Hostile and challenging reactions to European dominance at first took covert and oblique forms. Some of the best known were religious in character and avoided a direct assault on the political kingdom. Later, Africans have come forward claiming that they should run the affairs of their country alongside or in place of the Europeans. These newer political movements did not seek to abandon or reject the institutions through which Europeans had controlled Africa. There has been little demand for a return to the pre-colonial Africa or any radical abandonment of the form of colonial territories. Rather the claim was that Africans were now prepared to behave like the Europeans who had been taking responsibility for political and administrative control of African territories.

The basis of colonial government by Europeans had legally lain with the mother countries and been clothed in various constitutional and statutory instruments like the Foreign Jurisdiction Act for the British territories. But the essentials lay in the sociological status of Europeans as a dominant elite. The legitimacy of such a government in an aggressively political setting could not be secure. It was always vulnerable to claimants of the right to represent the popular masses being governed. White men could hardly make such a claim without the embarrassments of paternalism.[3] Effective African nationalism came with the emergence of Africans who could present themselves as

[1] J. Clyde Mitchell, "Africans in Industrial Towns in Northern Rhodesia," *H. R. H. The Duke of Edinburgh's Study Conference 1956,* vol. II.

[2] *Cf.* V. G. Pons, Nelly Xydias, and Pierre Clement, "Social effects of urbanization in Stanleyville, Belgian Congo," in *Social Implications of Industrialization and Urbanization in Africa South of the Sahara,* UNESCO, 1956, pp. 229–492.

[3] It may be one indicator of their political uncertainty of touch that the Belgians alone tried to elevate paternalism into an explicit doctrine of colonial government. *Cf.* G. E. Brausch, "Le Paternalisme: une doctrine belge de politique indigène," *Revue de l'Institut de Sociologie* [Solvay], 1957.

equipped to do what European governors and administrators had been doing and also to represent "the people." Once they did so, a new and ultimately irresistible competitor for legitimate authority was on the scene. The new authority might for a time be badly served by unsure or incompetent African leaders but it could not long be constrained.

For there to be effective African leaders, there had to be a mobilization of their popular support. The masses of the African population had to be in some way "politicized," and this process has normally taken forms not comfortably within the institutionalized range of political expression. By this I mean to say the masses were not at first and typically drawn into political action as voters in campaigns or as engaged observers of established governments. Particularly in the British territories, there was an attempt gradually to introduce the principles of representation and elections into the government of these territories. There were African members of the Legislative Council of the Gold Coast as early as 1886. Initially appointed, these African representatives have been ultimately elected in varying ways, with gradually widening franchises. This policy may be seen as a controlled and deliberate set of moves toward "politicizing" Africans. But the nationalistic movements have outrun any such controlled tutelage. Julius Lewin is undoubtedly too harsh when he writes that the legislative councils of the British territories were ". . . facades, rather than forums," and decries executive councils as "embryonic cabinets where the inner secrets of policy-making are still carefully guarded from African scrutiny."[4] For many new African leaders, these institutions have been schools of responsibility but they have not had pride of place in the political education of the masses. African political awareness has come more characteristically in the movements of protest, with meetings and demonstrations on the margin of legitimate political activity as the classic settings. Listening to long-winded orators in the beer halls of Northern Rhodesia, or waiting all day Sunday in an outdoor gathering of the unfranchised for a late afternoon speech from Tom Mboya or some other leading Kenya politician have been characteristic experiences. Passionate speeches to enthusiastic crowds that take the whole existing structure of government as a target of criticism—these have been the germinating expression of African political life.

Cause and effect become badly jumbled in the complex movement of African nationalism. The rapidity of the African conquest of self-rule and independence is at once a cause and a consequence of the process I have depicted. Had Africans come to political consciousness more gradually through becoming aware of political institutions and

[4] *Central African Examiner,* December 6, 1958, pp. 15–16.

their internal processes, learning of "the issues" (like the ideal voters of American liberals) in the contexts of these institutions, the forces created by enthusiastic responses to African leaders in public meetings might not have had such a free sweep. But conversely, rapid change meant little chance for the slow maturing of a response to institutions that needed much adapting if they were to be at all suited to African control.

Authoritarianism in the new African states is a particular cause and consequence of the rapid changes. It is—perhaps paradoxically—a feature of government in which there is basic continuity across the great shift from colonial to African control. For the colonial governments in Africa, however benevolent, responsible and well-meaning they may have been, were not democratic governments in the sense that we know them in the Western world. As I have stressed, colonial administrations did not have their mandate from the governed. They might, and typically did, work through indigenous African authorities at local levels and consultation went on at all levels, including the general territorial administration. But in the end they responded not to the dictates of the electorate but to the judgments of a governor and his advisors. There was little experience of direct and legitimate challenge to the authority of the administration. The District Officers or *commandants de cercle* who ruled the territories were, as Delavignette put it, "chiefs" rather than simple administrators.[5] They were police officers, magistrates, and omni-competent executives who might cajole and listen to complaints, but who in the end "told people what they were to do." A considerable measure of discretion was inseparable from diffuse and multiple powers so that one finds African nationalists today arguing that the arbitrariness of power they are accused of had ample precedents in colonial rule.

The Africans who have emerged as leaders of their people have an authority differently based but similarly diffuse. Winning leadership in the context of enthusiastic movements, they have taken on heroic stature in the eyes of their followers. Men like Azikiwe and Awolowo in Nigeria, Nkrumah of Ghana, Nyerere in Tanganyika, or Sékou

[5] Robert Delavignette, *Service Africain*, Paris (Gallimard), 1946, p. 31: "L'administration coloniale territoriale a un caractère d'humanité positive que prend une allure d'autorité révolutionnaire. Chargée d'introduire un régime nouveau dans la politique et l'économie du pays, concentrée dans quelques Européens, qui ne peuvent communiquer que par intermédiaires avec la masse de leurs administrés . . . et qui sont sépareés d'eux par le genre de vie, la forme de pensée, le mode de travail, comment ne serait-elle pas révolutionnaire et autoritaire? . . . Il y a dans l'administration coloniale térritoriale un principe interne qui lui est propre: l'autorité personnelle de l'administrateur et, en dernière analyse, la personnalité dans l'art de commander."

Touré in Guinea have the claim to authority of men whose qualities are thought to be beyond those of ordinary men. In the term Max Weber taught us and that is now being widely applied by Africanists, they are "charismatic" leaders. It was a part of Weber's analysis to stress that charismatic authority lacks the clear definition and bounds of legal, constitutional authority, and the application to Africa seems to be supported by the facts. Thus the "authoritarianism" we now see in Africa derives in part at least from the very nature of the authority through which it has been possible for Africans to grasp control of their own affairs.

Lest all of this discussion rest doubtfully in generality, or appear more personal and original than it in fact is, I venture to illustrate with a case from recent African history that has benefited from a lucid analysis.

AN ILLUSTRATION: NYASALAND

The disturbances in Nyasaland that attracted the world's attention in 1958 and 1959 arose from a confrontation of established colonial authority with the pervasive new authority of a nationalist leader. It will be recalled that Dr. Hastings Banda, "the most distinguished of Nyasas," returned to Nyasaland in July 1958 after an absence of many years in South Africa, the United States, Great Britain, and Ghana, during which he acquired a medical education, practiced his profession, and became known and respected among Africans from his own and other territories. He returned at the request of members of the African National Congress in Nyasaland and was immediately accepted as their leader in Nyasaland. Subsequent to his arrival, there was a series of public disturbances; force was used to disperse African crowds, and on the third of March, 1959, a state of emergency was declared and numerous leaders of the African National Congress were arrested. There was an immediate and vigorous reaction to this governmental move. A series of disturbances broke out all over the country in which 41 lives were lost and 68 persons were wounded by gunfire. In subsequent actions, aiming at restoration of law and order in the country, additional lives were lost. The Nyasaland Government issued a White Paper in which it alleged, among other things, that a plot to murder members of the Government had existed.

These events brought strong reactions in the United Kingdom and a commission was appointed by the Secretary of State for the Colonies, Mr. Alan Lennox-Boyd, to investigate the disturbances and the events leading up to them. The commission had four members, all British, under the chairmanship of Sir Patrick Devlin, and in the usual fashion, has come to be known as the Devlin Commission. In its report, this Commission remarks that the Government of Nyasaland "was a benevolent despotism."[6] It stresses the benevolence but points up the conflict between the despotism and the attitudes of a small minority of politically active Nyasalanders who had challenged the Government. The Commission notes that provision for the election of a few Africans to the Legislative Council had not altered the character of the Government. They describe the probable disappointment of the devisors of this constitutional arrangement:

No doubt it was hoped that the five Africans in the Legislative Council would treat the four years of the Legislature's life as a sort of probationary period during which they would put the African viewpoint with moderation and make a thoughtful contribution to a formulation of policy which remained the exclusive responsibility of the Government; this was their chance to learn how to run the estate which would someday be theirs. Instead of that, they have behaved as if they were the opposition in a full-fledged democracy whose duty it was to harass and criticize the Government. Their speeches are largely designed as propaganda to be printed in Hansard at Government expense; Hansard has become a best seller among educated Africans. But the forms of government and the attitude of the Government towards its subjects are still essentially paternal. The leaders of Congress have been pouring new wine into old skins.[7]

When Dr. Banda arrived on the scene, he intensified the issue by establishing contact with the people in enormous crowds amidst immense enthusiasm. His speeches were made in English and their content was moderate but their delivery was highly emotional and arousing. The Commissioners remark: "We have listened to the recordings of some of them and they are the speeches of a demagogue."[8] The Devlin Commission absolves Dr. Banda of many of the charges against him. They nevertheless argue that the effect of his appearance and his oratory was to present a sort of radical challenge to the Nyasaland Government such as would not be the case in the appearance of an ordinary political leader in a democracy. The Commission illustrates and then proceeds to analyse the challenge both to Europeans and to the traditional African authorities through whom they worked:

[6] Report of the Nyasaland Commission of Inquiry, *Cmnd. 814*, (H.M.S.O., 1959), p. 16.
[7] *Ibid.*, p. 16.
[8] *Ibid.*, p. 27.

In a democracy, politicians are frequently scoffed at. If one were referred to as "a little boy of twenty-five years direct from Oxford" no one would worry. But when Dr. Banda referred to District Commissioners in these terms (not an individual but the genus) it was thought by the Administration to be dangerous. A District Commissioner cannot afford to be jeered at or insulted in public; if that is tolerated, it would lead to a loss of authority which would be fatal. Many unofficial Europeans consider that the same thing applies to them . . . Government in Nyasaland is based on respect for authority and this applies to the Chiefs as much as to the Europeans. "Contempt" of a chief is an offense that he can punish. Party demonstrations against a chief hostile to Congress might well amount to contempt . . . The respect which by native tradition and custom is paid the chiefs is something which the Government is most anxious to preserve; one of the things about Congress which most disturbed the Government was the practice of stirring up disrespectful demonstrations against loyal chiefs. The Government's attitude is that the chiefs should be above politics . . .[9]

In these contexts, criticism of established authority was regarded, rightly or wrongly, as a radical rejection of authority. The Commission goes on:

If, for example, Dr. Banda attacked the enforcement of the Agricultural Rules, then must it not be that he did not want them observed? If so, then was not the African confronted with a choice between obedience to Dr. Banda and obedience to the Government? The African did not think of Dr. Banda as a party leader whose policies happen to be opposed to those of the Government; they thought of him as a national leader setting up his authority against that of the Boma (the seat of government).[10]

Tragic conflict was latent and scarcely avoidable:

The real case against Dr. Banda is not that he ever advocated disobedience . . . we do not think that he ever did—but that he refused to realize that disobedience was the inevitable consequence of what he was saying and doing . . . Congress behaved as if Nyasaland was capable of functioning as a democracy in the fullest sense and that the Government was holding things back. The Government, on the other hand, became increasingly intolerant of any opposition on Western and democratic lines because it considered it tantamount to the setting up of a rival

[9] *Ibid.,* pp. 16–17.
[10] *Ibid.,* p. 17.

*authority . . . This conflict of thought and feeling between a govern-
ment that is still paternal in outlook and an opposition that is not yet
as mature as it believes itself to be is no doubt a common feature in the
emergence of democracy all over the world.*[11]

The recent history of other African territories has not, I think,
differed in essentials from the case of Nyasaland. Governments whose
powers were not seen as explicitly and carefully defined, or subject to
open critical opposition, have been challenged and then inherited by
Africans. Diffuse respect for an alien elite has been replaced by enthusiastic devotion to charismatic African leaders, through a period of
struggle and crisis that is dangerously brief in many cases. Charges of
colonial blindness and selfishness on the one hand or of African im-
petuosity and heedlessness on the other hand are too common nowadays. Seen against an appreciation of human frailties and an analysis
of the forces with which leaders have had to deal, the wonder may be
that the great change has been as well-paved as it has in cases like
Ghana, Nigeria, and some of the French-speaking territories.

There are obviously other roots of the authoritarianism and the
distaste for open opposition we now see in African governments. It is
not to be taken for granted that a single African leader will readily
establish control over a whole territory. There are notoriously great
differences among the African peoples who were swept into one political entity by the colonial partition of Africa. Once political expression
is possible for Africans there is a good chance that it will give voice to
these differences. Well-tried machinery for accommodating opposition
among African leaders is no more present than it is for the transition
from European to African control. There are now abundant examples
in Africa of the flaring of tribal and other hostilities once European
control is lifted. Adding to the examples already given, one notes the
tribal form of most parties in the ex-Belgian Congo and the resulting
tragic violence in Kasai, Katanga, and elsewhere; the uncomfortable to
unsafe position of migrants like the Dahomians over much of French
Africa and the sharpening of measures against Southerners in Northern
Nigeria. New possibilities of expression of internal differences make
new demands for effective control by a government. Countries like
Ghana that have taken strong measures have pointed to the ruthlessness
of their opponents as justification—and with much plausibility. There
seems little doubt that African governments have graver problems of
security than the colonial governments had—they are more intimately

[11] *Ibid.*, p. 21.

involved in potentially explosive African differences. These, one ventures to think, are some of the realities behind the ideology of national unity and one-party systems which Western observers often find so disquieting. What role contemplation of models East and West may play invites further attention, and doing so brings us to the international relations of the new African states.

NEUTRALISM, INDEPENDENCE, AND MATURITY

The analysis of the transition to African independence that I have given makes it sudden and reactive. The old structure of colonial societies is not abruptly destroyed; rather, places are exchanged in its fabric. Africans previously in a dependent and subordinate status throughout these societies have claimed the control of them for themselves. Lord Mountbatten recently said that he thought the Tanganyika army could not be fully Africanized for twenty years, this being the time he estimated it would take to make battalion commanders. Such a vision of Africans growing through slow and natural stages into calm and unaffected exercise of high stations and authority as Europeans did before them has not and cannot be realized. Long before, a critical mass of psychological reactions is exceeded and Africans bounce to the top.

To assume that the Africans now controlling African states are calmly confident of their capacity to run African societies unaided seems very doubtful. There are too many controverting facts—the lack of trained African professionals and technicians, and the continuing control of Europeans over most business organizations are among the potent ones. When Nkrumah and other African leaders have warned about the dangers of colonialism in covert forms, Western powers have often felt offended at the impugning of their good faith in granting independence. But anxieties of the sort must be seen as normal and real. It must be remembered that Africans and their new states remain weak and have only recently been the passive subjects of guidance by white men in most spheres. We should expect a need for emotionally tinged acts and assertions that plainly affirm independence. In the international political sphere, neutralism or open sympathy with the Communist world are natural expressions of this need. If there are dangers in it, there are also grave dangers of another sort in steadily proclaimed loyalty to the West. For this sort of loyalty threatens to undermine the bases of confidence in setting forth as an independent state.

Sympathy for the Communist world is thus in part reactive. But that there is also an intrinsic appeal of Communist models in ideology and in development policy cannot be doubted. Outside the Western world, Communism, after all, is an ideology that permits the pursuit of goals learned from an envied and respected West while being in apparent opposition to it. And it is some ideology of this sort that the African states need.

It will, therefore, be astonishing if the African states are comfortable partners of the Western world in the great game of international politics. There is more than discouragement in this prospect. For if the general analysis here is sound, a stage of fractiousness in the leadership of African states may be essential to their progress towards maturity as independent and responsible nations. By adopting an independent course Africans may have costly experiences. But they will at least be gaining experience in the exercise of independent responsibility. And through the exercise of responsibility lies the best course toward attaining a true maturity. In nations as in individuals, true independence can only be an attribute of maturity. Like anxious parents, the Western nations are now seeing the African nations go off rather headstrongly by themselves. They expect and will need further help about which they will often have to be gracelessly demanding. Guiding hands will have to be light, deft, and inconspicuous to be acceptable. But their absence will be resented and their ultimate effects not trivial.

Single-Party Systems in West Africa

RUTH SCHACHTER MORGENTHAU
Boston University

In this paper I propose to examine the tendency towards single-party systems in West Africa, particularly in relation to the social structure and the historical circumstances in which the parties emerged.[1] I shall therefore point up the distinction between "mass" and "patron" parties, and then consider the new single-party governments, most of them based on mass parties, in relation to the prospects of democracy in West Africa. My argument is that mass parties are created by African leaders out of the very liberating and egalitarian forces we in this country generally associate with democracy. Some of the mass parties encourage the growth of forces and institutions which may ultimately make possible the machinery of democratic systems familiar to us: as, for instance, competition for every citizen's vote by more than one organized team of candidates. At this stage of West African party history, it seems to me, the number of parties is far too simple a criterion upon which to decide whether or not a system is democratic.

General statements about parties in the new West African states can be made only tentatively. Significant rights to vote and organize parties came to West Africa only after the Second World War. Since then formal institutional change has taken place at a rapid pace. The constitutional framework in which the parties grew changed continuously. The franchise expanded until it became universal, the powers of African elected representatives grew by stages from consultative to legislative and eventually to executive, and the locus of political power shifted from London or Paris to Africa. Even so basic a feature of a political system as its territorial and international frontiers occasionally altered. For example, Upper Volta was reconstituted as a separate territory in 1947; and some eleven years later the federation of French

Reprinted from *The American Political Science Review*, LV (1961), 294–307, with the permission of the publisher.

[1] Evidence for this paper was gathered during field trips to West Africa, and is to be published in my *Parties of French-Speaking West Africa*. I am most grateful to Jeffrey Butler, Thomas Hodgkin, Richard Sklar and Immanuel Wallerstein for their valuable comments, and to Newell Stultz for his assistance.

419

West Africa was dissolved and Ghana had absorbed British Togoland. The Mali Federation, born in 1959, dissolved before it was two years old. The general points evident from an examination of party history over less than twenty years may turn out to be of minor importance in a later perspective.

All these are reasons for caution. Nevertheless, the parties are among the oldest national political institutions in West Africa, wholly Africanized long before the governments or the civil services (which still are not). Hence parties give better guidelines to African politics than those formal institutions of government which were set up by French and British colonizers at least in part as a condition for their recent political withdrawal, and are being changed by Africans after independence.

The majority of the new West African sovereign nations are based on single parties, likely to dominate for some time whether or not opposition parties are allowed to exist alongside. Most of their governments are founded on mass parties: Ghana, Guinea, Ivory Coast, Mali (formerly Soudan), Senegal, Togo and—with qualifications—the Eastern and Western Regions in the Federation of Nigeria. Without the pressure these mass parties exerted on the French or British colonial authorities, it is doubtful whether the colonial era in West Africa would have ended quite so soon. Perhaps, indeed, the nationalist drive of these particular mass movements, linked with the rapid decline of European power, carried along towards independence in 1960 even those states in which mass parties have not yet emerged: the Northern Region of Nigeria, the Islamic Republic of Mauretania, and (with qualifications) Niger and Upper Volta, which are also single party systems, but based on parties of the "patron," "cadre," or "personality" types.[2] In Dahomey, however, government rests on an unstable alliance of parties, both of the mass and patron types, still regional and not territorial in scale.

Successive post-war electoral results in West Africa make obvious another clear trend: the only sharp changes in party majorities took place prior to independence, and were from patron to mass party majority; never the reverse. An apparent exception was Ivory Coast, where the *Parti Démocratique de la Côte d'Ivoire* (PDCI) rode to power in 1946, immediately after Africans were able to organize parties legally. Between 1949 and 1952 it lost a series of elections and by-elections, but only because the French administration had tampered with the ballot.

[2] "Patron" parties and "parties of personalities" are terms employed by Thomas Hodgkin, author of *Nationalism in Colonial Africa* (London, Muller, 1956). "Cadre" party is used by Maurice Duverger in his *Political Parties* (London, Methuen, 1954).

Officially, then, some candidates of the allied patron parties of Ivory Coast won, but the PDCI resumed its monopoly of offices as soon as the voters could register their choice freely once more.

I. MASS AND PATRON PARTIES

The main distinction between mass and patron parties lies not in the social origins of aspiring national leaders, and not in the scale of party organizations. It lies rather in the reply to the questions: How are the national leaders related to the rest of the population, and on what groups and with what ideas and structures did they build their parties? The distinction is perhaps best seen first at the local branch level.

Mass parties generally sought the adherence of every single individual. They wanted to enroll each man, woman, and even child, and so they had to establish local branches with headquarters, regular meetings and elections for branch leaders. Examples are the *Parti Démocratique de la Côte d'Ivoire* or the *Parti Démocratique de Guinée* (PDG) of Guinea. The patron parties usually terminated their structure simply with the adherence of influential notables or patrons; these were mostly the officially recognized "chiefs" or their direct representatives. Examples are the *Union Nigérienne des Indépendants et Sympathisants* (UNIS)*[3] of Niger, the *Parti Progressiste Soudanais** (PSP *sic*), the *Bloc Africain de Guinée** (BAG) or with qualifications, the *Northern People's Congress* (NPC) of Nigeria. Most patron parties did little to reach every individual in the community, and relied upon the "patrons" for their local influence. A defection from the local branch of a mass party rarely led to the disintegration of the branch. But the defection of a local notable from the patron party seriously weakened it in the locality.

Mass parties, such as the *Parti Démocratique de Guinée* of Guinea, the *Union Soudanaise* (US) of Mali, the *Convention People's Party* (CPP) of Ghana, the *Action Group of Nigeria,* the *Union Progressiste Sénégalaise* (UPS) of Senegal, the *National Council of Nigeria and the Cameroons* (NCNC), the *Parti Démocratique de la Côte d'Ivoire* of Ivory Coast, and the *Comité de l'Unité Togolaise* (CUT) of Togo counted their numbers in the hundreds of thousands. First organized around an anti-colonial platform, they claimed to "represent 'all the people'; to embody the national will . . ."[4]

Several structural concepts elaborated by Duverger and applied to Moroccan parties by Rézette[5] can be usefully employed in connection

---

[3] Parties indicated with an * have gone out of existence.
[4] Hodgkin, *op. cit.,* p. 144.
[5] R. Rézette, *Les Partis politiques marocains* (Paris, Colin, 1955).

with the tropical African parties. At least for a time, most mass parties were strongly articulated, relatively disciplined and called forth considerable direct participation from members, in varying degrees roughly indicated, in descending order, by the sequence of their listing above. The leaders of these parties emphasized organization partly because they opposed the established authorities and could not use established institutions. They usually created parallel women's and youth organizations. They published newspapers, set up central and regional headquarters, hired permanent staff, distributed membership cards, charged dues, and especially before independence, synchronized activities and shared personnel with African trade unions. The more effective their organization, the more mass party leaders were in a position to implement their decisions. *Union Soudanaise* and *Parti Démocratique de Guinée* leaders, for example, regarded their mass parties as "weapons"[6] designed to achieve independence and economic development with the greatest speed possible.

In contrast, most patron parties—*Parti Progressiste Soudanais**, for instance, and *Union Nigérienne des Indépendants et Sympathisants**— were weakly articulated, comparatively undisciplined, with little if any direct membership participation. This difference in structure between mass and patron parties is one of several reasons why, though mass parties took the place of patron parties with a regularity suggesting a definite pattern, so far no mass party has ever been replaced by a rival in free election.

Closely related to structure was the pattern of authority within the party. Not all but some of the mass parties had both institutionalized and collective leadership, such as the *Union Progressiste Sénégalaise,* the *Action Group of Nigeria,* the *Union Soudanaise* and the *Parti Démocratique de Guinée.* Elections were fairly regular; officers gave some account of their stewardship to the members; discipline was given serious attention; a predetermined procedure was followed when important decisions were to be made. Patron parties, and a mass party such as the *Parti Démocratique de la Côte d'Ivoire* after 1950, had essentially personal leadership; leaders, either as individuals or as a group, made decisions and reconciled conflicts in ways unfettered by pre-arranged rules. The parties with institutionalized leadership could deal far more smoothly with the problems posed by renewal and succession.

For an understanding of the authority pattern within the parties a

[6] David E. Apter and Carl G. Rosberg, "Nationalism and Models of Political Change in Africa," *The Political Economy of Contemporary Africa,* Symposia Studies Series No. 1, The National Institute of Social and Behavioral Science, George Washington University, 1959, p. 8.

modified notion of charisma is sometimes useful,[7] provided it is not understood simply as "the polar opposite of formal and traditional bonds,"[8] or taken to mean the total "absence of any defined hierarchy."[9] Thus some, but not all, mass party top-level leaders—Sékou Touré of the *Parti Démocratique de Guinée* and Mamadou Konaté (d. 1956) of the *Union Soudanaise*—enjoyed a type of charisma which was limited both by the constitutional procedure they themselves insisted upon within their mass parties, and by the power exercized to a greater or lesser extent by other groups and individuals within the party. Other leaders, particularly of patron parties—such as Fily Dabo Sissoko of the *Parti Progressiste Soudanais** and Sourou Migan Apithy of the *Parti Républicain du Dahomey** (PRD)—used their charisma comparatively unchecked by procedure, though limited by the power and influence of the "patrons." This was also true for some mass party leaders, such as Félix Houphouët-Boigny of the *Parti Démocratique de la Côte d'Ivoire*. Still other leaders, like Lamine Kaba of the Kankan region of Guinea, enjoyed charisma only within a locality considerably smaller than a territory. Their gift, usually recognized by only one ethnic group, came to be regarded as a threat to national party discipline. The notion of charisma, denoting extraordinary qualities ascribed to an individual, is a useful starting point for further investigation. But it is only a starting point; perhaps sharper than the idea Carlyle expressed with "Find in a country the Ablest Man . . . raise him to the supreme place . . . what he tells us to do must be precisely the wisest, fittest . . ."[10]

The distinction between mass and patron parties has implications beyond those already discussed—local branch organization, size of membership, patterns of authority, and structure. It illuminates also variations in social composition, methods and function. Before turning to these, however, we must look somewhat more closely at the total society in which West African parties sought support.

II. MODERN AND TRADITIONAL ELEMENTS

The West African societies in which ten new sovereign states emerged between 1957 and 1960 were at an earlier stage of economic and social

---

[7] David Apter, *The Gold Coast in Transition* (Princeton, Princeton University Press, 1955).

[8] Max Weber, "The Sociology of Charismatic Authority," *From Max Weber*, H. H. Gerth & C. Wright Mills, eds. (London, Routledge & Kegan Paul, 1952), p. 250.

[9] Peter Worsley, *The Trumpet Shall Sound* (London, MacGibbon & Kee, 1957), p. 271.

[10] Thomas Carlyle, "The Hero as King," *On Heroes and Hero Worship* (London, Ward & Lock, 1900), p. 262.

history than the retiring colonial powers. The specific figures are less reliable than the generalizations they are designed to illustrate. As a result of the reforms extended after the Second World War, the vote became universal in a society where—on very rough average—fifteen per cent could read or write, perhaps three per cent were regular wage earners, and another three per cent were employed away from their villages. Considerably more than half the people's efforts still went into subsistence activity outside the exchange economy.[11] In Europe, by contrast, the vote became general only after almost everyone was deeply involved in the market economy. Indeed, not even the middle classes could vote until after the emergence of the "commercial civilization from the feudal, the society based on contract from the society based on status."[12] Not so in West Africa. Although there is an educated elite— mainly clerks, teachers, nurses, doctors, lawyers, and low-level techni-cians—only Senegal, Ivory Coast, Ghana, and southern Nigeria have a growing minority of literate Africans self-employed in trade, transport, and farming for export.

Several hundred different ethnic groups make up the approximately sixty million inhabitants of the new West African nations. The educated minority is almost alone in seeing a clear interest in maintaining the present territorial frontiers, or in enlarging them, and in preventing tribal separatism from fragmenting the new nations. With a few excep-tions, the existence of this elite, its size and even its distribution accord-ing to ethnic and geographic origins, were due to the forces of economic and social change accompanying the arrival of the Europeans in West Africa. Much more economic activity took place in the coastal and forest belt of West Africa, and the proportion of people educated from that region is far greater than from the savannah and *sahel* belts. This caused trouble both for parties and for nations. Northern Nigerians, Ghanaians, and Ivory Coasters, for example, resent having too many party organizers, too many civil servants, and too many government leaders come from the southern regions of their countries. Some seeds of the 1958 riots against Dahomeans in the Ivory Coast were planted before the war, when the French West African educational system trained an unusually high proportion of them.

The political facts of colonial rule, and then the democratic reforms extending over some two decades, sped up the process whereby the modern layer of African society acquired the lead politically, even

[11] See Elliot Berg, "The Economic Basis of Political Choice in French West Africa," [this volume], esp. Table I on p. [610].

[12] Colin Clark, *The Conditions of Economic Progress* (London, Macmillan, 1951), p. 567.

though it was still so small a minority. The European powers enlarged the scale of West African political units from the many tribal to the present territorial ones. Together with their new technology they introduced or reinforced secular values such as equality and merit, weakened traditional religious sanctions, and overthrew kinship as the main determinant of rank. Although the British believed in indirect rule and the French in direct rule, in varying degrees they both undermined the secular authority of the pre-European authorities.

There were few areas in which the presence of the Europeans did not add yet another dimension to the already thorny issue of succession. Pre-war "native authorities," or members of the *commandement indigène*—the official "chiefs"—did not necessarily also have a traditional claim to high rank. These categories seem to have overlapped most in the savannah region of the western Sudan, where such historic pre-European empires as Mali and Ghana existed, and where in the nineteenth century the Europeans could not install their administrations until they had defeated the warrior-kings, Samory Touré and the sons of Hajj Umar Tall. The official "chiefs" were no regular mobile civil servants recruited by standards of merit; few were literate; they were for the most part stationed among their kinsmen. In time, these official "chiefs" constituted a new stratum of the population in the country-side, with a sense of corporate identity transcending the limits of their different ethnic groups. They were aware that the postwar reforms affected the "prestige of the chiefs, precedence, deportment, decoration, housing, salaries."[13]

This awareness developed farthest in Northern Nigeria, in Mali, Niger, and the plateau and savannah regions of Guinea. It became the basis for the more successful "patron" parties, including those now behind the single-party governments of Northern Nigeria, Niger, and Mauretania. In Mali and Guinea also, the patron parties which won in the postwar elections until defeated, in 1956, by the *Union Soudanaise* and the *Parti Démocratique de Guinée* mass parties respectively, were based on these "chiefs." It was therefore in these territories particularly that the struggle against the colonial power barely masked another struggle, most acute in the countryside, between traditionalists and modernizers. In Mali and Guinea the mass party leaders, as soon as they were in a position to do so, consolidated their electoral victory by doing away altogether with the official "chiefs" and replacing them with regular civil servants, assisted by elected village councils. In Niger and Northern Nigeria, however, the challenge to the "chiefs," though already offered

[13] From the electoral manifesto of September 5, 1945, issued by the *Parti Progressiste Soudanais* leader, Fily Dabo Sissoko.

by the respective opposition parties—*Sawaba* and the *Northern Elements Progressive Union* (NEPU)—has not yet been successful.

Even before the war educated Africans rather than traditional or official "chiefs" were increasingly sought out by their kinsmen to help them settle controversies with the Europeans and their laws. After the war, by the order in which they came as well as by their content, the reforms in West Africa helped the educated elite to assume the political initiative. (The recent history of the Congo illustrates, by contrast, the importance of this by-product of a reform phase preceding total independence.) In West Africa, most people took it for granted that Africans elected to postwar representative posts would know how to read and write in English or French—if only to talk to the Europeans who had promulgated the reforms. Moreover, in most territories the franchise was initially weighted in favor of those who were able to identify themselves in the records kept by the colonial power—which meant the literate and those earning money, mainly the people in the regular civil service, and only to a lesser degree those recognized as candidates for official "chief." The reforms gave the educated Africans legal channels for organizing the expulsion of the colonial power. They had reason to want to. Most of them lived in towns, saw Europeans often and were directly affected by the discrimination—racial, cultural, social and professional—which characterized the prewar colonial system.

The postwar reforms strengthened the position of the educated elite further by synchronizing political developments in areas of unequal political pressure, and by forcing even those traditional leaders who could still count upon the following of their ethnic groups, as in Mauretania or Northern Nigeria, to select educated "front men" for the new elective offices. Moreover, because the reforms extended over approximately two decades before full independence came, aspiring leaders had time to build records as nationalists, to champion opposition causes in the countryside, to build parties, and so anchor their authority to some degree. Nationalism gave the educated elite a powerful theme: to make all Africans once again masters in their own land. With a few exceptions this educated elite, rather than the traditional aristocrats or official "chiefs," got the credit for expelling the European colonizers.

Major or minor parties, mass or patron, these educated men staffed them. They provided the candidates for the new government offices after the war, they took the seats in legislative assemblies, in cabinets, and public corporations; they filled the senior civil service posts. A majority of them were of the first generation in their families to read or write a language other than Arabic. They had been trained in schools designed to produce only subordinates for Europeans in that phase of colonial history when all senior posts were reserved for Europeans. Many were only primary school graduates; a minority—significantly larger in southern Ghana and Nigeria, which were richer, than in French-speaking Africa—went to secondary school. Only a tiny number graduated from universities.

Since most university places only opened up to West Africans after the war, few graduates were available to take the first offices. Nearly all of these had to content themselves with second-level posts, usually in the civil service. Some, indeed, were in the peculiar position of working under African ministers who were contemporaries, but who had failed the secondary school or college entrance examinations—which had left them free to take part in the crucial first years of postwar political activity, and so to become "founding fathers." The mass franchise, in effect, added yet another reason why, for the modern elite, the standards of success in the schools of the Europeans were often the reverse of the standards of success in African elections. Under the prewar conditions of total European control, the most educated generally acquired the highest of the subordinate offices open to Africans. But after the war, when the villagers acquired the vote and so became arbiters in the competition for power among members of the elite, those with only a primary school education often spoke the language of the people and exhibited talents which appealed to the villagers.

While the state schools helped weaken ethnic and historic antagonisms, they also created new cleavages among the educated elite, which in some territories acquired some political significance. For example, in postwar Guinea most of those who had been prewar students in the dominant French West African secondary school, the École Normale William-Ponty, wanted to keep the only paying jobs open to them. These were invariably in the civil service and so they had little alternative, prior to 1956, but to go into "administrative" parties. Most of them joined one of the officially preferred regional patron parties. The mass party in Guinea, the *Parti Démocratique de Guinée,* was led by products of the lower state schools, who accused Ponty graduates of "betraying the masses," and called them "valets of the administration." In Gold Coast (now Ghana) also, political and educational cleavages were to some degree superimposed when the "Standard VII boys" joined a radical breakaway from the more highly educated leaders of the *United Gold Coast Convention** (UGCC) and built the *Convention People's Party.* In Ivory Coast, by contrast, Ponty graduates took the lead both in the regional "patron" parties, and in the mass party—the

Parti Démocratique de la Côte d'Ivoire. There Ponty graduates found alternatives to administrative employment in cocoa and coffee farming. Consequently in Ivory Coast political cleavages did not relate closely to differences in the diplomas achieved by members of the elite.

Apart from levels of education, differences of generation also made for cleavages among the elite, such as those which divided the Senegalese leaders of the *Bloc Démocratique Sénégalais** (BDS)[14] from the leaders of the Senegalese federation of the *Section Française de l'Intérnationale Ouvrière** (SFIO);[15] or the young organizers of the *Convention People's Party* from the older leaders of the *United Gold Coast Convention.** There are differences in ideology too: Marxist-inspired for the *Parti Démocratique de Guinée* and the *Union Soudanaise;* a blend of Catholic and socialist political doctrine for many leaders of the *Union Progressiste Sénégalaise.* These differences are sharpest in the minor parties organized by university trained graduates: dissident-marxist for some leaders of the *Parti du Régroupement Africain* (PRA) —*Sénégal;* close to orthodox Communism for the leaders of the Senegalese *Parti Africain de l'Indépendance* (PAI); an Africanized version of Emmanuel Mounier's French Catholic social doctrine for those participating in the *Mouvement Africain de Libération Nationale* (MLN). There were also differences in status, distinguishing in Senegal, for example, the prewar privileged "citizens" in the SFIO* from the "subjects" in the *Bloc Démocratique Sénégalais;** the former had earlier access to education, more wealth often from the peanut trade, and higher jobs in the civil service.[16]

These differences within the modern elite were balanced, however, by a certain common outlook. They conceived of themselves as Africans rather than Malinke, for example. Their common experiences in schools, jobs, and in the money economy, in prewar town associations, and with colonial administration gave them a homogeneity. But no such common outlook linked all the elite to the mass of the population. Instead, a separation gradually developed, most marked among people several generations or several decades removed from the village, *e.g.,* the "citizens" of Senegal or many of the French- or British-trained university graduates. Africans building parties to bridge this gulf after the war had to work with peoples mostly ignorant of French or English. Yet these were the languages expressing the modern constitutional decisions, including the decisions to introduce the universal franchise. Few had ever been to a large town and most had never lived in one;

[14] Forerunner of the *Union Progressiste Sénégalaise.*

[15] In 1958 both groups merged into the *Union Progressiste Sénégalaise.*

[16] For further details, see Kenneth E. Robinson's excellent chapter, "Senegal," in *Five Elections in Africa,* edited by him and W. J. M. Mackenzie (Oxford, 1960).

almost all handled money rarely and lived far from roads or railroads. The African organizer who came into a village to solicit votes was at the same time a transmitter of news of a modern world. This world was symbolized by the airport located perhaps fifty miles from the village, if the distance is reckoned in physical mileage; but several hundred years away if the distance is plotted against the timetable of European economic and social history.

Grass roots politics are different from national politics in most parts of the world, and particularly great in Africa. The educated elite are few in number and disproportionately distributed over even the most important of the many ethnic groups and regions of various types. The gap is large between the traditions which inspired the formal governments of the new nations and the pre-European institutions. To some extent most people continue to relate themselves to political parties through a "screen of kinship," a fact which made it necessary for all successful parties—mass or patron—to develop skill in "ethnic arithmetic" when selecting leaders and candidates. This skill is at the core of the new African parties' methods of approaching the important work of social integration.

III. THE INTEGRATING FUNCTION

In illuminating the functions of the parties, the mass-patron distinction again has meaning. Patron parties fulfilled only the minimum tasks assigned to parties by the formal institutions; they integrated only the patrons. With the possible exception of the *Northern People's Congress,* these parties were interested in an individual only insofar as he happened to be included in the franchise; they provided candidates for election and the minimum machinery for bringing the voter to the polls. They paid little attention to the function of political education, and barely explained the context of the postwar reforms to the population.

By contrast, the functions of mass parties were far more complex and varied. On occasion, before they acquired government responsibilities, mass parties disregarded—indeed replaced—the existing legal institutions. To the extent that for a time they substituted, or proposed to substitute, their structure for that of the state—that they developed their own ways of administering justice or of keeping order—these parties filled a revolutionary function. (Though in West Africa, unlike Cameroun or Algeria, none waged guerrilla war.) For some time the population considered them, far more than the legal institutions conceived in London or in Paris, to be legitimate. By agreeing to work at least partly within the postwar representative institutions, therefore, these parties legitimized the formal structure, rather than *vice versa*. Coincidentally, these parties acted as national "melting pots," educating people as Africans. Insofar as they provided a new social framework for people no longer firmly rooted in a stable ethnic tradition, they can be termed "parties of social integration."[17] They and their cultural affiliates were interested in everything from the cradle to the grave—in birth, initiation, religion, marriage, divorce, dancing, song, plays, feuds, debts, land, migration, death, public order—and not only in electoral success.

An analysis of the modern and traditional status and ethnic origins of national and local leaders shows how the mass parties performed this integrating function. This analysis is particularly important, since the achievement of independence in West Africa allowed shifts in the distribution of power not only between Europeans and Africans, but also within African society—between the modern and traditional elites, within each of these groups, and in the links connecting them with the mass of the population.

Perhaps the best approach is the relatively simple question—what group or sub-group predominated in the major parties? Trade unionists predominated within the *Parti Démocratique de Guinée* and were of great significance in the *Union Soudanaise* and the (outlawed) *Sawaba* mass party of Niger. African planters formed the *Parti Démocratique de la Côte d'Ivoire,* and people associated with the cocoa export trade were influential in the *Action Group of Nigeria.* The educated former "subjects" constructed the *Bloc Démocratique Sénégalais** to challenge, in effect, the "citizen"-led socialists. All these dominant groups were in the modern categories of the population, a feature all mass parties had in common and shared with only those few "patron" parties that were based on a prewar town elite.

Who predominated in those patron parties resting on important village personalities? The distinction between mass and patron parties, in relation to local party structure, was less neat in fact than in definition. When first organizing, aspiring mass party leaders did not disdain to accept the backing of an important local personage—an official chief, a traditional aristocrat, a Muslim *marabout* or an animist sage. But partly because most mass parties were born after the war either as or out of anti-colonial "congresses,"[18] locally important persons in West Africa connected with the colonial establishment usually held aloof until the mass party was itself becoming the establishment. Then many "shifted their rifles from one shoulder to the other."[19] Most important local

[17] Sigmund Neumann, *Modern Political Parties* (University of Chicago Press, 1956), p. 404.

[18] Hodgkin, *op. cit.,* p. 144.

[19] Madeira Keïta, "Le Parti unique en Afrique," *Présence Africaine,* février-mars, 1960, pp. 19–20.

personages without modern education who became identified with the mass parties during the height of the independence struggle—*la lutte anti-impérialiste*—had special reasons for lining up against the colonial administration, usually connected with a local quarrel over chieftaincy, prestige or property. Many rivals to the official "chiefs," at the village or regional level, joined the mass parties at an early stage. However, when such a personality became included locally within the mass party, the methods of the mass party worked to control his local influence, to make of him but one among many. There were, of course, variations in degree, related to mass party structure and to the type of tribal political organization.

Where there was an educated urban middle class, also identified both for cultural and economic reasons with the colonial power, its members hesitated too before becoming associated with the radical, anti-colonial mass parties, usually initiated by younger, less educated men, less acceptable to the Europeans. The clearest examples of this were in Senegal and in Gold Coast (Ghana). The prewar "subjects," shortly after they acquired the vote in 1945, broke from the "citizen"-dominated SFIO* of Senegal to organize their *Bloc Démocratique Sénégalais**. Similarly in Gold Coast the younger, more radical men broke from the *United Gold Coast Convention** to organize the *Convention People's Party*.

Thus in some areas, in spite of their many differences, a prewar town elite holding the highest positions permitted to Africans in the colonial system, and the official "chiefs" already conscious that the presence of the Europeans stabilized their position, made common cause in patron parties against mass party leaders. The lineup of "haves" against their "have not" challengers was evident in the epithets exchanged at election time. Urban patron party leaders called mass party leaders "vagrants" (Guinea), "veranda boys" (Ghana); in the countryside patrons underlined that their rivals were "slaves" or "strangers." Mass party leaders, for their part hurled labels like "union of featherbedders" at the patron party leaders.

In varying degrees, the nationalist struggle helped stir up "loyalty" issues, national and local, frequently with the result of providing yet another cause for disintegration in an already fragile society. For where they could, those lower on the traditional or modern social scale used the issue of nationalism to strengthen their own position through the mass parties. And those with privileges to lose, as in Niger or Nigeria, showed signs of preferring rule by the Europeans to rule by the *talakawa* (commoners in Hausa). Especially in the countryside, showing loyalty to the mass party when it was under pressure from the colonial power, was one way to compensate for a weak claim to belonging to the local ethnic group—for the immigrant *dioula* ("strangers") in Ivory Coast to show they were as loyal, for example, as the *originaires* who first came to the area.

With so few in the educated elite, and a subtle network of kinship connecting leaders and followers, it was logical that leaders of both mass and patron parties organized on a territorial scale should have gone through the first and simplest stage of "ethnic arithmetic": they kept a rough correspondence between the ethnic origins of leaders and followers. This correspondence is at least as important in Africa as in Boston or New York City politics. Defeating a patron party which has not been through this first stage was relatively easy for mass party leaders—as when, the *Bloc Démocratique Sénégalais** used "favorite sons" in the Casamance region of Senegal, to defeat the SFIO* which was locally (as well as territorially) dominated by Wolof and Lébou from Dakar or Saint-Louis. Leaders who tried to build national parties failed when they did not have among their ranks representatives of the most important ethnic groups. The Socialist party of Guinea was in this category. It grew from the Fulani club at the École Normale William-Ponty and never really succeeded in broadening its ethnic base, even though it underwent several important changes, from an ethnic to a nationalist ideology. Too many of one ethnic group, too few of another, caused jealousies and difficulties for any party. The *Parti Démocratique de la Côte d'Ivoire* had relatively little trouble with ethnic separatism from the Baule, while the *Convention People's Party* had considerable difficulty with the Ashanti. These two ethnic groups, traditionally related, occupy similar historic and geographic positions in their respective states, produce most of the coffee and cocoa and so have the most wealth. The PDCI from the beginning had Baule associated with them through the person of their leader, Félix Houphouët-Boigny; while in Ghana the CPP started, and except in the revolutionary years 1949–1950 remained, without similar support among the Ashanti. They are conscious of losing power to southerners, and "young men" "on occasion lament with their more conservative elders the present absolute reversal of Ashanti fortunes."[20]

While patron parties' leaders, once through this first simple phase of "ethnic arithmetic," generally stopped their calculations there, the leaders of mass parties had taken that as a point of departure. They tried to use their party organizations in order to awaken a wider, national sense of community. They appealed to particular categories existing within or cutting across ethnic groups—a technique suitable to re-

[20] Dennis Austin and William Tordoff, "Voting in an African Town," *Political Studies* (Oxford), June 1960, p. 131.

cruiting in a mobile, changing society. Youth and women were of course two such categories which mass parties emphasized heavily. As already noted, in many villages mass party organizers went to rivals of official "chiefs"; from these they discovered local grievances. They often appealed to rural underprivileged groups. For example, the *Parti Démocratique de Guinée* first gained a following in the Fouta Djallon plateau not among the Fulani majority, but rather among the "captives" living in the ancillary villages (*roundé*). They appealed to rural scribes, whose modern skills set them apart, and to those who had travelled, often "strangers" who were among the most recent immigrants to a flourishing agricultural area. In some areas they went to veterans—in Ghana, for example, and in Senegal. They sought out religious dissidents—Harrists in the Ivory Coast, Hamallists in Mali. In some areas they found Muslim proselytizers opposed by the "chief"—either because he was animist, or because though Muslim he nevertheless felt his secular position under attack. They found camel drivers, chauffeurs, transporters, and peddlers—such as the *dioula* traders of Western Upper Volta, Mali, Guinea, and Ivory Coast, or some "Hausa" traders of Ghana and Nigeria. (Many of these in fact came from families with a tradition as middlemen in the trans-Saharan trade before it declined under trans-Atlantic competition.) Finally, they appealed to those who earned money income for growing coffee, cocoa, peanuts or bananas, and had become restless with tradition; to young men who no longer listened to the old; and to women who made money trading in the marketplace. People responded to the mass party organizers' appeals against established authorities.

People in these non-ethnic social categories were still in a minority, to be sure; most of them had some roots in a tribal community and they too wanted party leaders of roughly similar origins to their own. Mass party leaders were well aware they needed associates who were kinsmen of those they sought as followers, even while many rejected the principle that ethnic considerations should enter into the selection of party office holders. Indeed, conflicts among ethnic groups were often sharper in mass than in patron parties, since mass parties made a continuous attempt to propagate modern values and diminish the weight of ethnic exclusiveness. For example, after their 1956 victories, both *Union Soudanaise* and *Parti Démocratique de Guinée* leaders developed the habit of deliberately scrambling the ethnic origins of party propagandists and their audiences. Men from the Guinea coast campaigned in the forest and Fouta Djallon; men from Upper Guinea in the forest. All these tactics had the purpose of encouraging people to relate themselves directly to the party.

Conflicts between modern and traditional leaders were also often sharper in mass than patron parties since most mass parties were egalitarian by policy. The traditional upper-class standing of Sékou Touré or Modibo Keïta, for example, was important because of the high popular esteem given to them. The *Parti Démocratique de Guinée* began to make headway among the Fulani after Diallo Sayfoulaye, the son of an important Fulani chief, "like La Fayette . . . left his privileges to join the democratic cause."[21] Félix Houphouët-Boigny, in the militant years of the *Parti Démocratique de la Côte d'Ivoire* before 1952, used his prestige as official chief, and not only as a doctor and wealthy planter, in order to entrench the PDCI in the countryside. On the whole, they used their nobility to preach equality.

The majority of the national and regional leadership in patron parties is of traditional upper-class status, while the majority of the mass party national and regional leadership is of commoner origin. But mass parties have a surprisingly large number of people with high traditional status as the top national party leaders. And patron parties have an exceptionally large number of prime ministers, or officials holding the first post in the modern institutions, with low traditional status. (Is this a method of chiefly control, reminiscent of their habit, at the turn of the century, of sending not their own but sons of slaves to the schools of the Europeans?) Alhaji Abubakar Tafawa Balewa, the Northern Nigerian designated by the *Northern People's Congress* to become Prime Minister of the Federation of Nigeria, is of low traditional status. So is Joseph Conombo, who until 1956 was deputy to the French National Assembly from Upper Volta, elected through a patron party based on the Mossi chiefs. So was Yacine Diallo (d. 1954), Guinea deputy to the French National Assembly representing the then dominant patron party alliance, and more specifically the Fulani chiefs. So is Hubert Maga, Prime Minister of Dahomey, who represented a regional patron party strong in Northern Dahomey. It is as if "princes" fear least the competition of "captives"; while villagers, first hearing equality preached, learn fastest from "princes."

Thus within mass parties, not only ethnic origins but also ethnic status continue to count, often causing more conflict precisely because mass party ideology usually ignores or challenges these differences. Yet men with high modern but low traditional qualifications—Ponty graduates of *griot*[22] descent, for example, lawyers descended of "captives"— were rarely put forward by local mass party branch members as candidates for elective office. In varying degrees, mass party national leaders

---

[21] *La Liberté*, PDG newspaper, December 22, 1955.
[22] Traditional caste resembling medieval troubadours.

usually maintained a continuous pressure in favor of such nominations, as of West Indians and other "strangers," to prove they believed in equality. (Precisely so as to be able to maintain this pressure, mass party leaders often preferred multi-member to single-member constituencies in legislative assembly elections. Where ten seats were to be filled, local branch members were more inclined to accept some candidates that national headquarters designated, than where only one seat was involved.) Though they tried much harder than patron party leaders, mass party leaders did not always succeed in avoiding institutionalizing ethnic differences. So in the long run, friction among ethnic groups in Ivory Coast may have been intensified by the *Parti Démocratique de la Côte d'Ivoire's* decision to organize local branches on an ethnic, rather than a neighborhood principle. This distinguished the PDCI local structure from that of most other mass parties. The *Union Soudanaise,* the *Parti Démocratique de Guinée,* and the *Union Progressiste Sénégalaise,* for example, made strenuous efforts to mix ethnic groups at the local level—and did so at least to the extent that neighborhoods did. The PDCI decision was a recognition of the way people actually communicated in Ivory Coast, a concession to reality, unwillingly made by many educated leaders because they knew they might need to assemble their followers rapidly. It was challenged by a PDCI Congress resolution in 1959, as yet not implemented.[23]

The various methods used by mass and patron parties further illustrate the differences between them. Patron parties adopted methods respectful of established authority. They rarely called mass meetings and until 1957 generally avoided the techniques of protest, offered few if any personal services to supporters, and were little concerned with party symbols. The mass parties, prior to achieving government majorities, employed techniques related to their revolutionary, legitimizing, educational and social integration functions. Demonstrations, strikes, boycotts and occasional violence were revolutionary techniques. The parties paid considerable attention to the creation of new national symbols: insignias, colors, slogans, party cloth for women to wear. The *Action Group of Nigeria* even hired American public relations advisers. Mass party choices of symbols and slogans were based on sound insight into popular responses, and repetition is at the heart of African oratory, as of drumming and dance.[24] "Vote the elephant; he is wise and never forgets." The *Parti Démocratique de Guinée* and the *Parti Démocratique de la*

---

[23] *Abidjan-Matin,* June 18, 1959. See A. R. Zolberg, "Effets de la structure d'un parti politique sur l'intégration nationale," *Cahiers d'études africaines,* October 3, 1960, p. 140 ff.

[24] Unless otherwise indicated, I recorded the citations in Africa.

Côte d'Ivoire painted the elephant on walls and roofs and streets and cars. In the savannah, however, the *Union Soudanaise* never made much of the fact that the elephant was its symbol also; for there *Union Soudanaise* opponents said with effect, "the elephant eats your crops and leaves you destitute." The *Action Group of Nigeria* adopted the palm tree as its symbol of the "life more abundant." Elaborating on the meaning of the *Bloc Démocratique Sénégalais* * party colors, Léopold Senghor of Senegal wrote "Green is for the Muslim majority, the color of the Prophet's flag; green is for the Christian minority, the color of hope; green is for the animists, the symbol of youth and the irrepressible force of Black Africa."[25] And using the elimination of forced labor to their ends, aspiring mass party *Union Démocratique Nigérienne* *[26] leaders of Niger whose ballot carried the picture of a camel, warned people not to vote for the patron *Union Nigérienne des Indépendants et Sympathisants* * party which had a yellow ballot bearing the picture of a stick and a basket. "Vote for the camel, and you will be as free as he," they said, well acquainted with that ornery beast. And they added, "The yellow ballot is a stick and a basket; if you vote for it forced labor will come back." The *Northern People's Congress* made *salama*—"peace"—its slogan. Prayers were often connected with party ceremonies, and so a libation was poured in connection with *Convention People's Party* and *Parti Démocratique de la Côte d'Ivoire* meetings, or the Fatiha (opening *sura* of the Koran) was intoned prior to some *Parti Démocratique de Guinée* meetings.

Personal oratory was one of the most effective educational techniques. Campaigning against the Guinea regional patron parties during 1954–6, Sékou Touré explained, "I am Diallo the shepherd from the Fouta, I am Mamba the planter from Nzerekore, Keïta the rice grower from Siguiri, Soumah the fisherman from the coast, I am African, I am every man." Both because they believed it, and because the "important people" in the countryside opposed them, most mass party organizers preached equality. "Vincent Auriol and Lamine both die if they go hungry." Or, "three men want to go to Bamako. The governor goes by plane, Mamba by bicycle, Yacine on foot. Who arrives first?" "The governor," shouts the crowd. "Next?" "Mamba." "Then?" "Yacine." In such dialogues leaders communicated the idea that the environment accounts for most human differences.

The identification of the mass party with the community before independence was emphasized not only by party sponsorship of dances,

---

[25] *Condition Humaine, Bloc Démocratique Sénégalais* * newspaper, November 30, 1948.
[26] The forerunner of *Sawaba*.

festivals, songs, receptions, by party organization of weddings or funerals, but also by the existence of an informal party social security system which resulted in support for indigent partisans, legal advice for imprisoned militants, payment of medical bills for the sick, food and housing for families of party widows or grass widows, as well as automatic hospitality for party-sponsored travellers. On occasion the mass party could count on free labor even for the construction of bridges, roads and schools—on popular good will that the *Parti Démocratique de Guinée* and *Union Soudanaise* leaders termed human investment—*investissement humain*—and included in their inventory of economic resources.

IV. DEMOCRACY AND THE SINGLE-PARTY SYSTEM

The nationalist struggle strengthens the position of the educated elite in largely traditional societies and encourages the elite to knit into mass parties the forces for change and dissent, both traditional and modern. There is not yet evidence to show that the trend from patron to mass party majority continues after independence. The distinctions between and among mass and patron parties turn on differences in degree, and some parties fall between the two categories. Is the *Parti Démocratique de la Côte d'Ivoire,* for example, losing its mass party characteristics and becoming a patron type? The efficiency of its organization has declined, as has its interest in social equality; there have been many signs of rising discontent; it has been increasingly unable to cope with ethnic separatist pressures. The *Northern People's Congress,* on the other hand, because of its growing emphasis on mass recruitment, may be moving towards the mass party type. Despite these transitional cases the distinction between types is useful.

It is useful in considering the now popular question: how far are the West African single-party systems democratic? I use "democratic" to mean, roughly, that decisions are made with general consent, according to established procedures, in harmony with such values as social equality, and under conditions in which opposition can be expressed. It is difficult to argue that West African single-party systems resting on patron parties are or are becoming democratic, notwithstanding variations in degree. Northern Nigeria has been mentioned. Least in Mauretania, somewhat more in Niger and Upper Volta, can significant evidence be found of general consent, of social equality as a value, or of opportunity to express opposition in the dominant party. The main opposition groups are outlawed. Of the single patron-party states it is easier to argue they are moving towards military dictatorship.

In the present phase of West African party history, there is more evidence that the single-party systems based on mass parties are moving towards democracy. There is, first, the element of widespread consent. During at least a brief period the territorial and party communities were indistinguishable; the mass party reflected the "general will." This was usually just prior to taking over responsibility for governing, but after using to advantage the fact of being in opposition. Discontent was the common denominator. Typical of the instructions national mass party leaders gave to local leaders were, "Go and talk to the peasants in the field." "Tell Abdoulaye his daughter cannot be forced to marry the old chief." "Tell the peasants not to sell their crops at that ruinous price." "Defend Pango's palm trees against destruction by the administrator." "Speak up for Binta's right to cultivate the land the chief claims." While not all the questions were settled, villagers found a national platform in the mass party which they had never known. Mass party organizers sought out grievances, expressed them in the market-place, coordinated them. They blamed European rule for forced labor, taxes, abuses of official "chiefs," racial discrimination, poverty. Out of these grievances they welded their massive demonstrations against colonial rule. Most patron party leaders were too linked with the established authorities to play this muckraking role.

Muckraking paid. Mass party membership was open to all, and practically all sought to acquire it. This characteristic of recruitment distinguished West African states based on mass parties from states based on single parties confining their membership—as most fascist or Communist parties do—to a selected group. The widespread influence and number of followers of the mass parties at their peak, their national character long before the institutions of government were controlled by Africans, their success in acquiring the credit for the national revolution —all these bore out the mass party claim to represent the entire population. This helps explain why many West African mass party leaders saw little contradiction between claiming to be democratic and insisting on the existence of only a single, mass-based party. It is the African version of that "sole and central power which governs the whole community, by its direct influence,"[27] which de Tocqueville observed in the nineteenth-century American idea of the state.

The prospect of democracy in West African mass party states is enhanced, second, by party organization and procedure. Mass parties, at their best, have developed the organization which can publicize and encourage the mass discussion of important issues. Local branches involve the many rather than honor the few, and mass party leaders

[27] *Democracy in America* (London, 1952), pp. 550–51.

try to use traditional organizations in order to reach individuals. They are often more effective than the civil service. Leaders are chosen by voting. In the thoroughly organized mass parties, institutionalized leadership was also collective. Set procedures were followed for the making of decisions and leaders were expected to report back. Thus the mass parties reenforced the African version of responsibility.

Mass parties strengthened democratic forces, in the third place, to the extent that they encouraged social equality. The modern elite, themselves in favor of such values as merit rather than birth as the determinant of rank, were in a stronger position in the mass party states. Moreover, most mass party leaders rose from lower positions both in the modern and the traditional social scale, and used their new power in favor of social equality. Though they had to employ both ethnic and status "arithmetic" to bridge the gap between the educated and the mass of the population, mass party leaders, unlike patron party leaders, did so in a manner to blur ethnic differences and weaken status differences.

The fourth contribution of mass parties to the prospects of democracy is setting conditions in which opposition is possible. Among the elite, there is enough consensus about the rules of the political game to make it possible for them to disagree without coming, too often, to blows. After all, in prewar Senegal, as in nineteenth-century Britain or present Southern Rhodesia and South Africa, the vote, and controversies among the several parties, remained confined to a few who spoke the same language and fought for similar interests. In the long run in Africa, restricting the franchise to a privileged few is a greater threat to democracy than the existence of but a single party. At the present stage of African social history, the mass party organization makes it possible for people to disagree within it, without necessarily triggering incidents endangering the rule of the elite and the stability of the state. Confining disagreements to the issues at hand is difficult in a society where only the members of an educated elite born of different ethnic groups are able to speak directly to each other in French or English. Even where the organization of a mass party is a "spider's web"[28] villagers often have different ideas than national leaders. Sékou Touré spoke of this to the Fifth Congress of the *Parti Démocratique de Guinée* in September 1959:

. . . democracy, within our Party, is not a democracy of clan or family, but a basic democracy to which the entire population contributes di-

[28] The term is frequently used by the *Union Soudanaise* secretary general, Modibo Keïta.

rectly and freely . . . the old forms of social democracy anchored in the villages often influence the party militants, who believe themselves authorized to violate the new individual forms prescribed within the PDG. Therefore at each new election for officers, dissensions arise within the Movement. This occurs because we have not yet accomplished our work.[29]

As long as kinship is an important link between the educated and their rural constituents, divisions among the elite on such constitutional matters as federalism, independence, or the position of "chiefs," is often taken by their kinsmen as a signal for settling entirely unrelated traditional issues over land, women or water. This was one of the dynamic factors behind the Kumasi riots which accompanied the *Convention People's Party-National Liberation Movement** (NLM)[30] controversy about constitutional matters after 1956. A similar dynamic helped to explain the Ivory Coast incidents of 1949–51. In the relatively integrated societies of North America or Western Europe, pluralism is quite rightly counted among the democratic virtues. In Africa today, it is rather a vice.

These four points back up the argument that West African states based on dominant mass parties are moving towards democracy. West Africans justify their insistence on a single party on yet other grounds—that a national emergency exists. The struggle for independence is "not the concern of a day, a year, or an age; posterity are virtually involved in the contest. . . . "[31] These words of Tom Paine's reflect the African sense of history.[32] Africans argue the plural "party system under imperialist domination is synonymous with a sterile division that profits only those who want to see to it that their privileges continue."[33] This is the logic of a community at war, considering an *administratif* to be like a "quisling." Most Africans carry their sense of urgency into the post-independence era, and consider unity necessary in order rapidly to "install the apparatus of the State, at the service of economic development, of social and cultural development."[34]

[29] *Official Report* (Conakry, 1959), pp. 43–4.
[30] After 1957 the United Party.
[31] "Common Sense" in *The Political Writings*, Vol. 1, Investigator Office (Boston, 1856), p. 33.
[32] For a most interesting discussion of the new history of West Africa, see Immanuel Wallerstein's paper delivered to the 1960 meeting of the American Sociological Association, "The Search for National Identity," mimeographed.
[33] Alexander Adandé, "In the Phase of National Reconstruction the Fusion of Parties Becomes a Categorical Imperative," address at the Congress for Cultural Freedom Conference, Ibadan, March 1959, mimeographed, F/413, p. 3.
[34] Madeira Keïta, *op. cit.*, p. 9.

While there is good evidence for the argument that West African states based on dominant mass parties are moving towards democracy, there is also evidence of forces moving against. How does a mass party continue to reflect the "general will" after independence? The full responsibilities of government have already brought out centrifugal forces—opposition within the mass parties from its youth, labor and traditionalist affiliates. Some officials have used their public office for personal gain. There have been signs of ethnic separatism, particularly on international frontiers. Rural friction intensified between "strangers" or *dioula* and the original owners of tribal lands. It appears, as Thomas Hodgkin claims, that the logical consequence of self-determination is anarchy. Yet perhaps even a greater threat to democracy is the fear of anarchy, making new African governments as quick to pass Preventive Detention Acts as the United States was to adopt the Alien and Sedition Acts in 1798.

What opportunity is there in the mass party states to express disagreement? This varies. *Within* the mass parties the greatest opportunity appears to exist in the best organized ones. So far discussion is widespread and frank—within the *Parti Démocratique de Guinée* and the *Union Soudanaise,* for example—and leaders have on many occasions been outvoted on important issues. Not only individual disagreement is possible under the party umbrella, but also organized disagreements by *tendances*—such as trade union, youth, student and cultural organizations, even the civil service. In the less highly organized mass party states, such as Ivory Coast, the Eastern Region of Nigeria, Senegal and Togo, these modern associations tend to be foci of opposition outside of the mass party, though not necessarily calling themselves parties.

The opportunity to express opposition through rival political parties also varies. In no West African mass party state is *all* organized opposition to the dominant party directly excluded by law, though specified parties or types of parties are outlawed in most states. It is excluded in effect, however, where it is a matter of doctrine to insist on the single party, the *parti unique,* and on its identity with both the popular will and with the state. It is less excluded where leaders justify the single party for empirical reasons as a *parti unifié,* making common cause in the present national emergency. Where single-party states are based on patron parties, opposition groups exist which are already or potentially mass parties; at least in Niger, Northern Nigeria, and to less extent Upper Volta these have considerable momentum behind them. But in mass party states, from among what groups has organized opposition come? There are "one-man shows" such as the *Union Démo-*

*cratique et Sociale Africaine** of Guinea or the *Front de Libération Noire** of Ivory Coast; rump groups left over from mergers or reorganizations, like the post-war *Parti Socialiste Sénégalais** and the "expatriate" groups such as the *Parti de la Libération de la Côte d'Ivoire* in Guinea; these have simply curiosity value and generally exist only for a short time. Limited staying power also characterizes parties like the *Parti de Solidarité Sénégalaise,* built by disaffected "clan leaders" and other rural personalities. Numerous ethnic minor parties exist in the countryside, such as the *Union Dogon** of Mali, or the Socialists among the Bété of Ivory Coast. When ethnic parties are based on urban areas, their supporters usually belonged to the tribes which originally owned the land—the *Rassemblement Démocratique Sénégalais* among the Lébou of Dakar, for example.

Standing alone these ethnic parties have little potential on the national scene. But they might have in inter-state politics if, for example, Guinea leaders used as an instrument of pressure the loyalty to the *Parti Démocratique de Guinée* of ethnic groups living on the frontiers of Liberia or Sierra Leone. Or there might be a future in federal politics if well organized teams of educated leaders synchronized the discontent among minority groups—as the *Action Group of Nigeria* has done in the North and the *National Council of Nigeria and the Cameroons* has done in the West of the Federation. The political history both of Nigeria and the former French West African federation suggests that federalism adds to the prospects for organized opposition groups. Partly this is because the desire to control the federation offers mass party leaders dominant in one region incentives to seek support in another. Furthermore the desire to work together in a federation is a reason why leaders of the dominant party in one region may at least hesitate before repressing opponents having political support in another region.

Most significant are opposition groups among "young Turks," mainly town-dwellers differently educated or younger than the men leading the dominant parties: JUVENTO in Togo, *An Nahda al Watenia al Mauritania* (Party of the National Renaissance of Mauretania), *Parti du Regroupement Africain-Sénégal,* and the *Parti Africain de l'Indépendance* of Senegal. With the possible exception of the PAI, these avant-garde groups had no conscious elitist theory governing recruitment, but in practice their audience is still confined to the modern elite, to youth and student and trade union groups. Particularly when the party in power is of a mass type, most of these groups alternate between opposing it, and joining it in order to constitute a "party within a party." These "young Turks" are nationalists and modernizers.

They have little appetite for ethnic, separatist opposition of the type loosely allied in the *United Party* of Ghana.

The "young Turks" constitute the actual or potential national, not ethnic, opposition. They might be joined, eventually, by breakaway groups from among the "founding fathers."[35] As long as the elite is small, the civil service is likely to absorb the most newly educated strata of the elite—and dominant parties will brook no partisan opposition from within the civil services. On economic development depends the growth of the modern strata of African society in large enough numbers, and spread evenly enough across ethnic groups, to permit opposition party leaders to calculate in ethnic and status "arithmetic." The chance of opposition groups eventually displacing in elections the dominant mass parties in the single-party states, may increase as the "national emergency" ends. Independence is mostly acquired. Now in West Africa, unity for economic development is the order of the day.

There are, in the mass party states of West Africa, obstacles to the growth of democracy, as in most other parts of the world. But on balance, to a much greater extent than the colonial governments which they succeeded, the mass party states rest on popular consent, strengthen procedures and institutions on a scale essential for accomplishing the tasks of the modern democratic state, reflect egalitarian values and leave room for the expression of opposition. So far, the mass party states have used to good effect the emphasis on

union, a word like friendship, goodness, an abstract thing having no face, raising no concrete image in the mind. It goes into all sauces; it accommodates itself to irreconcilables.[36]

[35] Julius Nyerere suggested this in "Africa's Place in the World," *Symposium on Africa* (Wellesley College, Wellesley, Mass., 1960), pp. 162–3.
[36] *La Liberté,* November 23, 1954.

The Use of Power

K. W. J. POST

University of Ibadan

In 1951 the three major Nigerian political parties were given an opportunity to gain power in a system which was intended to put one group firmly in control in each Region. We have seen that this had a powerful attractive effect during and immediately after the elections, with independents and even members of rival parties declaring for the party which seemed strongest.[1] The constitutional changes of 1954 gave more power to the governing parties—removed central control over Regional legislation, for example—and so enhanced the power of each party in its own Region. In their dealings with their opponents and the ordinary electors the major parties did not hesitate to insist that they were "the party in power" in their own Regions. It was a slogan used as much in the election of 1959 as in previous elections, even though that was a Federal, not a Regional election. As a result, it was commonly believed that the various parties would use their control of the Regional governments to preserve and increase their own power, and the wealth and influence of their supporters. Such a belief was a great incentive to cleave to the party in power, and it undoubtedly helped to keep the parties together after 1951, while their actual organizations were still being developed.

It may be noted that each Regional government had gradually acquired a number of public boards by 1959 which could be used as a means of dispensing patronage to party worthies. The various Housing Corporations, Information Services, Cinema Corporations, Library Boards and Printing Corporations had their quotas of members who were active politicians. This was made more obvious by the occasional appointment to these Regional bodies of party stalwarts from outside the Region: in 1959 there was, for instance, an Eastern member of the Western Region Housing Corporation, and a Western member of the

Reprinted from *The Nigerian Federal Election of 1959* (London: Oxford University Press for the Nigerian Institute of Social and Economic Research, 1963), pp. 55–66, with the permission of the author, the publisher, and the Institute. Several minor contextual changes have been made.

[1] *The Nigerian Federal Election*, pp. 26–55.

Eastern Printing Corporation. The first was the Leader of Action Group's Zone A in the East, and the second was President-General of the Zikist National Vanguard, an auxiliary of the NCNC. It was not unknown for a prominent party member to be given a place on one of these boards as compensation for failing to secure nomination in a Regional or Federal election. A man who had been successively a teacher, a Public Works Department timekeeper, a soldier, a railway-man, and the proprietor of an institute for the healing of the sick through the "psychic sciences" found himself appointed to the Cinema Corporation. In any case, a politician appointed to one of these bodies would be expected to pay a percentage of his salary to the party.

Control of the Regional governments did not give the major parties an opportunity merely to appoint members of public boards; they were also able to influence the decisions of a number of bodies which had very considerable sums of money at their disposal. The Marketing Boards, which came under the control of the Regional governments in 1954, had large reserves, the result of their purchase of cash crops from the farmers at a guaranteed price each season and sale of them on the world market at a price which for a number of years was considerably higher than that paid to the farmer. Various Finance and Development Corporations were empowered to spend money, drawn from these re-serves and other sources, on projects designed to increase the economic activity of Nigerians and promote the welfare of the people. In addition to this the new Regional governments were in a position to spend large sums of money, even before 1954, on projects such as road-building. The opportunity for a share in the funds thus disbursed was a powerful incentive to the new men to continue to support the party in power. The Action Group and NCNC thus contained extremes among their members. At the highest level could be found a group of men who might, in fact, lose money by neglecting their businesses or professions for the sake of politics, but who found their reward in the power and prestige of office and in the feeling that they were helping their people. At the local level could be found the small contractor who hoped by showing zeal for the cause to be given work by the local council which his party controlled.

It is impossible to assess how far government boards showed fa-vouritism towards members of the party which controlled them. It was commonly believed in 1959 that this was the case, but widely held be-liefs are not necessarily true ones. Nevertheless, there is frequently a close connexion between business and politics in modern political sys-tems, and such was the case in Nigeria. As in other countries, it is diffi-cult to isolate these connexions in detail, but enough evidence is available to enable us to see some of the connexions between governments, parties and private business.[2]

In general any remarks which are made will apply to the South, but not to the North. The origins of the Northern People's Congress and the social forces which it represented differed in important respects from those of the Action Group and NCNC.[3] There were business interests in the NPC in 1959, but they showed no signs of becoming as dominant as their Southern counterparts.

In the South politicians were often also businessmen and would frequently go into business with one another. In September 1952, for instance, the Aboki Trading Company was formed in Lagos; its directors were Kola Balogun, a lawyer and National Secretary of the NCNC, and F. S. McEwen, a school proprietor and principal, and at that time prominent in the NCNC Youth Association and Lagos politics in general.[4] Again, in April 1955 the Ideal Commercial Syndicate was formed in Sapele. Two of its three directors were Chief Gabriel Ekwejunor-Etchie, a prominent local Action Group leader, and Chief Arthur Prest, Action Group Federal Minister of Communications from 1952 till 1954. When the latter began to move away from the Action Group (he was finally expelled in November 1957) he ceased to be a shareholder and was replaced by a relative of Chief Ekwejunor-Etchie and the Secretary of the Action Group branch in Sapele.[5]

There were not only business connexions between individual politicians. The parties themselves were part of rival business and financial structures which existed to make money for the individuals concerned and provide financial backing for the parties. When Dr. Azikiwe returned to Nigeria in 1937 he set out to build up for himself a commercial empire based on the Tinubu Properties Ltd., which speculated in Lagos real estate, and on the *West African Pilot*, the chief organ of the nationalist movement. In 1948 the Tinubu Properties Ltd. became the African Continental Bank, which was re-formed as a public company in June 1950.[6] The directors were Dr. Azikiwe, his father, and his sister; of 111,935 ordinary shares issued by the end of 1954, Dr. Azikiwe held

[2] Much of the information which follows is taken from the returns of public companies kept at the Federal Ministry of Commerce and Industries in Lagos, and published periodically in the *Nigerian Trade Journal*. The author is deeply indebted to Mr. J. D. Nyhart for allowing him to draw on his research files.

[3] This point is elaborated in *The Nigerian Federal Election*, pp. 38–43 and 50–55.

[4] McEwen succeeded Balogun as National Secretary in November 1957.

[5] At the time of the Federal election of 1959 the latter was Organizing Secretary for Action Group in Warri Division.

[6] For general information about Nigerian banking at the time when the parties were forming see W. T. Newlyn and D. C. Rowan: *Money and Banking in British Colonial Africa*, Oxford Studies in African Affairs, O.U.P., 1954, Chapter V.

28,000 and his father, sister, and her two young daughters, 4,000 each.[7]
By 1956 Dr. Azikiwe's companies included the Nigerian Real Estate
Corporation Ltd., Nigerian Commodities Ltd., Suburban Transport
Ltd., African News Agency Ltd., Nigerian Printing Supply Co. Ltd.,
Nigerian Paper Co. Ltd., the African Book Co., Zik's Enterprises Ltd.,
the *West African Pilot* Ltd., and Associated Newspapers of Nigeria.[8]
As Mr. B. J. M. MacKenna, Q.C., put it in his opening speech as counsel for the Foster-Sutton Tribunal, which was set up in 1956 to examine
the affairs of these companies and the African Continental Bank, "The
principal use made of the public deposits [in the Bank] was to finance
the Zik Group of companies.[9]

By 1955 these companies had lost at least £98,000 and five of them
showed deficits over their original capital. In all 56 per cent (£321,000)
of the Bank's total funds had been loaned to one or other of Dr.
Azikiwe's companies, the main function of which was to produce the
Pilot, his chief political organ. Some £170,770 of these loans and over-
drafts had been guaranteed by two Eastern businessmen, L. P. Ojukwu
and N. M. Ugochukwu.[10]

In 1955 the African Continental Bank was insolvent, with a ratio
of cash held to customers' deposits of about 8 per cent. The Banking
Ordinance of Nigeria, which came into force on May 22nd, 1952, gave
all banks three years in which to qualify for a licence, which depended
on a liquidity ratio of 30 per cent. On May 20th, 1955, an agreement
was made by the Eastern Region Finance Corporation to invest £800,000
in the Bank; the money had come from the Eastern Region Marketing
Board, and was part of a transfer of £2,000,000 from the funds of the
Marketing Board to the Finance Corporation. At this time, Dr. Azikiwe
was Premier of the Eastern Region, and L. P. Ojukwu was Chairman
of the Marketing Board. This injection of capital raised the value of
the Bank's shares from nothing to 14s. 10d. each, and it was the demand
by E. O. Eyo, an Ibibio and an erstwhile lieutenant of Dr. Azikiwe,

[7] The information on Dr. Azikiwe's businesses is mainly drawn from the *Proceedings of the Tribunal Appointed to inquire into Allegations of Improper Conduct
by the Premier of the Eastern Region of Nigeria in Connection with the Affairs of
the African Continental Bank Limited and other Relevant Matters,* Lagos, Federal
Government Printer, 1957. Details of shareholdings in the Bank are in paragraphs
5,525–35, page 205.

[8] In 1959 the last group included the *Southern Nigeria Defender* (Ibadan),
Nigerian Spokesman (Onitsha), *Eastern Sentinel* (Enugu), *Eastern Nigeria Guardian*
(Port Harcourt), and the *Daily Comet* (Kano).

[9] This view was confirmed by Dr. Azikiwe in his evidence before the Tribunal:
see paragraphs 22,043–4, page 826.

[10] Details of the position of each company can be found in the evidence of
Mr. S. P. Wilkins, the chartered accountant who acted on behalf of the Tribunal,
more especially paragraphs 5,500–5,524, pages 204–5.

that this be investigated which led to the setting-up of the Foster-Sutton Tribunal.[11]

This, then, was the complex financial and business substructure upon which the NCNC was based. The various companies and the African Continental Bank were used to finance its newspapers. Dr. Azikiwe used his own personal fortune, made from his business ventures, to help finance the party; at the Jos Convention in December 1952, for instance, he donated £5,000 in cash and revenue-bearing securities to party funds.[12] Alternatively the Bank would make loans to the party for special purposes, like the one of £50,000 at 4 per cent interest which was revealed during the proceedings of the Tribunal.[13] Sometimes, however, the relationship would apparently be a purely business one; in 1954 Zik's Enterprises made a profit of about £8,000 from the sale of party buttons to NCNC. Above all, the dangers of mixing politics and business are very apparent. In 1955 the Bank and most of Dr. Azikiwe's businesses were virtually bankrupt, and had to have a large transfusion from Eastern Government funds, which fortunately for the party were controlled by the NCNC, in order to restore them.

The financial position of the party and the businesses in 1959–60, the year in which the NCNC was called upon to make its greatest effort to win power at the centre, was obscure. The companies tended to publish their balance sheets several years late, and an interlocking system of loans and shareholdings disguised the individual position of each. The sales of the *Pilot* appeared to be declining.[14] Private sources —often, however, opposition ones—in the East would quote figures of indebtedness to the African Continental Bank—£350,000 for the *Pilot*, £150,000 for the NCNC itself. In his report to the Annual Convention held in Lagos on September 10th and 11th, 1960, the National Secretary, F. S. McEwen, confirmed the shaky financial state of the party. Between January 1957 and July 1960, that is in the period which included the Federal election of 1959, the NCNC had spent approximately £1,200,000. In the same period its income "from all sources" had "not exceeded" £500,000.[15] The position of the party would have been even worse had it not been able to draw on the credit of the African Conti-

---

[11] See the evidence of Mr. Wilkins, paragraphs 5,190–212, page 195.

[12] In all £25,000 was raised on this occasion.

[13] See the evidence of Mr. Wilkins and E. O. Eyo, paragraph 5,366, page 200, and paragraphs 12,925–36, page 487. The money was to form a campaign fund for the Western Regional election of 1956.

[14] A notice appeared in the issue of September 17th, 1959, for instance, saying that because of "difficulties in collecting dues and unco-operative attitudes of Registered Readers" in Zaria these would be discontinued, and the paper could now be bought only from hawkers.

[15] F. S. McEwen, *NCNC on the March*, the NCNC National Headquarters Bureau of Information and Publicity, n.d. page 14.

nental Bank, a credit which from May 1959 was that of the NCNC controlled Eastern Region Government. In that month the Eastern Minister of Finance announced that the Bank had been completely taken over by the Eastern Region Development Corporation.[16] The Chairman of the Corporation, L. P. Ojukwu, was to be Chairman of the Bank, and F. S. McEwen the Acting General Manager.

The Action Group was also based upon a group of banking and newspaper concerns, the National Bank of Nigeria Ltd., the Amalgamated Press of Nigeria Ltd., and Allied Newspapers Ltd. The Amalgamated Press published the main party organ, the *Daily Service,* and in October 1959 launched the new *Sunday Express.* Allied Newspapers was a company set up in February 1959 to publish a chain of newspapers which the Action Group was establishing in all three Regions.[17] Its Managing Director was Editor-in-Chief of the *Daily Service.*

The National Bank was one of the oldest Nigerian banks. It was incorporated in Lagos as a private company in February 1933, with a nominal capital of £10,000. In September of the same year the Mutual Aids Society, a loans company, was incorporated with it. By 1951 it was banker to the Federal Cocoa Marketing Board (since superseded by Regional Boards) and had accounts from the United Africa Company, Elder Dempster, G. B. Ollivant, and other expatriate enterprises. Its paid-up capital in that year was £38,220, deposits amounted to £870,540 and loans, advances, and other accounts totalled £762,170.[18] Thus in 1951 it differed from the African Continental Bank in being an enterprise run according to purely commercial principles and with a large number of shareholders, most of them with small blocs of shares. From 1951, however, it became associated with Action Group. Two of its six directors in 1959 were Dr. Akinola Maja, for many years a leading Lagos businessman and known in the Action Group as "Father of the Party," and Alhaji S. O. Gbadamosi, the party's Federal Treasurer. The biggest single shareholder was the Western Region Marketing Board, which the Action Group Government had directed to invest £1,000,000 in the Bank in October 1955.[19] The next largest holding was that of a Lagos moneylending firm, with 27,470 shares. The balance sheet of the

[16] *Daily Times,* May 7th, 1959.

[17] This group included the *Mid-West Echo* (Benin), *Eastern Observer* (Onitsha), *COR Advocate* (Uyo), *Middle Belt Herald* (Jos), *Northern Star* (Kano), and the *Bornu People,* published in Jos but intended for Bornu. More on these will be found in Chapter VIII, [*The Nigerian Federal Election of 1959*]. In addition there was the *Nigerian Tribune* (Ibadan). This was published by the African Press Limited, which existed before the Action Group, until July 1st, 1959, when it was transferred to the Allied Newspapers group.

[18] Newlyn and Rowan, op. cit., pages 106–7.

[19] In April 1961 the Government of Western Nigeria took full control of the National Bank.

National Bank for 1958–9 indicated the total assets as £16,070,916 and the profit for the year as £43,851. The years since 1951 thus showed a considerable increase in the Bank's business.

One of its interests was in the Amalgamated Press. Among the shareholders of this Action Group publishing company, according to its latest returns in 1960, were Obafemi Awolowo and S. L. Akintola, who together owned a block of 1,000 shares. T. A. Odutola and Akinola Maja were also shareholders, along with such original members of the party as Akanni Doherty, A. A. Akinsanya, and S. O. Shonibare. The major shareholder, however, was the National Bank, with 53,700 shares, the result of loans to the company of £45,000 in 1954 and £115,000 in 1956.[20] Like its NCNC counterpart, the Amalgamated Press ran at a loss; by 1959 it had apparently lost £158,950 altogether. The Action Group was fortunate in having a bank connected with it whose credit was strong enough to enable the party's major newspaper to appear despite this handicap.[21]

We have now seen that each major Southern party was supported by a bank, which in particular was responsible for keeping the party's main newspaper alive, and that each bank had in the past received a very substantial injection of public money from government agencies, the respective governments being controlled by the different parties. This raises the whole intricate question of the use made by each party of the funds of the various Regional Marketing Boards, Finance Corporations, and Development Corporations. Constant allegations of favouritism and corruption were a normal part of Nigerian political life, but never proved.[22] The Foster-Sutton Tribunal provided the one instance of an investigation into the use of such funds, and it concluded that the action of the NCNC Government in putting public funds into the African Continental Bank was not a desirable one. This did not prevent Dr. Azikiwe from winning a massive majority at the election he called in the Eastern Region shortly after the report of the Tribunal appeared.

The whole matter is obscured by the fact that many of the Southern politicians were also successful businessmen. If it was the function of the

[20] Of the thirteen other shareholdings, one was that of the Service Press, which was absorbed by the company in 1953, the five non-Action Group directors being dropped (the sixth was Akinola Maja). Another was held by Chief Akintola in his own name alone. A third was held by Mrs. Awolowo.

[21] In August 1960 the Amalgamated Press entered into partnership with Roy Thomson, the owner of newspapers in Canada and Great Britain, and replaced the *Daily Service* with the *Daily Express*.

[22] In April 1960, for instance, Chief T. A. Odutola was awarded £1,000 damages by a Lagos High Court in a libel action against the *West African Pilot* and its editor. It had been alleged that his loans from the Western Region Development Board had been given for political reasons.

public boards to encourage Nigerian enterprise, then often these were the men who would be encouraged if economic factors alone were considered. Popular opinion, for what that is worth, held strongly to the view that there was discrimination against businessmen who happened to hold political views different from those of the Government of the Region. Certainly the various boards in each Region had been brought under the control of the governing party, the Eastern and Western since 1954, the Northern rather later.[23] Some of the loans made to prominent politicians were, in fact, made before this development, but the knowledge that he was in debt to the Government's Finance Corporation for a considerable sum must have been a powerful factor in deciding a man's allegiance, as would be the hope of further loans in the future. Not only this, but in at least one case, in the West, a prominent politician who had been loaned a total of £4,250 by the Development Board before his party took control of it had the interest on the loan waived later. Without going into the vexed question of morality, it may be concluded that there was a general failure in Nigeria to distinguish between public, party, and private financial interests, and that this gave the parties the opportunity to increase their own strength in a number of ways. One last example of the relationship between private enterprise, public money, and political profit may be given. This was the series of loans made by the Western Region Marketing Board to the National Investment and Properties Co. Ltd., a real estate and construction company formed in Lagos in April 1958. The four shareholders, with 25,000 shares each, were Akinola Maja, S. O. Gbadamosi (Action Group Federal Treasurer), S. O. Shonibare (Action Group Federal Publicity Secretary), and Alfred O. Rewane, Chief Awolowo's political secretary. The loans totalled £2,300,000, the share capital of the company being nominally £100,000. Amongst other ventures the company provided the £20,000 to set up the new Action Group newspaper chain, Allied Newspapers, in February 1959.

Business then added another dimension to politics in Nigeria in 1959. It created new interests and relationships, new allegiances and obligations. It helped to bind together the major parties more closely, to attract to them the support of people who hoped thus to advance their business careers. Of the major Southern parties the Action Group had perhaps the soundest business basis, drawing on a wider range of successful entrepreneurs. Once more the Northern People's Congress differed from the other two. It had no bank of its own, and the new Bank of the North, founded in 1960, may have been intended to fill that gap. The delay in the gaining of Regional independence for the

[23] The Northern Region Development Corporation had an expatriate official as chairman until March 1957.

North and the more prolonged dependence upon expatriate officials held back the assertion of political control over the public boards. The NPC had no newspaper publishing company of its own, though the setting up of one was discussed as early as October 1953.[24]

Finally, the different roles played by merchants and businessmen in the ranks of the NPC, the Action Group, and the NCNC may be noted. In the Southern parties they played a vital part, filling some of the most important offices, both in the national hierarchy and in local organizations. In the North, however, they did not on the whole enjoy great political influence.[25] This is not to say that they were not wealthy men. In 1937 Margery Perham remarked that in Kano

The richest are the sellers of kola nuts and those who may by courtesy be called lodging-house keepers. Some years ago it was estimated that one of these made £15,000 a year.[26]

To these had been added by 1959 dealers in cotton, groundnuts, and hides and skins, the vital primary products in the Northern economy, transport owners and cattle dealers. One of the last-mentioned in Jos paid £2,100 income tax for the year 1958–9. Despite this, the traditional limitation upon the position of merchants in Hausa-Fulani society still held good. Traditionally wealth could earn respect, but it could not buy rank, so that the political activity of the merchants was restricted to using their surplus wealth to finance the emirs in their wars and display and the lesser officials in their various schemes to further their careers. The merchants still fulfilled this function and they now also helped to finance the activities of the NPC.[27] A typical instance of the latter is to be found in a report of a speech by the President of the Kaura Namoda Northern People's Congress branch, praising a trader who had donated the money to build a local party headquarters, and another wealthy local trader who was a patron of the party.[28] In the emirates merchants

[24] The main newspapers in the North were the *Nigerian Citizen* and the *Gaskiya Ta Fi Kwabo,* published by the Government's Gaskiya Corporation. They were not prone to take an anti-NPC line. In February 1961 it was announced that the NPC and a "Federal Press Company" were about to launch the *Daily Mail.*

[25] There were a few notable exceptions. Ibrahim Musa Gashash, an important Kano merchant and businessman, became Northern Region President of NPC in 1952 and a Northern Minister in 1956.

[26] *Native Administration in Nigeria,* op. cit., page 84.

[27] For a modern example of the former function see M. G. Smith, *The Economy of Hausa Communities of Zaria,* Colonial Research Studies No. 16, London: H.M.S.O., 1955, p. 58.

[28] See the *Nigerian Citizen,* October 1st, 1958. The second trader appeared in U.A.C. advertisements as an example of what co-operation with that firm could do. In 1959 he was the NPC candidate in Kaura Namoda constituency and lost to NEPU.

did not usually hold key offices in the party, however, either at a national level or in the local organizations.

In the Middle Belt areas, where the same traditions did not apply, the situation was different. There the structure of society as it was developing in 1959 more closely resembled that of the South. Businessmen and merchants played a leading part in local organizations and also often dominated the NPC branches with which such organizations were affiliated; Jacob Obande, the Idoma businessman whose commercial interests were, in fact, focused on Enugu, rather than Kaduna, is an example of such a local NPC leader. Taken as a whole, however, it is true to say that wealthy Northerners had been slow to adopt the business form of the limited company, the type of association which most easily allowed for preference shares, mortgages, loans from public boards, and the other means by which political relationships could be translated into business terms. This, and the traditional limitations upon their political activities in Hausa-Fulani society, had been sufficient to prevent them from becoming as influential in the NPC as in the other major parties.

This continuing emphasis upon traditional authority illustrates the basic difference between the Northern People's Congress and the major parties of the South in 1959. The "new men" of the Eastern and Western Regions were the men who controlled the NCNC and the Action Group after 1951, and used them as instruments to try to mould the new economic, social, and political developments in these Regions to their own advantage, feeling this to be the advantage of all. The leaders of the Northern People's Congress were men who derived their influence from their association with traditional forms of government and traditional status in society, which they and their predecessors managed to accommodate to the exigencies of British rule with as little modification as possible and no change in the real balance of power. In its origins and aims the NPC showed its chief interest to be the preservation of the position of these men in their respective Native Administrations, though it must not be thought that the party necessarily opposed all development and change. Where the NPC had no traditional authority to build on it was weak, as will be seen in connexion with the dispute in the Jos branch in 1958.[29] The leaders of all three major parties had as one vital factor in their conduct the use of their parties as a means of ensuring their own high status. The fact that the society of Southern Nigeria was dynamic, changing rapidly under various pressures, and the society of Northern Nigeria comparatively static, its leaders resistant to radical change, goes very far towards explaining the basic differences between the major parties in 1959.

[29] See *The Nigerian Federal Election*, pp. 130–131.

PART FIVE

Forging Territorial Unity

II

Some Reflections on the Role of a Political Opposition in New Nations

DAVID E. APTER

University of California, Berkeley

1. THE ROLE OF A POLITICAL OPPOSITION

The role of a political opposition has proved ambiguous in most newly independent nations. New governments rarely see the necessity for a regular opposition party nor do they always accept the idea of opposition as a normal feature of government. There are many reasons why this is so. Most new nations have come into being after a prolonged period of struggle with colonial authorities which has caused nationalist leaders to monopolize loyalties. Also, opposition groups having themselves been associated with nationalism at some stage of their existence, often have an anti-government reflex common to those whose political actions have been aimed at changing the fundamental character of a country rather than accepting well established rules of political life and working within them. Indeed, many opposition leaders in new nations regard the new government much as they did their colonial predecessors, i.e., as basically illegitimate.

Considering such factors as these, we shall seek to show that an opposition in new nations needs a more limited and specialized role in order to safeguard its position and gain widespread acceptance. A great deal of discretion and responsibility is required on the part of those in the community whose views differ substantially from the government's. The key features of this role will be the subject of this paper.

In order to understand why an opposition needs to find a limited but indispensable role, we must recognize the special difficulties facing political leaders after independence. New nations are plagued with almost the entire range of political problems known to man. They are beset by an accumulation of immediate and often mundane tasks such as building up adequate medical, health, educational, transport, and

Reprinted from *Comparative Studies in Society and History*, IV (1962), 154–168, with the permission of the author and the publisher. A version of this paper was read at a Seminar held by the Congress of Cultural Freedom, Ibadan, Nigeria, March 1958.

other services, as well as improvement of housing, food supplies and other basic necessities beyond the subsistence level. To state this more sharply, in most of these countries per capita caloric intake remains far below that considered necessary for ordinary labor. Vivid in the minds of many political leaders are memories of the days when, not so long ago, they slept on the verandah and suffered from want of food and shelter. Some political leaders rose from poverty and obscurity to power in a short time. Politics is their only profession. For them to go out of office is, in effect, to become unemployed.

Concern with the role of a political opposition thus appears to many such political leaders as an academic exercise, divorced from the realities of life, or at best suitable for wealthy countries where political life is less stern and the future more secure.

We shall seek to show that this evaluation of political opposition is shortsighted, even though understandable. In the day-to-day bread and butter politics of a nation, an opposition can help to determine the success or failure of a government wrestling with its problems. A political opposition is neither a luxury nor a danger. If it performs its functions well, an opposition can be of crucial service both to the government of the day, and to the people of a new nation.

In the West the idea of opposition is not often questioned. It is assumed to facilitate representation and channel diverse demands into constructive paths. This view is by no means common elsewhere. The western view of democracy as the open competition of political parties catering to diverse public needs and thereby transforming demands into policy, is not wholly accepted in most new nations. Since theirs is rather a perspective of struggle, political leaders do not regard struggle as at an end when independence is achieved. Instead they ask the public to work together for the "higher" phase. This might be liberation of a continent from colonialism, as is the aim of Ghana, or integration of a single nation out of several autonomous states as is desired in the Middle East and in parts of former French West Africa.[1] In addition most new nations are anxious to industrialize. Whatever the obstacles, industrialization is attractive to political leaders. The urge is great to catch up with the West and modernize economic and social institutions. Whether cast in the role of crusader, or anxious to produce economic growth, political leaders easily accept the view that a political opposition is troublesome and dispensable, restricting the pace of development, at least in the early years following self-government.

Hence, when we look at many nations which attained independence since the war, the outlook for the opposition appears bleak. In Burma

[1] Such as the Sahel-Benin Entente.

charges of party corruption and selfishness led to the army taking over government. It was the army rather than politicians who swept the squatters from the cities, and distributed food to the hungry. In its zeal and efficiency, the army made the politicians look like foolish men, more proficient at scrutinizing monastic texts than dealing with the problems of the day. Facing similar problems, Indonesia is riddled with factionalism. Political party conflict can be found in every organized sector of life; in the army, the trade unions, the civil service and even in clan and village organizations. The country is so divided by party conflict that even "guided democracy" is impossible to achieve. If anything, opposition there is all-pervasive. Even the government is a coalition of oppositions.[2]

In the Sudan, the independence of the nation was challenged by political groups retaining strong ties with Egypt. The army took over in part to safeguard newly won autonomy. Even in Ghana, where the opposition has certainly not been extinguished, the entire executive committee of the Accra branch of the opposition United Party was put under preventive detention.

Fear that opposition will produce factionalism, corruption, and separatism is pervasive in new nations. The opposition is often blamed for producing a situation which in fact is inherent in the post-independence period of a nation. When the cement of nationalism is weakened a new basis for social solidarity must be found. Independence is an act of parliament or a stroke of the pen. Then the real difficulties begin. There is far more to self-government than a simple administrative transfer of power. Power is left to the nationalists like gold dumped in the streets, and many are bruised in the hectic scramble to gather it up again to place it in the strong box of the nation where it can be used for public good.

New governments have a tendency to set impossible goals for themselves. To accomplish many of the objectives which they attempt to achieve, "human obstacles" have to be overcome. Some of these obstacles derive from the traditional conservatism of people who are loath to change familiar ways. But nationalist political leaders, fresh from their victory against the colonial powers, want to show the world what they can produce with freedom. They desperately desire to breathe a new vitality into their corner of the world. Hence no new nation is without its dramatic and expensive development plan. Set for five years or ten, emphasizing industry, or agriculture, or mining, each new nation

---

[2] See Herbert Feith, *The Wilopo Cabinet, 1952–1953; a Turning Point in Post-Revolutionary Indonesia* (Ithaca: Modern Indonesia Project, 1958), pp. 165–193.

seeks to fulfill the grand plan which will produce net growth, steady economic savings, high levels of investment, and material benefits for all.

Impatient of the men in the villages who push the soil with outmoded implements and cling to rural ways, the new emphasis is upon discipline, education, and innovation. Unity is the demand of the hour—and cooperation. Join the party and the nation can be free and prosperous. A house divided cannot stand.

About such matters there is no "wrong" or "right" view. At the moment of independence the need for unity is great. It is easy for responsible leaders in government to take the view that an opposition simply magnifies grievance and exploits differences. Those who won independence know that it was not granted because of the kindness of colonial officials. Fought for by those willing to risk and dare, power has been captured by the nationalists; and having won it they intend to hold it by almost any means. The result is known. Rare indeed is the responsible opposition which can prosper in such a political climate.

2. TYPICAL PATTERNS IN NEW NATIONS

New nations tend to have either a great many parties, or a single dominant party with the opposition purely nominal. The Sudan was an example of the first, with the two main parties divided over the issue of closer union with Egypt. Government was a shaky coalition between large and small parties. India and Ghana are examples of the second. They possess a large mass "Congress-type" party which grew out of the nationalist movement, while competing parties remain small and relatively helpless.

In the first instance, competition between the parties characteristically weakened the unity of the state. Indeed few examples of a successful post-independence multi-party system can be found among the new nations except Israel and Nigeria. Others show a growing public dislike of party government. There develops a characteristic desire for a strong man who will be powerful and pure, leading the nation to harmony and achievement.[3] Hence it becomes possible for a single well organized group to be popularly preferred to several political parties. This is particularly so when bitter rivalry between parties divides the public. The greater the rivalry, the more people with passionate political attachments wish for an end of party conflict; but they are less willing to accept the dominance of any party other than their own. Hence they may look to an outside force (army, civil service)

[3] See E. Shils, "The Concentration and Dispersion of Charisma," [this volume, pp. 389–406].

to save them from themselves. Excessive fear of tyranny thus produces oligarchy.

Where there is a dominant party of the congress type and a nominal opposition, factionalism and intraparty intrigue become the prevailing political style. Politics then is similar to that in a bureacracy, where each party official builds up his own support inside the party and seeks to outmanoeuvre the others.

To avoid this, mass party leaders attempt to impose discipline under the guise of fraternalism. Effectively organized, the single mass party system can become the weapon of change and discipline in a society. For example, political leaders in Ghana were struck with the Liberian system where the True Whig Party has prevailed for many generations. Conflict occurs within the ranks, but the party presents a united front to outsiders. Hence conflict and difference do not appear to challenge the unity of the party. Loyalty to the party becomes loyalty to the state.[4]

Political leaders in single mass party nations often discover that political opposition has not disappeared but is latent and underground. If, in order to prevent this, government tries to control information, public opinion (or expression of it), voluntary associations like trade unions, etc., democracy itself becomes hopeless. Often using the phrases of democratic socialism to mask a power position, government becomes the "organizational weapon" and seeks to eliminate all groups which might challenge its power. To oppose then becomes identified as an act of treason. In such circumstances, opposition must, of course, go underground. When the government becomes alive to its presence, it declares that the opposition is engaged in treason, sabotage and other acts against the state.

3. THE FUNCTIONS OF AN OPPOSITION

The problems which we have discussed are not only of concern to the leaders of governments in new nations. They are also problems for the opposition. Both need to discover issues which are popular but which will not so divide the public as to generate mutual contempt between citizens. The opposition must oppose but not obstruct. Both must nourish and preserve society by helping to transform private demands into acceptable public policy. To enlarge on this theme it is necessary to discuss the functions of an opposition in more specific terms.

---

[4] This view is shared by other observers. For example, Pye indicates that "the fact that the ruling party in most non-western countries identifies itself with an effort to bring about total change in the society makes it difficult to limit the sphere of political controversy." See Lucian W. Pye, "The Non-Western Political Process," [this volume, p. 377].

A. INTEREST REPRESENTATION

The opposition has an important task in representing *interests* which have been overlooked by the majority party. Otherwise groups in the population whose interests have not been effectively represented, can become discontented. One feature of democratic government is that while it cannot appease all interests simultaneously, it will not, for long, continue to give advantage to one group over another. The long-run prospect of equal treatment for all thus kindles an interest in government on the part of the public, and creates a faith that government will deal, sooner or later, with the problems that plague them. Increasingly the public takes an interest in its government.

Still another factor enters here. Let us make a distinction between values and interests. Values are the basic beliefs and attachments held by the public. Interests are the immediate desires which they wish to satisfy. A belief in freedom or equality is a value. A demand for assistance to cocoa farmers, or for an irrigation system, or for a local council is an interest. Interests and values are, of course, related, and the ensemble of interests is one means of judging values. However, value conflict is a different matter from that of interest conflict. The latter is competition between groups for getting their demands met. If, for example, a government is to engage in development planning, interest groups will try to indicate types of development of immediate concern and benefit to them. They may ask for a scheme to be sited at points most beneficial to them. Value conflict, on the other hand, involves fundamental beliefs about what is right and wrong. *Value conflict challenges the foundations of society as a moral order, because at the value level, such conflict cannot be reconciled except by victory in a power struggle.*[5]

The task of an opposition, then, is to express interests as the basis for the perpetuation of the values to which it adheres, rather than to oppose government on value grounds. It can do this by advocating the interests of those who feel themselves aggrieved, and by suggesting alternative policies to the government. If, for example, it is proposed to create a semi-industrial area by the use of forced savings, planned allocations of the labor force, and the commitment of resources which might otherwise be available for other schemes, opposition might arise from the population affected by the program. Ancestral land might be violated for example, or control over land hitherto vested in a particular group might be upset. Pursuing the original plan at the expense of the wishes of the local people might engender value conflict. Government, taking as its primary value the need to produce material benefit and

[5] See Bertrand de Jouvenel, *Sovereignty,* trans. J. F. Huntington (Chicago, 1957), pp. 265–266.

equality for all people, might assume that the original plan is of critical importance in achieving this. If in its zeal it rides impatiently over the interests of the local population, the opposition might well charge that individual rights are being trampled underfoot, and that liberty is impaired. There develops value conflict. Value conflict produces rupture in social behavior between people who become scandalized at one another's behavior, impairing, often irreparably, the relations between them. Government can easily leap to a position of repairing the damage by eliminating the aggrieved group in the interests of harmony and progress.

Hence, the opposition has a fundamental role to play here. It needs to act as a mediator, formulating and representing diverse interests in such a way that tact and compromise become the style of political life, rather than strife and persecution. The reconciliation of interests is one important means to this end.

B. PROVISION OF INFORMATION

Another important function of an opposition is to provide otherwise unavailable *information* to government about public reaction to a particular official policy. In this respect, the opposition keeps the government informed about the consequences of official policy.

This function is particularly important in those nations dominated by a single mass party. The assumption here is this. Where the leadership in control of government is aggressive, impatient and progress-minded, the government soon begins to lack information, because the party itself becomes identified with the state. People will not care to make known their opposition to government leaders or the local followers of the dominant party because the risks might be too great. For example, a farmer who wants a loan for developing his farm might well understand that an agricultural loans board is dominated by people from the majority party who would be less likely to give favorable judgment on his application if they knew he belonged to an opposition. The same is true for families with children seeking scholarships from the government, or jobs and sinecures. The majority party controls all the patronage and all the avenues of opportunity. Political cynicism begins to spread and the public becomes adept at producing "spontaneous support" for the leaders even if in their hearts they despise them. This is a kind of political corruption which is far more harmful than such characteristic forms of corruption as misappropriation of funds, because society is then based on delusion and deception.

Indeed, if dissatisfaction remains hidden, only to break forward in sporadic but bloody intervals, the government sits on a powder keg. Its own party gets information pleasing to the ears of government officials. The true state of affairs remains uncertain, and political leaders therefore seek to control the entire organized life of the community. To reduce the consequences of ignorance when they are denied information, government leaders use coercion. By this means they seek to avoid blame for mistakes, and so remain invulnerable at the polls.

An opposition which indicates important centers of controversy and dissatisfaction is thus performing a valuable task. If people can freely ventilate their grievance by allowing the opposition to voice them, government is thereby provided with a knowledge of sensitive changes in public opinion and can modify its policies accordingly. This helps to make political goals more realistic, and avoids that kind of political ignorance which produces coercion. Just as the fluctuations in the glass of a barometer indicate information about the weather, so the rise and fall of support to an opposition indicates to government the effectiveness of its policies.

C. EXERCISING CRITICISM AND PROVISION OF ALTERNATIVES

The opposition has the responsibility of providing *criticism* and posing useful alternatives to government policies. This function, properly performed, helps government to set goals best qualified to produce public satisfaction. On matters of budget, welfare and other major concerns, criticism keeps the government responsive to the public and aware of weaknesses in its program. This is a classic function of an opposition and does not require extended discussion here.

The three functions, representation of interests, provision of information, and constructive criticism, are the main contributions of an opposition. We shall see how these three functions relate to representative government.

4. OPPOSITION AND DEMOCRACY

An opposition capable of performing the functions we have listed is instrumental in preserving the structure and spirit of representative government if these functions operate within three important spheres. The first involves the *values of democracy* itself, the second refers to *conciliar or parliamentary control over the executive,* and the third *involves effective representation.*

Our conception of democracy is of a political system committed to democratic values, conciliar control, and representation, especially through universal adult suffrage.

All democratic systems possessing these characteristics are, in the actual practice of government, operated by a party system. Competing parties can make each of these spheres active and meaningful, or they can dull them and make them inoperative. Hence, in this sense, democracy depends upon the performances of political parties.

Israel, with a responsible multi-party system has been operating effectively in all these spheres. Ghana, for a time threatened with conflict over values, especially those pertaining to individual rights, seems now to be most effective in the first and third spheres, with conciliar control rather ambiguous. There was a time in 1957 when twenty-seven members of the backbench of the Convention Peoples Party, the government party, threatened to bolt to the other side. Government took strong action to bolster up temporarily fading fortunes and has emerged triumphant. At the moment conciliar control would appear to be weak. Other nations as well, show a mixed picture. In few can it be said that democracy is flourishing—but there is no doubt that democratic values are the dominant mode of politics. Even in Pakistan or the Sudan, there remains a strong commitment to democratic values even if, for the moment, conciliar control is in abeyance. Indeed in both those countries there remains a strong possibility that the political parties, having been chastened by the unexpected intervention of the military, will be restored to life when the army considers the moment propitious.

Political parties play the key role in the way these three spheres of democracy can work.

5. THE PRESERVATION OF VALUES

Political values are a reflection of preferences and beliefs and therefore underlie the formal or constitutional appearances of government. Political values must be shared and accepted by the people who need to be willing to support them. Confusion over political values can destroy the consensual basis for a viable nation.

To breathe life into representative institutions requires genuine commitment to democratic values. These provide the rationale for this relatively complex political form. No system can survive on purely instrumental grounds. Values become the basis for emotional feeling about the society itself. Values are the symbolic expression of political right or wrong.

What are the values with which we are particularly concerned? Those most characteristic of democracy are the product of four hundred years of struggle in the West. First there was struggle against religious orthodoxy. Orthodoxy was identified as a form of repression and dogma. *Liberty* was viewed as freedom of thought. Next, the idea of liberty was extended to include *individualism,* and the political rights of men. This took the form of struggle against autocratic monarchs. *Political equality* subsequently led to demands for economic equality with an emphasis on opportunity, fair shares for all, and public education. Through socialist criticism along these lines, and through nineteenth century notions of progress, democracy thus acquired an economic dimension distinct from private property. Today we have the notion "psychic inequality," a consequence of social inequality, and there are efforts to obliterate those characteristics of a social order which breed feelings of inferiority and shame.

Although it took the West centuries to identify and realize these values, new nations strive to achieve them simultaneously. Modern nationalism is a demand for their realization. The problem is, however, that effort to achieve one can controvert the others. A paradox emerges. Overwhelming emphasis upon any one set of the values which are characteristic of democracy leads to a denial of others. The historical experience of the West was largely a process of realizing, *in turn,* each of the values we have identified. To achieve them all simultaneously is immeasurably more difficult.

Ghana, for example, emphasizes expansion of opportunity. Political leaders wish to emancipate people from ignorance and to utilize their talents. By this means they seek to restore respect to Africans and give people of color in all nations, including South Africa and the United States, courage to fight discrimination. Ghana also wishes to demonstrate through her own achievements after independence that the colonial powers cannot presume to judge the welfare of others and decide when a country is ready for independence. Ghanaians know that the best way to achieve these objectives is by demonstrating progress in Ghana. There is concentration on economic growth while attacking tribalism, separatism, and rural backwardness. Conflict has been produced between those anxious to achieve "progress" and those whose ways are more set in favor of custom and tradition and who, if they are not bewildered, become antagonistic to government policy. Values are challenged because liberty and freedom have become practical questions of liberty and freedom for whom. These are no longer regarded as inalienable rights. From a government point of view the question is whether or not a part of the population is free to jeopardize the development of the country as a whole. The opposition charges that the majority cannot be allowed to ignore the minority on such issues. Each side challenges the legitimacy of the other's acts. Value conflict, hitherto incipient, can easily become open and manifest.

However, if we consider the case of Ghana further, it turns out that in practice, most of the conflicts over value are directly derivable from inadequate reconciliation of interests. Rarely has it been the case that what the people want, and what the government seeks to accomplish are as far apart as it appears. In performing its function, i.e., indicating to government what the interests of disaffected groups might be, pointing out the most crucial demands, communicating to government the depth of feeling and emotion involved, and proposing some compromise suitable for both groups, value conflict can be avoided through actions of the opposition.

This is not simply a matter of niceties. If there is value conflict government endangers its own success. Nothing is more desperate for progress-minded political leaders than to find that the public becomes not an asset, a pool of talent, and a reservoir of strength, but a weight to be shifted from one shoulder to the next, finally crushing those who are attempting to march forward with the burden.

Local support, and the transformation of interest conflict into satisfactory cooperation thus is possible if the opposition represents, communicates, and criticizes government policy. The public begins to share the burden of government. Otherwise plans worked out in Accra or Lagos or Cairo or Delhi, have a way of being just enough out of perspective that they have unanticipated consequences which jeopardize their success and perplex leaders. No plans are perfect.[6]

It can be argued that all this requires considerable nobility from political party leaders. Opposition leaders commonly complain in new countries that the opposition can scarcely perform its functions if its very existence is being threatened. Indeed, many of the differences which arise between government and opposition bear little relationship to problems of national progress. Quite the contrary, it is often the case that the government and the opposition shared much the same objectives in the past, i.e., national liberation and independence, and continue to support much the same aims. Often what is involved is personal conflict between men who share an intimate social environment. They know all about one another. The vulnerability of each is exposed, and exploited. It is by no means rare that when one side becomes politically dominant, the leader who is personally an anathema to members of the opposition taunts them and goads them with displays of power. In such instances the surge of resentment and bitterness which comes over the opposition leads it into acts which play directly into the hands of government. Engaged in that kind of struggle, each side pre-empts the "public interest" as their party interest.

The problem is especially acute where the opposition is a combination of brilliant and educated men joined with embittered renegades

---

[6] See the discussion on planning by W. Arthur Lewis, "On Assessing a Development Plan," *The Economic Bulletin, the Journal of the Economic Society of Ghana,* June–July 1959.

from the dominant party and with a sprinkling of confused traditionalists. Characteristically, oppositions in new countries are a blend of traditionalists, renegades and sophisticates. They fail to discipline themselves, perform erratically and inconsistently (although at times brilliantly), and do not give the government assurance that they can be relied on for responsible action.

Where the mass party is overwhelmingly preponderant numerically, the opposition is not only small in numbers, but often composed of an elite antagonistic to popular and diverse membership of a mass party. Quite often a form of "class" conflict is built into the relationship between government and opposition in which the latter is alienated by being deprived of a share in power. Meanwhile the former may have leaders who take pleasure in humiliating the self-titled aristocrats who represent all that the mass parties dislike.

If an opposition party is to survive in such a situation, it requires unusual discipline and self-control. Normally, however, such oppositions are incapacitated by their membership. Rarely can they resist personalizing the issues and maligning the motives of government leaders.[7]

A delicate tread is thus required, the more so because mass political organizations are themselves riddled with factionalism and easily threatened. The more powerful the mass party, the more intense will become intraparty intrigue and fighting. It is here that the mechanism of conciliar government becomes so important because among other things, a legislature and an election system help to transform conflict between parties by putting them in a forum in which the performance is open to the public. The public makes the ultimate decisions about which side is preferred. If government and opposition carry their conflicts outside of the parliament and into all the other institutions of the country, public and private, a struggle for pure power soon emerges. Power then inheres in the dominant party, rather than in the institutions of government, to be won and lost, in turn, through the normal vagaries of electoral fortune. And if the power of the state inheres in the dominant party, then value conflict is profound and violence and coercion lurk on all political paths.

6. CONCILIAR CONTROL OVER THE EXECUTIVE

The most burdensome problem for an opposition is to respect the legitimacy of government, when that government is dominated by a

---

[7] The question has been raised whether or not an opposition could survive at all. The assumption here is that such opposition members have the choice of nominal opposition or oblivion. The benefits of opposition are preferable to oblivion. Hence recruits to the opposition can be found, especially where they do have an impact on government policy.

party which the opposition finds abhorrent. When the distinction between government and party breaks down, then representative government is at end, because embedded in the idea of democratic government is the concept that the party is a conveyer of the people's will through the institutions of government, but is not the repository of state power.[8] Here lies one of the fundamental differences between democratic and autocratic political belief. In the former, there is a respect for the limitations of office, a belief that such office is temporary for any occupant.

The opposition has an important responsibility for preserving these ideas through its action in parliament. It needs also to perform its functions in ways helpful to government, and by doing so to facilitate the system of political representation.

An opposition has to strike that difficult balance between being an enemy and a contender for the government. If it poses a threat to a majority party such that it serves as a potential center of gravity, pulling members away from the majority party to the extent of destroying it, the opposition may be viewed as an enemy. We indicated that factionalism characterizes the mass party in power. The opposition can sometimes attract enough factions to split the dominant party. This is undesirable, because it encourages mass party leaders (especially those trained in doctrine which assumes the party is "everything") to void such threats through punitive action. Majority party leaders may be propelled toward coercion under the guise of populism and discipline. And, since the mechanism of coercion is an application of state power, i.e., police or courts, the institutions of government are brought into contempt. Neither the government nor opposition parties can long have faith in their own government under such circumstances.

On the other hand, the opposition has to pose enough of an electoral threat to the dominant party so that both develop party discipline. Although we do not have space to discuss it adequately, an underlying feature of representative government is the coherence and discipline by which parties are organized so that they can represent the public, decide policy, and put it into practice.

Party discipline is important not only for representative purposes, but it is crucial also in the sphere of conciliar control over the executive. The opposition which finds the difficult point of balance between threats to the government party and ensuring party discipline, will be respected and be able to carry out its functions in a parliamentary setting. The opposition can do this by:

[8] See D. E. Apter, and R. A. Lystad, "Bureaucracy, Party, and Democracy," *Transition in Africa,* ed. by Carter and Brown (Boston, 1958), pp. 42–43.

(1) convincing the government backbench of the correctness of opposition views on particular policy so that backbenchers bring pressure on their own party leaders; and (2) in rare circumstances, it can threaten the life of the government by a potential anti-government coalition with disgruntled government-backbenchers joining with the opposition to force a general election.

Parliamentary party discipline, however, has other effects. It promotes an atmosphere of constraint and propriety in the legislature so that reasonable discussion can prevail, despite moments when tempers become inflamed. Such a climate is necessary if the functions of an opposition are to be achieved. In such a climate issues can be more easily decided on the basis of general merit. Alternative policies can be more clearly phrased and made more comprehensible to the people themselves. In this way parliament itself can become more meaningful to the public, which expects so much from a new government and its leaders.

It takes a delicate combination of forces to produce a climate of respect for the institutions of government and a situation where issues can be made more clear, so that a concept of the public interest gradually can become identified.

If such a pattern begins to take root, a whole series of subtle constraints upon the arbitrary power of the executive can be exercised, even when there is a preponderant government majority in parliament. Instead of "cabinet dictatorship," responsible government can develop. And instead of multi-party factionalism arising (as is often the case where parties are evenly divided) the government has assurance of a strong enough majority to carry through its program.

Party discipline then gives rise to coherence. Coherence allows policy alternatives to be posed in clearer fashion. Alternatives can provide government with knowledge of the best policies to carry out, and indicate necessary modification, and in the forum of parliament, ministers can be made more responsive to legislators. In this fashion, the opposition can preserve the second sphere of representative government, i.e., conciliar control. At the same time, it can reflect, more adequately, those interests of which the government may not be cognizant, and help to prevent unforeseen political difficulties.

7. REPRESENTATION

Representation, the third sphere of democratic government, is as important as the other two. Political party competition, i.e., the struggle between the party in power and the opposition, is the life blood of democracy. Indeed one observer argues that "the democratic method is that institutional arrangement for arriving at political decisions in which individuals acquire the power to decide by means of a competitive struggle for the people's vote."[9]

By electoral means leaders are selected, a mandate for a program provided, and the public participates in the process of government. It is in competing for elections that the three functions of an opposition are carried out at the public level. They must seek out interests which they think are popular and which reflect public feeling. They need to communicate this to the public by arranging their program and ideas in a package which shows the public at a glance what the contents are. Finally, the opposition attempts to sharpen the responsibilities of the electorate by criticizing the program and policies of the government and pointing out weaknesses and failures.

Hence, the representative aspect of government, underwritten by electoral competition, requires an opposition which is allowed to perform freely. Under these conditions generalized factionalism in the country becomes crystallized into main groups. And one of the practical rules of politics which works out in normally functioning democracies is that *when there is open party competition and free elections, both parties, government and opposition, seek the support of the large middle spectrum of voters,* i.e., those who comprise the bulk of the voting population. Hence, gradually, both parties draw closer together in their ideology and their programs to the point where relatively minor differences become the issues on which elections are fought. This is the experience of every successful parliamentary system.[10]

Nor is it difficult to see why this is the case. If we take the simplest possible case, a government with a "radical" program, and an opposition with a "conservative" program, we find that in real terms, most people in the country conform to neither one extreme nor the other, but fall somewhere in the middle. That is, they are in favor of some "radical" policies and some "conservative" ones. On the other hand, the extremists on either end of the political spectrum have no hope of winning elections themselves.

The important electoral factor is the middle group and in making coherent appeals to them, neither the government nor the opposition can have an extreme program. Hence the importance of free party competition—*it does not divide where all political parties are respon-*

[9] See J. A. Schumpeter, *Capitalism, Socialism and Democracy* (New York, 1942), p. 269.

[10] There are, of course, exceptions. Where the middle spectrum does not show an identity of interest or is very small, political parties exacerbate differences. The Third and Fourth French Republics are good examples of what can happen.

sible—but instead exerts a constant pull on the parties drawing them together. It neutralizes the extremists.[11] Thus party competition is basically not divisive, as is commonly thought, but most often unifying instead.

The forms of disunity which characterize governments in new nations are thus often premature. Equally, an opposition which fears and mistrusts the government of the day helps to magnify the fears of a majority party leadership that the opposition, in its efforts to achieve power is out to destroy all. In those first years of self-government both sides need to recognize how absolutely necessary each is to the other.

8. CONCLUSION

We have indicated the challenge to opposition which has appeared in almost every new nation. Opposition, we have tried to show, is essential if the problems of governing new nations are not to engulf those in public office and impel them to coercive solutions. In representing interests, providing information, criticism and alternative policies to government, the opposition can aid government in the three critical spheres of a democratic system, namely, preservation of a belief and acceptance of democratic values, helping to control the acts of the executive by conciliar control and advice, and giving coherence and meaning to the representative system.

In addition, by serving as a rallying ground and focal point for grievance, a responsible opposition can transform potential disenchantment with government into positive channels, preventing apathy, and avoiding cynicism about democracy.

New nations need more than bargaining power to gain the respect of the world. They need to demonstrate positive achievement. A responsible opposition can help win the struggle for unity, freedom, social betterment, and racial equality.

[11] Where government is composed of the extremists these generalizations are of course inoperable. Rarely is it the case in new nations that extremists do in fact run the government.

Intellectuals, Public Opinion, and Economic Development

EDWARD SHILS
University of Chicago

I

Economic development in the West proceeded, until the latter part of the nineteenth century, without the aid of the intellectuals. Neither the innovators in technology nor the enterprisers and managers of industrial firms were highly educated, nor did they interest themselves in intellectual matters. The world of finance contained a few exceptions to this proposition, such as David Ricardo, Samuel Rogers, and George Grote, but it, too, moved without the aid of economists or other professional or avocational intellectuals. The graduates of universities stood aloof from the practical work of commerce and industry in their countries; they went into scholarship, into theology and the church, into administration (first in Germany and then gradually in the rest of the countries of Europe), into medicine and the law, but they did not enter into the central stream of the economic life of their countries. Even in Great Britain, where the intellectuals' interest in economic life was greatest, their participation in the conduct of economic affairs was minimal. In France, a little was owed to a handful of important businessmen with St. Simonian sympathies, but that was about all. In Germany, a higher education and intellectual interests were practically guarantees against sympathetic participation in creative economic activity; and in the United States, the great enterprisers were neither educated nor intellectual.

Fortunately, at the time there was no need for intellectuals in economic life. A tradition of inventive and artful craftsmanship, especially in the engineering trades and those closely related to it, and indomitable ambition and resourcefulness among businessmen provided the motors for the enormous economic progress of Europe from the six-

Reprinted from *World Politics*, X (1958), 232–255, with the permission of the author and the publisher. Acknowledgment is due to the Congress for Cultural Freedom, Paris, under whose auspices this paper was prepared.

teenth to the end of the nineteenth century. Here and there a great physicist or mathematician invented a machine which found application in industry, but for the most part their mechanical inventions were toys; by far the great majority of practical technological innovations was produced by men who worked within the traditions of a trade, as entrepreneurs or employees. The nurture of technological development through the deliberate cultivation and application of science came only at the end of this period. It was only in the present century, above all in the chemical field, that the graduates of institutions of higher learning began to play a significant part in industry, by virtue of the specific knowledge and the scientific outlook which were absorbed by them in courses of technological and scientific study. Only in the twentieth century have great laboratories of scientific research, pure as well as applied, been established by large corporate enterprises and trade associations. Plastics, synthetic fibers, light metals, jet propulsion—these and many other advances characteristic of modern industrial technique have been made through research conducted by graduates of departments of physics, mathematics, chemistry, metallurgy, aeronautics, etc., of the great universities and technical colleges. Important innovations in industrial and commercial organization have been promoted by engineers and mathematicians trained in the law schools of the great universities. Even so, a large part of the driving force of contemporary industrial development in the countries which are improving their efficiency and are substantially raising the standards of living of their people—for example, Canada, the United States, Belgium, Italy, and Western Germany—still comes from outside the educated classes. Enterprise still draws its ethos from traditions which are not widely shared by the intellectuals.

The situation of the newly emerged countries, such as India, Indonesia, Burma, Malaya, Ghana, and Ceylon, is rather different. These countries are without innovating craftsmen in industry or innovating, risk-taking, industrial entrepreneurs. Their craftsmen, however skillful, work within definite and restrictive traditions, and require close supervision when confronted by new problems; their industrial entrepreneurs on a larger scale have been chiefly foreigners, while their own big businessmen find their talents drawn to commerce and finance. The dramatic initiative for industrial development in these countries draws little sustenance from the strata which in Europe and America created an industrial ascendancy. The most enthusiastic support for industrialization and modernization comes from those who have been in contact with the West, either in Europe or America or through its intrusions and representatives in their own countries. The accepted contact with the West has been predominantly through Western educational institutions and Western-founded or Western-inspired colleges and universities at home. The type and scale of industry which the educated seek are those now existing in the West (including the Soviet Union). The undramatic germination of small-scale industrial enterprises from the efforts of ambitious independent craftsmen arouses neither their attention nor their admiration. The proponents of industrialization and modernization—although not necessarily the sole or even most effective agents—are largely intellectuals, and their conception of industrialization is largely that of intellectuals without technological education or experience of economic responsibility. In most of the new countries, prevailing opinion does not believe that industrial development will come about through the processes that produced it in the West. Planning, governmental initiative and even management, the deliberate application of scientific outlook and procedure to industrial problems—these are the means which are expected to raise the level of industrial output and efficiency. This view rests in some measure on a derogatory conception of businessmen as either exploitative foreigners or money-grubbing, short-sighted, native manipulators of financial combinations. There is no confidence in their constructive powers, and in their willingness to take risks, or even in their readiness to add to their wealth through industry. In fact, of course, this disesteem for business enterprises derives from a deeper disesteem for their function and activity as such. The intellectuals' traditional distrust of the man of business is in part a religious matter, in part a product of the scope and strength of the kinship system. Whatever the source, it seems clear that the ruling groups in new countries are not inclined to entrust much of the responsibility for their industrial advance to private businessmen.

The alternative source of personnel for industrial progress therefore must necessarily be the intellectuals—the university-trained government official, the scientist, and economist, the engineer with a systematic training at a technological college rather than an empirical training at the workbench.

Economists well trained in both theoretical and applied economics are even more integral to the promulgation and execution of schemes for economic development in the newer countries than they are in long-established countries with a large stratum of experienced and forceful businessmen. A country like the United Kingdom, which decided to launch itself into governmentally planned economic life after the Second World War, could supplement an able civil service with a substantial body of experienced businessmen, and it could draw into government service a group of university-trained economists who had hitherto been engaged in teaching, research, and writing in universities and independent research institutes, and for economic periodicals. The poorer countries have no such resources. The more fortunate among them have a small number of high-grade economists taken from the universities and the civil service. They have very few businessmen to enlist into their service (and even if they had them they would be reluctant to use them). The less fortunate lack nearly all these resources. Their most vigorous personalities have chosen politics as a career. Their most acute minds are already in administration. They have very few industrialists conducting large-scale operations.

These new countries could all use more highly qualified economists, economist-administrators, and statisticians than are available at present. Their vast schemes of construction—hydroelectric installations, factories, railways, etc.—all require engineers trained in higher technological institutions. The improvement of their agriculture requires research and extension work which will demand men with appropriate university training. Moreover, the aspiration in almost all the new countries for a "welfare state" can be met only if there are far larger numbers of well-trained teachers at every level from primary to university, whose activities will range from rarefied intellectual analysis to extra-mural work in villages in the hinterland; of physicians and social workers; and, as literacy spreads, of journalists, scenario writers, authors, and critics. Programs of economic and social progress will thus depend for their fulfillment on the executive action of large numbers of intellectuals.

Perhaps never before in world history have intellectuals had such responsibilities and opportunities for the exercise of authority and creativity within the central institutions of their own societies. The need is for men of practical judgment and factual curiosity, with a capacity to appreciate small increments of growth and to understand the complexities and intractabilities which creative economic activity confronts. Yet the qualifications of the intellectuals for these grandiose tasks and possibilities are problematic. There are ample lawyers, bachelors of arts with moderate literary interests, and a fair number of polemical and hortatory publicists. Among the numerous intellectuals, there are scattered a small number of men who are first class by the highest standards. They work against great disadvantages.

II

The newly emergent countries in Asia are the heirs of a powerful intellectual tradition, predominantly religious. The religious sage has thus enjoyed the highest esteem, and the religious conquest of the self, or individuality, has been one of the highest goods, if not the highest. Nonattachment to the objects of this world and purification of the spirit by avoidance of the gratifications offered by contact with living and nonliving material objects have been central features of the tradition of intellectual activity in these countries. Moreover, because the religious component has been so preponderant in the cultural tradition, much of the most refined intelligence has been devoted to the interpretation of texts. The traditional institutions of learning have concentrated on the exegesis of sacred texts. The experience of everyday social intercourse, the experience of the craftsman and reflection thereon, and curiosity about the world of natural phenomena, physical and biological, have been absent from the range of activities of the traditional intelligentsia in these countries.

At present the traditional intellectuals, such as the *pandits* in India, are looked upon with condescending pity or outright contempt by the modern intelligentsia in these countries. What the traditional intelligentsia regards as sacred, its modern counterpart regards as superstition or triviality. There is little contact between these two sections of the intellectual classes. Their modes of life, their intellectual satisfactions and curiosities seem to be poles apart. Nonetheless a deeper affinity exists between them, with important implications for economic development.

The affinity is evident in the theoretical and literary tendencies of the modern intelligentsia in the underdeveloped countries. There are many reasons why the novel has not flourished in non-Western countries other than Japan, but one reason is a deficiency in the sense of concrete everyday reality. Naturalistic description of ordinary situations and concreteness of recall are both scantily developed in novels and biographies in the economically underdeveloped countries. This is one expression of a state of mind that reaches far beyond the literary world. How few study engineering or natural sciences, especially the experimental biological and physical sciences, in relation to those studying humanistic subjects! The readiness to immerse oneself in empirical enquiry—which has enough of its own dangers, as we see in America—and especially in the disciplines that require field work, is strikingly scant among the best minds in the educated classes in most underdeveloped countries. How vast is the disproportion between those who have taken degrees in the arts, in law, and in commerce, and those studying science and engineering! Wherever in the economically underdeveloped parts of the world there is an established university system, it is flooded with candidates for arts degrees for whom there will be very few opportunities for employment, and who would have little to contribute to economic development even if there were such opportunities.

This situation is in part attributable to the impact of the West. The Western rulers created secondary schools, universities, and colleges in countries like India, Burma, and Indonesia, to supply the needed middle- and lower-level civil servants, the highest positions being reserved for their own nationals or for the persons of local origin who had met the highest intellectual requirements of the metropolitan university system. Subsequently, when colleges were founded by local initiative, before and after independence, they were of the same sort. These colleges were not intended to make men into scientists and engineers. This was so in part because in the nineteenth century the chief colonial power, the United Kingdom, did not produce scientists and engineers in its own universities and did not think that it was the task of universities to do so. It was also a result of the absence of employment opportunities for native engineers and scientists. To the extent that the then dependent countries were industrialized, their higher technical personnel were imported from the metropolis. There was no incentive or stimulant to the growth of a technological sensitivity in the educated classes, and so no scientific or engineering tradition could find its nutriment.

The origins of the relative indifference toward the intellectual and practical mastery of nature and of the relatively weak feeling for concrete reality can thus be seen to be rooted both in the older traditions of each country and in the recent traditions established by the method of domination employed by the foreign ruler. Because of these traditions, the educated classes of the underdeveloped countries, however much they believe in the saving graces of science and technology, have a largely literary or ideological relationship to them. In practice, being an engineer or an applied scientist—to say nothing of an effective businessman—counts for less in the eyes of the educated than a good humanistic education.

Moreover, although there has been a revival of appreciation for the inherent qualities of traditional art, music, sculpture, and religious philosophy, there is still more prestige attributed to a thorough familiarity with the culture of the West, even in India and other Asian countries possessing traditional cultures of universal value. It is not only the man who has studied at Oxford, Cambridge, Heidelberg, or Paris —or even Cambridge, Massachusetts—who is deferred to but the person who, whether he has studied abroad or not, is intimate with the contents of *The New Statesman* and *The Economist,* who knows about

Bertrand Russell, T. S. Eliot, Hemingway, Sartre, Graham Greene, Camus, Auden, and Faulkner, who is at home in the conflicts within the British Labour Party and in the plays of Christopher Fry. Even among scientists in these countries, work seems to be done for an invisible jury of scientists in England, the United States, and Germany, while other scientists working in the same fields at home are less frequently thought of or referred to. This location of the intellectual center of gravity in foreign, indeed Western, countries, might—and to some extent should—be attributed to a more realistic or more refined appreciation of the superior quality of scientific, literary, and philosophical work in the West. This is, however, by no means the only reason for the displacement of the intellectual center of gravity; if it were, it would not injure the cause of national improvement and economic development. It is because this displacement fundamentally arises from xenophilia that it harms the culture, science, and economy of the underdeveloped countries.

The coexistence of xenophilia with fervent nationalism does not diminish its pernicious consequences. Indeed, extremist nationalism is often an unconscious expiation for guilt-generating but status-enhancing xenophilia. The harmfulness of xenophilia does not lie in its alleged "separation of the intellectuals from the people," for which the intellectuals in backward countries are often criticized by intellectuals themselves, by political leaders who are antagonistic to them, and by foreign observers.

Intellectuals in all countries are "separated from the people," and so they should be. No society can have its indispensable division of labor if the different skills which it requires are not also associated with differentiated tastes and outlooks. No society would be worthy of even the slightest respect if it did not allow people to be somewhat separate from each other; even totalitarian regimes, which demand homogeneity of taste and outlook, must permit some of these differences, this separateness, however unwillingly. Xenophilia is injurious because it manifests and fosters a severely deficient empathy for the states of mind of one's fellow-countrymen, a lack of intimacy with the social and material environment, and thus, at bottom, a form of blindness to the capacities and incapacities of one's fellow-countrymen, to their problems, and to their disposition to rouse themselves to do something about them. It expresses and reproduces the feebleness of the sense of affinity that unites a population into a modern nation. This "social scotoma" is not in the first instance a product of Westernization; it is a product of a hierarchical society in which the higher castes and classes have little feeling for those beneath them; it is furthered by the still undissolved cleavages which are generated by an overwhelmingly strong system of extended kinship. It is also a product of the religious tradition of non-attachment, which the more advanced religions of Hinduism, Buddhism, and Islam praise as the highest good, and which their vital existence in still very tangibly religious cultures renders into a frequently encountered reality. Whatever its causes, its result is the existence of educated classes with little understanding of the real problems of their native lands and the real states of mind of their countrymen.

A common reaction against xenophilia has been populistic nationalism. The aspiration for national independence was impelled by populistic nationalism, which persists and is renewed in independence. The intellectual vices of oppositional politics which were inevitable under the conditions of colonial politics, revolutionary or reformist, are sustained partly by their own tradition and partly by the mutual distrust of populistic, nativistic politicians and intellectuals with a Westernized education, outlook, and style of life. Both sides invoke "the people" to [put] down their antagonists. This beslavering of the uneducated, this praise of the "wisdom of the humble" and of the sagacity of the ancestors are often hypocritical, but at least as often they are sincere. Either way, however, they bring no improvement in the situation. They simply prolong the predominance of generalities and nebulous standards and ideals which, though they may be ineradicable from the political platform, contribute little to the hard work of making economic institutions function effectively. Where realism of perception and judgment is required, the creation of passionately espoused illusions is no better than indifference and disregard. Populism and traditionalism—which often buttress each other—both inhibit the self-confidence of those with modern education, and enfeeble the development and application of the knowledge and outlook necessary for modernizing society.

From the point of view of the needs of a new society which would combine economic progress with democracy and individual liberty, the xenophilia and nationalism of the intellectuals are equal hindrances. Both are unrealistic and both apply vague clichés, which were appropriate enough for an opposition with no prospect of constitutional access to power, to situations in which differentiated and specific judgment and a "feeling for the concrete situation" are called for. Neither is capable of that patient, detached scrutiny of situations in a mood free from the preconceptions and preoccupations connected with rigid and remote principles. Without that kind of scrutiny, the constructive, matter-of-fact assessment of achievements and shortcomings, which is indispensable to the realistic formulation of policy and its sound administration, is not very likely to develop.

III

Fruitful economic development, which will not only result in increasing the absolute numbers of metal lathes or planing machines or shipping tonnage, but which will contribute, through a self-generating, autonomous process, to raising the productivity and standard of living of the nation, requires, in addition to capital and skilled manpower and natural resources, adaptable and realistic judgment in economic enterprise and in the criticism of economic policy and practice. Ordinarily in the discussion of economic development through planning, stress is laid upon the adequacy of quality and quantity of planning and administrative personnel. This is a just emphasis and the first part of this article has been directed to an examination of certain inherited obstacles to such adequacy. But sufficient attention has not been paid to the machinery and personnel for critical evaluation of what the planners and administrators have done. Insofar as this problem is treated at all, it seems to be taken for granted that the government will do its own evaluation, or that foreign experts will be called in by the government to assess the effectiveness or the balance of various development projects, or even the scheme of development as a whole.

This does not seem to be sufficient. The government, especially where it claims to be democratic and seeks to foster democratic institutions as well as economic progress, should not be its own sole judge. Such it will be, however, if it monopolizes the machinery, personnel, and opportunity for factual evaluation of past activities and prospective plans. Nor can foreign experts be relied upon for such assessments. They will usually lack the concrete sense of the situation without which there can be no realism and, furthermore, they will too often flatter the government in that disingenuously condescending way which Western experts have of patting the heads of their colleagues in the economically underdeveloped countries. A country which aspires to practice democracy must actually practice it. This means that evaluation and criticism must be carried on by independent organs within the country, staffed by independent personalities of the same culture as those they criticize.

It is not sufficient that the planners and the executors of the plans should be well-educated and hard-headed, well-schooled in economic theory and experienced in economic administration. With all these qualities and with good will, too, those who make plans and try to carry them out acquire a vested emotional interest in what they are doing. They tend to gloss over their failures, to overlook obstacles and in general to avoid self-criticism necessary for better action in the future. There are extenuating reasons for this: the senior officials with the experience and the vantage point which would enable them to formulate a coherent and realistic view are ordinarily so very heavily burdened that they have neither the time nor energy to muster unaided the detached and comprehensive outlook required. (There are not enough highly qualified men to go around, and the vast overstaffing at the lower levels of the government service does nothing to mitigate this.)

Furthermore, practically all of the higher civil servants and economic advisors are intellectuals by training and disposition. They are modern in their outlook and Western in their cultural orientation (if not necessarily in their politics). As such, they tend to be distrusted by the politicians, who though often intellectuals themselves are more populistic and even demagogic, and therefore critical of those who have studied abroad, who live in a more or less Western style at home, and whose university and intellectual attainments are often higher than their own. In addition, the administrators are often at a psychological disadvantage vis-à-vis the politicians, because while the politicians were fighting for national independence, many of the higher administrators were serving the foreign ruler in the civil service or in educational institutions dominated by foreigners. The administrators are sensitive to the commonly held and frequently expressed criticism directed against them on these grounds, and this weakens their will to oppose the often unrealistic aspirations of their political superiors. For all these reasons, effective self-criticism within the government is bound to be insufficient. And since so many of the new countries wish to move in a more or less socialistic direction, the criticism which the competitive market and bankruptcy provide in the system of private capitalism cannot be effective. Hence, detailed and constructive criticism from outside the government—in other words, an effective public opinion—is an imperative condition of sound and not merely quantitative economic progress.

Although the economic planning in the Soviet satellite states of Eastern Europe failed in part because of the burden of Soviet exploitation of these "colonial" economies, the failure was aggravated by the fact that the planners and higher administrators were deprived of the benefit of independent criticism which could have made them more aware of their errors and the means of overcoming them. This kind of critical public opinion needs freedom from government control or censorship—and in most of the new countries outside the area of Communist rule, this freedom exists sufficiently. It also needs something more than freedom from external sanctions. It needs well-trained intellectuals who are interested in politics whatever their professional *expertise,* it needs shrewd economists and sharp-witted, actively enquiring minds with a sense of responsibility, with practical acumen, and a strong devotion to the well-being of their country which stops short of doctrinairism and fanaticism—such people are in short supply everywhere, and especially so in underdeveloped countries. It needs, moreover, the institutions of critical opinion—an economically independent press, sound research organizations within and outside universities, and civic and interest associations, as well as a parliament which by its debates and enquiries will inform that part of the citizenry which is concerned with affairs beyond the tip of its nose. These institutions too are inadequately developed in the new and economically underdeveloped countries.

In almost all these new countries, the short supply of talented and trained intellectuals is accentuated by the large-scale operations of the governments. The best are taken into the government at larger salaries, with higher prestige and better conditions of service than they could find in universities and colleges, on newspapers and reviews or in native-owned private business. In consequence, the instructed public opinion in the middle classes and in the country at large is disarmed at its very center, when, thanks to the heritage of cultural and political traditions, that center was weak enough to begin with.

The chief organs of an instructed public opinion—of a critical attitude which shares the general objectives of the government, feels a tie of solidarity with it and wishes it well as one wishes oneself well—are the press, parliament, the universities, and civic and interest associations. Where the wireless broadcasting system is in the hands of the government or a public corporation, it requires a great deal of subtlety and sophistication on the part of the broadcasting administrators to attain a stage where criticism of government actions is permitted; this stage has not yet been attained in underdeveloped countries. The press —both the newspaper and periodical press—must carry the heaviest burden of responsible criticism and the instruction of public and governmental opinion.

The other burdens of the press in these new countries are so great, however, that they can scarcely carry the last straw, which is the government's pre-emption of so many of the best publicists, actual and prospective, and their consequent removal from journalistic circulation. Some of the other burdens are perfectly well-known—for example, the high illiteracy rates and the poverty of the mass of the population, which restrict the circulation of newspapers and therewith the income from sales and advertising by private business. Newspapers as a result exist usually on a very narrow margin, and come to depend on government advertisements or announcements for a larger share of their advertising revenue than is the case in the West. One resounding instance of sanctions imposed by a provincial government against a single critical newspaper by withdrawal of advertising goes a long way: most other newspapers become extremely cautious about criticizing the government on points about which it is sensitive. It also makes for circumspection in enquiring closely into such subjects. Even the economically strongest newspapers are cautious about giving the hospitality of their columns to well-informed critics, however responsible and cogent, when they wish above all not to have trouble with the government.

The poverty of the press also means that, for the vast majority of journalists, salaries are poor. The press consequently finds it difficult to attract and retain high-grade young men. Staffs have to be kept small, with the result that there cannot be sufficient specialization to develop the *expertise* necessary for useful evaluation and criticism of economic programs. In addition to these immediate impediments to the formation of an instructed, constructively critical, responsible public opinion, there are others which are more deeply rooted in the past. In the first place, the state of nonattachment to the objects of the phenomenal world, a product of the great traditions of some of the new countries, is expressed in journalism as factual uninterestedness. It is not that false facts are deliberately presented—although that is not infrequent; rather there is lacking that avidity for facts, that deep curiosity to know "what, where, when," which marks the good journalist and also the high-caliber analyst and commentator on current events.

This unfactual disposition is reinforced by journalistic traditions inherited from the period of the struggle for national independence. Aside from the foreign-owned and foreign-edited newspapers and periodicals, the main style of the press during the time of foreign rule was hortatory and polemical. The meticulous search for details and matter-of-fact analysis were not regarded as necessary or appropriate, except among a restricted band of liberal nationalists whose patrician liberalism was swept away with the rest of the Victorian inheritance by the more populistic nationalism which came to the fore in the second quarter of the present century. Denunciation in rhetorical grandeur and perpetual complaint about all manner of iniquities were poor preparation for discriminating appraisal and criticism. The outsider who does not face the possibility that his party might come to power does not develop the empathy for the concrete problems which afflict the person holding the responsibility of office. Journalism in colonial countries was the service of a higher cause, not a profession or a business, and the journalism of the underdeveloped countries bears that mark today. Editors do not on the whole expect their reporters to dig for facts; they could not find reporters who could dig for facts, even if they wanted

them to do so. Reporters do not think that they are called upon to un-
earth facts as part of their job; they feel their explorations are over
when they have been given a briefing or a "handout" by a government
press officer. As a result, the press tends to be stuffed with reports of
speeches by cabinet ministers and members of parliament, and with the
substance of official releases. Leaders and turnover articles are not based
on ample study of the details of governmental or private economic
policy and activity. They tend to be very general and either affirmative
or denunciatory, without differentiated argument. Even significant reports, very factual in character, by parliamentary enquiry committees
find no response in the press because they are not in harmony with the
tradition of the profession, which still finds it easier to write about
Western foreign policy and the misbehavior of white people toward
colored people than about the day-to-day problems of the societies
themselves.

It should also be said that the governmental machinery for making
detailed information available is not always very useful. The reports of
parliamentary proceedings take a very long time to appear in print. Reports of governmental departments and public corporations appear only
after much delay and hard to come by. The government even seems
sometimes as if it does not want its actions to be critically analyzed,
thus continuing the practices of the foreign rulers.

There are other obstacles to the emergence and effectiveness of responsible criticism of governmental policies in the new countries. Even
if the full supply of facts were accessible, responsible sympathizers with
these policies would be reluctant to criticize the government in public.
The most secure as well as the most unstable of the new states are feeling their way amidst great difficulties, and some of their more circum-
spect intellectuals appreciate their national independence too much to
wish to give the appearance, above all to foreigners but also to their
own public, of "letting the side down" by public criticism. They are
aware that their new state rests on weak foundations which are recur-
rently shaken by traditionalistic and communal loyalties, and on an
impoverished and depressed peasantry, and they wish to avoid anything
that would enfeeble the authority of the government or hamper its efforts to create a vigorous consensus in support of its steps to improve
the economic life of the country. This reserve on the part of some of
the very best-informed and most intelligent intellectuals in the newly
established nation is accompanied by the hierarchical traditions of the
society, which endow those in authority with charisma and thus make
it unthinkable to criticize them. (This traditional attitude, which
heightens sensitivity to the charismatic component of authority, is also

responsible in a great many cases for much irrational, unfactual criticism, since the new ruling institutions are bureaucratic and untraditional and therefore lacking in the preponderantly charismatic quality which is prized in religious cultures.)

In the press of the new countries, there is no dearth of abusive criticism. Some comes from sensation-mongers, some from those who wish ill to the government, some from disappointed idealists whose struggle for national independence was motivated by deep ethical feelings and an ideal of a dignified national existence which has not yet been realized. Practically none of this criticism is matter-of-fact or well-informed about the dreadfully difficult problems of trying to govern a disunited, traditionalist population by methods appropriate to modern unified countries. Abusive criticism is like the barking of an ill-natured dog; it is heeded only when it is expressed by a party or an interest group strong enough to do political damage. It is never looked to as a source of welcome and helpful guidance. The hostile critics, even those who share the general aims of the government, lack both the factual sense and the facts themselves on the basis of which realistic assessment could be made and constructive suggestions offered.

Against this background it will easily be seen how little opportunity the planning officials and administrators have to receive sympathetic and thoroughly informed criticism from intellectuals, who although outside the government are not so much outside the world of official concerns that they are unaware of the massive facts and the imponderable matrix in which the facts rest.

Likewise, the aid which the press could give to legislators in following the work of the executive and in forming a picture of the true state of affairs in the country is not given, and the information and assessment which the politically interested public needs are not provided.

IV

An effectively critical and independent evaluation of economic policies and practices cannot ever be fully carried out by the newspaper and periodical press. Much of the work of the press in this regard depends on more basic enquiries such as could be conducted, and in some countries are conducted, by the staffs of independent universities and colleges, and research institutes. The views of these scholars, in the form of journal articles, monographs, books, lectures and seminars, and newspaper and periodical articles, can contribute greatly to the guidance and to the critical understanding of governmental action. The formal convocation of university intellectuals as consultants and advisors on governmental economic activities is no substitute for these other forms of expression of opinion, however desirable and important it is in itself. Such occasional drawing-in of the better university economists and anthropologists can provide, under favorable conditions, a more detached and broader perspective which the planners and administrators cannot get themselves. Fruitful consultation is possible, however, only where the consultants can draw upon a rich stock of knowledge which they have accumulated through their own and other scholars' research.

This is not the place to discuss in detail the sad condition of the institutions of higher learning in the new countries. The teachers are overworked, underpaid, and disesteemed; they have very poor libraries, they have little time, facilities, or energy for research, and neither they nor their superiors expect them to show any independence in initiating or conducting research on important subjects.

Unlike the situation in the West, the academic life in the new countries has no real tradition of detached factual research on issues of importance to the public good. The work of the Oxford Institute of Statistics, the Cambridge Department of Applied Economics, the National Bureau of Economic Research, so closely connected with Columbia University; the continuous stream of individual studies by qualified university economists, sociologists, and political scientists, of the problems, policies, and activities of concern to the government; and the research publications of para-academic institutions like the National Institute of Economic and Social Research in London, the Acton Society in London, the Brookings Institution in Washington—these have no counterparts in the new countries. The small Gokhale Institute of Economics and Political Science in Poona is almost unique in underdeveloped countries for its intellectual independence from government and for its empirical bent. The Council of Economic and Industrial Research in New Delhi, although formally independent, seems to be largely confined by its terms of reference to problems referred to it by the Government of India. Such a framework of problem selection, although it need not damage the probity of the enquiry, certainly deprives the government of the advantages of more detached study of plans for economic development.

There is at present virtually no tradition of impartial social research outside the universities in the new countries, and the Committee on Research Programs of the Planning Commission (in India), UNESCO, and other agencies seem blamelessly to be doing very little to foster it. Nor is the prospect for improvement very bright. Because the universities and the government draw from the same stream, the universities are about as hard put to it as the press to create a tradition of detached factual analysis of governmental economic policy and practice. If a young man is very outstanding in his academic career at home, he either goes abroad to continue his studies or he is taken into the government. When a well-trained young man comes back from a Western university with an advanced degree and with some training in rigorous analysis, a respect and feeling for concrete facts, and an ability to investigate and interpret economic situations, he is usually offered a post in a ministry and also one in a college or university. If he accepts the former he will probably enjoy, in addition to a higher salary, greater prestige, the feeling of helping his country in the immediate future, and the stimulating company of other persons of outstanding intellectual and cultural qualifications. If he accepts the university or college post, he will have, in addition to a poor salary—sometimes very much lower than the governmental salary—a dreary round of teaching and routine duties, and a library very inferior to the library of the Ministry; the Ministry gets the important books from London and New York as soon after publication as modern transportation allows, while the college or university libraries get them several years later, if at all. He will, furthermore, have older colleagues who are jealous of his intellectual attainments and ambition and who are unable or unwilling to provide stimulating intellectual companionship. If he teaches in a college he will usually have no research facilities, and if he ever produces manuscripts under such difficult conditions he will usually go out-of-pocket in order to get them typed. And once typed, their publication in book form faces almost insuperable obstacles in the form of the tiny reading public and the disorganized state of the publishing world. So in most cases the government appointment is accepted, and, apart from a small and wholly admirable group of distinguished exceptions, the colleges and universities become the receptacles of the leftovers and the second class. Few indeed are the outstanding young men who leave government service for the university; far more go the opposite way. And so the cycle goes, reinforcing itself with every completion.*

Again the result is the same as in the case of the press. The government's planning activities are deprived of a realistic and well-informed scrutiny which, while understanding the difficult problems the government is up against, tries from a wider and more detached point of view to indicate where the plans went wrong and what the planners can do to avoid such errors. Under present conditions, officials do not learn to benefit from criticism emanating from the universities; instead they maintain a secretiveness and touchiness which is injurious to efficiency in economic life and to political democracy. The press, parliament, and the public, which, at several removes, could assimilate the knowledge

---

* Since this article was written, a revolution in African higher education has begun.—W.J.H.

created by university research, go without the factual sustenance that public opinion needs if it is to keep government from persisting on a faulty course.

V

Frequent and considerable though its shortcomings might be, parliamentary politics contributes valuably to the formation of public opinion. It does so, however, only through a continuing scrutiny and criticism of government and the consequent pressure on government to justify its actions in a reasoned manner. The reporting and comment on the ensuing debate in the press and the due notice of it in the more literate sections of the political public enter into the obscure channels through which public opinion is formed. In the underdeveloped countries, parliamentary life suffers either from the overwhelming preponderance of one major party, as in India, or from a plethora of smaller parties, no one of which has a sufficiently large majority to provide stable government and none of which can offer sound opposition. In most underdeveloped countries, legislators of the majority parties—and this applies to much of the minority, too—have demonstrated their merits in the heroism and sacrifice of the campaign for national independence, rather than in particular professions and occupations requiring solid knowledge and responsibility in taking risks and running complex economic organizations. Even where their original educational attainments were high, years of political agitation, imprisonment, and the rough and tumble of oppositional journalism and politics left them standing where they were in their early twenties. Their equally gifted contemporaries who went into administration gained the advantage of elaborate knowledge and political experience. In the conflict which occurs in all governments between the civil servants and the legislators who would control them, and which is aggravated under conditions of underdevelopment and large-scale governmental economic operations, the legislators are at a disadvantage. They need all the help they can get from intellectuals in journalism and in the universities. Unfortunately that help is not forthcoming. For the most part the intellectuals in the press and the universities are unable to give it—for the reasons already examined—and their dispositions toward politicians are so unfriendly and derogatory that they would not give it if they could.

In some respects the backbench legislator of the ruling and the opposition parties, the party politician, is as much disesteemed by the intellectuals of the underdeveloped countries as is the businessman. In any conflict between, on the one side, the few outstandingly charismatic political leaders who led the national struggle, and the civil service, and, on the other side, the ordinary legislator who was only a local or second-rank figure, the sympathies of the intellectual outside the government are with the former. The press and university intellectuals do little to aid this ordinary legislator. At the same time, because of their lack of curiosity, their lack of routine civil courage, and their "unfactuality," the intellectuals can do little to curb, by the force of exposure to the public eye, the improper pressures on the civil service which the ordinary legislator sometimes exercises on behalf of communal, religious, and even entirely private ends.

Thus, not only does public opinion not receive the benefits that can be conferred by a lively and self-confident parliamentary life, but parliamentary life itself suffers from the insufficient quality of the intellectuals who are left to the press and the institutions of higher education after the civil service has picked them over.

VI

In the countries which have undergone a slower and more decentralized development than the underdeveloped countries are contemplating, parliament and press and the independent intelligentsia were joined by a mass of voluntary associations which sought to prevent abuses and to further their own aims. Such civic and interest associations are lacking in the underdeveloped societies. The modernization of these societies before independence was only partial and not very autonomous. The civil service and universities, which were the chief elements of modernity, were created and controlled by the foreign ruler; the only autochthonous modern institutions of public life were the oppositional press and agitational political movements. Large-scale native business enterprises, native ecclesiastical and philanthropic organizations, and public activities on behalf of any ends other than national revival and independence were absent. So political leadership in these sectors of society, which in modern Western countries plays an important part in the formation and expression of public opinion, was not called into existence. Local political life was either part of the struggle for national revival and independence or it was entirely traditional. The seedbed of modern civic life was scarcely prepared under colonial conditions.

Where modern interest organizations do exist, as in the case of manufacturers' or merchants' associations, they find it difficult to put their case in public. The atmosphere is unfavorable to their representations, and intellectuals are reluctant to enter their employ because they think that the service of business is a betrayal of the ideal. Communal

and political associations express their demands more by personal repre
sentation and by public demonstration than by public debate and
analysis. Thus although the underdeveloped countries are not free from
pressure groups, their pressure groups do not express themselves through
organs which would contribute to the improvement of the quality of
public opinion.

This immense gap must be filled by intellectuals if it is to be filled at
all. Intellectuals in underdeveloped countries must provide the administrative leadership and *expertise* which the traditions and situations of
their countries, and their own prejudices, have thrust upon them. They
must also create the public opinion and furnish the external *expertise*
and judgment without which the plans of their governments will go
astray.

This, however, can be done only if some of the intellectuals who
are first-class in their native capacities and their attainments are not
drawn into government or even into politics. It can be done only if,
outside the circles of governmental authority, there are strong circles of
able intellectuals well-endowed by nature, training, and experience to
understand, appreciate, and criticize the undertakings of their governments, within the framework of a fundamental sense of affinity.

The more distinguished intellectuals who enter governmental administration acquire their practical experience and sharpened judgment. To their excellent endowment, they add the sobering and
toughening knowledge which comes with responsibility for the day-to-
day management of affairs. A tiny handful in private business and a
number not much larger in journalism and the universities possess
equal capacities and attainments. But the great majority of intellectuals
in the underdeveloped countries are alienated from the centers of public
life. They are disillusioned and unhappy about the course of events.
They feel great ideals have been deserted for the sake of trivial advances.
In part their disillusionment is a response to the real difficulties of independent national existence, in part a product of the confrontation of
the vague and heroic idealism of opposition by the obduracy of reality.

VII

If the underdeveloped countries are to move in the direction to which
they aspire, they must deal economically with their material resources.
They will be able to do so only if they husband and cultivate their
intellectual resources more effectively.

The task is terribly arduous and the territory is uncharted. Difficult
though economic development is, there are precedents which give guid-

ance. Intellectual development, which will pay due attention to the requirements of science, scholarship, and preparation for public service and which will try to do by deliberate arrangement what in the West for better or for worse has taken care of itself, is even more difficult; there are fewer precedents and more indeterminate factors. What we say now, even more than what has gone before, should be taken as a contribution to an opening of the problem rather than as a set of specific recipes.

In order for public opinion to work effectively, the critics must somehow feel their fundamental parity with those they criticize. The critics must not be rankled by feelings of exclusion and inferiority. Resentment which comes from a sense of being excluded and dependent inhibits frankness and darkens the power of reason. Hence central and provincial governments should attempt, insofar as it lies in their powers, to foster a sense of autonomy and self-esteem in the press and in the institutions of higher learning. This can be done in part by the studious avoidance of political pressure or the use of the powers of patronage which intentionally or unintentionally influence the free expression of publicistic or academic opinion. For example, appointments to senior positions should be made by boards which are entirely independent of the government. They should include academic persons from outside the state and, in some cases, even outside the country. More than this, financial and fiscal policies which can make the press and universities more economically self-sufficient should be pursued. For example, tax exemptions for advertising in newspapers and periodicals should be increased, and additional tax allowances should be made for private gifts to universities above specified amounts.

A further requirement in the same direction is the establishment of a greater parity of status between the higher civil service and the universities. The traditional respect for the scholar and teacher in Asia is a valuable asset which has become dilapidated as a result of the reverence in which powerful secular authority is held; it is most desirable that it be renewed in an appropriate modern form. The renewal of a tradition is, however, one of the least manageable of tasks. A rather roundabout approach which would have other favorable consequences would involve an improvement in the intellectual quality and financial rewards of the academic profession, at least on its higher reaches.

One or two first-class universities or colleges should be maintained with salary levels and conditions of service comparable to those which the higher civil service provides for equally qualified persons. This would prevent the government from making off with the best brains in the academic world. It would make the academic career just as attractive financially and intellectually as the higher civil service and would thus provide a base on which the informed assessment and criticism of economic policies and trends could be developed. It is imperative to create a combination of Nuffield College, All Souls College, and the London School of Economics, which would provide intellectually stimulating society, ample opportunity and facilities for research, and enough teaching to raise up, by a first-rate intellectual discipline, a future generation of persons who would be at home in their own countries while having mastered the best that the most advanced countries can offer in the social sciences.

The absolute quantity of intellectuals of good quality in any underdeveloped country could conceivably be increased if the students who go to Western countries for advanced degrees could be better prepared before departure and better supervised during their periods of foreign study. At present there are many young people from the underdeveloped countries studying in Britain and the United States, representing a considerable investment of foreign exchange and of capital gifts made available by foreign governments and private institutions. Much of this seems to be poorly employed at present. Many of the students from underdeveloped countries are ill-adjusted in the countries to which they come, they idle away more of their time than seems necessary, and they conduct their studies in a half-hearted way. Would it not be possible for a University Grants Committee in each of the underdeveloped countries to establish, in cooperation with the major universities to which their students go, a better system of supervision and guidance than exists at present? Deans of Students and "foreign-student advisors" who know nothing of the background of their charges and the problems that await them at home are hardly in a position to encourage the student to make more efficient use of his intellectual opportunities during his sojourn abroad.

Another useful measure would be the assimilation of retired senior civil servants into university teaching and research. The senior civil servants are among the most valuable intellectual resources in the underdeveloped countries, and it is wrong to allow them to rusticate when they retire. Many of them are at the height of their powers, and not only their keen intelligence but their general culture and their shrewd and experienced judgment of the current scene would be invaluable additions to university life and, through it, to educated public opinion.

The principle of a permanent higher civil service, which has been adopted in the new countries from the British model, has a great deal to commend it. It builds corporate morale and guarantees integrity and efficiency. Yet, from the point of view of bringing an outside perspective into government and of making outside criticism more concrete and more pertinent, some modification might be in order. Might it not be desirable to assign senior civil servants who have the appropriate desires and aptitudes to research or journalistic work or to teaching for periods of a year or two at a time, and then let them resume their posts at levels and seniorities which they would have enjoyed had they not taken leaves of absence? Such an experience might give economist civil servants a more critical perspective on the economic state of their country, and it would correspondingly instruct those with whom they came in contact during their "outside" period. A system resembling this, under the sponsorship of the Commonwealth Fund, is already in operation, sending civil servants of the Administrative Class abroad for study and research. The scheme proposed here would send them into the "foreign territory" of industry, journalism, or the university in their own countries, or other underdeveloped countries with problems similar to their own.

A parallel series of measures with respect to the press should be encouraged by the government, since it is desirable that journalists—as well as professors of the social sciences—should improve their understanding of economic life, and that they should be enabled to judge policies and actions in the framework of the real problems facing their country. The chances for this improvement would be enhanced if journalists—and professors—were given opportunities to participate in governmental and private economic enterprises as regular staff members with appropriate responsibilities, for periods of a year or two at a time, returning afterwards to their newspapers or universities at the levels of seniority or rank they would have attained if they had not left.

The quality of journalists in the new countries would be improved if a system like the Niemann Fellowships were devised. This would allow opportunity for advanced academic study and research to those journalists who have shown most independence and intelligent persistence in pursuing some problem in the economic and political life of their countries. Once more advanced university centers are built up in the new countries, then the Fellows should be attached to these institutions rather than to Harvard, the London School of Economics, and the like.

However excellent the fundamental good sense of enquirers in the fields of government and economics, if they do not have adequate statistical and other descriptive data at their disposal their comments can scarcely rise above the level of generalities and edifying counsel. Governments should therefore develop more adequate reporting practices, making it easier for journalists and research workers to learn, independently of government press officers, just what has been going on in their economies. Civil servants should be allowed to give to journalists or qualified research workers all information which need not be kept secret on grounds of military security. Departmental reports and those of Parliamentary Commissions of Enquiry should be published promptly and should be readily available. Indeed, an overhaul of the government printing department and its system of public distribution is very necessary in many underdeveloped countries.

To meet the economic needs of the underdeveloped countries and, as a by-product, to create a "technological" state of mind, advanced technical training should be carried on in centers on the style of the Massachusetts Institute of Technology, the Zürich Eidgenossische Technische Hochschule, or the California Institute of Technology. Each large new country ought to make an effort to establish one of these institutions, spending sizable sums of money if necessary to attract outstanding teachers of engineering and scientific subjects and providing them with facilities for research. (Smaller countries should form such institutions by confederation on a regional base, either with each other or with their larger neighbors.) If this were done, there would not only be an adequate supply of technologists for economic development but there would begin a diffusion of the practical, matter-of-fact attitude which often accompanies the more specifically technical skills. Both of these are important for economic development and for political stability.

All these measures and many others which ought to be devised and instituted are intended to unify the different sections of the intellectual classes of the new countries, to make them more realistic in their attitudes, more appreciative of the real problems faced by their countries, more aware of their heavy responsibilities in the titanic undertaking of promoting economic and social development. If any of those proposals were to succeed only in bringing about the uncritical affirmation of governmental policies by journalists and professors, then it would be a failure, because uncritical affirmation is as useless a guide to realistic action as undifferentiated and ignorant nagging. These are the two temptations which menace the good sense of intellectuals in all countries, and not least in the newer ones. They must be equally avoided if standards of living are to be raised and freedom fortified.

A Theory of Corruption

Based on a Consideration of Corruption in the Public Services and
Governments of British Colonies and ex-Colonies in West Africa

M. McMULLAN
London

There is some corruption in all governments and in the public services
of all countries. Some countries, however, suffer from a greater degree
of corruption than others. Only very recently and in only a handful of
countries has such corruption been so far reduced as to be practically
negligible, that is to say so far reduced that it does not normally enter
into a citizen's relations with his government. In most countries throughout most of their known history such corruption has been an accepted
feature of life. In extreme cases today it can be a major obstacle to
economic development and a major cause of political instability. It
deserves attention for its intrinsic interest as part of the "pathology" of
bureaucracy, for its practical importance for the political and economic
development of the poorer nations of the world, and for the contribution that an analysis can make to sympathetic understanding of what
may otherwise be a repulsive feature of some societies. In this paper I
try to relate the corruption observed in the British Colonies and ex-
colonies of West Africa to the social conditions and histories of those
countries and to make some tentative generalisations from a comparison
of conditions there and in other parts of the world.

I am not asserting that these West African territories are peculiarly
given to corruption; there are many countries in the world where
the governments are more corrupt and many more where they were
equally corrupt in the recent past; the choice of these countries is
dictated only by the accident of the writer's own experience.

THE EFFECTS OF CORRUPTION

Understanding is desirable, but it is wrong to underrate the evil consequences of widespread corruption. People sympathetic to African and

Reprinted from *Sociological Review*, IX (1961), 181–201, with the permission
of the author and the publisher.

other nationalist movements are sometimes tempted to brush aside corruption as being a "passing phase" of no real political or social importance. Whether it is a "passing phase" or not in West Africa I do not know, though I shall give reasons for thinking that it is at least not a phase that will pass quickly; but I am certain that it is of real political and social importance. Some of the evils which widespread corruption may be expected to bring are:—

1. Injustice. This needs no explanation.

2. Inefficiency. In countries where the general standard of technology is low this is a serious matter. Railway accidents are caused by Station Masters corruptly agreeing to load logs that are too heavy for the wagons. Patients in hospitals may be denied treatment they require or bribe nurses to give them treatment they want (in West Africa usually injections), but which may be unsuitable for their condition. Corruption in making appointments may be relatively unimportant in a country where the general standard of competence is high, but in West Africa, where professional and technical competence is still rare, corruption results in the appointment of unsuitable people and the waste and frustration of the right man.

3. Mistrust of the government by the citizen. This is peculiarly serious where the government is anxious to carry out a programme of economic development for which the enthusiasm of the population needs to be enlisted. It also increases the difficulties of enforcing criminal, revenue, and other laws.

4. Waste of public resources. Corruption in the government involves the ultimate transfer of public funds to the pockets of politicians or officials. The businessman who has to bribe to get a government contract ultimately charges the bribe to public funds.

5. Discouragement of enterprise, particularly foreign enterprise. Corruption adds an incalculable hazard to the normal thickets of bureaucratic procedure. The final bribe is never paid. Investors and entrepreneurs are dismayed and frustrated, and may find that the unofficial cost of starting an enterprise is too great for it to be profitable.

6. Political instability. In a country where there is a great deal of corruption, political attacks on people in positions of power are easy to mount and easy to get popular support for. Much of the political history of some unfortunate countries could be told as the "ins" being accused, correctly, by the "outs" of corruption; popular indignation at the corruption causing the replacement of the "ins" by the "outs," who in turn become corrupt and are attacked by a new group of "outs." This process could be demonstrated in detail from the history of some

local government bodies in West Africa during the past ten years. At the national level it can lead either to political chaos, or

7. Repressive measures. It may be easier to deal with the accusations of corruption than with the corruption itself.

8. Restrictions on government policy. I recall a conversation with an American doctor who was an admirer of the British National Health Service. "No such service would at the moment be possible in my home State," he said, naming the State; "the civil service is too inefficient and corrupt to be capable of running it." A corrupt civil service and police force restricts the range of policies available to a government.

EVIDENCE

There is one preliminary problem which must be faced but cannot be solved; the problem of evidence. Arguments and statements about corruption cannot be demonstrated by factual or statistical evidence of the type normally acceptable as a basis for political or sociological generalisation. There are plenty of reports, histories and trial records[1] exemplifying corruption in different countries, but corruption is not a subject which can be investigated openly by means of questionnaires and interviews. Even if it were, in principle, possible to quantify the phenomenon, there would be no practical possibility of doing so. The reader is asked to accept as a premise of the argument of this paper that there is more corruption in these West African countries than in, for instance, the United Kingdom. This is a view based on my own observations over a decade, broadly shared by other well placed observers and supported by public expressions of concern by indigenous political and religious leaders in West Africa.[2] But it cannot, nor can many of the other statements in this paper be proved in the ways in which statements about less disreputable aspects of society can be proved. Cor-

---

[1] In West Africa, the Nigerian Governments have published some very useful reports of Enquiries into allegations of corruption, e.g. *The Report of the Commission of Enquiry into Port Harcourt Town Council*, Government Printer Enugu 1953; *The Report of the Enquiry into the Allocation of Market Stalls at Aba by P. F. Grant*, G.P. Enugu 1955; dealing with activities at a higher level there is the *Report of the Tribunal Appointed to Enquire into Allegations of Improper Conduct by the Premier of Eastern Nigeria in Connection with the Affairs of the African Continental Bank, Ltd.*, G.P. Lagos 1957. From Ghana there is the *Report of the Commission of Enquiry into Mr. Braimah's resignation and the Allegations Arising therefrom*, G.P. Accra 1954. For similar phenomena in another colonial territory, see *Commission of Enquiry into Matters Affecting the Public Service*, G.P. Kuala Lumpur 1955.

[2] E.g., President Nkrumah's announcement that the Ghana Government would set up a permanent Commission to investigate all forms of corruption and to receive complaints about it (*Ghana Today*, 22 June, 1960).

ruption still awaits its Kinsey report. This difficulty must be recognised but we cannot refuse to discuss important topics simply because the best type of evidence is not available.

DEFINITION

I shall not attempt a comprehensive or legally precise definition of corruption,[3] and will content myself with the common understanding that a public official is corrupt if he accepts money or money's worth for doing something that he is under a duty to do anyway, that he is under a duty not to do, or to exercise a legitimate discretion for improper reasons. Institutions have official aims, the human beings that work them have personal aims. The ideal relation between the individual and the institution is that the individual should be able to satisfy his personal aims in harmony with, and while forwarding, the official aims of the institution. It is nothing to the Home Office that the prison warder has six children to feed, but the prison warder is acting legitimately in working as a prison warder so that he can feed his six children with his salary. Should he find his salary insufficient, however, and take money from the prisoners for doing them favours, he will be described as corrupt. He will be using his position in the prison to forward his personal aims in a way which conflicts with the official aim of the institution. There is a conflict between the attitudes and aims of a corrupt official and those of the service, and an equally important divergence between the attitudes and aims of the member of the public who induces the corruption of the official, and the aims and attitudes of the society as a whole. These divergencies may be defined by reference to the laws and regulations in which the official aims and attitudes are set out.

THE ARGUMENT

The corruption discussed here is, by definition, illegal. People break laws because they do not accept them, or because they have other interests or desires which they prefer or are impelled to follow. Some laws in a society find almost universal acceptance, other laws are broken by

[3] In England there are a large number of laws against corruption. The most comprehensive definition is that in Section 1(1) of the Prevention of Corruption Act 1906, which includes not only corruption by public officials, but also similar behaviour by any agent or employee. Of course the type of behaviour which is the subject of this paper is not in West Africa or anywhere else confined to public officials. Similar behaviour is common among the employees of private companies, educational institutions, etc.

large numbers of people. Head-hunting, for instance, is illegal in New Guinea and in France, but the laws against it are more often broken in New Guinea than in France. Obviously the law against head-hunting in New Guinea is further from the popular attitude towards that activity in New Guinea than is the similar law in France from the popular attitude there. If there is greater corruption in West Africa than in Denmark the popular attitude towards corruption in West Africa must be different from that in Denmark.

Thus far is tautology. The problem is to identify the reasons for the popular attitude. The argument of this paper is that a high level of corruption is the result of a wide divergence between the attitudes, aims and methods of the government of a country and those of the society in which they operate, in particular of the procedures and aims of the government which put particular groups of the population at a special disadvantage: that therefore the different levels of corruption in different countries depend on the extent to which government and society are homogeneous.

PRE-COLONIAL SOCIETY

The question of how far corruption can be said to have existed in pre-colonial times in West Africa, and how far present corruption is the result of the persistence of attitudes from that time, is an extremely difficult one. To discuss it adequately would require far greater knowledge of those societies than I can pretend to, and a great deal of space if due regard was to be had to the variety of social and political structures which existed. I shall, therefore, make only three points about pre-colonial society: points which are possibly obvious, but which are too important to be taken for granted.

1. Pre-colonial West African societies were familiar with conflicts between personal aims and official or social aims, hence their laws and customs and the punishments and other sanctions by which they were enforced, *but* although men wielded political power, judged causes, led armies, and collected taxes, their functions were less precisely defined in relation to those activities than they are in the bureaucratic governments of colonial and post-colonial times. The judicial functions of a chief were not sharply distinguished from his familial function as arbitrator and peacemaker, or his political function as a leader concerned with the manipulation of power, so that impropriety in the exercise of his judicial function, such as favouritism, could less easily be attributed to him as corruption than in the case of a modern magistrate whose sole function is to judge. To say this is to come near to saying

that, as there was no public service in pre-colonial West Africa, there could be no corruption of it, but this is not quite accurate. In fact, examples could be given of behaviour clearly recognisable as corrupt (and recognised as such in the pre-colonial society) from the histories and legends of the peoples concerned. Such examples might be expected to be most common among the larger and more articulated political systems such as those of Northern Nigeria,[4] which had evolved many bureaucratic features long before the advent of the colonial bureaucracy.

2. A man may, of course, be bribed with a horse, a woman, or a gun as effectively as with a roll of notes, but the possibilities and utility of bribery obviously increases with the growth of a money economy. In pre-colonial West Africa, money played a relatively minor part, though its importance varied from place to place. To take an extreme instance: in an area where the people lived at subsistence level and, as would be likely, had a political structure almost without full-time professionals, there would be neither the need for, nor the means of, bribery. Even more important perhaps, is the availability of the sort of goods and opportunities on which to spend money, that makes money of greater value than any other single commodity. This is relevant to the claim that the Communist Government of China has greatly reduced corruption in that country, once notorious for it. Obviously, corruption must lose much of its attraction if there is little on which to spend the proceeds, and the acquisition of wealth is in itself (quite apart from the question of punishment for law-breaking) looked on with disfavour. Only in a money economy and a society which allows a good deal of freedom to individuals in disposing of their property, loosely speaking a capitalist economy, will the types of corruption we are dealing with be widespread.

3. In considering the relationship between corruption and traditional society in West Africa, observers often isolate the customary exchanges of gifts as the element in traditional life which has led to the growth of corruption in modern times. While not denying the relevance of customary gift exchange to bribery, the facility with which a bribe may be disguised as a customary gift, and, indeed, the genuine ambiguity of customary gifts in some traditional contexts, it is, in my opinion, wrong to isolate one feature of traditional life in this way. There were and are many features of the traditional way of life which, in the context of colonial and post-colonial society, contribute to the prevalence of corruption. My argument is that it is this clash of old customs, atti-

---

[4] I can claim no direct acquaintance with Hausa Histories or folk-tales but Hausa friends assure me that bribery is a not uncommon theme or incident in them. It seems to figure much less in Akan legends and tales.

tudes, etc., with the new forms of government that gives rise to corruption. The customary gifts are just one example. Other examples are easily found; the extended family system which leads to the overburdening of an official with family responsibilities so that his pay is insufficient, his family and tribal loyalties which obscure his devotion to the national community, the absence of an established class system which makes it hard for the official to cultivate the aloofness which perhaps must, for most people, be the accompaniment of official integrity.

CORRUPTION IN COLONIAL AND POST-COLONIAL TIMES

In modern times my thesis concerns the disharmony between the government and the traditional society on which it is imposed and which it seeks to change. Specifically, of course, this modern government was in West Africa the colonial bureaucratic government. It was alien to West Africa in obvious ways: it was controlled from a distant land, and the controllers were subject to pressures and had aims often quite unrelated to the situation in West Africa; its key men were foreigners, often with little understanding of West African society, usually with no understanding of the indigenous languages, while its junior officials recruited from the indigenous peoples struggled to find a balance between their alien masters and the demands of their own people. The disharmonies were innumerable, and I shall consider only two of the most important; the first typical of an economically underdeveloped country, second of a type found universally but which can be seen particularly clearly in West Africa. Before dealing with these, however, there is one important general topic.

THE CLIMATE OF CORRUPTION

Some years ago, I was escorting an African judge from the court in which he had just sentenced a murderer to death, to his car. The large crowd which had assembled to hear the case lined the path, cheering and dancing to express their pleasure at the verdict. One phrase was shouted over and over again, and was eventually taken up by the whole crowd and chanted in chorus. The judge asked me if I understood what it meant, and I said that I could catch the first words, "You're a good judge . . ." but could not understand the rest. "What they are shouting," said the judge, "is 'You're a good judge, we thought you had been bribed, but you haven't.'" With that he got into his car and was driven away.

No one there was surprised. A wryness of tone was the judge's only comment on the compliment that he was being offered. No one in the crowd saw any reason to disguise the implication that there would have been nothing surprising if the judge had been bribed. We were all living in a country where corruption was a very normal part of the scene and the assumption of corruption was part of everyone's equipment for his daily business.

Such a climate of corruption is in itself an important factor. There is a continuous interaction between the willingness of people to pay bribes and the willingness of officials to receive them. People normally behave in the way that the people they live with behave. In a society with a high level of corruption, hardly any citizen can carry out his business, avoid trouble with the government, and generally get through life comfortably, without acquiescing to some extent at least in the prevailing corruption. There are not a few such societies in the world, and persons from more fortunate countries must, when visiting them or doing business with them, conform (or at least acquiesce), unless they prefer empty gestures which will inconvenience themselves to no useful purpose. At the other extreme, in an ideally uncorrupt society, the single corrupt man would offer to give or receive bribes in vain.

DIVERGENCIES BETWEEN GOVERNMENT AND SOCIETY

The two examples of divergence between governments and West African society in Colonial and post-colonial times which I shall discuss are:—
    (a) that between a literate government and an illiterate society, and
    (b) that arising from laws in conflict with popular attitudes.

(A) LITERATE GOVERNMENT IN AN ILLITERATE SOCIETY

Colonial rule in West Africa was and is the rule of an illiterate society by a literate government. The government operates in accordance with and by means of written rules and regulations. No one who cannot read and write can hope to occupy effectively any position in the public service. Entry into even the lowest grades is only for those who can read and write. Not only is reading and writing essential, but reading and writing *in English,* a foreign tongue. The majority of the population is illiterate and has little or no understanding of English. (Literacy and understanding English, are in these countries, almost synonymous). Friction between the literate public servant and the illiterate population is inevitable, and is, of course, greatest at the base of the public service pyramid, where functionaries and contacts with the public are most numerous, and it is at this level that the greatest *volume* of corruption occurs (the amount of damage done and money involved may well be greater at higher levels). Between the public and the functionaries with whom they most often deal, there is a constant flow of presents and bribes, given willingly or unwillingly, pressed on the official or extorted from the public.

Many examples of this process could be given (and it should be borne in mind that the public service in economically underdeveloped and colonial territories is of infinitely greater importance as the main channel of social initiative and the main route of personal advancement than it is in countries like Britain), but as an example of literate government operating in an illiterate society and how it differs from the same situation in an almost wholly literate society like our own, consider the confrontation of a police constable and a farmer. The farmer is barefoot, and the policeman is wearing a pair of large, shiny boots, and this difference may stand as a symbol of their relative ability to protect themselves in modern West Africa. The police constable is literate, he has learnt (at some pain perhaps) not only to adapt himself to a specific set of rules and regulations, but to wield them against others; he is an authority on the law, at least at his own level; he can arrest the farmer, or report him, and he has, again at his own level, innumerable official and semi-official contacts with officers of other branches of government service. The farmer is relatively [naive]. He is uncertain of the exact contents of the various laws that affect him, and uncertain how he stands in relation to them. He knows he should have a licence for his shotgun but cannot be sure that the one he has is still valid, or if the clerk who issued it cheated him with a worthless piece of paper. He knows he should have paid his taxes, but he has lost his receipt, and anyway there is something called a tax year, different from a calendar year, which "they" keep on changing, so perhaps he should have paid some more anyway. Even if he feels sure that he has committed no crime, he cannot defend himself against the policeman. To complain to the constable's superior would not be much good in the face of the *esprit de corps* of the police. He can defend himself only by going to some other member of the literate class, a letter writer perhaps, or if the case is really serious, a lawyer, but has none of the skills necessary to choose a competent practitioner, and he may be so misunderstood that his real case is never put. Even if he has a good case and wins, it may not do him much good. All the policeman's colleagues will know about it and sooner or later, of course, he *will* break a law. Much better give the policeman what he is asking for, or if he is not asking for anything, better give him something anyway so that when something does go wrong, he will be more likely to be nice about it. *A man does not*, says the Ashanti proverb, *rub bottoms with a porcupine.*

Consider for a moment a similar scene in, say, the prosperous county of Sussex. In Sussex the farmer would be as well if not better educated than the policeman, and will know those parts of the law which affect him better than does the policeman. The farmer may be himself a magistrate or a local government councillor, or know magistrates and councillors and perhaps the Chief Constable socially. For *this* policeman to demand money from *this* farmer for doing him a favour or not doing him a disfavour would be a laughable miscalculation.

This contrast may be overdrawn, but serves to make the point. The illiterate man entangled in the toils of a literate government is under a disadvantage for which practically nothing can compensate him, but wealth can help.[5] Sometimes the West African farmer, in addition to his other disabilities, would be poorer than the policeman, though the pay of a police constable in West Africa is not high; but if he were a cocoa farmer, a rubber farmer, a coffee farmer, or not a farmer at all, but one of the large number of persons who, although illiterate, make more money than a police constable, then the temptation for the farmer to compensate himself for his lack of power and knowledge by use of his money becomes clear. Equally clear are the opportunities for an ill-paid policeman to turn his power over wealthy illiterates into a supplement to his pay. This exchange of wealth for power, and power for wealth, is, of course, the typical pattern of corruption.

The phenomenon of a literate government in an illiterate society arose in West Africa with the imposition of colonial rule, but it does not, of course, pass with the coming of independence. The independent governments in Nigeria and Ghana are quite as much committed to literate government as was the colonial regime; indeed, since independence, departments, officials, laws and regulations have multiplied at a great rate. The removal of this particular disharmony cannot be achieved by the abolition of literate government, but only by the abolition of illiteracy in the society.

(B) THE OPERATION OF THE LAW

My second example of persons and groups put under a disadvantage by official policy and thereby becoming a source of corruption is the operation of certain laws. All laws put certain persons under a disadvantage, i.e., those who do or wish to do what the laws forbid. Such persons are a source of corruption in every country.

[5] It is worth mentioning here that in many countries with a largely illiterate population the defence of the unlettered man against government officials is often an important function of political parties. Here the illiterate is buying protection in exchange for his vote or his general support for the party.

But laws differ:—

    (i) in the extent to which public opinion supports them;

    (ii) in the ease with which their breach can be detected;

    (iii) in the profits to be made by breaking them.

    (ii) and (iii), of course, stem to some extent from (i).

If a man tries to land an aeroplane in a suburban garden he will find:—

    (i) that all the neighbours are anxious to assist the police;

    (ii) that his transgression has become instantly notorious;

    (iii) that the financial rewards are not impressive.

If he tries to sell alcoholic drinks after hours he will find:—

    (i) that many members of the public will be very pleased;

    (ii) that it can often be done without the police getting to hear of it;

    (iii) that it is a source of financial profit.

Obviously, it is breaches of the law of the second sort which are most likely to be a source of corruption. Laws regulating gambling and drinking, for instance, usually have little general support from the population, will be broken by otherwise law-abiding citizens, are difficult to enforce, and frequently broken. They tend to bring all laws into disrepute, and, by the creation of a large class of persons vulnerable to legal action at the hands of the petty officers of the law, they encourage corruption. An extreme example of this type of law was, of course, prohibition in the United States. Post-war rationing in the United Kingdom had similar consequences, fortunately on a smaller scale, but will remind us that such laws are occasionally necessary whatever the price that must be paid for them.

Let us return for a moment to our Sussex policeman. Is there any group of people with whom his relations are similar to the relations of his West African confrere with the West African farmer? The answer is Yes. There are, first of all, the professional criminals, those who habitually break the law. Such people he can harrass, and they find it very hard to strike back at him, however unjustly he may beset them. Criminals are a notorious source of corruption in any police force. Next, and perhaps more important, as they usually have more money than the criminal classes proper, are people who engage in trade and activities where the line between legality and illegality is so fine, and the regulations so complex, that they are always in danger of unwittingly committing an offence, nearly always being tempted to commit one, and can therefore plausibly be accused of an offence at almost any time.

Notable examples are public-house keepers, bookmakers and motorists.[6] Any government must, and does, put some activities out of bounds; each time it does so, however, it puts some of the population at a disadvantage and anxious to defend themselves by corrupting those whose duty it is to enforce the laws.

For obvious historical reasons, these West African territories have an unusually large number of laws which, by the criteria I have suggested, are likely to give rise to corruption. A colonial regime, especially one like the British, responsible to a representative government in the metropolitan country, is bound, and indeed most people in the metropolitan country regard it as duty bound, to frame its laws with more regard to British than West African standards of desirable behaviour. Particularly during the early years of colonial rule, the colonial governments were more responsive to British than to West African pressure groups. For instance, the abolition of slavery was brought about by a popular agitation in Britain, but brought the British Government's representatives in West Africa into conflict with powerful and traditionally respectable elements of African society. Another example is the rules which arose from the British Government's adherence to the Geneva Convention restricting the sale of spirits to the inhabitants of protectorates. These may have been excellent, but did not spring from West African conditions or West African demands, and were consequently a source of conflict and alienation between rulers and ruled. The enforcement of these laws was, of course, sporadic and uncertain, so lightly were the territories administered and policed. Many of the difficulties that might have arisen from the imposition of alien laws were avoided by the sheer impossibility of enforcing them, and the wide discretion given to District Officers to adjust the intentions of the Statute Book to the realities of the local situation. But not all conflict could be avoided. The Second World War, for instance, produced a great many laws intended to regulate economic activity. Without adequate means to enforce such regulation, and without any understanding by the population of why such regulation was desirable, laws of this sort served mainly to corrupt the officers charged with their enforcement. An excellent example is the Exchange Control laws. Introduced during the war, when the Imperial Government understandably required all sterling territories to have approximately similar laws con-

---

[6] In West Africa lorry drivers are always complaining about extortion by the police. It is often alleged that the police on road patrol simply collect a toll from all passing lorry drivers. If the driver refuses to pay it is, of course, never difficult for the police to accuse them of some driving offence or to find some detail of their lorry that does not conform to the, inevitably, complex regulations.

cerning the import and export of currency, etc., they were practically unenforceable against the indigenous merchants who crossed and recrossed the unpatrolled and often undefined land frontiers of West Africa. At the same time, "smuggling" of currency was, and still is, profitable and completely devoid of any "criminal" stigma; after all, the evasion of currency regulations was widely practised in the United Kingdom, where the population had much more reason to appreciate the need for them. Still, the law was there, and was, through honest zeal, malice, or with intent to extort, spasmodically enforced, so that many who regarded themselves as honest merchants were vulnerable to attacks from officers of the law, and under the necessity of buying them off. Trade across the frontier in West Africa is often extremely profitable, and these laws became a serious focus of corruption for enforcement officers. At some customs stations a *pro rata* tariff was extracted by the officials from those travellers who wished to import foreign currency, but were too lazy to walk through the bush with it.

Once again, this type of conflict between the government and society first arose with colonialism, but it does not disappear with the coming of independence. President Nkrumah's government, for instance, is more strongly committed to the transformation of Ghanaian society than the colonial regime ever was, and this transformation is bound to involve acute strains between the laws and the behaviour of the ordinary Ghanaians. This is particularly true, of course, of laws controlling economic behaviour in one way or another, inevitable when a government is committed to developing the country as rapidly as possible. High taxation, for instance, will enrol many normally honest people into the semi-criminal ranks of the tax evaders. Any form of direct control of rare resources has the same effect.[7] No society can be transformed without laws that go against the interests and accepted behaviour of some people in it; these laws will set up the sort of conflicts which give rise to corruption. A wise government might be expected, while recognising this regrettable fact, to limit such laws to what it regards as absolute essentials. Such attractive possibilities as the prohibition of nudity, polygamy, or football pools might be thought to be unnecessary additions to the strains and frictions which will be imposed by a nationalist government's essential programme.

[7] The allocation of Market Stalls by Local Government Councils in West Africa is a regular cause of scandals. The trouble is that these exceedingly valuable properties are usually let at rents greatly below what they are worth. The difference inevitably transforms itself into bribes. The simple device of charging as much rent as the traders would be prepared to pay does not, perhaps understandably, commend itself to the Councillors and officials.

THE SUBJECTIVE ELEMENT

As I said earlier, there is a constant interaction between the willingness of officials to receive bribes and the willingness of the public to give them. It is part of the general conflict between the aims and methods of the government and the society which is being governed that the subjective attitude of many officials in these countries should not be in harmony with their objective rôles. The official rôle is not one indigenous to West Africa, but an import from another society where it has grown up flanked and buttressed by many attitudes and social forces missing in its new environment. Many West African officials have successfully adopted and internalised the qualities required for their rôle, but it is not surprising that many have not been completely successful. The West African official, subject to pressures of which his British colleague knows nothing,[8] is caught and squeezed precisely at the point of conflict between the colonial (or post-colonial) government and the indigenous society. The British official in West Africa is an overseas projection of a well established and understood mode of metropolitan behaviour, protected by traditions of aloofness, and difference, and the approval of those that matter most to him (other British officials) from the alien pressures of West African society. This subjective aspect of the question, the question of the individual morality, is of great importance, and I shall touch on it again when I discuss possible remedies for corruption.

HIGH LEVEL CORRUPTION

I have so far been dealing mainly with corruption at the lower levels of the government, the level at which hundreds of petty officials enforce the laws on the general public. Corruption at a high level, corrupt behaviour by Cabinet Ministers, Judges, Ambassadors, presents different though related problems. A Cabinet Minister who accepts bribes is trading his power for money just as surely as is the police constable, but we are here moving out of the realm where sociological generalisation is *necessarily* useful. A Cabinet Minister may be corrupt in any society, but this may have much more to do with his individual circumstances than any generalisation that can be made about the society. Yet most informed people would agree that these West African territories are more troubled by corruption among Cabinet Ministers or their like than is, say, Denmark. This fact can be related to certain features of these societies.

[8] See Chinua Achebe's novel *No Longer at Ease,* William Heinemann Ltd. 1960, for an excellent description of these problems.

(a) A climate of corruption in a society will affect Ministers as well as policemen, and, perhaps more important, will lead to public condonation of corruption by Cabinet Ministers. It is a most disconcerting feature of these societies that ordinary citizens will believe, and recount, the most fantastic stories, some of them palpably untrue, of corruption among their leaders, with no or very little sense of indignation. Even when official enquiries have disclosed instances of undoubted corruption, this has often had no effect on the political careers of the persons involved.

(b) Politicians in West Africa do not come from an established patrician class. Most of them are "new men" and have therefore had no opportunity to develop standards different from the rest of society, such as can develop in a particular class or group, and are not personally wealthy (at the beginning of their careers at least). Elevation to Cabinet rank therefore presents them at once with new needs for money (see (c) below), and new opportunities for acquiring it by trading their power for the wealth of others.

(c) As Ministers in a British-type parliamentary regime, they are playing rôles not well suited to their own education or to the society in which they are expected to play them. I will give two examples:—

(i) The sharp distinction that has grown up in Britain between the purposes for which public funds can and cannot be used creates special difficulties in a West African context. In England in Henry VII's day the King's money was the King's money, and was used for forwarding the interest of his government in every way. Subsequently there grew up a constitutionally important but by no means wholly logical distinction between those functions of the government on which public money could be spent, and those functions (e.g., the organisation of public support) for which politicians organising themselves in parties were expected to find finance elsewhere. In England, money for political parties is available from the large funds accumulated by businesses or Trade Unions, but in West Africa such sources are not available. As in most other parts of the world, standard subscriptions from ordinary party members are not sufficient to finance this important aspect of government. Governmental corruption, "kick-backs" on profitable contracts, the sale of profitable or prestige-giving appointments, are an obvious source of party funds. A great deal of the corruption at ministerial level in West Africa is to be explained along these lines, and in these cases really amounts to a transfer of public funds from one type of political expenditure (i.e., legitimate by British criteria), to the other type, i.e., party political expenditure.

(ii) In Britain, the distinction between the official and private capacities of the holders of high office is widely understood and accepted. As a private person, a Minister of the Crown is not expected to be particularly hospitable or lavish in his hospitality. In West Africa, if a man holds high office, he is often expected to entertain his relations, tribesmen, political supporters, for such generosity may be a condition of continued political eminence.

(d) The desire for wealth, for whatever purpose, is reinforced in many cases by a sense of the impermanence of the new status. It is not easy for a man who has risen from poverty to eminence and riches in a few years, as many African leaders have done, to feel confident that the present affluence will continue. The widespread stories of secret bank accounts in Switzerland and other foreign countries are, if true, to be accounted for by the desire to hoard against possible lean years ahead.

THE FUNCTION OF CORRUPTION

What is the social function of corruption in West Africa? Although damaging to official ideals and aims, it is clearly not a subversive or revolutionary phenomenon. It is rather an emollient, softening conflict and reducing friction. At a high level it throws a bridge between those who hold political power and those who control wealth, enabling the two classes, markedly apart during the initial stages of African nationalist governments, to assimilate each other. At the lower level it is not an attack on the government or its instruments by the groups discriminated against, but an attempt by them to reach an accommodation by which they accept their inferior status but avoid some of its consequences. In spite of the damage it does to a government and its policies, it may be of assistance in reducing resentments which might otherwise cause political difficulties. This useful role can be demonstrated by the semi-official recognition given by the British colonial regime to a practice which in the United Kingdom would be classified as corrupt—the acceptance of gifts from local chiefs by District Officers. This well-established, well-known, but never, for obvious reasons, officially recognised practice, grew from the traditional custom of presenting gifts to chiefs when approaching them with requests for favours. It was tolerated by the colonial regime, albeit in a limited form, because of its value for that regime. The colonial District Officer was, to most of the chiefs of his district, an unpredictable alien, wielding wide, undefined, powers according to incomprehensible criteria, whose arrival in the local rest house was often a cause of alarm. The courtesies of the offer and acceptance of gifts of eggs and chickens brought this alarming official some way into the chief's familiar world, threw some bridge across the gulf which separated the two men, and created a relationship in which the inevitable frictions were softened by a personal familiarity and a traditional context. This was, of course, of great value to the District Officer in doing his job, and was therefore tolerated by the colonial authorities. A similar softening of what might otherwise be an intolerable relationship between the official and the people he deals with can result from more heinous dealings. Indeed, the greater the corruption the greater the harmony between corruptor and corruptee.

APPLICATION AND DEVELOPMENT OF THE ARGUMENT

I cannot attempt a detailed application of my tentative thesis to other societies, but on a superficial view it seems to have much to recommend it. Countries such as the Scandinavian States, with a marked homogeneity of society, are, it is generally agreed, fairly free from corruption. The shortcomings in this respect of the U.S.A. can be related to its large immigrant populations and its second class races. The role of immigrants in the corruption of big city politics is a commonplace of American political science.[9] The corruption in Spain, Portugal and some Middle Eastern countries might be explicable in terms of the wide divergence between the very wealthy classes, who have a considerable voice in government, and the general poor. Despotic and dictatorial government might be found to be more likely to produce and indeed to protect corruption than forms of government more responsible to the views of the ruled. A theoretically interesting limiting case is that of slavery. Slaves are a group under an extreme disability, with an obvious need to protect themselves. Under many forms of slavery, however, they have no money or other means to corrupt their overseers. The extreme degrees of disability therefore may not result in corruption, as they remove the means of protection. The optimum conditions for corruption, according to this theory, surround a group under a harsh disability but still possessed of considerable wealth—a Jewish moneylender in a 19th century Polish ghetto, for instance—a Negro bookmaker in an Arkansas town—a wealthy brothel-owner in London. These conclusions do not seem to be contradicted by what we know of the facts.

REMEDIES FOR CORRUPTION

Responsible leaders in West Africa often make statements denouncing the prevalence and the dangers of corruption and not infrequently

[9] The classic statement is, of course, in Lincoln Steffen's *The Shame of the Cities* and his autobiography.

launch campaigns to "root it out."[10] I am unaware of any such campaign which has had any lasting effect, or indeed has even led to many prosecutions. Various remedies from prayer to flogging have been suggested, but none has been seriously tried.

Draconian programmes for combating corruption are sometimes elaborated. These involve extremely heavy punishments together with a highly-trained, well-paid corps of *agents provacateurs*. The combination of the two is supposed to alarm all potential corruptors or corruptees so much that they are frightened ever to offer or accept a bribe for fear of being denounced. Unfortunately, such violent police pressure unsupported by public opinion would be quite likely to result in an *increase* of corruption and of blackmail. The *agents provocateurs* themselves would have to be members of the society in which they were operating and it is hard to imagine that such a job would attract persons whose integrity would be beyond doubt. Frequent change of personnel would be required so that large numbers of such *agents* would be needed, making it even more difficult to ensure a high standard. Their opportunities for blackmail would be immense, and it is easy to see that such a campaign could only lead to unpleasantness far outweighing any possible beneficial result.

Given the continued desire by the governments of the West African countries for rapid economic development and general modernisation, conflicts fruitful of corruption will continue and are indeed almost certain to increase so that no immediate improvement is at all likely. It will be a long time before the societies are remoulded and homogeneous with the government; even total literacy will take considerably more than a generation. Does this mean that there is nothing useful that can be done except to wait for the slow evolution of the society?

The answer is, I think, that a great many useful things can be done, but none which will have dramatically rapid results. To achieve anything at all, of course, the leadership of the country concerned must regard the problem as really important, and be prepared on occasion to sacrifice political advantage by, for instance, making an example of a corrupt Minister even though he has a politically useful following in the country. Given such leadership, and it cannot be taken for granted that it is always available, the following measures suggest themselves:—

[10] After this paper was written, President Nkrumah announced (see *Sunday Times* of April 19th, 1961, for a report by Mary Dorkenoo) new measures directed particularly against corruption among M.P.s and party officials. The tone of the announcement would seem to indicate that this new campaign will be conducted with some vigour.

(a) Exemplary proceedings against Ministers or other important functionaries to publicise the government's determination;

(b) A slight increase of police pressure against corruption at all levels;

(c) A fairly low-pitched but steady and continuous educational effort in schools, colleges, and in the newspapers, and by other means of publicity. Not just a short and violent campaign, but one continuing over years and becoming a normal part of all educational processes.

(d) Most important of all, a special effort with the public service. This is the most hopeful line of approach and might produce relatively quick results. If I am right about the effect that development and modernisation will have on these societies, there is no hope of removing the public servant's opportunities for corruption. It may, however, be possible to train him not to take advantage of his opportunities. Small groups of people can be trained to have different standards in some respects from those of the generality of people, and in any society this is a normal feature of specialisation; each specialised group has special standards in respect of its own work. By educational pressure and disciplinary measures it should be possible to raise the standard of the public service. Such a policy could only succeed, however, if service conditions and salaries were good and the status of the service high.

(e) Careful scrutiny of existing and projected laws to eliminate those that tend to increase the opportunities for corruption unnecessarily.

It will be seen that I have not included in this programme any reference to religious or social emotions sweeping through the population. Such events are, however efficacious, not usually to be invoked by statesmen.

CONCLUSION

In conclusion, I should like to emphasise two points.

1. In the West African countries under consideration, the colonial regime is the obvious historical source of the conflict between the government and the society. It is not suggested that similar conflicts cannot arise without colonialism, or that colonialism is exceptionally potent as a cause of corruption. There are countries which have never been colonies in the sense in which the word is used of West Africa, where corruption is much greater than it is in these countries. Moreover, as 1 have indicated, the succession regimes there are committed to a far more thoroughgoing programme of change than their colonial predecessors,

so that the conflicts productive of corruption may be intensified after independence. Moreover, corruption under the colonial regime was limited by the presence of colonial service officials whose standards were those of the British public service. It is not yet certain how far an indigenous civil service can have the same effect.

2. Corruption is an evil, but the avoidance of corruption cannot be more than a subsidiary aim of government policy. If my thesis is correct, colonialism and the modernising westernising policy of succession governments give rise to corruption—but this, in itself, is not a condemnation of colonialism or a modernising policy. Governments must frequently act in ways which result in conflicts fruitful of corruption. The means of control, forced purchase and rationing necessary to deal with a local famine, for instance, are always productive of corruption, but no one would hesitate to pay this inevitable price when people are threatened with starvation. What one may, however, hope, is that a consciousness among policy makers that corruption is a phenomenon with causes that can be understood, will lead to a choice of methods designed to minimise corruption, and to an understanding of the need to strengthen factors working against it—the most important of which is the subjective integrity of the public service.

Vision of Africa

TOM MBOYA
Minister of Labor, Kenya

A vision of Africa—present and to come—is impossible without being armed with a background and history of Colonial Africa—its impact, effects, and the problems it has generated for the future Africa.

Despite its force as a stimulus to Africa's economic development, colonialism has been the biggest hindrance to the development of the indigenous people. Under colonial rule, little attention has been paid to the need to invest in education, health, technical training, and general community development for Africans. Partition of Africa and the use of territories as sources of raw materials for metropolitan economies have not allowed the planning of continental or regional development. Instead, colonial divisions have treated each territory in isolation from others.

Africans are convinced that economic and social conditions cannot be considered apart from their political setting. Self-government and independence open great possibilities for economic and social development. Self-government permits people not only to embark on development programs serving purposefully the needs of their own country which they know best, but also enables them to establish relations with other countries on the basis of equality and to coordinate progressively the economy of their country with those of others. Full economic and social emancipation is not possible without political emancipation. Above all, it is through becoming masters of their own fate that the energies of the people are fully released for the arduous task of economic and social development.

The subjection of a people, in any form, including forced labour, apartheid, or colonialism under the guise of assimilation, is wholly inimical to economic and social development. This is the answer to those who argue that African territories must wait until they have a viable economy and have acquired enough experience before they demand freedom.

Reprinted from James Duffy and Robert A. Manners (eds.), *Africa Speaks* (Princeton: D. Van Nostrand, 1961), pp. 21–27, with the permission of the author and the publisher.

This argument for delay, which smells of a passive betrayal of democracy, ignores the fact that experience has shown that it is only after independence that most countries have embarked on large-scale economic and educational projects, and that in all cases it is only after independence that the world has begun to be conscious of a country's economic and social problems. In fact, the foundations for stable government have been laid only after independence, which makes nonsense of the plea of colonial governments that they are training Africa for self-government. In every case colonial powers have left their African territories only when the organized pressure of the people has made it impossible for them to govern without serious consequences.

In addition to the suggestions: "Caution," and "Go slow," opponents of African freedom have raised other objections. While most of the opposition arises from those who fear that independence will cost them status, economic advantage, or other special privilege, I would like briefly to consider the questions that are posed time and again by non-Africans:

For example, questions have been raised regarding the methods that may be employed by nationalists in the effort to achieve independence. Concern has been expressed regarding the use of violence especially where colonial powers fail to yield to nationalist demands soon enough. It is relevant and important to consider the disadvantage of violence both in terms of the immediate suffering to which it exposes the people and country and also in terms of the possible psychology it may build in the minds of the people, i.e. that even after independence some may have the tendency to resort to the same methods in an effort to replace their leaders or Government. To this extent the December, 1958, Accra Conference resolves to use non-violent positive action. Nevertheless attention must be drawn to the words of that great English reformer, John Bright, who declared in 1886:

"I have never said a word in favour of force. All I have said has been against it—but I am at liberty to warn those in authority that justice long delayed, or long continued injustice, provokes the employment of force to obtain redress. It is the ordering of nature and therefore of the Supreme that this is so, and all preaching to the contrary is of no avail. If men build houses on the slopes of a Vesuvius, I may tell them of their folly and insecurity, but I am not in any way provoking, or responsible for, the eruption which sweeps them all away. I may say too that Force, to prevent freedom and to deny rights, is not more moral than Force to gain freedom and secure rights."

Secondly, there are those, perhaps affected by the guilty conscience which the general record of Western colonialism must unfortunately lead to, who fear that Africans may yield to the temptation to victimize minorities—particularly the formerly dominant whites—when independence is gained.

To these critics it is necessary to point out two main facts. A look at all independent African states shows a positive desire to accelerate the rate of economic development. To a large extent such development is dependent on foreign capital and skill. Business, commercial and industrial interests seem not only to thrive but to expand in the independent states despite the fact that most of these are foreign-run and owned. This, of course, is not the same as dealing strictly with a European settler interest, and it is related to the second fact. The African in the so-called multi-racial areas is as anxious as his brothers elsewhere to accelerate the pace of development and will rely heavily on external capital and skills. It would be inconsistent therefore for him to adopt a deliberate and hostile policy of victimization based on colour.

But all these arguments apart, it must be realized that the mere delay of independence does not ensure ultimate security for settlers. On the contrary, such delay gives the impression that the settlers are the obstacle to African development, with the result that hate rather than friendship or understanding is generated. Consequently, it is more risky in the long run to move slower than faster. When all is said, it will always remain as a fact that no paper or other form of security is permanent unless buttressed by a fund of goodwill. Goodwill, on the other hand, depends on the relations that exist between the settlers and the indigenous people, and this in turn depends on how far the settlers identify themselves with the African course instead of that myth of white supremacy.

The African struggle for freedom cannot be stopped and need not be justified either. Mistakes are bound to be made, but these call for understanding rather than judgment and condemnation—after all, not even one of those powers who claim to be the champions of democracy have achieved perfection. America has a segregation problem at home. Britain has a colonial problem and a small race problem at home. France has a problem of democracy at home and Algeria on her conscience.

There are those who are interested in Africa merely because they fear she may fall victim of communism and join the Russian bloc. Such an attitude is not only negative but bankrupt and is poor salesmanship for democracy. Africa has urgent human problems to solve and must devote all her time and energy to this task.

Rapid changes are taking place in Africa. The decade now opening before us promises to be years that will see the end of all forms of colonialism in Africa. We may still have a South African problem, and the silent colonies of Angola and Mozambique may still be in the hands of Portugal, but most of Africa will be free.

After freedom comes the period of consolidation. This means the mechanics of governing, defining attitudes, and embarking on massive economic and social programs. Africa has to wage a bitter and in some places a bloody struggle for freedom. Her struggle has been based on moral issues and in defense of basic democratic human rights and fundamental freedoms. To these the new Africa must dedicate herself, for to fail to do so would be a betrayal of the concept of her own struggle. The African personality would be meaningless unless it were to be identified with the noble things Africa fought for. In addition, therefore, to exporting to the world the benefits of her newly won freedom and dignity, Africa ought to remain the symbol and reminder to the world of dedication to freedom and democracy. She has no history or ties that would embarrass her. She has a clean past and a new start, and instead of joining any of the present power blocs or forming just another bloc, she should concentrate on establishing her own personality in the context of dedication to basic individual freedom and civil liberties. India's freedom brought with it the concept of neutralism and non-alignment. But let Africa's entry bring with it this new and noble emphasis of dedication to freedom for the individual.

Freedom and independence cannot be defined merely as the defeat of colonialism, European domination, or external exploitation. It is true that Africa must beware of future subtler forms or attempts at encroachment on her freedom, but freedom must include freedom for the individual within the newly established states just as much as economic development must mean and include equitable distribution of wealth and social advancement for all people. This is a question which must be faced more and more, especially as increasing numbers of territories become independent. The people who fight for independence always look forward to the elimination of all forms of oppression and undemocratic behaviour with the advent of their own government. These hopes must be met and justified, for on this depends whether or not Africa can take the lead in getting the world to rededicate itself to freedom and undiluted democracy.

Too often people think of democracy in terms of British, French, or American parliamentary and institutional patterns. Such people reckon that Africa must therefore import a blueprint of similar institutions and all the paraphernalia that go with it. This attitude often tends to overlook the fact that in developing their institutions, Europe and America were influenced by the set of circumstances and conditions in which they were operating and developing. Without departing from the basic principle of individual political and civil freedoms, Africa must be free, during the period of consolidation, to determine what pattern of institutions would be suitable in running a democratic government in Africa. Critics of Africa have sometimes declared that democracy would not work because of illiteracy and because opposition parties are not yet in existence. Illiteracy is no bar to democracy—it may call for a departure from some of the pattern of institutions used elsewhere, but this does not mean democracy is abandoned. Opposition parties must develop not because the text books say so but rather as a normal and natural process of the individual freedom of speech and freedom to criticize government and the right of a people to return a government of their choice by use of the ballot box. Thus, in practice, when a country has just won its independence most of its effective leadership will have worked together as a team in the nationalist struggle and the new government will have pledged itself to serve the peoples' most urgent social and economic needs. Such a situation can only leave room for a very weak and small opposition often with less impressive leadership, at least in the initial period. Unless a split occurs in the ranks of the new nationalist government, this situation may continue for ten or even more years. This does not mean the abandonment of democracy, but it is a situation which calls for great vigilance on the part of the people in respect to their individual freedoms. The party in power has a heavy burden while the small and weak opposition must not be tempted to use violence or undemocratic means to compensate for her weakness or for her frustration when she fails to make herself heard on national issues.

This challenge is one which Africa must face up to, for it is the challenge before the new nations.

Like most of the underdeveloped areas of the world, Africa needs rapid economic development. She has to do this in the shortest possible time and often with very limited personnel and capital. While engaging in her new development plans, she has also to face up to the task of reconstructing her economy from the colonial structure to one suited to the needs of an independent state. This task is not made any easier by the East-West power competition, but Africa must avoid being involved in this competition and be free to further her effects through multilateral or bilateral economic arrangements with whatever country will supply her with her immediate needs on the easiest terms and without political or other strings.

In the process of economic reconstruction African states may have to think of broader ties with neighbouring states and possibly of a pooling of resources and coordination of efforts. Development of power, communication, and research are fields in which such action is immediately advisable. The establishment of the United Nations Commission for Africa is an important contribution in this respect.

Every African leader hopes that independence will remove colonial barriers and facilitate the growth of African unity and possibly one day a United States of Africa. All leaders would in fact like to work for such a development. But it would be naive not to recognize that a number of problems, including those of language, tribalism in some areas, poor communications and great distances, conflicting personalities and political opinions, etc. will have to be recognized and resolved. This calls for statesmanship and mutual respect and understanding of each others' genuine interest.

In the world setting, Africa is the challenge of the second half of the twentieth century. She has a potential and a future that is bound to influence world affairs more and more as her new nations emerge. She has her own personality, and this must begin to impress itself on other nations and to be recognized and accepted by them. World affairs are as much her concern as they are the concern of the so-called bigger powers. She has a much bigger investment in world peace than some nations, since her peoples' needs must be met urgently.

Africa's struggle is three-fold: political freedom, economic opportunity, and human dignity. When this struggle is won throughout the continent it will be her challenge to dedicate herself completely to these concepts for which she fought.

The African and Democracy

JULIUS NYERERE
President of the Republic of Tanganyika

By the end of this present decade the whole of the African continent will have freed itself from colonial rule. The African nationalist claims that the end of colonialism will mean the establishment of democracy. His present rulers, who have themselves shown little respect for democracy, are equally convinced that the African is incapable of maintaining a democratic form of government. They prophesy that the end of colonialism will lead to the establishment of dictatorships all over the African continent. This debate over the ability or inability of the African to be a democrat rages whenever the words "Africa" and "Democracy" are mentioned together.

I have chosen to join the debate, in this article, not because I want to take sides but because I believe the debaters have not bothered to define their terms. If they had done so, and particularly if they had cared to analyse the term "democracy," they would probably have discovered that their conceptions of democracy were totally different; that they were, in fact, wasting their time by arguing at cross purposes.

I think one of the first things one should beware of, in thinking of "democracy," is the tendency to confuse one's own personal picture of it—a picture which, if examined, will usually be found to include the "machinery" and symbols of democracy peculiar to the society with which one happens to be familiar—with democracy itself.

More than one attempt has been made to define democracy; probably the best, and certainly the most widely quoted, is that of Abraham Lincoln: "Government of the People, by the People, for the People." But I think the easiest way to eliminate the inessentials is to start by ignoring all such definitions and simply remember that the word means no more than "Government by the People." Now, if the ruling of a country is to be in the hands of the people of the country, the people must have some means of making their voice heard. It is obvious that not all of them can take a personal part in the actual legislation and

Reprinted from James Duffy and Robert A. Manners (eds.), *Africa Speaks* (Princeton: D. Van Nostrand, 1961), pp. 28–34, with the permission of the author and the publishers.

policy-making, so it is necessary for them to choose from among themselves a certain number of individuals who will 'represent' them, and who will act as their spokesmen within the government. This may seem so elementary as to need no such elaborate explanation as I have given it here; but is it? If it is, why do so many people claim that "Africans cannot maintain democratic government in their own countries once they become independent"? And why do they always explain their doubts by saying that "Of course no African government will tolerate an Opposition"?

I do not think anybody, at this stage of our history, can possibly have any valid reason for claiming that the existence of an Opposition is impossible in an independent African state; but, even supposing this were true, where did the idea of an organiz[ed] opposition as an essential part of democratic government come from? If one starts, as I have suggested, from the purely etymological definition of democracy it becomes clear that this idea of "for" and "against," this obsession with "Government" balanced by "Official Opposition," is in fact something which, though it *may* exist in a democracy, or *may not* exist in a democracy, is not essential to it, although it happens to have become so familiar to the Western world that its absence immediately raises the cry "Dictatorship."

To the Ancient Greeks, "democracy" meant simply government by discussion. The people discussed, and the result was a "people's government." But not all the people assembled for these discussions, as the textbooks tell us; those who took part in them were "equals" and this excluded the women and the slaves.

The two factors of democracy which I want to bring out here are "discussion" and "equality." Both are essential to it, and both contain a third element, "freedom." There can be no true discussion without freedom, and "equals" must be equal in freedom, without which there is no equality. A small village in which the villagers are equals who make their own laws and conduct their own affairs by free discussion is the nearest thing to pure democracy. That is why the small Greek state (if one excludes the women and slaves) is so often pointed out to us as "democracy par excellence."

These three, then, I consider to be essential to democratic government: discussion, equality, and freedom—the last being implied by the other two.

Those who doubt the African's ability to establish a democratic society cannot seriously be doubting the African's ability to "discuss." That is the one thing which is as African as the tropical sun. Neither can they be doubting the African's sense of equality, for aristocracy is something foreign to Africa. Even where there is a fairly distinct African aristocracy-by-birth, it can be traced historically to sources outside this continent. Traditionally the African knows no "class." I doubt if there is a word in any African language which is equivalent to "class" or "caste"; not even in those few societies where foreign infiltration has left behind some form of aristocracy is there such a word in the local languages. These aristocrats-by-birth are usually referred to as "the great" or "the clever ones." In my own country, the only two tribes which have a distinct aristocracy are the Bahaya in Buboka, and the Baha in the Buha districts. In both areas the "aristocrats" are historically foreigners, and they belong to the same stock.

The traditional African society, whether it had a chief or not and many, like my own, did not, was a society of equals and it conducted its business through discussion. Recently I was reading a delightful little book on Nyasaland by Mr. Clutton-Brock; in one passage he describes the life of traditional Nyasa, and when he comes to the Elders he uses a very significant phrase: "They talk till they agree."

"They talk till they agree." That gives you the very essence of traditional African democracy. It is rather a clumsy way of conducting affairs, especially in a world as impatient for results as this of the twentieth century, but discussion is one essential factor of any democracy; and the African is expert at it.

If democracy, then, is a form of government freely established by the people themselves; and if its essentials are free discussion and equality, there is nothing in traditional African society which unfits the African for it. On the contrary, there is everything in his tradition which fits the African to be just what he claims he is, a natural democrat.

It was possible for the ancient Greeks to boast of "democracy" when more than half the population had no say at all in the conduct of the affairs of the State. It was possible for the framers of the Declaration of Independence to talk about "the inalienable rights of Man" although they believed in exceptions; it was possible for Abraham Lincoln to bequeath to us a perfect definition of democracy although he spoke in a slave-owning society; it was possible for my friends the British to brag about "democracy" and still build a great Empire for the glory of the Britons.

These people were not hypocrites. They believed in democracy. It was "government by discussion" which they advocated, and it was discussion by equals; but they lived in a world which excluded masses of human beings from its idea of "equality" and felt few scruples in doing so. Today, in the twentieth century, this is impossible. Today the Hungarys, the Little Rocks, the Tibets, the Nyasalands, and the Bantustans must be explained away somehow. They are embarrassing in this century of the Universal Declaration of Human Rights. Man, the ordinary man and woman in the street or in the "bush," has never had such a high regard for himself; and the demi-gods who try to treat him as their inferior are conscious of his power—this power frightens them, and they are forced to try to explain away their crimes. Today the "people," whose right it is to govern themselves, cannot exclude any sane, law-abiding adult person.

There is no continent which has taken up the fight for the dignity of the common man more vigorously than Africa. In other countries men may shout "One Man, One Vote" with their tongues in their cheeks; in Africa the nationalist leaders believe in it as a fundamental principle, and the masses they lead would accept nothing less. "Equal Pay for Equal Work" is a catch-phrase in many countries which practise nothing of the kind; in Africa the leaders believe sincerely in the basic justice of this, and again their followers expect nothing less. In many countries which claim to be democracies the leaders come from an aristocracy either of wealth or of birth; in Africa they are of the common people, for if ever there was a continent where no real aristocracy has been built, whether of birth or of wealth, that continent is Africa. Tradition has failed to create it, and the spirit of the twentieth century will make it almost impossible for it [to] grow now. Indeed, it is one way of discovering the widely different conceptions we may have of "democracy" to listen to those people who would like to build a middle class in Africa "as a safeguard for Democracy!" To them, democracy is government by the middle class, albeit the masses may play their part in electing that government.

Add, then, to the African tradition her lack of an aristocracy and the presence of a moral concept of human dignity on which she is waging her struggle for independence, and place these in the setting of this century of the Declaration of Human Rights, and it becomes difficult to see how anybody can seriously doubt the African's fitness for democracy.

I referred earlier in this article to the "machinery" and the symbols of democratic government. Many of the critics of African democracy are to be found in countries like Britain or the United States of America. These critics, when they challenge our ability to maintain a democratic form of government, really have in mind not democracy but the particular form it has taken in their own countries, the two-party system, and the debate conducted between the Government party and the opposition party within the parliament buildings. In effect, they are saying: "Can you imagine an African Parliament with at least two political parties holding a free debate, one party being 'for' and one 'against' the motion?"

Ghana and Nigeria would be understandably annoyed with me if I were to answer such critics by saying that I *can* "imagine" such countries; for they exist, and they are not figments of my "imagination."

But let us suppose they did not exist. To the Anglo-Saxon in particular, or to countries with an Anglo-Saxon tradition, the two-party system has become the very essence of democracy. It is no use telling an Anglo-Saxon that when a village of a hundred people have sat and talked together until they agreed where a well should be dug they have practiced democracy. The Anglo-Saxon will want to know whether the talking was properly organized. He will want to know whether there was an organized group "for" the motion, and an equally well organized group "against" the motion. He will also want to know whether, in the next debate, the same group will be "for" and the same group "against" the next motion. In other words, he will want to know whether the opposition was organized and therefore *automatic,* or whether it was spontaneous and therefore *free.* Only if it was automatic will he concede that it was democracy!

In spite of its existence in Ghana and Nigeria, however, I must say that I also have my own doubts about the suitability for Africa of the Anglo-Saxon form of democracy. Let me explain:

In his own traditional society the African has always been a free individual, very much a member of his community, but seeing no conflict between his own interests and those of his community. This is because the structure of his society was, in fact, a direct extension of the family. First you had the small family unit; this merged into a larger "blood" family which, in its turn, merged into the tribe. The affairs of the community, as I have shown, were conducted by free and equal discussion, but nevertheless the African's mental conception of 'government' was personal—not institutional. When the word government was mentioned, the African thought of the chief; he did not, as does the Briton, think of a grand building in which a debate was taking place.

In colonial Africa this "personal" conception of government was unchanged, except that the average person hearing government mentioned now thought of the District Commissioner, the Provincial Commissioner, or the Governor.

When, later, the idea of government as an institution began to take hold of some African "agitators" such as myself, who had been reading Abraham Lincoln and John Stuart Mill, and we began demanding institutional government for our own countries, it was the very people who had now come to symbolize "Government" in their persons who resisted our demands—the District Commissioners, the Provincial Commissioners, and the Governors. Not until the eleventh hour did they give way; and free elections have taken place in most of our countries almost on the eve of independence.

The new nations of the African continent are emerging today as the result of their struggle for independence. This struggle for freedom from foreign domination is a patriotic one which necessarily leaves no room for difference. It unites all elements in the country so that, not only in Africa but in any other part of the world facing a similar challenge, these countries are led by a nationalist movement rather than by a political party or parties. The same nationalist movement, having united the people and led them to independence, must inevitably form the first government of the new state; it could hardly be expected that a united country should halt in midstream and voluntarily divide itself into opposing political groups just for the sake of conforming to what I have called the "Anglo-Saxon form of democracy" at the moment of independence. Indeed, why should it? Surely, if a government is freely elected by the people, there can be nothing undemocratic about it simply because nearly all the people rather than merely a section of them have chosen to vote it into power.

In these circumstances, it would be surprising if the pattern of democracy in Africa were to take—at any rate for the first few years— the shape familiar to Anglo-Saxon countries. It would be illogical to expect it to; but it is unjust to African democrats to assume, therefore, that their own pattern of democratic government is less dedicated to the preservation of the rights and freedom of the individual, an assumption too often made by the very people who have delayed the establishment of democratic institutions on this continent.

I have already suggested that the nearest thing to pure democracy would be a self-governing village in which all affairs were conducted by free discussion. But I have also said that the government of a nation must necessarily be government by "representation"; therefore there must be elections and discussion-houses or parliaments. As a matter of fact, in Africa the actual parliament buildings are necessary rather for reasons of prestige than for protection against the weather. (Our weather is quite predictable!)

The two essentials for "representative" democracy are the freedom of the individual, and the regular opportunity for him to join with his fellows in replacing, or reinstating, the government of his country by means of the ballot-box and without recourse to assassination. An organized opposition is *not* an essential element, although a society which has no room and no time for the harmless eccentric can hardly be called "democratic." Where you have those two essentials, and the affairs of the country are conducted by free discussion, you have democracy. An organized opposition may arise, or it may not; but whether it does or it does not depends entirely upon the choice of the people themselves and makes little difference to free discussion and equality in freedom.

PART SIX

A Larger Unity

Pan-Africanism, Negritude, and the African Personality

ST. CLAIR DRAKE
Roosevelt University

"Pan-Africanism," "Negritude," "African Personality"—these are expressions which, however remote and strange they may seem to our unattuned ears, carry rich meanings for increasing numbers of Africans. We widen and deepen our own understanding of Africa as we come to know what various types of people mean when they use these words, and how these expressions function as a part of the significant, but sometimes bewildering, ongoing contemporary African Revolution—a revolution which certainly has not yet reached its climax.

It should be noted, first, that it is impossible to discuss these terms and the concepts associated with them without repeated reference to Marxism, socialism, and communism. This is because the terms have been coined or refined by African intellectuals, and no intelligent African who has been reacting sensitively to his world during the last thirty years could avoid the confrontation and the dialogue with socialist thought and action.

For Africans who have lived in France or in French Africa, the political life around them has centered, at times, upon a dynamic interplay between Catholic, Socialist, and Communist parties and their affiliated unions. The people of the Left have also been those who have supported the anticolonial movements. (In fact, it is a matter of public record that one of former French Africa's most respected conservative politicians founded his local party with a strong "assist" from the French Communist Party and then, in 1950, made a deft disengagement. Sékou Touré's unions had a close alliance with the French Communist unions until he sounded a call, in 1956, for all African unions in Guinea to break away from all French unions, whether Catholic, Socialist, or Communist.)

Africans who have lived in England or in British Africa have seen that some of the strongest supporters of African independence have

Reprinted by permission, *Boston University Graduate Journal*, X (1961), 38–51. Copyright, 1961, by the Trustees of Boston University.

been members of a labor party which, I have been reminded more than once by African friends, enjoyed capitalist America's sustained financial and moral support, while it was nationalizing Britain's mines, banks, railroads, medical facilities, and even a part of the steel industry.

Africans in the Union of South Africa have not only been exposed to a hostile labor party which sponsored the Colour Bar Act in the mining industry, but also to European and Asian Communists who compete with a handful of white liberals for African attention. And in the Union, too, I suspect that communism has been made attractive by a government which legally defines protest against discriminatory laws as "statutory communism."

I shall add that the works of Marx, Engels, Lenin, Trotsky, and Stalin have been readily accessible to students in England and Europe.

I submit that it is the inquiring mind and not subservience to Moscow that leads to the lively interest which many Africans show in socialism and in nations that call themselves socialist. I think, too, that my subsequent discussion will reveal that Pan-Africanism, Negritude, and the African Personality function as intellectual and emotional anchors against winds of doctrine from both East and West which would blow Africans off the course they have set for themselves—being African! Indeed, for many Africans, exposure to a welter of competing socialist doctrines and nations is as confusing and disillusioning as dealing with scores of Christian denominations and several mutually antagonistic Western powers for the last hundred years has been.

I shall begin by discussing Pan-Africanism, the term which has been in use longest. It might help our discussion, however, if we start with a little mental geometric exercise. Let us, first, draw a large imaginary circle to denote Pan-Africanism in its broadest and most diffuse meaning as the tendency of some Africans and New World Negroes to unite their efforts in a common struggle to destroy the derogatory image of Africans and Negroes, which is a legacy of the slave trade, and to unite in the struggle against racial discrimination everywhere and for African self-determination. I call this *racial Pan-Africanism.*

Let us now draw a smaller circle within the larger one to define a more restricted set of meanings. As awareness grows among people throughout the continent of Africa of its vast potentialities and of the need for solidarity if independence and unity are to be attained as each new state emerges, what I call *residential or continental Pan-Africanism* also emerges. The emphasis here is upon uniting all Africans, *in Africa,* to pursue common goals. Emphasis upon this type of Pan-Africanism is replacing a former emphasis upon racial Pan-Africanism.

Finally, let us draw a small circle, in the middle of the other two, to denote the existence of groups of thinkers who try to elaborate systematic ideas about how the continent should be liberated and reorganized and what the relations of its people should be with other continents, with Europeans and Asians, and with the people of African descent everywhere. I call this *ideological Pan-Africanism*. Its main practitioners are George Padmore, Kwame Nkrumah, Sékou Touré, Léopold Senghor. The activities of people participating in all three circles make up *The Pan-African Movement* which has been in existence for almost a hundred years.

The history of the Pan-African movement is a fascinating story of the convergence of two streams of thought and action. One involves French-speaking Negroes, the other those for whom English is the medium of discourse. The term Pan-Africanism is itself the creation of a group of English-speaking intellectuals from Africa, the West Indies, and the United States, but it is now the common political language of both groups. It seems first to have appeared in print around 1900, when a West Indian lawyer convened a group of Africans and New World Negroes in London, to discuss common problems. A distinguished American Negro scholar, Dr. W. E. B. Dubois, convened the first formally organized Pan-African Congress in Paris in 1919. Dr. Dubois also convened the Second Pan-African Congress in London in 1921, and a third one met there in 1923, with a supplementary session in Lisbon organized by Liga Africa, an association of Angola and Mozambique Africans. Incidentally, shortly before this conference met, a Brussels newspaper denounced this Congress of 1923 as "an agency of Moscow and the cause of native unrest in the Congo," a statement as ironic as it was inaccurate, for in those days, Dr. Dubois was a leader of the liberal NAACP, and the few hundred intellectuals in the Pan-African movement had no mass base anywhere in Africa.

A Fourth Pan-African Congress met in New York in 1927. Most of the 200 delegates were American Negroes, but at least one Gold Coast Chief was among the delegates from abroad, for Casely Hayford, cofounder of the influential British West African Congress, had endorsed the program and pledged its support. This Congress planned a fifth one to be held in Africa itself, but the depression years shifted the American Negro leaders' attention to problems closer home. When it did meet, it was under different auspices—that of a group of Ideological Pan-Africanists which had been growing up in London between 1935 and 1945. The Fifth Pan-African Congress met in Manchester, England, in October of 1945. The organizing secretaries were a West Indian journalist, George Padmore, and an African graduate student in philosophy who had recently arrived from the University of Pennsylvania,

Kwame Nkrumah. The Chairman was Jomo Kenyatta. The 200-odd delegates were mainly African students and trade unionists. Dr. Dubois was invited from America to preside as "Father of Pan-Africanism." The mood was a militant one, with the African delegates insisting that the second World War must signal the end of colonialism as well as of fascism.

The delegates decided to go home to "ginger up" mass movements for self-determination that had already begun in Africa. They pledged each other to fight for complete political independence and a union of African states. The first country to be free would convene the Sixth Pan-African Conference. Kenyatta left for home in 1946, and Nkrumah left for the Gold Coast in 1947. Padmore, Peter Abrahams (the South African novelist), Ras Makonnen, a West Indian, and other members of the Pan-African Federation stayed in England to agitate, lobby, and serve as a clearing house for information. Richard Wright, the American Negro novelist, was the liaison with French African institutions in Paris.

By 1951 Ghana had secured internal self-government. By 1953 Kenyatta was under seven-year detention. In 1955 Padmore published a theoretical book called *Pan-Africanism or Communism?* to which Richard Wright wrote the introduction. After studying at Fisk University and Howard University in the United States, this sensitive and intelligent West Indian student had become a prominent leader in the international Communist movement. He broke from it in 1935, and his book explains why he came to the conclusion that the Soviet Union was using Africans for its own ends. He details the steps by which he arrived at a new conception of Pan-Africanism and ends the book with a summary of it:

In our struggle for national freedom, human dignity, and social redemption, Pan-Africanism offers an ideological alternative to Communism on the one side and Tribalism on the other. It rejects both white racialism and black chauvinism. It stands for racial co-existence on the basis of absolute equality and respect for human personality.

Pan-Africanism looks above the narrow confines of class, race, tribe, and religion. In other words, it wants equal opportunity for all. Talent to be rewarded on the basis of merit. Its vision stretches beyond the limited frontiers of the nation-state. Its perspective embraces the federation of regional self-governing countries and their ultimate amalgamation into a United States of Africa.

In such a Commonwealth, all men, regardless of tribe, race, colour, or creed, shall be free and equal. And all the national units comprising

*the regional federations shall be autonomous in all matters regional, yet
united in all matters of common interest to the African Union. This is
our vision of the Africa of Tomorrow—the goal of Pan-Africanism.*

When Ghana became independent in 1957, Nkrumah invited Padmore to come to Ghana to serve as his Advisor on African Affairs. Out
of conversations with Bourguiba of Tunisia and Nkrumah of Ghana
came plans for a Conference of Independent African States which met
in April of 1958. A new term appeared in the African political vocab-
ulary, "The African Personality." The opening paragraph of the Conference declaration read as follows: "We, the African states assembled
here in Accra, in this our first Conference, conscious of our responsibilities to humanity and especially to the people of Africa, and desiring to
assert our African Personality on the side of peace, hereby proclaim and
solemnly reaffirm our unswerving loyalty to the Charter of the United
Nations, the Universal Declaration of Human Rights, and the Declaration of the Asian-African Conference held at Bandung."

And so the African Personality symbolized the unified will of the
political leaders of these states to confront all other states with a common policy, a will determined by themselves and their supporters in
their own countries, and a policy determined always by the African
and not by the European, Asian, or American states. The ultimate
goal was an African political *presence* on the world scene, a continent
expressing itself as an entity in world affairs not only on matters of
war and peace, but on all issues. It was something which they expected
to grow. With twenty-eight African states, this African presence makes
itself increasingly felt.

For the African Personality to exert its maximum influence, however, every area of the continent would have to secure its sovereignty.
The Conference, therefore, authorized its delegates to support Algeria
in its pressure upon France at the United Nations, and the eight
member states pledged financial and moral support for a conference to
be convened to plan ways and means to widen the area of sovereignty
on the continent of Africa. This became the Sixth Pan-African Congress,
called the "All-African Peoples Conference," which met in Accra in
December of 1958. The Conference call had been prepared by George
Padmore and Nkrumah and the purpose of the meeting was stated as
follows: ". . . to formulate and proclaim our African Personality based
on the philosophy of Pan-African Socialism as the ideology of the African Nonviolent Revolution." Three hundred delegates from twenty-
eight countries representing sixty-two organizations were present. (It
may be noted that very few organizations of French-speaking Africa

were present, but that the representatives of the major parties were meeting simultaneously in Bamako trying to define the next steps in their relations with France and with each other.)

Nkrumah spoke at some length on his view of the African Personality, stressing the point that, while the concept had a cultural dimension, priorities should be given to the political dimension, to the pressure for independence within each African territory, and to the joint action on the world scene by the growing group of independent states. "An African Personality expressing itself through an African Community" was the way he put it. The conferees accepted the general point of view. They did not, however, commit themselves to "an African Personality based upon Pan-African Socialism." And on the question of "nonviolent revolution," the Conference resolution read: "Full support is pledged to all those in Africa who seek freedom through nonviolent means and civil disobedience, *and* to those compelled to retaliate against violence in order to attain freedom and independence. Where such retaliation is necessary, all legislation is condemned which considers those who fight for their independence as ordinary criminals."

The concept of continental Pan-Africanism, as defined by Padmore, and of the African Personality, as the term was used by the First Conference of Independent African States, are political concepts. They contain models to be lived up to, or to be attained. They are images of a desired high degree of solidarity. United Nations' votes are a useful measuring rod of attainment. South African apartheid evokes complete solidarity. On the Congo, however, African states *divide* into radicals, moderates, conservatives.

Implied in these concepts also is the idea that all men born or naturalized on the continent will recognize each other as Africans. This includes white men, too, "if they act right." "Acting right" means acceptance of economic, political, and social equality, and the idea of one man, one vote.

The concept of *racial* Pan-Africanism, as it has developed historically, deals with another dimension of reality, psychological and cultural —the desire of Negroes *everywhere* to feel confident and unashamed and even proud of their color, their hair, their lips, and of African cultures. The prejudice and propaganda of white men have destroyed this core of self-esteem or threatened it.

Continental Pan-Africanism offers a defense against neocolonialism and client relations with European states. Racial Pan-Africanism offers a defense of the citadel of the self for all who are fated to be identified with Negro Africa—West Indians, American Negroes, Africans. The concept of Negritude deals with these more subtle matters of the soul.

It is a product of French-speaking Negroes. British-speaking Pan-Africanism has a tendency to say, "Seek ye first the political kingdom, all other things shall be added unto thee." For almost a quarter of a century of Pan-African development, however, French-speaking Negro intellectuals did not bother about the political kingdom. They emphasized the primacy of other things. Since 1946 the two streams have been converging. By 1958 they were merging.

But let us examine briefly the development of Pan-Africanism among French-speaking Negroes. While Padmore was operating as the central figure in a group of English-speaking nationalist agitators in London between 1935 and 1945, a Senegalese intellectual, Léopold Senghor, was gradually emerging as the first among equals in a group of West Indian and French African poets, novelists, and essayists in Paris. They were exploring the *cultural* frontiers of Pan-Africanism. And like their British counterparts they, too, were trying to define their relationship to these socialist and communist movements which are an integral part of European culture.

Senghor, the African, had begun to reject the Marxist view of the world at about the same time that Padmore, the West Indian, was embracing it. In the late 1920s, as a student at the Sorbonne, Senghor had discovered the writing of a Haitian scholar, Dr. Jean Price-Mars, and the poems of an American Negro professor at Howard University, Dr. Alain Locke. He says the discovery was to him like finding a well in the desert. Here were men whose ancestors came from Africa singing the praises of what they called their "African heritage," while many educated Africans in Africa thought of nothing as good, or true, or beautiful that did not come from Europe, especially from France. Inspired by these New World Negroes he began to reflect on the values of Negro African cultures, while becoming a cultivated French savant, too. A few years later, a Haitian poet, Aimé Césaire, rejecting the values of both capitalist and communist societies, and protesting against the idea that Negroes were inferior because they had not developed an industrial and mechanical civilization, spoke in passionate defense of "those who never invented anything, who never conquered anything, but who, in awe, give themselves up to the essence of things," dancing ecstatically, drumming skillfully, telling tales rich with meaning, bringing wood to life with symbolism from their souls. He saw Negro Africans expressing something richer and deeper than riveters erecting skyscrapers or designers of machinery bending over their drawing boards. They were expressing their own inner genius which he called their Negritude.

Senghor, the poet, but also the scholar interested in philosophy, took the term, intellectualized it, and refined it. For him it was not that Africans had never invented anything. They had invented *other* things, but things whose value Europeans could understand and appreciate, too.

Negritude, as Senghor came to use the term, referred to that distinctive set of values and institutions which a people rooted in the specific environments of Negro Africa had developed through the centuries—an approach to the outer world and to human relations involving deep concern for the group, a devotion to spiritual values, and a certain "softness" and "gentleness" and "gracefulness" as opposed to the "hardness" and manipulative orientation of Europeans. He expresses this in superb poetic imagery. He felt that these were values in which Africans should take pride.

Change through intimate contact with the West was inevitable, but this did not mean that all African values must disappear or that Negro Africans should feel ashamed. Negritude had remolded Islam, had "softened" it. Why could it not do the same to Western culture? Senghor looked overseas to the descendants of Africans in the Americas for proof of the tenacity of Negritude. Despite distance and time and deculturizing influences, Senghor felt he could detect Negritude. In one of his poems he speaks of an element of gaiety and spontaneity which Negroes in Harlem bring to the "coldness" of New York. In his eyes they had preserved their Negritude. (Negritude survives better, perhaps, in Latin Catholic cultures rather than in Protestant Anglo-Saxon cultures, for the former type of cultures are more similar in ethos.)

Senghor turned seriously to politics after the second World War. He visualized a French Community which would give full scope in Africa for the expression of Negritude. He gradually began to move toward a position that independence and sovereignty were necessary goals. Today, the poet-philosopher is President of the Republic of Senegal.

Senghor explicitly rejects Marxism as a philosophy to guide African state-building. He rejects it on humanistic grounds and because he feels it is alien to the spirit of Negritude. But he also rejects Western capitalism as alien to the spirit of Negritude. Some kind of socialism based upon African realities is, for him, the path to Africa's future. We are fortunate that the American Society for African Culture has made available to the American public a pamphlet in English called *African Socialism* in which Senghor learnedly and forcefully states his position.

It is significant to note that those political leaders in Negro Africa who call themselves Marxist socialists incorporate aspects of the Negritude concept in their philosophical systems, although they do not use the term and may have come to the idea quite independently. Thus, Kofi Baako, the recently appointed Minister of Defense in Ghana, in a recent address analyzing the ideology of the Convention Peoples Party, defines the "African Socialism" to which it is dedicated as "a non-atheistic type of socialism adapted to African needs and conditions." But he insists that he is a Marxist too. Sékou Touré, the President of the Republic of Guinea, who also refers to himself as a Marxist, was reported in *Le Monde* for April 4, 1960, to have said: "Communism is not the way for Africa. The class struggle here is impossible. . . . The fundamental basis of our society is the family and the community." Or, upon another occasion, "Africa is essentially *'communocratic.'* Collective life and social solidarity give its inhabitants a degree of humanism which many people might envy." And for Sékou Touré, Africa always comes first, and for Negroes this means Black Africa. "Everyone," he has said, "must return to the cultural and moral sources of Africa, reintegrate his own consciousness, reconvert himself in his thoughts and actions to the values, conditions, and interests of Africa." Senghor would say it differently—"Everyone must accept the fact of his *Negritude*, and deliberately proudly."

Why, then, do Ghanaian and Guinean theorists insist upon retaining Marxism explicitly as a part of their concept of African Socialism? I suspect that it is because they are by temperament and experience activists, first, but philosophers, second, and poets not at all. They are interested, primarily, in the problem of teaching a new generation how the West conquered and controlled Africa; of the strategies of the African reconquest; of how the masses can be mobilized for the industrial "take off" in areas which are underdeveloped and largely illiterate; of how to analyze a situation in order to detect possible obstacles to their goals. They think that Marxist methods of thought and action taught them these things. It can teach others. But Aimé Césaire, the Haitian poet who coined the word Negritude, reminds us in an article in *Présence Africaine* on the "Political Thought of Sékou Touré" that "He is not trying to make Africa Marxist," but attempting to suffuse Marxism with Negritude. For him, political independence was a prize to be secured primarily so that Africans could be free to choose, to re-shape, and to reinterpret European values, and to be themselves. Aimé Césaire notes that Sékou Touré says of the future economic system of Guinea that "it must be worked out on the basis of the 'African Personality.'" With respect to education, its mission is "the rehabilitation and blossoming of the 'African Personality.'" Here is a concept in which the term refers to the ethos of African life, the spirit which suffuses African society, and to some of the customs and social arrangements which are characteristic of African life.

The recapturing of lost dignity is always Sékou Touré's main theme, and one road to it is by what he calls "the Africanization of action." He says, "Our unceasing efforts will be directed toward finding our own ways of development." This concept of African personality is not inconsistent with that of the Independent African States, but it goes farther by facing inward toward the African society as well as outward toward the world scene. On the cultural side, Africa may have many personalities, but each is nevertheless authentically African.

I must not end this discussion of Negritude without reference to an institutional expression of the spirit of Negritude. My distinguished colleague, Alioune Diop, might not refer to his venture in such fashion, but I plead "sociological license" in order to do so. In 1947 Diop and his colleagues began the publication of a journal, *Présence Africaine,* which, now published in both French and English, is indispensable for anyone who wishes to understand modern Africa. Among the original sponsors were André Gide, Albert Camus, and Jean Paul Sartre, whose article, "Black Orpheus," in the first issue is a classic statement of the more subtle implications of the Pan-African movement. The American Negro novelist, Richard Wright, soon joined the group. The Society for African Culture, which emerged to formalize the activities of the *Présence Africaine* group, convened the First Congress of Black Writers and Artists in 1956, with the blessings of UNESCO. Out of that meeting came the organization of an affiliate, The *American* Society of African Culture. In 1959 the Second Conference of Black Writers and Artists met in Rome.

The influence of *Présence Africaine* upon young people in the French-speaking areas of Africa has been highly significant. This magazine, for instance, opened a window on the world to those who eventually became the leaders of the nationalist movement in the Congo. By 1955 Diop in a now famous article, "Cultural Colonialism and Nationalism," was stressing the necessity for political independence if African cultural independence was to be assured. In 1959 a special issue dedicated to the Independence of Guinea stated one of the goals of *Présence Africaine* as being "to assist our friends . . . to understand the legitimacy of the African aspiration to independence and unity." When Padmore died, *Présence Africaine* memorialized him in "A Tribute to the Great Pan-Africanist"—the "spiritual father of Guinea" who "gave everything to Africa."

As one reviews the essays and poetry of *Présence Africaine,* he cannot avoid being impressed by the frank acceptance of a racial focus for Pan-Africanism which the editors and contributors show. They start from certain African realities, namely, that most Africans are viewed by the outer world as *black* Africans; that an image exists of *black* Africans as being inferior in intellectual capacity and as having inferior cultures; that this image is false and must be corrected. They do not wince at the word *black* nor apologize for being *black*. They do not narrowly define *black*. In practice they use the same definition as that employed in my native state of Virginia: "Any one with an ascertainable trace of Negro blood is a Negro." It is not the skin color in which they are interested, but the cultural products of those who are defined —and sometimes denigrated—as "Negro."

There are those who feel disquiet over the tendencies of African scholars and New World Negro scholars to express their feelings of cultural Pan-Africanism in organizational form. It seems to carry overtones of racism in reverse. But I think that Sartre, in "Black Orpheus," showed penetrating insight by coining a term which does not translate too well, "anti-racist racism." I would prefer "protective racial solidarity." As he points out, so long as race prejudice against Negroes exists, one can expect movements among them designed to clarify misunderstandings, protest disabilities, and to seek a common ground of action. This does not destroy their devotion to broad humanistic goals nor isolate them from their fellows. As Sartre says, it is a dialectical process. "Anti-racist racism" has as its goal the destruction of racism.

The term African Personality has caught on in West Africa, but not in the continental Pan-African sense. In popular usage, it reflects some racial Pan-Africanism and much Negritude. And despite the tendency of political leaders to confine the term to political matters, it has been taken up in popular usage to symbolize and give shorthand expression to a wide range of sentiments and aspirations. Scholars may protest, but the schoolboys and the semiliterate masses, the editors of magazines and newspapers, the producers of radio programs, and the speakers at political rallies in Nigeria and Ghana have a term which has "caught on." The popular meanings may be inferred from a few examples of the term's use.

A Ghana daily newspaper runs a regular feature of a picture of a girl in traditional dress; the caption reads, "The African Personality." An American visitor asks a college student why the busses and lorries carry slogans such as "Take Me Home with Care" or "Cry for Life but Not for Things" or "Holy Boy" or "Uncle Sam." He receives a laugh and an answer, "African Personality." Last December, an Englishman teaching in a secondary school in Ghana told me the story of a mischievous boy who, when he was reprimanded, flashed back, "No offense intended, Sir. I was just projecting the African Personality."

Certain verbs appear again and again with the noun. The African Personality is something that can be *proclaimed, formulated, asserted,* and *projected.* And for Sékou Touré, it is something that can be *rediscovered.* For some individuals, the term allows the expression of very serious sentiments. I cite a case from an experience at the Accra airport in Ghana. A Bristol Britannia 102 had just flown in with the Ghana flag on its tail and the words *Ghana Airways* on its side. Two trim hostesses disembarked and walked briskly toward the terminal followed by passengers of varied racial origins. A chauffeur whom I knew, who had had ten or eleven years of schooling, turned to me and said, pointing to the hostesses with an obvious sense of superiority, "See, we've projected the African Personality in the air. You Africans in America haven't done that yet." I had to grudgingly admit that what he said was essentially true. He reflected for a few moments. His mood changed. His next words had a tone of exasperation touched with bitterness. "Yes," he said, "our flag is painted on that plane. Those are African girls out there. Black men will soon be flying it. But we had to buy it from the white man. The white man still makes them." For him, as for most young Africans, the African personality will not be fully projected until *black* designers are designing airplanes and until *black* hands are turning them out in *black*-operated factories.

In the popular view, it is something American Negroes and West Indians are expected to have naturally. "Satchmo" is thought to have a lot of it. But white people may acquire it. I accompanied the fifty school teachers who went to Ghana under the auspices of the Peace Corps. Two of them won second prize dancing the "high-life" one night while relaxing during the on-the-spot orientation period. When I told the driver of my car, he grinned and said, "They're getting the African Personality."

Africa at the UN: Some Observations

JOHN H. SPENCER

Fletcher School of Law and Diplomacy

Within the space of less than six years, the African membership in the United Nations has increased from three to twenty-eight Members constituting the largest geographical group in the Organization.[1] Furthermore, as many as seven other territories may become independent and seek membership before the end of 1965.

I. THE RISE OF THE AFRICAN PRESENCE— FORMATION OF THE AFRICAN CAUCUS

This sudden and massive incursion of African states into the World Organization has naturally aroused curiosity concerning the role of these states within the United Nations and speculation with respect to their effect upon its functioning.

The African states can today amass, when they are fully united, some 26 percent of the votes in the General Assembly. Although this is not equivalent to the 39 percent position which the Latin American states had in the early years of the United Nations, it is nevertheless a major bloc of votes capable of exercising a pervasive effect upon Assembly proceedings. Over and beyond the mere votes alone, which thus far have often been widely divided save on clear-cut anticolonialist questions and certain broad matters in the realm of peace and security, the operation of the African caucus functioning in collaboration with the larger Afro-Asian caucus has become one of the principal factors in General Assembly politics.

The African caucus may be said to date from the establishment of an "informal working machinery" at the UN initiated by the First Conference of Independent African States meeting at Accra in 1958. It was only after the admission of the large number of new African states

Reprinted from *International Organization*, XVI (1962), 375–386, with the permission of the publisher.

[1] South Africa, which is not in the African caucus, is excluded for the purposes of this study.

in 1960, however, and the eruption of the Congo crisis, that the caucus became a major force in UN politics. As the Congo situation developed the African Members became both increasingly vocal and dexterous in political maneuvering. One measure of their influence was seen in their insistence upon the Secretary-General's accepting an Afro-Asian consultation committee on Congo affairs. Another was the vote taken at their demand on October 11, 1961, to censure the South African delegate for remarks in the General Assembly. On this occasion the African position resulted in a favorable vote of 67 to 1, with 36 states abstaining or "not participating." This was a vast change from a decade earlier when the General Assembly had at one point selected the Union of South Africa, over objections of the African states, as the representative of that continent to help achieve a solution of the Eritrea situation.

By combining their forces with the Asian states in the Afro-Asian caucus, which when united commands 47 percent of the Assembly vote, the African states have been able to increase even further their leverage in the proceedings of the General Assembly.

II. AFRICAN STANDS ON SOME ISSUES BEFORE THE GENERAL ASSEMBLY

Space does not permit a detailed review of the positions which the African states have taken in the multiplicity of votes before the General Assembly. Their stands have varied from time to time, depending upon circumstances, upon the type of question before the Assembly, and upon political influences of many kinds operating both within the group and upon its members from other sources. The record shows that most of the African states voted more or less closely with the Western powers on a wide range of issues when they first became independent. As time has passed group pressures, anti-colonialist sentiments, desires to demonstrate complete independence, and an "African view," as well as suasion by external arguments and blandishments, have led many of the states to part company with the Western delegations and to vote differently.

In glancing back over the record one can discern certain broad patterns of voting on colonial issues, as distinguished from questions involving the East-West struggle and from what might be termed "other questions" where neither colonial nor Cold War elements were at work.

Questions of "colonialism" are quite understandably capable of evoking a heated, emphatic, and vigorous show of strength against what is identified as the colonialist policy or action. This has been particularly evident where the action has related directly to African territory, as in the case of Portuguese Angola, or French evacuation from the Bizerta base in Tunisia. On the resolution at the fifteenth session calling for early termination of colonial rule generally, the African states spoke with a common voice. On the Algerian situation, on the other hand, the African states found it impossible to speak with a single voice or purpose. At the fifteenth session some of them, notably the members of the leftist and politically aggressive Casablanca grouping of states, including Ghana, Guinea, Mali, Morocco, and the United Arab Republic, bitterly condemned French policy and pressed hard for a resolution demanding a UN-supervised plebiscite in Algeria. Other states, especially those in the Brazzaville grouping of former French dependencies, were disposed, because of their associations with France, to resist such moves in opposition to the Casablanca grouping, while still others, identified with neither grouping, abstained, were absent, or voted on opposite sides.

The same transpired at the sixteenth session on the resolution calling for the neutralization of Africa with respect to nuclear testing. Most of the Brazzaville grouping abstained with France in the balloting.

On issues closely related to the Cold War, divisions have occurred among the African Members. Some have inclined to move progressively in the direction of an Eastward orientation, lining up their votes time and again with the Soviet bloc. This has been particularly characteristic of the Casablanca grouping. However, in such questions as disarmament, Tibet, Hungary, Cuba, and indeed, even on the Congo, the Casablanca group has not presented a united front. And one can even see tendencies on the part of such states as Liberia, Libya, the Sudan, and Ethiopia, which had previously been generally friendly toward the West, to cast their votes for Soviet-favored proposals, as in certain resolutions on summit talks, the Congo, and Cuba. On the other hand, members of both the Brazzaville and the Monrovia groupings have on many occasions voted in substantial numbers in the same way as the Western powers, or at least abstained and refused to vote against the West, as in the fifteenth session on the question of the admission of Communist China.

On the Congo question, a sharp cleavage developed among the African delegations. The members of the Casablanca grouping, in particular Guinea and Mali, on the one hand, pressed for strong, forceful measures by the UN to compel President Tshombé of Katanga Province to desist from demands for independence and to remain a part of a unified Congolese state. The members of the territorially closer Brazzaville grouping, on the other hand, were outspoken in opposition to the military operations of the UNOC (UN Operations in the Congo) forces and were often critical of UN activities in the area. For their part they were sympathetic to and supported the stand of Mr. Tshombé in favor of a loose confederation.

One could see in these postures, on the one hand, the fears of such leaders as Nkrumah and Touré that success on the part of Tshombé in rebelling against a central regime might give encouragement to resistance to their own totalitarian-like regimes and create a precedent for UN sanction of separatism. Members of the Brazzaville grouping, on the other hand, wished to forestall the rise of a potentially powerful, highly centralized regime in the heart of black Africa. They viewed Tshombé as a bulwark against a possible communist threat and as a stable element in the chaotic Congo political situation. Moreover, they disliked the spectacle of the UN intervening in what they considered to be a domestic situation. For what was done here could easily become a precedent for UN intervention in other internal disruptions or situations irrespective of the injunction in Article 2, paragraph 7, of the Charter against intervention by the World Body in "matters which are essentially within the domestic jurisdiction of any state." There was far more than a legal technicality at stake in the contrary positions taken by various African states on the Congo affair.[2] Nevertheless, despite this common attitude, the Brazzaville grouping, like the others, has failed to maintain a unified front on this problem during the fifteenth and sixteenth sessions.

On what might be generalized as "other questions," and even on matters that slip into the East-West struggle but are of distinct and direct vital concern to the African states per se, these countries have lined up with the West when they have found its position compatible with what they conceive to be their particular interests. Thus, in 1961, the African states were generally opposed to the Soviet Union's "troika" proposal for the Secretary-Generalship. Where their emotional desires for a peaceful world are brought into play they may find themselves in agreement with the Soviet bloc against the West, as happened at the sixteenth session on the draft resolution calling for an immediate nuclear test moratorium without international inspection pending conclusion of a general arms control agreement. On economic aid and development proposals looking toward larger expenditures or more liberal loan arrangements, the African states generally can be expected, out of what they conceive to be their own self-interests, to vote for

[2] For an incisive discussion of this problem see R. C. Good, "Four Tendencies at the United Nations," *Africa Report*, June 1961 (Vol. 6, No. 6); and "Congo Crisis: The Role of the New States," in *Neutralism*, published by the Washington Center of Foreign Policy Research, 1961.

larger, more costly programs than the Western powers are willing to accept. And many of them, faced as they are with the most difficult economic and financial outlooks, can be expected to cast their votes against heavier assessments or to resist making contributions for carrying out these programs.

III. ASSOCIATIONS WITH ASIAN STATES—INFLUENCE OF MEMBERSHIP IN AFRO-ASIAN CAUCUS

An important element in the activities of the African states at the United Nations is their participation in the larger Afro-Asian caucus. Although the Asian members are numerically fewer than the African, and although the principle of alphabetical rotation is followed each month in the choice of president, the pervasive influence within this caucus is unquestionably Asian. This development reflects several influences among which are the cumulative effects of the Bandung, the Afro-Asian, and the All-African Peoples Conferences, and the decisive support supplied by the Asian UN Members over the past decade to the emerging African group in their campaign for the admission of new Members from their continent. This has resulted in a generally close coordination between a substantial number of the African states, especially those forming the Casablanca grouping, and the Asian "neutralists," who often appear to be more pro-Soviet in their stance than genuinely neutral in the full sense of the term.

In view of all the subtle differences in the outlooks and policies of the various African and Asian states it is difficult to affix any hard and fast number to the Afro-Asian caucus members that are "pro-East," "pro-West," or "neutralist." During the fifteenth and sixteenth sessions of the General Assembly, voting alignments of Asian and African states on a number of highly political issues seemed to imply that a majority of these states were "pro-Eastern." But this interpretation can be deceptive. For not every time African states and the communist powers voted alike were the Africans voting *for* the Soviets; quite often it was the Moscow-controlled bloc trying to identify itself with Africans and Asians in order to insinuate the notion that Moscow is their true friend and supporter.

The voting margins have been too tenuous to permit the projection of any assured conclusions. On some of the most important contests at the fifteenth and sixteenth sessions substantial numbers, including some at least of the largest and potentially most effective leaders in the African scene, voted with the Western powers. Again, on some items the voting result was as much an identification of certain Western powers, especially the United States, with African positions and interests as vice versa. Thus, one must be careful in applying a "pro-West" label simply because of surface appearances of the voting tallies.

No hard and fast pattern is discernible as yet among the lists of abstainers on General Assembly votes. These vary with the issues presented and the diplomacy that goes on behind the scenes and within the UN walls. Somalia, Togo, and the Congo (Brazzaville) abstained on a high percentage of votes at the fifteenth and sixteenth sessions. About all one can say is that African states, like some others, are quick to take advantage of the protective camouflage which the international conference machinery can offer.

IV. THE ISSUE OF SELF-DETERMINATION

On no question have Africans felt more strongly than on self-determination. From the time that a sense of national consciousness began to stir among the African peoples, and leaders began to call for an ending of colonial ties, the concept of self-determination became the principal touchstone of African politics. Although this was not always spelled out in precise terms, the meaning was clear: sever the colonial rule, give the lands independence, let the African peoples decide for themselves what policies should be applied within their lands, within Africa as a whole, and what role their country should occupy in international relations. Along with this went, in many cases, resentments born of the sense of class consciousness, racial discrimination, and inequalities of social and educational opportunity which Africans so often experienced.

There is little question that the struggle for self-determination, and the need for friends and supporters within the United Nations on matters affecting the destinies of Africa, contributed to the coalescing of the African and the Asian states during the 1950's. For Asians too were preoccupied with similar issues in their own part of the world.

In the settlement of the problems of the former Italian colonies after World War II, including especially the assignment of Somalia to Italian trusteeship, Africans felt that African self-determination was at stake and they saw non-Africans making the decisions. Likewise, within the Trusteeship Council and in the General Assembly non-African combinations determined what should be done with respect to the trusteeships and the non-self-governing territories in Africa. All of these incidents, plus the struggles of Tunisia and Morocco for independence, together with hatred of the *apartheid* policies being pursued in South Africa against the black man, fired emotions and fed the urge to obtain the right of self-determination.

Viewed in the large, the long struggle for self-determination in Africa, both north and south of the Sahara, came to eventual fruition outside rather than within the United Nations. In a very real sense the UN was instrumental in advancing the independence of Somalia, Togoland, the Cameroons, and Tanganyika by means of the stimulus, pressures, and assistance brought to bear through the trusteeship system. The UN certainly aided Libya in achieving its independence and establishing its statehood. It would be foolhardy to say that the debates and resolutions in the General Assembly on the Tunisian and Moroccan questions in 1950–1951 did not play some part in hastening ultimate French agreement to their independence. And at the time of Suez, the actions of the special emergency session of the General Assembly in calling by an overwhelming vote for a cease-fire and the withdrawal of British, French, and Israeli forces from Egyptian soil, together with the establishment of the UN Emergency Force to take over at Suez and then to police the Gaza Strip, certainly were not an insignificant factor in preserving the independence and the integrity of Egypt.

For the vast majority of the newly-independent states, nevertheless, actions taken by Britain, France, and Belgium outside the Organization through collaboration or at last agreement with the nationalist leaders of the various lands were the decisive factor in their attainment of independence. It is understandable, therefore, that while the African states have been eager to become Members of the World Organization for the prestige, sense of equality, and economic and technical assistance which they may gain from it or through it, their leaders and people adhere to the view that their independence has been achieved largely through their own efforts rather than through the United Nations.

V. CURRENT CONCERN FOR STATUS QUO AND TERRITORIAL INTEGRITY

With the attainment of independence, the African states have now "crossed the divide" from the dynamics of "self-determination" into the area of status—that is, the maintenance of independence and of frontiers —and the protection of territorial integrity. Positions are now reversed. The concept of territorial integrity is a meeting place of the old quest for self-determination and the new concern for status quo. With this reversal comes a fear lest the United Nations should serve as a means or instrumentality to re-establish, in one form or another, the *"status quo ante."* And with this one sees the anomaly of certain Western states pressing for self-determination in Algeria, the Congo, and New Guinea over Afro-Asian opposition.

For many of the African states the problem has become transformed from the political issue of urging self-determination to the legal and political one of insisting on territorial integrity. Such a concept has no meaning in itself without the territorial definition supplied by the adoption of the existing boundaries drawn in the past by the colonial powers, however artificial they may be in terms of ethnic, economic, or geographic factors.

The magnitude of the dangers which may be involved in the further application of the principle of "self-determination" to peoples within the emerged states can be sensed in the facts that the Lunda, Chokwe, Bakongo, and Azande tribes extend far beyond the borders of the Congo into Northern Rhodesia, Angola, the Congo (Brazzaville), the Central African Republic, and the Sudan, respectively; that the Somalis lay claim to one-third of Ethiopia as well as to a substantial portion of Kenya; and that the Ewe cut across the frontiers of Ghana, Togo, and Dahomey. It is not without moment that President Sylvanus Olympio of Togo, who launched his career by serving as spokesman at the General Assembly for a Ewe national state, should now look with favor on the retention of the present non-ethnical boundaries of Togo.[3]

It is not surprising that African and Asian states supported and frequently invoke the provisions of resolution 1514, passed at the fifteenth session of the General Assembly, calling for respect for territorial integrity. Nor is it unusual that they should resist efforts to make Ruanda-Urundi into two separate states in accordance with the alleged desires of the populations rather than a unified state. It was in keeping with the same attitude that the majority of the Afro-Asian states opposed draft resolution A/L.368 presented at the sixteenth session by the Brazzaville group, and supported by the Netherlands, calling for the application of self-determination to the settlement of the problem of New Guinea. Speaking in opposition to this proposal the Indian delegate declared:

you cannot split up the peoples of any country. If you do that then what is there left? . . . Are we going to push this principle of self-determination, however good it might be, to destroy the integrity of States and to affect the sovereignty of countries?

And the Indonesian delegate affirmed that "the recent history of the Congo offers ample proof that full self-determination based upon regional or ethnical considerations only creates confusion and suffering for the people concerned."[4]

[3] S. Olympio, "African Problems in the Cold War," *Foreign Affairs,* October 1961 (Vol. 40, No. 1), p. 50–57.
[4] A/PV.1065, November 27, 1961.

Thus, the United Nations is faced with the seemingly paradoxical situation in which some African and Asian states that had formerly long and strenuously pressed for "self-determination" in North Africa now align themselves to block a proposal to that end offered by other African states. The piquancy and measure of the reversal are further revealed by the fact to which the representative of the Central African Republic made acidulous reference,[5] that the opposition to self-determination for New Guinea rested essentially on espousal of the Dutch colonial definition of the territories.[6] The position of the Brazzaville group has been almost equally clear; in 1961 it opposed a UN plebiscite in Algeria,[7] and through its leader, the representative of the Ivory Coast, it expressed support for the recognition of pre-existing colonial frontiers in Africa.[8]

Sensitive to press criticism of the ambivalent stand taken by some on the Congo situation, the Foreign Minister of Nigeria at one point observed:

Where, they said, is the principle of self-determination as regards Katanga? I said the following: how would you as an American like it if the State of New York or the State of California were to be cut off from the United States because the people wanted self-determination?[9]

Thus, following the example of the Latin American states in the

[5] "One of the principal arguments advanced in support of that thesis by Mr. Subandrio . . . is that when a colonial territory accedes to independence, its sovereignty should be exercised within the limits of the former colonial sovereignty. This is a principle which is doubtless quite just in most cases, but certain qualifications must be introduced when it is a question of territories whose peoples are not united by racial or cultural links or by common beliefs." A/PV.1065.

[6] "The right of self-determination applies, of course, to the entire population *of a colony as a unit and to the entire territory of a colony as a unit* [italics added] . . . The right of self-determination is not something to be applied to racial, cultural, or ethnic groups *within a colony.*" A/PV.1065, November 27, 1961, Subandrio, representative of Indonesia.

[7] "In our opinion, the problem of self-determination raises several awkward problems . . . We consider that we could never agree to the right of self-determination being exercised otherwise than for the whole body of the Algerian people and for the whole of the Algerian territory." A/PV.956, December 19, 1960, D'Aroussier, representative of Senegal.

[8] "At the moment of accession towards independence, in order to avoid internecine wars which might jeopardize the independence just acquired with such difficulty it was agreed to accept the territorial limits obtaining at that time." A/PV.1043, October 27, 1961. The political relations between the Congo (Brazzaville) and the Congo (Leopoldville), in general, and with respect to the provinces of Katanga and Leopoldville, in particular, cannot be ignored in this connection.

[9] A/PV.1031, October 10, 1961. See also opposition of the Sudan, itself a former beneficiary of self-determination. A/PV.1065, November 27, 1961, Ambassador Adeel on West Irian question.

nineteenth century, the African states, having won the struggle against colonialism, are now insisting upon respect of pre-existing colonial boundaries.[10] Ethiopia has long contended for the validity of the boundary line drawn between itself and the territory of Somalia by the treaty with Italy in 1908. Recently the representative of Liberia, the frontiers of which had been determined by agreements with colonial powers, cautioned others with these words:

We know that brothers and sisters were separated mutually by boundaries imposed to meet the requirements of the colonial powers. Much as we deplore those arbitrary acts, those boundaries have become fixed after a period of time and form all boundaries of the independent African States. What chaos, what confusion, what hatred could be engendered by each of the new African countries against each other were those boundaries to be changed or readjusted . . . My advice to my fellow African States, especially those that live in African States, is to let sleeping dogs lie.[11]

And in similar vein the Foreign Minister of Nigeria remarked at the sixteenth session:

I am not happy to listen in this Assembly and find one African State raising a question of a boundary dispute with another State here when in fact we can treat this as a domestic affair and deal with the matter at home. I am appealing to all concerned: African States, do not make speeches at this rostrum about boundary questions. That is why my country, in its foreign policy says, "Leave these territories as they are."[12]

Thus it appears that the General Assembly is not likely to become the forum in which decisions will be taken on controversies relating to boundaries in Africa if the African states can prevent it.

The same deep-seated concern for preserving their territorial integrity and independence can be said to underlie the suspicion with which some African states have viewed the activities of the Secretariat

[10] See Rupert Emerson, *From Empire to Nation* (Cambridge: Harvard University Press, 1960), Chapters VI and XVI.

[11] It would seem that the basic issue involved in the recent admission of Mauritania was less the threat to the territorial integrity of Morocco, as exploited by it in the discussions, than the threat to African boundary treaties generally if the colonial arrangements establishing the frontiers of Mauritania were to be drawn into question by the General Assembly through refusal to admit Mauritania to membership.

[12] A/PV.1031, October 10, 1961.

in the Congo and elsewhere. These actions have stirred fears lest the United Nations should intrude upon their independence or integrity, or should in effect re-establish a form of trusteeship in lands which have but recently emerged from this status. Thus, even before the Congo crisis, the proposal of the Secretary-General to establish a UN "presence" in Africa in the form of personal ambassadors, as previously attempted in the Middle East and Southeast Asia, evoked serious misgivings in African quarters.

The sudden interposition of the Secretary-General in the final phase of the boundary discussions between Ethiopia and Somalia in 1958 for the announced purpose of resolving the issues by his personal intervention was felt to be a factor contributing to the breakdown of negotiations and the failure to obtain a solution of this issue. Similarly, truce talks with the government of Katanga have produced periods of sudden opposition and obstructionism. There is a pervasive fear among African states lest the Secretariat be inspired to action along the lines of the late Secretary-General's political testament contained in the introduction to his last annual report.[13] If it is true that to a degree the General Assembly has assumed parliamentary powers, then the assertion of political and executive functions by the Secretary-General would exacerbate the fears already entertained with regard to the Assembly. Yet, such a course claimed the support of the late Secretary-General.[14]

The African states were, consequently, in the main laconic in their defense of the Secretary-General when at the fifteenth session he came under attack from the Soviet bloc for allegedly overreaching his powers. This did not preclude, however, their standing firm against Soviet machinations to replace the Secretary-General with a triumvirate that could be blocked at any moment by a veto from within the office by the Soviets or the West or a "neutralist." On the contrary, they used their persuasion and influence to elect an acting Secretary-General who albeit was from an Asian neutralist country. Although U Thant was known for active diplomacy on behalf of his country, he had not prior to his election publicly espoused the late Secretary-General's theory of executive-political leadership.

[13] See *International Organization*, Autumn 1961 (Vol. 15, No. 4), p. 549–563.
[14] In his view, the Secretary-General was "one in whom there would be combined both the political and executive functions of a President with the internal administrative functions that were previously accorded to a Secretary-General. Obviously, this is a reflection, in some measure, of the American political system, which places authority in a chief executive officer who is not simply subordinated to the legislative organs but who is constitutionally responsible alone for the execution of legislation and in some respects for carrying out the authority derived from the constitutional instrument directly." Dag Hammarskjöld, *The International Civil Servant in Law and in Fact* (Oxford: Oxford University Press, 1961), p. 11.

VI. CONCLUSION

The present attitude of many African states is scarcely one of unbounded confidence in United Nations operations. There is some hope, however, that the UN can be beneficial to these states, in helping them preserve their territorial integrity and in extending to them increased economic and technical assistance. The fact that the African states are able to work together with the Asian states on many questions has given them a measure of assurance that in the General Assembly at least their views can be registered with effect and that proposals which they deem inimical to their interests can be blocked. Conceivably, the transformation of some political questions into juridical ones, or at least their acquisition of a more highly juridical coloration than before, may well lead to disposition to refer some legal disputes relating to such matters as boundary lines to adjudication by the International Court of Justice. To the extent that this should occur in place of public debate and bloc voting in the General Assembly it would amount to a departure from reliance upon the Afro-Asian caucus with its numerous cross-currents and uncertainties.

For many problems regional institutions and solutions may serve a useful purpose in the African scene. The convening of no less than 25 regional conferences since 1957, and the recent organizational proposals of Casablanca, Monrovia, Dakar, and Lagos lend support to this hypothesis. A comment by President Youlou of the Congo (Brazzaville) exemplifies a feeling that is widely prevalent: "We cannot allow the fate of our brothers on the other side of the Congo to be decided quite arbitrarily by those who do not know their country and their spirit . . . Africa is our affair, our problems cannot, I repeat, be solved by any but ourselves, the great African family."

It is quite conceivable that African states which resent the discussion of African problems at the UN could accept to do so *en famille,* by "palaver" as it were, in regional meetings removed from the UN. Although the movement toward regionalism has already produced rival systems, the desire to find accord through regional channels cannot be gainsaid.

The success of the moderate elements at the Monrovia and Dakar gatherings in May and June of 1961, and the results achieved at Lagos in January 1962, give solid reason for encouragement. Fortunately the Lagos grouping constitutes the largest, and at the moment, the most active, regional organization.[15] For the near future regionalism can

[15] See Rupert Emerson, "Pan-Africanism," in [International Organization, XVI (1962)], p. 275–290; and Erasmus H. Kloman, Jr., "African Unification Movements," *ibid.,* p. 387–404.

perhaps afford a theater in which relations between the West and African states might be explored without the handicaps of protective coloration or parliamentary compromise that must almost inevitably appear when matters are being debated or voted upon within the United Nations. At the same time the United Nations can continue as a forum in which the African personality can be brought to bear upon world problems, whether in a unified or divided voice. It can provide an instrumentality for helping to keep or to restore peace, for mobilizing political pressures to speed the process of independence for the remaining colonial lands. And, of course, it is in the eyes of all Africans an indispensable channel for the funneling of economic, financial, and technical assistance for the realization of their aspirations of economic growth and cultural advancement.

Political and Regional Groupings in Africa[1]

CAROL A. JOHNSON

CONFERENCES OF INDEPENDENT AFRICAN STATES

FIRST CONFERENCE OF INDEPENDENT AFRICAN STATES

The First Conference of Independent African States, attended by representatives of the independent states of western and northern Africa (Ethiopia, Ghana, Liberia, Libya, Morocco, the Sudan, Tunisia, and the United Arab Republic), was held in Accra, Ghana, from April 15 to 22, 1958.[2] The purpose of the conference was: 1) to discuss problems of common interest; 2) to formulate and coordinate methods aimed at accelerating mutual understanding; 3) to consider means of safeguarding the independence and sovereignty of participating countries and of assisting dependent African territories in their efforts toward the attainment of self-government; and 4) to plan cultural exchanges and mutual assistance schemes.[3]

Foreign ministers headed most of the delegations participating in the meetings, which were presided over by Prime Minister Nkrumah of Ghana. In his welcoming speech at the inaugural session, Prime Minister Nkrumah pointed out that the conference marked the first time in history that representatives of independent states in Africa were meeting together with the aim of forging closer links of friendship and cooperation.[4] One of the main purposes of the conference, he continued, was to appeal to the Great Powers a) to make a supreme effort toward re-

Reprinted from *International Organization*, XVI (1962), 426–448, with the permission of the publisher.

[1] For additional information on this subject see Erasmus H. Kloman, Jr., "African Unification Movements," [*International Organization*, XVI (1962)], p. 387–404.

[2] "Accra Parley Demands End to Racialism, Foreign Rule in Africa," *Africa Special Report*, April 1958 (Vol. 3, No. 4), p. 1, 3–4, and 10–11. See also *The Manchester Guardian*, April 15 and 16, 1958; *The Christian Science Monitor*, April 17, 1958; and *Afrique Nouvelle* (Dakar weekly), April 28, 1958.

[3] *Official Handbook, Conference of Independent African States—April 1958*, Government Printer, Accra, Ghana.

[4] *Conference of Independent African States: Speeches Delivered at the Inaugural Session, 15th April 1958*, Government Printer, Accra, Ghana.

solving their differences and b) to let the African states work out their own destinies. In foreign affairs, he added, the independent African states ought to endeavor to follow a policy of positive nonalignment so as to enable them at any time to adopt measures which would best suit their national interests and promote the cause of peace. Turning to economic matters, Prime Minister Nkrumah urged the African states to explore trade possibilities between them, including the exchange of trade missions, while at the same time enlarging their trade with the rest of the world. Emphasizing that the African states should do their utmost to develop their own economies, he suggested nonetheless that they should welcome economic assistance offered through the organizations of the United Nations, as well as aid from outside the UN, as long as it did not compromise their independence. Succeeding speakers stressed the importance of establishing solid bases for continuing cooperation and of impressing upon the world the unity of the independent African states.

Of the eleven resolutions adopted by the conference, eight dealt with political matters, one with economic questions, one with cultural exchanges, and one with administrative machinery.[5] In the first group, with respect to foreign policy, the conference: 1) affirmed a number of fundamental principles, including loyalty to the UN Charter, settlement of all international disputes by peaceful means, and abstention from the use of collective defense arrangements to serve the particular interests of any of the big powers; 2) stated the conviction that all participating governments should avoid being committed to any action which might entangle them to the detriment of their interest and freedom; and 3) expressed the belief that as long as fundamental unity of outlook on foreign policy was preserved, the independent African states would be able to assert a distinctive "African personality" and speak with a concerted voice. With regard to the future of dependent African territories, the delegates, expressing the view that a definite date should be set for the future attainment of independence by each of the colonial territories: 1) called upon the administering powers (a) to take rapid steps to implement the provisions of the UN Charter and the aspirations of the people for independence, (b) to refrain from repression and arbitrary rule in territories under their control, and (c) to end immediately all discrimination; and 2) requested all participating governments (a) to

[5] See Conference of Independent African States: Declaration and Resolutions, 22nd April, 1958, Government Printer, Accra, Ghana. See also The Christian Science Monitor, April, 21, 1958; The Manchester Guardian, April 21 and 24, 1958; The New York Herald Tribune, April 21 and 23, 1958; The New York Times, April 22 and 23, 1958; and Afrique Nouvelle, April 25, 1958.

give all possible assistance to the dependent peoples in their struggle for independence, and *(b)* to offer facilities for training and educating peoples of the dependent territories.

Concerning Algeria, the resolution adopted by the conference urged France to recognize the right of the Algerian people to independence and self-determination, to withdraw her troops from Algeria, and to enter into immediate peaceful negotiation with the Algerian Liberation Front (FLN). It also appealed to France's allies to refrain from helping it in its military operations in Algeria; it recommended that participating governments instruct their UN representatives to consult with each other on Algeria and to solicit support for a just and peaceful settlement of the problem. With respect to international peace, a conference resolution, *inter alia:* 1) called upon the Great Powers to discontinue the production of nuclear and thermonuclear weapons and to suspend nuclear tests; 2) urged the UN to ensure that the African nations were equitably represented on international bodies dealing with the problems of disarmament; and 3) expressed concern, *inter alia,* over noncompliance with UN resolutions and the Palestine and South West Africa questions. Additional resolutions covering political matters: condemned racial discrimination and segregation; deplored outside interference directed against the independence, sovereignty, and territorial integrity of the independent African states; urged France to cooperate fully with the UN commissioner to ensure fair and democratic elections in Togoland; and, denouncing the use of military force against the unarmed people in the Trust Territory of the Cameroons under French Administration, appealed to the UN to intensify its efforts in helping the people of that territory to achieve their legitimate political aspirations.

The resolution concerning economic matters covered a wide range of proposals, including establishment of a joint economic research commission among the participating states, formulation of common policies on foreign investment, utilization of Africa's mineral resources in ways more advantageous to Africa's peoples, and possible eventual establishment of an African common market. In the cultural field, the conference formulated a number of proposals for the exchange of peoples and materials and recommended the conclusion of agreements for the promotion of cultural cooperation. Finally, with regard to administrative arrangements, the conference decided to constitute the permanent representatives of the participating governments at the UN as the informal permanent machinery for coordinating all matters of common concern, for examining and making recommendations on concrete practical steps in implementation of the decisions of the conference, and for preparing the ground for future conferences. A declaration issued by the conference summed up the views expressed in the resolutions.[6]

It was agreed that the Second Conference of Independent African States should be held at Addis Ababa, Ethiopia, within two years. In addition, according to press reports, *ad hoc* meetings of foreign ministers or experts to deal with problems as they arose were to be held when necessary.[7]

SECOND CONFERENCE OF INDEPENDENT STATES

A conference attended by high level representatives, mostly foreign ministers, of eleven independent African states plus delegates from several dependent territories met in Addis Ababa, Ethiopia, from June 14 to 24, 1960.[8] According to press reports, the independent states of Cameroun, Ethiopia, Ghana, Guinea, Libya, Liberia, Morocco, the Sudan, Tunisia, Togoland, and the United Arab Republic were represented by delegates; the Congo (Leopoldville), Nigeria, Somalia, and the Algerian provisional government were also granted full member status.[9] Among the guests were nationalist leaders from Northern and Southern Rhodesia, Kenya, Uganda, Tanganyika, South Africa, and South West Africa. In an opening address Emperor Haile Selassie of Ethiopia, noting that the conference was meeting at a time of crisis in the relations of the Great Powers, stressed that the breakdown of the East-West summit conference was a matter of concern to the African states since peace was essential to the prosperity and ordered progress of the African continent. Turning specifically to African questions, he emphasized the importance of stimulating increased cooperation in the spheres of trade and transport and urged the setting up of an African development bank.

The representative of Ghana proposed the establishment of additional African organizations, including a community of independent African states, a council for economic cooperation and development to coordinate the economic policies of the African countries and work

[6] Reproduced in *West Africa*, May 10, 1958 (No. 2143), p. 449.

[7] *The Manchester Guardian*, April 21, 1958.

[8] "African Political Leaders Confer in Addis Ababa," *Africa Report*, July 1960 (Vol. 5, No. 7), p. 5; "Independent African States at Addis Ababa," *West Africa*, June 18, 1960 (No. 2246), p. 697; "Addis Ababa Conference," *ibid.*, June 25, 1960 (No. 2247), p. 725; and Richard Pankhurst, "Independent African States at Addis Ababa," I and II, *ibid.*, July 2 and 9, 1960 (Nos. 2248 and 2249), p. 731, 769. See also *The Manchester Guardian*, June 16, 1960; and *The New York Times*, June 15, 20, and 26, 1960.

[9] *The Manchester Guardian*, June 16, 1960.

with the UN Economic Commission for Africa, a cultural council, a scientific research council, and a customs union based on the removal of trade barriers between African countries. The Nigerian delegate, on the other hand, cautioned that in the view of his delegation a union of African states was premature since it would involve "working from the top downward." He admitted, however, that there was a need for close cooperation between the independent African states.

The general themes of the conference were support for the independence movement throughout Africa and conviction that the African states should play a more significant role in international diplomacy. The conferees reached a series of decisions on two important issues discussed at the conference—Algeria and South Africa.

With respect to Algeria, resolutions called for a) negotiations between France and the provisional government for a cease-fire, and b) the introduction of self-determination. The conference also recommended continued diplomatic and material support for the Algerian liberation movement. With regard to South Africa, resolutions: 1) urged member countries to boycott South African goods and close their ports and airfields to South African transport; 2) requested member states to press the British Commonwealth to take all possible steps to secure the exclusion of the Union of South Africa from the Commonwealth; and 3) asked the Arab states to cut off all oil and petrol supplies to South Africa.

Other resolutions adopted by the conference: 1) invited the colonial powers to establish a timetable for the independence of their African territories; 2) urged the British government to take immediate steps to dissolve the Federation of Rhodesia and Nyasaland; 3) decided to establish a special fund to aid freedom fighters in Africa; 4) condemned nuclear tests in Africa; and 5) warned African states against economic neocolonialism, recommending the effective control of foreign firms in Africa.

On the question of cooperation among African states, the conference suggested the establishment of a council of African economic cooperation to organize a joint African development bank and a joint African commercial bank, as well as to devise other cooperative means of implementing and maintaining African economic unity. The conference also proposed the setting up of councils for educational, cultural, and scientific cooperation. The resolution on African political unity expressed the view that cooperation among the African states was essential for the maintenance of their independence and sovereignty, but deferred the question of any specific plan for unity to a later conference.

ALL-AFRICAN PEOPLE'S CONFERENCES

FIRST ALL-AFRICAN PEOPLE'S CONFERENCE

The First All-African People's Conference, a nongovernmental assembly attended by more than 300 political and trade union leaders representing 200 million Africans in 28 countries plus observers from Canada, China, Denmark, India, the Soviet Union, the United Kingdom, and the United States, took place in Accra, Ghana, from December 8 to 13, 1958.[10] The conference was called by a preparatory committee composed of representatives from eight independent states (Ethiopia, Ghana, Guinea, Liberia, Libya, Morocco, Tunisia, and the United Arab Republic); the 28 dependent and independent African countries participating were: Angola, Basutoland, Belgian Congo, Cameroons, Chad, Dahomey, Ethiopia, French Somaliland, Ghana, Guinea, Ivory Coast, Kenya, Liberia, Libya, Mozambique, Nigeria, Northern Rhodesia, Nyasaland, Occidental Afrique, Senegal, Sierra Leone, South Africa, South West Africa, Tanganyika, Togoland, Tunisia, Uganda, and Zanzibar. Mr. Tom Mboya, general secretary of the Kenya Federation of Labor, was reported to have been designated chairman of the conference by the preparatory committee.[11]

According to its organizers, the purpose of the conference was a) to give encouragement to nationalist leaders in their efforts to organize political independence movements, and b) to plan strategy for nonviolent revolution in Africa. In a speech opening the conference, Prime Minister Nkrumah listed four stages of political development to be sought by Africa's political leaders: 1) the attainment of independence; 2) the consolidation of independence; 3) the creation of unity and community among the free African states; and 4) the economic and social reconstruction of Africa.

Mr. Mboya warned, in addressing the assembly, that Africans would not tolerate any interference with the development of an African personality or any attempts to undermine the independence for which the African countries were fighting. Two themes underlay many of the speeches and deliberations of the conference, which dealt only with political matters and not with economic, educational, or social problems

[10] "People's Conference Plans Permanent Body," *Africa Special Report,* February 1959 (Vol. 4, No. 2), p. 3–7; and "Africa Lifts Its Voice," *Political Affairs,* February 1959 (Vol. 39, No. 2), p. 1–8. See also *The Christian Science Monitor,* December 9, 10, 12, and 15, 1958; *The Manchester Guardian,* December 9, 11, and 12, 1958; *The New York Herald Tribune,* January 4, 1959; *The New York Times,* December 4, 6, 9, 10, and 15, 1958; *The Times* (London), December 9 and 10, 1958; and *Afrique Nouvelle,* December 12 and 19, 1958.

[11] *Afrique Nouvelle,* December 12, 1958.

as such: 1) acquisition of political power by Africans, throughout the continent, as rapidly as possible; and 2) avoidance of "balkanization" of West Africa.

In addition to discussions in plenary, five committees were charged with the consideration of specific programs and the drafting of resolutions. The areas singled out for debate in committee were: 1) imperialism and colonialism; 2) racialism; 3) frontiers and federations; 4) tribalism and traditional institutions; and 5) establishment of a permanent organization.

The conference adopted numerous resolutions on the above-mentioned items.[12] It condemned racialism and discriminatory laws, citing the Union of South Africa, the Portuguese territories, and Rhodesia as examples of countries where racialism existed "in its extreme and most brutal forms," and deplored the alienation of the African's best land for the use of the European colonizers. In this area the conference recommended: 1) that states impose economic sanctions against South Africa in protest of racial discrimination there and withhold migrant labor from that country; 2) that no African state carry on diplomatic relations with any country on the African continent which practiced racial discrimination; 3) that immediate independence be granted to all African states in order to put an end to racial discrimination; and 4) that the mandate of South Africa over South West Africa be revoked, and that immediate steps be taken to grant independence to that territory. The conference also: rejected the Portuguese claim that her colonies were part of her metropolitan territory and demanded their immediate independence; condemned discriminatory practices in the Central African Federation; and urged the British government to end the state of emergency in Kenya, release political prisoners, abrogate all discriminatory laws, establish a common electoral role based on adult "one man, one vote" suffrage, and enact laws for the transfer of lands and rights to the African people.

Another resolution condemned imperialism and colonialism in any form and stated that the political and economic exploitation of Africans by Europeans should cease forthwith. The conference declared its full support to all fighters for freedom in Africa and suggested that African states should pursue in their international policy principles which would expedite and accelerate the independence and sovereignty of all dependent and colonial African territories. It also urged that the universal adult franchise be extended, and that a human rights committee of the conference be formed for the purpose of examining complaints

[12] Complete text of the resolutions reproduced in *Current History*, July 1959 (Vol. 37, No. 215), p. 41–46

of the abuse of human rights in every part of Africa and of taking appropriate steps to ensure the enjoyment of these rights by everyone.

The conference designated tribalism and religious separatism obstacles to the rapid liberation of Africa, to the political evolution of African countries, and to realization of the unity of the continent. It recommended that steps be taken by political, trade union, cultural, and other organizations to educate the masses concerning the dangers of these "evil practices," and that independent countries allow their governments to pass laws and distribute propaganda discouraging tribalism and religious separatism. A further resolution called upon the governments of independent countries to suppress or modify traditional institutions, since they were a barrier to progress.

Under the heading "frontiers, boundaries, and federations," the conference endorsed Pan-Africanism and declared its own ultimate objective to be the evolution of a commonwealth of free African states. In addition, it expressed support for the desire in various parts of Africa for regional groupings of states, but advocated that such groupings be based on the following three principles: 1) only independent states and countries governed by Africans should join together; 2) the establishment of regional groupings should not be prejudicial to the ultimate objective of a Pan-African commonwealth; and 3) adherence to any group should depend on the wishes of the people ascertained by referendum on the basis of universal adult suffrage. The conference resolution on this item denounced the artificial frontiers drawn by the imperialist powers, particularly those which cut across ethnic groups, and called for the abolition or adjustment of such artificial boundaries at an early date.

Finally, the delegates decided to establish the All-African People's Conference on a permanent basis with a professionally-staffed secretariat at Accra. The aims of the organization were to be: 1) to promote understanding and unity among the peoples of Africa; 2) to accelerate the liberation of Africa from imperialism and colonialism; 3) to mobilize world opinion against the denial of political and fundamental human rights to Africans; and 4) to develop the feeling of one community among the peoples of Africa, with the object of the emergence of a United States of Africa. The secretariat was charged with the task of organizing a similar conference every year.

In a closing speech, Prime Minister Nkrumah once again drew attention to the following goals: independence, creation of an African community, and economic and social reconstruction on the basis of African socialism. Calling for an all-African trade conference and a cultural conference, he pointed specifically to the role of African busi-

nessmen in the economic reconstruction of Africa. He reminded delegates that disciplined organization was the key for the attainment of
African independence. Chairman Mboya delineated the problems facing
the conference as: 1) colonialism; and 2) European minority elements
in East and southern Africa. The attitude and stand taken by the colonial powers, he warned, would determine whether Africans would be
driven to violence.

SECOND ALL-AFRICAN PEOPLE'S CONFERENCE

The Second All-African People's Conference was held in Tunis
from January 25 to 31, 1960; some 180 delegates from about 30 African
countries, including the Portuguese territories and the Union of South
Africa, and over 40 observers from China, Greece, India, the United
Kingdom, the United States, West Germany, and Yugoslavia attended.[13]
Opening the conference, President Habib Bourguiba of Tunisia appealed to Africans to eliminate artificial boundaries and unify the continent. He urged the attainment of independence by peaceful means but
expressed support for the use of arms where necessary.

These two themes—independence and unity—were re-echoed in the
speeches of other delegates. The conference devoted considerable discussion to the dangers of neocolonialism—economic dependence on the
former metropole, balkanization resulting in political vulnerability, and
affiliation of African institutions, particularly trade unions, with international bodies. Conferees criticized the French Community and the
European Economic Community as examples of the new form of imperialism. In addition, delegates stressed the desire of Africans to remain
outside the divisions of the Cold War and to keep their organizations
free from foreign influences.

Resolutions adopted by the conference: called for the independence
of all colonies; urged the break-up of the Central African Federation;
supported the Greater Somali movement aimed at uniting British
Somaliland with Somalia and parts of Ethiopia and Kenya; and demanded immediate independence for Kenya on the basis of "one man,

[13] "All-African People's Conference Convenes in Tunis," *Africa Report,* January
1960 (Vol. 5, No. 1), p. 6; "Tunis Conference Ends on Militant Note," *ibid.,*
February 1960 (Vol. 5, No. 2), p. 13; "All-African Peoples at Tunis," *West Africa,*
January 30, 1960 (No. 2226), p. 130; "All Africa People's Conference at Tunis,"
ibid., February 6, 1960 (No. 2227), p. 143; "African Voices in Tunis," *ibid.,*
February 13, 1960 (No. 2228), p. 177; Lorna Hahn, "Africans Meet in Tunis," *The
New Leader,* February 8, 1960 (Vol. 43, No. 6), p. 8; Catherine Hoskyns, "Tunis
Diary: An Impression of the Second All-African People's Conference," *Africa South,*
July–September 1960 (Vol. 4, No. 4), p. 104–111; and "Africans in Congress," I
and II, *The Economist,* February 6 and 20, 1960 (Vol. 194, Nos. 6076 and 6078),
p. 534, 728–730.

one vote," together with the release of nationalist leader, Jomo Kenyatta. The conference asked the African states to intensify the struggle for independence, and decided to set up a committee to coordinate aid from the independent countries to the nationalist movements. On Algeria resolutions were enacted which: 1) called for the creation of a corps of all-African volunteers to fight with the FLN; 2) requested all governments to pledge regular financial contributions to the Algerian insurgents; 3) invited all states to recognize the FLN government in exile; 4) appealed to the UN to impose peace in North Africa and to recognize an independent Algeria; and 5) sent a message to the United States government urging withdrawal of economic and military aid to France on the ground that such assistance was being used to prolong the Algerian War.

In terms of inter-African cooperation the conference agreed to establish an all-African trade union, with an autonomous African central organization. The details were left to an African trade union conference which was to meet in Casablanca, Morocco, in May. In the economic field, leaders were urged to wrest their respective countries from economic dependence on ex-imperialist countries and not to enter into any undertaking which would prejudice the move toward liberty and unity in Africa. Specific recommendations for further economic unity included the following: establishment of a transport company to provide better links between the African countries; creation of an all-African investment bank; and removal of customs and trade barriers wherever possible. On the social and educational level the conference approved a) the establishment of organizations to finance the training of students, technicians, and cadres, and b) the holding of an all-African youth festival and sports program. The conference also urged exchanges of teachers, students, technicians, and doctors.

Finally, delegates decided that the Secretary-General of the conference should be a full-time official, and re-elected Abdoulaye Diallo, Guinea's resident minister in Ghana, to that position.

THIRD ALL-AFRICAN PEOPLE'S CONFERENCE

From March 25 to 31, 1961, approximately 207 delegates representing 58 political and trade union groups from over 30 countries, together with a number of observers, attended the Third All-African People's Conference at Cairo.[14] The press noted that the resolutions adopted by the conference covered the following five general questions:

[14] George M. Houser, "At Cairo—the Third All-African People's Conference," *Africa Today*, April 1961, p. 11–13; and "All Africa People's Condemn Neocolonialism," *West Africa*, April 8, 1961 (No. 2288), p. 389.

1) liberation of African colonies; 2) new patterns of colonialism; 3) decolonization of Africa and reorganization of the liberation movement; 4) cultural, economic, and social development of the continent; and 5) African unity and solidarity.[15]

With respect to the liberation of African colonies, the conference recommended the creation of an all-Africa freedom fund committee to administer an African freedom fund.[16] The committee, which was to be composed of three representatives of independent African states and three of dependent territories, was to meet at least once every three months to study the financial needs of all the African countries struggling for freedom. The resolution also demanded the immediate withdrawal of all colonial governments from Africa and urged African freedom fighters to intensify their struggle. A second conference resolution denounced the following as manifestations of neocolonialism: puppet governments, foreign military bases, regrouping of states, balkanization, integration into colonial economic blocs, economic infiltration by a foreign power or economic entrenchment of the colonial power, and direct monetary dependence.[17] The resolution named the United States, West Germany, Israel, Britain, Belgium, the Netherlands, South Africa, and France as the main perpetrators of neocolonialism, and designated colonial embassies and "so-called foreign and United Nations technical assistance" personnel who "sabotaged" national development as agents of neocolonialism. It invited all independent African states to aid the liberation of the dependent African countries, and reaffirmed a determination to mobilize mass opinion against neocolonialism.

With regard to reorganization of institutional structures, the conference recommended at the political level 1) suppression of all discriminatory and reactionary institutions, and 2) reorganization of the judiciary and the administration.[18] At the economic level the following modifications were suggested: 1) subordination of the economy to the needs of national interests, through control over (a) exports, imports, and investments, and (b) production; 2) introduction of agrarian reforms; 3) creation of currencies and national banks; and 4) establishment of internal commercial links and lines of communication permitting profitable cooperation. At the cultural and social level the con-

[15] *La Bourse Egyptienne,* March 26, 1961, and *The Times* (London), March 30, 1961.
[16] All-African People's Conference, Cairo, March 1961, *Resolution on the Liberation of Dependent Countries.*
[17] All-African People's Conference, Cairo, March 1961, *Second Commission Resolutions.*
[18] All-African People's Conference, Cairo, March 1961, *Resolution, Reorganization of Structures and Liquidation of Remnants of Imperialism.*

ference demanded: 1) the reorganization of education with a view to establishing authentic African history; and 2) the organization of youth activities in the direction of sports, popular artistic education, and national construction. Concerning economic and social development, the conference proposed: 1) establishment of an interstate African transport company (land, sea, and air); 2) creation of an African investment bank; 3) signing of multilateral customs and foreign exchange agreements; 4) recognition of trade union rights and setting up of a council of states to control and examine cases involving the violation of the democratic rights of workers; 5) establishment of a common research institute to promote authentic African culture; and 6) creation of an African solidarity academy, offers of scholarships, and increases in cultural exchanges.[19]

Concerning African unity, the conference recommended the setting up of the following: 1) an African consultative assembly composed of members representing the parliaments of independent states, which would meet periodically to formulate a common policy of African states; 2) a council of African states to study and implement recommendations of the consultative assembly; 3) a commission of experts to elaborate a common economic policy in order to consolidate African political unity; 4) a commission of African commanders entrusted with the study and organization of a joint defense scheme; and 5) a cultural commission to formulate policy in the field of education and cultural exchanges.[20]

The conference also adopted resolutions on the following specific political issues: Algeria, Nyasaland and Rhodesia, Kenya, the High Commission Territories, Cameroun, Angola, Mozambique, Portuguese Guinea, South Africa, South West Africa, Ruanda-Urundi, the Congo, and the United Nations. The conference expressed support for the liberation movements in all the dependent territories discussed and urged the speedy accession to independence of these countries. With regard to Algeria, a resolution recommended that the African states increase their diplomatic and material support to the provisional government. The conference demanded the dissolution of the Central African Federation, and, with respect to Kenya, the release of Jomo Kenyatta. On Angola, the conferees recommended that the Afro-Asian Members of the UN engage all their efforts in obliging Portugal to apply the General Assembly resolutions on that territory and that the

[19] All-African People's Conference, Cairo, March 1961, *Resolution of the Committee No. 4.*

[20] All-African People's Conference, Cairo, March 1961, *Resolutions, Committee for African Unity and Solidarity.*

African states reconsider their commercial and diplomatic relations with Portugal. The resolution on South Africa called for the severance of diplomatic relations and an economic boycott; that on South West Africa demanded that the South African administration leave the territory forthwith. With regard to the Congo, the conference expressed support for the government presided over by Mr. Gizenga and urged the immediate implementation of all Security Council resolutions. Finally, with respect to the United Nations, a resolution called for reorganization of the Secretariat and revision of the Charter to conform with the current world situation.

BRAZZAVILLE POWERS

ABIDJAN

The first meeting of the twelve French-speaking African states which subsequently became known as the "Brazzaville group"— Cameroun, Central African Republic, Chad, Congo (Brazzaville), Dahomey, Gabon, Ivory Coast, Malagasy, Mauritania, Niger, Senegal, and Upper Volta—was held at Abidjan in the Ivory Coast in October 1960.[21] The meeting was organized by President Félix Houphouet-Boigny of the Ivory Coast for the purpose of discussing whether the independent African states could mediate or in some other way help bring the Algerian conflict to an end without alienating France. The final communiqué stated that the conference had examined the Algerian, Congolese, and Mauritanian questions, that all the countries attending would support Mauritania's application for membership in the UN, and that further meetings would be held.

BRAZZAVILLE AND DAKAR

The second meeting of the group took place in Brazzaville from December 15 to 19, 1960, at which time conclusions were reached on several critical current issues.[22] With respect to the Congo, the Brazzaville powers endorsed UN technical assistance to the region, but rejected long-term UN trusteeship, political intervention by other African

[21] Hella Pick, "The Brazzaville Twelve and How They Came to Be," *Africa Report,* May 1961 (Vol. 6, No. 5), p. 2, 8, 12, and 15, and "The Brazzaville Twelve," *Africa South,* April–June 1961 (Vol. 5, No. 3), p. 76–84; and "French-Speaking States Seek Common Policies," *Africa Report,* December 1960 (Vol. 5, No. 12), p. 12.

[22] "African Leaders Convene at Rival 'Summits,'" *Africa Report,* January 1961 (Vol. 6, No. 1), p. 11. See also note 21 above, and *The Manchester Guardian,* January 13, 1961.

states, or efforts by any of the Great Powers either directly or indirectly to recolonize the Congo. The communiqué stated the belief that a political solution in the Congo could be reached through a round-table conference representative of all Congolese political parties. On Algeria, the group rejected the demand for a UN referendum and urged French President de Gaulle to initiate negotiations with the FLN to end the Algerian war in 1961. The Brazzaville powers reiterated their support for the admission of Mauritania to the UN.

In addition, the Brazzaville communiqué dealt with long-term cooperation among the twelve with a view to developing a common foreign policy, more intensive economic and cultural cooperation, pooled diplomatic representation, establishment of a permanent secretariat, and possibly a common defense scheme. A detailed agenda was drawn up for the economic group which met at Dakar in late January and which, according to press reports, recommended the establishment of a joint economic secretariat whose task would be to ensure the smooth working of customs unions between group members, to coordinate development plans, including joint efforts for securing development capital, and to investigate the possibilities of price stabilization schemes.[23]

YAOUNDÉ

The press announced that at the third meeting of the Brazzaville powers, held in Yaoundé, Cameroun, in the final week of March 1961, delegates decided to establish an organization for economic cooperation, the *Organisation africaine et malgache de coopération économique* (OAMCE), with headquarters at Yaoundé.[24] In addition, the communiqué stated that the twelve heads of state had approved a project for pooling their air transport into a single system to be called *Air Afrique,* with headquarters in Abidjan.

Concerning current political problems, delegates, according to press reports, expressed approval for a proposal to send a military aide representing the twelve states to the Congo or for any other measure decided on at the Monrovia Conference to be held in May.[25] With respect to Algeria, the conference observed that the negotiations about to begin in Evian between representatives of the French government and the Algerian provisional government constituted an important step toward solution of the problem.

[23] *The Manchester Guardian,* March 27, 1961.
[24] *Le Monde,* March 31, 1961. See also *Africa Report,* June 1961 (Vol. 6, No. 6), p. 9; and *West Africa,* April 22, 1961 (No. 2290), p. 441.
[25] See below, p. [575–577].

Finally, delegates announced plans to draft a mutual defense pact at a later meeting and set Tananarive as the site for the next conference of the twelve.

TANANARIVE

The final communiqué of the Tananarive Conference, which met from September 6 to 12, 1961, observed that the conference marked the formalization of the plans and aspirations of the previous conferences of the twelve.[26]

The conference adopted the Charter of the African and Malagasy Union which stated as its aim the coordination of the foreign policy of member states in order to strengthen their solidarity, assure their collective security, assist their development, and secure peace both in Africa and Malagasy and in the world at large.[27] Membership was to be open to all independent African states, admission to be contingent upon the unanimous approval of member states. The charter provided for an "administrative" Secretary-General, who was to be chosen for a two-year term by a conference of heads of state and government. The secretariat was to be located at Cotonou, Dahomey, and the candidate for Secretary-General was to be proposed by the President of Dahomey. The general policy of the African and Malagasy Union was to be determined by the conference of heads of state and government, which was to meet twice a year, with special sessions to be called on the initiative of one state supported by the majority of the members of the Union. The charter also provided that between sessions meetings of the respective ministers, experts, or permanent representatives to the United Nations should be held as necessary. Decisions were to be determined by majority vote.

In the economic sphere, the conference adopted five protocols.[28] The first created a committee for economic and social development charged with studying the development plans of member states, with establishing an investment regime, and with considering the feasibility of a common price stabilization fund for member countries' products. The second created a permanent secretariat to the *Organisation africaine et malgache de coopération économique* established earlier at Yaoundé. The third set up a committee of foreign commerce to study all questions relating to customs cooperation and fiscal harmonization, including the possibility of establishing an African and Malagasy free

[26] African and Malagasy Union Tananarive Conference, *Communiqué Final,* September 12, 1961.

[27] *Complete Text of the Charter of the African and Malagasy Union Adopted at the Tananarive Conference, September 6–12, 1961.*

[28] African and Malagasy Union Tananarive Conference, *Communiqué of September 11, 1961.*

trade zone and of enlarging existing customs unions. The fourth created a committee for the study of monetary problems, whose prerogatives included examination a) of the balance of payments of each state with a view to proposing measures designed to eliminate deficits, and b) of the modalities of transfer of funds. The fifth established a committee of scientific and technical research, the functions of which were: 1) to gather, analyze, and distribute information of the scientific research institutes already existing in member states; and 2) to examine the possibility of setting up technical institutes at African and Malagasy universities.

In the area of defense, delegates signed a defense pact, to be ratified by the parliaments of the twelve states, which established a) a Supreme Council on which each of the parties to the pact was to be represented by a plenipotentiary delegate, and b) a permanent secretariat to be located at Ougadougou, Upper Volta.[29] The preamble reaffirmed the adherence of the signatories to the principles of the UN Charter and the desire of reinforcing existing ties among the parties on the basis of respect for their independence and of noninterference in international affairs. Operative articles of the pact stated, *inter alia:* 1) that parties to the pact would settle by peaceful means, in conformity with the UN Charter, all international differences in which they might become involved; 2) that the parties would consult each other on appropriate measures whenever the territorial integrity, political independence, or security of one of them was threatened; 3) that aggression aimed at one or more of them would be considered aggression against all, and that each, in the exercise of individual or collective defense recognized by Article 51 of the UN Charter would assist the attacked party; 4) that any action taken against one of the states would immediately be brought to the attention of the UN Security Council; and 5) that each of the parties assumed the obligation *(a)* of entering into no international agreement which would conflict with the pact, and *(b)* of seeking the prior accord of the parties for any new defense agreement.

In other areas of cooperation, on coordination of telecommunications between the twelve, the conference approved the creation of the *Union africaine et malgache des postes et télécommunications,* with headquarters in Brazzaville.[30] In addition, the conference adopted several conventions on juridical matters covering, *inter alia,* diplomatic representation, establishment, and judicial cooperation.[31]

[29] The text of the defense pact can be found in the *Journal Officiel de la République Malgache,* December 16, 1961.

[30] African and Malagasy Union Tananarive Conference, *Communiqué of September 8, 1961.*

[31] African and Malagasy Union Tananarive Conference, *Communiqué of September 9, 1961.*

With respect to current international problems, the conference discussed Berlin, disarmament, decolonization, Algeria, the Central African Federation, the Portuguese colonies, South Africa, the Congo, Ruanda-Urundi, New Guinea, and the United Nations.[32] The conference concluded that the Berlin crisis could be resolved only through negotiations between the four powers, and that the solution to the problem should be based on the principle of self-determination for West Berlin. With regard to disarmament, delegates expressed support for all proposals envisioning disarmament with controls and denounced the initiative of the Soviet Union in resuming nuclear tests. Representatives called for the acceleration of the process of decolonization and for the extension of economic and technical assistance to the newly-independent states. The group reiterated its position on Algeria, and insisted on the inalienable right of Africans in the Central African Federation to enjoy national independence. With regard to the Portuguese territories and South Africa, member states announced the intention of introducing resolutions in the United Nations calling for the breaking off of diplomatic relations. In addition, they stated that they would increase aid, material and moral, to the African nationalists in the Portuguese territories, and that they would propose revocation of the South African mandate over South West Africa. The conference expressed approval for the unity of the Congo (Leopoldville) but criticism of the involvement of the UN in Congolese internal affairs. With respect to Ruanda-Urundi, delegates asked for close UN supervision of the elections to be held in that territory; concerning New Guinea, the conference expressed support for application of the principle of self-determination. Lastly, the conference criticized use of the veto to exclude Mauritania from UN membership, and on more general questions relating to the UN, the conferees: 1) called for an increase in the membership of the Security Council and Economic and Social Council, as well as a more equitable geographical distribution of seats; 2) observed that creating a triumvirate Secretary-General would simply introduce the veto, which already existed at the level of decision, to the level of action; and 3) asked for a more equitable distribution of Secretariat posts.

CASABLANCA POWERS

A summit meeting of the Presidents of Ghana, Guinea, Mali, and the United Arab Republic, attended also by the Libyan Foreign Minister, the Ceylonese Ambassador in Cairo, and Premier Ferhat Abbas of the Algerian provisional government, was convened in Casablanca by King

[32] African and Malagasy Union Tananarive Conference, *Statement regarding International Problems.*

Mohammed of Morocco in early January 1961 for the purpose of co-ordinating policy on the Congo and of considering a suggestion for the formation of an African high military command.[33] Ethiopia, India, Indonesia, Liberia, Nigeria, Somalia, Sudan, Togoland, and Tunisia were invited but did not attend the conference. Excluding Ghana, all those states present which had troops with the UN Operations in the Congo (ONUC) had announced their intention of withdrawing them prior to the meeting.

In an opening address King Mohammed suggested five points to restore order in the Congo: 1) establishment of a permanent Congo committee appointed by the UN General Assembly to advise on measures to be taken in the Congo; 2) a conciliation conference of leaders of all parties in the territory; 3) a political truce; 4) increased UN material and technical aid; and 5) a call to African states to take the lead in helping the Congo. In the area of inter-African cooperation he proposed the creation of an African consultative assembly and of committees to coordinate African economic, cultural, and military policies, based on the following principles, *inter alia:* liquidation of colonialism; elimination of racial segregation; barring of nuclear experiments from Africa and of foreign intervention in African affairs; reaffirmation of African neutralism; consolidation and mutual defense of new African states; building of African unity; and action to consolidate world peace.

With regard to the Congo, the resolution adopted by the conference called for the release of Premier Lumumba and all other members of the elected government, the reconvening of parliament, the disarming of Colonel Mobutu's army, and the expulsion of all Belgians and others not under the UN Command. In addition, it renewed the threat to withdraw troops from the Congo unless the UN Command acted immediately to support the "central government," and reserved the right to take appropriate action should the purposes and principles which justified the UN presence not be realized. On other African questions, the conference pledged unconditional support for the Algerian provisional government, and denounced the Algerian referendum as well as all consultations unilaterally organized by France. On South Africa

[33] Harry B. Ellis, "Failure at Casablanca," *New Leader,* February 20, 1961 (Vol. 44, No. 8), p. 14–15; Margaret Roberts, "Summitry at Casablanca," *Africa South,* April–June 1961 (Vol. 5, No. 3), p. 68–74, "Casablanca 'Summit,' " *Venture,* February 1961 (Vol. 13, No. 2), p. 1–2, and "Pan-Africa and the Congo," *West Africa,* January 14, 1961 (No. 2276), p. 31; "African Leaders Convene at Rival 'Summits,' " *Africa Report,* January 1961 (Vol. 6, No. 1), p. 11; and "African Summit Meeting," *West Africa,* January 7, 1961 (No. 2275), p. 11. See also *The Christian Science Monitor,* January 3 and 5, 1961; *The Manchester Guardian,* January 9 and 13, 1961; *The New York Times,* January 1, 5, and 8, 1961; and *The Times* (London), January 9, 1961.

the conference reaffirmed support of resolutions adopted at previous African conferences calling for an economic boycott. Additional resolutions: 1) approved any action taken by Morocco for the recognition of her legitimate rights to Mauritania; 2) denounced Belgian attempts to divide Ruanda-Urundi into two states through "organized repression against the nationalist elements;" 3) named Israel an instrument of imperialism and neocolonialism in the Middle East and in Africa; and 4) condemned nuclear explosions in the Sahara.

With respect to the other aspect of the conference's deliberations, the question of the establishment of common African institutions, the conference formulated an "African Charter of Casablanca." The preamble, which enunciated the need for vigilance against neocolonialism, pledged the signers to a policy of nonalignment, called for the independence of all remaining colonial territories, declared the determination to discourage the maintenance of foreign troops and the establishment of bases which would endanger the liberation of Africa, and urged members to rid the African continent of political and economic intervention and pressures. The main body of the charter provided for the establishment of a permanent African consultative assembly, three permanent functional committees—political (heads of state), economic (ministers of economic affairs), and cultural (ministers of education), and a joint African high command, composed of the chiefs of staff of the independent African nations. Each of these bodies was to meet periodically to coordinate and establish common African policies. The functions of the joint African high command were to ensure the common defense of Africa in case of aggression against any part of the continent and to safeguard the independence of African states. Experts were to meet within three months to set the organizations in operation. The charter was signed by King Mohammed of Morocco and the Presidents of Ghana, Guinea, Mali, and the United Arab Republic; association was to be open to other African states.

According to press reports of September 1961, the proposed committees had begun operations.[34] The cultural committee, meeting at Tangiers in August, had arranged educational and research exchanges. The economic committee was studying plans for tariff reductions and schemes for African common markets.[35] The military committee had set up headquarters in Cairo, with General Mohammed Fawzi as commander-in-chief. Driss Slaoui of Morocco, who had been made Secretary-General of the group, had been charged with the task of establishing a permanent secretariat for the political committee in Bamako.

[34] *The Christian Science Monitor*, September 25 and 30, 1961.
[35] See below.

CONFERENCE OF THE AFRICAN ECONOMIC COMMITTEE

On July 17, 1961, a five-day conference of the economic committee instituted by the Casablanca Charter opened at Conakry, Guinea; the meeting was attended by delegates of Ghana, Guinea, Mali, Morocco, the United Arab Republic, and the Algerian provisional government.[36] In an opening address President Sékou Touré of Guinea called for the formation of a higher economic community of the Casablanca states with the immediate aim of harmonizing production and price policies and of making preferential reciprocal purchases.

The final communiqué of the session recommended the progressive removal of customs duties and trade quotas among the members states over a five-year period beginning January 1, 1962. The delegates also proposed the establishment of a payments union and an African development bank. Other topics discussed included the following: possibilities for closer commercial relations, coordination of economic planning, exploitation of natural resources, improvement of telecommunications, and a unified policy toward the Commission for Technical Cooperation in Africa South of the Sahara (CCTA). Formation of a joint air and shipping line were to be considered at a later conference.

At a follow-up meeting in mid-autumn 1961 delegates of the same countries announced plans for the establishment of a Pan-African Airways.[37] The five-day session of civil aviation and marine experts decided that an African civil aviation organization should be set up immediately, and that a draft project for the establishment of a Pan-African air carrier should be prepared. The proposed civil aviation organization was to collect data, prepare studies, and implement whatever plans might evolve from those studies.

Finally, press reports of April 1962 indicated that at a seven-day session of the economic committee in Cairo a series of agreements had been signed establishing an African payments union, an African development bank with capital of $30,000,000, and an African common market.[38] Under the common market scheme customs duties for members were to be reduced by one-quarter upon implementation of the agreements and were to be eliminated within five years. The chairman of the committee announced that the group would welcome any African state that would like to join.

[36] "Casablanca Economists Discuss Customs Union," *Africa Report*, August 1961 (Vol. 6, No. 8), p. 11–12; "Conakry," *West Africa*, July 22, 1961 (No. 2303), p. 799; and "Casablanca and Monrovia," *West Africa*, July 29, 1961 (No. 2304), p. 830.
[37] "Plan for Pan-African Airways," *West Africa*, November 4, 1961 (No. 2318), p. 1233.
[38] *The New York Times*, April 4, 1962.

The next meeting of the committee was to be held in Tangiers at the end of July.

MONROVIA POWERS

MONROVIA CONFERENCE OF HEADS OF AFRICAN AND MALAGASY STATES

Representatives of twenty independent African states [Cameroun, Central African Republic, Chad, Congo (Brazzaville), Dahomey, Ethiopia, Gabon, Ivory Coast, Liberia, Libya, Malagasy, Mauritania, Niger, Nigeria, Senegal, Sierra Leone, Somalia, Togo, Tunisia, and Upper Volta] met in Monrovia from May 8 to 12, 1961, to consider four major items: means of promoting better understanding and cooperation toward achieving unity in Africa; threats to peace and stability in Africa; establishment of special machinery to which African states might refer in case of disputes among themselves; and possible contribution of African states to world peace.[39] Ghana, Guinea, Mali, Morocco, the Sudan, and the United Arab Republic were unrepresented at the conference.

The keynote of the opening speeches was African unity.[40] President Tubman of Liberia, in a welcoming address, observed that although the idea of a universal political order was debatable at the current stage of African political experience, the necessity for better cooperation was obvious. He pointed out that the attainment of any form of unity had to be a voluntary process, and that political union could be more rapidly achieved where there was a community of economic interest, cultural cross-fertilization, and free social intercourse and association. In a reply to President Tubman's address, President Senghor of Senegal expressed the view that Africa could move faster toward unity than other continents because its values were founded on the spirit of union and not of division—on a mutuality which enabled Africans to reach agreements based not simply on a given community or individual interest. The essential condition for success, he suggested, was to emphasize cultural, technical, and economic cooperation rather than the agreement of political parties. He urged that the African states align

[39] "Pan-African Affairs," *Africa Digest,* August 1961 (Vol. 9, No. 1), p. 37; "The Monrovia Conference," *Africa Report,* June 1961 (Vol. 6, No. 6), p. 5; "The Monrovia Conference," *Présence Africaine* (Vol. 9, No. 37), p. 193–199; and "Independent Africa in Monrovia," *West Africa,* May 20, 1961 (No. 2294), p. 539. See also *The Christian Science Monitor,* May 10, 1961; *The Manchester Guardian,* May 12 and 15, 1961; *The New York Times,* May 8, 9, 12, 17, and 21, 1961; and *The Times* (London), May 9, 10, 12, 13, and 15, 1961.

[40] *Opening Speeches, Conference of Heads of African and Malagasy States, Held at the Centennial Pavilion, 8th–12th May, 1961,* Liberian Information Service, Monrovia.

themselves on the one hand as a group at the United Nations and, on the other, as a general organization for African cooperation.

Three major resolutions were adopted by the conference.[41] The first, which was concerned with the means of promoting better understanding and cooperation in Africa and Malagasy, established the following principles to govern the relationship between the African and Malagasy states: 1) absolute equality of states, whatever the size of their territories, the density of their populations, or the amount of their wealth; 2) noninterference in the internal affairs of states; 3) respect for the sovereignty of each state and for its inalienable right to existence and to the development of its personality; 4) condemnation of outside subversive action by neighboring states; 5) promotion of continent-wide cooperation, based on tolerance, solidarity, good-neighbor relations, periodic exchange of views, and nonacceptance of any one leader; and 6) unity—but not political integration—of aspirations and of action considered from the perspective of African social solidarity and political identity. The resolution also approved in principle the creation of an inter-African consultative organization to put into effect the above-mentioned principles, and suggested that it be established at the succeeding conference, which was to be held in Lagos, Nigeria. In addition, it decided: 1) that a technical commission of experts designated by the respective states should meet in Dakar within three months with a view to working out detailed plans for economic, educational, cultural, and scientific cooperation, as well as cooperation in communications and transportation among African and Malagasy states; 2) that all African and Malagasy states should recognize the desire to promote the revival of African culture and traditions; and 3) that all African and Malagasy states should make a special effort to introduce the study of French and English in addition to that of their respective national and official languages.

The second resolution, dealing with threats to peace and stability in Africa and the world, touched on the following items: dependent territories, Algeria, the Congo, Angola, South Africa and South West Africa, disarmament, Mauritania, and the UN. The conference affirmed its unanimous determination to give material and moral assistance to all dependent territories in order to accelerate their accession to independence. With regard to Algeria, the resolution appealed to the government of France and the provisional government of the Algerian Republic to conclude at the earliest date an agreement ending the war

[41] *Resolutions of the Plenary Sessions, Conference of Heads of African and Malagasy States, Held at the Monrovia City Hall, 8th–12th May, 1961,* Liberian Information Service, Monrovia.

and according to Algeria its independence and territorial integrity. Concerning the Congo, the conference reaffirmed its confidence in the UN, called on all African states to desist from hastily recognizing secessionist regions and from taking sides with rival groups, and condemned assassination and subversion as means for achieving political power. In respect of Angola, the resolution appealed to all African and Malagasy states to pledge their whole-hearted material and moral support to the Africans in that territory and called to the attention of world conscience the atrocities and repression to which the Angolese population was victim. Regarding South Africa and South West Africa, the conference: 1) condemned *apartheid;* 2) asked all African and Malagasy states to apply immediately political and economic sanctions, collectively and individually, against the South African government; 3) urged the African and Malagasy states to contribute by all possible means moral and material assistance to the Africans and Asians in South Africa; and 4) affirmed support for the decision of the UN Trusteeship Council requiring the South African government to acknowledge the authority of the Council as guardian of the mandate over the territory of South West Africa. On the subject of disarmament, the resolution appealed to the nuclear powers to stop nuclear explosions and the manufacture and stockpiling of nuclear weapons, requested the chairman to ask the Commission on Nuclear Disarmament, in session in Geneva, to use its best endeavors to secure the above-mentioned objectives, and took note of the assurances of the French government that it would cease all further nuclear explosions in Africa. Finally, in relation to the UN, the conference: 1) urged UN Members to assure a more equitable geographical distribution of seats in the Security Council and Economic and Social Council as well as to work for the enlargement of the Councils; 2) decided to send a cablegram asking Security Council members to vote favorably on the admission of Mauritania to the World Organization; 3) condemned any attempt to weaken or undermine the authority of the UN; and 4) recorded the intention of the African and Malagasy states to present a united front toward all world problems with which Africa might in the future be faced at the UN.

The third resolution, which bore on the settlement of conflicts between African states, recommended: 1) that disputes should be settled by peaceful means; 2) that a commission should be created to which litigations could be submitted; and 3) that a written appeal should be sent to the heads of state of Ethiopia and Somalia urging them to renew their efforts toward an early solution of their frontier dispute and any other problems.

MEETING OF EXPERTS AT DAKAR

Economists from nineteen of the twenty Monrovia Conference states (Ethiopia excepted) plus Libya met at Dakar from July 17–23, 1961, in pursuance of a recommendation adopted at the Monrovia Conference in May, and reached common agreement on sixteen draft resolutions covering economic, financial, social welfare, and other forms of cooperation.[42] The conference recommended: 1) the promotion of trade among African countries through regional customs unions and the progressive establishment of common external tariffs; 2) harmonization of development policies, including investment codes and conventions, creation of an investment guarantee fund, exchange of economic information, and coordination of economic research; 3) cooperation in communications, specifically, construction of a connecting network of national roads, establishment of a joint shipping company, and amalgamation of existing airways; and 4) steps to break down language barriers and harmonize educational systems. The resolutions also covered standardization of medical practices, definition of minimum qualifications, and setting up of veterinary training institutions.

The recommendations were to be presented to a second conference of Monrovia states, scheduled for Lagos, Nigeria, in September 1961.

LAGOS CONFERENCE

Representatives of twenty independent African states met in Lagos, Nigeria, from January 25 to 30, 1962, to discuss proposals for inter-African cooperation as well as current international problems affecting Africa.[43] Eight states—Ghana, Guinea, Libya, Mali, Morocco, Sudan, Tunisia, and the United Arab Republic—did not send representatives because the Algerian provisional government had not been invited to the conference; of these eight, Libya and Tunisia had attended the previous conference of the group at Monrovia. The Congo (Leopoldville) and Tanganyika were the only countries not represented at Monrovia that sent delegates to Lagos.

In an opening address to the conference Governor-General Nnamdi Azikiwe of Nigeria told delegates that the basic ideological difference

[42] *Africa Report,* August 1961 (Vol. 6, No. 8), p. 11; and *West Africa,* July 22, 1961 (No. 2303), p. 799, and July 29, 1961 (No. 2304), p. 817. See also *The Times* (London), July 24, 1961.

[43] Joseph R. L. Sterne, "The Lagos Conference," *Africa Report,* February 1962 (Vol. 7, No. 2), p. 3–6, 23; Margaret Roberts, "What Price for African Unity?" *Africa Trade and Development,* March 1962 (Vol. 4, No. 3), p. 9, 16; "Lagos and Addis Ababa Conferences," *Asia & Africa Review,* March 1962 (Vol. 2, No. 3), p. 6; and "The Lagos Decisions," *West Africa,* February 10, 1962 (No. 2332), p. 149.

between the Casablanca and Monrovia groups was the absence of a declaration by the Casablanca powers recognizing the right of African states to legal equality, to self-determination, to safety from interference in their internal affairs through subversive activities, and to the inviolability of their territories from external aggression. Governor-General Azikiwe expressed the view that public avowal of these principles was material to the question of African unity since a declaration of adherence to them calmed the fears of the smaller states that their stronger neighbors might have expansionist ambitions.

The theme of the conference was insistence upon noninterference and strict limitation of the fields of functional cooperation. Within these bounds, however, the conference took some specific organizational steps toward the coordination of activities. Delegates approved in principle a detailed charter for an Organization of Inter-African and Malagasy States, to be worked into final form at a foreign ministers' meeting later in the year. The charter was to come into effect when formally ratified by two-thirds of the independent African states. It provided for the following three principal organs: 1) an assembly of heads of state and government which would convene at least once every two years and at which resolutions would be approved by a two-thirds vote; 2) a council of ministers which would meet at least once a year and which could be called into emergency session in the event of a threat to peace and security; and 3) a secretariat which would have charge of the commissions and committees established by the council of ministers. The functions of the Secretary-General were carefully delineated; his independence of any member government was specifically cited. Among the activities envisioned in the charter were the following: 1) establishment of a special fund to finance regional development projects; 2) formation of a customs union; 3) setting up of a scientific training and research institute, one of the purposes of which would be to avoid duplication of educational resources; and 4) selection of committees to coordinate activities in such fields as culture, education, health, labor, social welfare, insect control, and agriculture. The conference decided to set up a standing committee of finance ministers. The committee, which was to be assisted by a permanent secretariat, was to be responsible for the pooling of statistics, the regulation of currency exchanges, the harmonization of tax structures, the stabilization of primary commodity prices, and the creation by stages of regional customs unions. The committee was also to undertake studies looking toward the establishment of a development bank and a private investment guarantee fund. In addition, the finance ministers were requested to report to the succeeding conference, to be held in six months at Addis Ababa, on the effects

a) of the European Economic Community (EEC) on the economies of the African states and b) of existing associations between a number of African states and EEC.

Delegates also discussed political issues such as colonialism, Algeria, and the United Nations. With respect to colonialism, a conference resolution urged independence for all territories at the earliest possible date. The conference stated that an immediate diplomatic and economic boycott should be placed on all colonial powers that refused to recognize the right of the indigenous majorities to self-determination and independence. The resolution on Algeria expressed the hope that the government of France and the Algerian provisional government would soon reach agreement on complete independence for Algeria. With regard to the United Nations, the conference suggested: 1) that the African and Malagasy Members form a distinct and independent group at the UN; and 2) that the group strive to obtain revision of the UN Charter toward equitable representation of the African and Malagasy states in the Security Council, the Economic and Social Council, and the Secretariat.

GHANA–GUINEA–MALI UNION (UNION OF AFRICAN STATES)

At a meeting in Accra, which took place from April 27 to 29, 1961, Presidents Kwame Nkrumah of Ghana, Sékou Touré of Guinea, and Modibo Keita of Mali signed a charter formally establishing a tripartite Union of African States.[44] The charter came into effect upon its simultaneous publication on July 1 in the capitals of Ghana, Guinea, and Mali after the three heads of state had met at Bamako, Mali, on June 26 in order to examine the extent to which decisions reached at their April meeting in Accra had been implemented.[45] The drafting of the charter evolved out of a decision announced by the three government leaders at Conakry, Guinea, on December 24, 1960, envisioning common diplomatic representation and the creation of committees to draw up arrangements for harmonizing economic and monetary policies.[46]

[44] *Charter for the Union of African States and a Joint Communiqué Issued Later after a Summit Conference between the Leaders of the Union*, Accra, Ghana, Government Printing Department. See also "Mali, Ghana, Guinea Sign Union Charter," *Africa Report*, May 1961 (Vol. 6, No. 5), p. 11; and "Accra Communiqué Causes Dismay," *West Africa*, May 6, 1961 (No. 2292), p. 495.

[45] "Ghana, Guinea, Mali Formalize Their Union," *Africa Report*, August 1961 (Vol. 6, No. 8), p. 11; and "End of an African Frontier," *West Africa*, July 8, 1961 (No. 2301), p. 751.

[46] "Ghana, Guinea, Mali Confer on Union," *Africa Report*, February 1961 (Vol. 6, No. 2), p. 10; and "The Osagyefo and Others." *The Economist*, December 31, 1960 (Vol. 197, No. 6123), p. 1366–1367.

The Union charter, which was to be open to signature to all African states that accepted its objectives and which designated the Union of African States as the "nucleus of the United States of Africa," sought: 1) to strengthen cooperation between the member states politically, diplomatically, economically, and culturally; 2) to pool the resources of member states in order to consolidate their independence and safeguard their territorial integrity; 3) to achieve joint collaboration for the liquidation of imperialism, colonialism, and neocolonialism in Africa and the building up of African unity; and 4) to harmonize the domestic and foreign policy of members in order to make their activities more effective. Included among the functions of the Union were to be the working out of a common domestic orientation of the member states, strict observance of a concerted diplomacy, organization of a system of joint defense, definition of a common set of directives relating to economic planning, and rehabilitation and development of African culture.

With regard to administrative arrangements, the supreme executive organ of the Union was to be the conference of heads of state of the Union. The conference, which was to meet quarterly, was to be preceded by a meeting of a preparatory committee whose task was to draft recommendations for the consideration of the conference. In addition, the charter provided that coordinating committees should be established among political, trade union, women's and youth organizations for the purpose of giving them a common ideological orientation.

In order to achieve harmonization of foreign policy, the charter proposed: 1) that, at each Union conference, policy directives should be decided upon and sent to all the diplomatic missions of member states; 2) that ambassadors and other heads of missions abroad should coordinate their activities through frequent consultation; and 3) that delegations to international gatherings should present a common stand. With respect to joint defense, the charter provided that member states should oppose any installation of foreign military bases on their soil, and that a common system of defense should be organized, based on the principle that aggression against one member state should be considered an act of aggression against other states of the Union.

In the economic field, the charter endowed an economic committee, to consist of a delegation of five members per state chosen from among the officials responsible for economy and finance in each state, with the task of coordinating and harmonizing the economic and financial policy of the Union states in accordance with directives jointly agreed upon. The committee was to hold two sessions each year and was to submit recommendations to the heads of state.

The provisions of the charter were to come into effect upon its simultaneous proclamation in the Union states. Modifications to the charter had to be approved unanimously by the conference of heads of state.

SPECIAL CONFERENCES

SANNIQUELLIE CONFERENCE

Meeting in July 1959 at Sanniquellie, Liberia, President Tubman of Liberia, President Touré of Guinea, and Prime Minister Nkrumah of Ghana pledged themselves to work together for the formation of a "Community of Independent African States."[47] To this end, they decided that a special conference should be held in 1960 after Nigeria, Togoland, and the Cameroons had attained independence. They agreed on the following principles to be presented to the projected conference as the basis for discussion: 1) Africans, like all other peoples, had an inherent right to independence and self-determination; 2) the name of the proposed organization should be the "Community of Independent African States;" 3) each state or federation which became a member of the Community should maintain its own national identity and constitutional structure; 4) each member should accept the principle of non-interference in the internal affairs of any other member; 5) the acts of states or federations members of the Community should be determined in relation to the essential objectives of freedom, independence, and unity of the African personality; 6) the policy of the Community should be to build up a prosperous African unity for the benefit of the peoples of Africa and of the world, and in the interests of international peace and security; 7) a main objective should be to help accelerate the independence of African territories subjected to domination; 8) the Community should set up an economic council, a cultural council, and a scientific and research council; 9) membership should be open to all independent African states and federations and to nonindependent countries upon their attainment of independence; 10) the Community should have a flag and an anthem, to be decided upon at a later date; and 11) the motto of the Community should be "Independence and Unity."

Before adjourning, the three government leaders also called for free elections under UN supervision before independence in the French

[47] *First West African Summit Conference, Held at Sanniquellie, Central Province, Liberian Hinterland, July 15–19, 1959.* Liberian Information Service, Monrovia; *Africa Digest,* November 1959 (Vol. 7, No. 2), p. 68; and *Africa Special Report,* August 1959 (Vol. 4, No. 7), p. 3–4. See also *The New York Times,* July 26, 1959; and *Afrique Nouvelle,* July 24, 1959.

Cameroons, and for inclusion of the Algerian question on the agenda of the forthcoming UN General Assembly session. They condemned *apartheid* and all other forms of racial discrimination and protested against French atomic tests in the Sahara.

MONROVIA CONFERENCE ON ALGERIA

In early August 1959 a five-day conference of foreign ministers from nine independent African states (Ethiopia, Ghana, Guinea, Liberia, Libya, Morocco, Sudan, Tunisia, and the United Arab Republic) was held at Monrovia, Liberia.[48] The main item on the agenda was the Algerian question. Specifically, the meeting was convoked to formulate joint African policies on Algeria, to mobilize Africans in support of the Algerian nationalists, and to take steps to end the war in Algeria. Previous to the conference, the provisional government of the Algerian Republic had been recognized by Ghana, Libya, Morocco, Sudan, Tunisia, and the United Arab Republic; in the course of the conference the representative of Guinea announced that his government would exchange ambassadors with the provisional government but that his country saw no need to go through the formalities of recognition since the rebel government had been in existence before Guinea became a state. The Algerian Minister of Information, who spoke as a full delegate at the conference, according to press reports affirmed that the provisional government was ready at any time to meet representatives of the French government on neutral territory in order to discuss a political settlement in Algeria.[49]

In his welcoming address President Tubman called on both the French and the Algerians to modify their extreme positions and asked the conference to develop a formula for negotiating a peaceful settlement of the problem. He suggested the possibility of mediation by friendly states or by the UN. President Tubman denounced French threats to break diplomatic relations with any state which recognized the provisional Algerian government, by stating that threats were "very weak substitutes for negotiations among nations."

The resolutions on Algeria adopted by the conference appealed to France to recognize the right of the Algerian people to independence, to withdraw its troops from Algeria, and to negotiate with the pro-

[48] *Africa Digest,* September 1959 (Vol. 7, No. 1), p. 38, and November 1959 (Vol. 7, No. 2), p. 68; "African States Unite on Algeria," *Africa Special Report,* August 1959 (Vol. 4, No. 7), p. 2–4; and Joan Gillespie, "Africa Conclave," *New Leader,* September 7, 1959 (Vol. 42, No. 32), p. 10–12. See also *The Manchester Guardian,* August 8, 1959; *The New York Times,* August 9, 1959; *The Times* (London), August 12, 1959; and *Afrique Nouvelle,* August 7 and 14, 1959.

[49] *Afrique Nouvelle,* August 7, 1959.

visional government to bring the war to an end. The conference called upon members of the North Atlantic Treaty Organization (NATO) to urge France to desist from using NATO arms in Algeria and requested African states to render material aid to Algeria.

Resolutions on other items adopted at the meeting included the following: 1) denunciation of any decision to conduct nuclear explosions in any part of Africa, with a specific protest against announced French atomic tests in the Sahara; and 2) condemnation of discrimination and segregation in all forms, particularly as practiced in South Africa, Kenya, and the Central African Federation. With respect to dependent territories, the conference heard petitioners from Angola, Cameroons, Nyasaland, Southern Rhodesia, and Uganda; it: 1) called on the conscience of the world and on the UN to help dependent territories achieve independence; 2) declared its support for African self-determination in Nyasaland; and 3) reaffirmed demands that the UN hold a plebiscite in the French Cameroons before the trust territory achieved independence.

PAN-AFRICAN FREEDOM MOVEMENT OF EAST AND CENTRAL AFRICA (PAFMECA)

MWANZA

PAFMECA was formed at a conference held in Mwanza, Tanganyika, from September 16 to 18, 1958, for the purpose of coordinating regional activities toward the achievement of independence for territories in East and Central Africa.[50] The conference, which was attended by representatives of political parties from Kenya, Nyasaland, Tanganyika, Uganda, and Zanzibar, considered the following issues: 1) the position of those present toward (a) the non-African minorities in Kenya, Tanganyika, and Uganda, and (b) the Central African Federation (Nyasaland, Northern Rhodesia, and Southern Rhodesia); 2) methods for achieving coordinated action among the nationalist movements in East and Central Africa and for pooling resources in a concerted drive against imperialism; and 3) the development of a fundamental philosophic creed for the emergent African nations.

Discussion resulted in the establishment of a freedom fund for East Africa and in the appointment of a "caretaker committee," under the

[50] "Pan-African Conference," *Africa Digest*, November–December 1958 (Vol. 6, No. 3), p. 90–91; and Gikonyo Kiano, "The Pan-African Freedom Movement of East and Central Africa," *Africa Today*, September 1959 (Vol. 6, No. 4), p. 11–14.

chairmanship of Mr. Francis J. Khamisi of Kenya, to coordinate nation-alist efforts and the programs of political organizations in the region. In addition, the conference adopted a freedom charter which declared freedom to be the birthright of every people and which denounced colonialism, trusteeship, partnership, *apartheid,* multiracialism, and white-settlerism as enemies of African freedom. The signatories dedicated themselves to the achievement of self-government throughout Africa and to the establishment of democracy under which there would be no discrimination, victimization, or segregation based on color, race, or religion—those of foreign origin who upheld the principles of parliamentary democracy, social justice, and equality would, either if they were citizens by birth or if they became naturalized citizens, enjoy the full rights and protections of a citizen. Signatories of the charter also pledged themselves to the UN Charter and to the Declaration of Human Rights. Poverty, ignorance, and ill health, the charter stated, could be eradicated only under self-government and international cooperation on the basis of equality and mutual benefaction. In addition, the charter: supported full industrialization and the enhancement of cooperative methods; called for control of the major means of production by the people themselves through democratically instituted governments; and demanded full recognition of trade union rights. Finally, the charter called for the establishment of Pan-African freedom movements in each territory in East and Central Africa.

On other issues, the conference expressed opposition to the Central African Federation which, it contended, had been created against the will of the Africans in the Federation. It also affirmed that at that juncture, i.e., prior to independence, the question of an East African Federation was irrelevant.

MOSHI

A second PAFMECA conference was held at Moshi, Tanganyika, in September 1959.[51] The delegates, representing the Belgian Congo, Kenya, Tanganyika, Uganda, and Zanzibar, unanimously approved a demand that "Africans should be given the right to govern themselves now" and denounced the repressive measures being applied against Africans in the multiracial areas of the continent.

The conference adopted resolutions on the Belgian Congo, Kenya, Nyasaland, Uganda, and South Africa, *inter alia.* The resolution on the Congo: 1) urged the Congolese voters to select in forthcoming elections candidates who would pledge themselves to securing full

[51] "East Africans Call for Self-Government," *Africa Special Report,* September 1959 (Vol. 4, No. 9), p. 2.

responsible government for the Congo by 1960; 2) asked the Belgian government to implement soon its promise of independence for the Congo; and 3) called on the Congolese people to beware of any Belgian *divide et impera* attempts. Regarding Kenya, conference resolutions demanded an end to the seven-year state of emergency and the immediate release of nationalist Jomo Kenyatta. The conference called on Kenyan African leaders in the Nationalist Party and the Independence Party to form a united African organization. With respect to Nyasaland, delegates requested the release of Dr. Hastings Banda and other Nyasaland African Congress leaders and the removal of the ban which had been placed on the Congress. A resolution urged that the Nyasaland Governor be relieved of his duties so that an atmosphere of "harmony and development" could be created. A resolution on Uganda asked the British administration to release all African political detainees and to take steps to ensure the observance of human rights and the rule of law. Representatives requested an inquiry into political disturbances in that territory. Concerning South Africa, the conference called for a world-wide boycott of South African goods and decided to bring to the attention of heads of state the "gross abuse of human rights" in South Africa. In addition, the conference asked transport unions in East and Central Africa to draft detailed plans for refusing to handle goods headed for or coming from South Africa.

In other actions, the conference denounced French plans for nuclear tests in the Sahara and appealed to Asian settlers in Kenya and Nyasaland to realize that keeping aloof from nationalist movements would be doing themselves a "great disservice."

ADDIS ABABA

Another PAFMECA conference, at which approximately 50 leaders representing both independent states and nationalist movements in East, Central, and southern Africa—as well as observers from other parts of Africa—were present, was held in Addis Ababa, Ethiopia, in early February 1962.[52] Ethiopia and Somalia were elected to full membership at the meeting. The nationalist parties of South and South West Africa, Basutoland, Bechuanaland, and Swaziland were also admitted, with the result that the title of the organization became henceforth the Pan-African Freedom Movement of East, Central, and South Africa (PAFMECSA).

[52] "Embryonic Alliance Emerges at PAFMECSA Conference," *Africa Report*, March 1962 (Vol. 7, No. 3), p. 14; and "Lagos and Addis Ababa Conferences," *Asia & Africa Review*, March 1962 (Vol. 2, No. 3), p. 6–7.

In terms of closer union, the conferees pledged themselves to work toward a federation of eastern Africa upon the accession to independence of Kenya, Uganda, and Zanzibar. Since Ethiopia and Somalia were to be included in the federation, the conference requested the East African Common Services Organization (EACSO) and the governments of Ethiopia and Somalia to initiate discussions on the extension of the East African common market and EACSO to those states.[53] The countries of Central and South Africa were also eventually to become members of the federation. In more immediate terms, the conference emphasized the need for cooperative efforts in the fields of transportation and communications and decided to hold in the near future a meeting of ministers of education to discuss means of cooperation in the latter field.

On other current political questions, the conference: 1) condemned *(a)* colonialist *divide et impera* policy, and *(b)* "maneuvers to subvert African unity . . . by encouraging . . . tribalism, regionalism, reaction, and opportunism;" 2) endorsed UN efforts in the Congo but called for additional UN pressure on the "fascist" governments of Portugal, South Africa, and Southern Rhodesia; 3) designated the preservation of the Federation of Rhodesia and Nyasaland and the failure of the British government to settle the constitutional crisis in Northern Rhodesia as threats to the peace and security of Central Africa; 4) called for the independence of the High Commission Territories of Basutoland, Bechuanaland, and Swaziland; and 5) reaffirmed previous resolutions condemning *apartheid,* demanded that the African states deny use of their ports and airfields to South Africa, requested curtailment of the flow of African laborers into South Africa from neighboring territories, rejected offers of self-government to the Transkei as an "insult to African people who are demanding complete and genuine freedom and independence for all of South Africa," and called for the immediate withdrawal of South African administration from South West Africa; 6) opposed the establishment or maintenance of foreign military bases in Africa; and 7) urged the French government and the Algerian provisional government to reach agreement at the earliest possible date. With respect to other international matters, the conference called for the cessation of the manufacture, stockpiling, and testing of nuclear weapons and for revision of the UN Charter in the direction of equitable geographical representation on the Security Council and other UN organs.

[53] See *The Future of East African High Commission Services: Report of the London Discussion,* June 1961, London, H.M.S.O., Cmnd. 1433.

Observations on the Political Regrouping of Africa

GEORGES BALANDIER

la Sorbonne

I

Decolonization involves more than the transfer of sovereignty (a development, and often an orientation, which is new as far as economic and social changes are concerned). It also raises the problem of political units and boundaries. The colonial powers established boundaries in a rather arbitrary manner, based upon the fortunes of conquest rather than African needs. African leaders are now concerned with the difficulties and necessities of regrouping.

Frequent African migrations (notably between the sixteenth and eighteenth centuries), brought about by warfare, economic needs (especially the search for productive land), and religious evangelism (such as the expansion of Islam), meant population instability. Other factors, principally the insufficiency of "techniques in utilizing area" (in the words of P. Gourou) and ethnic and cultural heterogeneity, caused large states (e.g., Ghana, Mali, and the Congo) either to disappear or to be limited in their capacity for large-scale organization. For example, J. J. Maquet's study of the Kingdom of Ruanda[1] reveals this weakness; only the central provinces are meaningfully involved in the state organization and have clearly submitted to the central power, whereas the outer provinces have retained many of their previous structures and much of their autonomy. Because of the above factors, it is easy to understand that the political boundaries of Africa are still uncertain and the nation-state does not have deep roots.

The more stable and permanent political entities are those coterminous with ethnic groups or clans which have relative permanence in a defined territory and in which the people are highly socialized. But

Reprinted from *Revue Française de Science Politique* (Presses Universitaires de France), X, 4 (December, 1960), 841–849, with the permission of the author and the publisher. Translated into English by William John Hanna.

[1] J. J. Maquet, *Le Système des Relations Sociales dans le Ruanda Ancien* (Tervuren: Musée Royal du Congo Belge, 1954); and J. J. Maquet and M. d'Hertefelt, *Elections en Société Féodale: une Etude sur l'Evolution du Vote Populaire au Ruanda-Urundi* (Brussels: Academie Royale des Sciences Coloniales, 1959).

because the membership of these ethnic groups or clans usually ranges only from a few thousand to a few hundred thousand, they can only be the basis of micro-states. Today, it is important to bring about a real change of scale, to organize sufficiently large political entities, and to make unifying forces prevail over particularistic tendencies. The latter requirement explains current attempts to reconstruct and exalt African history: the prestige of ancient Ghana is placed in the service of the decolonized Gold Coast, and that of Mali in the service of independent Soudan. (Unlike modern Ghana, modern Mali contains the sacred places and principal provinces of the ancient empire.) However, the emphasis on African history is not without danger; it can lead to the strengthening of African conservatism to the detriment of the politics of development and modernization, and it can reawaken traditional antagonisms such as the one between the Lulua and the Louba in Kasai Province of Congo (both large tribes proud of their former royalties).

II

The will to break with the colonial past does not make it possible, without grave risk, to ignore the geopolitical factors of colonization. It is within the framework of the new territories that the modernization of Black Africa began, economic solidarities developed, and modern political activity has been organized. This framework is important despite the existence of interterritorial political parties, notably in French-speaking Africa. The solidarity within the R.D.A., for example, has not prevented territorial divergencies from arising from the referendum and the problems of managing the French Community.

What are these geopolitical factors?

1. NEGATIVE FACTORS

Colonial expansion led to a division of Africa based upon the hazards of exploration and relative imperial strength. Critics of colonialism have not failed to point out the effects of this "surgical diplomacy" which, in the words of M. G. d'Arboussier, "separated peoples of the same ethnic origin and social structure, and brought together different ethnic groups and structures." Examples are not lacking. Ashanti-related groups are divided between Ghana (there, they are called Ashanti) and the Ivory Coast (Baoule, Agni); the former Congolese area is divided among Angola and the two Congo Republics; the remains of the former Lunda Empire are found in Angola, Congo (Leopoldville), and Northern Rhodesia. Such traditional ties are not by themselves sufficient to cause successful political regrouping, but

they can serve as pretexts. Thus, the image of the ancient Congo Kingdom has enabled the people of present-day Ba-Kongo areas to envision
a modern political state uniting all Ba-Kongo people.

A secondary point should also be mentioned. Colonization created
small territories whose continued separate existence is uncertain (e.g.,
Gambia, Togo, Dahomey), and sparsely populated territories whose
natural resources cannot fully be exploited (e.g., Gabon, with its
impressive mineral and forest resources, has a population of less than
500,000).

2. POSITIVE FACTORS

The artificial boundaries drawn by the European powers created
entities which now exhibit a degree of unity. These new entities are
more structurally elaborate than their traditional African counterparts
were before European intrusion. The elements of this structural elaboration include (a) partially developed modern communications and economic systems; (b) a unified administrative system; (c) the diffusion of
an international language (the colonizer's), facilitating communication
both internally (because the number of vernacular African languages
was consequently reduced) and with the outside world; and (d) new
population centers outside traditional milieux, encouraged primarily by
the development of wage-earners, which provided Africans with the
experiences of urban life.

Colonies have, in the final evaluation, acquired a personality and
brought about the partial fusion of heterogeneous tribal elements. For
example, even the most intransigent Cameroonian nationalists do not
dispute the existence of a Cameroon which has very precise boundaries,
viz., those established by the Germans. The nationalists have limited
themselves to an orthographic transformation, returning to "Kamerun"
to deny the break in colonial rule. The unity which has been brought
about by colonization is no longer contested, despite the differences
and tensions which exist between the people of northern and southern
Kamerun.

3. STRATEGIC POLITICAL FACTORS

European colonization and settlement (which also facilitated settlement by other minorities, especially Asian) has been very localized in
Black Africa. It has been concentrated in the South, and in some parts
of the center and the east. Everywhere, however, the consequences of
European intrusion have been similar: economic development managed
by Europeans who controlled the means of production (mines and
industries) or tried to protect themselves against eventual African com-

petition (e.g., by export agriculture in Kenya); social and juridical systems prejudiced against Africans (e.g., native reserves, color bars, different and unequal laws); and political regimes, which have tried to oppose any democratization.[2]

The privileged minorities, which in many areas are still well entrenched, have tried to preserve their advantages and their economic interests in the face of African claims of rightful ownership and demands for independence. The minorities' strategy has been simply to change the size of the relevant political unit so that they feel less vulnerable to these claims and demands. Two manifestations of this strategy can be distinguished.

(a) Fusion. The Central African Federation (the two Rhodesias and Nyasaland), with the Copper Belt as an economic link, illustrates the use of fusion.

(b) Separation. Political entities formed by colonization are broken up in order to create preponderantly white states and "residual" black African states. Some white leaders wanted to do this in the Central African Federation by making the two Rhodesias an industrialized white state and Nyasaland a black state with a backward economy. Now they are trying to settle for an independent white Southern Rhodesia. In the Republic of South Africa, the advocates of racial separation are creating all-black Bantustans within the country's borders. In the Congo, the temporary "independence" of Katanga resulted not only from indigenous differences, but also from the intervention of colonial powers and interest groups that wanted to establish a mining state under their indirect control.

III

It is easier to create the appearance of a state and affirm its sovereignty to the outside world than to constitute a national community and a stable polity. Decolonization poses this problem to African governments, and one way to classify them is according to the solution they adopt.

1. OPPOSITION TO BALKANIZATION

Boundaries created by colonization are contestable, and are contested, if only because they evoke a past which has been rejected. But the outlines of political units which might be substituted for the pres-

---

[2] For a general discussion, see P. Gourou and G. Balandier, "Les Problèmes Raciaux," *Encyclopédie Française*, XI (Paris: La Vie Internationale, 1957). For a case study by an African, see Jomo Kenyatta, *Facing Mount Kenya* (London: Secker and Warburg, 1953).

ent territories remain very vague. African nations are, in fact, only in the process of formation. I. Potekhin, the Russian Africanist, sees this with a clarity equal to that of his western colleagues.[3] Although the political map of Black Africa remains very fragile, African leaders tend to consider associations of existing states rather than a complete re-drawing of this map. Some leaders of the former A.O.F. want its federal structure to be restored in some way, but within the framework of new political conditions. The central government of Congo (Leopoldville) is now struggling to maintain territorial unity, but during the period of Belgian rule they condemned the anomalies of this very territory. Other examples of this phenomenon could be given. It can be explained in two ways.

(a) By raising the question of boundaries, ethnic loyalties could be stimulated which might develop into separatist nationalisms. This would risk weakening Black Africa by further balkanization, a develop-ment feared by most African leaders (notably President Senghor).[4]

(b) Major regrouping seems difficult to realize at the moment be-cause of the difficulty justifying them historically (traditions common to a large number of people are, with few exceptions, lacking) and be-cause of situations created by colonization (e.g., the proposed Congo state, a modern manifestation of the former Congo Kingdom, would have to overcome the reality of three existing states, the two Congos and Angola).

On the other hand, some regrouping is now being accomplished. These are easily justified by urgent economic needs, the importance of strengthening less viable states (e.g., those with small or scattered popu-lations, or meager resources), and the desire to consolidate African soli-darities. What are these regroupings?

2. REGROUPING BASED UPON HISTORICAL MOTIVES

In these cases the pre-colonial African past is exalted and supplies a mystical reference to a modern political unity. An illustration is provided by the Federation of Mali (Soudan and Senegal) which had, however, a very short existence. The historical heritage was not equally meaningful to each of the partners, and differences in interests and plans for development (social and economic) were sharp.[5]

---

[3] Potekhin, "De Quelques Problèmes Méthodologiques pour l'Etude de la Formation des Nations en Afrique au Sud du Sahara," *Présence Africaine*, XVII (December, 1957–January, 1958), 60–73.

[4] See L. S. Senghor, *Congrès Constitutif du P.F.A., Rapport sur la Doctrine et Programme du Parti* (Paris: Présence Africaine, 1959).

[5] President Senghor's remarks at a press conference held in Dakar on August 23, 1960, published by the Senegalese Information Service, supports this last point.

3. REGROUPING BASED UPON "REASON"

Because of the difficulties which have been experienced, some African political leaders have adopted an empirical approach, which at least ensures the emergence of some flexible functional groups. This is the case with the states of the Council of the Entente which, under the leadership of M. Houphouet-Boigny, is attempting to handle truly functional problems in common in order to ensure uniformity and co-ordination in administrative, financial, economic, and similar matters. This is also the approach that has been chosen by three of the countries which were in the A.E.F. (Gabon did not participate), but with less immediate results. At present, the empirical approach appears to be the surest and the best adapted to the period of transition.

Culture is also a possible basis for regrouping. Shortly before his accidental death, B. Boganda, founder of the Central African Republic, envisioned a Latin Africa composed of the A.E.F., Congo (Leopold-ville), and the Portugese territories. However, the project was utopian, for it took little account of political realities in central Africa. Nevertheless, it appears that colonization created more endurable solidarities (because of language, culture, ways of life, and so on) than one could imagine during the fights for independence. In West Africa, the separation between the Africa of English influence and the Africa of French influence is quite clear, in spite of the apparent good will towards unification. The latter have taken several steps towards association. The rapprochements envisaged (September, 1960) between the Ivory Coast, the Soudan, and Senegal, which appeared to be an agreement of reason between three former members of French West Africa (an agreement to which Guinea could ultimately subscribe), eventually did not materialize. But the conference held in Abidjan (October, 1960) initiated by President Houphouet-Boigny brought together almost all the states which had been French colonies and made it easier for them to formulate a common approach to the major problems of Africa.

4. REGROUPING BASED UPON IDEALISM

The mystique of African unity exerts the greatest power and enlists the greatest intellectual support for association. Pan Africanism represents the theoretical organization given to the mystique. The Union of Ghana and Guinea, established on November 23, 1958, is presented as one of the first concrete results of Pan Africanism, and it aspires to become "the vanguard of the United States of West Africa." In fact, it remains fragile and appears more the product of circumstances (Guinea's need to break its isolation after the referendum) than that of a Pan African doctrine. Because of this, the reticence of other states to join is understandable. For example, Nigeria seems to be more concerned with organizing its 35 million people (scattered in three weakly integrated regions) than participating in unions which, for the moment, are very vulnerable.

IV

Political evolution is most advanced in West Africa, but throughout the continent the process of transformation has not been completed. Regional associations remain unstable and competitive and developmental patterns are difficult to identify. However, one cannot fail to recognize the necessary basic stages or the central question which has emerged: How to change from traditional political units (often tribal or ethnic) to large political units (federal or confederal) without consolidating at the intermediate stage of the nation-state? The acceleration of history creates a telescoping of these stages, but can it ignore the logic of change?

Three other factors which affect the redrawing of Africa's political map should also be noted:

(a) The remaining links with the former colonial powers. Ghana, although a champion of independence and of African solidarity, belongs to the Commonwealth; and Dr. Nkrumah, in a speech to the Fifteenth General Assembly of the United Nations, attacked manifestations of colonialism more vigorously when they were outside the zone of British influence.

(b) The solidarity between countries of Tiers-Monde on the one hand, and the independent African states on the other.

(c) Affinities resulting from the choice of the same type of economic and social development, or the same conception of political democracy.

The remarks presented here show the difficult gestation period which the new Africa is undergoing, and how the outlines of tomorrow's political units are not yet clear.[6] Existing structures, divergencies of interest, rivalries—external influences too—explain the situation and why it is so uncertain.

[6] Cf. the series of articles by G. Balandier, "Les Mouvantes Frontières de l'Afrique," published in *Le Monde*, January 10, 11, 12, and 13, 1960.

The Politics of African Separatism

DONALD S. ROTHCHILD
Colby College

The advent of national self-determination in Africa is proving to be a shattering experience—not only to the ties of control previously exercised by the seats of empire overseas but also to the frail states which are now securing the attributes of sovereignty. "One can, indeed, argue," observes Professor Rupert Emerson, "that where deep-running ethnic diversity exists the introduction of democratic institutions is likely to have the effect of intensifying national distinctions and antagonisms since such institutions work to force a reconsideration of the definition of the 'we' into whose hands power is passing."[1] In no continent is the prospect of fragmentation more real than in Africa. If the events which have recently occurred in the Congo, the Mali Federation and elsewhere continue to form a pattern of separatism, they may cause historians of another era to look back and to classify this evolution as the "Repartition of Africa."

Although this paper deals specifically with disintegrative tendencies in Africa—searching wherever possible for general causes, I am aware, of course, that strong countertendencies are at work on that continent. The ideal of pan-Africanism is still adhered to. Yet the quickening pace of separatist activities indicates that the problem of building widely-based, regional institutions is becoming more and more complicated. What seems mandatory, if African unity is to become a reality, is a broadening of loyalties and a de-emphasis of differences. Past experience in Western Europe, for example, has made all too clear how often narrow loyalties (based on racial, religious and national fears of domination, a warped conception of self-interest, and an inability to thwart the forces of drift) have won out. It would be a tragedy for Africa to suffer a similar fate.

Before attempting to classify the main reasons for separatism in Africa, it seems necessary first to present some brief descriptions of this

Reprinted from *Journal of International Affairs*, XV (1961), 18–28, with the permission of the publisher.

[1] *From Empire to Nation: The Rise to Self-Assertion of Asian and African Peoples* (Cambridge: Harvard University Press, 1960), p. 222.

process in action. As recently as 1958, Basil Davidson praised France for establishing two large units in West and Equatorial Africa, thereby laying the framework for "the emergence not of 12 'nation states' but of two federations."[2] Subsequent events have demonstrated the speed with which schismatic tendencies have made themselves felt in present-day Africa. Guinea's independence, which was granted immediately after her people rejected the 1958 constitutional referendum, posed a challenge for the leaders of France's other African territories. How long could they delay the move toward complete national sovereignty, even though conciliatory gestures to Franco-African solidarity might be justified by economic necessities? The answer was soon forthcoming.

Since the Constitution of the Fifth Republic provided that a member state of the Community could either change its status or become independent by a resolution passed in the legislative assembly and approved by a referendum, the way was cleared for a rapid transformation of the French Community. In Equatorial Africa, attempts to establish a "confederal" union including the Central African Republic, Chad, Gabon, and the (ex-French) Congo were largely unsuccessful. Congolese leader Abbé Fulbert Youlou objected to losing his nation's individual representation at the United Nations, and wealthy Gabon feared the consequences of close economic ties with her neighbors. Thus Equatorial Africa is today a prime example of "Balkanization"; all four states are fully independent, and, while some efforts have been made to salvage a loose Union of Central Africa out of the present situation, the outlook for close interterritorial ties seems far from likely at this time.

In West Africa, the leaders of Senegal, Soudan, the Voltaic Republic and Dahomey decided to form the Federation of Mali, a project that ended in partial failure as both the Voltaic Republic and Dahomey withdrew from the scheme. Despite initial opposition from President de Gaulle and the Ivory Coast's Houphouet-Boigny, Senegal and Soudan went ahead with their federation plans and, on November 27, 1959, requested independence within the Community. Shortly afterwards, on June 20, 1960, French leaders displayed a change of heart and granted independence to Mali. Meanwhile Houphouet-Boigny and his allies formed a rival "Council of the Entente" consisting of the Ivory Coast, Dahomey, the Voltaic Republic and Niger. The "Entente" powers, not to be outdistanced by Mali's success, publicly requested, on June 3, 1960, that France transfer independence to each of the republics *before* negotiating Franco-African treaties of co-operation. Again France complied, and four new states were born in Africa. In the various joint

[2] *New Statesman,* LVI (August 9, 1958), p. 161.

communiqués issued after independence, the four "Entente" member states have agreed to establish common constitutional forms, diplomatic representation, and economic and technical policies. If these moves can lead to closer political links of a permanent nature, this would represent a great leap toward the goal of African solidarity.

Certainly the fate of the Mali Federation has destroyed all remaining illusions that the journey toward African unity will be an easy one. Senegalese leaders, oriented toward the West and less inclined to militant nationalism than their Soudanese partners, grew uneasy as federal Premier Mobido Keita, Soudan's strong man, moved to tighten his grip by seeking the office of federal president. The wealthier Senegalese feared that if Keita became president (an outcome virtually assured by Soudan's majority in the federal assembly), the powers of the federal government would be increased to the disadvantage of the Senegalese. Hence the latter talked of secession. Keita thereupon dismissed Senegalese Premier Mamadou Dia as defense minister of Mali and declared a state of emergency. Dia deposed Keita in retaliation and pulled Senegal out of the Federation. At first Soudanese leaders refused to concede that the Mali Federation had been disrupted, but when the United Nations admitted both Senegal and the Mali Republic to membership, they were forced to bow to the inevitable. Yet even these disheartening memories have deterred neither group from continuing to espouse the cause of African unity. Senegal's President Leopold Senghor has recently called for the creation of a union of the eight states of French West Africa, and Keita has thrown his support behind the pan-Africanist aspirations of President Nkrumah of Ghana.

A case of African separatism to achieve worldwide attention is Katanga Province's secession from the newly independent Republic of the Congo. Premier Moise Tshombe of Katanga had long threatened to make such a move. His mineral-rich province, which contributes more than half the revenues collected by the central government in normal times, is a bastion of Belgian enterprise. Belgian technicians, settlers, armed forces and commercial concerns (particularly giant Union Minière du Haut Katanga) have all played a key role in creating this prosperous *imperium in imperio* in the heart of central Africa.

Following the 1959 riots in Leopoldville, a number of Belgian settlers, aware of the meaning of the new barometer readings, joined Tshombe's *Confederation des Associations Katangaises* (the Conakat). Previously the tribally-based Conakat gained much strength from its opposition to alien Kasi intrusions into the political life of Katanga. Now the Conakat reflected settler influence by becoming even more determined in its espousal of loose ties with the other five provinces.

This new emphasis and composition in turn caused the Conakat to lose Baluba and other of its tribal supports. These groups broke away and formed the unitary-minded Balubakat Cartel, led by Jason Sendwe.

In the important provincial assembly elections held in 1960, the Conakat emerged victorious, but only by a slim majority. Consequently, when the Cartel boycotted the provincial assembly after the election, the Belgians found it necessary to change the assembly's quorum requirement from two-thirds to a simple majority. And Tshombe's inability to secure even this modified quorum for basic policy votes— including the one severing Katanga's relations with the rest of the Congo—has caused him real embarrassment. At least one observer has pointedly concluded that "the Government of Katanga continues on a basis of what looks like doubtful legality."[3]

Premier Tshombe made his announcement of independence less than two weeks after the Congo became a republic. The mutiny of the *Force Publique* presented him with a propitious opportunity to act. Katanga's premier feared the designs of Congo Premier Lumumba as well as a Belgian withdrawal from the country and decided that a "go it alone" policy was worth the risks involved. However, when international recognition of his action failed to materialize, Tshombe prudently modified his stand by announcing his support for a "United States of the Congo." Katanga's willingness to participate in such a confederation would hinge, he explained, upon the adequacy of the measures taken to circumscribe the power of the central government.

Once Premier Lumumba's government in Leopoldville lost its grip on the country, tribal warfare, widescale unemployment and panic ensued. Unilateral Belgian action to rescue their kinsmen remaining in the Congo and to restore order was regarded, in some quarters, as an attempt to regain imperialist control by backstairs methods. The crisis was one calling for international action, and the United Nations rose to the occasion.

In response to repeated calls for help from beleaguered Congolese authorities, a United Nations force was dispatched to deal with the turbulent situation. Secretary General Dag Hammarskjold and United Nations administrators in the field soon recognized four major responsibilities: that of warding off outside interference; that of preventing domestic disorder and warfare; that of preserving the country's unity; and that of rebuilding the economy. United Nations armed forces were immediately put to work patrolling major cities, guarding airports and public places, preventing tribal clashes, and arranging a cease-fire in

---

[3] Patrick O'Donovan, "In Tshombe's Katanga, Desperate Adventure in Sunday Calm," *Observer* (London), July 24, 1960, p. 7.

Katanga and South Kasai Provinces, where major fighting had broken out. Moreover, the Secretary General was able to make use of the presence of an international brigade in the Congo to hasten the withdrawal of Belgian troops from the area.

Sooner or later the entry of United Nations troops in the Congo was bound to affect the question of Katanga's secession. The disrupted Congo economy cannot be put in smooth-running order unless the mineral revenues of her richest province are used for the general welfare. Since the United Nations has the responsibility of rebuilding the Congolese economy, it must treat the Congo as a unit in order to achieve its purposes. Consequently, in all the debates on the Congo, Dag Hammarskjold has insisted on treating Katanga as part of the Congo while at the same time trying to encourage the Congolese to find the solution to their own problems. "I feel strongly," he told the Security Council on August 8, 1960, "that the United Nations would have failed in its mission if it maintained order while permitting democratic principles to be violated." He reconciled these two positions by personally leading United Nations forces into Katanga and by refusing, on the same occasion, to allow Lumumba to use these military units for any partisan ends. Congolese unity was therefore given a chance to develop, but no particular blueprint was imposed from the outside. In setting his standards of "independence, impartiality, objectivity," the Secretary General has made a real contribution to international government, but it remains to be seen whether self-determination and unity are to be coexistent in the Congo.

Moise Tshombe's successful defiance of Leopoldville's authority has encouraged other Congolese leaders to come out in favor of a less centralized form of government. During early August the increase in federalist ranks was noteworthy. The central committee of President Joseph Kasavubu's Abako party passed a resolution declaring their lack of confidence in Premier Lumumba's government, and a Leopoldville meeting of Abako sent a telegram to the Security Council charging that Lumumba was incapable of ensuring security in the country and urging that the Council consider a confederation along provincial lines as the only valid solution to the present crisis. It does not seem likely that Kasavubu would have been willing to risk open battle with Lumumba and his centralist allies unless he felt that the balance of forces was swinging in favor of some kind of federal compromise. Furthermore, Puna party, which plays a leading role in Equator Province, sent a telegram to the Security Council from its Leopoldville headquarters supporting confederation as the only possible basis for establishing stable government. And in South Kasai, provincial leader Albert

Kalonji proclaimed the independence of his "Mining State" and opened negotiations with neighboring Katanga with an eye to federation.

After Colonel Mobutu assumed power in mid-September and installed his caretaker government, a review of the basic law governing the Congo became possible. The federalists recognized their chance and made some moves to begin serious discussions of their constitutional problems. It seems evident that the time has come to give detailed consideration to the advisability of adopting a federal system. Not having adapted the political system to the existing clusters of power in the first place seems a mistake in planning. The unity of the Congo should be preserved, but the best means to that end may not lie in the most tightly-knit form of statecraft. "The Congo is too big, and its peoples too diverse, to be governed as a unitary state or even a tight federation," commented the *Manchester Guardian Weekly*. "M. Lumumba, who is the chief proponent of a strong centre, came to power . . . because he had more support than any other party leader. But he had less support than M. Tshombe, M. Kasavubu, and the other regional leaders combined."[4] If these federalist leaders could agree among themselves upon a satisfactory formula for dividing the power of the state between the regions and the central government, surely they have the numerical strength to bring their accord into effect. However, these men have yet to demonstrate a readiness to subordinate particular interests to those of the whole. No democratic solution to the problem of Congolese unity can be found where such a largeness of purpose is lacking.

Separatist tendencies are by no means a Latin African monopoly but are evident in British Africa as well. In the Federation of Rhodesia and Nyasaland, appeals to contract out of the union are made constantly. Both black and white nationalists advocate partition, though their motives are often diametrically opposed. To the vast majority of Africans in Nyasaland and Northern Rhodesia, the imposition of the Central African Federation in 1953 meant the extension of (white) Southern Rhodesian influence to the north. They resented this as a backward step which might, in effect, deny them a chance for future self-rule on the Ghanaian pattern. Consequently, they began a campaign aimed at the dissolution of the new federal structure. Because of their legitimate grievance against the practices of inequality within the Federation, these African nationalists seem to have paid scant attention to the economic advantages to be derived from union. Nyasaland in particular has benefited from funds made available to it by the

[4] Vol. 83, No. 4 (July 28, 1960), p. 8.

federal treasury. The amounts spent on education, public works and health have risen considerably above those of pre-federation times. Moreover, federation has helped Nyasaland to share in the good credit rating of her neighbors and to participate (albeit less intensively) in the industrial expansion now taking place.

Dr. Hastings Banda, leader of the African nationalists in Nyasaland, clearly places his people's self-rule above the economic advantages of Central African federation. He asserts, moreover, that the Nyasas will be able to transform their country into a "Central African Denmark" after independence. But if Nyasaland proves to be unviable, he then proposes to join his nation's fate with that of Northern Rhodesia, the Congo, Tanganyika and other like-minded lands. The one solution he rules out is to continue the present association with Southern Rhodesia. Thus he told a Dar es Salaam audience in the spring of 1960 that when he was approached by officials in Blantyre he refused self-government for Nyasaland within the Federation, "because I can never envisage Nyasaland as being self-governing within any federation with Southern Rhodesia. It would be merely a glorified provincial council."[5]

Partly in reaction to African demands for independence in Northern Rhodesia and Nyasaland and partly out of long-standing skepticism over the value of federation, the more extremist elements among the white population have mooted the idea of a breakup or a loosening of existing bonds between the territories. This is particularly noticeable in Southern Rhodesia. In the course of the general election held in that territory in 1958, the United Federal party leader, Sir Edgar Whitehead, observed that if African nationalism should gain the upper hand in the northern territories, Southern Rhodesia might be compelled to seek the shelter of South Africa. Subsequently, in 1960, he declared that unless the forthcoming review of the federal constitution met certain conditions, he would refuse to sign the agreement drawn up there and would resubmit the whole question of Southern Rhodesian participation in the Federation to the electorate. Mr. William Harper, leader of the segregationist-inclined Dominion party, expressed his opinions even more clearly. He doubted that his party's Central African Alliance plan (which would attach the Northern Rhodesian Copperbelt and the intervening railway line to an independent Southern Rhodesia) would elicit much support from any other quarter. Therefore he talked both of secession and the establishment of a looser type of federation between Southern Rhodesia and the "black states" of the north. In July, 1960,

[5] Quoted in *East Africa and Rhodesia*, May 19, 1960, p. 890.

after several important men resigned from the Southern Rhodesian branch of the Dominion party, a party caucus issued a policy statement backing its leader "in his fight for Southern Rhodesia first and his determination to go forward with his plan for an economic alliance with neighbouring territories as an alternative to Federation." The statement also emphasized that "the extreme course of the complete secession of Southern Rhodesia from the Federation will only be resorted to if the interests of Southern Rhodesia indicate that this step is unavoidable."[6]

It seems a certainty that all this deep-seated African and European hostility to the Central African Federation will exact some price when the forthcoming review of the Constitution takes place. In its recent report on the future of the Federation, the Monckton Commission called for an increase in the proportion of seats allotted to Africans in the central legislature, a broadening of the franchise, the inclusion of guarantees against racial discrimination, an expansion of the sphere of territorial activities and, quite significantly, the inclusion of a right of eventual secession. The commission argued that by granting the right of secession to each territory, political tensions would be eased, thereby reducing the likelihood of a breakup of the Federation.[7] Nevertheless, it is impossible to predict how these recommendations will fare during the review of the Constitution. And regardless of what the next stage may be, political pressure from various sources may cause the dismemberment of the federal edifice at some future time. If that should happen, one can only hope that economic hardship and South African expansion will not be the outcome.

It is not beyond the realm of possibility that the strains of union may also jeopardize the future of the Federation of Nigeria. Its form of federalism, including as it does three large, populous, semi-autonomous regions, hardly acts to discourage ideas of separatism, since each of the regions possesses all the normal prerequisites for nationhood. At various times leaders in all regions have threatened secession; yet it is important to bear in mind that these threats have come less and less frequently as the federal system has taken hold. Now that imperial control no longer exists, irresponsible actions could lead to unfortunate crises. Nigerians realize this. They are anxious to make their country a center of power and stability in Africa. Thus the premier of the North-

---

[6] *Rhodesia Herald,* July 29, 1960 as quoted in the *Federation of Rhodesia and Nyasaland Newsletter* for the week ending July 29, 1960, p. 3.

[7] See the *Report of the Advisory Commission on the Review of the Constitution of Rhodesia and Nyasaland,* Cmnd. 1148 (London: H.M.S.O., 1960), p. 101.

ern Region, Alhaji Sir Ahmadu Bello, recently took great pains to assure a New York audience: "There need be no fear that the emergence of Nigeria as an independent member of the British Commonwealth presages a time of turmoil or disturbances."[8] Leadership and co-operation are both evident. But perhaps the most effective countervailing force to future secessionist movements lies in the emphasis being placed at present on national loyalties, achievements and aspirations.

The foregoing record surely indicates that major obstacles stand in the way of African interterritorial consolidations. Some of these may be listed as follows:

(1) *Racial and tribal diversities.* The diversity of African peoples is a source of strength and excitement. Politically, however, it presents problems. In each emergent land various races and tribes must be integrated. The new "nation" must become the primary focal point of loyalty. In British Central Africa and in the Congo where loyalty to race and tribe, or both, are often placed before loyalty to country, the dismemberment of the state is facilitated. Therefore to expect wide territorial entities to flourish while the process of national integration is at an early stage is perhaps too much to hope for.

(2) *The reluctance of rich territories to join poorer neighbors.* African nations apparently find the sharing of wealth no easier than do their Western counterparts. Katanga Province's secession from the Congo, Gabon's unwillingness to be an integral part of a French Equatorial African confederation, and Senegal's discomfort over her close association with poorer and more populous Soudan all attest to the tension which results from the attempt to unite richly endowed lands with their less fortunate neighbors. Perhaps Nigeria's experience with revenue allocation could be of help in alleviating such fears. By allocating tax revenues to the central government and the regions according to a pre-determined ratio, a workable compromise has been reached. It seems possible that other African nations might learn from this experiment something which they can adapt to their needs.

(3) *Nationalism.* There are two dimensions in which to view African nationalism. In the first, the citizen is offered a wider focal point of loyalty than tribe, race or religion. Nationalism provides an alternative to intertribal, interracial and intercredal hostility, those ugly obstacles to good human relations in the "old" Africa. Thus a Ghanaian subject, swept up in the struggle for national freedom and dignity, is likely to identify himself primarily with his country's goals

[8] *Daily Times* (Lagos), July 8, 1960, pp. 1, 8.

and aspirations and not those of his Fanti people. In the second dimension, nationalism appears as the cause of new hostilities. Animosities are directed against other nations because of border disputes, ideological differences or offenses to national pride—to say nothing of its use for purposes of internal regimentation. Surely this projection of "tribalism" onto a wider screen is a tragic commentary on the alleged progress of our century. For just at the time when Europe seems to be growing out of its parochial differences, Africans are seizing upon the forms and expressions of nationalism with a resolute sense of mission. This is a process which doubtlessly cannot be avoided, but it is likely to impede the growth of durable federations.

(4) *Charismatic, dictatorial leadership patterns.* In multi-group societies struggling for national liberation, virtually the whole force of the community for once overcomes its differences (even if only temporarily) and unites behind the nationalist party, the spokesman for the people's salvation. The party leader expresses both the people's determination to be free of external control and the values they plan to maintain once victory is secured. While performing this role, the leader gains the mandate to rule from his countrymen. When one considers that the leader possesses the inner strength and firmness to lead the way to freedom, it is not surprising to find him carrying over the same qualities into the post-independence period. However, one of the consequences of this emerging pattern—a one-party state with a strong leader —is the compartmentalization of African political life. Politics becomes personalized and rigid, and this situation in turn makes the establishment of interterritorial federations more difficult. Accordingly, the Senegalese fear Keita's alleged authoritarianism, and Tshombe is distrustful of the overweening and communistic ambitions he attributes to Lumumba. Moreover, the competition between strong personalities may be the best explanation for the inability of the Ghana-Guinea Union to become a true federation.

(5) *International pressures.* With the cold war struggle between East and West obviously affecting the internal power struggle in the Congo, it seems hardly necessary to emphasize the significance of international pressures upon the fate of large territorial units in Africa. The delivery of Belgian military equipment to Tshombe's forces and the dispatch of Soviet aircraft and trucks to assist Lumumba's army are evidence of outside interest in the Congo's political affairs. But a less dramatic example of the effects of external pressures is also at hand. Most African nations find it convenient to stay within the franc or sterling zones after gaining independence. During imperial times they

built up complicated trade and fiscal relations from which they are now loath to disentangle themselves. Participation in these monetary blocs has the effect, however, of inhibiting inter-territorial trade and of making the political integration of contiguous territories more difficult. Hence the peanut farmer of the British territory of Gambia, who normally might be expected to prefer the higher-priced French zone, is not attracted to the idea of a Senegal-Gambian merger which would saddle him with heavy import duties, increased transportation costs, and an expensive market in which to purchase goods.[9] And as long as such bonds of interest between the emergent African land and the former imperial power remain firm, progress toward the uniting of Africa will be slowed.

(6) *Competition for capital.* Even in the wealthier territories of Africa, the development of industrial and agricultural potentialities is still at an early stage. African states need assistance in order to fulfill their goals, and they will often have to compete against each other in order to attract the necessary capital for their programs. Because of the great number of new states, the similarity of their economic problems, and the limitation of excess capital throughout the world, an intense competition for such capital seems likely to occur. Those territories which are most successful in finding the necessary capital to effect their plans seem unlikely to be enthusiastic over the sharing of their advantages with contiguous lands. And certainly such an attitude will not facilitate progress toward African federation.

The point cannot be made too often that there are few instances of federation occurring between sovereign countries. Where territories are associated in a working relationship before their independence, there exists a controlled situation in which adjustments can be made. Once independence is granted, however, the room for maneuver becomes much more limited. Secession, therefore, coming after sovereignty is granted, is likely to do lasting damage.

The fragility of modern Africans states, particularly federalistic ones, often encourages the founding of separatist movements. Separatist leaders seize upon the unstable situation to fight for what they see as their own interests. However, some loss of security and opportunity usually occurs on all sides. No doubt these leaders are fully justified in struggling against an externally imposed federation to which they have never given consent, but if satisfaction for just grievances can be ob-

[9] See R. J. Harrison-Church, "Gambia and Mali: 2," *West Africa,* July 2, 1960, p. 740.

tained within the context of a wider union, prudence might dictate a more accommodating attitude toward such associations.

Finally, what can be accomplished where territories possess a common heritage but are unable to cope with the centrifugal forces driving them apart? Perhaps the adoption of a less demanding organizational form might reduce the disruptive movements caused by a tight-knit political association. Thus the East Africa High Commission seems a healthy alternative, under the present conditions of East African life, to overly centralized unions or no unions at all. So long as African statesmen tailor the cloth of union to the state form to be fitted, they will be acting in a constructive manner.

The Economic Basis of Political Choice in French West Africa

ELLIOT J. BERG

Harvard University

Africans in French Tropical Africa have recently been called on to make several far-reaching political decisions. Two basic questions have been at issue: the nature of the relationship between France and the African territories, and the nature of relations between the African territories themselves. On the first question, the Referendum of September 28, 1958, on the Constitution of the Fifth French Republic gave Africans the choice between total independence and internal autonomy within "The (French) Community."[1] With regard to their mutual relations, the territories which made up the federations of French West and French Equatorial Africa could remain tied together politically, or they could sever all formal political connections among themselves; in French African political terminology, the second issue has been whether or not the individual territories should form "primary federations."

The issue of total independence or internal autonomy within "The Community" was temporarily decided at the 1958 Referendum, when eleven of the twelve territories of French West and Equatorial Africa voted to remain with France, Guinea alone choosing immediate independence. Since then several members of "The Community" have initiated negotiations with France for the full transfer of sovereign powers to local African governments, and the indications are that all French-speaking West Africa will be fully independent within the near future.

The outcome of the second question—political relations among the African territories—is not so clear. The trend up to now has been

Reprinted from *The American Political Science Review*, LIV (1960), 391–405, with the permission of the author and the publisher.

This paper is a revised version of one given at the Second Annual Convention of the American Society for African Culture, New York City, June 27, 1959. Much of the research on which the paper is based was done in Africa in 1957 and 1958, when the author was a Foreign Area Research Fellow of the Ford Foundation. The author is indebted to Dr. Ruth Schachter, African Research and Studies Program, Boston University, for many helpful comments and discussions.

[1] They also could choose to become departments of France, but this alternative was hardly relevant to the West African territories.

against the re-creation of primary federations. The federations of French West and French Equatorial Africa ceased their legal existence in April, 1959. Two of the former territories of French West Africa—Senegal and the Soudan—have formed the Federation of Mali. And, under the sponsorship of the Ivory Coast, four of the others (the Ivory Coast, the Upper Volta, Niger, and Dahomey) have decided to join together in a loose organization. All seven of the states of West Africa under French influence have, finally, agreed to enter a customs union. Aside from the Federation of Mali, none of these new arrangements (and this goes also for the Ghana-Guinea Union, another loose association) involves the cession of genuine power to a federal body; all attempts at closer union have failed, mainly because of the opposition of the Ivory Coast to the rebirth of federal government in French-speaking West Africa.

Many complex factors enter into the explanation of why most of French tropical Africa refused independence when it was offered, and why the newly autonomous African states in what used to be French West Africa are having difficulty in re-uniting themselves. The fact that the new French Constitution allowed them the possibility of choosing independence at any time in the future swung many leaders into the Community. The *mystique* that guided M. Houphouet-Boigny, leader of the Ivory Coast, his belief that Africans and Frenchmen could show the world a new path in racial and international cooperation, is fundamental in explaining the Ivory Coast's adherence to the French Community, and its reluctance to enter a federation with other West African states. On the other side, the very different ideas of M. Sékou Touré, Guinea's leader, on the future of Africa influenced Guinea's decision to take its independence. French action in the internal politics of some of the territories affected the outcome of the referendum, and considerations of internal political balance led a number of African leaders to decide against independence.

All these factors and others are pertinent in understanding the direction of political events in French-speaking West Africa. But underlying them is a set of economic circumstances which have given shape to the political decisions made; in West Africa, as elsewhere, political choice is conditioned by the nature of the economic environment in which it takes place. It is the purpose of this paper to outline some of the main features of this economic setting, and to explore their political implications. More specifically, we first examine the characteristics of French West Africa's pattern of economic development, and then consider the economic background to the problem of refashioning a federal state in what was formerly a colonial federation. In the final section we consider the role of economic factors in explaining the French African states' temporary refusal of independence when it was first offered, and in accounting for the difficulties of political re-integration among them.

I. THE PATTERN OF ECONOMIC DEVELOPMENT IN FRENCH WEST AFRICA

THE RELATIVE SPEED OF RECENT DEVELOPMENT

One of the striking aspects of the economy of French West Africa (FWA) is the extent of its development since the end of World War II. Between the turn of the century, when settled administration began in most parts of the area, and 1939, changes in the economic and social structure of the country were few. New ideas, new ways of doing things, new wants did begin to penetrate traditional society and prepare the way for future changes. But the going was slow and actual achievements few. A railway system was laid down, some roads were built, some African farmers took to coffee and cocoa growing in the Ivory Coast, and in Senegal Africans continued the export of peanuts which they had been growing for sale since 1850. In 1913 about 240,000 tons of peanuts were exported from Senegal, making up over half the total value of FWA exports. In 1938 some 370,000 tons were exported, and peanuts were still 45 per cent of the total value of exports that year; except for the increasing output of cocoa and coffee from the Ivory Coast the volume and structure of production in 1938 differed little from that of 1913. The territories of the interior—the Soudan, Niger, Upper Volta and Mauritania—remained largely outside the currents of modern economic life, except for their role as exporters of labor and cattle to the coastal areas. Even along the coast there was little industry, and practically none outside of Dakar in Senegal. No minerals were exported. Some 90 per cent of the population was bound up in a subsistence economy; only about 200,000 men (most of them temporary migrants) worked for wages, and of these fewer than 140,000 worked for private enterprises.[2]

The low-gear movement of the economy was matched by equally slow development on the social side. Relatively few Africans received any kind of education at all; fewer reached the secondary school level; a tiny handful got to the universities in France. In 1938 there were only 71,000 pupils in schools, or 3.2 per cent of the school-age population.

Then came the war, and after it a political and economic "new deal" in French Africa. Under it, the economy of FWA expanded at a

[2] Agence Economique du Gouvernement-Général de l'Afrique Occidentale Française, *Annuaire Statistique de l'Afrique Occidentale Française et du Togo, 1934–1935–1936* (Paris, 1937), p. 121. The source of other statistical data in this section is: Haut Commissariat de la République en Afrique Occidentale Française, *A.O.F. 1957; Tableaux Economiques* (Dakar, 1958).

TABLE I.

SOME INDICATORS OF DEVELOPMENT IN
FRENCH WEST AFRICA, NIGERIA, AND GHANA, 1956

	French West Africa	*Nigeria*	*Ghana*
(1) Population (millions)	18.8[a]	31.2	4.7
(2) Area (square miles)	1,800,000	373,000	78,800
(3) Exports per capita ($ U.S.)	18.2[b]	12.1	51.6
(4) Imports per capita ($ U.S.)	20.3[b]	13.7	52.9
(5) Percentage of total population engaged in nonagricultural wage-earning[c]	1.4	1.2	4.6
(6) Electricity consumption per capita (kwh)	7.7	7.3	49.0
(7) Road density (miles of road per thousand square miles of area)	27.1	99.2	49.0
(8) Number of inhabitants per automotive vehicle[d]	270	1,290	120
(9) Railway density (miles of railway track per thousand square miles of area)	1.4	15.1	7.0
(10) Per capita passenger miles travelled on railways	15	12	35
(11) Number of inhabitants per doctor[e]	33,000	54,000	25,000
(12) Percentage of school-age children attending schools[f]	13	37	86

Sources: French West Africa: *AOF 1957, Tableaux Economiques.* Nigeria: Federation of Nigeria, *Digest of Statistics,* Vol. 5, #3, 1956 and Vol. 7, #2, 1958; Federal Education Department, *Digest of Statistics, 1956;* Federal Department of Statistics, *Report on Employment and Earnings Enquiry,* September 1956. Ghana: *Digest of Statistics,* Vol. 7, #1, 1958; *Education Statistics, 1957; Economic Survey, 1957.*

[a] Recent sampling surveys have found a consistent understatement in previous population estimates. On the basis of the results of these surveys Government statisticians in FWA have unofficially re-evaluated FWA's 1956 population as between 22 and 24 million. (See Haut Commissariat Général à Dakar, Groupe d'Etudes des Comptes Economiques, *Comptes Economiques de l'Afrique Occidentale Française, 1956, Rapport #2, Inventaire des Ressources humaines en 1956* (Dakar, March 1959, p. 4). To the extent that these new estimates are more accurate than the official figures all the indicators in the table are of course overvalued.

[b] The official 1956 dollar-franc rate of exchange (175 cfa francs to $1 U.S.) is used in the conversion. Because the franc was considerably overvalued, the official rate inflates the real volume of FWA's exports and imports in dollar terms.

[c] The estimated nonagricultural wage-earning labor forces used in the calculation of these percentages are: FWA, 270,000; Ghana, 215,000; Nigeria, 410,000. Agricultural workers are omitted mainly because of the difficulty of estimating the number of sharecroppers and wage-earners at work for African farmers. These workers are more numerous in FWA and Ghana than in Nigeria.

[d] Trucks, buses, taxis and private cars.

[e] The Ghana figure refers to 1954.

[f] University students are excluded. Roughly, 2,000 FWA students were pursuing post-secondary studies, 1,300 Ghanaians, and 2,500–3,000 Nigerians.

rate unmatched in its earlier history. Between 1947 and 1957 coffee exports almost tripled—from 43,000 to 118,000 tons, making FWA (more precisely, the Ivory Coast) the world's third largest coffee producer. Cocoa exports during the same period increased from 28,000 to 76,000 tons. Peanut exports almost doubled, from 380,000 tons in 1947 to 710,000 in 1956. Secondary industry grew; food processing plants, flour milling and soap manufacture made their appearance for the first time or significantly expanded their capacity. Mining operations began in Guinea and in Mauritania. The urban population in the main towns expanded enormously: Dakar (in Senegal) and Conakry (in Guinea) doubled in size in 10 years; the population of Abidjan (in the Ivory Coast) tripled. The number of non-agricultural wage-earners doubled, and the total number of wage-workers increased at an even faster rate. Electricity production tripled during these years, a real beginning was made on the construction of a creditable road system, and the number of automobiles and trucks increased tenfold.

The economic achievements of the postwar period were not at the expense of social development, for the social services of the area expanded as well. The number of doctors serving FWA's people rose from less than 500 in 1946 to almost 650 in 1956, and the number of hospital beds increased from 10,000 to 20,000. Education began to touch substantial numbers of the school-age population for the first time. In 1947 only 128,000 were in school, out of an estimated school-age population of 2.4 million; in 1957 about 377,000 out of 2.8 million were in school. The rate of school attendance thus grew in 10 years from 5 per cent to over 13 per cent.

The increased rate of development since 1946 has not revolutionized FWA's economy. Over 80 per cent of its people still remain very largely within the subsistence sector of the economy. The exchange sector remains overwhelmingly devoted to the production of agricultural products for export; over 70 per cent of FWA's export earnings come from three crops (peanuts, coffee, cocoa). Its industry is still insignificant, as witnessed by the low percentage of its population in industrial employment. But during the postwar period all sectors of the economy experienced a high and increasing level of activity. The pace of economic change was quickened by more intense contact between the money economy and ordinary villagers. Most important, FWA was effectively endowed with the social and economic base from which future growth can take place, for a substantial amount of social overhead capital has come into being—roads, ports, bridges, communications facilities, schools, markets, hospitals, buildings, educated people.

In order to get some idea of FWA's location in economic space, some idea of its degree of advancement, Table I lists a number of measures of social and economic development. To show how FWA compares with its main West African neighbors the same measures are given for Nigeria and Ghana. As indicators of development the measures are very rough. The data on which some of them are based are extremely crude; in the case of wage-earners, for example, a substantial number of workers in each of the countries (agricultural laborers, domestic servants, and most of those employed in enterprises with less than 10 workers) are excluded because they have never been accurately counted or reported. Some of the other indicators require careful interpretation; road densities, for example, are based on the official figures of road mileage, all roads being included, even those of very questionable quality. If paved roads alone are taken, the comparisons are much less favorable for FWA, which had in 1956 less than 1500 miles of paved roads as against Ghana's 1650 miles and Nigeria's 3400 miles. Similar problems of interpretation arise for most of the other indicators. Despite these difficulties, however, the figures given in Table I do tell us a good deal about the three countries.

Two general conclusions emerge from the table. The first is that Ghana is well ahead of the others, an indication of the solid economic base underlying its political independence. The second is that FWA and Nigeria are not so far from one another in their relative degrees of development. It is mainly in the extent of education that Nigeria shows a clear superiority.

The difference is in fact greater than the table suggests. For there were in 1956 about 90,000 Europeans in FWA, while Nigeria had only about 15,000 (and Ghana under 10,000). The European presence inflates most of the indicators, since Europeans are heavy importers of consumer goods, intensive users of automobiles, consumers of much electricity, etc. Even the education statistics are affected by their presence, since in FWA European children attend local schools, while they usually do not in Ghana and Nigeria. So while the general conclusion holds, that FWA and Nigeria are in roughly similar stages of economic and social development, the advantage of Nigeria is greater than appears on the surface of the figures. The comparisons cannot therefore be taken as indicating relative degrees of *African* development within each country. Nor, for similar reasons, can the comparisons be interpreted to indicate relative degrees of preparedness for self-government. For it is not only in social and economic results that such preparedness must be measured; the ways in which these results are achieved are also important. And while in Nigeria and Ghana the sources of development—especially the sources of development funds—have been essentially internal, FWA has been heavily dependent on France, particularly for the capital investments that have given impetus to its recent growth.

DEPENDENCE ON FRENCH CAPITAL GRANTS FOR DEVELOPMENT EXPENDITURE

We noted above the considerable post-World War II expansion of FWA's basic transportation, communication, education and health facilities. The kind of real capital formation involved in the development of these facilities can, in principle, be financed in any country in one or both of two ways: the authorities can draw on domestic resources, either by restricting the current consumption of its citizens or—where possible—by utilizing unused resources already existing in the country, mainly the "leisure" of its citizens. Or the country can get help from abroad, help which will make it easier to bring idle resources into use or make it possible to transfer resources from other uses to capital formation, *e.g.*, roads, hospitals and schools. The former way is the hard way; it involves belt-tightening of one kind or another. Countries that can finance their development the second way are—in one sense at least—lucky; they don't have to sacrifice for development, either immediately by restricting their current consumption or later by not participating in the higher incomes that development brings with it.

French West Africa is in the second category. Its postwar development has been accompanied by relatively heavy doses of public capital investment, the greatest part of which has come in the form of grants from France. Between 1947 and the end of 1956 public capital investment in FWA totalled 170 billion 1956 cfa francs, or—depending on the exchange rate used—between $750 million and almost $1 billion.[3] Of this total, about 106 billion francs, or over 70 per cent, came from the French Treasury, most of it in the form of outright grants, and the rest

[3] The franc in which this sum is expressed is the colonial franc, the cfa franc as it is called, which exchanges for two French francs. The current rate of exchange between the cfa franc and the U. S. dollar is, since January 1959, about 247 francs to one dollar.

The data on which this estimate of investment is based come from *AOF 1957, Tableaux Economiques*, pp. 336 ff. Annual investments are given there in current francs; the total 1947–1956 investment in current francs is 155 billion. I have converted these current francs into 1956 francs with the deflator used by government statisticians in France and Africa (*Cf. AOF, 1957*, p. 340). This deflator consists of an index based on an average of French wholesale and retail price indices.

To translate the franc investments into a dollar equivalent is an uncertain operation. The official rate of the franc was kept at artificial levels throughout the postwar period; use of this rate to convert franc investments into dollars therefore substantially inflates their real value in dollar terms. This kind of problem is not of course unique to the franc; it arises in all currency conversions, particularly in a world of managed currencies. But the difference between the official exchange rate of the franc and its rate on the world's money markets was so large during the period under consideration that it seems essential to note it here. To give a more meaningful dollar estimate of public investments in FWA I have therefore converted the franc investments into dollars at two different rates of exchange, the official 1956 rate of 175 cfa francs to one dollar, and the average free market rate that year of 225 francs to one dollar.

in long-term, low-interest loans. To get some perspective on what kind of investment effort this represents it is enough to look at estimates of earlier public investment. Government statisticians in FWA have estimated that between 1903 and 1946 only 46 billion 1956 cfa francs flowed from French sources to public authorities in West Africa;[4] and all of this was composed of loans, not grants. This means that in 10 postwar years more than twice as much public capital investment took place in FWA as had been made in the 43 previous years. The fact that earlier public investments from France were repayable loans, while most of the more recent investments were outright grants, is not the least significant aspect of this contrast.

The extent of FWA's dependence on France for investment funds has been even greater than the above figures suggest. The territories have been able to contribute 30 to 35 per cent of the total public investment from their own resources only because France has paid for a substantial part of their ordinary administrative expenditures. The financial relationship between France and FWA is so complex, their economies and their administrations have been so integrated, that it is not easy to tell just how much of ordinary operating expenses has been covered by French contributions. The official estimates are that between 1950 and 1956 over 37 per cent of FWA's civil and military expenses were paid for by France.[5] The trend toward political autonomy between 1956 and 1959 did not decrease this percentage appreciably. Table II gives a breakdown of civil administrative expenditure for the fiscal year 1958. Of a total of about 55 billion cfa francs spent that year on normal running costs of civil administration in FWA, French sources contributed almost 27 per cent. If military expenditures were added, the percentage of French contribution to total civil and military expenses would be around 35 per cent.

The extent of this dependence on French help for ordinary expenses of government can nevertheless be exaggerated. Whether military expenditure can rightfully be counted as entirely essential is open to question. And if FWA were to be independent tomorrow it could surely do without many of the French administrative officers and other civil servants whose usefulness is equally open to question now. Furthermore, the pensions of retired civil servants and military personnel are fixed obligations assumed by the French government. Even after inde-

---

[4] *AOF, 1957,* p. 340.

[5] The total expenditure for operating costs, pension payments and the armed forces during this seven year period was 260 billion cfa francs, of which the French paid 97 billions. *AOF 1957,* p. 376.

TABLE II.

SOURCES OF EXPENDITURE ON CIVIL ADMINISTRATION, GENERAL AND LOCAL
BUDGETS, FRENCH WEST AFRICA, 1958
(Billions of cfa Francs)

i. Expenditures paid from locally raised revenues	40.6[a]
ii. Expenditures paid from French budget	14.25
Administrators and judges	1.9
State services	6.0
Civil and military pensions	3.5
Subsidies to local budgets for administrative expenses	1.65
Transfer to metropolitan budget of a part of salaries of French civil servants in FWA	1.2
Total civil expenditure	54.85

Source: Direction Générale des Finances, Dakar.

[a] Municipal expenditures not included. Includes a 6 billion franc contribution to the expenses of State services.

pendence France would continue to pay them as she is doing in independent Guinea. This is a substantial part (25 per cent) of the total French assistance to civil administrative expenditures. On the other hand, payments for military security are completely excluded from Table II; but an independent FWA would have to set up some military establishment, and this would require transfer of resources now being used elsewhere. In any case, the main point is that French help in subsidizing ordinary operating costs of government has allowed the FWA authorities to transfer resources to public investment which would otherwise have been required for normal administration. Directly or indirectly, therefore, most of the relatively heavy government investment of the postwar period has depended on French aid.

Many Africans have dismissed this kind of cataloguing of French aid to Africa as irrelevant, and have raised doubts as to whether Africa has really benefited from it. They argue that Africans themselves have had little to do with planning how the aid should be used, that the big French firms (the "colonial trusts") have drawn disproportionate profits from it, that projects have been badly chosen. And more recently there has grown up a doctrine which argues, in effect, that "it all goes back to France anyway, so Africa gets little good out of French aid."

Some of these criticisms are well founded. Economic planning has been done without sufficient consultation of African opinion. Projects have too often been undertaken as much for their value as splashy propaganda as for their economic utility; they have too often been heavy on luxury and esthetic appeal—architectural or engineering *tours de force* which are pleasing and impressive but which represent added costs that a poor country can ill afford.[6]

There is no room here to consider in detail the recent, and perhaps the most significant African complaint about French economic aid— that it does no good because "it all goes back to France." It deserves some consideration, however, because it serves as an ideological under- pinning for demands for independence: an obvious reply to the argu- ment that Africa needs French economic aid is that this aid doesn't help Africans and so there would be no loss in their dispensing with it.

As it is generally expressed, the argument is unsound; Africans seeking economic arguments for independence can find better ones. French aid does indeed return in large measure to French individuals and enterprises, but it does so in payment for factors of production which are used either in Africa or in France for African purposes. In any underdeveloped economy which is interested in capital formation at the lowest cost, a high proportion of investment funds will inevitably go to the hire or purchase of foreign factors—machines, raw materials, technical skills. The impact of the investment expenditure on the domestic economy is thereby reduced; in technical terms the investment multiplier is low because of heavy leakages in the form of imports. But the fixed capital created by the foreign factors remains within the country. It may be in the form of roads or buildings, or it may be in educated or trained people. It may even be in an increase in technical knowledge, as is the case with investments in research.

In one sense the "it all goes back to France" argument does have real meaning. The critics might be suggesting that local factors of pro- duction should have been used more heavily. In building roads, for example, more local labor and less imported French machinery could have been used. This would mean that more of every injection of in- vestment funds in Africa would be distributed as wages to Africans, and less as wages and profits to Frenchmen in the machine-making industry in France. It would mean a greater short-run rise in the national in- come of French Africa as a result of French aid. But it would also mean less capital formation in Africa. Building roads by means of unskilled laborers with shovels, for example, is more expensive (even where it is possible) than is road-building with modern machinery. It is not im- possible for a government to plan its development projects so as to maximize the use of domestic factors of production; there are places

[6] The Grand Council building in Dakar and the Abidjan bridge are two well- known examples. Less known but more striking is the airport at Bouaké; this airport in the center of the Ivory Coast services about two local flights a week, yet it is far more luxurious than the airport at Lagos (Nigeria) which has a local and interna- tional traffic over 20 times as heavy.

where it would be economic to do so. But in a situation where investment resources are being granted from abroad it is not a very practicable alternative; and given the conditions of labor supply in West Africa, it is not clear that it would be economically justifiable.

RELATIVELY HEAVY USE OF FRENCH LABOR

We have so far outlined two characteristics of FWA's pattern of economic development—its relatively rapid postwar growth, and its heavy reliance on French economic aid for its development financing. A third feature is the extent to which Europeans have been used in staffing the administrative bureaucracy and in the ranks of skilled and lower-level supervisory employees in the private sector of the economy. For a number of reasons, Africans in FWA have held an extremely small proportion of managerial responsibility in the country, even responsibility of a limited sort. While this is a general characteristic of all colonial societies, it has been particularly true in French Africa. On the one hand, Europeans of modest attainments were more plentiful in FWA than in most other parts of colonial Africa. And on the other hand, the number of skilled and educated Africans was insignificant until quite recently. As a consequence, neither in the administration nor in private employment were there many Africans above the level of junior clerks.

The picture was not very different in Ghana and Nigeria until 1946, except that those countries had a wider educational base on which to build. But after 1946 Africanisation in British West Africa moved forward at a lively pace. In FWA, despite the other postwar changes, administrative responsibility and skilled or technical work remained almost entirely in the charge of Frenchmen. To some extent this was not easily avoidable. It takes time for the educational pipeline to turn out trained people. Also, many talented and able Africans entered political life, thereby drawing off ability which might otherwise have risen in the private or administrative bureaucracies. But there is more to it than this. Africanisation moved forward especially slowly in FWA because the haziness of the ultimate outcome of the French-African relationship prevented serious thinking about an Africa without the French, and the nature of FWA politics between 1946 and 1958 made it difficult for African leaders to do much about it.

In the British West African territories there was never any question that independence would, sooner or later, become reality; in FWA, on the contrary, the question of the ultimate relationship with France, once the period of stewardship was at an end, had never been squarely faced. Under the constitution of the Fourth Republic the overseas territories were an integral part of the French Republic. Despite the territorial assemblies established in each territory since 1946, sovereignty resided in the French Parliament. No specified end to the French-African connection was in sight, and certainly no possibility of legal accession to independence.

After 1946 African political parties gained increasing control of political power within each territory. Except for some incidents in the Ivory Coast and Guinea, they did so peacefully, working always within the legal framework of the Fourth Republic. The steady and quiet construction of a local power base was accompanied by no open demands for independence. Such demands were outlawed; the general strategy of most African leaders was to consolidate their power without alarming French officials. "Independence" therefore was a nasty word, banned for a decade in polite political society. This meant that African political leaders could not prudently push an intense and systematic Africanisation program in FWA as their counterparts in British West Africa had been doing, especially since 1946.

The peculiar legal structure of the Fourth Republic added an additional complicating element to the Africanisation problem. According to law, a citizen of the French Union had the right of free circulation in all parts of that Union—much as, in this country, Puerto Ricans as citizens are free to move to New York City. This meant that, provided he could meet some nominal entry requirements, no Frenchman could be prohibited from coming to FWA. And as the postwar boom got under way, many Frenchmen did come; between 1946 and 1956 the European population of FWA rose from 32,000 to 90,000—the great majority being French nationals. Employment in Africa had a great appeal. Not only were wages good, conditions attractive and social upgrading inevitable, but there was also an extra feature that served as a special lure: because of the rate of exchange between the French and colonial francs, each franc saved in Africa could be turned into two francs at home. This gave many French nationals, particularly those of lesser skill or training, a splendid chance to put a little something aside. Among the 60,000 new European entrants into FWA during the decade after 1946 were sizeable numbers of men with little skill, the much-discussed *petits blancs* who too often knew little more, as a Dakar newspaper editor once put it, than that "two metropolitan francs equal one cfa franc." To a great extent these men filled the many posts of lower supervisory rank that qualified Africans might have taken over, had there not been Europeans present in such number. Why European employers and the administration were willing to employ Europeans when similarly trained Africans could have been found at much lower

FRENCH WEST AFRICA, 1956

Territory	Population millions[a]	Area 000 sq. km.	Exports[b]		Imports % of total FWA	Public[c] investment per capita 1947–1956 (cfa francs)	Electricity consumed (KWH per capita)	Rate of school attendance, % of school age	No. inhabitants per vehicle	No. of non-agricultural wage-earners
			% of total FWA	per capita (cfa francs)						
Senegal	2.230	197	35	9,500	52	10,000	41.6	24	Dakar: 15 Rest: 225	83,600
Mauritania	.616	1,086	—[d]	—	—[d]	4,000	.3	7	620	3,900
Soudan	3.643	1,204	—[d]	—	—[d]	3,600	2.3	8	650	27,000
Guinea	2.507	246	8.5	2,000	10	5,000	5.6	10	320	44,500
Ivory Coast	2.482	322	43.8	10,600	30	7,000	9.4	28	120	75,000
Upper Volta	3.326	274	1.7	300	—[e]	2,000	.8	7	1,050	21,000
Dahomey	1.615	116	4.3	1,600	8	4,800	1.9	28	350	15,000
Niger	2.336	1,189	6.7[f]	1,500	—[e]	1,800	1.1	3	850	13,000

Source: AOF, 1957, Tableaux Economiques, Dakar, 1958.

[a] Includes Europeans.

[b] Interterritorial trade and smuggling excluded.

[c] Does not include all public investment, but only that substantial part of the total which was distributed through FIDES, the development fund.

[d] Since most of the exports and imports of Mauritania and the Soudan pass through the port of Dakar, separate foreign trade statistics do not exist for these territories. Their trade is counted with that of Senegal. Mauritanian exports have been practically nil, but the Soudan's peanut exports are significant. The per capita export figure of 9,500 francs, given for Senegal, thus overstates the Senegalese contribution.

[e] Foreign imports for the Upper Volta pass through Abidjan, and those for Niger come through Cotonou. Separate foreign trade statistics therefore do not exist for these two territories, though export estimates have been made.

[f] The Niger territory's 6.7 per cent contribution to the total exports from FWA in 1956 is unusually large. The supported peanut price in Niger was substantially higher than in neighboring Nigeria, so thousands of tons of Nigerian peanuts were smuggled across the border for sale in Niger.

cost is a complicated matter; elements of inertia, race prejudice, strike insurance, social compatibility, and a frequently genuine belief that Africans were less productive, less responsible and less trustworthy—all these factors and others were important.[7]

For all these reasons, responsible posts in FWA have remained in the nearly exclusive control of Europeans. Where Ghana and Nigeria have hundreds of Africans in higher level administrative positions in the civil service, and some even in private industry, there are only handfuls of such men in FWA. In the civil service Africanisation has barely begun. There were about 42,500 civil servants in FWA in 1951, including some 5,300 Europeans. Only about 2,000 of these Europeans were doing genuinely higher level administrative or technical work, of the sort that normally requires higher education. About 30,000 of the 37,000 African civil servants were in the lowest classifications—the junior clerk grades; 5,500 were in the middle levels, in jobs for which teacher training school or some secondary school attendance is an entry requirement. The higher ranks of the service included 2,000 Africans, but most of these were connected with administration; they were African auxiliary doctors, midwives, pharmacists, veterinarians.[8]

By 1956 the situation had not appreciably changed. The size of the civil service had increased to about 56,000. Some few African university graduates had moved into the higher posts of the service. But there were still 5,500 Europeans in the middle ranks, in jobs requiring no more than secondary school training. Just how little real inroad the Africans had made in taking over the administrative machinery of their country is suggested by more recent figures for the Ivory Coast. In that territory in 1958 there were fewer than 20 high-level African administrative and technical officers.[9] The degree of Africanisation was greater in the civil services of Senegal and Dahomey, but more so in the middle levels than at the top.

What was true of the bureaucracy in government was even truer in private industry. Not only were managerial jobs closed to Africans but to an extent unmatched outside of white-settler Africa, Europeans and Africans were in open competition for lower-level jobs. A study of the major trading firms in Senegal in 1957 showed that the middle skill categories contained 600 Europeans and over 300 Africans. The ranks of sales clerks and secretaries were continually replenished by wives of

[7] Cf. E. Berg, "French West Africa," in Labor and Economic Development, Walter Galenson, ed. (New York, 1959), p. 258, note 110.

[8] Annuaire Statistique de l'Afrique Occidentale Française, Vol. 5, tome 3 (Paris, 1957), pp. 97–103; and information supplied by the Direction Générale de Personnel, Dakar.

[9] Information supplied by the Ivory Coast Ministry of the Fonction Publique.

French servicemen (or wage-earners) stationed in FWA.[10] In 1954 there were about 22,000 Europeans working for wages in FWA, some 14,000 of them in the private sector. Of these 14,000, about 4,700 were managerial people; the rest were classified as follows: 540 "ordinary manual workers"; 2,000 "qualified manual workers"; 6,000 "office workers."[11]

The presence of these Europeans in the labor market had two effects. It blocked African accession to a wider range of jobs, for many of the Europeans were doing work that could have been done by Africans; it therefore hindered the development of African skills and responsibility. But it also magnified another obstacle for Africans aspiring to positions of authority in private industry. Employers were prevented by inertia, and by fear of unloosing a host of racial problems, from placing Africans in jobs that might involve giving orders to Europeans. It is no surprise that of the 250,000 African wage-earners in the private sector for whom statistics were available in 1954, only 1,600 qualified as *cadres*—men of responsibility.[12] By 1957 there had been no significant change; some 2,100 Africans were listed as *cadres* in the private sector in that year.[13]

The point is sufficiently clear. Between 1946 and 1958 Africans in FWA secured political power within their territories. But the apparatus of government and the administration of private economic activity remained in the hands of Europeans. There were two kinds of Africans: political leaders—ministers, deputies and their aides—and the rest, who were still to an extraordinary degree the hewers of wood and the drawers of water. In the middle was a great void, filled by the Frenchman in Africa.

PROTECTION OF FWA'S EXPORTS IN FRENCH MARKETS

To the dependence on France for development funds and an (unwilling) dependence on Frenchmen for trained personnel must be added a third aspect of FWA's dependence on France, and a major characteristic of its economic development pattern: its close trade integration

[10] One of the most striking differences between pre- and post-independence Guinea is the disappearance of European shop clerks in the main stores. Because the military left, and with them their wives, relatively inexpensive European clerks are no longer available.

[11] *Annuaire Statistique de l'Afrique Occidentale Française,* Vol. 5, tome 2 (Paris, 1957), p. 128.

[12] *Ibid.* In the official classification of the wage-earning population, 489 Africans were classified as "management"; most (358) of these were in the motor transport industry. Of the 1641 classified as *cadres,* almost 20 per cent (302 men) were found in the railway administration, a government corporation.

[13] Haut-Commissariat Général à Dakar, *Comptes Economiques de l'Afrique Occidentale Française, 1956. Rapport No. II: Inventaire des Ressources humaines en 1956* (Dakar), March 1959, p. 50.

within the highly protected franc zone. Much more t[Belgian territories in Africa, the French areas have the protective wall of the metropolitan country. M (over 70 per cent in recent years) come from Fran same proportion of its exports are sold there. FW. high-price area. Because of restrictions on purchase FWA's residents have had to pay higher than world they import. And as a counterbalance, FWA's exp than world prices in French markets protected b exchange controls. For much of the postwar period thus sold at 15 to 20 per cent above world pric enjoyed the benefits of a 20 per cent French tari franc zone countries, and FWA's nascent food p been able to sell in France at prices substantial comparable imports from elsewhere.

It has recently become a favorite pastime "who overpays more," the French consumer of t African buyers of French goods.[14] The calculat (ignoring capital grants) France comes out ah argued—rightly—that prices in FWA are high prices of imports from France, both of consui ment. Whatever the relative benefits and the FWA producers are high-price sellers who h; the hot-house conditions of the franc zone. exports than of others. Cocoa already compe might not do too badly. But peanuts would h banana producers might well be pushed t suddenly to face the winds of open compet of tropical products in unprotected worl them very cold winds indeed. Though she face world competition on more even ter temporary dislocations would be considera

[14] *Cf.* Raymond Bertrand, "La construction e d'échange pour l'Afrique Occidentale Française 1956, pp. 280–307; and Pierre Moussa, *Les chan Franco-Africaine* (Paris, 1957), pp. 77–79. Wl Africa are taken into account the balance of ecoi Africa's favor. The extent of the advantage, in f in France, particularly after 1956. This protest the development of the doctrine known as "(journalist), which argued in effect that France on ungrateful colonies which would in any e articles by Raymond Cartier in *Paris-Match,* A also J. Ehrardt, *Le Destin du colonialisme* (P;

TABLE III.

SOME INDICATORS OF ECONOMIC DEVELOPMENT, TERRITORIES OF F

UNEVEN GROWTH AND THE ABSENCE OF A NATIONAL ECONOMY

We have so far described characteristics of FWA's economic development pattern that derive directly from its relation with France. What aspects of the internal development of the country have been fundamental in determining recent political behavior?

One of the most striking facts has been the great unevenness of FWA's development. In general, the coastal states of Senegal, Guinea, the Ivory Coast and—to a much lesser extent—Dahomey, have flourished, while the vast interior states of the Soudan, the Upper Volta, Niger, and Mauritania have been relatively little touched by modern economic advance. The geographical origin of export production gives some indication of this differential rate of growth. In 1951 the littoral fringe of FWA (the western parts of Senegal and Guinea and the southern parts of the Ivory Coast and Dahomey) grouped about 7 million people in 500,000 square kilometers. From this region came 91 per cent of the value of exports in that year; the "continental sector" of around 12 million people and 4 million square kilometers produced the rest.[15]

Table III illustrates the unequal development of the different territories by comparing a number of specific economic and social indicators in each of them. It shows how much more advanced in almost all respects are Senegal and the Ivory Coast. Slightly less than three-quarters of all non-agricultural wage-earners are found in Senegal, Guinea and the Ivory Coast; if agricultural wage-earners, sharecroppers and domestic servants were included, the proportion of the total FWA wage-earning population in those three territories would probably approach 90 per cent. Guinea, whose industrial advance has moved forward significantly since 1956, compares more favorably now than the table shows. Dahomey shines only in educational achievements; it has long done so, and this is why one of Dahomey's main exports has been its skilled and educated people. The gap between the richer and the poorer areas has been growing larger; development since the war has concentrated on the coastal areas. As the per capita FIDES investments given in the table show, Senegal and the Ivory Coast have benefited most. And available data on private investment suggest that Senegal, the Ivory Coast and Guinea have drawn the lion's share of it.[16]

A final feature of FWA's economic landscape is that a "national" economy has never developed to any significant extent. The productive coastal regions have been tied to the world market rather than to their

[15] See Speech of Governor-General Cornut-Gentille before the opening session of the Grand Council of FWA in Dakar, in *Procès-verbaux des délibérations du Grand Conseil, session extraordinaire, réunion de 21 mai 1954*, pp. 11 ff.

[16] *Cf. AOF, 1957*, pp. 363 ff.

TABLE IV.

INTERTERRITORIAL TRADE IN FRENCH WEST AFRICA, 1956

(Millions of cfa Francs)[a]

Exports From:	Imports Into:								External Trade[c]		Total Exports[b]
	Senegal	Mauritania	Soudan	Guinea	Ivory Coast	Upper Volta	Dahomey	Niger	Smuggled Exports	Recorded Exports	
Senegal	X	1,590	17,230	1,330	2,000	—	450	—	20	21,090	43,690
Mauritania	1,090	X	1,400	—	—	—	—	120	—	—[d]	2,490
Soudan	5,590	60	X	500	890	2,050	—	—	20	—[d]	9,230
Guinea	300	—	210	X	240	—	10	—	320	5,070	6,160
Ivory Coast	370	—	1,100	340	X	4,830	90	—	550	26,290	33,570
Upper Volta	—	—	450	—	1,910	X	70	—	—	1,000	3,430
Dahomey	170	—	—	20	90	—	X	1,240	1,010	2,630	5,150
Niger	—	—	80	—	—	—	990	X	—	3,940	5,010
External Trade[c]											
Smuggled Imports	—	370	50	370	70	80	1,000	230	X	X	1,920
Recorded Imports	34,780	—	—	6,640	18,450	1,580	3,720	1,570	X	X	60,020
Total Imports[b]	42,300	2,020	20,520	9,200	23,650	8,540	6,320	3,150	2,170	66,730	—

Source: Haut-Commissariat-Général à Dakar, Groupe d'études des comptes économiques; *Comptes économiques de l'Afrique Occidentale Française, 1956,* Rapport No. VI, *Echanges interterritoriaux* (Dakar, March 1959), Table 38.

[a] All figures and totals are rounded.

[b] Discrepancies due to rounding.

[c] These figures refer to trade with countries outside of French West Africa, including trade with neighboring non-French territories in West Africa. The estimates for smuggling are very approximate; the figure of 70 million francs for smuggled imports entering the Ivory Coast seems to be particularly underestimated.

[d] The total of the external (non-FWA) trade of the Soudan and Mauritania is imputed to Senegal.

own hinterlands or to each other. The territories of the interior send to the coastal and forest regions some of their food (mainly cattle and fish) and manpower. They receive in return European import goods; cola nuts and bottled beverages are about the only important domestically produced commodities which the regions near the coast export to the interior.

Table IV shows the pattern of interterritorial trade in FWA. These statistics are crude; measuring interterritorial trade is extremely difficult, since FWA has always formed one free trade area and West African frontiers are in all cases very permeable. Nonetheless, the figures do indicate the direction and probable order of magnitude of trade between the various territories.

The table suggests the existence of four separate economic units in FWA: the group Senegal-Mauritania-Soudan; Guinea alone; the Ivory Coast and the Upper Volta;[17] and Dahomey and Niger. Only the Soudan, because of its central geographic position, engages in noticeable commerce with both the Senegalese bloc and the Ivory Coast. The Soudan turns both ways in the labor market too, for it sends its men to work in both Senegal and the Ivory Coast.

Because an unknown but probably substantial amount of interterritorial trade is not included, Table IV understates the magnitude of the exchanges that occur. On the other hand, the degree of interpenetration of the territorial economies is less than the estimates in the table show, since much of the estimated trade does not reflect territorial specialization, but results rather from reliance of the territories of the interior on the ports of the coastal states. Since Mauritania and the Soudan rely on the port of Dakar, the Upper Volta on Abidjan, Niger on Cotonou, a substantial portion of the trade between coastal and interior states represents transit trade only.

The slight extent of interterritorial coastal trade is a good indication of the absence of a unified "national" economy. Of Senegal's total exports in 1956, less than a tenth went to Guinea, the Ivory Coast and Dahomey, and only about 2 per cent of its total imports came from these territories. The Ivory Coast sent less than 2 per cent of its exports to the other coastal territories, and took only a tenth of its imports from them. Guinea likewise sent less than 2 per cent of its exports to the other coastal territories, while receiving slightly less than a fifth of its imports from them.

The failure to develop more of a national economy has many

[17] The Upper Volta, and to a lesser extent the Niger Republic, also have connections with Ghana, exporting migrant laborers and cattle and importing cola nuts, European manufactures and cash remittances.

causes, but perhaps the most important is the nature of the transportation system. The railway network in FWA was built not to tie the territories together but to draw the products of the interior to the seaports. Railways run from each main port (Dakar, Conakry, Abidjan, Cotonou) into the interior, and end there, as unconnected with the others as spokes in a hubless wheel. The road system which might conceivably bind the various spokes together has in fact never done so. Road transport in the interior tends to be expensive, and the cheapest way—sometimes the only way—to move goods from territory to territory is by sea. But sea transport is costly too; the rate structure of French shipping lines has made "inter-colonial" shipping relatively much more expensive than shipping from France to any of the "colonial" ports. These high shipping charges, in the absence of an internal road network, have worked against the development of any territorial specialisation. The best example is cement; there is a cement plant in Senegal, but none elsewhere in FWA. The Senegalese plant has not captured the whole FWA market, however, because high transport costs make Senegalese cement, delivered in Abidjan or Conakry, almost as expensive as French cement shipped from Marseilles. It is the same with flour. Heavy costs of shipment from Dakar to Abidjan have encouraged the establishment of a flour mill in Abidjan despite the fact that at Dakar a large flour mill operates at less than capacity. Thus the transportation system has encouraged in each of the territories a kind of autarchic development; it has not bound them together through specialisation and increased trade.

II. POLITICAL ECONOMY OF FEDERALISM IN FRENCH
WEST AFRICA

The features of FWA's economy outlined above have obvious and direct political implications. We will consider their bearing on the two most important political questions in the area: the problem of political unity among the various territories of French-speaking West Africa, and the choice between total independence and continued attachment to France.

Due to the "accident" of French colonial administration, disparate and separate economic units were forged together into one political body, the Federation of French West Africa. For the French the creation of the Federation was in part an administrative convenience. It enabled them to run general overhead coordinating services more cheaply, and it satisfied the French penchant for centralized government. But it was something else too. It was a financial necessity, a pooling device aimed at relieving the French Treasury of the charge of administering the poorer territories of the area.

In the very early days of the French occupation each of the territories was financially autonomous, and the poorer territories were subsidized by the *métropole*. But in 1900 a new finance law was adopted in Paris, laying down the principle of economic self-sufficiency for the colonies—the principle, that is to say, that the colonies would no longer receive economic help from France, and that like the British colonial territories they would in fact begin to contribute to their own administration and defense. The poorer territories, however, could never carry on unaided, much less contribute to general expenses of French administration. So the Ministry of Colonies decided to group the richer with the poorer territories into one administrative unit—the federation of FWA. By making the richer areas pay for the poorer, the principle of colonial self-sufficiency could be made operative. In 1904, therefore, the French set up the federation and in 1905 endowed the federal government with its own budget, the General Budget of FWA. Its essential purpose was to centralize much of the revenue and expenditure of the territories. Senegal, Dahomey and Guinea would henceforth replace the French Treasury as the source of support of the Soudan, Niger and other areas of the interior.

It is understandable that the richer territories did not like this at all. Senegal, then the most developed by far of the territories, was the scene of violent anti-federalism.[18] Dahomey was no less disturbed, and even in Guinea, then hardly a land of milk and honey, there were objections to the new financial arrangements.[19] The reasons for these protests are not hard to find. In the early days, as more recently, the revenues of the General Budget came from customs duties—taxes on exports and imports. And Senegal, Dahomey and to a lesser extent Guinea, were the sites of most of the exporting and importing. The burden of support of the entire Federation therefore fell on the traders and residents there. Table V shows that Senegal and Dahomey accounted for about 80 per cent of the total exports and imports in 1920. In the 1930s Dahomeyans no longer had that cause for complaint; by then Dahomey was no longer a major contributor to the revenues of the General Budget. Discontent persisted in Senegal until the end of the 1920s,[20] but the crash of peanut prices in the depression and the eco-

[18] *Cf.* R. L. Buell, *The Native Problem in Africa* (New York, 1928), Vol. 1, p. 933.

[19] A. Arcin, *Histoire de la Guinée Française* (Paris, 1911), p. 719. The main objectors, it should be noted, were not Africans but rather the European traders.

[20] Buell, *op. cit.*, p. 934.

TABLE V.

RELATIVE IMPORTANCE OF DIFFERENT FWA TERRITORIES IN FOREIGN TRADE,
SELECTED YEARS

| | *Imports (per cent of total)* | | | |
	Senegal Mauritania Sudan	Guinea	Ivory Coast Upper Volta	Dahomey Niger
1920	61	9	10	20
1938	62	11	19	8
1947	70	8	15	7
1956	52	10	30	8
	Exports (per cent of total)			
1920	66	7	13	14
1938	50	13	27	10
1947	54	11	26	9
1956	35	9	46	11

Source: AOF, 1957; Tableaux Economiques, p. 127.

nomic advances of the Ivory Coast reduced the sources of Senegalese displeasure; by the end of the 1930s the Ivory Coast was carrying a good part of the common burden. The economic surge of the Ivory Coast really began to weigh heavily in the postwar period, when the expansion of its cocoa and coffee production, coupled with high prices for those items, made the Ivory Coast the chief contributor to the general support of the federation. By 1957 the Ivory Coast was producing 46 per cent of the export income of FWA, as against 35 per cent for Senegal and the Soudan combined.

The Ivory Coast's economic outdistancing of the other territories contributed heavily to creating the political tensions which led to the ultimate disintegration of the federation of FWA. The Ivory Coast has been the main African agent in the destruction of the federal government, and the main opponent of any new federation. The Ivory Coast position rests on a profound sense of economic grievance—that it has been, as its leaders say, the cow that the other territories never tired of milking. The basis for this sense of injury lies in the recent history of federal finance in the country.

Duties on imports and exports were, as we have seen, the source of most internally raised government income in FWA. Establishment of these duties and the distribution of income derived from them was a federal function. Aside from the relatively small portion set aside for development expenditure, the revenues raised by the federal government were divided into two main parts. One portion was used by the federal government to finance its services. The second was distributed to the eight territories of the federation for their own use. In most recent years the portion spent by the federal government was about 50 to 60 per cent of the total; the federal government, that is, provided over half of the total government services in FWA. In 1956, for example, the federal government had about 35 billion francs for administrative expenditure; it spent 19 billion itself, and distributed the rest to local budgets.[21]

How the revenues of the federal government were distributed to the local budgets was obviously a matter of prime concern to all the territories. Rebates and subsidies from the federal government made up 35 to 50 per cent of the total government income of the richer territories such as the Ivory Coast and Senegal, and as much as 90 per cent of the government income of the poorer territories.

According to a Law of August 29, 1947, the revenue remaining in the General Budget after the expenses of federal services had been met was to be divided among the territories in accordance with what is known as the "Derivation Principle": each territory should receive in the form of a rebate an amount proportionate to its contribution to the revenues of the General Budget—essentially, that is, according to the importing and exporting each territory accounted for in the given year. In fact, however, the amount of rebate and subsidy each territory received was the subject of annual negotiations in the Grand Council, the federal assembly in Dakar. And as it turned out, the poorer territories always came out best. The Derivation Principle gave way to a redistribution principle.

Table VI shows what part of federal revenues was derived from each territory and what each territory received from the federal budget in the way of subsidies and rebates in 1949 and 1954. Revenues derived from economic activity in the Ivory Coast rose spectacularly in that period. It was the source of about 37 per cent of the total receipts collected by the General Budget in 1954, while it received only 18 per cent of the total federal rebates distributed to the territorial budgets. A somewhat greater portion of receipts originated in Senegal in 1954 (39 per cent as against 37 per cent from the Ivory Coast), but in contrast Senegal received almost 30 per cent of the total rebates. Whatever the relative distribution of the burden between them, it is clear from the

---

[21] Actually it distributed only 12.6 billion to local budgets; 3.5 billion went to municipal and special budgets within the territories. These figures have been calculated from the budgetary estimates in *Annuaire Statistique de l'Afrique Occidentale Française*, Vol. 5, tome 3, pp. 106 ff.

TABLE VI.

Territorial Contributions to and Receipts from Federal Budget of French West Africa, 1949 and 1954

| | Federal Receipts by Territorial Origins | | | | Federal Subsidies and Rebates to Territories | | | | Net Contribution of Territories to Federal Budget | | Per Capita Contribution to Federal Budget[b] |
| | (millions of francs) | | % of total | | (millions of francs) | | % of total[a] | | (millions of francs) | | (francs) |
	1949	1954	1949	1954	1949	1954	1949	1954	1949	1954	1954
Senegal	5,810	11,840	45.6	38.7	1,000	1,600	24.4	29.4	4,810	10,240	4,590
Mauritania	150	730	0.1	0.2	320	560	7.8	10.3	−170	170	28
Sudan	440	1,030	3.5	3.4	660	500	16.0	9.2	+220	530	15
Guinea	1,040	2,520	8.2	8.2	390	580	9.5	10.6	650	1,940	1,773
Ivory Coast	3,000	11,170	23.4	36.5	730	990	17.8	18.0	2,270	10,180	4,560
Upper Volta	210	690	1.6	2.3	320	340	8.3	6.2	−110	350	11
Dahomey	920	1,750	7.2	5.7	410	580	10.0	10.6	510	1,170	670
Niger	350	800	2.8	2.6	280	300	6.8	5.5	−40	500	21
Unspecified	970	740	7.6	2.4							
Totals	12,740	30,620	100.0	100.0	4,100	5,450	100.6	99.8	7,700	25,080	

Source: Compiled from budget data in *Annuaire Statistique de l'Afrique Occidentale Française,* Vol. 5, Tome 3, p. 83, 106 ff. All francs are cfa francs.

[a] Errors due to rounding.

[b] Per capita contributions are slightly underestimated, due to the use of 1956 population figures in their calculation.

table that these two territories were bearing most of the costs of central administration in FWA; all the other territories except Guinea made only token contributions.

Senegal's large contributions to the federal budget was not a cause for dissatisfaction among Senegalese leaders. Senegal was, after all, the seat of federal government. Public administration was one of its main industries; the return on its contribution was direct and tangible. Ivory Coast leaders, on the other hand, felt that they were paying too much for too little, and that in addition the Ivory Coast was subsidizing not only the poverty but also the financial laxity of the other territories. Each year at budgetary sessions in the Grand Council the Ivory Coast representatives defended the Derivation Principle in the allocation of rebates. Each year they were voted down. The negotiations were always unpleasant for all parties. Ivory Coast representatives were in the uncomfortable position of being rich and surly defenders of the law and their own self-interest. The accumulated frustrations and resentments built up during these years certainly enter in no small way in explaining the present recalcitrance of the Ivory Coast leaders regarding federation with other West African states.[22] The Ivory Coast is willing to cooperate with other states. It is even willing to give them economic aid. But it does not appear ready to enter any constitutional arrangement which involves loss of control over its finances.

III. ECONOMIC FACTORS IN THE DECISION ON INDEPENDENCE

We have already detailed the extent to which FWA has been dependent on France for money, for men and for markets. Evidently, this dependence is of prime importance in understanding the decision of most French African territories to remain within the French Community. When, quite suddenly, African leaders were given a chance to opt for immediate independence they hesitated to accept the possible economic consequences. Their civil services, on the upper and middle levels, were still almost entirely manned by Frenchmen. Their economic resources were insufficient to allow any substantial investment for development, and there was no good reason to believe that adequate help would come from non-French sources to allow them to maintain anything like the rate of investment that had characterized the 1946–1958 period. The break-up of the federation of FWA, furthermore, meant that the poorer

---

[22] Nigerian experience in the field of federal finance has been different from that of FWA. In Nigeria the center has not acted as an agency for substantial redistribution of income from the richer (southern) regions to the poorer north. On the contrary, some evidence indicates that for some time a redistribution took place from the north to the other regions. *Cf. Report of the Commission on Revenue Allocation*, Nigeria, 1951, p. 72.

territories could no longer count on the traditional support of the richer ones. For these poorer areas, independence from France would have meant severe cutbacks even in the ordinary services of government. For all the territories, independence involved the possible loss of protection in French markets and perhaps the need to seek new outlets for their exports.

There is no need to embroider this theme of African economic dependence on France; its significance is clear. There is, however, one aspect of the matter that deserves some further attention: the effect of the economic environment in producing a psychological unpreparedness for independence among African elites.

After 1945 African political parties won increasing control over their territories. But as their internal political control grew, so did their economic dependence on France; economic integration developed as fast as political decentralization. For this reason among others French Africa came to live in a kind of economic never-never land, a place where economic decision-making was unnecessary—key decisions were made in France—and economic responsibility not a serious concern. FWA's investment funds came from France. Its exports sold in protected French markets. Its internal price level was determined by French prices. Even the wage scales of its civil servants depended on French civil servants' wages.

In this environment there was little thought about some final reckoning, come Independence Day. No one encouraged such thought, since independence was not openly and frankly regarded as the ultimate outcome of the French-African relationship. No impetus nurtured a sense of economic responsibility, in the absence of any need for hard economic thinking. In fact, the political drives until 1956, drives which centered on obtaining *equality* with Frenchmen, only accentuated the economic problem. The demands for equal pay for equal work in the civil service, for example, operated to load the budgets of FWA with heavier wage bills than most poor governments can afford. But it didn't matter. The important consideration was equality, not economics.[23]

Given this heritage it is no wonder that when the option for independence was unexpectedly presented in 1958, most African leaders were not prepared to take it, particularly since they had the alternate possibility of taking it later when they were more ready. For independence would have meant a radical break with the economic past, a hand-to-hand dealing with the economic facts of life for which French Africa and French African political leaders had little training.

[23] *Cf.* E. Berg, in *Labor and Economic Development*, pp. 232 ff.

IV. CONCLUSION

To underline the economic factors which have played a part in shaping political developments in French-speaking West Africa is by no means to explain everything. Lines of economic determination are loose. Men moved by strong passions and great ideas may step beyond them, particularly when profound psychological and ideological forces are at work, as they are in questions involving political independence in colonial situations. Even if all African leaders in ex-FWA were convinced that independence necessarily involved severe cutbacks in rates of economic growth and in current standards of living, most would still prefer it to *permanent* political dependence on France. So except for possible ties of a Commonwealth type, the separation of French-speaking West Africa from France is certain to occur, whatever its economic consequences.

That it did not take place in 1958 was due to many causes, not all of them economic. Senegal, despite the vulnerability of its peanut-based economy, might have chosen the path of immediate independence if its modern leadership had been in fuller control of the countryside. And the Niger territory, perhaps the feeblest economic unit in all of West Africa, might well have voted for independence if French influence had not been brought strongly to bear there during the September referendum. Nor are the decisions of the Ivory Coast and Guinea wholly reducible to economic terms. The Ivory Coast, despite its dependence on French markets for its coffee, is ex-FWA's soundest economic entity. Yet it most decisively turned its back on independence in 1958. About Guinea, it is only possible to say that economic and other conditions were more permissive there, allowing it to opt for independence with slighter risks than in most of the other territories: it was highly organized politically; it was not greatly dependent on aid from the other FWA territories through the federal budget; its mining boom was attracting new injections of foreign capital; its economic future was hopeful.

The same combination of economic and other factors that in the 1958 referendum led most African leaders to accept temporarily a status short of full independence is now leading them to negotiations with France, negotiations looking toward independence on terms that will retain French economic assistance.

On the question of internal political re-integration in French-speaking West Africa—a more important question in the long run than the timing of total independence—economic factors are even more fundamental. We have seen how the lack of economic community in FWA and the unequal geographical distribution of income provoked problems of federal finance and contributed, especially through the actions of the Ivory Coast, to the destruction of the old federation. Largely as a result of its fiscal experience the Ivory Coast is the most "anti-federalist" of the former FWA states.

In taking an anti-federalist stand, Ivory Coast political leaders risk placing their territory outside the ideological mainstream in French-speaking West Africa, for African unity is the most powerfully attractive political idea in this part of the world. But the sense of economic grievance runs deep in the Ivory Coast, and it exists on all levels of society. There are few sections of articulate Ivory Coast opinion which do not feel that their territory has been exploited by its ex-partners in the federation. Africans in other parts of French-speaking Africa tend to regard this as simply another manifestation of the "bourgeois" mentality dominant in the Ivory Coast. So it may be. But whatever it is called it has long roots, and there is no obvious reason why it should not for some time continue to dilute that like-minded sense of common African interest on which political unification must depend. Whatever happens to M. Houphouet-Boigny and his vision of a French-African Community (and recent events suggest that it will survive, if at all, only in the form of a loose association of independent states) the Ivory Coast is likely to remain one of West Africa's most unwilling candidates for political union with neighboring African states.

Name Index

(Names of contributors to this volume are capitalized, and the page numbers of their articles are in italics.)

Subject Index

logical, 9–15, 176–191, 217; reaction to, 10–18; sociological, 216–217; stress and strain of, 26; in style of life, 4, 9, 42, 107; theory construction and, 127; uneven, 3–10, 226, 424. *See also* Economic change

Charisma, 29–30, 35, 37, 186–187, 365–369, 389–406, 413, 423, 488–489; attenuation of, 35–36, 387; concentrated in ruling elite, 30, 390; criticism and, 484–485; encouraged by new elites, 29–30, 181; imperial, 302; and modern surrogate objects, 30, 392–393; and post-charismatic politics, 387; sensitivity to and change, 391; and shared image of concentration, 30, 390; and sycophant purges, 368. *See also* Political messiahs

"Checks and balances," 33, 38

Civil service: "collaboration" with Europeans in, 481; efficient but not economic, 398–399; as neutral non-party government, 459–460; politicization of, 32–33

Civility: underdeveloped, 35, 209–210, 389, 478–479

"Civilizing" Africans, 2, 21, 161

Class. *See* Social status

Cliques, 375–376

Coercion, 33–34, 463, 467–468

"Collaboration," 12, 178, 180, 211

Collective goals, 79

Colonial. *See* Imperial

Colonial stereotypes, 1, 47

Commercialization, 7–8, 221–222

Common identity: and African unity, vii, 39–40, 58, 562

Communication, 5–6, 86, 88, 93–97, 213, 309, 326–327, 378–379, 385–388, 405, 414

Communism, 530–531, 533, 536, 538

Community: decision-making in, 23–24; 328–329; development of, 33, 311–315

Comparative analysis, vii, 64–66

Conakry. *See* Conferences

Conferences: Abidjan (Brazzaville Group, 1960), 567, 593; Accra (First All-African People's Conference, 1958), 39, 516, 534, 546, 560–563; Accra (First Conference of Independent African States, 1958), 39, 167–168, 534–535, 542, 555–558; Accra (Union of African States, 1961), 580–582; Addis Ababa (African Heads of States, 1963), 39, 41; Addis Ababa (PAFMECA, 1962), 586–587; Addis Ababa (Second Conference of Independent African States, 1960), 558–559; Bandung (Afro-Asian Solidarity, 1955), 167, 546; Brazzaville (Brazzaville Group, 1960), 567–568; Cairo (Afro-Asian Solidarity, 1957), 167, 546; Cairo (Casablanca Economic Committee, 1962), 574; Cairo (Third All-African People's Conference, 1961), 546, 564–567; Casablanca (Casablanca Group, 1961), 571–573; Conakry (Casablanca Economic Committee, 1961), 574; Dakar (Brazzaville Economic Group, January 1961), 568; Dakar (Monrovia Economic Group, July 1961), 578; Lagos (Monrovia Group, 1962), 578–580; Monrovia (Conference on Algeria, 1959), 583–584; Monrovia (Monrovia Group, 1961), 575–577; Moshi (PAFMECA, 1959), 585; Mwanza (PAFMECA, 1958), 584–585; New Delhi (Afro-Asian Group, 1949), 167; Sanniquellie (Community of Independent African States, 1959), 43, 582–583; Tananarive (Brazzaville Group, 1961), 569–571; Tunis (Second All-African People's Conference, 1960), 546, 563–564; Yaoundé (Brazzaville Group, 1961), 568–569

Congo (Brazzaville), 24, 108, 111–112, 117, 139–140, 145–146, 197, 547, 549, 567–568, 570, 575, 589, 596

Congo (Leopoldville), 1, 6–7, 16–17, 24, 43, 103, 105, 108, 115, 117–119, 153, 168, 173–174, 186, 199, 221–223, 237–238, 297, 407, 416, 426, 535, 539, 558, 560, 578, 589, 595, 597–601, 603–604; continental concern about, 543–545, 549–550, 552–553, 566–568, 572, 576–577, 585–587, 592–593

Consensus, 126, 380–381

Continuity: of European and African rule, 19, 28–29, 412, 484; of old and new Africa, 18–25, 86, 102–103, 215. *See also* Tradition

Corruption, 22–23, 293, 328–329, 450, 495–514; charisma and, 36, 402; defined, 498; functions of, 510–511; high-level, 508–510

Council of the Entente, 593, 596–597, 608

Counter-elites, 29

Cross-pressures, 9, 22–23, 121, 280–281,

litical behavior and, 322–323, 373; types of, 66–76. *See also* Centralized chiefdoms

Traditionalism: and change, 254–277; defined, 255; types of distinguished, 256

Traditionalist movements, 210

Travel, 6, 116, 220; gap in, 6; imperial needs and, 6, 626; new perspectives and, 6, 405

Tribalism. *See* Ethnic group identifications

Tunis. *See* Conferences

Uganda, 19, 21, 30, 104–105, 186, 189, 221, 224, 229, 254, 256, 263, 267–268, 270–271, 277–278, 284, 289, 294, 558, 560, 584–587

Underdevelopment: as a problem of independence, 26

Unemployed. *See* Opposition

Unequal treatment: of Africans, 11, 13, 182, 217, 426. *See also* Europeans

Union of African States, 580–582

United Nations: African states at, 542–554; nationalism and, 15, 164–174, 183–184, 187, 542–587 *passim;* problems of compared with African unity, 1

United States: and nationalism, 15, 232

Unity: cross-pressures and, 9; goal of, 459; traditional, 48–49. *See also* Forging territorial unity

Upper Volta, 51, 54, 298, 419–420, 433–434, 437, 441, 567, 570, 575, 596, 608–609, 622–625, 628, 630

Urban-rural: gap between, 7, 373, 377–378; link between, 148

Urbanization. *See* Towns

Values. *See* Perspectives

Vertical divisions, 4–9, 327, 380, 478–479

Vested interests: African unity and, 42–43, 592, 600, 603, 605, 631, 634; economic development and, 480; forging territorial unity and, 26–27

Voluntary associations, 7, 10, 25, 34, 51–52, 92–93, 143–146, 210–211, 320–321, 323–326, 374, 377, 382–384; criticism, public opinion, and, 482, 489–490; economic, 211; link with nationalist movements of, 212; nationalism and, 10, 213; political socialization and, 10

Voting. *See* Elections

"White man's burden," 161

Women: as a factor in elections, 358; station of, 111

World view: in politics, 374–375

Xenophilia, 14, 478–479. *See also* Europeans as reference groups

Yaoundé. *See* Conferences

Youth: and opposition, 36, 39, 380, 442–443

Zanzibar, 37, 560, 584–585, 587